Novels
for Students

National Advisory Board

Novels
for Students

Presenting Analysis, Context, and Criticism on
Commonly Studied Novels

Volume 23

Sara Constantakis
Project Editor

Foreword by Anne Devereaux Jordan

THOMSON
GALE

Detroit • New York • San Francisco • San Diego • New Haven, Conn. • Waterville, Maine • London • Munich

THOMSON
™
GALE

Novels for Students, Volume 23

Project Editor
Sara Constantakis

Editorial
Anne Marie Hacht, Ira Mark Milne

Rights Acquisition and Management
Jacqueline Key, Shalice Shah-Caldwell,
Timothy Sisler

Manufacturing
Drew Kalasky

Imaging
Leitha Etheridge-Sims, Lezlie Light, Mike Logusz

Product Design
Pamela A. E. Galbreath

Vendor Administration
Civie Green

Product Manager
Meggin Condino

ISBN 0-7876-6946-6
ISSN 1094-3552

Printed in the United States of America
10 9 8 7 6 5 4 3 2 1

Table of Contents

The Informed Dialogue: Interacting with Literature

When we pick up a book, we usually do so with the anticipation of pleasure. We hope that by entering the time and place of the novel and sharing the thoughts and actions of the characters, we will find enjoyment. Unfortunately, this is often not the case; we are disappointed. But we should ask, has the author failed us, or have we failed the author?

We establish a dialogue with the author, the book, and with ourselves when we read. Consciously and unconsciously, we ask questions: "Why did the author write this book?" "Why did the author choose that time, place, or character?" "How did the author achieve that effect?" "Why did the character act that way?" "Would I act in the same way?" The answers we receive depend upon how much information about literature in general and about that book specifically we ourselves bring to our reading.

Young children have limited life and literary experiences. Being young, children frequently do not know how to go about exploring a book, nor sometimes, even know the questions to ask of a book. The books they read help them answer questions, the author often coming right out and *telling* young readers the things they are learning or are expected to learn. The perennial classic, *The Little Engine That Could, tells* its readers that, among other things, it is good to help others and brings happiness:

"Hurray, hurray," cried the funny little clown and all the dolls and toys. "The good little boys and girls in

the city will be happy because you helped us, kind, Little Blue Engine."

In picture books, messages are often blatant and simple, the dialogue between the author and reader one-sided. Young children are concerned with the end result of a book—the enjoyment gained, the lesson learned—rather than with how that result was obtained. As we grow older and read further, however, we question more. We come to expect that the world within the book will closely mirror the concerns of our world, and that the author will *show* these through the events, descriptions, and conversations within the story, rather than *telling* of them. We are now expected to do the interpreting, carry on our share of the dialogue with the book and author, and glean not only the author's message, but comprehend how that message and the overall affect of the book were achieved. Sometimes, however, we need help to do these things. *Novels for Students* provides that help.

A novel is made up of many parts interacting to create a coherent whole. In reading a novel, the more obvious features can be easily spotted—theme, characters, plot—but we may overlook the more subtle elements that greatly influence how the novel is perceived by the reader: viewpoint, mood and tone, symbolism, or the use of humor. By focusing on both the obvious and more subtle literary elements within a novel, *Novels for Students* aids readers in both analyzing for message and in determining how and why that message is communicated. In the discussion on Harper Lee's *To*

Kill a Mockingbird (Vol. 2), for example, the mockingbird as a symbol of innocence is dealt with, among other things, as is the importance of Lee's use of humor which "enlivens a serious plot, adds depth to the characterization, and creates a sense of familiarity and universality." The reader comes to understand the internal elements of each novel discussed—as well as the external influences that help shape it.

"The desire to write greatly," Harold Bloom of Yale University says, "is the desire to be elsewhere, in a time and place of one's own, in an originality that must compound with inheritance, with an anxiety of influence." A writer seeks to create a unique world within a story, but although it is unique, it is not disconnected from our own world. It speaks to us *because* of what the writer brings to the writing from our world: how he or she was raised and educated; his or her likes and dislikes; the events occurring in the real world at the time of the writing, and while the author was growing up. When we know what an author has brought to his or her work, we gain a greater insight into both the "originality" (the world of the book), and the things that "compound" it. This insight enables us to question that created world and find answers more readily. By informing ourselves, we are able to establish a more effective dialogue with both book and author.

Novels for Students, in addition to providing a plot summary and descriptive list of characters— to remind readers of what they have read—also explores the external influences that shaped each book. Each entry includes a discussion of the author's background, and the historical context in which the novel was written. It is vital to know, for instance, that when Ray Bradbury was writing *Fahrenheit 451* (Vol. 1), the threat of Nazi domination had recently ended in Europe, and the McCarthy hearings were taking place in Washington, D.C. This information goes far in answering the question, "Why did he write a story of oppressive government control and book burning?" Similarly, it is important to know that Harper Lee, author of *To Kill a Mockingbird,* was born and raised in Monroeville, Alabama, and that her father was a lawyer.

Readers can now see why she chose the south as a setting for her novel—it is the place with which she was most familiar—and start to comprehend her characters and their actions.

Novels for Students helps readers find the answers they seek when they establish a dialogue with a particular novel. It also aids in the posing of questions by providing the opinions and interpretations of various critics and reviewers, broadening that dialogue. Some reviewers of *To Kill A Mockingbird,* for example, "faulted the novel's climax as melodramatic." This statement leads readers to ask, "Is it, indeed, melodramatic?" "If not, why did some reviewers see it as such?" "If it is, why did Lee choose to make it melodramatic?" "Is melodrama ever justified?" By being spurred to ask these questions, readers not only learn more about the book and its writer, but about the nature of writing itself.

The literature included for discussion in *Novels for Students* has been chosen because it has something vital to say to us. *Of Mice and Men, Catch-22, The Joy Luck Club, My Antonia, A Separate Peace* and the other novels here speak of life and modern sensibility. In addition to their individual, specific messages of prejudice, power, love or hate, living and dying, however, they and all great literature also share a common intent. They force us to *think*—about life, literature, and about others, not just about ourselves. They pry us from the narrow confines of our minds and thrust us outward to confront the world of books and the larger, real world we all share. *Novels for Students* helps us in this confrontation by providing the means of enriching our conversation with literature and the world, by creating an *informed* dialogue, one that brings true pleasure to the personal act of reading.

Sources

Harold Bloom, *The Western Canon, The Books and School of the Ages,* Riverhead Books, 1994.

Watty Piper, *The Little Engine That Could,* Platt & Munk, 1930.

Anne Devereaux Jordan
Senior Editor, TALL
(Teaching and Learning Literature)

Introduction

Purpose of the Book

The purpose of *Novels for Students (NfS)* is to provide readers with a guide to understanding, enjoying, and studying novels by giving them easy access to information about the work. Part of Gale's "For Students" Literature line, *NfS* is specifically designed to meet the curricular needs of high school and undergraduate college students and their teachers, as well as the interests of general readers and researchers considering specific novels. While each volume contains entries on "classic" novels frequently studied in classrooms, there are also entries containing hard-to-find information on contemporary novels, including works by multicultural, international, and women novelists.

The information covered in each entry includes an introduction to the novel and the novel's author; a plot summary, to help readers unravel and understand the events in a novel; descriptions of important characters, including explanation of a given character's role in the novel as well as discussion about that character's relationship to other characters in the novel; analysis of important themes in the novel; and an explanation of important literary techniques and movements as they are demonstrated in the novel.

In addition to this material, which helps the readers analyze the novel itself, students are also provided with important information on the literary and historical background informing each work. This includes a historical context essay, a box comparing the time or place the novel was written to modern Western culture, a critical essay, and excerpts from critical essays on the novel. A unique feature of *NfS* is a specially commissioned critical essay on each novel, targeted toward the student reader.

To further aid the student in studying and enjoying each novel, information on media adaptations is provided, as well as reading suggestions for works of fiction and nonfiction on similar themes and topics. Classroom aids include ideas for research papers and lists of critical sources that provide additional material on the novel.

Selection Criteria

The titles for each volume of *NfS* were selected by surveying numerous sources on teaching literature and analyzing course curricula for various school districts. Some of the sources surveyed included: literature anthologies; *Reading Lists for College-Bound Students: The Books Most Recommended by America's Top Colleges;* textbooks on teaching the novel; a College Board survey of novels commonly studied in high schools; a National Council of Teachers of English (NCTE) survey of novels commonly studied in high schools; the NCTE's *Teaching Literature in High School: The Novel;* and the Young Adult Library Services Association (YALSA) list of best books for young adults of the past twenty-five years.

Input was also solicited from our advisory board, as well as from educators from various areas.

From these discussions, it was determined that each volume should have a mix of "classic" novels (those works commonly taught in literature classes) and contemporary novels for which information is often hard to find. Because of the interest in expanding the canon of literature, an emphasis was also placed on including works by international, multicultural, and women authors. Our advisory board members—educational professionals—helped pare down the list for each volume. If a work was not selected for the present volume, it was often noted as a possibility for a future volume. As always, the editor welcomes suggestions for titles to be included in future volumes.

How Each Entry Is Organized

Each entry, or chapter, in *NfS* focuses on one novel. Each entry heading lists the full name of the novel, the author's name, and the date of the novel's publication. The following elements are contained in each entry:

- **Introduction:** a brief overview of the novel which provides information about its first appearance, its literary standing, any controversies surrounding the work, and major conflicts or themes within the work.

- **Author Biography:** this section includes basic facts about the author's life, and focuses on events and times in the author's life that inspired the novel in question.

- **Plot Summary:** a factual description of the major events in the novel. Lengthy summaries are broken down with subheads.

- **Characters:** an alphabetical listing of major characters in the novel. Each character name is followed by a brief to an extensive description of the character's role in the novel, as well as discussion of the character's actions, relationships, and possible motivation.

  Characters are listed alphabetically by last name. If a character is unnamed—for instance, the narrator in *Invisible Man*—the character is listed as "The Narrator" and alphabetized as "Narrator." If a character's first name is the only one given, the name will appear alphabetically by that name.

  Variant names are also included for each character. Thus, the full name "Jean Louise Finch" would head the listing for the narrator of *To Kill a Mockingbird,* but listed in a separate cross-reference would be the nickname "Scout Finch."

- **Themes:** a thorough overview of how the major topics, themes, and issues are addressed within the novel. Each theme discussed appears in a separate subhead and is easily accessed through the boldface entries in the Subject/Theme Index.

- **Style:** this section addresses important style elements of the novel, such as setting, point of view, and narration; important literary devices used, such as imagery, foreshadowing, symbolism; and, if applicable, genres to which the work might have belonged, such as Gothicism or Romanticism. Literary terms are explained within the entry but can also be found in the Glossary.

- **Historical Context:** This section outlines the social, political, and cultural climate *in which the author lived and the novel was created.* This section may include descriptions of related historical events, pertinent aspects of daily life in the culture, and the artistic and literary sensibilities of the time in which the work was written. If the novel is a historical work, information regarding the time in which the novel is set is also included. Each section is broken down with helpful subheads.

- **Critical Overview:** this section provides background on the critical reputation of the novel, including bannings or any other public controversies surrounding the work. For older works, this section includes a history of how the novel was first received and how perceptions of it may have changed over the years; for more recent novels, direct quotes from early reviews may also be included.

- **Criticism:** an essay commissioned by *NfS* which specifically deals with the novel and is written specifically for the student audience, as well as excerpts from previously published criticism on the work (if available).

- **Sources:** an alphabetical list of critical material used in compiling the entry, with full bibliographical information.

- **Further Reading:** an alphabetical list of other critical sources which may prove useful for the student. It includes full bibliographical information and a brief annotation.

In addition, each entry contains the following highlighted sections, set apart from the main text as sidebars:

- **Media Adaptations:** a list of important film and television adaptations of the novel, including source information. The list also includes stage adaptations, audio recordings, musical adaptations, etc.

- **Topics for Further Study:** a list of potential study questions or research topics dealing with the novel. This section includes questions related to other disciplines the student may be studying, such as American history, world history, science, math, government, business, geography, economics, psychology, etc.

- **Compare and Contrast Box:** an "at-a-glance" comparison of the cultural and historical differences between the author's time and culture and late twentieth century/early twenty-first century Western culture. This box includes pertinent parallels between the major scientific, political, and cultural movements of the time or place the novel was written, the time or place the novel was set (if a historical work), and modern Western culture. Works written after 1990 may not have this box.

- **What Do I Read Next?:** a list of works that might complement the featured novel or serve as a contrast to it. This includes works by the same author and others, works of fiction and nonfiction, and works from various genres, cultures, and eras.

Other Features

NfS includes "The Informed Dialogue: Interacting with Literature," a foreword by Anne Devereaux Jordan, Senior Editor for *Teaching and Learning Literature* (*TALL*), and a founder of the Children's Literature Association. This essay provides an enlightening look at how readers interact with literature and how *Novels for Students* can help teachers show students how to enrich their own reading experiences.

A Cumulative Author/Title Index lists the authors and titles covered in each volume of the *NfS* series.

A Cumulative Nationality/Ethnicity Index breaks down the authors and titles covered in each volume of the *NfS* series by nationality and ethnicity.

A Subject/Theme Index, specific to each volume, provides easy reference for users who may be studying a particular subject or theme rather than a single work. Significant subjects from events to broad themes are included, and the entries pointing to the specific theme discussions in each entry are indicated in **boldface.**

Each entry may have several illustrations, including photos of the author, stills from film adaptations, maps, and/or photos of key historical events, if available.

Citing Novels for Students

When writing papers, students who quote directly from any volume of *Novels for Students* may use the following general forms. These examples are based on MLA style; teachers may request that students adhere to a different style, so the following examples may be adapted as needed.

When citing text from *NfS* that is not attributed to a particular author (i.e., the Themes, Style, Historical Context sections, etc.), the following format should be used in the bibliography section:

"Night." Novels for Students. Ed. Marie Rose Napierkowski. Vol. 4. Detroit: Gale, 1998. 234–35.

When quoting the specially commissioned essay from *NfS* (usually the first piece under the "Criticism" subhead), the following format should be used:

Miller, Tyrus. Critical Essay on *Winesburg, Ohio. Novels for Students.* Ed. Marie Rose Napierkowski. Vol. 4. Detroit: Gale, 1998. 335–39.

When quoting a journal or newspaper essay that is reprinted in a volume of *NfS,* the following form may be used:

Malak, Amin. "Margaret Atwood's *The Handmaid's Tale* and the Dystopian Tradition," *Canadian Literature* No. 112 (Spring, 1987), 9–16; excerpted and reprinted in *Novels for Students,* Vol. 4, ed. Marie Rose Napierkowski (Detroit: Gale, 1998), pp. 133–36.

When quoting material reprinted from a book that appears in a volume of *NfS,* the following form may be used:

Adams, Timothy Dow. "Richard Wright: Wearing the Mask," in *Telling Lies in Modern American Autobiography* (University of North Carolina Press, 1990), 69–83; excerpted and reprinted in *Novels for Students,* Vol. 1, ed. Diane Telgen (Detroit: Gale, 1997), pp. 59–61.

We Welcome Your Suggestions

The editor of *Novels for Students* welcomes your comments and ideas. Readers who wish to suggest novels to appear in future volumes, or who have other suggestions, are cordially invited to contact the editor. You may contact the editor via e-mail at: **ForStudentsEditors@thomson.com.** Or write to the editor at:

Editor, *Novels for Students*
Thomson Gale
27500 Drake Road
Farmington Hills, MI 48331–3535

Literary Chronology

1819: George Eliot is born Mary Ann Evans on November 22 in Arbury, Warwickshire, England.

1872: George Eliot's *Middlemarch* is published.

1874: W. Somerset Maugham is born on January 25 in the British Embassy in Paris.

1880: George Eliot dies of heart failure on December 22 in London, England.

1912: William J. Lederer was born on March 31 in New York City.

1918: Eugene Burdick was born on December 12 in Sheldon, Iowa.

1928: Anita Brookner is born on July 16 in London, England.

1929: Imre Kertész is born on November 9 in Budapest, Hungary.

1932: Joanne Greenberg is born in Brooklyn, New York.

1935: Carol Shields is born on June 2 in Oak Park, Illinois.

1937: Thomas Pynchon is born on May 8 in Glen Cove, Long Island, New York.

1940: James Welch is born on November 18 on the Blackfeet reservation in Browning, Montana.

1943: Michael Ondaatje is born on September 12 in Colombo, Sri Lanka.

1944: W. Somerset Maugham's *The Razor's Edge* is published.

1947: Salman Rushdie is born on June 19 in Bombay, India.

1947: Duong Thu Huong is born in Thai Binh, Vietnam.

1952: Michael Cunningham is born on November 6 in Cincinnati, Ohio.

1953: Alice McDermott is born on June 27.

1958: William J. Lederer and Eugene Burdick's *The Ugly American* is published.

1964: Joanne Greenberg's *I Never Promised You a Rose Garden* is published.

1965: Eugene Burdick dies on July 26.

1965: W. Somerset Maugham dies on December 16 in France.

1973: Thomas Pynchon's *Gravity's Rainbow* is published.

1974: James Welch's *Winter in the Blood* is published.

1981: Salman Rushdie's *Midnight's Children* is published.

1984: Anita Brookner's *Hotel du Lac* is published.

1988: Duong Thu Huong's *Paradise of the Blind* is published.

1990: Imre Kertész's *Kaddish for a Child Not Born* is published.

1992: Michael Ondaatje's *The English Patient* is published.

1993: Carol Shields's *The Stone Diaries* is published.

1998: Alice McDermott's *Charming Billy* is published.

1998: Michael Cunningham's *The Hours* is published.

2003: Carol Shields dies of breast cancer on July 16 in Victoria, British Columbia, Canada.

2003: James Welch dies of a heart attack on August 4.

Acknowledgments

The editors wish to thank the copyright holders of the excerpted criticism included in this volume and the permissions managers of many book and magazine publishing companies for assisting us in securing reproduction rights. We are also grateful to the staffs of the Detroit Public Library, the Library of Congress, the University of Detroit Mercy Library, Wayne State University Purdy/ Kresge Library Complex, and the University of Michigan Libraries for making their resources available to us. Following is a list of the copyright holders who have granted us permission to reproduce material in this volume of *Novels for Students* *(NfS)*. Every effort has been made to trace copyright, but if omissions have been made, please let us know.

COPYRIGHTED MATERIALS IN *NfS*, **VOLUME 23, WERE REPRODUCED FROM THE FOLLOWING PERIODICALS:**

Christianity and Literature, v. 50, summer, 2001. Reproduced by permission.—*Commonweal*, March 27, 1998. Copyright © 1998 Commonweal Publishing Co., Inc. Reproduced by permission of Commonweal Foundation.—*Durham University Journal*, v. LXXXVII, July, 1995. Reproduced by permission.—*Essays on Canadian Writing*, v. 53, summer, 1994. Copyright © 1994 Essays on Canadian Writing Ltd. Reproduced by permission.— *Explicator*, v. 50, summer, 1992; v. 60, summer, 2002. Copyright © 1992, 2002 by Helen Dwight Reid Educational Foundation. Both reproduced with permission of the Helen Dwight Reid Educational Foundation, published by Heldref Publications, 1319 18th Street, NW, Washington, DC 20036-1802.—*Harper's Magazine*, June, 1999 for "The Reanimators: On the Art of Literary Graverobbing" by Jonathan Dee. Copyright by Jonathan Dee. Reproduced by permission.—*Hungarian Quarterly*, v. 43, winter, 2002. Reproduced by permission.—*Journal of Popular Culture*, spring, 1976. Copyright © 1976 Basil Blackwell Ltd. Reproduced by permission of Blackwell Publishers.— *Literature Interpretation Theory*, v. 13, 2002. Copyright © 2002 by OPA (Amsterdam) B.V. All rights reserved. Reproduced by permission of Taylor & Francis Group, LLC., http://www.taylorandfrancis.com.—*Nemla Italian Studies*, v. XXI, 1997 for "Italy and the Ruins of Western Civilization: Michael Ondaatje's 'The English Patient'" by Mark A.R. Kemp. Copyright © 1997 by Nemla Italian Studies. Reproduced by permission of the publisher and the author.—*Publishers Weekly*, v. 241, February 28, 1994. Copyright © 1994 by Reed Publishing USA. Reproduced from Publishers Weekly, published by the Bowker Magazine Group of Cahners Publishing Co., a division of Reed Publishing USA., by permission.—*SAIL: Studies in American Indian Literatures*, v. 8, summer, 1996 for "When Critical Approaches Converge: Team-Teaching Welch's 'Winter in the Blood'" by Jim Charles and Richard Predmore. Reproduced by permission of the authors.—*Women's Review of Books*, v. 11, May, 1994 for "'The Stone Diaries'" by Gail Pool. Copyright 1994 Women's

Review, Inc. Reproduced by permission of the author.—*World Literature Today, summer-autumn*, 2001. Copyright © 2001 by World Literature Today. Reproduced by permission of the publisher.—*Yale Review*, spring, 1959. Copyright © 1959 Basil Blackwell Ltd. Reproduced by permission of Blackwell Publishers.

COPYRIGHTED MATERIALS IN *NfS*, VOLUME 23, WERE REPRODUCED FROM THE FOLLOWING BOOKS:

Burt, Forrest D. From *W. Somerset Maugham.* Twayne Publishers, 1985. Copyright © 1985 by G.K. Hall & Company. Reproduced by permission of The Gale Group.—Carden, Mary Paniccia. From "Making Love, Making History: (Anti) Romance in Alice McDermott's 'At Weddings' and 'Charming Billy'," in *Doubled Plots: Romance and History.* Edited by Susan Strehle and Mary Paniccia Carden. University Press of Mississippi, 2003. Copyright © 2003 by University Press of Mississippi. All rights reserved. Reproduced by permission.—Hellmann, John. From *American Myth and the Legacy of Vietnam.* Columbia University Press, 1986. Copyright © 1986 Columbia University Press, New York. All rights reserved. Republished with permission of the Columbia University Press, 61 W. 62nd St., New York, NY 10023.—Loss, Archie K. From *W. Somerset Maugham.* Ungar Publishing, 1987. Copyright © 1987 by Archie K. Loss. All rights reserved. Reproduced by permission of The Continuum International Publishing Group.—Malcolm, Cheryl Alexander. From *Understanding Anita Brookner.* University of South Carolina Press, 2002. Copyright © University of South Carolina 2002. Reproduced by permission.—Ruoff, A. Lavonne. From "Alienation and the Female Principle in 'Winter in the Blood,'" in *Critical Perspectives on Native American Fiction.* Edited by Richard F. Fleck. Three Continents Press, 1993. Copyright © by Three Continents Press 1993. All rights reserved. Reproduced by permission.—Sanders, Ivan. From "The Hungarian Identity of Nobel-Laureate Imre Kertész," in *The Treatment of the Holocaust in Hungary and Romania During the Post-Communist Era.* Edited by Randolph L. Braham-Randolph L. Braham. The Rosenthal Institute for Holocaust Studies, 2004. Copyright © 2004 by Randolph L. Braham. All rights reserved. Republished with permission of the Columbia University Press, 61 W. 62nd St., New York, NY 10023.—Sands, Kathleen M. From "Alienation and Broken Narrative in 'Winter in the Blood,'" in *Critical Perspectives on Native American Fiction.* Edited by Richard F. Fleck. Three Continents Press, 1993. Copyright © by Three Continents Press 1993. All rights reserved. Reproduced by permission.—Velie, Alan R. From "'Winter in the Blood' as Comic Novel," in *Critical Perspectives on Native American Fiction.* Edited by Richard F. Fleck. Three Continents Press, 1993. Copyright © by Three Continents Press 1993. All rights reserved. Reproduced by permission.

Contributors

Bryan Aubrey: Aubrey holds a Ph.D. in English and has published many articles on twentieth-century literature. Entries and original essays on *Hotel du Lac, Paradise of the Blind, The Razor's Edge, The Ugly American,* and *Winter in the Blood.*

Tamara Fernando: Fernando is a writer and editor living in Seattle, Washington. Entry and original essay on *The English Patient.*

Joyce Hart: Hart is a freelance writer and author of several books. Entry and original essay on *I Never Promised You a Rose Garden.*

David Kelly: Kelly is an instructor of creative writing and literature in the Chicago area. Entry and original essay on *Midnight's Children.*

Melodie Monahan: Monahan has a Ph.D. in English and operates an editing service, The Inkwell Works. Entries and original essays on *Middlemarch* and *The Stone Diaries.*

Wendy Perkins: Perkins is a professor of American and English literature and film. Entries and original essays on *Charming Billy* and *The Hours.*

Scott Trudell: Trudell is a doctoral student of English literature at Rutgers University. Entry and original essay on *Gravity's Rainbow.*

Carol Ullmann: Ullmann is a freelance writer and editor. Entry and original essay on *Kaddish for a Child Not Born.*

Charming Billy

Alice McDermott
1998

Charming Billy (1998), Alice McDermott's most celebrated novel, focuses on the tragic life of Billy Lynch, an Irish American who comes of age in New York City during the later part of the twentieth century. It opens at his funeral where several of his friends and relatives gather to recall Billy's life within his tight-knit Irish Catholic, Queens community. As they come to offer support to his long-suffering widow Maeve, they celebrate his poetic, gentle soul and mourn his descent into the alcoholism that eventually killed him.

As McDermott weaves together the sometimes contradictory stories from those who have come to remember Billy, she presents a heartbreaking portrait of unrequited love and a masterful depiction of an Irish community that revels in its traditions and remains loyal to its members. In her chronicle of Billy's attempts to realize his dreams and the tragic result of his failures, she creates a poignant tale of love and loss and the tension between romantic illusions and reality.

Author Biography

Alice McDermott was born on June 27, 1953 to Mildred Lynch McDermott and William J. McDermott, who, like Billy in *Charming Billy*, worked for Con Edison. Alice was raised in a middle-class Irish Catholic family in the suburbs of Long Island, New York. She attended elementary school at

Alice McDermott © Jerry Bauer. Reproduced by permission

St. Boniface in Elmont, Long Island, and high school at Sacred Heart Academy in Hempstead, both typical Irish Catholic schools run by the church. Though she never knew her grandparents since both of her parents had been orphaned, her family became a part of the Irish Catholic community in suburban Long Island. Many of her novels reflect her upbringing there during the 1950s and 1960s.

When McDermott was young, she began developing her talent as a writer by writing stories in a notebook. These stories served as self-expression and compensation for her being overshadowed by two outspoken older brothers. After graduating high school in 1971, McDermott attended the State University of New York (SUNY) at Oswego. Her parents were not supportive of her desire to be a writer, since they worried that she might struggle financially. She did, however, find encouragement from her instructors at SUNY, especially from her first mentor Paul Briand, who taught her to be a disciplined writer.

McDermott graduated with a bachelor of arts degree from Oswego in 1975 and moved to New York City where she worked briefly as a clerk-typist for Vantage Press, a job that supplied material and inspiration for her first novel, *A Bigamist's Daughter*, published in the early 1980s. After New York, McDermott pursued a master's degree in fiction writing at the University of New Hampshire. There, she met her second mentor, Mark Smith, who built her confidence in her writing and encouraged her to start sending out her manuscripts for publication.

By 1979, McDermott had completed her master's degree and had her first short story, "Simple Truth," published in *Ms.* magazine. During this time, she also worked as a lecturer and taught English at the University of New Hampshire. A romance developed there with a research neuro-scientist named David Armstrong, whom she married on June 16, 1979.

A Bigamist's Daughter (1982), which focuses on the past's influence on the present, received decent reviews. After this first novel, McDermott and her husband moved to La Jolla, California, where she briefly taught at the University of California. Her second novel, *That Night* (1987), received rave reviews and was a finalist for the National Book Award, the Pulitzer Prize, the PEN/Faulkner Award, and the *Los Angeles Times* Book Award. After moving back to the East Coast with her husband, McDermott again became a finalist for the Pulitzer Prize in fiction with her next novel, *At Weddings and Wakes* (1993).

Charming Billy, published in 1998, was her most popular novel and won her the most acclaim. It won the 1998 National Book Award and spent several weeks on *The New York Times* best-seller list. As of 2005, McDermott and her family live in Bethesda, Maryland, where she manages to balance a life of raising children, engaging in volunteer work, teaching, and writing.

Plot Summary

Part 1

Charming Billy spans three generations of Irish Americans living in Queens, New York, from World War II to the end of the twentieth century. The narrator, whose first name is not given, is the grown daughter of Billy's best friend and cousin, Dennis. She has come home to support her father after Billy is found dying in the street. She begins the story at a funeral party in the Bronx, in 1982, where forty-seven friends and relatives have gathered to mourn and to reminisce about Billy Lynch.

Dennis takes charge of the arrangements for Maeve, Billy's widow, making sure that the party runs smoothly. The narrator begins her description of Billy, an alcoholic who greatly taxed those who loved him, which includes everyone in the room. At this point, Dennis's daughter shares the narrative with various members of the party, who offer their personal memories of Billy.

Their talk turns to Eva, the girl whom Billy loved first and hoped to marry. He met her one summer on Long Island after he and Dennis returned from the war. Eva had been helping her sister Mary with her duties as a nanny for a wealthy family on the island. At the end of the summer, Eva went back to Ireland with Billy's ring to wait for him to have enough money to send for her. After taking on a second job, Billy sent $500 to her. Kate, Billy's sister, remembers that Mary called Dennis soon after and told him that Eva had died of pneumonia, which Dennis then relayed to Billy. It was a blow that the relatives thought he would never endure.

Eventually, he met and married Maeve, whom many thought would be his salvation, but the narrator notes that she "was only a faint consolation, a futile attempt to mend an irreparably broken heart. A moment's grace, a flash of optimism, not enough for a lifetime." They then discuss and argue about his drinking, which increased over the years into full-fledged alcoholism. His sister Rosemary insists alcoholism is a disease and so was not a result of his weakness, but Dan Lynch argues that he would not have drunk himself to death if Eva had not died, noting that Billy had told him "that every year was a weight on his shoulders."

At the end of the party, Dennis admits to his daughter, "Here's the most pathetic part of all. Eva never died. It was a lie." He then takes over the narrative to tell Billy's story, moving back and forth from past to present. He explains that what Mary had actually told him was that Eva had married her hometown sweetheart and kept Billy's money to make a down payment on a gas station. Dennis, fearing that Billy would be devastated by that news, determined that it would be easier for him to think that she died than to know she rejected him for another man.

Dennis tells his daughter that Billy found out that he had lied when Billy decided to make a trip in 1975 to Ireland, where he found Eva married with four children. He admits to her, "it's a bad business. A lie like that," and notes that neither he nor Billy ever told anyone the truth about Eva.

Media Adaptations

- An audio version of the novel read by Roses Prichard is available as of 2005 from *Books on Tape*.

Dennis then describes how hard it was for him when his wife died.

Part 2

Dennis's daughter takes over the narrative, explaining that the Long Island house where Dennis and Billy first met Eva and Mary had been owned by Mr. Holtzman, her grandmother's second husband. She describes her grandmother in her father's words, "the most unsentimental woman he had ever known or heard of," with a single-minded devotion to the truth. Yet, she had convinced Dennis to try to bring Billy out to the Long Island house again, sure that the experience would help him get over Eva.

The narrator moves back and forth in time, filling in bits of Billy's story as it was connected to the Long Island house. She explains that when Billy came back from his trip to Ireland, he came to the house and told Dennis that he saw Eva there. The narrator then goes back to the time when Billy met Eva, noting that he fell in love with her immediately. His natural ability with children helped him impress her as he picked up one of the children in her charge who was crying and calmed him.

Eva became part of his vision of Long Island, representing to him a "golden future," an Eden. As the narrator recreates her version of Billy's proposal to Eva, she suggests that Eva was reluctant to promise to return to the United States, but Billy kept insisting that he would earn enough money to bring her entire family over as well.

The narrator then begins a long story of her grandmother's life, including her need to find something better for herself than the hard lives many Irish immigrants had found in America. Her grandfather, Daniel, had fallen in love with her grandmother, Sheila, in much the same way as Billy had with Eva—immediately. Sheila agreed to marry Daniel because he adored her and because he would be able to provide her with her own home.

Part 3

Back in the present, Dennis tells his daughter that he got Mr. Holtzman to advance Billy the money to send Eva because it was taking Billy too long to save it. He admits that he got caught up in Billy's vision of the future and so decided then that when Billy married Eva, he would marry her sister Mary. Soon after, Mary told Dennis that Eva had married her childhood sweetheart in Ireland, and Dennis later broke off his relationship with Mary.

During this period, Maeve had summoned up the courage to go into Holtzman's shoe store, where Billy had been working to earn the money for Eva. Maeve had fallen in love with him. Billy responded sympathetically to Maeve, who had lost her mother when she was eight, and eventually the two married. The narrator describes the difficult life Maeve had lived, tending her alcoholic father and then later, taking care of Billy as his own alcoholism slowly destroyed him.

The narrator then returns to the present, as Maeve and some of those who had attended the funeral tell sad and humorous stories about Billy as they sit with her at her home. The narrator imagines how difficult it must have been for Billy to live with "the disappointment that lingered at his heart's core" all those years after he lost Eva, and how he drank to forget that disappointment.

The narrator notes how hard it was for Maeve to take care of him and the many nights she had to call Dennis for help in picking Billy up off the floor and getting him up to bed. In the present, Dan and Dennis discuss Billy's character and assess his relationship with Maeve. Dennis remembers the sorrow he felt over the death of his own wife.

Dennis then relates the details Billy told him about his meeting with Eva and he and his daughter try to evaluate Billy's life. The narrator closes with a brief description of meeting her husband, the son of Holtzman's boarder at the Long Island house, and notes that her father eventually married Maeve. After trying to assess her father's and Billy's lives, she closes with an assertion that what is real and what is imagined does not make, "when you [get] right down to it, any difference at all."

Characters

Mr. Holtzman

Mr. Holtzman is Dennis's stepfather and Sheila's second husband. He adores Sheila and is a good provider for her, but he is stingy to others, always denying that he has much money, even though his shoe business is quite profitable. He asks Dennis and Billy to fix up his Long Beach house, where Billy meets Eva, and later, under Dennis's urging, agrees to lend the $500 Billy wants to bring Eva back to the United States.

Billy Lynch

Billy is the focus of the novel as his friends and relatives gather at his funeral to mourn him and to try to understand what led him to drink himself to death. While they all show great loyalty and sympathy for his memory, the narrator notes that Billy had "at some point, ripped apart, plowed through, as alcoholics tend to do, the great, deep, tightly woven fabric of affection that was some part of the emotional life" of all of them.

His friends and relatives, however, focus primarily on their fond memories of Billy: his loyalty, his perseverance, his kindness, and his poetic soul, displayed in the poetry he would recite by memory and his romanticism, which, McDermott suggests, along with his trusting nature, eventually destroyed him.

Billy charmed people with his affectionate nature and his ability "to find whomever he was talking to bright and witty and better than most." He drew out others' charm "with his own great expectations or simply imagined it, whole cloth." Billy had a "need to keep in touch, to keep talking, to be called by name when he entered the crowded barroom, slapped on the back." Yet, he had "half the life taken out of him" when Eva died. Dennis concludes, "for all the love he'd poured out for friends and family for all the years that he lived, he was never . . . loved sufficiently in return," at least not by Eva "whose love he most sought."

Daniel Lynch

Daniel Lynch, Dennis's father, has a similar personality to that of Billy, except exaggerated. The narrator notes that from the moment Sheila married him, her home was not her own. He opened it to anyone who had emigrated from Ireland and needed a place to stay. Daniel "had bankrupted himself and estranged his wife and filled their tiny apartment with far-flung relatives from the other side: simply to know this power, this expansiveness" of giving to others something that they desperately needed.

Danny Lynch

Danny Lynch, another cousin, offers opinions about Billy at the funeral that often provide an alternate view of him. When Rosemary insists, for example, that Billy's alcoholism was caused by genetics and that he would have drunk himself to death even if he had not had his heart broken by Eva, Danny contradicts her, noting how heavy the burden of unrequited love was for Billy.

Dennis Lynch

Dennis Lynch is Billy's cousin and was his best friend. Ironically, he may have destroyed Billy by lying to him about what happened to Eva. When Dennis tells him that Eva died of pneumonia instead of running off with a childhood sweetheart, he helps Billy perpetuate his romantic vision of her and the sense that destiny had cheated him. Dennis tells Billy the lie because of his desire to protect his friend, but he does not think carefully about his inability to recognize reality.

Dennis helps his daughter put the pieces of Billy's story together in an effort to get as accurate a portrait as possible, and also, most likely, to try to assuage his own guilt about telling the lie. He tries to get a clear vision of Billy, but his view inevitably becomes subjective. Dennis admits that he must at times also believe in a romantic vision of reality, which makes the hardships of life so much easier to endure. The narrator concludes that Dennis's and Billy's faith "was no less keen than their suspicion that in the end they might be proven wrong. And their certainty that they would continue to believe anyway."

Kate Lynch

Kate Lynch, Billy's older sister "whose memory had already proven keen," provides yet another view of her brother. She also offers her opinion of Eva, which contradicts Billy's vision of her.

Maeve Lynch

Maeve, Billy's wife, was a homebody, "a plain girl, but determined," which she proves when she decides that she wants to marry Billy. In an effort to see him as much as possible, she finds excuses to return to Holtzman's shoe store where he works, at one point, throwing her father's shoe away so they would have to make the trip. Her plainness had honesty to it, "[a] kind of beauty that was not

a transformation of her simple features but an assertion of them, an insistence that they were no more than what they appeared."

She displays endurance, patience, and loyalty both to her father and then to Billy as the two succumbed to the devastation of alcoholism. She was typical of her generation "wedded to the widowed father." Two important factors in her life—her mother dying when Maeve was young and growing up with a policeman for a father—had given her "some sense early on of the precariousness of life, the risk taken by simply walking out the apartment door."

The relatives suggest that if she did not have her father to take care of, she would have become a nun. Dennis and Dan also doubt if she would "have known what to do with a sober man, with the full force of the affection of a sober man who'd never loved another." McDermott does not make it clear whether Maeve was "Billy's salvation, or at least his second chance" or whether no one could have saved Billy from self-destruction.

Rosemary Lynch

Rosemary Lynch, Billy's sister, is sympathetic to Maeve and determined that Billy's destiny was shaped by his genetic propensity for alcoholism.

Sheila Lynch

Sheila Lynch, Dennis's mother, provides a counter to Billy's romanticism in the novel. She married both of her husbands not for love, but for financial security and, especially, a home of her own. According to Dennis's father, Sheila was "the most unsentimental woman he had ever known or ever heard of." The narrator notes that "she was a Geiger counter for insincerity, phoniness, half-truths."

Dennis was reluctant to bring Billy home after he fell in love with Eva since his mother "sought truth so single-mindedly that under her steady gaze exaggeration, self-delusion, bravado simply dried up and blew away, as did hope, nonsense, and any ungrounded giddiness." Her devotion to logic and clear thinking prompted the community to turn to her for advice when she got older. Yet, she also displayed a softer side as she aged, at one point insisting that Dennis take Billy back to Long Island to help him get over Eva.

Narrator

The narrator, whose first name is never given, returns to Queens to help her father, Dennis Lynch, grieve for his best friend. As she listens to his and others' stories of Billy, she tries to gain an objective vision of the man, which is made easier by both her link to the family and her outsider status. She becomes McDermott's voice as she walks the thin line between illusion and reality that is at the heart of Billy's story. At the end of the book, she reveals that she has married the son of Holtzman's Long Island tenant.

Themes

The Development of Love

Billy's love for Eva develops out of his romanticized vision of the world. Billy has the soul of a poet, often reciting poems by Yeats and jotting down notes to his friends about extraordinary things he has seen or qualities in them that he appreciates. Dennis notes that Billy had "a tremendous willingness to find whomever he was talking to bright and witty and better than most." This eagerness to see the beauty around him prompts him to fall in love with Eva on a beach in Long Island, which had become a magical place for him. He fell in love with her "before she had even come clearly into his view" and then he promptly fell in love with a vision of his future, which, he was certain would be Edenic.

Maeve falls in love with Billy for quite a different reason. She has no romantic visions of him and their life together, knowing what it is like to live with an alcoholic. Dan Lynch concludes that Maeve wanted Billy because he fit the pattern of her life. She had become comfortable in her role as caregiver and supporter in her relationship with her father and recognized that she could fulfill the same role with Billy. Put together, these two patterns of falling in love suggest that the initial attraction can be generated by what a person seeks idealistically or, by contrast, by a person's attraction to the known and familiar, even when those are not necessarily positive.

Unrequited Love

Both Billy and Maeve suffer the painful consequences of unrequited love. While at one point, Billy jokes to Eva that their story is right out of *Romeo and Juliet*, he cannot deny the heartache that he has endured as his love for her became a weight on his shoulders that drove him to drink himself to death. Dennis concludes that "Billy wanted too much," but Billy's romantic vision of Eva compelled him to yearn for nothing less.

Topics for Further Study

- Some reviewers have noted a similarity between Jay Gatsby and Billy Lynch. Read *The Great Gatsby* (1925) and then write an essay comparing and contrasting Gatsby and Billy, their dreams, and the historical/cultural influences on them.

- Investigate alcoholism and in a PowerPoint presentation, note its causes and treatment.

- Maeve's story is presented from Dennis's and Dennis's daughter's point of view. Rewrite the scene at Maeve's house after the funeral luncheon from her point of view.

- If you were to provide illustrations for the novel, what would you depict? Compose a drawing or painting that represents an important element of Billy's story.

Unlike Billy, Maeve quietly accepted the fact that he did not truly love her. She gave up her life for him, Dennis notes, in order to support his dream, hoping "the world would somehow turn out to be just the way he believed it to be." She hoped that "he'd turn out to be right in the end, with all his hanging on to the past. All his loyalty to the dead." When his dream eventually destroyed him, his death almost destroyed her as well.

Loyalty and Support

Many other characters in the novel besides Maeve offered Billy their loyalty and support. Those who gather at his funeral spend their time praising Billy and his gentle humility and kindness as they forgive his destructive behavior. His drunkenness often caused them to banish him until he sobered up, but ultimately, they all did what they could to ease his pain. Yet, not all efforts to help Billy ended positively. Dennis's inability to see his relative and best friend suffer led to the lie that may have destroyed Billy. Maeve's quiet acceptance of his alcoholism also may have ultimately encouraged his destructive impulses.

Style

Multiple Narratives

The novel presents an intricate narrative design made up of stories told by friends and relatives who have come together to remember charming Billy. Rand Richards Cooper writes that this is "a stealthily ambitious work" in its "surprising experiments in form and voice." These "elusive" storytellers not only add pieces to Billy's story; they also, Cooper notes, "stand looking back through the one-way window of assimilation at the lives their parents and grandparents lived." At times, they tell separate stories, and at other times they "compress their talk into a group monologue." Interspersed with these monologues are moments of thoughtful reflection, which Cooper deems to be a reflection of McDermott's "elegiac impulse."

The central narrator is Dennis's daughter, who has come home to Queens to help her father grieve for his dear friend. She is connected to the family enough to understand all of the lives that have been linked by Billy, but she is distant enough to provide a more objective perspective on these resonant and nostalgic tales. She gets many of the details of Billy's story from her father, however, who expresses his view of Billy, which complicates her task. She must fill in the blanks herself, by sifting through the multiple narratives she hears at the funeral in order to present a portrait of Billy that is as accurate as possible.

Historical Context

World War II

The world experienced a decade of aggression in the 1930s that culminated in World War II (1939–45). This global conflict resulted from the rise of totalitarian regimes in Germany, Italy, and Japan. These militaristic regimes rose to power as a result of the Great Depression experienced by most of the world in the early 1930s and from the conditions created by the peace settlements following World War I, specifically the Treaty of Versailles which severely limited Germany and held it responsible of huge debts incurred by World War I. The dictatorship established in each of these three countries encouraged expansion into neighboring countries. In Germany Adolf Hitler strengthened the army during the 1930s with the clear intention of gaining control of other European countries.

In 1936 Benito Mussolini's Italian troops took Ethiopia. From 1936 to 1939 Spain was engaged in civil war involving Francisco Franco's fascist army, aided by Germany and Italy. In March 1938 Germany annexed Austria and in March 1939 occupied Czechoslovakia. Italy took Albania in April 1939. One week after Nazi Germany and the U.S.S.R. signed the Treaty of Nonaggression, on September 1, 1939, Germany invaded Poland. World War II officially began when, on September 3, 1939, Great Britain and France declared war on Germany after a German U-boat sank the British ship *Athenia* off the coast of Ireland. Another British ship, *Courageous*, was sunk on September 19. All members of the British Commonwealth, except Ireland, soon joined Britain and France in their declaration of war.

On December 7, 1941, Japan attacked the U.S. naval base in Pearl Harbor, Hawaii. As a result of the four-hour attack, approximately 2,400 Americans died and 1,300 were wounded. The next day, the United States declared war on Japan. On December 11, 1941, the United States declared war on Germany and Italy after receiving a declaration of war from the two countries. The total number of European casualties by the end of the war in 1945 was approximately 40,000,000. Over 400,000 Americans died.

Irish Emigration

Thousands of Irish men and women immigrated to the United States during the nineteenth century to escape poverty and famine of their native land. The United States became a dream for these people who fled these hardships along with English oppression as they packed themselves tightly into what were referred to as coffin ships due to the hostile living conditions on board, heading for a new home. Initially, their experience of being in the States, however, did not live up to their vision of the good life. Most settled in their arrival ports and were soon herded into the city's tenement sections, from which they had little chance of escape. Each major city, including New York, had its Irish or shantytown where, due to their poverty and prejudice against them, the Irish lived in shacks. Ridiculed for their dress and their accents and blamed for increases in the crime rate, these foreigners were often greeted with "No Irish Need Apply" signs when they looked for employment.

During the twentieth century, however, standards of living improved for Irish immigrants as their children adapted to the new world. Sons born in the United States became plumbers, policemen, and carpenters and settled with their families along the East Coast, especially in Boston and New York. Later, third and fourth generation American-born and educated Irish entered politics and other white-collar professions.

Critical Overview

Reviews of the novel have been overwhelmingly positive. Rand Richards Cooper in his article for *Commonweal* considers *Charming Billy* to be Mc-Dermott's "most challenging [novel] to date" and "incorrigibly digressive, brash with time, intricately layered and crammed full of life."

One of the most highly lauded qualities of the novel is McDermott's style. Cooper notes her narrative expertise when he writes: "The Christian echo of a redemptive, sacrificial quality to Billy's passion could be heavy-handed. But McDermott guards against bathos by making those mourners who explicitly construe Billy as a Christ figure *themselves* seem heavy-handed." A reviewer for *Publishers Weekly* insists that this "poignant and ironic story" is filled "with dialogue so precise that a word or two conjures a complex relationship." The review concludes: "McDermott's compassionate candor about the demands of faith and the realities of living brings an emotional resonance to her seamlessly told, exquisitely nuanced tale."

Cooper also praises the novel's realism: "McDermott isn't content merely to describe a texture of consciousness; she wants to create it, taking the density of Irish Catholic working-class family life, and pressing it into the very molecules of the novel." Starr E. Smith in *Library Journal* adds that the "series of vividly drawn episodes" provide the reader with "an accessible narrative distinguished by strong characterizations and a marked sense of place." In his review for *American Libraries*, Bill Ott determines the novel to be "a heartbreaking story" and notes its accurate depiction of alcoholism. "For a tippler," Ott insists, "the line between charming and pathetic is a thin one. McDermott's genius is that she straddles that line beautifully."

Father John Molyneux, writing for *U.S. Catholic*, finds the novel's themes inspirational: "As the mourners form Billy's tragic story, it becomes a gentle homage to all the lives in their community fractured by grief, shattered by secrets, and sustained by the simple dream of love." Molyneux suggests that through the novel, McDermott challenges "us to recognize the goodness and decency of our family members without sentimentalizing them."

Criticism

Wendy Perkins

Perkins is a professor of American and English literature and film. In this essay, Perkins examines the tensions between illusion and reality in the novel.

Alice McDermott's celebrated novel, *Charming Billy* opens at a funeral luncheon, where forty-seven friends and relatives gather to mourn and to reminisce about Billy Lynch in a Bronx restaurant that could have been taken from a scene in an Irish play by John Millington Synge. The setting, however, is not the only touch of the Irish in the novel. The particular sensibility that Alice McDermott infuses throughout *Charming Billy* reflects what John Millington Synge calls in his preface to his play, *The Playboy of the Western World*, a "popular [Irish] imagination that is fiery and magnificent, and tender." The Irish penchant for employing the imagination in the telling of stories becomes the focus of the novel as McDermott explores the lure of the creative rendering of experience as well as its inevitable clash with reality.

As Billy's friends and relatives gather together at his funeral, each of them feels compelled to tell "the story of his life, or the story they would begin to re-create for him this afternoon." Their versions often conflict with each other, as they focus on love and loss, delusion, and reality. Thrown out of focus by time and private agendas, their colorful stories ask a central question that examines the book's title. Was Billy a charming personality or is the portrait that is created a charming recreation of him? McDermott delineates this tension between imagination and reality when, at the end of the first chapter, after she has given voice to several of these stories, she ends with the truth about the central lie of the book—Eva, the love of Billy's life, never died.

Rand Richards Cooper in his article for *Commonweal* writes: "McDermott frames Billy's life story in ironies, stinting neither the cost nor the complexity of his romanticism." Billy's cousin, Dennis reveals the irony that sets the tone for the entire book when he tells the others about his first view of Billy's corpse. He notes that Billy's face was "bloated to twice its size and his skin was [so] dark brown" from alcoholism that Dennis could not recognize him at first, insisting when he saw the body, "But this is a colored man." This amalgam of illusion and reality begins the novel's examination of Billy and its illustration of the difficulties inherent in the attempt to gain an objective view of reality.

Much of the talk at the funeral focuses on Billy's drinking and its cause. The guests argue over whether Billy's alcoholism was inevitable, springing from an Irish propensity for drink or from his tragic love for Eva. Dennis and his daughter, who as the central narrator tries to weave together all of the stories about Billy into an accurate portrait of him, wrestle with a more complex issue concerning Billy's love for Eva. Was Billy destroyed by Eva's failure to return from Ireland or by Dennis's lie about her having died? Would Billy have been able to accept Eva's rejection more readily than her untimely demise? As Dennis and his daughter struggle to find answers to these questions, they explore the complex nature of illusion and truth and ultimately the vagaries of human destiny.

The question about the effect of the lie becomes central as McDermott dismisses the insistence that Billy's fate was determined by his heritage. Billy's sister Rosemary argues that "Billy would have had the disease whether he married the Irish girl or Maeve," concluding "[e]very alcoholic's life is pretty much the same." Cooper notes, however, that those characters such as Rosemary who blame genetics "come off as pinched and zealous proponents of our era's mistaken urge to collapse tragedy into (mere) pathology: a reductively pragmatic approach, McDermott clearly believes, to the mysteries of human existence."

McDermott adds a nice ironic touch to the discussion the members of the funeral party have of Billy's drinking when she notes the connection between "the drinks in their hands and the drink that had killed him." Yet, she concludes, the enjoyment of the drinks is redeemed "in the company of old friends, from the miserable thing that a drink had become in his life." The gathering of these friends helps redeem "the affection they had felt for him, once torn apart by his willfulness, his indifference, making something worthwhile of it, something valuable that had been well spent, after all." This then becomes the motive of McDermott's storytellers, to discover that valuable essence to Billy, which will prove that his time and theirs "had been well spent, after all."

> The portrait that emerges most clearly of Billy in the narrative is that of a fragile romantic, ultimately destroyed by his unrequited love for a young Irish girl."

The portrait that emerges most clearly of Billy in the narrative is that of a fragile romantic, ultimately destroyed by his unrequited love for a young Irish girl, which he claimed to his cousin Dan, was every year, every hour "a weight on his shoulders." Dennis explains to his daughter that he decided to lie about Eva's fate to try to ease Billy's suffering, claiming, "better he be brokenhearted than trailed all the rest of his life by a sense of his own foolishness." Yet, Dennis remains conflicted about what he has done. Noting the fine line between illusion and reality that was walked by his community, he notes the "audacious, outlandish" nature of the lie and concludes that "the workaday world, the world without illusion (except Church-sanctioned) or nonsense (except alcohol-bred)," the world of the Irish Catholics in Queens, "didn't much abide audacious and outlandish. Not for long, anyway."

Dennis's lie caused Billy to maintain a romantic vision of Eva, one that was constructed by him from the first moment he met her. While the relatives at the funeral cannot agree on whether she was beautiful, and his sister Kate claims that she was "a little chubby," to Billy, she was an angel. The first time he saw her, his nearsightedness caused him to see "her as a mirage of smeared color . . . a mirage that perhaps only wild hope and great imagination could form into a solid woman." He fell in love with her "before she had even come clearly into his view." That afternoon "he fell in love with the rest of his life," which he envisioned now as a "golden future," an "Eden." Billy could not recognize that "adrift in the same world that held their fine future there was accident and disappointment, a sickening sense of false hope and false promise that required all of God's grace to keep at bay."

McDermott refuses to provide a clear, objective portrait of Billy, including any answers concerning the consequences of his devotion to his

What Do I Read Next?

- John Millington Synge's 1907 play *The Playboy of the Western World*, which addresses the theme of illusion and reality, focuses on the reception given to Christy Mahon, as he wanders into a small Irish village, declaring that he has just murdered his father.

- Frank McCourt's *Angela's Ashes*, published in 1996, is an award-winning novel that traces the lives of a poor family in Ireland headed by an alcoholic father.

- McDermott's *A Bigamist's Daughter* (1982) focuses on the impact of the past on the present.

- In *Irish America* (2001), Maureen Dezell chronicles Irish Americans' lives from the 1840s to the beginning of the twenty-first century.

romanticized image of Eva. Dennis recognized the need to devote oneself to an imaginative vision of reality when he gave Billy the money to send for Eva. He understood then "what Billy's fine dream, Billy's faith, was going to come to. But he also saw, in his own . . . romantic heart, that its consummation would become a small redemption for them all." Yet later, Dennis insists that it was better for Billy to discover the truth about Eva so that he "didn't go through his whole life deceived about it. Didn't die thinking about some lovely reunion in the sweet hereafter." Ultimately, McDermott leaves open the question of whether the truth or the illusion about Eva caused Billy to drink himself to death.

McDermott also refuses to take a definitive stance on the effect that Maeve had on Billy's life. At one point, the narrator insists that "her presence in the shoe store was Billy's salvation, or at least his second chance," but by the end of the paragraph, after an attempt to analyze whether the clearly plain Maeve had perhaps a "certain beauty," she concludes that "Maeve was only a faint consolation, a futile attempt to mend an irreparably broken heart. A moment's grace, a flash of optimism, not enough for a lifetime."

The narrator does, however, come to some conclusions. She recognizes the human capacity to believe and to be deceived, and determines, "you can't have one without the other, each one side of the other." In her final assessment of Billy and ultimately of human nature, she concludes that, as with all those gathered together to remember Billy, their faith "was no less keen than their suspicion that in the end they might be proven wrong. And their certainty that they would continue to believe anyway." Billy becomes for them an almost mythical emblem of human frailty as well as a courageous romantic who refused to give up his dreams.

In *Charming Billy*, McDermott deftly illuminates the interpretive gifts of the Irish and the subsequent tension they can produce between imagination and truth. Ultimately, the lure of the dream cannot be reconciled with objective reality, yet, she suggests, we can recognize its ephemeral nature and still persist in reaching out for it, as if "what was actual, as opposed to what was imagined, as opposed to what was believed, made, when you got right down to it, any difference at all."

Source: Wendy Perkins, Critical Essay on *Charming Billy*, in *Novels for Students*, Thomson Gale, 2006.

Mary Paniccia Carden

In the following essay excerpt, Carden explores how McDermott treats "the romance plot's function in the formation of histories and identities" in Charming Billy.

Charming Billy centers in the conflicted imbrication of romance and anti-romance, [and] its multiple interpretations of romance-as-history produce a complex set of responses. Narrated by the unnamed daughter of Dennis Lynch, the title character's cousin and closest friend, the novel begins at Billy Lynch's funeral luncheon. *Charming Billy* moves between 1945 and 1991, as the narrator explores the story of Billy's tragic romance and the ways it has defined not only a common Irish past but also future American generations. Gathered in "a small bar-and-grill" located in the Bronx, which "might have been a pub in rural Ireland." The mourners struggle with the meaning of Billy's life and death. He had been an alcoholic who "had, at some point, ripped apart, plowed through . . . the great, deep, tightly woven fabric of affection that was some part of the emotional life, the life of love, of everyone in the room." In order to "mak[e] something worthwhile" of their investment of affection and faith in him, they must make "something worthwhile" of his romantic story, and by extension of their own "li[ves] of love." According to Dennis Lynch's adult daughter, "You could not redeem Billy's life, redeem your own relentless affection for him, without saying at some point, 'There was that girl.'"

Billy meets Eva, "the Irish girl," on Long Island as he and Dennis enjoy their post–World War II "hiatus . . . between their lives as they were and whatever it was their lives were to become," repairing a cottage belonging to Mr. Holtzman, the man Dennis's mother married after his father's death. In *Charming Billy,* the Long Island house functions as a nexus of competing meanings around love. Dennis's mother is capable of "deflat[ing] the most romantic notion with a single word." She has "no patience for poetry, Broadway musicals, presidential politics, or the pomp of her religion . . . under her steady gaze exaggeration, self-delusion, bravado simply dried up and blew away, as did hope, nonsense, and any ungrounded giddiness." To her the cottage represents stability, not romance; to Dennis and Billy it stands for the perfect union of the two. Having "been here, just like this, all the while [they] had been locked in the adventure and tedium of the war," it represents a bridge to prewar normality and to the security of love and family.

At the beach, the cousins encounter two Irish au pairs; Dennis lays immediate claim to Mary, leaving her sister Eva for Billy. Billy "fall[s] in love" with her "before she had even come clearly into his view." At their next meeting he falls "in love with the rest of his life, and that was better still." It seems to him that like the cottage, "this golden future . . . had been part of the same life he'd been living all along." Unable to see Eva "clearly," Billy imagines her as a kind of fetish of an extended Irish American history. In this space of upper-class privilege, Billy's "golden future" extends the possibilities of his working-class fathers, combining continuing immigration from Ireland with movement up the American social ladder. Billy starts toward this future by asking Eva to stay in the United States. She, however, feels impelled to return to her family in Ireland, prompting Billy's offer to bring them over, as well:

> "That's how my father's family did it. Dennis's father came over first and then brought over his six brothers and his sister, and Lord knows how many more."
>
> . . . "I'll send for you," he told her. . . . "as soon as I save the money I'll send for you. I'll bring you back. Can I do that?"

" *Charming Billy* oscillates between hope and disappointment in heterosexual romance as a controlling metaphor."

> She shook her head only slightly and . . . whispered, "There's still my family."
>
> "I'll send for them, too," he said, and because he heard her laugh a little, perhaps saw her smile, he added, laughing as well, "I'll send for them all, your parents and your sisters and the next-door neighbors if you want me to. Does your town have a pastor—I'll send for him. A milkman? Him too. . . . Is there a baker you're particularly fond of? Any nuns? Cousins? We'll bring them over. We'll bring them all over."

This, he believes, is "what his life had held for him all along"; successful romance with "the Irish girl" would reestablish continuity by replicating his family's model for "creating a future." Like *At Weddings and Wakes, Charming Billy* presents romantic love imbricated with the hopefulness of immigrant dreams and the possibilities of America, a romantic love that stands as metaphor for the historical processes that create Irish Americans.

But Billy receives word that Eva has died of pneumonia in Ireland and later marries the "plain" Maeve, a union that seems "a futile attempt to mend an irreparably broken heart. A moment's grace, a flash of optimism, not enough for a lifetime." Billy's cousin and drinking partner, Dan Lynch, believes that had Eva lived, the family would be gathered to evaluate "'a different life.'" While Dan figures Billy's alcoholism in direct proportion to his loss, Billy's sister Rosemary points to the many alcoholic members of the extended Lynch family and argues that alcoholism "'isn't a decision, it's a disease, and Billy would have had the disease whether he married the Irish girl or Maeve.'" Her assertion that "'every alcoholic's life is pretty much the same'" opposes Dan's view of Billy's romantic agency, his manly loyalty to one true thing.

While Rosemary focuses on Billy's "genetic predisposition" to alcoholism, to a fate he carried "in his genes," Dan insists "'Say he was too loyal. Say he was disappointed. Say he made way too much of the Irish girl. . . . But give him some credit . . . for having a hand in his own fate. Don't say it was a disease that blindsided him and wiped out everything he was.'" This exchange encapsulates the narrative conflict between romance and anti-romance, consent and descent, random fate and truths there all along. Billy's romantic plan to bring Eva, her family, and most of her village to America recapitulates the process of immigration that his community celebrates as the source of their own lives. His plan has failed, but his loyalty upholds the values and priorities that produced the Lynch family in America. While *At Weddings and Wakes* focuses on immigrant sorrow as outcome of history and model for romance, *Charming Billy* posits romance as the primary metaphor for the community itself, regardless, to some extent, of outcome.

Billy's romantic immigrant plan encapsulates communal history in its connections to the community's other hero, center of its other privileged romantic narrative—Dennis's father, Daniel Lynch. Continuously importing relatives from Ireland, Daniel replays an immigrant romance that makes him his community's patron "saint" and revered patriarch. When Billy "cri[es] in his beer that he would not have [Eva's] boat fare by summer," Dennis remarks, "'You're more like my father than my father was.'" "'In this family,'" Billy responds, "his glass to his heart, 'you couldn't say a kinder word.'" Even the outwardly cynical Dennis believes "in his own (his own father's) romantic heart" that the "consummation" of Billy's Irish romance "would become a small redemption for them all." Perhaps this desire to redeem the lives constructed by Daniel Lynch's immigrant dream is behind the lie that Dennis tells Billy, a lie that both perpetuates and ends Billy's romance. Eva did not die young, beautiful, and tragic in Ireland. Instead, she marries a "hometown boy" and uses Billy's passage money for a down payment on a gas station. Dennis invents Eva's death because he believes it would be "better" for Billy to be "broken-hearted" than "trailed all the rest of his life by a sense of his own foolishness." His lie preserves the model of masculinity central to the community's Irish American romance with history by preserving the dignity of the would-be patriarch.

The potential redemption Dennis had invested in Billy's successful conjunction of immigration and heterosexual romance occurs at the gaps in Daniel Lynch's story. His father had been a fisher of men, providing new life in a better place, a role that may have "made him Holy Father to a tenement's worth of Irish immigrants but kept his wife and son mostly impoverished and never—what

with one wetback mick after another being reeled in from the other side and slapped down on their couch—alone in their own home." Daniel's romanticized status is contradicted by the "dark fairy tale" Sheila Lynch tells. Orphaned and alone, she marries Daniel hoping for security and recognition, but instead finds continuing dislocation in "one- and two-bedroom apartments that also served as permanent way stations for an endless string of penniless Irish immigrants." Sheila wakes on "her second morning as a young bride" to find two such immigrants asleep on the floor and "never had [Daniel's] attention all to herself again." Daniel's primary love interaction is with the new arrivals who provide the rewards and satisfactions of his life; his immigrant romance supersedes their romantic couplehood. Dissenting Daniel's myth, Sheila teaches her son the dangers of romantic illusion "in the same careful and loving way another mother might tell a child that the aspirin was not candy and the laundry bleach not fruit punch." So when Dennis prevents Billy from revealing his "rabid infatuation" to Sheila, he protects not only Billy but also his own investment in Billy's dream, a dream that would renew and repair the romantic narrative disputed by his disappointed mother.

Billy misinterprets Dennis's suppression of the Irish girls, assuming that Dennis feels guilty for having had sex with Mary. *Charming Billy* continually reminds us that Dennis also had an Irish girl, insistently referencing an anti-romantic counter plot to Billy's story. But even as his experience shadows Billy's deferral of sexual fulfillment in immigrant desire, Dennis is seduced by Billy's "sweet romance." Romance, it seems, is contagious in all its incarnations: after getting Billy the job and loan that will enable him to bring Eva to America sooner rather than later, Dennis "understood for the first time why . . . his father had bankrupted himself and estranged his wife and filled their tiny apartment with far-flung relatives from the other side simply to know this power, this expansiveness. Simply to be able to say, as he said to Billy that day . . . 'Here you go.' Here's your life." Caught up in this power, he decides to "give [Mary] a ring on the day Billy married Eva." When Mary summons him unexpectedly, he believes she is pregnant and resolves to "marry her immediately," but also realizes that she represents "a future that he only understood now he never honestly wanted." After she delivers the news of Eva's defection, he ends their relationship. Dennis's failed romance with "Irish Mary" highlights the element of chance in Billy's relationship with Eva (what if Dennis had picked Eva instead?) and illustrates Dennis's ambivalent reception of his father's legacy. Mary stands at/as the start of another potential chain of immigrants, positioning Dennis to continue the work his father began. In the story he tells Billy he banishes her to Ireland, space of dead dreams.

Dennis is "stunned" at the "audacity" of his lie, well aware that "the workaday world, the world without illusion (except Church-sanctioned) or nonsense (except alcohol-bred) that was the world of Irish Catholic Queens New York, didn't much abide audacious and outlandish. Not for long, anyway." But although his lie might seem outrageous, its effect is conservative—it preserves his community's romantic view of its history and adjoins its other ordering narratives. Even Dennis falls back on the view of Billy as a tragic hero of romance; as he tells his daughter the truth after the funeral luncheon, he adds that " 'when Billy sets his heart on something there's no changing him. He's loyal. He's got this faith—which is probably why he drinks.' " Dennis, as we have seen, is not alone in this view. In *Charming Billy,* alcohol, romance, and religion converge on multiple levels.

A reviewer of *Charming Billy* characterizes Billy as a "priest of romance, a person who gave to earthly love the priest's loyalty to the divine" (LeClair 27). Romance, like religion, necessitates a leap of faith, an assurance of permanence that promises enduring meaning and reward. When Billy kisses Eva for the first time, it "[is] like inhaling the essence of some vague but powerful alcohol" imbued with "the dark flavor of desire . . . for something he couldn't give a word to—for happiness, sure, for sense, for children—for life itself to be as sweet as certain words could make it seem." Despite the powerful intoxicating effect of love (and gin), he also knows that "adrift in the same world that held their fine future there was accident and disappointment, a sickening sense of false hope and false promise that required all of God's grace to keep at bay." Aware that romance might not be capable of withstanding a cold and random world, Billy seeks the supplement of grace—divine love—as its mirror and affirmation.

As the day of Billy's funeral draws to a close, Dennis's daughter holds a drink (poured symbolically for Billy) and observes that "each sip raised a kind of veil that was both a warmth across the cheeks and a welling in the eyes. A way of seeing, perhaps. Perhaps the very thing that Billy would have found so appealing, had the drink been his." This "way of seeing" alleviates the discordance between faith and disillusionment, between the promise of love and the

experience of loss. When Billy drinks, he experiences "the force of his faith . . . a force he could only glimpse briefly while sober." It becomes "clear and steady and as fully true as the vivid past or the as-yet-unseen but inevitable future. . . . Drunk, when Billy turned his eyes to heaven, heaven was there." Dan Lynch, who insists on the sanctity of Billy's loyalty to Eva, compares him to a priest who sacrifices all to enter "so fully into his faith that it changes the very fabric of his life." In these interconnected locales of faith, the "way of seeing" offered by alcohol, the hopefulness of grace, and the promise of love keep fear and loneliness at bay by offering the assurance that individual lives matter.

While Billy might appear as a "priest of romance," McDermott and her narrator have one eye fixed on the contradictions of such a position—they come clear to Billy himself during his trip to Ireland to take the pledge. Dressed as a priest in order to carry a friend's license and drive his rental car, he sets out to visit Eva's grave. Instead, he finds himself visiting with Eva in her gas station/lunch room. Thirty years later, their summer on Long Island seems "part of a story now, and as a story, it was nothing any of them had truly lived." But, a "married priest," Billy did "truly live" an illusion, and his masquerade reflects his competing identities: true to Eva and to Maeve, romantic hero and maudlin drunk, a "priest of romance" face-to-face with his "thirty years of misdirected prayer." His broken romance, it turns out, was not a matter of fate but of choice; Eva chose Ireland. Her enduring shadow-romance with her hometown boy relocates love to the space Billy's community has left behind, throwing the romance of American lives—the foundation of Daniel's myth—into dispute. Marrying, having children, working in her small business, Eva lives a life quite similar to the life Billy offered. For his part, Billy does not stop drinking, does not tell anyone but Dennis about his encounter with his dead love, and does not die hoping to find Eva in "the sweet hereafter," as his community believes. Billy has defined himself through his romantic faith, and dies with the knowledge that he has lived under false assumptions.

These assumptions are never abandoned by his community, despite the almost universal anti-romance which characterizes their lives. Dan Lynch, a reduced version of his namesake, clings to "the story" that he never married because he "was such a connoisseur of beauty and behavior that no flawed wife could have pleased him and no flawless one could have been found." Sheila glories in her marriage of security, viewing Holtzman as "the embodiment of good sense, practicality, relief, the soundest investment she had ever made." When she rents the Long Island cottage, site of Billy and Eva's projected honeymoon, her tenant's marriage falls apart. Dennis believes that "Mr. West would not have left his wife and three sons" if Sheila "had not been there offering a furnished rental at a year-round, reasonable rate." Billy's sister Kate endures years of browbeating from her aspiring-lawyer husband and is now bejeweled and manicured but alone. Bridie "from the old neighborhood" had "a crush on Billy" when she was young, a crush that "everyone" knew about; Billy, however, deflects her unrequited love by insisting that she "would have married Tim Schmidt if he'd lived." But Tim Schmidt died in the war and the man she later married suffers from advanced Alzheimer's disease.

The narrator incorporates these and other stories into her reconstruction of Billy's, positioning ideals of romantic love beside unfulfilled desire, empty promises, and bitter disappointments. Her own parents' romance, she believes, "ran the typical course from early infatuation to serious love to affection occassionally diminished by impatience and disagreement." Their love, she feels, "is a given," but she also believes that "there were months, maybe years, when their love for each other might have disappeared altogether and their lives proceeded only out of habit or the failure to imagine any other alternative." This acknowledgement of the mundane, even tedious, course of love integrates romance into the "nine-to-five" life that, according to Sheila, makes individuals "what [they] really [are]: one of the so many million, just one more." Dennis views "wife children house" as "the extent of his success," and, like his father before him, is "depend[ed] upon" by "scores of friends and relatives." At bottom, this life does not seem substantially different from the future he rejected with "Irish Mary."

But this "good-enough . . . typical kind of mid-twentieth-century marriage . . . suddenly blossomed into something else in the year [Claire Lynch] was dying," when the narrator's parents claim "their love, their loyalty to one another" as the source of their lives' fulfillment. As love and loyalty become "no longer a matter of chance or happenstance but a condition of their existence no more voluntary or escapable than the pace of their blood," Dennis and Claire view "their meeting, their courtship, their years raising children, every ordinary day they had spent together" as "merely the running start they had taken to vault this

moment. To sail, gracefully and in tandem, across the abyss." Affirming heterosexual union as completeness, their renewed love ameliorates failures, inadequacies, and twists of fate. Here, romance makes something "triumph[ant]" out of ordinary lives, after all.

However, this narrative of successful, satisfying romance, Dennis and his daughter understand, has been belatedly imposed over a sometimes unruly and open disappointing experience. After his wife's death, Dennis could not

> convince himself that . . . the assurance that they had achieved something exclusive, something redemptive in the endurance of their love, had been any more than another well-intentioned deception, another construction, as unbelievable, when you came right down to it, as the spontaneity of a love song in some Broadway musical, the supposedly heartfelt supplication of a well-rehearsed hymn, the bearing any one of Billy's poems . . . had on the actual way any of us lived from day to day.

> He could not convince himself then . . . that heaven was any more than a well-intentioned deception meant to ease our own sense of foolishness, to ease pain.

Taking stock of his life with Claire, Dennis rejects the romantic symmetry that, like the promise of heaven and his lie to Billy, serves to redeem our standing as just "part of the crowd." Later he recants, telling his daughter that " 'it was only a brief loss of faith' " and that he " 'believe[s] everything now. . . . Again.' " "Of course," she notes, "there was no way of telling if he lied."

Even this ambivalent success is withheld from Maeve, whose name, "ironic[ally]," means "intoxicating one." Her childless marriage to Billy seems firmly situated in the realm of anti-romance, only marginal "compensation . . . for what he had lost." "Without [Billy]," Maeve "would have become a nun," and "having chosen this part," she "stand[s] steadily by as his future was formed for her." She tends to Billy as she had to her alcoholic father, and now holds "in her memory . . . a thousand and one moments she would never recount, things he had said to her, terrible things he had done, ways she had seen him (toothless, incoherent, half-clothed, bloodied, soiled, weeping) that she couldn't begin to tell." Maeve's sisters-in-law praise her "loyalty," her "patience" and "endurance," but most of the characters view this form of loyalty as anti-romantic.

Dennis's daughter considers the postcard Billy sent Maeve from Long Island after the Ireland trip. The card—a picture of "Home Sweet Home in East Hampton" with the salutation *beautiful friend*"— may encode an ironic commentary on the romance associated with the Long Island cottage or a transformation of the anti-romance associated with Maeve, an honoring of other forms of constancy. Possibly, it demonstrates Billy's late acceptance of "yet another life, the one that had been waiting for him all along, even while he'd been busy imagining his life with Eva." Or it might simply represent Billy's tendency toward the poetic. The card encapsulates the contradictions of Billy's life, an uneasy balance between his romantic mythos—represented in his loyalty to Eva—and his prosaic life—represented in his loyalty to Maeve. The "Home Sweet Home" card and its inscription in any case illustrate a powerful component of Billy's charm—his ability to make the unbeautiful beautiful, to narrate his life and the lives of others through poetry and prayer, through the language of love and faith. Despite his ugly death and the anti-romantic realities underlying his love story, Billy remains an attractive romantic figure who embodies his community's view of history.

The narrator cannot determine what her father intends that she understand from their exchanges about Billy, Sheila, and Claire, seeing in him "either the near-triumph of faith or the nearly liberating letting go of it." It is also unclear why she repeats the story, interposed with those of other members of the community, to her husband and children. Dennis's daughter met her husband—a son of the Long Island tenant—in the same area Billy met Eva, but is "spared the memory of a first conversation on the same sunny bay beach." Although she and Mr. West's son disavow the conventions of romantic love, "world-wise, open-eyed, without illusion," they "truly believed" then and "would believe on and off again for the rest of [their] lives" that the "whole history of Holtzman's little house" was, "with [their] own meeting, redeemed." This belief positions their romance as the culmination of the familial and cultural histories that the house represents; this, she implies, is what their lives held for them all along. Because we know virtually nothing about the narrator's love relationship, her references to it add another level of complexity to the ambivalent textual view of romance: her (patchy) love plot both echoes and disavows Billy's and her parents'.

Observing that "the claim to exclusivity in love requires both a certain kind of courage and a good dose of delusion," she articulates history as a series of coincidences: "Irish Mary . . . would have been happy enough to accept my father's ring . . . had Eva not chosen to stay in Ireland. . . . My mother's first fiancé would have married her

gladly . . . if my father hadn't beaten him home." The narrator acknowledges similar factors of chance in her meeting with her husband, but also suggests that at their first greeting their children "must have pricked up their ears." Dennis's daughter evokes a fated romantic couplehood to describe her relationship with her husband, yet notes that "there are a hundred opportunities . . . for a sense of falsehood to seep in, for all that we imagine as inevitable to become arbitrary, for our history together to reveal itself as only a matter of chance and happenstance, nothing irrepeatable, or irreplaceable, the circumstantial mingling of just one of the so many million with just one more." As she tells her family's stories of (anti)romance, she acknowledges that love, the thing that we imagine distinguishes us from "the so many million," is the very thing that makes us the same.

Remembering and revising the foundational narratives of her Irish American community, the narrator reviews their lessons about love and history, about meaning and truth in human lives, but finds no satisfying answers. *Charming Billy* concludes with the surprising and (to the narrator, at least) anti-romantic news of Dennis and Maeve's marriage. Dennis and his daughter do not examine this relationship in light of his earlier talk of truth and lies, leaving her to wonder "was it penance . . . compensation for an old and well-intentioned lie, for the life it had deprived her of? Or was it merely taking care. . . . A hand held out once again to whoever happened to be nearby." She does not consider that this might be what their lives had held for them all along. While the narrator does not perceive Dennis and Maeve's relationship as an alternate, perhaps more realistic, expression of love, McDermott leaves this possibility open. Nothing that her father's "capacity for sympathy was no less than Billy's for self-denial," the narrator concludes that "their faith . . . was no less keen than their suspicion that in the end they might be proven wrong. And their certainty that they would continue to believe anyway." Here, the narrator makes an unacknowledged transition, combining the lines of "faith"—romantic and religious—established through the text. Fusing faith in God's redemptive plan with faith in redemptive heterosexual union, she transfers both to a level of mystery that seems to transcend logic, philosophy, even experience.

Dennis says, "'every one of us is living proof . . . that it's a powerless thing, this loving one another, nothing like what [Billy] had imagined. Except in the way it persists.'" He marries Maeve in the church he attended during the Long Island hiatus, renamed from "St. Philomena's" to "Most Holy Trinity." Philomena had been "tossed out of the canon of saints . . . because some doubt had arisen about whether or not she had actually lived." Dennis's daughter, however, is not convinced that "in that wide-ranging anthology of stories that was the lives of the saints—that was, as well, my father's faith and Billy's and some part of my own—what was actual, as opposed to what was imagined, as opposed to what was believed, made, when you got right down to it, any difference at all." While the narrator views the romance that structures individual lives and cultural histories as "imagined," even illusory, she also finds that its "actual" truth or falsity does not diminish its force as "belief," as epistemological foundation of the various faiths that give lives meaning.

We have been taught that those who do not learn from history are condemned to repeat it. In McDermott's novels, as well as in a much of Western literature and culture, romance, which is endlessly repeated, stands as history. McDermott's characters understand their Irish American history as a reflection of the promises of the heterosexual romance plot, which creates the possibilities of their lives. Here, history is romance and romance is history. But this equation labors under the constant pressure of anti-romance, of the failure of heterosexual union to provide the transcendence it promises. The pervasive anti-romance of *At Weddings and Wakes* denies the power of love to redeem individual lives, while *Charming Billy* oscillates between hope and disappointment in heterosexual romance as a controlling metaphor. If romance stands as the historical screen upon which we project our lives, then McDermott's narrators have stepped briefly behind it. The screen, once dislodged, does not completely return to its original position, leaving the projection to play into the darkness behind. Fixed and de-centered, present and absent, true and false, romance-as-epistemology evokes yet continually defers solid meaning in individual lives and cultural histories.

McDermott "writes beyond the ending" (DuPlessis 5) by insisting that romance never resolved itself and that happily-ever-after dreams continue to recede before us. Love—situated as the privileged source of balance and stability for individuals and cultures—produces abiding uncertainty. In *At Weddings and Wakes* and *Charming Billy* McDermott melds romance and history into a single story, a story that is both necessary to individual and cultural self-definition and "nothing any of them had truly lived." Her novels center around

efforts to sort "truth" from "story," but demonstrate that such a distinction is finally impossible, that those epistemological "truths" which structure our lives are a function of story. And romance is the story we seem to know best.

Source: Mary Paniccia Carden, "Making Love, Making History: (Anti) Romance in Alice McDermott's *At Weddings* and *Charming Billy*," in *Doubled Plots: Romance and History*, edited by Susan Strehle and Mary Paniccia Garden, University Press of Mississippi, 2003, pp. 3–23.

Rand Richards Cooper

In the following essay, Cooper reviews McDermott's previous works, then discusses the "wildly discursive" style of Charming Billy *and the reason for the "elusive, anonymous quality of McDermott's narrators."*

One of the pleasures of going back to a talented writer's early work is finding the promising failure, the intriguingly bad book.

Alice McDermott's first novel, *A Bigamist's Daughter* (1982), told the story of a Manhattan vanity press editor romantically involved with one of her luckless writers. Burdened with backstory, plot contrivances, and stilted dialogue ("Some love goes even beyond the lover himself. . . . Love that's like a spiritual life, like pure faith. . . ."), the novel was a classic case of a writer fighting her own strengths. It was bad in the way some clothing is bad: it just didn't fit. Bent on a single point-of-view protagonist, McDermott restrained a powerful storytelling impulse and ended up making her characters speak her own themes. She used awkward plot moves to steer the novel toward what she really wanted to write about, namely, not her heroine's present but her past—a child's perception of the physical world and the stubborn mysteries of adulthood. *A Bigamist's Daughter* was ostensibly a smart '80s novel about a woman finding her strength. But trapped inside it was very different book, less breezy and ironic, more lyrical and backward-looking, and far less narratively conventional.

McDermott's subsequent career has been a matter of setting this trapped book free. *That Night* (1987), a sparkling, swooning evocation of a lost era, related the events of a summer evening in a 1960s Long Island suburb, when a gang of hot-rodding town toughs, attempting to steal away their leader's girlfriend, does battle with the fathers of the neighborhood. The story is told, retrospectively, by a nameless narrator who watched the rumble as a ten-year-old, and whose own adult identity is subordinated to her role as witness to the past—in effect, a stand-in omniscient narrator, telling the story and its ramifications from all angles. The close focus on one event enabled McDermott to range widely through time, and in and out of the various characters as well, creating the novel's blend of tight control with lyrical expansiveness, and giving vent to a sensibility at once rapturous and haunted.

If *That Night* discovered its author's preoccupations—memory and the world of the child, the character of community, the power of desire, the evanescence and permanence of time, the ironies of fate—*At Weddings and Wakes* (1992) pushed them further. The novel studies an Irish-Catholic family in New York, circa 1960, through the eyes of two girls and a boy brought on weekly visits from their home on Long Island to their grandmother's apartment in Brooklyn, where through endless afternoons the children's mother and three aunts pour out decades of pent-up disappointments, hopes, and recriminations. Though the fate of one of the aunts figures as a recurring fugue theme, the novel is less plotted than painted. The coffee table with its doily, plastic flowers, and dish of sugared almonds; the family photographs; everything draped and dim and airless, and from the next room the muffled sound of someone sobbing: it is an achingly detailed tableau of lace-curtain Irish despair.

At Weddings and Wakes is the only novel I can think of told from a third-person-plural point of view, a narrative built on "The children saw . . ." and "To the younger girl it seemed that. . . ." Yet the children's individual identities are strangely blurred; we barely learn their names, and other than a few parenthetical asides which sweep us decades ahead, we get no glimpse of their subsequent, adult lives and selves. This too is an extension of an impulse already evident in *That Night*. Indeed, an odd disjunction between the extravagant detail of her descriptive writing and an unwillingness to individuate the point-of-view character has figured increasingly as a hallmark of McDermott's style. Reading *At Weddings and Wakes* is a bit like being carried to a window on the shoulders of anonymous porters. Inside is a world where wedding-party bands play "Galway Bay" as men tell stories of Gentleman Jimmy Walker or a voice calls out "Sweet Jesus, don't mention Parnell!"; where children are taught the lives of the saints by nuns with names like Sister Illuminata. *At Weddings and Wakes* took the lyrical sadness of *That Night* and joined it to something like ethnography. Written in a lovely prose that quivers at the brink

> **The mildly deprecating irony McDermott reserves for what might be called post-Irish life suggests ambivalence about the trade-offs that come with breaking free of one's roots."**

of sentimentality—this is a writer who can make even a door, "easing itself closed with what sounded like three short sorrowful expirations of breath," seem wistful—it is a nostalgic and immaculately detailed valedictory to a vanishing corner of Irish Catholicism.

McDermott's new novel, *Charming Billy,* is her most challenging to date—incorrigibly digressive, brash with time, intricately layered and crammed full of life. Set in 1983, *Charming Billy* focuses on three days following the funeral of Billy Lynch, WWII veteran, long-time employee of Con Edison, and lifelong resident of Irish-Catholic New York (Queens, to be exact). Through the reminiscences of family and friends we meet an incurable romantic who drank himself to death at sixty: a Billy who charms older ladies in restaurants; calms a woman's baby by murmuring Yeats's "Down by the Sally Gardens"; writes notes on napkins to send to the priest; calls his cousin and best friend, Dennis, in the middle of the night to rail drunkenly against death and the passing of all things. It is a rousing, tender rendition of that stock Irish figure, the poetic rogue in love with his sorrows. Is that a breviary in Billy's jacket pocket, or a flask?

Behind his sorrow lies a tale of deception and lost love. McDermott takes us to Long Island in the summer of 1945, where Billy meets and courts a young Irish nanny named Eva. Back in Ireland, she agrees to marry him, accepts the money he saves to send for her passage—and then is heard from no more. Through a go-between Dennis uncovers the banal truth (Eva has married another man and used the $500 to open a gas station), but tells Billy instead she died of pneumonia. The impulsive lie inaugurates Billy's decades of grieving devotion to her memory—he eventually marries, but stays true in his heart to Eva—and places in the novel's foreground the proposition that a life of deluded passion is better than one of clear-eyed disillusion.

Critics have likened McDermott to Joyce; but there's also a lot of F. Scott Fitzgerald in this novel—Billy an Irish workingman's Gatsby, Eva his Daisy, and Ireland itself, perhaps, the green light over the water. Like Gatsby, Billy conflates romance with poetry; kissing Eva on the beach in 1945 he feels, McDermott writes, "a desire for life itself to be as sweet as certain words could make it seem. . . ." But McDermott frames Billy's life story in ironies, stinting neither the cost nor the complexity of his romanticism. First there are the ravages of alcohol and its punishing toll on the body: the downside of poetry is, literally, morbidity. Then there's the fact that Billy's tragedy is founded on a lie. And for whose benefit? His goodness of heart gets soaked up by friends and relatives whose hurting he does for them: he loves and loses; he keeps the faith.

The Christian echo of a redemptive, sacrificial quality to Billy's passion could be heavy-handed. But McDermott guards against bathos by making those mourners who explicitly construe Billy as a Christ figure *themselves* seem heavy-handed. Still, those who dismiss Billy's suffering as the "genetic disease" of alcoholism—there's an Uncle Ted, an evangelical AA member—come off as pinched and zealous proponents of our era's mistaken urge to collapse tragedy into (mere) pathology: a reductively pragmatic approach, McDermott clearly believes, to the mysteries of human existence.

Charming Billy is a stealthily ambitious work of fiction. Under the cover of a realist's reverence for descriptive detail and a romance writer's duty to affairs of the heart, McDermott conducts surprising experiments in form and voice. At times she's content simply to sit her characters around a table and quote speaker after speaker, or to compress their talk into a group monologue of page-spanning paragraphs that reads like an unedited transcript. Elsewhere, her narrator steps forward with pronouncements that have a Jane Austen-like ring: "In the arc of an unremarkable life, a life whose triumphs are small and personal, whose trials are ordinary enough, as tempered in their pain as in their resolution of pain, the claim of exclusivity in love requires both a certain kind of courage and a good dose of delusion." An elegiac impulse plays freely with her sentences, lending a curious, huffing quality:

> He had, at some point, ripped apart, plowed through, as alcoholics tend to do, the great deep, tightly woven fabric of affection that was some part of the emotional life, the life of love, of everyone in the room.

How lonely they all seemed to me that night, my father's family and friends, lonely souls every one of them, despite husbands and children and cousins and friends, all their hopes, in the end, their pairings and procreation and their keeping in touch, keeping track, futile in the end, failing in the end to keep them from seeing that nothing they felt, in the end, has made any difference.

There's a fine line between the exquisite and the laborious, and such writing risks becoming a parody of lyricism. There's something almost willful in the baroque extravagance of McDermott's style. It's as if she feels her previous books haven't gone far enough, that this time she's determined not merely to write *about* loss, but to take it down into the basic structures of the novel itself, fashioning a syntax of melancholy, a prose that gasps with sadness and doubles back on itself like the tangled contingencies of fate.

So too with the profusion of characters and their stories. *Charming Billy* seems wildly discursive, chronicling not merely the principal players in Billy's life, but much of the large supporting cast as well. You may find yourself flipping back to check which Daniel Lynch this is (there are two) or whose Uncle Jim worked at Edison back in '37; or wondering how you got onto the story of Billy's cousin's mother's Great-Aunty Eileen. Who *are* all these people? Again, McDermott isn't content merely to describe a texture of consciousness; she wants to create it, taking the density of Irish Catholic working-class family life and pressing it into the very molecules of the novel. It's as if the welter of names and stories—or rather our resistance to it—reveals our own attenuated capacity for family life. Reading *Charming Billy* one feels at times something like the strangeness, the scratchy bewilderment, of things perceived across a cultural divide.

Which brings us, finally, to the narrator. *Charming Billy* is told by the daughter of Billy's cousin Dennis, but through much of the novel you'd hardly notice it. She's a rather ghostly presence, never named, often present in the room but listening far more than talking. Only in the margins of the story do we get the skimpiest hints at her own life: a college graduate, married, living in Seattle with her children and husband. Readers of McDermott's last two books, recognizing yet another version of the trademark stealth narrator, may wonder, why not simply dispense with her altogether? Why bother to bring the narrator in as an actual character if you're not going to fill her out? It would be easy enough to toss the crutch aside and let an omniscient narrator take the slow drift back through the decades of Billy's life.

But there's a reason for the elusive, anonymous quality of McDermott's narrators. Third-generation Irish Americans situated at the end of a progression that goes urban New York, suburban Long Island, Somewhere Else, they stand looking back through the one-way window of assimilation at the lives their parents and grandparents lived. It is a crowded picture, replete with emblems of a no-frills urban Irish Catholicism; a funeral party over roast beef and boiled potatoes; characters with names like Mickey Quinn or Bridie "from the old neighborhood" (famous for her pound cake, made with a full pound of butter); men who stop after work at Quinlan's for a quick drink before Friday Mass and who call their wives "Mama"; apartment living rooms where the brocade sofa with its plastic slipcovers stands beneath a framed copy of the Irish Blessing as a new widow sobs in grief, and the Monsignor, stopping to offer solace, is welcomed with awe and deference, like a movie star.

For better and for worse, this is the life of ethnic and religious community—loud, close-knit, restrictive. And it is a life McDermott's point-of-view characters have left behind. In *Charming Billy* the narrator's few comments about herself make clear who she is: "I married Matt and we headed off to Seattle. Lives of our own, we said. Self-sacrifice having been recognized as a delusion by then, not a virtue. Self-consciousness more the vogue."

Lives of our own, we said. The mildly deprecating irony McDermott reserves for what might be called post-Irish life suggests ambivalence about the trade-offs that come with breaking free of one's roots. Yes, things are gained: mobility, a change of scenery, freedom—including sexual freedom—education and professional status, and so on. But much gets lost. To shrug off the burdens of group identity is also to shrug off ferocious attachments; and McDermott's novels express doubt about whether, as ties attenuate and the old neighborhood sinks further into the past, anything as vivid and nourishing will take their place. The grand struggle to wrest one's self from the group delivers her protagonists to this deeply American paradox: that getting a life of your own brings a diminished sense of who you are. Hence the ghostly narrators. *Charming Billy* bids farewell both to Billy and to

his entire way of life, its nameless narrator sent back to inspect a world where everyone owned a piece of you from one where identity rests on the still more perilous ground of self-discovery. Who *is* this person looking back with such regret and longing?

Source: Rand Richards Cooper, "Charming Alice: A Unique Voice in American Fiction," in *Commonweal*, March 27, 1998, pp. 10–12.

Sources

Cooper, Rand Richards, "Charming Alice: A Unique Voice in American Fiction," in *Commonweal*, March 27, 1998, pp. 10–12.

McDermott, Alice, *Charming Billy*, Random House, 1999.

Molyneux, Father John, Review of *Charming Billy*, in *U.S. Catholic*, November 2004, p. 33.

Ott, Bill, "Tipplers," in *American Libraries*, March 2000, p. 85.

Review of *Charming Billy*, in *Publishers Weekly*, October 6, 1997, p. 73.

Smith, Starr E., Review of *Charming Billy*, in *Library Journal*, November 1, 1997, p. 116.

Synge, John Millington, Preface to *The Playboy of the Western World*, in *The Playboy of the Western World and Other Plays*, Oxford University Press, 1998, pp. 96–97.

Further Reading

Charles, Ron, Review of *Charming Billy*, in the *Christian Science Monitor*, November 28, 1998, p. 18.
　　While Charles praises McDermott's technique in the novel, he ultimately finds its theme cynical.

Griffin, William D, *The Book of Irish Americans*, Crown Publishing, 1990.
　　This illustrated book chronicles the immigration of seven million Irish to America and their more than 40 million descendants.

Milam, James Robert, and Katherine Ketcham, *Under the Influence: A Guide to the Myths and Realities of Alcoholism*, Bantam, 1984.
　　The authors present a comprehensive overview of the causes and treatment of alcoholism.

Skow, John, Review of *Charming Billy*, in *Time*, January 12, 1998, pp. 87–90.
　　Skow declares the novel to be shrewd in its sketch of lower-middle-class Irish life.

The English Patient

Michael Ondaatje

1992

The English Patient tells the stories of four individuals whose lives come together at the end of World War II in an abandoned Italian villa: Hana, a 20-year-old nurse from Canada who seeks refuge from the proliferation of wartime death; Kirpal (Kip) Singh, a 25-year-old "sapper," or bomb dismantler, from India who is a member of the British Army; David Caravaggio, a friend of Hana's father who worked as a spy during the war and was severely disfigured while a captive of the Germans; and Hana's patient, a severely burned man whose identity is the mystery at the heart of this novel. Each of these characters finds him or herself far away from home, displaced by the war, and each of them finds a quiet refuge in the abandoned Italian villa to reconstruct their lives. While Hana and Kip eventually develop a romantic relationship, Caravaggio becomes more and more obsessed with the patient's true identity: Caravaggio believes that the patient may not be English, as everyone assumed, but a Hungarian who worked as a spy for the Germans. Interspersed into the story of the lives of these characters together in Italy are each character's clear recollections of the past, including the patient's hallucinatory memories of a torrid love affair, of desert exploration, and of friendship and betrayal. The novel becomes a collage of memories that explores themes of war, nationality, identity, loss, and love.

Michael Ondaatje, previously known as a poet, received immense critical and popular acclaim for *The English Patient*. The book earned The Booker Prize for best novel of 1992.

Author Biography

Poet and novelist Michael Ondaatje is perhaps best-known for his novel *The English Patient*, which focuses on an international group of characters isolated together in an abandoned Italian villa at the end of World War II. The novel explores themes of nationhood, identity, and displacement; the exploration of such themes seems to have arisen from Ondaatje's own life experiences. He was born in Colombo, Sri Lanka, on September 12, 1943, to parents Philip Mervyn Ondaatje and Doris Gratiaen. Ondaatje's family was what is known as Burgher—a minority but affluent class of people descended from the South Asian island's non-British European colonists. He spent his early childhood in Sri Lanka; after his parents divorced, he moved with his mother and siblings to England. He subsequently moved to Canada, where he attended the University of Toronto, graduating with a bachelor's degree in 1965. His experience of inhabiting several countries throughout his life, and his multi-ethnically influenced childhood, have greatly informed and shaped the themes of his writing.

Ondaatje started his writing career as a poet—in fact, his primary focus as a poet greatly influences the style of his prose. His first collection of poems, *Dainty Monsters*, was published in 1967. His first work of prose, *Coming through Slaughter* (1976), is an experimental biography of New Orleans jazz legend Buddy Bolden. In the latter part of the 1990s, Ondaatje published *Handwriting*, a collection of poetry (1998) and the novel *Anil's Ghost* (2000), which is about the violent civil war between the Sinhalese government and the Tamil separatists in Sri Lanka. Ondaatje had written about Sri Lanka previously in the critically acclaimed memoir *Running in the Family* (1982), in which he recounts his family's history in Sri Lanka, colonialist life on the South Asian island, and his own childhood.

The English Patient (1992) was awarded the Booker Prize for that year, and became a bestseller, making Ondaatje one of Canada's most famous writers and the most well-known writer of Sri Lankan origins. *The English Patient* was adapted as an Academy Award–winning film in 1996.

Since 1970, Ondaatje has been a member of the faculty of the Department of English at Glendon College at York University, in Toronto. Ondaatje also serves as the editor of Brick, a Literary Journal, for which his wife, Linda Spalding, is also an editor. The journal is published twice a year out of Toronto.

Michael Ondaatje   © Christopher Felver/Corbis

Plot Summary

Chapter 1: The Villa

Near the end of World War II, a young Canadian nurse, Hana, is living in an abandoned Italian villa with a severely burned patient. Hana had decided to stay behind with her patient, who was too fragile to move, after her hospital regiment moved on. Hana does not know the patient's identity, but she tries to piece together his story from his fragmentary hallucinations. She thinks he is English.

Hana passes her time by reading to the patient from the villa's large library, as well as cleaning, gardening, and perusing books by herself. The war has left her emotionally scarred.

The patient remembers crashing a plane in the desert. A tribe of desert people find him and tend his badly burned body. They transport him across the desert as they care for him. As he heals, he serves them by identifying European-made weapons found hidden in the desert.

Chapter 2: In Near Ruins

Caravaggio, who knew Hana through her father in Canada, seeks her out at the villa. Hana had learned six months earlier that her father was killed in the war; Caravaggio knows of his death as well.

Media Adaptations

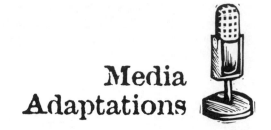

- An audio edition of *The English Patient*, narrated by Michael York, was issued by Random House in 1993.
- A film version of *The English Patient*, directed by Anthony Minghella, was released in 1996. It won several Academy Awards, including Best Picture, Best Director, and Best Supporting Actress for Juliette Binoche, who played the character of Hana.

Caravaggio, a former thief who worked as a spy during the war, tells Hana that his thumbs were cut off by the Germans after they captured him. When he wonders why they stopped at his thumbs, Hana tells him it is because the Germans were being forced to retreat from Italy.

Chapter 3: Sometime a Fire

A Sikh sapper (military explosives specialist), part of a British regiment, joins the group at the villa. The Sikh sets up his tent at the villa gardens. He is there with a sapper regiment to defuse the bombs of the area, which the Germans have left everywhere in the wake of their retreat.

Sometime after his arrival at the villa, Kip is working with intense concentration on defusing a bomb just outside the villa; coming upon a "trick" in the bomb's wiring he finds himself in need of assistance, and yells for help. Hana runs out and assists him, in spite of the danger to herself, until Kip successfully defuses the bomb. They curl up together, exhausted, in their very first moment of intimacy.

That evening, Caravaggio brings home a pilfered gramophone, and the foursome have a small celebration in the patient's room. Kip suddenly leaves when he hears an explosion; another sapper, Hardy, had been killed while trying to defuse a bomb. Kip returns hours later and finds Hana still in the patient's room. He crosses the room to be with her, snipping the wires of the patient's hearing aid so the patient will not hear them.

Chapter 4: South Cairo 1930–1938

Told from the point of view of the patient, this chapter consists of fragments of the patient's past: he had been part of an inter-European expedition mapping the Libyan deserts before World War II. In 1936, Geoffrey Clinton, a young Englishman, joins the patient's company in the desert, bringing with him his new, young wife, Katharine.

Chapter 5: Katharine

Told mostly from the point of view of Katharine Clifton, this chapter is a series of short accounts of the genesis of her relationship with the patient: her dreams of him; their somewhat violent lovemaking; awaking in their room in Cairo to the sound of morning prayers. He, in the meantime (although he has told her to claim no ownership over him), grows more and more obsessed with her and more and more disturbed by having to pretend in public that their relationship does not exist. She insists, for the sake of her husband's sanity, that they end the affair. The separation is heartbreaking for both of them, but neither lets the other know.

Chapter 6: A Buried Plane

Caravaggio believes that the patient is the Hungarian Count Ladislaus de Almásy, a desert explorer who helped the Germans navigate the deserts on numerous occasions. Caravaggio knows everything about Almásy because he had tracked his movement across the desert. Despite Hana's protestations, Caravaggio drugs the patient into a hallucination to get to the bottom of his identity.

In 1939, Geoffrey Clinton had attempted a murder/suicide by trying to crash his plane into the patient in the desert. Katharine was in the plane with him. He did not hit the patient, but Clifton was killed and Katharine severely wounded; the totaled plane left the patient and Katharine with no transportation out of the desert. The patient leaves Katharine in a desert cave and goes on foot in search of help. The patient is taken captive because the dessert is now a war zone, and he is thought to be a spy for the Germans. He is only able to return to Katharine years later. When he reaches the cave, he finds her body and carries her from the cave to a hidden plane. While flying out of the dessert, the plane catches fire, burning the patient, and then crashes.

Chapter 7: In Situ

Kip was the second son in his family. Although it was traditional for the second son to become a doctor, he enlisted in a Sikh regiment instead and was shipped to London, where he was selected by Lord Suffolk as part of a new sapper regiment. Kip was 21 years old when he joined the regiment, and he highly valued the intimate friendship he developed with Lord Suffolk and his assistants, Miss Morden and Mr. Fred Harts, especially because his experience with the rest of the army had been one of social alienation because of his race.

Kip tells Hana of the bomb that exploded and killed Lord Suffolk, Miss Morden, and Mr. Harts; however, he does not discuss their deaths at all. Rather, his story concentrates on his own efforts in continuing Lord Suffolk's failed attempts to dismantle a new type of bomb, which he succeeds at after much suspense. In the meantime, Kip tucks away the memory of his friends, so as not to let his anguish disturb his work. He does not share his grief with Hana.

Chapter 8: The Holy Forest

Hana, Caravaggio, and Kip lead a quiet and private life, together in the villa, with the patient. They bring a ladybug from the garden for the patient to look at; they play hide-and-go-seek in the darkness of the library.

Chapter 9: The Cave of Swimmers

Told in the first-person voice of the patient, as he speaks to Caravaggio during a morphine-induced conversation, the patient continues to fill in more details about his past with Katharine Clifton. He finds himself secretly falling deeper and deeper in love with Katharine, and after she had been in their company for more than a year, it is Katharine who initiates their affair by casually informing him that she wants him "to ravish" her.

The patient's story segues into recollections of his good friend Madox who had been with him in the desert for ten years. Madox returned to England after the war broke out and the desert group was forced to disband. While at church with his wife, during a sermon praising the war, Madox shot himself to death.

The patient shifts into speaking in a third-person voice about Almásy and Katharine Clifton in Cairo, leading Caravaggio to wonder who he is speaking as now. The patient does not ever admit that he and Almásy are the same person.

Almásy brings Katharine, injured from the plane crash, to the Cave of Swimmers, and leaves her there to go for help. He walks through the desert until he comes to an English base at El Taj. The English soldiers there take him captive, thinking

that he is an enemy spy because of his Hungarian name. He is unable to return to Katharine until, years later, he begins transporting German spies across the desert. When he returns to her, he cradles her decomposing body in the silence of the cave.

Chapter 10: August

Kip is in Naples in October, 1943, where a German soldier who turns himself in confesses that the harbor is wired with thousands of bombs that will explode when the city's power is turned on. The city is evacuated except for 12 sappers. They spread throughout the city and conduct the work of dismantling and re wiring until the hour that the electricity is to return. Kip waits in a church until the electricity comes back. No bombs explode.

Back at the villa at the present moment, Kip storms angrily into the patient's bedroom, pointing his gun angrily at him. He has just heard that the United States has bombed Hiroshima. The realization of the injustice of the American and British-led policies against the non-Western countries of the world forces Kip to question why he, as a Sikh, is fighting a British war. He walks out on the patient, on Caravaggio, and especially, on Hana.

Sometime after Kip leaves, but before her patient dies, Hana writes a letter to her stepmother, Clara, in which she openly discusses the death of her father, Patrick, for the first time. The letter represents a catharsis for Hana.

Years later, Kirpal Singh, now a doctor in India with a wife and children, sits and thinks about Hana, who is now in Canada. Hana, in her kitchen in Canada, knocks a glass from the cabinet. At that same moment, Kirpal Singh catches a fork in midair, which had been dropped by his daughter, symbolizing a metaphysical connection between Hana and himself, though they are separated by the politics of their nations and the physicality of their continents.

Characters

Count Ladislaus de Almásy
See The English Patient

David Caravaggio
A middle-aged Canadian of Italian descent, Caravaggio, who was a professional burglar in Toronto, had joined the war effort as a spy for the Allies in Italy. He is an old friend of Hana's father,

and when he hears that she is staying in an abandoned villa with a burn patient, he joins her there after his release from the hospital. His thumbs had been cut off while he was held captive and tortured by the Germans immediately prior to their retreat from Italy. He has developed an addiction to morphine.

Caravaggio, like the patient, represents a father figure to Hana. He is concerned about her health and safety and often tries to convince her to leave the abandoned villa. Hana remembers him as having been a gregarious and confident man, but the war and the torture have broken his spirit. He and Hana often sadly reminisce about their lives in Toronto before the war. Caravaggio is also a sort of a nemesis to the patient, as he is obsessed with the patient's true identity: he believes that the patient is not an Englishman but a spy who worked for the Germans. Because of his obsession with the patient's identity, he drugs him again and again into lucid hallucinations in order to pry his story from him. By the end, however, the patient's tragic story has removed any trace of Caravaggio's anger towards him.

In a novel that takes the futility of war on as a major theme, Caravaggio is a personification of this futility. As well as being the most vocal about his disdain for the war and its waste, his maimed hands are both evidence and symbols of its futility.

Geoffrey Clifton

An Englishman of high social standing, Geoffrey Clifton joins Almásy, Madox, and the rest of the Geographical Society desert expedition during the last days of his honeymoon with his new wife Katharine. He is a pilot with a good-natured personality; his wife is the apple of his eye, and he constantly boasts to the company of her beauty. It is later revealed that Clifton is a spy for the English government, keeping tabs on the international band of desert explorers.

Although Almásy and Katharine attempt to keep their affair a secret, Clifton eventually learns of the affair. On a trip back to the desert to retrieve Almásy, Clifton attempts to crash his plane into him; he misses Almásy but kills himself and mortally wounds Katharine.

Katharine Clifton

Fifteen years his junior, Katharine Clifton becomes Almásy's lover for a relatively brief and turbulent time. They had become acquainted during the Geographical Society expeditions in the Libyan desert, which Katharine's husband took her to during the last days of their honeymoon. She becomes enamored with the desert, and her growing interest in the desert is matched by her growing interest in Almásy, who is also secretly falling in love with her. She initiates the secret, and often somewhat violent, sexual affair, but the pressure of keeping it secret, coupled with her guilt, causes her to break it off—a move that breaks Almásy's heart, though he would not admit it to her.

When Clifton crashes his plane into the desert in an attempt to kill Almásy, he kills himself and mortally wounds Katharine. Almásy leaves her in a cave while he goes for help; she dies when he is unable to return to her. Katharine's death is the patient's greatest source of anguish. His inability to save her is the ultimate reason he renounces his identity.

The English Patient

The identity of the English patient is the crux of the mystery at the heart of this novel; his identity remains somewhat ambiguous even to the end of the novel. Burned beyond recognition, the patient is introduced to the young Canadian nurse, Hana, in an Italian hospital. She stays on with him at an abandoned Italian villa after her hospital regiment moves on. Through several fragments of his mostly hallucinatory monologues that pepper the novel, it is revealed that this patient, whom everyone believes to be an Englishman, was part of a Geographical Society expedition to map the Libyan desert. During his time in the desert, he meets and falls in love with Katharine Clifton, the young wife of his colleague Geoffrey Clifton. They commence a violent affair and break it off, only to have Clifton, in a fit of jealousy, attempt to kill them both by crashing his plane in the desert. Clifton is killed, and the patient leaves the severely injured Katharine in a desert cave until he can return with help. By this time, World War II has broken out, and he is captured by the English, who assume he is a spy for the Germans. He is unable to save Katharine. Two years go by before he is able to return to the cave and retrieve Katharine's body.

The patient was kept from saving Katharine because, by virtue of his name, the English assumed he was allied with the Germans. That he is thought to be an enemy by the British because of his non-Anglo name is the root of the patient's refusal to identify himself or align himself with any nation. The patient is a man of great historical and geographical knowledge, and a great passion for the desert. Both the death of his friend Madox and the death of Katharine cause him enough anguish to not be able to face his memories, except in the stupor of the morphine injections that Caravaggio administers.

Hana

Twenty-year-old Hana is originally from Toronto and was sent to Italy with the Canadian army as a nurse. The overwhelming trauma she experiences and witnesses during the war leaves her severely scarred emotionally: the experience of caring for scores of dying soldiers; receiving news of her father's death in France; becoming pregnant and having to terminate the pregnancy all leave her scarred. While working in an abandoned villa that has been transformed into a hospital, she meets a patient who is burned beyond recognition. When her regiment moves on, Hana remains at the villa alone with the patient. Later, she is joined by David Caravaggio and Kip the sapper, with whom she eventually develops an intimate relationship.

Hana idealizes her patient; she finds a fatherly type of comfort with him and regards him as a "despairing saint." Her idealism, in spite of her emotional anguish, is evident in her attitude towards nationalism and race; when Caravaggio questions whether the patient is English or is in league with Germany, Hana states that it does not matter what side he is on. Hana also idealizes Kip, whom she is drawn to for comfort and whom she also regards as a sort of saint. Her observations of him reveal an adoration of his beauty; however, her mild obsession with the brownness of his skin and with his long, dark hair seems to have more to do with a universal idea of beauty and less to do with their difference in race.

Unfortunately, Hana's idealism did not affect Kip, who left her ultimately because she, as a Canadian, is associated with the West and with what he comes to regard as its violent racist policies against non-Western cultures.

Hana does, at the end of the book, achieve a catharsis that none of the other characters seem to: she writes a letter to her stepmother, Clara, informing her of the details of her father's death and discussing, for the first time, her own grief. Finally able to openly acknowledge her father's death, Hana achieves an emotional healing.

Hardy

Hardy is an Englishman and a member of Kip's sapper regiment in Italy. Unlike the other English sappers, who are reluctant to show the senior-ranking Sikh respect because of his race,

Hardy is enthusiastic in following Kip's orders. Kip and Hardy form a friendship. Hardy is killed while attempting to defuse a bomb. His sudden death is an indirect factor that propels Kip towards starting a romantic relationship with Hana.

Mr. Fred Harts

Fred Harts is Lord Suffolk's chauffeur and constant companion in his bomb disposal work. Together with Lord Suffolk and Miss Morden, the threesome is known as the Holy Trinity. Mr. Harts is killed along with Suffolk and Morden while defusing a bomb in 1941.

Kip

See Kirpal Singh

Madox

An Englishman and a member of the Geographical Society, Madox is Almásy's closest friend, having spent ten years charting the African deserts with him. The Geographical Society, an international band of explorers stationed in the desert and away from the political tensions of Europe, seems to transcend the boundaries of nationalism. The group is disbanded because of the commencement of World War II, which sadly transforms the desert into a war zone. Madox returns to England and ends up committing suicide. The patient, heartbroken at his friend's death, says that Madox "died because of nations."

Miss Morden

Miss Morden is secretary to Lord Suffolk and accompanies him during every bomb dismantlement. When Lord Suffolk chooses Kip to join his sapper regiment, Miss Morden becomes the only English woman to truly befriend Kip. He cherishes her friendship and views her as a sort of mother figure; she takes him to plays and, during one touching instant, daubs him with cologne to calm him during a bomb disposal. Her death by explosion, along with Fred Harts and Lord Suffolk, is a great source of anguish to Kip.

Kirpal Singh

Kirpal (Kip) Singh, as a sapper in the British army, is part of an elite and unique unit handselected and trained in bomb disposal. It is extremely technical and dangerous work. Kip is a Sikh originally from India, which is a colony of Britain at the time the novel takes place. His vehemently anti-British brother is jailed for refusing to join the British army; Kip joins in his place and is sent to London. He acquires his nickname, Kip (which he is called throughout most of the novel), from the British soldiers who derived his name from some kipper grease that got on some of his reports.

Kip faces discrimination in the army that, while it allows him to be a soldier, disbars him from social activities; that is, until he is befriended by his mentor in the sapper unit, Lord Suffolk, and his assistants, Miss Morden and Mr. Harts. Kip becomes Lord Suffolk's right-hand sapper, and he regards Lord Suffolk as a father figure. Indeed, Kip values these three English people as though they were family, and he is emotionally shattered when they are suddenly blown up by a bomb. Rather than facing his anguish at their deaths, he tucks away their memories—an act he compares to Peter Pan packing away his shadow—and heads to Italy with another sapper unit. Here, he encounters Hana, with whom he commences a romantic relationship, and the patient, with whom he forms a fast friendship, based on their similarities in taste, knowledge, and personality.

During his time in Europe, Kip falls in love with Western culture, especially that of the English. He constantly hums the Western tunes he learns through his portable radio headset; he adores English tea and condensed milk; later, in Italy, he finds himself in awe of the vast frescoes of the churches.

In the meantime, Kip's own non-white racial background is a constant factor in his relationship to the European world he now inhabits; his race is represented especially by the constant repetition throughout the text of the description of his "brown skin." The consciousness of his color is ever-present and represents his racial difference as a significant factor in his life—even during the intense, life-and-death moments of bomb disposal.

The character of Kip is very much a mirror of the character of the patient: the patient himself often refers to Kip as a younger version of himself. He also refers to the both of them as "international bastards," based on their life experience of straddling different national and ethnic cultures, seeming to not be bound in spirit by the tenets of just one national identity. However, for Kip, the patient's idealized "international" identity is shattered by the American bombing of Hiroshima. This act of violence by what Kip calls a "white nation" against a "brown nation" destroys Kip's previous idealization of the West, Europe, and especially the Britain; it makes clear to him the exploitation by these colonial nations of the non-Western peoples of the world. His explosive anger at the Americans' celebration of the nuclear bombing of Japanese civilians, and his subsequent, very sudden exit from both the villa and from Hana's life, forms the climax of the novel.

Lord Suffolk

Lord Suffolk, an English gentleman, is the head of an experimental bomb disposal unit as part of the British Army. He chooses Kip as a member of his elite sapper unit; Kip eventually becomes his top sapper. Lord Suffolk, along with his constant work companions Miss Morden, his secretary, and Mr. Fred Harts, his chauffeur, are known as The Holy Trinity. Kip becomes especially close to Lord Suffolk who, as his mentor, becomes a father figure to Kip. Lord Suffolk is killed in 1941 by a bomb, and his sudden death is a great source of sadness for Kip.

Themes

War

The English Patient is centered around the events of World War II, but markedly absent from its narrative is any mention—save the bombing of Hiroshima, which has great personal significance to the character Kip—of any of the major action or history of the war itself. Rather, it focuses on the personal experiences of war of the four main characters and, in doing so, portrays war as an endeavor that results not in glory, but destruction and, ultimately, betrayal to those who take part. Hana's letter to her stepmother Clara at the end of the novel most clearly states the betrayal of the war towards those who joined its efforts; Clara was the only one of Hana's family not to join the war effort, and Hana asks of her, "How were you not fooled like us?" What Hana—and the others—were "fooled" by was the sense of honor and duty that drove each of them to join the war effort. Hana, Kip and Caravaggio have all voluntarily left their own countries to join the Allied forces in Europe, but the novel focuses on what the war took from these characters: Caravaggio is horribly maimed; Hana loses her father, her lover, and her child; Kip, who joined the British army out of a sense of loyalty to England and the West, not only loses his best friends in a bomb disposal, but in the end is betrayed by the West by the bombing of Hiroshima, which he views as an act of blatant racism. The patient himself, who wanted nothing

Topics For Further Study

- The film version of *The English Patient* has several differences from the original novel. Watch the film after reading the novel. Compare and contrast the differences in the plot and the characters. Why do you think these changes were made and how do they change the overall story? Take a chapter or event from the book that was not in the film, and write a scene for it. How would you have fit this scene into the film?

- At the end of the novel, Hana writes a letter to her stepmother, Clara, and discusses in detail the death of her father, Patrick. This letter signifies an emotional healing on Clara's part because she had previously been unwilling to acknowledge his death. Kip and Caravaggio, also, have been emotionally wounded by the events of the war. Do you think that, like Hana, either of them achieved a sense of healing by the end of the book? Write a letter, in the voice of either Caravaggio or Kip, that reflects what you believe their state of mind is by the end of the novel.

- Kip's brother is jailed in India for refusing to join the British army. At this time, India is a colony of Great Britain. India would gain independence only two years after the end of WWII, in 1947. Kip's brother is a protestor against the British presence in India. Write a research report on the independence movement in India. Who were the key figures? How is the British influence still seen in India today? What has been the impact of Indian culture on the British?

- *The English Patient* is actually a sequel to an earlier novel, *In the Skin of a Lion*, which takes place in Canada and includes the characters of Hana and Caravaggio. Read *In the Skin of a Lion*. What are the thematic elements in the earlier novel that carry over to *The English Patient*? How do you feel Hana and Caravaggio have changed as characters? Based on your reading of *In the Skin of a Lion*, how do you think their lives would have played out if they had never gone off to war?

- The bombing of Hiroshima by the United States is, to Kip, an unforgivable act of violence that he believes is fueled by racism. Kip is also angry over the way that he hears the bombing reported over the radio. Research news clippings on the bombing of Hiroshima, from the time of the bombing to the present time. How is the bombing reported? What is the tone? Is the bombing condoned? Is there ever a sense of injustice or wrongdoing that would reflect Kip's feeling? See if you can find news sources from different countries regarding the bombing. How have different cultures responded to the bombings? What is the lasting impact on those cultures today, specifically in Japan?

---

to do with the war, is unable to save Katharine as a direct result of the conflict and is forced to take sides; he also loses his best friend, Madox, who commits suicide as a direct result of the war. None of the characters exit the war with a sense of honor or glory; as Caravaggio notes angrily, "The armies indoctrinate you and leave you here and they f—— off somewhere else to cause trouble, inky-dinky parlez-vous."

Nationhood and Identity

The patient says to Hana that the idea of nations is one that deforms people. The novel *The English Patient* explores the attempt of the characters to transcend the constrictions of nationhood, and their helplessness and inability to do so because of the greater power of politics, government, and the war that surrounds them.

In the desert, the patient and his international band of friends had no need or desire to label themselves according to their nationality; being in the desert—removed, at that time, from the politics of Europe—they were able to forego their labels of nationhood. However, the war brought the politics of Europe to the desert; it forced the disbandment of the Geographical Society and therefore, symbolically, put an end to the patient's dream of transcending nationhood. The patient's best friend, Madox, shoots himself rather than be forced to ally himself with Britain against other men simply because of their nationality. Most tragic of all is the very fact that it is the patient's name, and the nationhood it implied, that kept the patient from saving Katharine's life. The English soldiers stationed outside the desert took him prisoner rather than help him rescue Katharine, simply because his Hungarian name denoted an association—albeit nonexistent—with their enemy. In the end, the patient is only able to shed his identity through the literal loss of his face, as he is severely burned beyond recognition.

Kip, too, attempts to transcend the constrictions of nationality by attempting to straddle both his Sikh culture and the Christian British culture; his attempt at assimilation into British culture is especially symbolized in his adoption of the nickname given him by the British soldiers—throughout the book, he is known as "Kip" rather than "Kirpal Singh." For Kip, however, transcendence is even more impossible because of his Asiatic race: he, a member of the British army's elite sapper unit, is indelibly marked as Indian by the very color of his skin, the "brownness" of which is evoked repeatedly throughout the novel. Even in the heat of dismantling a bomb, he is still conscious of the brownness of his skin and, therefore, his status as an outsider. Kip originally joins the British army with the conviction that he can transcend the superior racism of the British, and therefore gain acceptance, simply by ignoring the laws, written and unwritten, that impinge upon his personal freedom. However, by the end of the novel, it is the bombing of Hiroshima—an act of extreme violence that he views as motivated by the racism of the white West against Asia—that makes clear to Kip that he cannot escape the racism with which the West would regard him. He leaves the British Army and returns to his own nation, resuming his name, Kirpal Singh. Although he loves her, that Kip leaves Hana behind denotes that he completely gives in to the labeling of nationality that he had so desperately tried to overcome: he leaves because he associates Hana, as a white Canadian, with the racism of the West.

Trauma, Personal Grief, and Healing

The novel, in its focus on the private, internal lives of each of the characters through their personal memories, examines the effect of trauma and, in the case of Hana, the progression from trauma, through denial, to acceptance.

The narrative of the novel is often propelled by the characters' dealing with anguish: for example, the English patient finds himself unable to face the death of Katharine, and his emotional shock and inability to fully face her death is reflected in the very narrative structure of the novel: his conversation and hallucination greatly alters as he begins to either speak or think about her. For example, the chapter "Cairo 1930–1938," the patient is speaking with Hana of his past and discusses the beginning of his affair with Katharine; throughout this chapter, he speaks in the first person. However, during his drugged conversation with Caravaggio he is eventually forced to confront the circumstances surrounding her death. The patient's narrative style shifts considerably: rather than speaking in the first person, he begins to speak in the third person of Almásy (the patient's true name), causing Caravaggio to wonder whether the patient is speaking as himself or as another person. This third person narration disconnects the patient from the person of Almásy and thus from Almásy's pain, making it the only way possible for him to discuss Katharine's death. The patient's hallucinations and refusal to acknowledge his true identity allows him to keep separate from his personal anguish and, therefore, to not have to face it fully. As he says to Hana, "Death means you are in the third person."

But, while the patient does not seem to receive a respite from his grief except through his own eventual death, Ondaatje uses the character of Hana to show redemption through acceptance: Hana's character development is one from debilitating grief and denial, to healing and acceptance. Throughout the novel she refuses to acknowledge the death of her father, even going so far as to tell the patient that he is alive in France. The entrance of Kip into her life, and the happiness and comfort he brings her, helps Hana to be able to feel happiness again. Although in the end Kip leaves her, Hana is left with the ability to move on in her life. Her transformation is evident in the letter she writes to Clara at the end of the novel, in which she is finally able to openly discuss her father's death.

Geography

Hana, in her letter to her stepmother Clara at the end of the novel, writes, "Do you understand the sadness of geography?" Hana is discussing her sorrow at being unable to be with her father, Patrick, while he died in France and she was tending soldiers in Italy. Here, her sorrow is a helpless sorrow aimed at the impossibility of transcending the physical space of geography. In *The English*

Patient, the physical geography of the earth symbolizes nationhood and the separateness that it forces between people. During their courtship, Hana constantly imagines Kip as an extension of his continent and as the embodiment of all of India. Indeed, their relationship is consistently described in terms of the geography they represent: for example, an intimate moment between Hana and Kip is described: "Hana now received this tender art, [Kip's] nails against the million cells of her skin, in his tent, in 1945, where their continents met in a hill town." The climax of the novel occurs when Kip, unable to separate Hana from the West he has come to despise, leaves her and returns to India. Hana returns to Canada; their retreat to their respective homes is as impossible a separation to surmount as the larger, political forces that drove them apart.

However, Ondaatje creates an ending that is almost magically surreal, allowing Kip and Hana to transcend the physical space of geography: as Hana, in Canada, knocks a glass from a shelf, Kirpal Singh reaches down to catch a falling fork in India. This ending to the novel seems to leave the hope that there is indeed a plane that transcends the constraints of both the political and the physical world.

Style

Setting

The novel takes place during World War II. The timing of the novel is integral to several of the themes it explores, including the role of nationhood in the identity of the individual, and the illusion of the honor of war.

Setting the novel during World War II also gives Ondaatje a backdrop through which to examine the effect of the colonialism of Britain on the world policies of the United States in later years: World War II marked the end of Britain's powerful colonial era, and the rise of the United States as the new world power. The emergence of the United States as the world power is metaphorically represented, in the novel, by the bombing of Hiroshima. Through the character of Kip, Ondaatje shows how the American rationale to bomb Japan with the atomic bomb is directly related to the racist colonialist philosophy of Western superiority that especially characterized the British Empire's rule over its non-Western colonies.

The large part of the action of the novel takes place in both an abandoned Italian villa, where the lives of the four main characters converge, and in the North African deserts prior to the start of World War II. The abandoned villa is a ruin, seemingly frozen in time. The paintings of a garden on the walls of the patient's room seem to blur the boundaries of internal and external physical space within the villa: this, combined with its removal from time, create an idealized space for the four main characters to attempt to remove themselves from the reality of the war and the politics of nations that surround them. The "boundary-lessness" and timelessness of the villa is also echoed in the desert: the patient and the other members of the Geographical Society find sanctuary in the desert from the political conflicts of their individual nations, as well as a freedom from the labels of their nationalities. However, both of these sanctuaries prove unable to withstand the greater machinations of the politics of nations; eventually, the war encroaches upon both sanctuaries, forcing the inhabitants to either choose sides, or to eventually die. Through the portrayal of the powerlessness of these sanctuaries against the war, Ondaatje seems to show the powerlessness of the individual against the greater political movements of nations.

Collage

The English Patient employs a narrative structure that is not, like the majority of novels, based on the chronological order of the events around which its story is built, but is rather structured like a collage. It is constructed largely of the recollection or retelling of numerous, non-sequential memories of each of the four main characters. This collage of recollections is interspersed between the main action of the story, which includes both the love story between Hana and Kip, and the uncovering of the patient's true identity by Caravaggio. Using this collaged and multi-voiced structure allows Ondaatje to do a number of different things.

By providing a collage of episodes, rather than being tied to a strict chronological structure, Ondaatje is able to reveal each of the character's private memories, most specifically those memories that they would not share with anyone else. For example, Kip's friendship with Lord Suffolk and Miss Morden is revealed only through the flashback of his memories. The personal effect of anguish is a major theme of the novel, and through revelation of each of the characters' most private memories, Ondaatje not only provides vital background information for each character but is able to specifically explore the source of each character's most private grief, as well as how they are either able or unable to come to terms with it.

The collage of memories, all told from the point of view of each specific character, also provides the novel with a number of varied points of view. For example, because Ondaatje—having abandoned chronology in the structuring of this novel—is not constricted by time, he is able to include the voice of a dead character—that of Katharine. Her perspective, given in the chapter "Katharine," on the stormy relationship she has with the patient, provides an intimate portrait of the character of the patient that would otherwise not be revealed.

The non-linear and multi-voiced, collage-like narrative structure of the novel is echoed by the patient's copy of Herodotus's *The Histories*, into which the patient has pasted his own personal writings and observances, as well as clippings from other books and magazines. Like the collage the patient has created with the histories by interspersing personal anecdotes and the writings of others between the pages of the story that Herodotus tells, Ondaatje has created a collage of multi-voiced narrations and experiences. This non-linear and multi-voiced, collage-like narrative structure, then, becomes more than a narrative device. It represents an alternative to the way that history itself—also traditionally recorded in a strictly chronological manner—can be written, providing a framework for a form of written history that takes into account more than one perspective.

Historical Context

The English Patient is set largely in Italy at the end of World War II and features characters from Africa, Europe, Canada, and India. The war is the direct cause of the convergence of the main characters—Kip, Hana, Caravaggio, and the patient himself—at a bombed-out villa in Italy, several months before the war's end. The international nature of the relationships between the characters, and the effect of the war on the characters as individuals and in their relationships to each other, is integral to the development of the novel, particularly the theaters in which the war was played out, and the bombing of Hiroshima that punctuated the war's end.

World War II was a direct result of the failure of the outcome of World War I to provide a satisfactory environment for peace: Germany, who was the loser of World War I, was left in complete economic turmoil, and the terms of the Treaty of Versailles—the treaty that marked the end of World War I—left the country with little recourse for reconstruction or growth; and both Italy and Japan, who were victors of World War I, were highly dissatisfied with the spoils of war they were awarded. Eventually, these three countries formed the Axis powers that faced off with France, Great Britain, the USSR, and the United States, which formed the Allied powers in World War II.

Before the commencement of World War II, both Italy and Germany adopted a totalitarian form of government known as fascism, militaristic in structure and centered on a dictator. The rise of fascism in Germany occurred with the installment of Adolph Hitler as Germany's dictator in 1933, who offered promises to overthrow the Treaty of Versailles and restore German power by annexing its surrounding countries. Earlier in Italy in 1922, Benito Mussolini became that country's fascist dictator. Concurrently, Japan, which had already long established a military government, began the process of invading and taking over China.

In 1938 Hitler began his quest to conquer Europe with the forced annexation of Austria, an event that was backed by Italy and not stopped by France or Great Britain, who were surprised by Germany's show of sudden power. World War II officially began when Germany invaded Poland, a country that had a mutual protection agreement with France. The act of aggression against Poland caused both France and Great Britain to declare war on Germany on September 1, 1939. In the coming years, Germany proceeded to invade much of Europe, including France itself.

The grisly hallmark of Hitler's reign in Germany and his actions in World War II was the mass extermination of Jews and other minority groups in concentration camps, which has come to be known as the Holocaust. His aim was creating what he saw to be a "pure" German state.

The United States, which had taken an isolationist stance and was reluctant to become involved in another large-scale conflict in Europe, managed to stay out of the war until December 7, 1941, when the Japanese launched an attack on the military base at Pearl Harbor in Hawaii, provoked by the United States' freezing of Japanese assets that threatened to cripple that country's economy. The United States entered into a war with fronts both in Europe and in the Pacific Ocean.

The involvement of Great Britain in the war brought in people to the war in Europe from its commonwealth territories and its colonies all over the globe, including Canada—an independent state that nevertheless has strong ties to Great Britain—and India, which was still under British colonial control. The physical theater of war also extended outside of Europe to the colonies of France and Great Britain in Africa, as seen in the novel. In *The English Patient*, the war was one that brought many people from all over the globe to fight to defend lands they had never seen, and the sense of disconnectedness brought on not only by the act of war, but of fighting in a foreign land, is a major theme of the novel. Likewise, especially for India, Indians were at once fighting to defend the British Empire, while at home a burgeoning independence movement was taking hold—only a short 2 years after the end of WWII would India force Britain to give it independence, in 1947. The tension between Great Britain's control over India, its movement towards independence, and the complex results of the racism that characterized the imperialist attitude of the English towards the native people of the Indian subcontinent whom they governed, is especially played out in the character of Kip and his own attitude towards the West, which profoundly changes by the end of the novel.

Although in the early years of the war the triumph of the Axis powers seemed imminent, by 1941, with the involvement of the United States, the tide had begun to turn in favor of the Allies, with the British, Canadians, and Americans taking Italy in the summer of 1943. On June 6, 1944, which is known as D-Day, Allies surprised the Germans and took the beaches of Normandy, finally beginning the reclamation of France; the Allies succeeded in breaching the German border in the Spring of 1945. May 8, 1945, known as V-E Day, Germany officially surrendered.

The atomic bomb was dropped by the Americans on the Japanese cities of Hiroshima and Nagasaki on August 6 and August 9, 1945, respectively, killing an estimated 240,000 people. Japan formally surrendered on September 2, 1945.

World War II was especially characterized by the prominence of new and more lethal technology, most notably the atomic bomb. In terms of loss of life and destruction of property, World War II is the most destructive in history. It was the framework for the use of the most horrific weapon that humankind had ever created; it was the theater of the gruesome genocide of the Jews by the German Nazis. It was characterized by air raids that took the lives of many civilians. It left the once powerful British Empire and the overall economy of Europe in shambles, providing a power gap into which the United States and the USSR became the new superpowers, touching off a new era: the cold war between the capitalist democracy of the US, and the communist USSR.

Critical Overview

Although Michael Ondaatje had published several collections of poetry and novels prior to *The English Patient*, it is this novel that propelled him into worldwide fame as a writer. *The English Patient* was a bestseller in 1992, the year that it was published and received highly favorable reviews in the major North American newspapers. He was awarded the Booker Prize in 1992, sharing this prize for Best Novel with Barry Unsworth's *Sacred Hunger*. Ondaatje was the first Canadian to be awarded this prize.

Ondaatje was previously known as a poet, and the critics picked up on the influence of poetry on the narrative style of *The English Patient*. A review in *MacLean* found the poetic influence a strength of the novel. John Bemrose wrote:

> Michael Ondaatje . . . who began his writing career as a poet, has managed to recast the traditional novel in his own peculiar way, so that the measured dance of his poetic rhythms and images leads the reader ever deeper into a story. His new novel, *The English Patient*, is one of the finest Canadian novels ever written . . . Ondaatje has somehow found a way to give an abstract narrative the illusion of physical presence. That accomplishment also depends on his masterly command of rhythm.

While the novel received almost entirely highly favorable review by the general readership, it has also held its own as a subject for critical literary interpretation during the 13 years it has been in publication, providing in its unconventional construction a rich critical source for narrative studies, and in its subject matter, a source for post-colonial literary studies, among other subjects.

Criticism

Tamara Fernando

Fernando is a writer and editor living in Seattle, Washington. In this essay, Fernando examines how the narrative structure of The English Patient *serves as a criticism of traditional historiography.*

Ralph Fiennes as the English Patient and Kristin Scott Thomas as Katharine Clifton in the 1996 film version of The English Patient   The Kobal Collection. Reproduced by permission

In *The English Patient*, the title character is a nameless, severely burned man cared for by a young nurse at the end of World War II. His only possession is a copy of *The Histories* by Herodotus, into which he has pasted his own writings as well as clippings from other books, creating a collage of knowledge, observations, and unrelated events.

As the patient discusses his love of *The Histories* with Hana, his nurse, he says of Herodotus:

> I see him more as one of those spare men of the desert who travel from oasis to oasis, trading legends as if it is the exchange of seeds, consuming everything without suspicion, piecing together a mirage. "This history of mine," Herodotus says, "has from the beginning sought out the supplementary to the main argument." What you find in him are cul-de-sacs within the sweep of history.

Like the patient's personal version of *The Histories*, Ondaatje's novel is a collage; its narrative structure is not based on chronological events but is constructed largely of numerous non-sequential

memories and experiences of the four main characters. This non-linear narrative structure, however, is more than a narrative device. It is through this use of non-linear narration that Ondaatje not only tells the personal stories of the four main characters of the novel, but deconstructs the way history itself is recorded, narrated, and understood.

The "cul-de-sacs" and "the supplementary to the main argument" that so interest the patient in the quote given above are the occurrences and points of view that existed and do exist outside of the chronology of a history (what the patient calls "the main argument.") This idea is illuminated by Amy Novak's essay on the narrative structure of *The English Patient*, in which she discusses the traditional process by which history is written—that is, the act of historiography. She summarizes the philosopher Hegel's influential theory of historiography thus:

> According to a received Hegelianism, which still informs conventional thinking about the past, History is constructed as a linear movement, through erasure,

What Do I Read Next?

- *In the Skin of a Lion* (1987) is the prequel novel to Ondaatje's *The English Patient*. Set in Canada between the World Wars, the novel features the characters Caravaggio and Hana, who are important figures in *The English Patient*, but focuses mainly on Hana's father Patrick. The novel shares some of its major themes with *The English Patient*, including the examination of personal grief and anguish.

- Like *The English Patient*, Ondaatje's novel *Coming through Slaughter* does not stick to a chronological narrative but rather pieces together the life of jazz legend Buddy Bolden through a collage of imagery and anecdotes. It was first published in 1976.

- Ondaatje's *Anil's Ghost* (2000) is set in Sri Lanka, Ondaatje's native country. The novel is about the work of a forensics specialist sent by the United Nations to investigate the brutal civil war that tore the island nation apart for the better part of the latter twentieth century.

- Ondaatje's memoir *Running in the Family* (1982) is an account of two trips he took to his native country of Sri Lanka and, through the stories he learned during these trips, is an account of his family's history and his own childhood.

- Ondaatje has published several collections of poetry since the late 1960s. *The Cinnamon Peeler: Selected Poems* (1989) is a collection of previously published poems.

- *The God of Small Things* (1997), the 1998 Booker Prize–winning novel by Indian writer Arundhati Roy, examines both personal grief and loss, as well as the inescapable power of government, politics, and society over the individual. The novel takes place in mid-twentieth century Southern India during a time of political unrest. Told through the eyes of two children, it portrays the taboos of caste and sexuality that pervaded their society.

- Nobel Laureate V. S. Naipaul's novel *The Mimic Men* (1967), which features a character of Indian descent who lives in the British Caribbean, examines, through the dysfunctional and globe-trotting life of the main character, issues of identity pertinent to a Third World shaped by British colonialism.

- *For Whom the Bell Tolls* (1940), one of Ernest Hemingway's best-known novels, is set during the civil war in Spain. It is a tale of camaraderie in wartime that ultimately portrays war as futile and destructive, rather than honorable and just.

---

toward an already predetermined meaning. . . . In order to ensure this coherency of this totality, contradictory moments that do not record the present's coming to Being are erased or expelled from signification.

In other words, the conventional practice of historiography is the telling of history chronologically, that "linear movement" to which Novak refers. That chronology, by its very nature as a linear progression, is therefore singular in its point of view not only of the past, but of the state of the present to which the historical narrative is pointing. The singularity of the point of view of a chronologically written history, in order to remain coherent, eliminates any occurrence or

interpretation that not only does not contribute to a forward-moving chronology, but offers a contradiction to that singular, linear point of view. These "erasures" are indeed the supplementary, the "cul-de-sacs" to which the patient refers in the quote above.

History looms large in *The English Patient*; the novel takes place during World War II, which is, arguably, the event given the most significance in the commonly known historiography of the twentieth century. But the most familiar stories and people named in the commonly held historiography are strangely absent from this novel. Instead, it seems that Ondaatje seeks to tell what can be called a "supplemental" history of World War II, one that focuses

> "The linearity of history is inaccurate because it does not allow for the natural fact of multiple, and opposing, points of view in society."

on the private stories of four characters profoundly affected by the war, on those types of stories that would be cast aside as Novak's erasures. Ondaatje's abandonment of the mainstream history is not merely evident in the subject of his novel, but is manifested in the very structure of the novel itself. Like the traditional historiography that Novak discusses above, the traditional structure of a novel—a chronological plot with a beginning, middle, and end—is linear. But Ondaatje wrote *The English Patient* not as a linear, chronological story. It is built from individual scenes, collaged in a non-sequential order, from both the main characters' respective pasts and their present lives together at the Italian villa.

This can be seen in, for example, the progression of Chapter 8, "The Holy Forest." This chapter, a non-linear collection of stories, abandons chronology in its construction and therefore does not give the reader a sense of the movement of time, either forward or backward. These self-contained accounts include: the careful delivery of a ladybug to the patient from Kip; a discussion among the characters of Indian sarongs; Hana recording her thoughts in a book; an extended section detailing a single bomb disposal carried out by Kip and his assistant sapper Hardy, which delves not only into Kip's state of mind while defusing a bomb, but provides intricate specifics of the technicalities of his job; Kip and Hana washing their hair; almost six pages of Kip, Caravaggio, and Hana playing hide-and-go-seek in the darkened villa; Hana and Kip laying in his tent, recalling his childhood.

Each of these small episodes is what the patient referred to as the "cul-de-sacs," the "supplements" of history. They do not contribute to the forward movement of chronologically ordered historiography, but are rather encapsulated in themselves. However, the fact that these stories do not denote a forward motion in time does not mean at all that they do not develop. Rather, Ondaatje has

skillfully woven together these seemingly self-contained episodes into a composite, like a quilt made of many pieces. The reader comes away from Chapter 8 with a clear sense of the intimacy developed between the characters during their days together at the villa, with a sense of the refuge from the war they take in each other, and the way that their lives are constantly subject to the strong undercurrent of the threat of sudden death during wartime. With the wartime experiences of the four characters—noticeably away from the battlefield and away from the more familiar theaters of World War II—Ondaatje does succeed in creating a narrative that veers completely away from the overarching action of the war.

The abandonment of chronology not only allows for the inclusion of the supplementary stories (additional stories deemed unnecessary to the linear plot), but it also allows for the inclusion of points of view that are not, as Novak noted, allowable within the constraints of chronology. Ondaatje is able, because he is not constrained by the element of time, to provide the point of view of a character who is dead. Chapter 9: "Katharine" is told in the third-person voice but from the specific point of view of Katharine Clifton, the patient's dead lover.

Throughout the novel, the reader is given clues to the patient's past through his fragmentary, hallucinatory memories, and slowly the reader learns the tragic story of his affair with Katharine Clifton, and her subsequent death. However, by including a chapter told from the point of view of Katharine, the reader is given a perspective on the affair that would never have surfaced strictly from the patient's own recollections and interpretations. Through this chapter, readers learn that about his self-righteous talks, his pompous insistence on refusing to be beholden to their relationship, her feeling of extreme guilt for being unfaithful to her husband. With such details that only Katharine's point of view could provide, this chapter not only provides additional details about the nature of the affair that is at the heart of the mystery of this novel, but also provides a perspective on the patient that further develops his character.

This inclusion of Katharine's point of view gives voice to a character who would otherwise, within the constraints of a strict, forward-marching chronology, be silent. She is a character who is already dead by the time the novel's present time commences. In fact, even in the writing of a linear historiography, the biggest flaw is the very fact that, by its nature, it leaves existing but competing points of view out of the narrative, thereby rendering these points of view silent. Novak relates that the philosopher Ernesto Laclau goes so far as to call traditional history an "ideological fantasy" that "[conceals] the fundamental split or antagonism around which the social field is structured." The linearity of history is inaccurate because it does not allow for the natural fact of multiple, and opposing, points of view in society.

Ondaatje's nonlinear narrative construction goes farther than simply being an alternative narrative device. It becomes a physical criticism of the chronological writing of history that is inaccurate and incomplete in that it omits and erases. That the novel is a critique of the writing of history is strongly evident not just in its alternative structure, but in its content—in particular, at the climax of the novel, when Kip discovers that the United States has dropped the atomic bomb on Hiroshima.

Kip, an Indian Sikh and a loyal member of the British army, is horrified, enraged, and disillusioned by the bombing of Hiroshima's civilians by the United States, an act he sees as motivated by a racist sense of superiority of what he terms the "white nations" over the "brown nations." But what is interesting about this scene in the novel is that Kip can hear, over the radio, the immediate construction of a narrative that excuses this blatant act of violence. He says to his friends: "I'll leave you the radio to swallow your history lesson. . . . All those speeches of civilization from kings and queen and presidents. . . . Listen to the radio and smell the celebration in it."

Two opposing points of view are portrayed in this scene: Kip's anger at the racist motivation and violence of the atomic bombing, and, represented by the radio broadcast's "celebration," the immediate interpretation by the Allied forces of the bombing of Japanese civilians as a just measure to bring an end to the war. This broadcast represents the creation of a historiography to describe the bombing as it is happening. By the end of the war, the United States will emerge as the victor and, therefore, will be the dominant interpreter of history. Kip's opposing point of view, representing the members of "brown nations" facing the exploitation of the more powerful West, will become one of the erasures, a valid voice rendered silent by the chronological writing of history.

The bombing of Hiroshima represents a turning point for Kip's character, and therefore a climax in the novel: it is the occurrence that propels him to leave the villa, leave the British army, and even to leave Hana. As a climactic point in the novel, Kip's interpretation of Hiroshima seems to be the point to which the novel was leading—not only in its development of characters and plot, but in its very structure. For Ondaatje, through the character of Kip, is offering a sharp criticism not only of the bombing of Hiroshima, but of the very historiography that excuses the bombing and, by its exclusive nature, would render any opposing viewpoint silent and, therefore, written out of existence. This criticism extends not only through the characterization and actions of Kip, but through the very structure of the novel itself. In its success in creating a non-linear narrative made from what the patient terms "cul-de-sacs" and what Novak terms the "erasures" of history, Ondaatje's novel calls for no less than a new paradigm of historiography, away from the chronological and therefore exclusive, and towards a model that seeks to include opposing interpretations and myriad voices.

Source: Tamara Fernando, Critical Essay on *The English Patient*, in *Novels for Students*, Thomson Gale, 2006.

Susan E. Hawkins
and Susan Danielson

In the following essay excerpt, Hawkins and Danielson examine how the film version of The English Patient *"erases the geopolitical stakes at issue" in the novel to sustain a Western imperialist view of World War II.*

> In the end it is always the ruling classes, bourgeois certainly, but above all aristocratic, that long mourn the empires, and their grief always has a stagey quality. Benedict Anderson

The public reception of the film *The English Patient* (1996) constitutes a particularly notable example of America's allegiance to the unquestioned story about World War II, one that constantly rationalizes the "ending" and thus reaffirms a continued commitment to a politics of liberal consensus. Arguably this century's most powerful cultural myth, the narrative of western sacrifice, heroism, and ultimate triumph in the "Good War" tacitly informs Anthony Minghella's version of this story and accounts in part for the film's extraordinary popular and critical success. The fact that the film's release followed closely upon the heels of the Smithsonian's National Air and Space Museum's (NASM) decision to effectively cancel the *Enola Gay* exhibit in January 1995 provides a larger historical and cultural intertext within which to read the film's American success. By substituting passion for history, Minghella erases the geopolitical stakes at issue in Michael Ondaatje's 1992

Naveen Andrews as Kip and Juliette Binoche as Hana in the 1996 film version of The English Patient

© Tiger Moth/Miramax/The Kobal Collection

Booker Prize–winning novel and instead nostalgically celebrates western imperial adventures in the African desert.

In order to effect such an enormous transformation, Minghella makes two crucial editorial decisions. First, he refuses the novel's all-important climactic moment, "the reaction of the characters in the monastery to the news of the bombing of Hiroshima" (Katz 138). In so doing, he displaces Kip's (Naveen Andrews) reaction to that horrific news onto his reaction to the death of his sergeant and friend, Hardy (Kevin Whately). This historical elision is covered over by Minghella's second major editorial decision, to privilege the obsessive, adulterous love story between Katherine Clifton (Kristen Scott Thomas) and Count Ladislaus de Almasy (Ralph Fiennes), controlled by the latter's point of view. Such a refocused lens foregrounds traditional masculine fantasies of desire—for the secrets of the desert, the unattainable woman, the unknowable other—and repeats yet again an old story of mythic romance dependent upon hackneyed orientalist tropes. While such decisions os-

tensibly were made, according to the film's editor, Walter Murch, in the interest of both economy and "weight," their ideological implications reveal a reactionary sexual and nationalist politics. For in the grammar of the film, white Anglo-European men such as Almasy, Hardy, Madox, and Clifton emerge as the ultimate victims of World War II, their "suffering" and deaths serving as an opaque screen for millions of war dead, Asian as well as European.

In this way, Minghella's film rescripts the Anglo-American myth of the "Good War," the European war, and muffles the unresolved controversies concerning the Pacific front. In this construction of history, Americans serve as the unquestioned heroes in both Europe and Asia and the Japanese as aggressive war mongers. For their infamy at Pearl Harbor and its exposure of American vulnerability, and to save Americans from the slaughter that would follow any invasion of Japan, the myth argues that Japanese more or less deserved atomic obliteration. Any other reading would call into question American decisions and raise the specter of racist motives. As in the Smithsonian's decision to replace the original *Enola Gay* exhibit with a highly revised exhibit plan "that eschewed controversy" (Thelen 1029), film critics and most book reviewers collude in the culture's preference for nostalgia and historical misprision in which Americans can once again rest in the familiar and comforting story, the story without those A-bombs as an ending.

That the film figures such a preference becomes clear through the sheer critical and emotional excess surrounding its reception. From Siskel & Ebert to *Time* to *The New Yorker,* key modifiers occur again and again—"ravishing," "voluptuous," "beyond gorgeous," "epic." This is a "big film" (Corliss 82), "an old-fashioned movie-movie—extravagantly romantic" (Ansen 72). The crown, however, for the most enthralled reviewer, must go to Anthony Lane of *The New Yorker:* "[N]othing in recent cinema [. . .] had prepared me for the palpitating shock of 'The English Patient' [. . .]. Man to man, this is awfully close to a masterpiece" (118,121).

While film critics waxed eloquent over Minghella's "masterpiece," American book reviewers had expressed lukewarm responses to the novel; in particular, they almost universally rejected the ending which is set in motion by the bombing of Hiroshima and Nagasaki. At one extreme, this rejection figures itself through total denial, for example in Linda Hutcheon's six-column review article, "The Empire Writes Back," in *The Nation.* In her reading, which obviously points to issues of empire and its others, she at *no point* mentions Hiroshima or Nagasaki. Most often, however, the critics reject that portion of the novel with either a dismissive shrug, "a political ending for an apolitical book" (Balliett 162), or with a "structural" objection: "the author's designs become almost too insistent" (Iyer 72); the "dissonant political note" "seem[s] an error of literary, if not political, judgment" (Bell 73–74). At the other extreme from outright denial, reviewers clearly express their rejection regardless of the magazine's ostensible politics. Writing in *The New York Review of Books,* Hilary Mantel finds nothing to admire. Aside from "underrealized characters," "colossal, crushing ironies," and plot in all the wrong places, the novel's explicit critique of western motives for dropping the bomb constitutes "a crude polemic [. . .] exploding into the final pages of the book" (22;23). Craig Seligman, writing in *The New Republic,* moves closer to the actual source of

> **Ondaatje's novel, however, chooses to do more; it disrupts representations of the desert and of Europe from its opening chapters. . . ."**

discomfort radiating out from the novel's flashpoint:

> And though there's no dismissing the elements of racism in the bombing, only a sentimentalist would feel comfortable lumping Japan with "the brown races" of the Third World. [. . .] The destruction of Hiroshima doesn't implicate us as Westerners—it implicates us as human beings [. . .].(41)

No matter what position they occupy on the political spectrum, the reviewers' message throughout reads loud and clear: Ondaatje goes too far when he has Kip assert an alternative perspective on America's historic decision. In the novel's most emotional and terrifying moment, Kip hears the news of the bombing on his radio headset. Outrage and shock galvanize him. He awakes to the reality of his own position as a colonial subject, as a brown man in a white world. At this moment, he speaks as his father's son and his brother's comrade rather than as an admirer of "all things British":

> Americans, French, I don't care. When you start bombing the brown races of the world, you're an Englishman. You had King Leopold of Belgium and now you have [f——ing] Harry Truman of the USA. You all learned it from the English [. . .].

Just as Hutcheon erases the bombings responsible for the deaths of a quarter of a million people, Seligman refuses the United States's real and hostile treatment of the Japanese and Japanese Americans. Seligman's insistence that the United States was not "lumping Japan with the 'the brown races' of the Third World" ignores a long, bad chapter in American history that, beginning in the mid-nineteenth century, includes the following: the deployment of Asian exclusion laws; the United States Supreme Court's 1916 denial of American citizenship to Takao Ozawa "because he was 'clearly' 'not Caucasian'" (Takaki 208); and, most shameful, the shipment of thousands of Japanese-American citizens to concentration camps after Pearl Harbor.

While Ondaatje's novel directly challenges the liberal anticommunist consensus that still informs cold war discourse, Minghella makes a different choice. Despite his avowed purpose to "dramatize the individual in the midst of world-historical events," his representations of the "historical" aspects of World War II merely function as the vehicle for "the catastrophic love at the heart of it all" (qtd. in Thomson 43). By substituting passion for history and dramatizing doomed love, his film is powered by the usual motor for classical romance whether it be medieval or Gothic or Hollywood forties. Thus, melodrama, a term invoked enthusiastically in numerous film reviews, serves as a financially viable and emotionally satisfying vehicle that works through clear generic conventions.

Oriental Time, Desert Romance, Pre-national Bodies

In his opening sequence, Minghella replicates the imperial gesture implicit within orientalist discourse through his construction of the landscape as feminine and sexually unconstrained. His North African desert functions as the "permissible" space for impossible love, heterosexual as well as homosexual. This desert world and its evocation of the hidden and exotic—the Cave of Swimmers, sudden sandstorms, Bedouin tribes—establishes the archaic, timeless narrative within the film, cinematically determined as the most powerful and arresting.

We are drawn immediately into this world as we watch a hand paint sepia-colored strokes of delicate swimmers on what appears to be parchment. The imagery suggests flight which links the opening sequence to the next, that of the lovers flying over the desert. Only later, after the discovery of the Cave of Swimmers, do we know that this is Katherine's hand, painting examples of the ancient figures on the cave's walls. This image subtly dissolves into a stylized, undulating pattern like softly folded material. The swimmer fades into shadowy superimposition, gradually transforming into another shadow, that of a tiny toy-like plane as it moves across what we now recognize as sand dunes, the camera panning up above the cockpit, giving us a view of two figures. This sequence establishes one of the film's major visual echoes and locates the lovers within this register of beautiful swimmers, exotic desert places, sensuous curves, and flight. Cinematically the mysterious, undulating images and unknown locale exist prior to our knowledge of what we might term, for the sake of simplicity, the "realistic" or "historical" register in the film signified by gun fire.

The plane, at first clearly dwarfed by the vast and feminized desert, now fully enters the historical frame as screaming German voices break the airy idyll and violent blasts of anti-aircraft fire interrupt the calm suspension of the plane's movement. These two separate images, the first visual and oriental, the second aural and occidental, converge through the unwitting agency of the couple in the plane. Only later do we learn that Katherine, one of the plane's occupants, is already dead. The remainder of the film will explain for us how she and its other occupant, Almasy, arrived at the convergence of the archaic calm of the desert and the insistent violence of contemporary Europe, here shatteringly dramatized by the plane's fiery explosion. Almasy's body, burned beyond recognition, survives the plane's explosion to become, ironically, the site for multiple national and moral misrecognitions of, and in, that Europe. A double irony we don't believe the film intends is that the cartographer Almasy achieves in the emblematic wreckage of his own body one of his greatest desires, a world without recognizable, national borders. Reduced to dust and voice, or "toast" as he quips to the officer in the Italian field hospital, his body signifies, on one level, the death throes of an older European, patrician imperial attitude. Similarly Almasy's "amnesia" allows him to resist his caretakers' various desires to read him, to contain him within an identifiable European discourse with an identifiable role in the European war that has led them all to this place. His determination to transcend nationalist borders in the midst of a nationalist war motivates the couple's final undoing.

The classical romance theme that develops through the film's continual flashbacks conflates imperial and sexual desire. In this desert realm the colonial impulse both masks and allows the potentially disruptive consequences of adultery and homosexuality. Here white men can transcend "legitimate" borders of nation states, heterosexuality, and marriage. In a crucial sequence, Almasy sketches a map as his Bedouin guide compares the outline of the desert cliffs to a woman's spine. This map metaphor rehearses a comparison found throughout orientalist discourse: "The geology and topography of the land, then, is explicitly sexualized to resemble the physiology of woman" (qtd. in Shohat 675). In his quest to map Katherine, Almasy will ask Madox for the name of the little hollow at the bottom of a woman's throat. In naming the spot, he writes the map. Aurally echoing the opening sequence, the conference between Almasy and the guide is interrupted by an airplane's droning engine. Clifton (Colin Firth) and Katherine are flying into the base camp for the first time. Later, just as the Muslim guides gather for one of their daily prayers, Almasy breaks from the rest of the group and struggles up the rock face he had sketched in the previous scene. He stops, raises his head, and then deliberately places his hand into an ancient stone hand-print, a perfect fit. The scene ends as he proceeds to discover the cave and its ancient drawings of swimmers while the Bedouins continue their chanting in the background. The cave has been waiting to be discovered by its true, its "natural" owner, the man whose hand fits the mold, whose key fits the lock.

After Almasy's discovery, the rest of the exploration team moves equipment into the cave. As Almasy enters, he sees his colleague, Bermann, comforting a young Muslim guide who has bumped his head on the stone walls. Soon after, in a ride back to base camp, Bermann engages in a sexual flirtation with the guide who is perched, like a monkey or a bird, atop the jeep they are driving. Bermann turns to Almasy and asks, "How do you explain to someone who has never been here feelings [. . .] which seem quite normal?" And just as the Count answers, "I don't know," the young man flies off the roof into the sand as the jeep careens out of control and crashes. This calamity provides the occasion for the next calamity, the launching of the affair between Katherine and Almasy.

Minghella's creation of this entire sequence refigures orientalist clichés of the most pernicious sort—the exotic desert provides yet again a space of unconstrained social, libidinal, and sexual freedom. Only here can Bermann engage in his homoerotic desires, only here may Katherine and the Count begin an affair that defies the boundaries of "civilized" Europe. For the young Bedouin's body, Katherine's body, and the Cave of Swimmers constitute prenational bodies, entities ultimately incapable of resisting European invasion. While Minghella's text clearly posits an equivalency between interracial homosexual desire and illicit heterosexual desire, only Katherine will be sacrificed for such desire.

The Cave of Swimmers (the Gilf Kebir), which will become Katherine's death chamber, represents the film's preeminent symbol of archaic time. Now devoid of the water the name Gilf Kebir invokes, the walls are peopled by swimming figures, suggesting that sometime in the remote past even this desert space was fluid and life-giving. That Katherine dies here, quite literally killed by her husband as he crashes his plane just outside the Cave of Swimmers, completes the identification between Almasy's two quests: to map the desert and to map

her body. The opening flight over the desert becomes, in retrospect, not only a funeral cortege for Katherine but for the entire post-Enlightenment project to possess the other. Insofar as Katherine, with her continual desire for water—the green gardens of England—is aligned with the swimmers she paints, Almasy's quest for her is a quest for a life which cannot be supported in the present. Archaic life-present death. Romance traditionally posits this equivalency, for their love in its impossibility is already an anachronism. It can no more survive than Bermann's attachment to the young guide can survive outside the desert, or the gentlemen of the International Sand Club can survive the devastation of World War II. Aspiring to join the nomadic world of their Bedouin guides, the Europeans gathered on this quest long to reenact a pre-national, protohistorical moment of discovery, yet every space they enter insists not only that such desire can never be fulfilled, but that the final victim of their quest will be the very persons/places they wish to map.

Occidental Time, Historical Romance, Modernist Bodies

The fiery explosion of Katherine and Almasy's plane which initiated the retrospective narrative is intercut with the film's narrative present, Italy, 1944, and Hana's (Juliette Binoche) experience of the war. Here too the setting exhibits a kind of exoticism, redolent of the past, but it is European and medieval rather than archaic and mythical. The bombed-out monastery that Hana chooses as "her" place in which to watch over the English patient suggests Gothic overtones, alludes to a world of sacred books and knights, painted gardens now exposed to the elements. In other words, this is a classic and "tame" war-torn Europe, its familiar tourist territory established through long-shots of the monastery's Renaissance architecture. And it is in this familiar albeit damaged space that Minghella attempts to script a romance in contrast to Almasy's obsessive desire for Katherine. Despite Minghella's reduction of their presence in the movie, Kip and Hana, as a couple, reflect the novel's evocation of an utterly different, one might even say, contemporary relationship, one based on mutual recognition and awareness of difference, and an evolving realization of the other as an object of desire. The film retains Kip's rescue of Hana from the wired piano, the mined garden, and her insistence on helping him dismantle it. She has hacked off her hair in slapdash fashion while Kip carefully maintains his traditional, long hair bound up in a turban. Hana admires the beauty of his un-done hair as she watches him wash it outside in the garden. She goes to his bed; he does not go to hers. However, in the chapel scene, so radically revised and expanded from the novel it may be called "original," Minghella conveys the delicacy of their relationship and its differences from Katherine's and the Count's. While it echoes the Cave of Swimmers in terms of a darkened, interior space, it also puts Kip in the role of guide as he orchestrates the logistics for the purpose of surprise and pleasure. When Kip hoists Hana up into the nave of the chapel to observe the remains of western culture's art, the frescoes lit by flares, Hana becomes the living swimmer/flyer rocking back and forth on the pulley device he anchors. She sees the art because of the flare's controlled fire, and the entire event becomes his gift to her which she accepts openly, joyfully.

However, the film ends by reinserting Hana and Kip into the narrative conventions of western romance, thus undoing the contrast between the two couples that it had set up and developed in the first half. Once again this emphasizes Minghella's decided move away from the novel's central perspective. Two scenes illustrate this point dramatically. The first locates Kip's motivations for leaving the monastery within his loyalty to the Allied project and western individualist ideology, not, as in the novel, with his sudden and complete recognition of the western racism in which he has been complicit. In the film, he breaks from Hana and their life at the monastery after the bomb they hear explode in the local village kills Hardy, his sergeant and partner. Kip, a Sikh, colonial subject, and lieutenant in the British Army, functions throughout the film as a bomb disposal expert; his job is to undo the arbitrary destructiveness of the Allied and Fascist forces. Despite his incredible expertise, he is powerless to save Hardy who, in celebrating the European war's end, has drunkenly climbed to the top of a statue. At the moment of the explosion, Kip is celebrating with Hana; they are clearly in love; they are dancing, and he is too caught up in his own life to care deeply enough about his English friend. Although Kip's departure from Hana and the monastery occurs as a consequence of orders to ship out, his emotional estrangement from Hana cannot be separated from his guilty recognition of what he sees as his own self-absorption. Hardy's death registers as Kip's personal failure; he must leave Hana in order to redeem himself for having failed to save Hardy.

Minghella's creation of this sequence functions as the film's preeminent example of historical displacement. As Walter Murch indicates (we hope naively), "the film just didn't seem to want to accommodate [the bombings of Hiroshima and Nagasaki]; Hiroshima intruded as an extraneous political event [. . .]" (Katz 138). For those of us familiar with the novel and with the material events themselves, such displacement posits, perhaps unwittingly, a version of filmic essentialism in which film and romance are "naturally" equivalent and political critiques of western adventurism are dismissed on ostensibly aesthetic, apolitical grounds. Thus Ondaatje's insistence on the horror of atomic warfare through Kip's recognition of western imperial racism and his decision to find a home among the world of his father and brother are disavowed. Instead, once again the film substitutes passion for history; in this case personal guilt is borne, not by the westerners who planted the land mines that killed Hardy, but by the East Indian man who has spent the war defusing such bombs. While Kip's despair over Hardy's death strikes the audience as touching and tragic, Minghella's exploitation of their homosocial bond is inflected by the lost-buddy motif found in every war movie every made. Thus, unlike Bermann's flirtation with the Bedouin youth, Kip's attachment to Hardy is coded within the conventions of heterosexual romance, the "Good War" narrative contextualized as it always is within the tropes of personal sacrifice and national honor.

The film's final scenes complete the undoing of the early contrast between the two couples, continuing to silence the powerful transformation Kip undergoes in the novel. Rather than projecting the narrative forward into the potentially new world, one in which Kip can be at home in India and find productive life-affirming work as a physician-healer-father, the film loses sight of Kip as he roars away from the monastery on his motorcycle. In the last scene, Hana and Caravaggio also abandon the monastery by climbing into a waiting truck, the camera zooming in on Hana as she turns to smile wistfully at a young girl seated beside her. They are returning home to Toronto. Just prior to this scene, however, a clear conflation between Hana and Katherine occurs as Hana reads Katherine's last letter to Almasy, pasted into the back of his beloved copy of Herodotus's *Histories*. Hana's voice dissolves into Katherine's, Hana's image flickers into Katherine's. Visually and aurally Hana reenacts the ending of the obsessive romance, speaking Katherine's dying words for Almasy: "[W]e are

Ralph Fiennes as the English Patient in the 1996 film version of The English Patient

© Tiger Moth/Miramax/The Kobal Collection/Bray, Phil

the real countries, not the boundaries drawn on maps by powerful men." Minghella's choice here suggests that, despite the differences in her relationship to Kip, Hana is in some way the inheritor of Katherine's romantic destiny.

Although Hana's departure suggests great confidence and self-possession, the film's layered editing—Katherine/Hana/young girl—reaffirms passion even as its own logic has attempted to do something else. For after Hana's smile, her acknowledgment of the younger generation and the camera's momentary look at the possible future, the film cuts from her face back to the initial image of the lovers in the plane flying across the desert and then cuts back to Hana's face and the sun through the trees, the end. The future, as such, is replaced by the past, by an image of endless flight over endless desert over endless time; in short, the romantic nationalism embodied through Katherine and Almasy's affair is here resuscitated and reaffirmed. This image constitutes Hana's consciousness, what she carries with her as she leaves. Doomed romance triumphs and the triangulation of the three women suggests their essential similarities, still Woman above all, whose project is romance, not to be disrupted by the exigencies of history, racism, or atomic bombs.

Through its focus on the romance of Almasy and Katherine, the film continuously reasserts the clichéd opposition between the idealized, primordial space of the desert with its unmapped terrain and mysterious peoples; and the realistic, industrial west with its gunfire and planes, its noisy and destructive invaders of that ahistorical realm. In the midst of World War II, Almasy attempts to map a middle ground between the oriental and occidental. But his desire, this space he longs for, is without foundation. He and Katherine have no place to land. For Minghella, and for those who find nostalgia more seductive than history, this irony and their tragedy are more than sufficient for a film. Ondaatje's novel, however, chooses to do more; it disrupts representations of the desert and of Europe from its opening chapters; the Arabs are already part of an ancient history and culture; they live in the present and tend to the downed Almasy not out of selfless generosity (read: "noble savage") but for his knowledge of guns; colonizers such as Almasy and his friends are part of the cultures that drop atomic bombs on people of color. And Kip, far from remaining enthralled in western politics, returns home to India.

Source: Susan E. Hawkins and Susan Danielson, "The Patients of Empire," in *Literature Interpretation Theory*, Vol. 13, 2002, pp. 139–53.

Mark A. R. Kemp

In the following essay excerpt, Kemp examines "Almásy's allegorical role as functionary of imperial Europe relative to Kip's 'Oriental'" in The English Patient.

Additionally, they are the flames of the burning plane and body of the Hungarian count, turned North African explorer, turned Nazi collaborator, turned "English patient." Almásy, like the Villa San Girolamo itself, is a repository of Western knowledge. "I am a man who can recognize an unnamed town by its skeletal shape on a map. I have always had information like a sea in me." Almásy's narrative unfolds like an archive establishing epistemological authority. That it does so as often through more aggressive forms of mastery signals the violence underlying the "innocent" accumulation of knowledge. That is, in Ondaatje's text, Almásy emblematizes the ruthless accumulative function of imperialist orientalism that Said inventories and that Mary Louise Pratt more benignly terms "planetary consciousness." With its bombed clutter of beaux arts and belles lettres, the villa thus makes an apt place for Almásy's final days.

As his identity emerges, we ask: *Why must the patient be "English"?* Certainly the assumption of his Englishness on the part of both characters and readers permits them to sustain their trust and sympathy long enough for the text to prolong the mystery and build the erotic tale offered as an "explanation." But opening up the mystery through the reconstruction of a dubious narrative means unmasking the English patient and his deeds. He is amnesiac or reticent; either way, there are gaps and contradictions in his story. His narrative unreliability serves to complicate our emotional response to Almásy. Because of the emphasis on the love story in the movie, our sympathies for Almásy make his collaboration with the Nazis more troubling. Hence the controversy over "the real Almásy's" wartime-activities that erupted shortly after the release of the movie, in which a number of historically-minded critics and viewers were incensed both by inaccuracies in the movie (as if it were a documentary) and by the heroization of a figure whose work for the Nazis allegedly resulted in deaths. I am arguing, however, that Ondaatje's text leads us instead to question Almásy and thereby perceive his complicity in politics even before the war, when he was engaged in supposedly "innocent" scientific exploration. Ondaatje may have chosen to base his character on a historical person to ensure a degree of reader responsibility

for the text. In other words, a clearly marked grounding in demonstrable historical figures and events might discourage the tendency to discredit the truths of the text because it is "only fiction."

Ondaatje understands history itself as "fictional" in the sense that it is a reconstruction and, therefore, unreliable narrative. Herodotus becomes the key source for Almásy and Ondaatje not only because he is the "first historian." According to Almásy, Herodotus' history works by "piecing together a mirage," a "supplementary to the main argument. . . . What you find in him are cul-de-sacs within the sweep of history—how people betray each other for the sake of nations, how people fall in love." The primary record besides Almásy's suspect memory is the "commonplace book" he has assembled from the fragments of his life—"maps, diary entries, writings in many languages, paragraphs cut out of other books"—and glued into a worn copy of Herodotus' *Histories*. From this text, his lover Katharine has pointedly read the famous story of Candaules and Gyges, implicitly casting herself in the role of the queen whose naked body King Candaules vainly insists on showing off. Katharine's husband has brought her to North Africa for their honeymoon and seems also to need to parade her. In thus offering herself to Almásy, the Gyges of their story, she replicates the tale, showing how "words . . . have a power" to stimulate passion and to change the course of history.

As history, Almásy's desert romance begins in the objective tone of official accounts, then gives way to grandiose jingoism:

> By the mid-1930s the lost oasis of Zerzura was found by Ladislaus de Almásy and his companions.

> In 1939 the great decade of Libyan Desert expeditions came to an end, and this vast and silent pocket of the earth became one of the theatres of war.

Only from an arrogantly Eurocentric perspective can oases be "lost" and territories "silent." Empire and economics are subtly mystified: "All human and financial behaviour lies on the far side of the issue being discussed" by the explorers at their Royal Geographic Society meetings back in London. Yet having stated the disinterested nature of these scientific expeditions, the narrator then quotes an English explorer discussing methods for "irrigation and drainage of the Nile Delta." Not only do the geographers alter the terrain and its indigenous culture in the course of their studies, they do so for the material gain or political administration of a colony. Sending fossils to the British Museum and naming geological features seem to us benign and necessary acts. The geographers' contributions to colonial projects become less benign when, for example, their maps acquire military utility. "This country," Almásy realizes too late, "had I charted it and turned it into a place of war?"

His anguish argues his innocence. But scattered observations in his narrative suggest he is not so innocent of the consequential power exercised in the desert, even by gentlemen explorers. He proclaims too vociferously the "nationlessness" of his scientific community in the Sahara. "All of us . . . wished to remove the clothing of our countries. . . . We disappeared into landscape." Yet, "some wanted their mark" on the desert, and one explorer "even wanted a tribe to take his name, and spent a year on the negotiations." Escaping "nations" indicates the imperial privilege of free movement even while the traveler imposes borders and names. The same explorer who wishes to adopt or "father" a tribe has a fancy, it turns out, for bondage and children: among the maps and family photos in Fenelon-Barnes's tent, Almásy discovers, "under the covers . . . a small Arab girl tied up, sleeping there." Here again is one of those cul-de-sacs that apparently lead nowhere (the paragraph and its image end in a blank space). But, Ondaatje wishes to remind us, such apparent dead ends really constitute crucial sites in "the sweep of history." While Almásy lets such revelations slip only to discount them through his subsequent silence, his hasty dodge to more important subjects, Ondaatje lets the gaps and abrupt leaps in narrative function ironically. Like the more complicated moment in which Almásy identifies guns for the Bedouins who have rescued him from his burning plane but remains obstinately silent about the North Africans' resistance against the European presence (even implicitly denying it), the incident with the Arab child allows Ondaatje to comment on realities that Almásy's own narrative conceals. Here, the native is literally covered up, but also simultaneously infantilized and sexualized, taken for an animal (Almásy first thinks the lump under the blanket is a dog), and commodified.

Almásy's self-representation accords perfectly with the accounts of "anti-conquest" that Mary Louise Pratt describes in her study of scientific and travel narratives, *Imperial Eyes*. Pratt argues that those writings employ, in contrast to "older imperial rhetorics of conquest," the simultaneously passive and possessive "strategies of representation whereby European bourgeois subjects seek to secure their innocence in the same moment as they assert European hegemony." Most of these writers were supported in their scientific schemes for

> **Ondaatje's text leads us instead to question Almásy and thereby perceive his complicity in politics even before the war, when he was engaged in supposedly 'innocent' scientific exploration."**

classifying nature or discovering the source of a river by home governments and private investors, thus making them "handmaidens to Europe's expansive commercial aspirations" (Pratt 34). *The English Patient* hints at such motives while portraying the "innocence" of the explorers.

Like Kurtz in *Heart of Darkness,* Almásy is a composite European, a Hungarian educated in England who speaks German and Arabic and writes books in French. In making him an "English patient," the novel lays England and Englishness out on the table, anaesthetized and dreaming of past glory. When it comes to nurse Hana's reading to this worldly "English" traveller and map-maker, what better book than Rudyard Kipling's *Kim?* A tale of colonial power and national loyalties, it serves as a crucial intertext to *The English Patient*'s exploration of identities and boundaries. Kip—obviously a combination of Kipling and Kim—has treated Almásy as the old lama, Kim's spiritual mentor and traveling companion, but also sees him as quintessentially "English" when he laments:

> I sat at the foot of this bed and listened to you, Uncle. . . . I grew up with traditions from my country, but later, more often, from *your* country. Your fragile white island that with customs and manners and books and prefects and reason somehow converted the rest of the world. . . . You and the Americans converted us.

Note the multiple allegorizations in this passage. Almásy represents England, Kip India, and with the global power shift the war is bringing, the others can now stand in for America. For Kip has heard of the U.S.'s act in Japan, and has come first to the English patient with his blame and his gun. "Here . . . listen to what you people have done," he accuses:

> American, French, I don't care. When you start bombing the brown races of the world, you're an Englishman. You had King Leopold of Belgium and now you have [f——g] Harry Truman of the USA. You all learned it from the English.

Because of the atomic explosions, Japan must now signify "Asia" for Kip—Japanese depredations in Asia obviated by Kip's necessary pan-Asian anti-Westernism.

How has his "voyage in," as Edward Said has called the gravitation of colonial subjects to the metropolis and the "hybrid cultural work" (*Culture* 244) that results, turned into this abrupt "voyage back"? In his colonized double consciousness he always sees himself ironically as "a man from Asia who has in these last years of war assumed English fathers, following their codes like a dutiful son" (Ondaatje 217). But, as he tells Hana, he also likens himself to one of the bombs he has to dismantle, on which "there is always yellow chalk scribbled. . . . Just as there was yellow chalk scribbled onto our bodies when we lined up in the Lahore courtyard" for their army physicals. He has thus been constructed and deployed as a sort of human missile to seek and destroy. But just as landmines can be equally hazardous to the people they are designed to protect—we have recently relearned this lesson in Kuwait and in Bosnia, where mines continue to kill or maim thousands per year—so can people made into weapons explode in "friendly" faces. Kirpal Singh's explosion shocks the other characters in *The English Patient* and many readers as well, particularly those who require psychological "realism" from their novels rather than the play of complex tropes and intertextualities. That *The English Patient* demands to be read as allegory is signalled from the outset by its title. The true "patient," that is, is not an Englishman but Englishness or, rather, the historical essence associated with England in its relations with the world.

But Ondaatje's novel deals more broadly with loyalties and how they influence history. Caravaggio first puts into words the problem of the futility of political loyalties:

> The trouble with all of us is we are where we shouldn't be. What are we doing in Africa, in Italy? What is Kip doing dismantling bombs in orchards, for God's sake? What is he doing fighting English wars?

Kip has avoided such questions. To survive, he has adopted the requisite invisibility of the Indian colonized subject that his brother, imprisoned for his anti-colonial activism, has refused. Kip prefers to slip across lines, "switch allegiances" like his namesake Kim, to the extent that he perhaps forgets his own identity. Almásy calls him "fate's fugitive" and hints at an avenging role for him: "Kip is my David," he remarks when commenting on the Italian Renaissance artist Caravaggio's

painting "David with the Head of Goliath." Why is Ondaatje's Caravaggio, whose first name is David, not Almásy's David? After all, he has come to hunt down the collaborator Almásy, and some of the narrative impetus comes from Caravaggio's relentless interrogation of the patient. Yet this David—who even works as a painter for a time in his appearance in Ondaatje's earlier novel *In the Skin of a Lion* (1987)—is no giant-slayer. Or, if he is, which giant is ambiguous; in his travels through Italy, he horribly witnesses a David-and-Goliath clash: "As he lay there the mined bridge exploded and he was flung upwards and then down as part of the end of the world. He opened his eyes and there was a giant head beside him." Caravaggio imagines this head—surely a decapitated statue—as somehow his victim, perhaps belonging to a person whose name he thinks he has divulged under torture to the Germans. He may feel himself to be as complicitous as Almásy. Perhaps it is this guilt and not his pity for Almásy's story of Katharine's death that makes Caravaggio excuse him in the end.

The principal confrontation, then, is between Kip and Almásy. They confront one another as friends, brothers, enemies, all within the narrative economy of historical allegory. That allegory depicts the advent of the "Third World," both in its militant form, the wars of decolonization, and its peaceful form, the "Non-Aligned Movement." The latter, a collective of Asian and African nations that first met in April 1955 in the Indonesian city of Bandung, created the name "Third World" to describe those states not militarily aligned with either the U.S. or the Soviet Union. The Third world therefore originated with the birth of the Cold War in August 1945 (although that term too did not come into use until three years later). As a contest of ideologies, the Cold War remapped the world and fought its battles for influence and economic or territorial control in the small ex-colonial states like Cuba and Vietnam.

> [Kip] feels all the winds of the world have been sucked into Asia. He steps away from the many small bombs of his career towards a bomb the size, it seems, of a city . . . he had brought out the photo of his family and gazed at it. His name is Kirpal Singh and he does not know what he is doing here.

Kip realizes his loyalties are no longer tenable after Hiroshima and Nagasaki. Such historical consciousness is, of course, impossible: Kip cannot know in August 1945 the real significance of the A-bomb, nor the global political changes it will initiate. Only readers, with the advantage of historical irony and some awareness of postcoloniality, can understand the meaning of that moment. His reaction, then, should be read as an allegorical one, in which the representative figure of colonial dependency becomes politically conscious and acts accordingly. Fleeing by motorcycle through the Italian campagna reverses Kip's earlier advance northward. As Italy recedes behind Kip, India and a struggle for independence that would be won only two years later and which Kip will presumably join lie ahead. He carries with him the burden of his decision; and, like Benjamin's angel of history, the spectre of the English patient "sits on the patrol tank facing him, the black body in an embrace with his, facing the past over his shoulder." Similarly, Africa, with its as yet "nationless" society and imperial privilege, recedes into nostalgia for Almásy—and for the "English" spirit of empire he represents.

Source: Mark A. R. Kemp, "Italy and the Ruins of Western Civilization: Michael Ondaatje's *The English Patient*," in *Nemla Italian Studies*, Vol. XXI, 1997, pp. 131–55.

Stephen Scobie

In the following essay, Scobie explores poetic imagery in The English Patient *and how Ondaatje uses it to manifest the themes of fire and desire.*

I: A Man Falls, Burning, from the Sky

This image—arresting, violent, beautiful—occurs towards the beginning of Michael Ondaatje's Booker Prize–winning novel *The English Patient*. For Ondaatje himself, quite literally, it was this image that began the novel. He has explained in an interview, "I usually begin books in a dream-like—no, that sounds a little esoteric. But I had this little fragment of a guy who had crashed in the desert. I didn't know who he was, or anything" ("In the Skin" 69).

It is typical of Ondaatje that he would begin his book with an image, rather than a character or a plot; his sensibility as a writer is grounded in poetry, and all his "novels" may be described as poetic novels. As his international reputation has grown, and as reviewers in Britain and the United States have attempted to introduce his previous work to their readers, even *The Collected Works of Billy the Kid* has been described as a novel. That is a very loose description, but it is symptomatic of the way in which Ondaatje's approach to narrative by way of the image has been assimilated, sometimes misleadingly, into more conventional categories. *Billy the Kid* is in fact a mixture of genres—prose narrative, lyric poem, collage text, and illustrated text—but it is perhaps best summed

> " All of the characters in *The English Patient* are bound together by love and loss, by absence and desire. At the centre of the pattern, controlling it by her terrible absence, is Katharine Clifton. . . ."

up by its seldom quoted subtitle, *Left Handed Poems*. Poems, that is, that come to you in a devious manner, like the reversed photographic negative that first gave rise to the legend that Billy the Kid was a left-handed gun. A gunman's poems; sinister.

Often, then, a critical response to Ondaatje's novels will have to adopt the techniques of talking about poetry as much as, if not more than, the techniques of talking about fiction. An examination of patterns of image, symbol, and metaphor will lead the reader into the book as readily as a more conventional investigation of characterization or plot. Over the years, Ondaatje has moved closer to the stance of a traditional novelist, and *The English Patient* is perhaps his most accomplished novel so far, but it is still an image that engenders and dominates the book.

This image, of a burning man falling into the desert, has all kinds of symbolic or mythological resonances (Lucifer, for instance, falling into hell—and the third page of Ondaatje's novel does cite the Miltonic phrase "the war in heaven"), but it also poses obvious questions of narrative. "I didn't know who he was," Ondaatje confesses, so the business of the novel becomes the telling of a story to explain who he was. How did he get there? Why was he burning? What happened next?

So a story begins, and unwinds compellingly before us; and as Ondaatje slowly, deviously circles the plot back towards its opening/climactic image, the moment when a man falls burning from the sky, the narrative grips us with a kind of horrified awe. At the same time, a series of related images—of fire, scars, mutilated hands, bombs, warfare and healing, desert esoterica—plays itself out with the precision of an extended poem. And out of these two matrices, of plot and image, emerges also a cast of four characters, each of them a strongly drawn individual, yet each of them also balancing, mirroring, and complementing the others, so that their total seems greater than the sum of their parts. These four characters together form another image: a constellation, perhaps, of the four elements. But especially fire.

II: "The Streets of Asia Full of Fire"

Fire dominates the novel, right from the English patient's first account of his crash: "I fell burning into the desert. . . . I flew down and the sand itself caught fire. [The Bedouin] saw me stand up naked out of it. The leather helmet on my head in flames." A later revisiting of the same scene provides an even more vivid image: "Then his legs are free of everything, and he is in the air, bright, not knowing why he is bright until he realizes he is on fire." (The intertextual echo is, surely, the line from Thomas Nashe: "Brightness falls from the air" [283]).

But not only the English patient is haunted by fire. The nurse Hana is devoted to caring for him at least in part because, as we learn only late in the novel, her own father died of burns: *So burned the buttons of his shirt were part of his skin, part of his dear chest.*" The thief Caravaggio, escaping his torturers, rests for a moment on a bridge, but the bridge explodes. "Light was pouring into the river. He swam up to the surface, parts of which were on fire." Caravaggio's ascent through burning water thus parallels and inverts the English patient's fall through burning air. The mined bridge links Caravaggio to the fourth character, Kip, whose whole element is fire: he works as a sapper, defusing bombs, in daily and imminent danger of going up in flames. Another passage describes one of Kip's colleagues who "had been working in a shaft with frozen oxygen and the whole pit had suddenly burst into flames. They hauled him out fast, already unconscious in his harness." Thus the image pattern extends: a burning man rising from the ground to meet the burning man who falls from the sky. And the man who swims to the surface of a burning river. And the man who dies of burns in a dovecote. . . .

The insistence on fire may be followed in two directions: the political and the personal. *The English Patient* is vitally concerned with the interaction between private identity public events, and with the inescapable intrusions of geopolitical forces into people's lives. The Italian villa in which the four characters gather is (or they try to make it be) a refuge from history, a place where the war is over. But the war is not over; and the observant reader will realize that the date of the action is moving inexorably closer to August 1945, to Hiroshima and Nagasaki.

Some critics have seen the sudden reference to Hiroshima at the end of the novel, and Kip's violent reaction to it, as clumsily handled: too abrupt, too unprepared for, too simplistic in its judgement that "They would never have dropped such a bomb on a white nation." (At a purely realistic level, it certainly seems implausible that any contemporary radio broadcast could provide Kip with enough details for him to react, as he does, with the full horror of a post-nuclear sensibility; but everything about the novel has surely indicated to the intelligent reader that the logic of the imagery will take precedence over any strict adherence to the conventions of realism.)

This criticism has been especially strong in the United States. As I indicated in my first endnote, an earlier version of this essay appeared in *The World and I,* a monthly magazine put out by the *Washington Times.* Each month, its book section features one text, publishing extensive extracts and three or four review articles; in February 1993, the featured book was *The English Patient.* This choice does not seem to have gone down well with the "Editor and Publisher" of *The World and I,* Morton A. Kaplan, who devoted his editorial to a bitter attack on Ondaatje's novel, principally on the grounds that it gives a historically inaccurate account of what Kaplan argues was the entirely justifiable decision to drop the atomic bomb on Hiroshima ("War often forces cruel choices," and so on):

> Fine writers such as Mark Twain or Herman Melville portrayed serious faults in society and character without stooping to hatred of their own society. Self-hatred is not a constructive emotion. And it is not fine or even good or acceptable literature to pander to this nonsense. That the author has undeniable talent only makes the perversion of those talents more deplorable. (17)

The tone of outrage here would be comic if it were not so "deplorable." The line about "hatred of their own society" suggests that Ondaatje is some kind of race traitor; the impulse to censorship is barely held in check in the notion that some forms of literature are not "acceptable"; the idea that literature should express only "constructive" emotions is equally disturbing; and the proposition that Mark Twain is a more historically accurate writer than Michael Ondaatje is simply ludicrous. (One wonders what Mr. Kaplan makes of that paragon of historical accuracy, William Shakespeare.)

But what gives Kaplan's rant its special piquancy is the fact that it is entitled, without even the benefit of quotation marks, "The English Patient." Richard Van Oort has commented on this bland appropriation:

> Kaplan becomes a player on a stage that Ondaatje's novel has already pre-inscribed, has already predicted. No doubt Kaplan feels he is a reader of Ondaatje's novel, but it seems to me that the novel reads Kaplan, indeed, reads us all, in the sense that it invites us to master its narrative while at the same time confounding our attempt to master it. . . . Kaplan is not so much the victorious critic and interpreter of Ondaatje's failed novel, but the victim, "the patient" *par excellence*. . . . The production of narrative implies a teller and a listener. In traditional psychoanalytic terms, the patient is the teller of a faulty narrative, which the analyst, the listener, must interpret to produce the correct, intelligible, consistent, truthful narrative. Clearly, this is the role Kaplan sees himself in: the sane, intelligent, objective analyst filling in the unfortunate gaps in the English Patient's failed and faulty narrative. But does it not seem strange that a novel that foregrounds the act of narrative representation as a dialogical construct, as dependent upon the context of its telling, should be reprimanded in this manner for neglecting to represent the facts, for failing to represent the one and only true narrative?

Van Oort's comments are relevant not only to the question of the novel's historical accuracy or responsibility, but also to a wider question—to which I shall return in my third and fourth sections—of the *reading* of the English patient (and of *The English Patient*). For the moment, however, I would just like to emphasize his point that Kaplan's reaction, in its naïve literalism, again assumes that the book ought to be approached as a realistic novel rather than as a poetic narrative in which, as I said earlier, the logic of the imagery takes precedence over the logic of characterization. It is this logic of imagery that I see right from the start of the novel. So my reaction to the charge that the Hiroshima theme is introduced clumsily or abruptly is twofold: first, I believe that it *is* prepared for, if only subliminally, both by the progression of the dates and by the pervasive imagery of fire; and, second, I feel that it has to be abrupt, it has to have the quality of an intrusion, to shatter the sanctuary the novel has provided for its readers no less than the villa for the characters.

The imagery of fire culminates in Kip's horrific vision: "he sees the streets of Asia full of fire. It rolls across cities like a burst map, the hurricane of heat withering bodies as it meets them, the shadow of humans suddenly in the air. This tremor of Western wisdom." This image echoes all the way back to the very first sentences of the novel, where Hana senses "a buckle of noise in the air." The picture of Hana's dead father, with the buttons of his shirt burned into his chest, is reminiscent of photographs of the victims of Hiroshima. Immediately before Kip hears the news, he is remembering the story of how the electrical system of Naples had been mined, so that "When power was turned on, the city would dissolve in flames." If the English patient is indeed, in one symbolic association, Lucifer, the falling angel expelled from heaven, then the brightness that falls from the air has always been the hanging fire of nuclear apocalypse.

III: "I Wanted to Erase My Name"

But the imagery of fire also extends in more personal directions. As the English patient himself proclaims, in a passage Hana reads from his diary, "the heart is an organ of fire." Thus, the imagery of fire extends to the intricate patterns of personal relationships presented in the novel. Love, too, burns and consumes; love, too, falls, bright, from the sky.

All of the characters in *The English Patient* are bound together by love and loss, by absence and desire. At the centre of the pattern, controlling it by her terrible absence, is Katharine Clifton, whose death forms the awful secret of the English patient's memory, and of the novel's plot. It is in their affair, presented in a series of short, intense, almost hallucinatory scenes, that the fire of the heart burns brightest. But her death becomes a literal fire, which burns away every trace of her lover's identity, leaving him as an anonymous patient in an English hospital. This anonymity, this willed (or faked) loss of identity, fulfils what had already been his conscious desire:

> *Ain, Bir, Wadi, Foggara, Khottara, Sbaduf.* I didn't want my name against such beautiful names. Erase the family name! Erase nations! I was taught such things by the desert. Still, some wanted their mark there. . . . Fenelon-Barnes wanted the fossil trees he discovered to bear his name. He even wanted a tribe to take his name, and spent a year on the negotiations. Then Bauchan outdid him, having a type of sand dune named after him. But I wanted to erase my name and the place I had come from.

The "mark" of the name is like an inscription on the blank page of the desert—or like a scar on the blank page of the body. So the English patient's desire to erase his name leaves him indeed nameless, professing ignorance of his own identity, and with his body reduced by fire to one all-encompassing scar. It is an ironic and bitter reversal of figure and ground: leaving no mark or scar upon the desert, he has become all scar, all mark. And is thus himself unreadable.

Or else, perhaps, multiply readable. As Van Oort comments,

> The English patient is at once signified and signifier: he is, on the one hand, a burnt body, devoid of demarcation, a black hole completely unreadable; but for that very reason he becomes a signifier infinitely interpretable, an anonymous text to be read. . . .

The patient's anonymity, and his (un)readability, make him the perfect blank screen onto which the other characters can project their own devious passions. Patient, passive, he receives the identities they desire him to have. He is the *English* patient: the subject, that is, of a language, of a discipline. (This book will be studied, patiently, by the patients of English, the academic students of English.)

Katharine's death leaves an absence in him too, an absence that he refuses to fill by reclaiming any name. So Hana, obsessively nursing him as her only patient, sees him as the image of every man who has died under her care in the course of the war; and, most obviously, she sees him as Patrick, her father, dying of burns. Kip, who insists (against Caravaggio's mounting body of evidence) that the patient is in fact English, also sees him, by virtue of his Englishness, as a dead father. For Kip, the patient represents Lord Suffolk, his patron in the bomb-disposal squad, who also died in a moment of fire. And, at a wider level of political allegory, the English patient and Lord Suffolk (who eats Kipling biscuits) both stand for the paternal relation of England to India, the imperialist power celebrated in Rudyard Kipling's *Kim* and rejected here by Kip.

More complex is Caravaggio's projection of desire onto the English patient. Caravaggio is a thief, but an unorthodox one, often distracted by the personal idiosyncracies of the people he is robbing. In a sense, he steals not so much their property as their identities. (In the earlier novel *In the Skin of a Lion,* there is a strangely evocative scene in which Caravaggio enters a house at night only to watch a woman reading by lamplight. The scene is duplicated by his first sight of Hana in *The English Patient.*) Working as a spy in the war, he steals and creates identities. "[H]e had been trained to invent double agents or phantoms who would take on flesh. He had been in charge of a mythical agent named 'Cheese,' and he spent weeks clothing him with facts, giving him qualities of character." It is this desire, for the theft of identity, that Caravaggio now turns on the English patient. Feeding him morphine in stronger and stronger doses, Caravaggio

elicits a confession in which the English patient becomes the central figure in one of Caravaggio's spy dramas.

At this point, Ondaatje's narrative becomes complicit with Caravaggio's desire. Whether Caravaggio's version of the English patient's identity is true or not scarcely matters, but what does matter is the fact that the story he tells satisfies, precisely, the need for story. It answers the questions implied by Ondaatje when he remarks, "I didn't know who he was, or anything." So, even as the English patient slips into talking about himself in the third person, the supposedly authoritative third-person narrative of the novel begins to refer to him by the name, Almásy, that Caravaggio has ascribed to him. The English patient becomes the character that both Caravaggio and Ondaatje will him to be—indeed, insofar as Almásy goes along with Caravaggio's decoding, he becomes also the character that he wills himself to be. No less than the other characters, Almásy projects a fiction of identity onto the blank screen of his own burned body.

As I stated earlier, there is a further, political dimension to this projection of identities onto the English patient. It is Kip, most of all, who wants the English patient to be English—so that he can project onto him all the ambivalences of his response to the imperial centre, both his colonial emulation of the English master (Lord Suffolk) and his postcolonial rejection of the English warmonger (complicit in the bombing of Hiroshima). But as Ondaatje allows his narrative to align itself with Caravaggio's version, it also undermines any such easy postcolonial reading. The English patient may represent the centre of Empire, but as a patient he is no longer an active force, and as Almásy he is no longer even English. Englishness is thus written out of the novel; always already, the centre is empty. Always already, there is *only* the post-.

IV: Cradled within the Text

In this pattern of personal relationships, then, there is a recurrent theme of deferral or substitution. Each character deflects his or her true desire through the image of another, and the English patient especially—passive, nameless—becomes their screen. But in his story, too, in the tragic memory of his affair with Katharine Clifton, there is a similar displacement and deferral. He first falls in love with Katharine when he hears her read aloud the story of Candaules and Gyges.

Candaules was an ancient king who was so proud of his wife's beauty that he did not believe that any other man could even imagine how beautiful she was. So Candaules forces his friend Gyges to view her naked, as if his own belief in her beauty could only be authenticated at one remove, by another man's testimony. But the queen sees Gyges in his hiding place, and later tells him that he must either kill Candaules or else die himself. Gyges does kill Candaules, marries the most beautiful woman, and becomes a great king.

As Katharine reads the story, she allows the clear implication that she is the queen, her husband, Geoffrey, is Candaules, and the English patient must play the role of Gyges. But the novel allows for other parallels too. It is Geoffrey, rather than the English patient, who attempts to kill his rival; and it is Caravaggio who most often plays the role of spy, watching women from secret places. The characters of the ancient story shift around, according to the characters' desires. One narrative projects itself onto others. A preexisting story affects the course of stories still in progress. As the English patient (deep in his morphine dream) explains it to Caravaggio:

> So the king is killed. A New Age begins. There are poems written about Gyges in iambic trimeters. He was the first of the barbarians to dedicate objects at Delphi. He reigned as King of Lydia for twenty-eight years, but we still remember him as only a cog in an unusual love story.

> [Katharine] stopped reading and looked up. Out of the quicksand. She was evolving. So power changed hands. Meanwhile, with the help of an anecdote, I fell in love.

> Words, Caravaggio. They have power.

Katharine reads the story of Gyges and Candaules out of a copy of Herodotus's *The Histories.* It is a book that the English patient has carried with him for years, and he not only reads it, he writes in it. "It is the book he brought with him through the fire—a [book] that he has added to, cutting and gluing in pages from other books or writing in his own observations—so they all are cradled within the text of Herodotus." This image may be read as a dramatization, on Ondaatje's part, of the ideas that critical theorists would designate as "supplementarity" or "intertextuality."

As it is set out by Jacques Derrida, the "supplement" stands in a paradoxical relationship to its "original." It presupposes both that the original is complete in itself, a finished work to which any addition must come from the outside, as a supplement; and, simultaneously, that the original is *incomplete,* that it contains within itself an emptiness or lack that the supplement comes to fill. For

the English patient, Herodotus's *The Histories* is both complete (the act of cutting and pasting in pages from other books foregrounds itself as the addition of something extraneous) and incomplete (what he writes into the text responds to a lack, and a demand, that the text already exhibits). In thus supplementing the text of Herodotus, the English patient is duplicating the supplementary nature of the original; he quotes Herodotus as saying, "This history of mine . . . has from the beginning sought out the supplementary to the main argument." As Derrida phrases it, "One wishes to go back *from the supplement to the source:* one must recognize that there is a *supplement at the source*" (304).

The idea of intertextuality has been one of the mainstays of recent literary theory. Far more than simply influence or allusion, intertextuality is both an active interaction between texts and the sense that the possibility of such interaction is the precondition for the very existence of a text. In *The English Patient,* Ondaatje translates this theoretical concept into literal images. The English patient writes his own observations into the blank spaces of Herodotus's pages. Hana does the same, for books are "half her world"; she pulls down volumes at random from the library shelves and makes notes about the men who share her life.

> She opens *The Last of the Mohicans* to the blank page at the back and begins to write in it.

> *There is a man named Caravaggio, a friend of my father's. I have always loved him. . . .*

> She closes the book and then walks down into the library and conceals it in one of the high shelves.

Cradled within the text, Hana confesses and hides what she cannot declare. Cradled within the text of Herodotus, the English patient falls in love with Katharine Clifton. Cradled within the text, Michael Ondaatje's novel quotes unceasingly: *Kim, The Last of the Mohicans, The Charterhouse of Parma,* John Milton, Christopher Smart, Anne Wilkinson. Cradled within the text, books (like everything else) become weapons. Caravaggio remembers a German spy who used Daphne du Maurier's *Rebecca* as a codebook with which to report on English troop movements. For Kip, booby-trap bombs can be found anywhere: in the metronome of a piano, in "the spines of books." Kip reads the bombs he defuses as he would a particularly difficult, intricate (and dangerous) text.

Words have power; words are dangerous. A book is what you take with you through the fire.

V: Punching the Glass

It is characteristic of Ondaatje that he should thus celebrate the power of words (the lover's power, the poet's power) in images that simultaneously suggest their destructive potential. In previous novels and poems, he has shown his fascination for the fine and uneasy balance between creation and destruction, between the book as revelation and the book as booby-trap bomb, blowing off the unwary reader's hands. *The Collected Works of Billy the Kid* explores the parallel between the artist and the outlaw, and the "works" are both poems and killings. *Coming through Slaughter* portrays a musician who goes mad at the height of a parade, and collapses into silence. Ondaatje is fascinated by these figures, though in his poems he also distinguishes himself from them, holds them at arm's length:

> Why do I love most
> among my heroes those
> who sail to that perfect edge
> where there is no social fuel
> Release of sandbags
> to understand their altitude—("White Dwarfs" 70)

As a writer, Ondaatje is drawn to the moment when balance collapses, the moment when his characters lose their fine control; but of course he himself, in the precision of his work, always maintains his own balance, his own control.

In many of these works there is a recurring image of damaged hands. For both Billy (the gunfighter) and Buddy (the cornet player), the hands are the vehicle of artistic work. Buddy dreams of smashing his hand into glass, of raising his wrist into the path of a circling overhead fan, of crawling over barbed wire. At the moment of his death, Billy's hand smashes through a window and his arm goes "manic." The moment the hand goes through the glass is, in Ondaatje's imagery, the moment the self-destructive artist most fully declares himself, both as artist and as victim—victim of the violence he evokes in those around him, and victim also of the violence within himself, within his own art.

Though none of the characters in *The English Patient* is explicitly an artist, they all share the same fascination with esoteric knowledge and detailed manual skills. And the same imagery recurs. The thief Caravaggio, dependent on his hands for his breaking-and-entering skills, loses both his thumbs, and the mutilation reduces him to a state of helplessness akin to Buddy Bolden's silence. The injuries from which Katharine dies include a broken wrist. As his plane crashes, the English patient "thrusts his hands up against the cockpit glass. . . . Begins punching the glass, cracking it, finally breaking it, and the oil and the fire slop and spin everywhere." Having broken the glass, he falls, burning, from the sky.

But there is also, in this novel, healing. While Caravaggio and the English patient remain lost, locked in their world of morphine and pain, Hana and Kip slowly, tentatively, reach beyond the war. Near the end of the novel, there is an image of Hana, "her hands in her pockets now, the way Kip loved to see her walk. So relaxed, as if she had put her arms away for the night, now in simple armless movement." But this image is benign in comparison to Caravaggio's ruined hands or Katharine's broken wrist: Hana's hands are simply put away for the night. In the morning they will again be a nurse's hands, moving over the patient's burned body.

Similarly, for Kip, there is a moment when, defusing a bomb, he realizes that "If he were wrong, the small explosion would take off his hand." But the explosion does not come for Kip, at least not in this form, and our final image of him is one that combines his manual dexterity with an instinctive, unspoken connection between himself and Hana, persisting across years of silence and continents of separation. Hana is in Canada, a figure unknown now even to her author; Kip is in India, working as a doctor, and is a husband and father.

> And so Hana moves and her face turns and in a regret she lowers her hair. Her shoulder touches the edge of a cupboard and a glass dislodges. Kirpal's left hand swoops down and catches the dropped fork an inch from the floor and gently passes it into the fingers of his daughter, a wrinkle at the edge of his eyes behind his spectacles.

Left-handed catch. Left-handed poems. A novel that comes from the left hand of history, out of the sinister heart of fire.

Source: Stephen Scobie, "The Reading Lesson: Michael Ondaatje and the Patients of Desire," in *Essays on Canadian Writing*, Vol. 53, Summer 1994, pp. 92–106.

Sources

Bemrose, John, Review of *The English Patient*, in *Maclean*, Vol. 105, No. 42, October 19, 1992, p. 71.

Novak, Amy, "Textual Hauntings: Narrating History, Memory, and Silence in *The English Patient*," in *Studies in the Novel*, Vol. 36, No. 2, Summer 2004, pp. 206–32.

Ondaatje, Michael, *The English Patient*, Knopf, 1992.

Further Reading

Herodotus, *The Histories*, Oxford University Press, 1998.
In *The English Patient*, the title character's only possession is a copy of *The Histories* by Herodotus. Herodotus, who lived during the 5th century B.C., is widely regarded as the father of the study of history. *The Histories* records the customs and practices of peoples of what is today known as the Middle East; the book also covers various wars between the Greeks and Persians.

Keegan, John, *The Second World War*, Penguin Books, 1990.
A chronology of World War II, this one-volume history also includes chapters specifically devoted to the details of such components as weapons production and espionage.

Kipling, Rudyard, *Kim*, W.W. Norton, 2002.
First published in 1901, *Kim* is the British author Rudyard Kipling's masterpiece novel. Set in British colonial India, it is the story of an Indian-born British boy who lives among the native people of India and becomes a follower of a Tibetan Buddhist monk. Ondaatje makes numerous references directly to this novel in *The English Patient*.

Said, Edward, *The Edward Said Reader*, edited by Moustafa Bayoumi and Andrew Rubin, Vintage Books, 2000.
Edward Said was one of the most influential figures in the field of post-colonial studies, especially pioneering the study of the effect of colonialism on the reading and writing of literature. *The English Patient*, especially through the character of Kip, broaches many of the themes of identity that post-colonial studies examine: this collection is a worthy introduction to Said's works on the subject.

Gravity's Rainbow

Thomas Pynchon

1973

Thomas Pynchon's 1973 novel *Gravity's Rainbow* is one of the landmarks of American fiction. Set in the final months and aftermath of World War II, it focuses on a search for German "V-2" rockets, which were the world's first guided missiles, as well as the wartime atmosphere in London and the postwar atmosphere in Germany and France. Particularly important to this narrative are American Lieutenant Tyrone Slothrop and his quest to find one particular, mysterious rocket called 00000, as well as Slothrop's search for his identity and the conspiracy surrounding his childhood and military career. The novel includes such a great number of characters, subplots, historical flashbacks, and governmental-corporate conspiracies, however, that it resists an accurate summary and relentlessly poses questions about the nature of history, Western culture, and reality itself. These questions apply not just to World War II history but to the Vietnam War, the American civil rights movement, and other events that occurred while Pynchon was writing the novel in the 1960s and early 1970s.

Because of its immense and complex scope, *Gravity's Rainbow* is recognized to be an extremely difficult novel to read and understand. In fact, some readers and critics have claimed that it is utterly incomprehensible and unreadable. Important characters and storylines often diverge, disappear entirely, or turn out to be merely fictional, and many readers have found it necessary to use companion literature or reread the eight-hundred-page novel multiple times. As one is reading the novel,

however, it is important to remember that its difficulty and obscurity arc critical aspects of its meaning: Pynchon is invested in a thorough critique of post-World-War-II society. To Pynchon, the complexity and obscurity of *Gravity's Rainbow* highlights the confusion, dismay, purposelessness, and overwhelming technological escalation of the contemporary world.

Author Biography

Little is known of Pynchon's personal life because of his deliberate reclusion. He refuses to participate in interviews with the media, and only his closest and most trusted friends know where he lives. In fact, more is known about Pynchon's ancestors than Pynchon himself. His ancestor William Pynchon was a Puritan writer who arrived in America in 1630 but returned to England after a tract he wrote was declared heretical. Pynchon also had a prominent ancestor and namesake who was a reverend and scholar in nineteenth-century New England, and another branch of his family contained prominent stock brokers before the market crash of 1929.

What is known about Pynchon is that he was born in Glen Cove, Long Island, New York on May 8, 1937, son of an industrial surveyor and Republican politician. In 1953, Pynchon entered Cornell University to study in its engineering physics department, but he changed to the college of arts and sciences during his second year and then dropped out of college to serve in the Navy. Pynchon returned to Cornell in 1957 to complete a degree in English, and he became friends with the writer Richard Fariña, who died in a tragic accident in 1966. While at Cornell, Pynchon may have been influenced by the famous Russian American novelist Vladimir Nabokov, who was an English professor there. In any case, Pynchon wrote his first short stories while studying there.

In 1960, Pynchon went to work as a technical writer for Boeing Aircraft in Seattle, Washington, and remained there for two and a half years. He published his first stories in 1960, and his first novel *V.* was published in 1963 to considerable critical acclaim. Complex and erudite, *V.* focuses on Herbert Stencil's obsessive quest to discover the person or thing his father's diary refers to simply as "V." Pynchon's second novel, *The Crying of Lot 49* (1967) uses the second law of thermodynamics (regarding entropy) as a metaphor for social de-

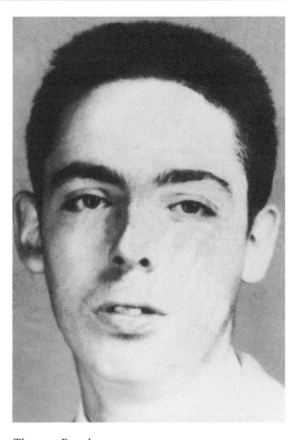

Thomas Pynchon   UPI/Corbis-Bettmann

cline. *Gravity's Rainbow* was published in 1973, and Pynchon's next novel, *Vineland*, which did not appear until seventeen years later, was generally considered a disappointment. *Mason and Dixon* (1997) is a fantasy about the formative years of the United States, and like Pynchon's other novels it fascinates some critics and frustrates others.

Plot Summary

Part 1: Beyond the Zero

Gravity's Rainbow has traditionally been broken into numbered episodes based on the novel's unnamed sections that are divided by lines of seven squares. Episode 1 of part 1 takes place on December 18, 1944, with Pirate Prentice watching a German V-2 rocket approach London. Pirate makes a "Banana Breakfast" for his troops and goes to receive a message from his superiors in Greenwich. In episode 3, Teddy Bloat photographs the desk of American Tyrone Slothrop in ACHTUNG headquarters (a special operations unit of the British military), interested in a map of London with stars marking Slothrop's sexual escapades. Episode 4 describes Slothrop's girl-chasing in London, his childhood, and his Puritan ancestry.

Roger Mexico and Jessica Swanlake reveal their love and attend a séance in episode 5. The perspective then shifts to describe Pirate's memories of his service in the Persian Gulf and of a woman he loved and lost. Episode 6 describes Roger and Jessica's relationship, and the pair drive to meet Dr. Pointsman. Pointsman's foot gets stuck in a toilet bowl as he and Roger try to capture a dog on the site of a bombed-out house. In episode 8, Pointsman talks about Pavlovian psychology with Kevin Spectro, and they discuss what Slothrop's map has to do with the German rockets. The rockets seem to be distributing in a random sequence as Roger predicts, but Slothrop's map suggests that each of his sexual adventures occurs on the site of a rocket blasts, some time before it hits. As a child, Slothrop was conditioned and later de-conditioned by Dr. Laszlo Jamf to become sexually excited at loud noises, and Pointsman comes to believe this is why he can anticipate the rocket strikes.

In episode 9, Roger and Jessica sleep in their house that has been ordered abandoned, and a voice from Jessica's perspective describes conversations between Roger and Pointsman about statistical versus deterministic views of the rocket strikes. Episode 10 describes Slothrop's hypnotic vision in a London hospital in which he is chased by African Americans down a toilet and then enters a cowboy story. Pirate decodes a message in episode 11 that, it later becomes clear, means that the British government has taken Katje Borgesius out of Holland. Episodes 12 and 13 describe Pointsman, Brigadier General Pudding, and other staff at the mysterious government project called "The White Visitation," which will be involved in manipulating and controlling Slothrop.

In episode 14, Katje is filmed in order to condition Pointsman's octopus, Grigori. The episode flashes back to Katje's period with Captain Blicero and his sexual slave Gottfried and tells the story of Katje's colonial ancestor Frans van der Groov. In episode 15, Slothrop is released from the hospital (which will later be hit by a V-2 rocket) and goes to have sex with a girl named Darlene in an East London flat. Episode 16 contains vignettes about Roger and Jessica, and episode 17 journeys through Pointsman's beliefs and fantasies about his psychological discoveries through Slothrop.

Episode 18 introduces Carroll Eventyr and his supernatural connection to a man killed during a 1930 Berlin street riot. The next episode continues a discussion of Berliners in the years before Hitler, such as Leni Pökler and her frustration with her husband Franz's devotion to science. Episode 20 describes the Christmas Eve party at The White Visitation. Slothrop is at a casino on the French Riviera, being watched by Pointsman's operatives. Episode 21 is a Boxing Day (the day after Christmas) scene with Roger and Jessica visiting Jessica's sister and her family.

Part 2: Un Perm' au Casino Hermann Goering

In the first episode of part 2, whose French title means "A Furlough at the Hermann Goering Casino," Slothrop saves Katje from Octopus Grigori and begins to have paranoid suspicions. Slothrop spends the night with Katje, and the next morning she arranges for all of his clothes and papers (his identity) to be stolen. In episode 3, Slothrop begins studying rocket science, and Katje gives him a subtle warning before she departs for England. In England, Katje is ordered to keep the director of The White Visitation, Brigadier Pudding, under Pointsman's control by acting as his sexual dominatrix.

Slothrop discovers evidence of a corporate conspiracy in episode 5, as well as elements connecting his childhood conditioning to a mysterious rocket project (Rocket 00000). At a party he meets a profiteer named Blodgett Waxwing who confirms his suspicions about the octopus episode, and he decides to escape and meet Waxwing in Nice. Slothrop learns of his friend Tantavity's death in episode 7, and he flees for Nice, becomes involved with a group of Argentine anarchists, ditches the Secret Service agents who are following him, and assumes the identity of English war correspondent Ian Scuffling. In episode 8, the Nazis have surrendered and Pointsman, Roger, Jessica, and Katje meet at a seaside resort to discuss their plans for Slothrop.

Part 3: In the Zone

Slothrop has traveled from Switzerland to Nordhausen, Germany, and continues to investigate connections between his childhood conditioning by Laszlo Jamf, a plastic called Imipolex G, and Rocket 00000. He also meets a new lover, Geli Tripping, who is the girlfriend of the Russian operative Tchitcherine. In episode 2 Slothrop investigates the rocket factory "Mittelwerke" but is chased and nearly caught by Major Duane Marvy. Episode 3 discusses Enzian, the leader of a Black rocket team called the Schwarzkommando, and Herero culture. In episode 4, Slothrop escapes to Berlin in a hot-air balloon, and episode 5 discusses Tchitcherine's background.

In episode 6, Slothrop has been in occupied Berlin for several weeks and has taken up with Margherita (or Greta) Erdmann. He assumes a new identity, "Rocketman," and raids the house occupied by President Harry Truman, recovering six kilograms of hashish before Tchitcherine captures him. The series of episodes that follow provide background information about Tchitcherine's interest in Slothrop, Slothrop's relationship with Greta, Greta's marriage and her daughter Bianca, and the firing of Rocket 00000. In episode 12, Slothrop delivers the hashish to the underworld character Säure and continues his sexual relationship with Greta.

In episode 13, Horst Achtfaden is interrogated by Enzian and the Hereros about the Schwarzgerät (or S-Gerät), which will turn out to be a compartment inside Rocket 00000 made of the plastic Imipolex G (which was invented by Dr. Jamf) and intended to hold a person. In episode 14, Slothrop and Greta travel to a resort town and get on a ship called the *Anubis* where Greta meets her daughter Bianca. Slothrop has violent sex with Bianca and, in episode 16, a story about Japanese Ensign Morituri reveals that Greta has child-murdering tendencies. Episode 17 delves further into Greta's history and adds to Slothrop's knowledge of Rocket 00000. Slothrop falls off the ship in a storm and is picked up by Frau Gnahb, who brings him to "Springer," or Gerhart von Göll. Springer agrees to obtain the Schwarzgerät for Slothrop, but Springer is abducted by Tchitcherine.

In episode 20, Klaus Närrisch leads a raid to free Springer and is captured during the escape. Episode 21 describes Enzian's plans to launch Rocket 00001 in order to stop the tribal Hereros from committing suicide. In episode 22 Slothrop boards the *Anubis*, where he discovers Bianca's dead body, and he disembarks to travel through the Zone towards the location of "Operation Backfire," the British rocket research center. Katje watches a film in episode 23 that contains an implanted message suggesting that she leave The White Visitation. In episode 24, Katje and Pirate tour a version of hell.

Slothrop treks across Germany in episode 25 until he meets a young boy searching for a lemming. He encounters Major Marvy but escapes him

because he is disguised as a Russian officer. Slothrop warns the Hereros that Marvy plans to raid the Schwarzkommando, and Marvy waits with Tchitcherine before the attack. In episode 28, Slothrop assumes the role of "Plechazunga" (a pig-hero), escapes a raid, and meets Franz Pökler. Pökler tells him about Laszlo Jamf, and episode 30 discusses Slothrop's uncle Lyle Bland, who participated in the scheme to sell Slothrop to Jamf.

In episode 31, Slothrop is at Operation Backfire, where two British medical officers are preparing to castrate him. Meanwhile, a plane is on its way to drop the atomic bomb on Hiroshima. Slothrop escapes and has sex with Leni Pökler, and because Major Marvy has put on the Plechazunga suit, he is mistaken for Slothrop and castrated. In episode 32, Tchitcherine worries that his government will destroy him, and two rich Londoners discuss Pointsman's failure with Slothrop, the Conservative plan to destroy blacks, and their own homosexuality.

Part 4: The Counterforce

In episode 1, Slothrop finds the long-lost kazoo of his childhood and Pirate Prentice flies to Germany. Roger Mexico discovers in episode 2 that Jessica has left him for her husband Jeremy, and he joins the "Counterforce" of Pirate, Katje, and other discontented characters who want to find Slothrop and dismantle the "Man," a corporate-governmental conspiracy. Episode 3 is a paranoid vision about a colonel and a conspiracy in the power and light industry. In episode 4, Katje meets Enzian, and they discuss Blicero and the launch of Rocket 00000. Episode 5 notes what happened to Miklos Thanatz after he was thrown off the *Anubis*; by the end of it, Thanatz has told the Schwarzkommando what he knows about Rocket 00000.

Amidst the myriad of events in episode 6, Slothrop discovers that the United States had dropped the atomic bomb. Episode 7 reveals that the Soviets have allowed Tchitcherine to track his half-brother Enzian in order to find the Schwarzkommando themselves. In episode 8, Jessica tells Roger that she is planning a family with Jeremy, and the Counterforce (now joined by Brigadier Pudding's spirit) comes to believe that Rocket 00000 was fired due north. Episode 9 discusses Geli Tripping's continued search for Tchitcherine and then reveals Gottfried kneeling before Blicero in the days before the launch of Rocket 00000. In episode 10, Enzian and the Schwarzkommando, having avoided a number of attacks, prepare to launch Rocket 00001. Geli finds Tchitcherine in episode 11, and her magic blinds Tchitcherine just as he is about to confront Enzian. The final episode fragments into sixteen scenes, including Gottfried's ascent inside the Schwarzgerät compartment of Rocket 00000, and the novel concludes in a 1970 Los Angeles theater that is about to be destroyed by a missile.

Characters

Horst Achtfaden

Achtfaden is an aerodynamics man who worked on the Schwarzgerät. Enzian and the Schwarzkommando capture him and interrogate him in part 3, episode 13.

Beaver

See Jeremy Swanlake

Lyle Bland

Slothrop's uncle Bland participated in the scheme to sell Slothrop for use in Laszlo Jamf's experiments.

Captain Dominus Blicero

Dominus Blicero is the code name of Lieutenant Weissmann, the controller of Rocket 00000 and a Nazi arch-villain. He is a sadomasochist who keeps a boy named Gottfried along with Katje Borgesius as sexual slaves, and by the end of the novel the reader learns that Blicero has launched Gottfried in the Schwarzgerät section of Rocket 00000. Blicero thinks of this grand plan as a form of sexual sacrifice by which he is able to transcend his existence and become a true lord of death.

Critics have argued that Blicero is meant to represent a spirit of death, and he seeks to dominate and destroy people as a force that is somewhat like death itself. This interpretation explains perhaps why Slothrop, who is obsessed with and possibly in love with death, spends the entire novel searching for Blicero (and Gottfried). Blicero also represents a number of political ideas, however; for example, his sexual domination and destruction of Gottfried is connected to the Nazi Holocaust. Blicero (or Weissmann, which means "white man" in German) is also responsible for bringing Enzian to Germany and is representative of white supremacist ideology. Katje describes his appearance as dominated by his yellow teeth: "long, terrible, veined with bright brown rot."

Teddy Bloat

Bloat is a British soldier and a participant in Pointsman's conspiracy against Slothrop. He is a friend of Tantavity's and Slothrop's until Slothrop discovers that Bloat is spying on him at the Hermann Goering Casino. Bloat is promoted to major upon his return, and he may have had something to do with Tantavity's death.

Seaman Bodine

Seaman Bodine is "an American sailor [of the U.S. destroyer *John E. Badass*] with an orangutan look to him." He convinces Slothrop (as Rocketman) to recover his six kilograms of hashish without telling him that it is outside President Truman's house, and he appears in part 3 to help Slothrop escape in a Red Cross van from Pointsman's operatives.

Katje Borgesius

Katje is a spy and lover who takes on a variety of complex roles in the novel. She is Blicero's slave, along with Gottfried, until she departs and meets with Pirate Prentice, who tells her she can work at The White Visitation. Pointsman then assigns her to seduce Slothrop, which she does and then arranges for his identity to be stolen, but before she returns to England Katje subtly warns Slothrop of the conspiracy against him. Back at The White Visitation, Pointsman assigns Katje to act as Domina Noctura, the dominatrix of Brigadier Pudding in order to keep him in line. Finally, Katje joins the Counterforce to find Slothrop and discover what happened to Rocket 00000.

Katje is a mysterious character in the sense that her motivations and employer are never entirely clear. Some evidence suggests that she may be involved with Enzian in some way, for example, although this is never fully explained. Katje is from Holland and has Dutch colonial ancestors. She is very attractive and blonde, but she knows that "inside herself . . . she is corruption and ashes," and she is connected in some way to the Holocaust. Nevertheless, Katje appears to have genuinely warm feelings towards Slothrop and some of her other lovers.

Hilary Bounce

A rocket scientist from Shell International Petroleum, Bounce teaches Slothrop about aerodynamics and raises Slothrop's suspicions about an international corporate conspiracy.

Emil Bummer

"Once the Weimar Republic's most notorious cat burglar and doper," Bummer (known as Säure) is an underworld figure involved in Slothrop's adventures in the Zone. Säure is responsible for putting Slothrop in touch with Springer.

Ronald Cherrycoke

Cherrycoke is a "noted psychometrist" for Psi Section (a special operations unit of the British military focusing on paranormal psychology).

Clayton Chiclitz

Chiclitz is a sidekick of Major Marvy and a character from Pynchon's earlier novel *V*.

Christian

Christian is a companion of Enzian. He is extremely angry at Enzian and Josef Ombindi for their treatment of his sister Maria and her husband Pavel, but he follows Enzian after they find Pavel.

Darlene

Darlene is one of Slothrop's lovers in London.

Reverend Paul de la Nuit

De la Nuit is a "chaplain and staff automatist" for the British.

Sir Stephen Dodson-Truck

Dodson-Truck is a Pointsman operative with a pompous Oxford accent.

Oberst Enzian

Enzian is the half-brother of Tchitcherine and the leader of the Schwarzkommando. Half European and half Herero (a tribe from a former German colony in Africa), Enzian joins the ranks of the Otukungurua in order to carry out the quest of the Herero "Revolutionaries of the Zero." He comes to lead the Black rocket task force of the Schwarzkommando, whose goal is to launch Rocket 00001. Enzian is brought to Germany and trained by Blicero, but at some point he seems to stop carrying out Blicero's orders. Enzian is consumed with his feud with Tchitcherine as well as his own interests, and by the end of the novel he has apparently launched himself in a replica of Rocket 00000 as a kind of sacrificial ritual to avoid tribal suicide among the Herero.

Bianca Erdmann

Bianca is Greta's young daughter who is tortured and raped by many men. Slothrop has sex with her and, in a way, falls in love with her before he falls out of the *Anubis*. She dies a gruesome death on the ship after this, and Slothrop later finds her body.

Greta Erdmann

Also known as Margherita or Gretel, Greta is one of Slothrop's more maniacal lovers. She was a star in German horror/pornographies, she is into sadomasochism, and she has a tendency towards violence against children. She is searching for her daughter Bianca while she is with Slothrop, and she is married to Miklos Thanatz.

Carroll Eventyr

Eventyr is a psychic and The White Visitation's "resident medium," and he later joins the Counterforce in search of Rocket 00000.

Osbie Feel

Osbie is a secret cameraman for ACHTUNG (he tapes Katje and possibly has a relationship with her) and later a member of the Counterforce to find Slothrop. He cuts a somewhat comical figure, becomes a heavy drug user, and gets a tattoo of Porky Pig.

Milton Gloaming

Gloaming is a member of Psi Section who is involved in a word-counting project.

Frau Gnahb

Frau Gnahb is the "apple-cheeked lady" who picks up Slothrop after he falls off the *Anubis*. She calls herself the "queen of the coastal trade" (Slothrop calls her "unbalanced"), and she helps Slothrop by taking him to Springer.

Otto Gnahb

Frau Gnahb's son, Otto helps Slothrop rescue Springer from the Tchitcherine.

Gottfried

Gottfried is Blicero's passive slave who is launched in the Schwarzgerät of Rocket 00000. He succumbs to Blicero's incessant sexual domination of him, and Blicero sacrifices Gottfried in a kind of magic ritual in which he destroys his sacred sexual object.

Rollo Groast

Groast works in various capacities for the British.

Myron Grunton

Grunton worked for the BBC, helped to form the Schwarzkommando, and worked for The White Visitation.

Dr. Laszlo Jamf

Dr. Jamf is the scientist who conditioned Slothrop when he was young and invented the plastic Imipolex G (used to make the Schwarzgerät). Although he never appears in the novel, Dr. Jamf is one of the key characters to understanding the plot, particularly as it relates to Slothrop and his paranoia. Jamf conditioned Slothrop to get an erection at any loud noise, then de-conditioned him, and Pointsman believes that this de-conditioning is responsible for Slothrop's anticipation of the striking point of V-2 rockets. Despite his importance, however, there is some suggestion in the novel that Dr. Jamf is simply a figment of Slothrop's imagination.

Ludwig

Ludwig is a "surprisingly fat kid of eight or nine" who is searching for his lost lemming when he meets Slothrop.

Maria

Maria is Christian's sister who has been mistreated by Josef Ombindi's Empty Ones.

Major Duane Marvy

A fat, racist American major, Marvy leads a technical intelligence team that hunts Slothrop throughout the Zone. Slothrop narrowly escapes from him (in a hot air balloon) after encountering him at an occupied German rocket factory and escapes him again while disguised as a Russian officer. Later, Marvy is caught in a British raid of a brothel, mistaken for Slothrop, and castrated by Pointsman's operatives.

Roger Mexico

Mexico is a statistician at Psi Section and the lover of Jessica Swanlake. Mexico endures a conflict between his work and his lover throughout part 1, wishing with Jessica that the war would end, and he is something of an anti-Pointsman figure because he believes strongly in the randomness of statistics. In part 4, he realizes that Jessica is working for Pointsman, devotes himself to the Counterforce, and plays a prominent role in the effort to find Slothrop.

Kurt Mondaugen

Mondaugen is an electrical engineer who works with Pökler, for Blicero.

Ensign Morituri

Morituri is an ensign in the Japanese Imperial Navy who alerts Slothrop to Greta's capacity for violence. He was in kamikaze training, but he could not stomach it and came to Germany as a Japanese liaison.

Clive Mossmoon

Mossmoon is a plastics expert who is probably gay.

Scorpia Mossmoon

Scorpia is a racist Briton who has an affair with Pirate.

Lieutenant Oliver Muffler-Mafflick

Tantavity, as he is called, is Slothrop's good friend until he dies mysteriously. He shares an office with Slothrop and travels with him to the Hermann Goering Casino, and he has a tendency to get drunk and be mischievous. After Slothrop returns to England he discovers that Muffler-Mafflic has died, and this information drives Slothrop to flee to Nice.

Klaus Närrisch

Närrisch is a slightly crazy rocket guidance expert who worked with Achtfaden on the Schwarzgerät. He has a "lumpy nose, stoop, week's growth of orange and gray whiskers, and oversize leather trenchcoat with no trousers on underneath." Närrisch meets Slothrop on Frau Gnahb's ship and leads a raid to free Springer, but Tchitcherine captures him.

Domina Noctura

See Katje Borgesius

Josef Ombindi

Ombindi is the leader of the "Empty Ones," which is another name for the Herero of Enzian's Otukungurua.

Andreas Orukambe

Andreas is a Schwarzkommando cohort of Enzian.

Dr. Edward W. A. Pointsman

Ned Pointsman is a Pavlovian doctor at The White Visitation who forms plans to manipulate Slothrop's life. At first he believes Slothrop can be used to predict V-2 rocket strikes, and, more importantly for him, he thinks he will win the Nobel Prize based on his discovery of Slothrop's psychological condition. Most of Pointsman's attempts are botched or go awry, however; he begins to lose touch with reality, and he ends up in disgrace. Part of his problem is that he believes there is a conspiracy against him and the seven other Pavlovian doctors who are in possession of a book about behaviorism, all of whom seem to be dying.

Franz Pökler

Pökler is a German chemical engineer whom Blicero (as Lieutenant Weissmann) blackmails into working on the Schwarzgerät by holding his daughter Ilse in a concentration camp. Pökler is allowed to see Ilse (or a different girl pretending to be Ilse) once a year, and this begins to drive him insane. He finally quits the "game" of continuing to work efficiently, visits the concentration camp where his wife and daughter were kept, and tells his story to Slothrop.

Ilse Pökler

The daughter of Franz and Leni Pökler, Ilse is an innocent child who is put into a concentration camp and probably abused in order to keep her father under control. Towards the end of the novel, however, there is the suggestion that Ilse survives and is not used as a sex object. Ilse is mysteriously connected to Bianca Erdmann, and Slothrop wonders whether they are the same child.

Leni Pökler

Lena is Franz Pökler's wife, the lover of Peter Sacha, and a Nazi sex slave. She is involved with anti-Nazi intellectuals before the war, she is held in a concentration camp, and after the war she is a prostitute who has sex with Slothrop under the name "Solange."

Dr. Porkyevitch

Porkyevitch is a scientist in charge of conditioning an octopus named Grigori in order to manipulate Slothrop into loving Katje.

Graciela Imago Portales

"International eccentric" Graciela is one of the Argentine anarchists.

Captain Geoffrey Prentice

Known as "Pirate," Prentice is a British intelligence officer who later joins the Counterforce. He stars in the opening scenes of the novel, but he turns out to be important mainly because of his mysterious working relationship with Katje. Pirate is the one to sign Katje on at The White Visitation, and later they work together in the Counterforce.

Brigadier Ernest Pudding

An eighty-year-old veteran of World War I, Pudding is in charge of The White Visitation. He has delusions about his own importance, he has an intense desire for sadomasochism, and he disapproves of Pointsman's plans for Slothrop. Pointsman keeps him under control, however, by sending Katje to be his dominatrix, and Pudding dies of an infection after eating Katje's feces. Pudding later appears as a spiritual member of the Counterforce.

Walter Rathenau

A German foreign minister who was assassinated in 1922, Rathenau was an architect of conspiratorial government control policies. The Psi Section attempts to communicate with him in a séance.

Géza Rózsavölgyi

Rózsavölgyi is a Hungarian scientist who works with Pointsman at The White Visitation.

Peter Sachsa

"Habitually cool and sarcastic," Sachsa works at The White Visitation and is Leni Pökler's lover.

Säure

See Emil Bummer

Gustav Schlabone

Gustav is a composer, instrumentalist, and "Säure Bummer's frequent unwelcome doping partner." He is involved in the postwar underworld scene.

Max Schlepzig

Schlepzig is a former German film star and an alternate identity of Slothrop.

Ian Scuffling

See Tyrone Slothrop

Webley Silvernail

Silvernail is an audiovisual expert at The White Visitation.

Broderick Slothrop

Slothrop's father, Broderick sold his son to Dr. Jamf's experiments in exchange for Harvard tuition.

Tyrone Slothrop

Slothrop is, as far as there is one, the main character of the novel. He is a lieutenant in the

United States Army on assignment in London during World War II, and the bulk of his efforts are spent trying to find the Schwarzgerät and uncover its connection to his childhood trauma. Slothrop's goals and desires change greatly in the course of the novel, however. When Franz Pökler asks him whether the Schwarzgerät is "really all you're after?" Slothrop replies, "Don't know." He is extremely promiscuous and a classic sufferer from paranoia, seeing connections in everything. Indeed, he comes to believe that the war and his entire life are run by a group of conspirators. The novel provides much evidence to support this paranoia, although sometimes Pynchon casts doubt about whether various key events, such as Slothrop's romantic encounters or various military operations and conspiracies in which he is involved, are real or imagined.

Slothrop is descended from a long line of Puritan American ancestors, about whom he frequently muses. When he was young, his father and uncle sold him for use in Dr. Laszlo Jamf's scientific experiments, which condition him and then de-condition him to have an erection when he hears a loud noise. Slothrop's involvement with Jamf is perhaps the key reason why he is such a valuable commodity to British, American, and Russian forces. Special forces units search for him throughout the novel, but he narrowly avoids them and their plans for him by employing a series of disguises and alternate identities. After losing his identity at the Hermann Goering Casino, Slothrop takes on the identities of the film star Max Schlepzig, the war correspondent Ian Scuffling, the superhero Rocketman, and the German pig-hero Plechazunga. By the end of the novel, Slothrop's identity seems to have disintegrated altogether, and it is unclear what becomes of him.

Solange

See Leni Pökler

Dr. Kevin Spectro

A neurologist and one of Pointsman's cohorts, Spectro is killed by a V-2 rocket strike.

Der Springer

See Gerhart von Göll

Francisco Squalidozzi

Squalidozzi is the leader of a group of Argentine anarchists seeking refuge in postwar Germany.

Jeremy Swanlake

Jessica's husband, Jeremy, also called "Beaver," is a British officer working at Operation Backfire.

Jessica Swanlake

Jessica is Roger Mexico's passionate lover until she leaves him permanently for her husband. She turns out to be working for Pointsman, and her betrayal of Mexico sends him over the edge.

Tantavity

See Lieutenant Oliver Muffler-Mafflick

Vaslav Tchitcherine

Tchitcherine is Enzian's half-brother, who is obsessed with finding Rocket 00000 and destroying Enzian and the Schwarzkommando. Although he has drifted into this rather personal mission, he is a Soviet intelligence officer, and Russian intelligence officers are tracking him in order to locate Enzian themselves. Tchitcherine "comes from Nihilist stock," had a dour boyhood, and is characterized as a "mad scavenger." Although there is a dramatic build-up to his confrontation with Enzian, Tchitcherine is bewitched by Geli Tripping's magic and passes right by Enzian without recognizing him.

Miklos Thanatz

Thanatz is Greta Erdmann's husband and Bianca's father. He is involved in sexual practices, including incest with his daughter; was involved in the firing of Rocket 00000; and is captured by the Schwarzkommando in part 4.

Geli Tripping

Geli is Tchitcherine's lover, but she has an affair with Slothrop as well. She believes she is a witch and seems to possess some sort of magic which she uses to distract Tchitcherine from his mission to confront his half-brother.

Trudi

Trudi is the blonde lover of Gustav who is involved in Säure's orgies.

Franz van der Groov

Van der Groov is Katje's ancestor who is involved in the destruction of the dodo bird on the Dutch colonial island of Mauritius.

Gerhart von Göll

Von Göll, or "Der Springer," is a German "film director turned marketeer" who helps Slothrop locate the Schwarzgerät. Säure puts them in touch by giving Slothrop Springer's symbol, a white chess knight, and Klaus Närrisch leads Slothrop on a mission to rescue Springer from Tchitcherine.

Blodgett Waxwing

Waxwing is a phony identity specialist who provides Slothrop with the documents for his disguise as Ian Scuffling.

Verbindungsmann Wimpe

Wimpe is a German spy as well as a chemist and drug manufacturer. He comes into contact with Tchitcherine and travels to the United States after the war.

Themes

Death, Paranoia, and Metaphysics

Pynchon addresses a kaleidoscope of themes in *Gravity's Rainbow*, but he continually returns to ideas related to metaphysics, a branch of philosophy that studies fundamental questions of reality and existence. The novel questions what is real, how one is able to discern reality, and whether there actually is any reality at all. Its complex plot can be seen as a search for causes of death and a quest to discover who or what it is (if anything) that controls the world.

The search for death and its causes is a key theme in the novel, and it is focused on the myriad of efforts to discover and understand German V-2 rockets. In charge of the ultimate V-2 rocket is "Dominus Blicero," whose name is intended to mean, lord of death. Blicero fires Rocket 00000 from the region of northern Germany where, according to the African special forces team building it, death resides. The main character involved in the search for the rocket is Slothrop, who is characterized by his obsession with death and his tendency to be drawn to it. Like his search for the rocket, Slothrop's search to understand and possibly reach death becomes hopelessly confused. Nevertheless, Pynchon uses Slothrop to suggest that Western civilization is obsessed with death and seems to focus all of its efforts on destroying life in massive quantities as well as, in a sense, discovering the true nature of death.

Slothrop is not concerned simply with discovering the nature of death, however; he is a victim of paranoia obsessed with finding the nature of the beings that control everything in his life and in the world. Given that the novel suggests that multinational companies such as Shell and General Electric ran both sides of World War II, Pynchon seems to be sympathetic to this view. The paranoid view of the world that maintains there is a malevolent plan deliberately being acted out contrasts with the anti-paranoid view of the world that maintains events are caused by a series of coincidences and there is no conspiracy.

The opposing views of paranoia and anti-paranoia are important to Pynchon's views on metaphysics because this opposition seems to be a metaphor concerning whether any common forces (good or evil) hold the world together or whether the world is a collection of random and meaningless events. By the end of the novel, however, Pynchon's views on paranoia remain unclear. He suggests that humans are constantly trying to determine the nature of reality, death, and existence, but never necessarily coming to any conclusions. He may also be suggesting that corporate and government conspiracies actually exist and are involved in efforts, coordinated or uncoordinated, to wipe out individuality and control the world.

War and Technology in the Late-Twentieth Century

Gravity's Rainbow examines themes of war and technological advances from the beginning of World War II through the Vietnam War. Pynchon is concerned about the enormous and complex technologies for destroying human life that have proliferated since World War II. His novel seems to point out that late-twentieth-century mechanisms of destruction threaten not just life but identity and selfhood because they alienate people from their uniqueness and their concepts of who they are. Nearly every character in the novel is drawn from his/her true life and identity (Roger from Jessica, Brigadier Pudding from his sexual fulfillment, Slothrop from his literal identity and his home) because of war and technology. Pynchon may be suggesting that the effects of war and conflict are disastrous, violent, and far-reaching due to late-twentieth century technological advances.

Race, the Holocaust, and the Civil Rights Movement

Racism is a common element in many of Pynchon's key storylines, and Pynchon considers the theme of race within the setting of World War II as well as the 1960s U.S. civil rights movement. The quest to find Enzian's African Schwarzkommando is perhaps the most prominent of the plotlines in

Topics For Further Study

- Some of *Gravity's Rainbow* is historically factual and some is not. Research an important aspect of the plot such as the German rocket program, and write an essay that discusses what is historically accurate and what is fictional about the event or series of events in question. Also discuss Pynchon's efforts at satire and supposition about history, including what poses as history but is not necessarily factual.

- Give a class presentation about the history of conspiracy theory during the 1960s and early 1970s, when Pynchon was writing *Gravity's Rainbow*. While you are doing your research, keep in mind the assassinations of John F. Kennedy and Robert Kennedy, the scandals and cover-ups of the Nixon administration, hostility towards the U.S. civil rights movement, and theories about United States involvement in the Vietnam War.

- Write an essay about the scientific advances of the World War II era and their long-term effects. Include applications of mathematics in breaking or forming codes, advances in aerodynamics, the race to create an atomic bomb, machine technology, radar, and other innovations to which *Gravity's Rainbow* refers.

- Lead a class discussion about postmodernism and post-World-War II American literature. Prepare yourself by reading about postmodern theory and acquainting yourself with the most influential American writers of the late-twentieth century. How did literature change in the 1950s, 1960s, and 1970s? What were some of the most important foreign influences on the American literary scene? How does Pynchon fit into the various movements, texts, and ideas of his era?

which Pynchon explores race relations. Characters such as Slothrop and Tchitcherine are obsessed with racial difference, and their obsessions trace back to childhood traumas involving racist conditioning. Blicero and others are also prejudiced against Jews, and Pynchon writes openly about the horrors of the Holocaust. Much of Pynchon's black and white symbolism and allusion (Geli Tripping's white magic or the imagery surrounding Domina Noctura, for example) emphasizes that racism is widespread, formidable, and dominant in postwar Western culture. Pynchon also connects racist ideology to capitalist and governmental conspiracies such as that of the German company IG Farben, which used concentration camp labor to produce chemicals, one of which was the Zyklon-B rat poison used in the gas chambers to exterminate Nazi prisoners.

Globalization and Empire

Gravity's Rainbow analyzes globalization and empire both in their political dimensions and in their tendencies to destroy individual identity. Politically, Pynchon examines and critiques empires ranging from the Germans and their dealings with the African Hereros, to Dutch colonial Mauritius, to British, Russian, and American plans for world domination. As depicted in the novel, empire building is a means of subjugating another culture and controlling the lives of everyone living in it. Additionally, Pynchon outlines a widespread conspiracy in the non-governmental arena of capitalist globalization. The novel suggests that war is a means for companies such as Shell and General Electric to continue the business of buying and selling, with no regard for human life and little tolerance for individuals who want to control their own destinies.

Style

Fact and Fiction

Pynchon's novel is full of historical and cultural allusions from all over the world, and many of them are historically accurate details. Characters such as Walter Rathenau, numerous World War II episodes, corporate references to Shell, General Electric, and the German chemical company IG

Farben, and stories from colonial Germany, Holland, and Russia are all based on thorough historical research. However, Pynchon often mixes these elements of historical fact with fiction, so it is difficult to tell what has been invented and what has been taken from factual historical accounts.

Pynchon's allusions to history provide an interpretation of the events themselves, and they place his thematic and philosophical ideas into historical context. His ambitious claims about the nature of reality and the important questions he raises about postwar culture are grounded in multi-layered references to historical realities, some of which are anachronistic and some of which are subtly altered. Pynchon uses the blend of the historically accurate world and his fictional world that operates within and around it to challenge the reader's beliefs about history, reality, and Western culture. The result is a pastiche of interminable references and implications that make *Gravity's Rainbow* both a convincing and challenging historical and cultural document.

Fragmentation

Gravity's Rainbow is famous for its almost impenetrable difficulty. Plot lines are extremely difficult to follow, important characters disappear for five hundred pages at a time, and the novel does not have any sustained character studies (even Slothrop disappears toward the end). The narrative perspective is often extremely unclear, and the characters (including Slothrop) seem able to discover their true roles in the complex postwar world. Perhaps most importantly, the reader is never sure what is real and what is imagined: evidence at various points suggests that even central events, such as Slothrop's romantic encounters, Dr. Laszlo Jamf, and the Schwarzkommando's quest to build Rocket 00001 are simply imagined fantasies. The pervasive confusion and fragmentation are key parts of the stylistic method by which Pynchon creates an overwhelming and challenging world where certainties do not exist.

Historical Context

The United States in the 1960s and Early 1970s

Life in the United States during the time in which Pynchon wrote and published *Gravity's Rainbow* was marked by dramatic social change and turbulent conflict. The civil rights movement,

a term which normally refers to the effort to end discrimination and segregation against African Americans, reached a climax in the 1960s. In the South, sit-in campaigns at segregated businesses, the integration of black students into segregated schools and colleges, and demonstrations against discrimination were met with extraordinary violence. Police tactics such as releasing dogs and spraying high-powered fire hoses on groups of high school students focused national attention on leaders such as Dr. Martin Luther King Jr. (1929–68). One year after King's "I Have a Dream" speech at the 1963 March on Washington, D.C., President Lyndon B. Johnson (1908–73) signed the Civil Rights Act, but race relations continued to be strained and black rights organizations diverged in their missions and beliefs.

In addition to the turbulence surrounding the civil rights movement, the United States was shaken in the 1960s by a series of high-profile assassinations as well as the country's increased involvement in Vietnam, that extended from 1957 to 1975. President John F. Kennedy (1917–63) was murdered in 1963, and Dr. King and presidential candidate Robert Kennedy were killed in 1968. Some theorists have alleged that the assassinations of John and Robert Kennedy were conspiracies. Meanwhile, the United States escalated its military involvement in Vietnam, having instigated a draft and committed to a full-scale war by the mid-1960s. The war was an extension of the cold war (a competition in stockpiling arms engaged in principally by the United States and the U.S.S.R.), and many of its horrors were brought home to televisions in the United States.

The dramatic developments of this period shocked many Americans and contributed to a rise in social activism. There was a massive opposition campaign against the Vietnam War that continued into Richard Nixon's presidency and contributed to the U.S. withdrawal in defeat from the country. At the time *Gravity's Rainbow* was published, Nixon was involved in the Watergate scandal (1972–75) that led to the surfacing of cover-ups, corruption, criminal acts, and conspiracy on the part of the president and his administration.

World War II

World War II, which began in the late 1930s and continued until 1945, was the largest and most devastating conflict in human history. Its causes included the economic desperation in Germany following World War I and the rise of ambitious military governments in Germany, Italy, and Japan.

Compare
&
Contrast

- **1940s:** The United States sends great numbers of soldiers to fight in World War II on the side of the Allies.

  1970s: The United States fights the Vietnam War, an escalation of cold war tensions with the Soviet Union.

  Today: As of 2005, the United States Army continues to fight in Iraq after having invaded the country based on the false claim that it was stockpiling weapons of mass destruction.

- **1940s:** World War II finally lifts the United States out of the Great Depression (1929–39), and soldiers return home to start families in great numbers.

  1970s: The Vietnam War ends, Richard Nixon resigns, the postwar economic prosperity in the United States dwindles due to energy crises and industrial competition from Asia.

  Today: The United States economy remains strong despite the downturns following the September 11, 2001 terrorist attacks.

- **1940s:** Tensions begin to show between Western capitalist countries, including Britain, France, and the United States, and communist countries, including the Soviet Union and China.

  1970s: The cold war is at its height, with very poor Soviet and U.S. relations, although Richard Nixon fosters diplomatic relations with Communist China.

  Today: The cold war ends, Russia is a capitalist country, and the United States is the world's only superpower.

The principal parties of the war were the Allied Powers (including Britain, the Soviet Union, and later the United States) and the Axis Powers (principally Germany, Japan, and Italy), and the war was fought on two fronts: in Europe and in Asia and the South Pacific. In the late 1930s, Japan invaded China, and later it fought the United States and the Soviet Union. Adolf Hitler's fascist government invaded Poland in 1939, and the German army made rapid advances in Europe until it controlled France, Norway, and much of Eastern Europe and the Balkan region. Hitler attempted to invade Britain in 1940, and when this failed the Nazis began an extended bombing campaign of London, called the Blitz. Meanwhile the Soviet Union took control of countries, including Finland and Romania, and Hitler staged a surprise attack on Soviet armies in 1941, breaking a non-aggression pact.

The United States entered the war in 1941 and sent reinforcements to Europe while Nazi armies were preoccupied on the eastern front. Britain continued to endure severe bombing campaigns, but the Allied invasion of Normandy in 1944 helped turn the tide of the war. From this point until Germany's surrender, Allied armies remained on the offensive, and Soviet soldiers invaded Berlin in April of 1945. When the Allies liberated continental Europe, they found evidence of the Nazi Holocaust in which millions of Jews, Catholics, homosexuals, and others had been murdered in concentration camps. In August 1945, the United States dropped two atomic bombs on Japan, and Japan soon surrendered. The climate in postwar Europe was characterized by increasing tensions between capitalist and communist victors. Areas occupied by the Soviets became communist countries while Allied-occupied countries became capitalist, Germany was divided into eastern (pro-Soviet) and western (pro-Allied) countries, and Berlin, which is wholly located in the eastern sector, was itself divided into capitalist and communist sections that were later separated by a massive concrete wall.

Critical Overview

Gravity's Rainbow received very positive reviews in the press and among academic critics, although some critics have maintained that the novel is

Aerial view of the London blitz of 1940, during World War II © Hulton-Deutsch Collection/Corbis

incomprehensible. Edward Mendelson (quoted in John Stark's *Dictionary of Literary Biography* entry on Pynchon) writes, "few books in this century have achieved the range and depth of this one. . . . This is certainly the most important novel to be published in English in the past thirty years." In his influential 1973 essay "Rocket Power," Richard Poirier stresses Pynchon's historical importance and argues that the book is "a profound (and profoundly funny) historical meditation on the humanity sacrificed to a grotesque delusion—the Faustian illusion of the inequality of lives and the inequality of the nature of signs." The novel was disqualified from winning the Pulitzer Prize because the advisory board deemed it unreadable and obscene, but it won the National Book Award in 1974.

Subsequent criticism has dealt with various issues, including the novel's significance to postmodern theory and its historical and political analysis of the late-twentieth-century Western world. In his 1982 essay, Tony Tanner discusses the experience of reading the novel and how Pynchon fits into American literary history: "[Pynchon] is a key contemporary figure in the great tradition of those who extend the possibilities of fiction-making in arresting and enriching ways—not in this

or that 'Great Tradition,' but in the great tradition of the novel itself." Dwight Eddins, meanwhile, explores the religious aspects of the novel: "The basic conflict of *Gravity's Rainbow*, the dialectic that finally structures the novel, is a religious one. It is marked by mystical and supernatural manifestations on both sides, by the presence of fanatical devotees, and by a drive for nothing less than metaphysical dominance." Margaret Lynd's 2004 essay, by contrast, emphasizes the novel's scientific issues: "The power that science has acquired over the past four centuries to determine the scope and parameters of human possibility dominates the multiple themes of *Gravity's Rainbow*." These critical perspectives are examples of the wide variety of critical approaches to the novel.

Criticism

Scott Trudell

Trudell is a doctoral student of English literature at Rutgers University. In the following essay, Trudell argues that sexuality and illicit sexual affairs are key topics by which Pynchon develops his critique of postwar culture in Gravity's Rainbow.

A common motif in the diverse and complex array of events in *Gravity's Rainbow* is the affair, or the brief sexual relationship, that is usually extramarital or illicit in some way. Characters are constantly having sex, running off together, cheating on their partners, and becoming carried away by their forbidden fantasies. Frequently, they engage in violent, sadomasochistic acts that include rape and pedophilia—acts that led the Pulitzer Prize advisory board to deem the novel obscene. Affairs often involve spying on the part of one or even both parties, and lovers have a tendency to leave or betray each other based on their roles in one of the novel's many plots and conspiracies. From Mexico's affair with Jessica to Katje's sadomasochistic control of Brigadier Pudding to Blicero's sexual domination of Gottfried to Slothrop's pedophilic sex with Bianca, illicit relationships are among Pynchon's most frequent devices.

Pynchon uses sexual affairs in his thematic agenda for a variety of reasons, including as a twist on the conventional tool of the romantic encounter as a way to drive the plot (this allows Pynchon to build up and then betray his readers' expectations). Sexuality, particularly illicit or deviant sexuality, is especially important in the characterization of Slothrop, whose identity is based on his frequent sexual acts as well as his sexual desire for death itself. Perhaps the most important role sexuality plays in the novel, however, is to develop and underscore Pynchon's central message that late-twentieth-century humanity is obsessed with securing its own violent destruction, both literally and in terms of its metaphysical identity.

The novel's numerous sexual affairs are, among other things, authorial tricks that involve the reader in a straightforward, coherent, and traditional narrative which Pynchon then completely undercuts or eliminates, forcing the confused reader to speed off on a completely different storyline. Affairs perform this function well because they immediately create a series of traditional expectations for a reader: the common convention of the love story in which two characters meet and fall in love, often working together to solve a mystery or achieve a positive resolution to the crux of the plot. This sort of love story was particularly common in American films of Pynchon's era, a medium to which the novel refers frequently. Unlike a formulaic film or a predictable love story, however, Pynchon first complicates the affair by rendering it forbidden or illicit, then overturns readers' expectations about how it fits into the greater plot and finally abandons the relationship entirely.

> Pynchon argues that postwar culture is like Slothrop or Dominus Blicero in the sense that it sacrifices what is most private and most sacred to it in a kind of self-obliterating ritual that destroys all forms of identity and purpose."

Brief, illicit sexual encounters are particularly common to Slothrop, Pynchon's main character. Slothrop's promiscuity is perhaps his defining personality characteristic, and it is one of Pynchon's favorite tools to rapidly jolt the reader into a new narrative mode and move the plot forward. In a sense, Slothrop's affairs are connected to the V-2 rocket strikes on London not because they anticipate them according to any scientific rules of behaviorism, but because the rockets metaphorically represent the incessant shocks to identity and purpose that occur because of technological and cultural modernity. In Pynchon's worldview, rapid escalations in technologies of mass destruction have changed the way people live and conduct relationships. By disorienting the reader and transferring the action to a string of distinct affairs, Pynchon underscores the lack of purpose in postwar life and the deep confusion that characterizes late-twentieth-century Western culture.

Slothrop is an appropriate character to demonstrate Pynchon's vision of modern life because he is an anti-hero, someone whose identity has been stolen, who is hopelessly separated from his home, and who has very little knowledge or understanding of his goal and purpose in the postwar world. His past affairs completely disappear from his life (another reason that the image of V-2 rockets destroying their locations is an apt metaphor) with no possibility of lingering attachment or comfort. Perhaps his most heartfelt or loving attachment is, perversely, to the young girl Bianca, and she dies a gruesome death on the ship where they met and had sex. Taken as a whole, Slothrop's hopeless and isolating affairs define his identity as an absence of identity because they contain no possibility for

What Do I Read Next?

- Pynchon's short novel *The Crying Lot of 49* (1967) is more direct and readable than *Gravity's Rainbow*. Its southern California detective story progresses, though, from clarity to disorder.

- Vladimir Nabokov's 1955 novel *Lolita* is the shocking and enthralling story of a professor's illicit relationship with a pre-pubescent girl.

- John Keegan's *The Second World War* (1989) is an authoritative single-volume resource about World War II.

- *Catch 22* (1961) by Joseph Heller tells the story of a World War II bombardier named Yossarian who struggles to ensure his own survival in a world in which bureaucracies utterly control people's destiny.

---

sustained human contact. This is particularly true because they are generally sadomasochistic, violent, or socially unacceptable.

Pynchon also uses Slothrop's sexual affairs as a technique to prepare the reader for Slothrop's disappearance in part 4 of the novel; the fragmentation of Slothrop's character is the natural result and unavoidable outcome of his incoherent, unstable identity. Readers are surprised by Slothrop's disappearance because Pynchon sets up the novel as a mystery and readers expect mysteries to be solved, but irresolution and dismay are the only possible results of Slothrop's problematic sexuality. His love life is as unsolvable as the corporate-governmental mystery/conspiracy working against him; neither has any hope of being exposed, uncovered, or resolved.

Nevertheless, Pynchon teases the reader by tracing this conspiracy back to Slothrop's childhood conditioning by Laszlo Jamf, explaining Slothrop's importance to the many corporate and governmental agents searching for him on the basis of his unique, manipulated sexuality. Insofar as there is a root solution to the mysteries of the novel, it is connected to Slothrop's childhood and his sexual conditioning. In fact, all of Slothrop's military and conspiratorial adventures are related to his sexuality. His sexual adventures precede the rocket strikes, his erections are related to the rockets, his searches and missions always involve the objects of his lust, his lovers are frequently also the lovers of key governmental agents (including Tchitcherine, Blicero and Pökler), and he is betrayed and manipulated by lover-spies such as Katje. Slothrop's promiscuous sexual identity becomes increasingly violent, obscene, and illicit until he is having sex with little girls and literally turning into the pig Plechazunga, and eventually it is utterly fragmented and destroyed.

In his entry on Pynchon for the *Dictionary of Literary Biography* John Stark argues that *Gravity's Rainbow* is preoccupied with developing a "culture of death," and he points towards a comment in the final episode of the novel that Slothrop "might be in love, in sexual love, with his, and his race's, death." This sexual connection to Pynchon's central theme of death is shared (among other characters) by Dominus Blicero, whose represents the spirit of death in the novel (even his name is a conflagration of German and Latin that means "Lord of Death"). Blicero's obsessive sadomasochistic domination of Gottfried and his ultimate murder of Gottfried by placing him inside Rocket 00000, are extreme examples of the desire to explore and control death—a desire that Slothrop also feels.

The sexual obsession with death in *Gravity's Rainbow* is, in part, a reference to Sigmund Freud's theory of the "death drive." Freud believed that there is an unconscious desire to die in human psychology which, like Buddhist philosophy, seeks to reach a void or a state of non-existence. Although Pynchon suggests that this desire exists and is an extremely important force, he frames it as a socio-cultural phenomenon as opposed to the kind of innate desire described by Freud. In fact, the novel's entire structure is designed to emphasize that modern, post-World-War-II Western culture is obsessively dedicated to the sexual violation and destruction of the human race. This nihilistic desire to rape or sexually dominate humankind extends to humanity's conception of itself and its metaphysical convictions about its purpose. Pynchon argues that postwar culture is like Slothrop or Dominus Blicero in the sense that it sacrifices what is most private and most sacred to it in a kind of self-obliterating ritual that destroys all forms of identity and purpose.

An alternative example of Pynchon's suggestion that the death drive is a cultural phenomenon of the postwar world is the illicit relationship of Roger and Jessica. These two characters (not Slothrop) are the protagonists of part 1, and the reader is invested in the success of their relationship, which is one of true love according to the conventional rules of romance. Their relationship is a sanctuary from the war, and it is the opposite of the trend towards death, nihilism, and the destruction of humanity that the war represents. They are, in a sense, the great hope of the novel, and their relationship signifies a trend away from death. According to the narrator's dramatic claim in part 1, episode 6, "They are in love. F—— the war."

It is no coincidence, therefore, that Roger and Jessica disappear for five hundred pages around the time that the war ends, and, when they finally reappear, they separate permanently and bitterly. Roger discovers that Jessica was, in fact, working on behalf of Pointsman, and he goes slightly crazy, urinating on Pointsman's desk before dedicating himself (like Slothrop) to finding Rocket 00000. The fact that Roger and Jessica's relationship ends in this way suggests that the culture of destruction has become permanent, the "war" (in the conspiratorial sense of a mechanism for buying, selling, and destruction) is interminable, and humanity is actively seeking to destroy itself.

Slothrop's experience parallels Roger and Jessica's. As the novel progresses and humanity moves closer to the cataclysmic event of the atomic bomb, Slothrop gets further and further away from his home and from any sense of self-understanding. He seems to be discovering some kind of truth about himself and his childhood, but in fact the solution to the mystery of Slothrop's sexuality (and the mystery of the corporate-governmental conspiracies of the novel) is ironic. Laszlo Jamf turns out to have been quite probably nothing more than a figment of Slothrop's imagination, and the deviant string of sexual affairs slowly end as they become increasingly obscene. Slothrop's journey of self-discovery, as far as it is one, leaves him with no identity at all; it only leads

him to a nihilistic vision of purposelessness and despair. Sexuality, particularly illicit sexuality, is the key to understanding the vast and mysterious conspiracy of the novel, but this key does not actually uncover or solve the mystery; it simply reinforces Pynchon's message that the postwar world is an immense mechanism for self-obliteration and death.

Source: Scott Trudell, Critical Essay on *Gravity's Rainbow*, in *Novels for Students*, Thomson Gale, 2006.

Christine Turier

In the following essay, Turier identifies sources for the octopus and Pointsman in Gravity's Rainbow.

The bizarreness of the image of the octopus Grigori's attack on Katje in *Gravity's Rainbow*, together with the orchestration of that attack by the mad Pavlovian Pointsman, stamps it with a typically "Pynchonian" uniqueness. Yet it is not the singular product of an eccentric imagination but another example of Pynchon's extreme eclecticism. For the octopus combines two radically different sources: one, that of early Japanese art; the other, the field of neurobiology. The image of a woman being "attacked" by a giant octopus is, in fact, not uncommon in early Japanese art. It is best known in the West through the rendition of Katsushika Hokusai. Reproduced as "The Dream of the Fisherman's Wife" in Lucie-Smith's *Eroticism in Western Art,* it is also widely represented in texts on Japanese *Ukiyo-e,* especially those concerned with Hokusai, in the West the best known of the *Ukiyo-e* school. Hokusai's rendition portrays a naked woman swooning in the arms of "twin incubi" between rocks and sea. Her lower torso is enveloped by the "giant" octopus, and the tentacles of the smaller octopus encircle her neck.

What is most notable about this image, besides its eroticism (certainly not out of place in Pynchon's text), is the ambiguity of the woman's reaction to the "attack"; does she swoon from terror or ecstasy? It is an ambiguity also present in Pynchon's portrayal of the scene; is Katje truly afraid or a knowing and willing participation in the "attack"? It is not her scream that is heard on the beach but that of "one of the dancers." She thanks Slothrop afterward, with "[n]ot a tremor in the voice." Yet, during the attacks we see her "... already half in the water, ... trying to cry out, but the tentacle, flowing and chilly, barely allows her windway enough to breathe." Slothrop becomes mesmerized by her hand clutching his shirt, causing it to furrow "in tangents to her terror." As well, we know as readers that it was the film taken secretly in Osbie Feel's kitchen that was used to condition Grigori. Paradoxically though, and in contrast to Slothrop's reaction to Grigori—"wow it's a *big* one, holycow"—her comments betray a cool detachment bordering on familiarity with the octopus—"They are very optical aren't they. I hadn't known"—as well as a genuine surprise that it should attack her: "It *saw* me. Me. I don't look like a crab." Nevertheless, as with Hokusai's print, which exudes eroticism, not terror, the intuition comes out in favor of the woman's participation. The ambiguity of Katje's response is not lost either on Slothrop: "Structure and detail come later, but the conniving around him now he feels instantly, in his heart."

In relation to Pynchon's use of the octopus, however, it is not only this image which has antecedents. The suggestion that Pointsman might find the available Grigori a more suitable subject for experimentation than either Slothrop or the more conventional canine ones has, as does much of Pynchon's reference to science, a sound empirical base. Spectro's summary of the advantages of octopi as subjects (". . . docile under surgery," survival of "massive removal of brain tissue," and the reliability of their unconditioned response) is in fact extremely accurate. His assertion that there is "[n]o limit to the things you can teach them" is more than just the punchline to a parodic joke at the expense of psychological research (not to mention Pointsman himself). Joke though it is, the octopus has often been used in research into the structure and functioning of the brain. British anatomist J. Z. Young, during the late fifties and early sixties, pursued extensive research into brain function using cephalopods. His book *A Model of the Brain* documents the results of his work. Young used in his research both trained (that is, conditioned) and untrained octopi. His subjects also "stuffed" themselves "with crab meat"; their learned tasks also involved attacking "strange moving figures." Besides the attributes outlined by Spectro, the structure of the cephalopod's nervous system makes it an ideal subject for the study of the brain. Octopi have limited sensory inputs— they are very "optical." In addition to vision, they have only chemo-tactile receptors in the arms. They are entirely without hearing or an effective sense of smell. They possess a limited response range, that is, to attack or not to attack. These attributes, together with the size of their nerve fibers, make the study of brain function in

> **"** The implications of the assault upon the female by "the brain" are an area that has so far been completely overlooked.**"**

cephalopods a much simpler task than it is in the more complex vertebrates, while the similarity of their optical system to that of vertebrates (including humans) makes the comparison of brain function a viable one.

The similarity between Young and Pointsman, however, does not end here. Pavlov and Pointsman's search for the mechanical/physiological root of behavior is echoed by Young: "I believe that it will be possible to find some changes in certain specific places after each learning occasion." Some 230 pages later, he acknowledges that "there is still no definite knowledge of what this change is" but goes on to speculate on where it might be found. Young states, "Whatever process operates in learning it seems likely that it involves the choice between two or more possibilities. It is usually assumed that this choice is made by some form of *facilitation* [my emphasis] in the pathway that has been excited." Young, however, finds preferable the idea that "learning occurs by the *elimination* [my emphasis] of the unused pathways," a hypothesis that bears a strong resemblance to Pointsman's idea of "spot's of inertia."

One further point of significance, which links both sources of the octopus in *Gravity's Rainbow*, is the observation by Young that because the "octopus's central nervous system is less completely centralised than that of vertebrates" it "might be said to 'think with its arms.'" The idea of the octopus as "all brain" is certainly reinforced in Hokusai's image. That science and technology ("the brain") represent central thematic concerns in *Gravity's Rainbow* is well documented. Yet the implications of the assault upon the female by "the brain" are an area that has so far been completely overlooked.

Source: Christine Turier, "Pynchon's *Gravity's Rainbow*," in *Explicator*, Vol. 50, No. 4, Summer 1992, pp. 244–46.

A German V-2 rocket ready for launching on a launching pad somewhere in Germany © Corbis

Sources

Eddins, Dwight, "Orphic Contra Gnostic Religious Conflict in *Gravity's Rainbow*," in *Modern Language Quarterly*, Vol. 45, No. 2, June 1984, pp. 163–90.

Lynd, Margaret, "Science, Narrative, and Agency in *Gravity's Rainbow*," in *Critique*, Vol. 46, No. 1, Fall 2004, pp. 63–80.

Poirier, Richard, "Rocket Power," in *Thomas Pynchon's "Gravity's Rainbow": Modern Critical Interpretations*,

edited by Harold Bloom, Chelsea House Publishers, pp. 11–20; originally published in *Saturday Review of the Arts*, Vol. 1, No. 3, March 3, 1973.

Pynchon, Thomas, *Gravity's Rainbow*, Viking Penguin, 1973.

Stark, John, "Thomas Pynchon," in *Dictionary of Literary Biography*, Vol. 2: *American Novelists Since World War II, First Series*, edited by Jeffrey Helterman, Gale Research, pp. 411–17.

Tanner, Tony, "*Gravity's Rainbow*: An Experience in Modern Reading," in *Thomas Pynchon's "Gravity's Rainbow": Modern Critical Interpretations*, edited by Harold Bloom, Chelsea House Publishers, pp. 69–83; originally published in *Thomas Pynchon*, Methuen, 1982.

Further Reading

Hawthorne, Mark D., "Pynchon's Early Labyrinths," in *Critique*, Vol. 25, No. 2, Spring 1998, pp. 78–93.

Hawthorne's essay discusses labyrinths as they are constructed and presented in Pynchon's fiction, focusing particularly on *Gravity's Rainbow*.

Hume, Katherine, *Pynchon's Mythography: An Approach to "Gravity's Rainbow,"* Southern Illinois University Press, 1987.

Hume tracks Pynchon's use of the myth of Orpheus in *Gravity's Rainbow*. A prodigious musician, Orpheus is granted the right to bring his wife back from the dead but breaks the agreement by looking back for her, thus losing her forever.

Newman, Robert D., *Understanding Thomas Pynchon*, University of South Carolina Press, 1986.

This broad discussion of Pynchon and his works is basic, readable, and accessible.

Weisenburger, Steven, *A "Gravity's Rainbow" Companion: Sources and Contexts for Pynchon's Novel*, University of Georgia Press, 1988.

Weisenburger's guide to Pynchon's novel is an indispensable resource for first-time and repeat readers. It includes plot summary information and thoroughly researched notes about important or confusing details and references.

Hotel du Lac

Anita Brookner
1984

Hotel du Lac, by British novelist Anita Brookner, was published in 1984. Brookner's fourth novel, it won the Booker Prize, Britain's most prestigious literary award. As a result of her first three novels, Brookner had won a reputation for writing about the difficulties faced by middle-aged, single, lonely women, and *Hotel du Lac* follows this pattern. It also owes something to the genre of popular romance novels; its heroine, Edith Hope, is a successful writer of such novels. She has been dispatched by her friends in London to a hotel in Switzerland because of an unfortunate lapse on her part, although the reader is not initially informed about what the lapse was. Edith intends to use her temporary stay to finish her latest romance novel, but instead she spends much of her time observing and interacting with the other hotel guests, who include a rich and glamorous but self-centered elderly widow and her daughter; an upper-class young woman who suffers from an eating disorder; a lonely, old and deaf countess; and an enigmatic man named Mr. Neville. The self-effacing, quiet Edith, a romantic soul whose relationships with men are less than satisfactory, spends much time thinking about how a woman ought to behave in order to satisfy her longings for love, as well as recalling in painful detail the reasons for her banishment. In the end, Edith receives a proposition from Mr. Neville that forces her to think deeply about what she really wants in life and whether she is prepared to compromise her ideals.

Anita Brookner © Jerry Bauer. Reproduced by permission

Author Biography

Novelist and art historian Anita Brookner was born on July 16, 1928, in London, the only child of Newson and Maude Brookner. Her father, who was born in Poland and was Jewish, was a company director, and her mother, also Jewish, was a former professional singer. Her father encouraged her to read, and she was reading the novels of Charles Dickens from the age of seven.

Brookner was raised in the London suburb of Herne Hill and attended James Allen's School for Girls in Dulwich. Her adolescence was not a happy one, however. Not only was her parents' marriage a stormy one, but she grew up in the shadow of the Nazi persecution of the Jews, since the family home was often filled with Jewish refugees from Europe.

Brookner attended King's College, London, from which she graduated with a bachelor of arts in history in 1949. She received a Ph.D. from Courtauld Institute of Art, London, in 1953. After this she spent three years studying in Paris on a French government scholarship before teaching art history at Reading University from 1959 to 1964 and at the Courtauld Institute from 1964 to 1988, where she specialized in eighteenth- and nineteenth-century French art. In 1967, Brookner became the first female Slade Professor of Art at Cambridge University. She has written a number of books about art history, including *Watteau* (1968), *The Genius of the Future* (1971), *Greuze* (1972), *Jacques-Louis David* (1980), and the essays contained in *Soundings* (1997) and *Romanticism and Its Discontents* (2000).

Brookner did not turn to novel writing until she was in her fifties. She once told an interviewer, Olga Kenyon, that she began to write fiction out of boredom and the wish to review her life. Her first novel, *A Start in Life*, was published in 1981. (In the United States it was published as *The Debut*.) Since then, Brookner has published novels at the rate of one novel a year. Her fourth novel, *Hotel du Lac* (1984) won the Booker Prize, Britain's most coveted literary award, and established her reputation on both sides of the Atlantic.

Brookner's novels include *Family and Friends* (1985); *A Misalliance* (1986), published in the United States as *The Misalliance* (1987); *A Friend from England* (1987); *Latecomers* (1988); *Lewis Percy* (1989); *Brief Lives* (1990); *A Closed Eye* (1991); *Fraud* (1992); *A Family Romance* (1993), published in the United States as *Dolly* (1994); *A Private View* (1994); *Incidents in the Rue Laugier* (1995); *Altered States* (1996); *Visitors* (1997); *Falling Slowly* (1998); *Undue Influence: A Novel* (1999); *The Bay of Angels* (2001); *The Next Big Thing* (2002), which won the Booker Prize and was published in the United States as *Making Things Better* (2003); and *The Rules of Engagement* (2003).

Brookner was made a Commander, Order of the British Empire (CBE) in 1990. She is a Fellow of New Hall, Cambridge, and has received an honorary doctorate from Smith College in the United States. As of 2005 she lives in Chelsea, in West London.

Plot Summary

Chapters 1–4

Hotel du Lac begins in late September at a quiet, respectable hotel in Switzerland, where Edith Hope, a thirty-nine-year-old English writer of romantic novels, has just arrived. Edith's friends have persuaded her to take a month's break away from her home in London, since they consider her, for some reason as yet undisclosed to the reader, to be in disgrace.

Edith hopes to be able to finish her latest novel while staying at the hotel, although her first act upon arrival is to write to David, the married man with whom she is having an affair. At dinner that night she observes the hotel guests. She notices a slender Englishwoman and her small dog, Kiki; a silent countess, Mme de Bonneuil; and a glamorous, energetic English lady who appears to be in her sixties (it later transpires that she is seventy-nine) and her daughter. Edith's observations of and interactions with these and other guests, and her consequent reflections on her own life, form the substance of the novel.

After dinner, the glamorous lady invites Edith to join them. Mrs. Iris Pusey is a wealthy widow from London who regularly comes to the Hotel du Lac with her daughter Jennifer for the sole purpose of going on shopping expeditions for luxury items, such as fine clothes and jewelry. The conversation between Mrs. Pusey and Edith is entirely one-sided, since the older lady talks only about herself. Edith does not mind this, however, since she has no desire to share information about herself. Edith's observation of Mrs. Pusey sparks her reflections about what kind of behavior is most becoming to a woman, since the outgoing, confident Mrs. Pusey is the complete opposite of the quiet, self-effacing Edith.

Edith also notices the closeness and affection between Mrs. Pusey and Jennifer, and this observation leads her to recall her own very different relationship with her mother, Rosa. In her youth in Vienna, Rosa had been beautiful and flirtatious. But soon after her marriage to a university professor she became bored and frustrated. However, when her husband died in his early fifties, Rosa went to pieces, becoming even more unhappy and unreconciled to her fate.

Edith also recalls David, and how they met at a party given by her friend, Penelope. Edith and David exchanged very few words at the party, but David then came to her house several hours later, as she guessed he would, and they almost immediately went to bed together.

Chapters 5–8

That night, Edith does not sleep well. In the morning, she talks to Monica, the slender Englishwoman, for the first time. She wonders why Monica is staying at the hotel and thinks she may be recently bereaved or convalescing from an illness. Later she meets another guest, Mr. Neville, a tall man in a gray suit and panama hat. He invites her for a walk, during which he reveals that he knows she is a writer whose pen name is Vanessa Wilde.

In the evening, Edith hears a scream coming from the corridor. She rushes to the Puseys' suite, fearing Mrs. Pusey has had a heart attack, only to find that the scream was uttered by Jennifer at the sight of a spider. Mr. Neville is in the process of scooping the spider up and throwing it out of the window.

Edith writes to David, telling him she has discovered that Monica, her new friend, suffers from an eating disorder and appears to subsist entirely on cake. Monica is also infertile, and her wealthy, titled husband, whom she hates and fears, has sent her to the hotel to get well so she can produce a child for him.

Mr. Neville takes Edith to lunch in a small restaurant high above the lake. He tells her that he owns an electronics firm and that his wife left him several years ago. But he is content being single, since this leaves him free to please himself rather than be concerned about the happiness of another. He believes that selfishness leads to a simple and enjoyable life, and he urges Edith to be more self-centered. Edith knows there is something wrong with this argument, but she does not dispute it with him. She finds him intelligent and even good-looking. They talk about love, and Edith says that she cannot live fully without it. Mr. Neville disputes this position, saying that what she needs is not love but social position and marriage, which he apparently believes is possible without love.

Later at night, Edith writes to David, giving him an account of Mrs. Pusey's boisterous seventy-ninth birthday party earlier that evening, which had continued until midnight. Edith left the party feeling out of sorts. She now remembers her own birthday parties when she was a girl. She made her own cake, and for once enjoyed a semblance of family life as she thinks it ought to be lived. Still feeling uneasy, she recalls the events that brought her to the hotel.

Chapters 9–12

Edith had agreed to marry Geoffrey Long, a worthy but dull man whom she had met at one of Penelope's parties. She agreed to marry him because she thought that at the age of thirty-nine, it would be her last chance. She had given up hope of ever getting what she really wanted. But on the day of the wedding, as her chauffeur-driven car approaches the Registry Office where groom and guests are assembled, she changes her mind and asks the chauffeur to drive on to the nearby park. When she later returns to her house, everyone is indignant, and Geoffrey accuses her of making him a laughing stock. She hands him back his ring and says good-bye. Later that day, David comes to visit her, and she tries to make a joke of the entire incident. Meanwhile her friends, especially Penelope, are making arrangement to send her away to the Hotel du Lac in disgrace.

Back in the present, there is a commotion in the hotel before breakfast the next day. Mrs. Pusey is upset when she finds Alain, a young member of the hotel staff, in Jennifer's room, even though all he has done is deliver breakfast.

Later, Edith meets Monica in a café. Monica tells her that Mr. Neville has taken a fancy to her and that he is very wealthy, although neither fact holds any interest for Edith.

On a chilly day in October, Mr. Neville takes Edith on a day trip on the lake. Over lunch, he unexpectedly asks her to marry him. He says he can offer her social position and security, companionship and shared interests, and that he needs a wife he can trust. He argues that such a marriage is in her own interests, even though he admits that he does not love her and knows that she does not love him.

Later that day, Edith decides to accept his proposal. She writes to David, saying it will be her last letter to him. She explains that she is to marry Mr. Neville, and there is no reason why she and David should meet again. She also reveals that she has not mailed any of her previous letters to him. At six the next morning, she is going to the front desk to buy a stamp when she sees Mr. Neville discreetly leaving Jennifer's room. This solves the mystery of the closing door she had vaguely heard several times in the early morning; she now knows that Mr. Neville has made a habit of staying the night with Jennifer. She tears up her letter to David and makes a reservation for the next flight to London.

Characters

Alain

Alain is an eighteen-year-old boy who works at the Hotel du Lac. He takes his responsibilities very seriously and is upset when Mrs. Pusey implies that it is somehow improper for him to bring Jennifer her breakfast in her room each morning.

Comtesse de Bonneuil

Comtesse de Bonneuil is an elderly woman who is staying as a guest at the hotel. Edith thinks she has a face like a bulldog. Mme de Bonneuil is completely deaf and says almost nothing, spending her time sitting around on her own and reading the newspaper. She lives at the hotel even though she has a beautiful house near the French border. The problem is that she does not get along with her daughter-in-law, whom she despises, and her son suggested that she move out of the house and into the hotel. She did as he asked because she is devoted to him and does not want him to be happy, but in doing so she has condemned herself to a life of loneliness.

Mrs. Dempster

Mrs. Dempster is Edith's cleaning lady at her home in London. Edith considers her dramatic and unreliable.

Edith Hope

Edith Hope is a thirty-nine-year-old writer of romance novels. Writing under the name of Vanessa Wilde, she has been modestly successful, with substantial sales of her five lengthy novels. Edith is the daughter of a professor and is a quiet, unassuming, diffident kind of woman. She does not dress in very fashionable clothes, and people sometimes tell her she looks like Virginia Woolf. Edith describes herself in typically modest terms: "I am a householder, a ratepayer, a good plain cook, and a deliverer of typescripts well before the deadline; I sign anything that is put in front of me." However, in spite of her apparently passive exterior, Edith is a highly intelligent woman with a sharp wit and a keenly observant eye. It is just that she does not choose, for the most part, to reveal herself to other people, preferring to talk to them about themselves rather than say much about her own life and thoughts.

Edith is single, but she is having an affair with a married man named David. She is in love with him but only sees him twice a month on average, and sometimes less. What she really wants is to be happily married, but she knows that David will never leave his wife. There is no one else available who fulfils her longing for romantic love. Her more extrovert friend Penelope often tries to fix her up with one of her own men friends. It was one such friend, Geoffrey Long, who courted Edith and persuaded her to marry him, but she could not go through with it and jilted him on the wedding day. Edith cannot settle for friendship and companionship with a worthy man; she must also have in the relationship the spark of love and deep tenderness. It is only love, or the hope of it, that keeps her feeling fully alive.

Banished to the Hotel du Lac following the debacle with Geoffrey, Edith is both fascinated and repelled by Mrs. Pusey, who seems to have achieved everything that Edith has failed to achieve and who in terms of her personality is Edith's exact opposite.

M. Huber

M. Huber is one of the owners of the Hotel du Lac, which is a family-run hotel. Officially, he has retired, but he still plays an active role in the business.

Geoffrey Long

Geoffrey Long, a kind, affable but rather dull man, assiduously courts Edith after the death of his mother. She agrees to marry him because he offers her a home and security, and all her friends tell her that he will make an excellent husband. But Edith jilts him on the wedding day.

Penelope Milne

Penelope Milne is Edith's friend, although Edith does not hold her in great affection. More outgoing than Edith, Penelope often tries to set Edith up with men of her acquaintance. Penelope is not married but feels no need to be. She flirts with men and has relationships with them but also regards them as enemies, creatures she can conquer whenever and if she chooses to do so. Penelope is loud in her disapproval of Edith's jilting of Geoffrey Long and instrumental in packing her off to the hotel in Switzerland.

Monica

Monica, a tall, very slender upper-class Englishwoman, is a guest at the hotel. She suffers from an eating disorder and appears to live mostly on cake, feeding much of her hotel food to her small dog, Kiki. Edith decides that Monica is what Mrs. Pusey would call a fortune-hunter: she married for money. But her marriage is a desperately unhappy one. She appears to be infertile, and her husband, Sir John, whom she loathes, has sent her to the hotel in order to get well so that she can produce an heir for him. If she should fail, he will divorce her. But Monica is not the kind of woman to go quietly. Her manner is defiant and belligerent. She plans to humble Sir John into keeping her, or, if she is unsuccessful, to ruin his reputation. Monica is also a snob; she despises men such as Mr. Neville and Mrs. Pusey's late husband, as well as Sir John, because they all made their money through trade, which she considers vulgar.

Philip Neville

Philip Neville is a guest at the hotel. In his fifties, he is an intelligent man of few words, although he chooses those words carefully. He is fastidious and well-dressed, and he pays courteous attention to the ladies at the hotel. He is also wealthy, the owner of an electronics factory, but he says he prefers to spend time on his farm. He tells Edith that his wife left him some years ago for another man, and he claims that now he enjoys his life because being single allows him to behave selfishly. The only person he has to please is himself. He takes an interest in Edith and surprises her by asking her to marry him. He proposes what he thinks of as an enlightened kind of arrangement, based on shared interests and companionship: she gains social position and security in exchange for allowing him the freedom to pursue affairs with other women, should the opportunity and desire arise. Edith fears that he is heartless and in some ways dislikes him, but she agrees to his proposal, until she discovers that he has been carrying on a discreet affair with Jennifer at the hotel.

Iris Pusey

Iris Pusey is a seventy-nine-year-old blond English widow who is staying at the hotel with her daughter Jennifer. She is wealthy and glamorous and likes to spend her time shopping for luxury goods. She is well-dressed, extroverted, and extremely self-centered. She adopts Edith as a confidante but is so narcissistic that she talks only about herself and shows no interest in Edith's life. Mrs. Pusey loves to be the center of attention, makes grand entrances into the dining room, and makes sure she gets maximum attention from the waiters. Edith finds her interesting and is drawn to her confident, self-assured, charming manner. Mrs. Pusey appears to be everything Edith is not, having made a successful marriage with a husband who, so she says, adored her and bought her whatever she desired. She glories in being ultra-feminine and getting what she wants out of men with ease.

Jennifer Pusey

Jennifer Pusey, Iris Pusey's unmarried daughter, is about the same age as Edith, but she looks younger. Jennifer is devoted to her mother, with whom she goes on shopping expeditions, but she does not have much to say for herself. When she is around her mother, she behaves, at least in Edith's view, like a small girl. Jennifer is attractive and rather plump and dresses expensively in a way that emphasizes her sexuality. At various moments

Edith notices that Jennifer's pants are maybe a little too tight, as is her jersey, and she also wears skimpy nightgowns. It later transpires that Jennifer is carrying on a discreet affair with Mr. Neville.

David Simmonds

David Simmonds is an auctioneer, the head of the family business. He is married and has children, and he is also Edith's lover. They met at a party given by Penelope. David is a self-indulgent man who does not deny himself anything. Edith remarks on his constant appetite, and she keeps her house full of food in order to satisfy it. David appears to be fond of Edith but not as fond of her as she is of him, and he has no intention of leaving his wife. She fears that he is not as interested in her as he once was.

Priscilla Simmonds

Priscilla Simmonds, David Simmonds's wife, is tall, blond, and good-looking. Edith sees her at a party once and observes her as sexy and confident but also argumentative and discontent.

Harold Webb

Harold Webb, Edith's literary agent, is a mild and scholarly man who looks like a country doctor. He is kind and seems genuinely concerned about Edith's welfare. He advises her to spice up her books by making them more modern and sexy, but she does not listen to him.

Themes

Loneliness and Isolation

The novel explores the different kinds of loneliness in several of the female characters who are guests at this quiet hotel in the off-season. The fact that they are staying at such a place at such an unpopular time suggests that they are in some way out of the mainstream of society.

First and foremost is Edith Hope. Unmarried but still searching for love, Edith has to make do with a relationship with a married man that produces more loneliness than intimacy. Even though David is at the center of her emotional life, she manages to see him only occasionally, and she feels that she hardly knows him. Each time he leaves, she feels that he has gone forever, and she endures many "empty Sundays" and "long eventless evenings" without him.

At the hotel, Mrs. Pusey and Jennifer recognize Edith's loneliness immediately when they see her, and they pity her because of it. In part, her loneliness arises because of her reserved temperament. Since her work as a writer is solitary, and she is by nature quiet rather than gregarious, she does not form close friendships easily. She goes to dinner parties not because she enjoys them but out of a sense of social duty. She is also under no illusions about her friendships, knowing that while she is away at the hotel, none of them can be trusted to get in touch with her.

In a sense, Edith is a person who waits for life to come to her, rather than going out and seizing it. She is more of an observer than a doer, and this pattern tends to create distance between her and others. Her solitariness is sharply contrasted with the gregarious, outgoing nature of several other characters, such as Penelope, David, David's wife (the briefly glimpsed Priscilla), and Mrs. Pusey, all of whom appear to have found their place in life and society and are quite content with it.

A second lonely character is Monica, who mixes little with the other guests. She reveals her state of mind early in her first conversation with Edith. "It's so nice to have someone to talk to," she says. Like Edith, whose loneliness in part stems from her frustrating relationship with her lover David, whom she sees only seldom, Monica's loneliness is due to her unsatisfactory relationship with her husband, who will divorce her if she is unable to produce a child. She also longs for the child she seems unable to conceive and feels condemned to loneliness and exile.

A third lonely character, and perhaps the loneliest of them all, is the Comtesse de Bonneuil. Once again, the problem stems from her relationship with a man, in this case, her son. Mme de Bonneuil lives at the hotel because she failed to get along with her daughter-in-law, so her son suggested that she move out of their house. Her son visits her once a month, but other than that takes no interest in her. Since Mme de Bonneuil agreed to his wishes because she did not want to make him unhappy, her loneliness results from her act of self-sacrifice. Her situation is that of an old person who appears to have outlived her usefulness, and her isolation is compounded by her total deafness, which makes communication very difficult for her.

The Search for Love

Although she is still unmarried at the age of thirty-nine, Edith refuses to renounce the search for love. She admits to Mr. Neville that she cannot be fully herself without love; it is vital for her existence: "I cannot think or act or speak or write or

Topics For Further Study

- How does *Hotel du Lac* parallel popular romance novels and how does it differ from them? Do romance novels offer merely escapist entertainment or do they embody some truth? Do they show what men and women really desire and how they really behave? Read a novel by Barbara Cartland and then write an essay comparing it to *Hotel du Lac*.

- In a work of literature, a foil is a character that sets off another character by contrast. They may react to similar situations very differently, for example. Discuss how foils are used in *Hotel du Lac*. Examples might include Mrs. Pusey, Penelope, and Mme de Bonneuil as foils for Edith.

- Research what makes a successful marriage. On what basis do people select their future partners?

Are all successful marriages based on romantic love? How important is companionship? Then make a chart in which you evaluate the relationship Edith has with David as compared to the potential relationship she might find with Mr. Neville.

- *Hotel du Lac* is not considered a feminist novel, even though it features a female protagonist and many female characters. Why should this be? Does the novel express a view of the world incompatible with feminism? Is Edith a rather old-fashioned woman in her attitudes to what women want? Write a feminist critique of *Hotel du Lac*, using Showalter s work, *A Literature of Their Own: British Women Novelists from Brontë to Lessing*, as one of your references.

---

even dream with any kind of energy in the absence of love. I feel excluded from the living world." Her idea of happiness, she continues, is to spend the day alone, reading and writing, secure in the knowledge that the man she loves will be returning in the evening. What she craves is not the passion and ecstasy of romantic love, but what she calls "the simplicity of routine."

It is this desire for domesticity that persuades Edith twice within a year to accept proposals of marriage, even when she does not love the man concerned. She convinces herself that if she cannot have the deep love she wants, she can at least accept the offer of companionship and security for which she has an equal longing. But in the case of Geoffrey Long, she realizes, in the nick of time, that marriage to a man whom she neither loves nor deeply respects—it is the sight of his "mouse-like seemliness" as he waits for her at the Registry Office that convinces her she cannot go through with it—will bring her no happiness. In the case of Mr. Neville, when she sees him emerging from Jennifer's room she realizes that the bargain she has struck with him, under which she would acquire social position and respectability in exchange

for his freedom to pursue love and sex elsewhere, is distasteful to her.

In both cases, Edith's essentially romantic nature, the existence of which she denies in her conversation with Mr. Neville, will not allow her to make a sterile compromise in the name of security. In the end, she elects to continue her affair with David, even though it is in so many respects an unsatisfactory relationship. David, unlike Geoffrey Long and Philip Neville, will never marry her, because he will never leave his wife. His relationship with Edith is one-sided in the sense that she means far less to him than he does to her. For David, Edith appears to be little more than an easy source of sex and food. (She notes his voracious appetite and how pleasurable it has been for her to cook for him.) But she loves him, nonetheless, and the fact that she has someone at least peripherally in her life whom she can address as "My dearest," and write lines to such as "You are the breath of life to me," means more to her than the promise of a more socially acceptable relationship devoid of passion. Her need to cling to David because he is all she has is a testament at once to the preciousness of love, that she will accept such an imperfect version of it, and to Edith's great loneliness, that she can find nothing better.

Style

Setting

The setting, by a large lake in Switzerland, plays an important role in the novel. The imagery associated with the lake is of mist, fog, and grayness. The opening sentence sets the tone: "From the window all that could be seen was a receding area of grey. It was to be supposed that beyond the grey garden . . . lay the vast grey lake, spreading like an anaesthetic towards the invisible further shore." The grayness reflects the dull, somber, dispiriting nature of Edith's life at this time; it lacks color and vitality. The simile in which the lake is compared to an anaesthetic expands on this parallel, suggesting life dulled of feeling and sensation.

The image of grayness recurs often in the novel, as when Edith takes her trip on the lake with Mr. Neville, and "the grey mist . . . encompassed the lake as far as the eye could see." That grayness is used to reflect Edith's mood is clear when she thinks to herself, of a particularly depressing moment during her stay, "Now she was as grey as the season itself."

Not all the days are gray, however. There are times when the landscape is "full of colour and incident," and these are the times when Edith's mood tends to change. When she lunches with Mr. Neville high above the mists of the lake, the weather is brighter and clearer, and Edith is no longer "the mild and careful creature that she had been on the lake shore." In the higher air, she is "harder, brighter, more decisive, realistic, able to savour enjoyment, even to expect it."

The imagery of grayness in Edith's present location is contrasted with the nostalgia with which she recalls her house in London. She remembers the "sharpness of the scents" as she sits in the garden as evening comes on, and the quality of the light at sunset, which "was of such very great interest to her she would put down her book just to watch it fade, and change colour, and finally become opaque and uninteresting." Her home acts as a pleasant refuge from the world, whereas the gray lake is an uncomfortable reminder of its realities.

Point of View

The novel is told almost entirely from Edith's point of view. This is done mostly in the third person, but also, in the three letters Edith writes to David, in the first person. Occasionally, and very briefly, the narrative switches to a male point of view, including that of M. Huber, Edith's gardener, David, and Mr. Neville. This form of narrative is known as selective or limited omniscience, in which the narrator enters the mind of a limited number of characters (in this case, mostly a single character).

Limiting the point of view almost exclusively to Edith is effective because it brings out Edith's introspective nature, in which she is constantly examining her own feelings and situation in life. The tiniest fluctuations in her mood and perceptions are noted. As she sits in the deserted salon, for example, "she felt her precarious dignity hard-pressed and about to succumb in the light of her earlier sadness."

The point of view also brings out the fact that Edith is an observer of life. She witnesses events as much as participates in them. She is also subject to error, as when she misjudges the ages of Mrs. Pusey and Jennifer, only gradually arriving at the truth. She also makes misjudgments about Mme de Bonneuil and Monica, which lead her to remark wryly to David, "So much for the novelist's famed powers, etc." She means famed powers of observation, which reminds the reader not only of the subjectivity of perception—people are as they are perceived to be, and objective truth is hard to establish—but also of the fact that Edith herself is a writer, a creator of fictional characters.

Historical Context

Women's Movement and Feminist Literature

The modern women's movement that began in the 1960s produced an upsurge in literature by and about women. In the United States this was stimulated by the publication of Betty Friedan's *The Feminine Mystique* in 1963. In Britain, the publication of Doris Lessing's *The Golden Notebook* (1962) raised similar issues about the status of women and the expectations they had about their lives. Germaine Greer's *The Female Eunuch* (1970) and Kate Millet's *Sexual Politics* (1970) were also influential in what was called at the time "consciousness-raising" for women. Such books encouraged women to organize politically and lobby for equal pay in the workplace, for abortion rights, and for freedom from sexual harassment and sex discrimination. According to Elaine Showalter in her important work of literary criticism, *A Literature of Their Own: British Women Novelists from Brontë to Lessing* (1977, rev. 1999), the pace of the women's movement were slower in the United Kingdom than in the United States. The British movement produced no charismatic leaders, and the media was slower to publicize the movement. Some

Compare & Contrast

- **1980s:** Harlequin, the largest publisher of romance fiction in the world, sells romance books in a hundred international markets; the books are translated into twenty-three languages. Harlequin has an estimated twenty million readers in North America and fifty million around the world.

  Today: According to Romance Writers of America, romance novels are read by fifty-one million people in the United States each year and account for 49 percent of paperback book sales. Sales amount to over $1 billion yearly. The genre is rapidly diversifying to reflect the realities of contemporary women's lives. Heroines may be single mothers or divorced women, for example, and "hen lit" features older heroines. Romantic suspense, in which the heroine not only finds romance but also solves crime, is increasingly popular. Other sub-divisions include paranormal/science fiction romance and gay romance.

- **1980s:** In Britain, the 1980s are a more conservative decade than the 1960s and 1970s. The Conservative government of Margaret Thatcher promotes free market reform, privatizes state-run industries, checks the growth of the welfare state, and reins in the power of the trade unions. The start of the AIDS epidemic in 1981 makes people more cautious in their sexual behavior.

  Today: The Conservative Party is no longer in power, having been ousted in 1997 by the Labour Party. From 1997 to 2005, Prime Minister Tony Blair wins a record three successive general elections for Labour, but in 2005, the Labour Party's majority in Parliament is sharply reduced. This change is partly a result of the unpopularity with the British public of the war in Iraq, in which the British government is a strong supporter of U.S. policy.

- **1980s:** British women writers begin to experiment with new forms and ideas beyond realism. These include popular genres such as detective fiction, science fiction, romances, thrillers, and horror. British black writers and British writers of Asian descent produce some of the "richest and most innovative" writing in Britain, according to Diana Wallace. However, some of the optimism of earlier decades gives way to pessimism about the future as ideals of liberation collide with what may actually be possible in an imperfect world.

  Today: Discussing contemporary British women's literature, Elaine Showalter in the revised edition of *A Literature of Their Own: British Women's Novelists from Brontë to Lessing* points out that the pioneering themes and metaphors typical of women's fiction from the 1970s onward have become part of every female writer's repertoire. She also notes that British literature by women has become less insular, with strong American and European influence, and less homogenous in style. This development reflects the contemporary global culture. Women writers are no longer limited to the social and domestic but participate in the literary mainstream "as postmodern innovators, politically engaged observers, and limitless storytellers."

British feminists also scorned television and newspapers because of the media's perceived distortions. However, as Showalter noted, by the late 1970s, the English movement was beginning to catch up. Laws guaranteeing equal rights for women were passed, and women's studies programs sprang up in universities.

As noted by Diana Wallace, in "'Writing as Revision': Women's Writing in Britain, 1945 to the Present Day," in the 1970s and 1980s there was also a boom in women's publishing in Britain, since "[f]eminism provided a theory and a language which many writers found enabling." Many women's presses were formed, starting with Virago in 1973 and followed by

The Women's Press, Onlywomen, Pandora, Sheba, and Honno. These presses often published work by women that mainstream publishers turned down.

According to Nicci Gerrard, in *Into the Mainstream: How Feminism Has Changed Women's Writing*, the dominant form of the emerging genre of feminist women's fiction in the 1960s and 1970s was domestic realism, as produced by Lessing and other authors such as Margaret Drabble, Iris Murdoch, Marge Piercy, and Marilyn French. Gerrard notes that

> For the first time, women's experiences were treated as central and significant: it mattered that daily and domestic details were recorded; that shopping and cooking, nappies and sleepless nights, menstruation and sexual desire, heterosexual and homosexual relationships were written about from a woman's point of view.

Such novels reflected women's lives as they were really lived and helped to create a sense of solidarity between women, giving many the courage to change unsatisfactory lives.

Gerrard points out that during the 1980s, there was a plethora of what she calls "feminist confessional" novels about "female suffering in a patriarchal world (sexual abuse, inequality, rape, pregnancy and abortion, the trap of motherhood and female conditioning)." However, she also points out that many leading British writers of the period, including novelists Antonia Byatt, Maggie Gee, and Emma Tennant, eschewed the feminist label, arguing that to accept it would imply that their work had a narrow ideological agenda rather than being an expression of a deeper level of artistic consciousness.

It has often been pointed out that Brookner's novels seem to be written against the prevailing feminist trend. In *Hotel du Lac*, for example, the heroine Edith Hope is not only a writer of popular romance novels (and thus implicitly unsympathetic to the goals of feminism), but also seeks romance and domesticity as her ultimate happiness. Her career as a writer, although moderately successful, seems to take second place in her mind. She wants what a woman is traditionally supposed to want: a man and a home. Patricia Waugh points out how unsuited Brookner's heroines seem to be for life in the contemporary world: "Their moral strengths function as weaknesses in the patriarchal, consumerist, and acquisitive world of the post-1960s, and they themselves internalize this disparaging view of their qualities, resulting in a perpetually low self-esteem."

Flora Alexander reaches a similar verdict about Brookner's work. She writes of Brookner's "detached and wary" attitude toward feminism. Brookner "does not see in feminism any remedy for the problem that she understands best—the problem of wishing for things, such as affection and family life, that by chance have been denied."

It is this inwardness of Brookner's work, the fact that she does not engage contemporary social and political issues, that makes her work in the 1980s untypical of the prevailing trends in women's fiction. Perhaps that is why *The Cambridge Guide to Women's Writing in English* defines her work as "in the tradition of English psychological fiction."

Critical Overview

The awarding of the 1984 Booker Prize, Britain's most prestigious literary award, to Brookner for *Hotel du Lac* sparked some controversy. Although the style and structure of the novel were generally admired, some critics felt that the judges were playing safe, rewarding a traditional kind of novel at the expense of more innovative work. However, reviews in Britain were positive, and *Hotel du Lac* quickly became a bestseller. Over fifty thousand copies were sold within the first five months of publication.

In the United States, the novel was also a bestseller, although critical reaction was mixed. Walter Clemons, in *Newsweek*, described it as "impeccably written and suffused with a pleasing, sub-acid wit," but he also thought it inferior to similar novels by Elizabeth Bowen and Christina Stead.

Anne Tyler, in the *New York Times Book Review*, had a more positive verdict, declaring the book to be Brookner's "most absorbing novel," partly because in contrast to earlier Brookner heroines, Edith Hope is "more philosophical . . . more self-reliant, more conscious that a solitary life is not, after all, an unmitigated tragedy." Tyler points out, as other reviewers do, the general uneventfulness of life at the hotel, but she seizes on the contrast between Edith and the Puseys, who "come to stand for all that Edith has missed (or dismissed) in her life," as conveying the central meaning of the novel. Edith comes to see through their superficiality, leading Tyler to the conclusion that though the Puseys may be, to use the analogy that Edith employs, the hares who always beat the tortoises in the race of life, the author intimates "that it's sort of silly even to run the race, let alone to win it."

The reviewer for the *New Yorker* also delivered a positive verdict, commenting that "Miss Brookner has the art to give us characters who have character, and the intelligence and the vocabulary and the grace of style . . . to bring them menacingly to life."

Lake surrounded by mountains, Switzerland © Paul Linse/Corbis

Less enthusiastic was Adam Mars-Jones, in the *New York Review of Books*, who argued that the success of the novel depended on "its heroine's being convincingly vulnerable, a softly complex creature likely to be trampled by a brutal world." But while acknowledging that Edith's temperament is "so thoroughly self-punishing that she doesn't actually need to be treated badly in order to generate the demure agony that is her recurrent emotion," Mars-Jones noted that Edith is in fact made of sterner stuff; her supposed weakness and helplessness are belied by her intelligence, her powers of observation, and her cutting remarks about others, including her friends. According to Mars-Jones, Edith prefers it if her friends underestimate her and do not recognize her power.

A hostile review came from the pen of Robert Jones, and was published in *Commonweal*. Jones complained that the novel was "humorless," with "stock characters and . . . lifeless prose," and suffered from a paucity of ideas. His conclusion was that *Hotel du Lac* "is the kind of fiction that often wins awards because it gives the illusion of being 'literary' without unsettling us by its vision or eliciting any response but a sigh of received ideas."

Views such as that of Jones have been very much in the minority, however. In the twenty years that have elapsed since Brookner wrote *Hotel du Lac*, she has written another nineteen novels, but *Hotel du Lac* is still generally regarded as one of her finest, if not her very best.

Criticism

Bryan Aubrey

Aubrey holds a Ph.D. in English and has published many articles on twentieth century literature. In this essay, he discusses the conflict in the protagonist between romanticism and realism, and how Brookner subverts the stereotypes of the popular romance novel.

A number of reviewers offered the opinion that *Hotel du Lac* was merely a more sophisticated version of a pulp romance, a "Harlequin Romance for highbrows," as Martha Bayles put it in *The New Republic*. For Angela McRobbie, in Britain's *New*

What Do I Read Next?

- Brookner's novel, *The Misalliance* (1987), like *Hotel du Lac*, features a lonely middle-aged heroine and the inner conflicts she tries to overcome. Blanche Vernon has been deserted by her husband of twenty years, whom she still loves. Struggling to find meaning and purpose in her newly solitary existence, she strikes up a friendship with Sally, a carefree young woman. Through Blanche, Sally, and other female characters, the novel offers a contrast between two different types of women: the dutiful, trustworthy, and reliable and the superficial, selfish, and irresponsible.

- English novelist Margaret Drabble's *The Radiant Way* (1987) follows the lives of three middle-aged, well-educated women in 1980s England. The title is ironic, since life in England during the Thatcher era is presented as anything but radiant. All the women experience losses of some kind or another, such as divorce, loss of job, or bereavement. The texture of the novel is rich and rewarding, full of social and personal detail, and ranging across the entire fabric of the nation.

- *Excellent Women* (1952) by Barbara Pym has been hailed as one of the finest English comic novels of the twentieth century. Pym has often been compared to Brookner, and in this novel she explores the lives of women in 1950s London. Like the heroines in many of Brookner's novels, Pym's protagonist is a rather self-effacing unmarried woman in her thirties. She lives a quiet life until a new couple moves into the apartment below hers, disrupting old relationships and bringing in new ones. As with all Pym's novels, *Excellent Women* is distinguished by its gentle wit and astute observations of the lives of women, and of men, too.

- *Loving with a Vengeance: Mass-Produced Fantasies for Women* by Tania Modleski (1984) analyzes popular entertainments aimed at women, such as romance and Gothic novels and soap operas. Modleski argues that popular culture shapes women's understanding of themselves but the desires so produced cannot be satisfied within a patriarchal world.

Statesman, "The slow sorrow with life which finds temporary release in the strong-jawed hero is here displaced into a more upmarket world." Brookner herself told interviewer Olga Kenyon that when she started writing the novel, she "simply wanted to write a love story in which something unexpected happened, and in which love really triumphed." Of course, when a writer begins to write, the mysterious process of creativity takes over, and what emerges in the final version is often very different from what the writer may have had in mind at the beginning. *Hotel du Lac* is far from being a story in which love triumphs. There is not a single relationship described or alluded to in the entire novel that would fit such a description. Instead, Brookner produced a subtle novel which plays with and subverts the romantic stereotypes embodied in the popular romance genre. For all its romantic underpinnings, *Hotel du Lac* reaches for a more hard-nosed view of reality, but one which does

provide some hope for the future for its lonely protagonist.

One of Edith Hope's most noticeable qualities is her diffidence. Since she has no confidence that her desires in life will be met, she has difficulty asserting herself and allows other people to shape her actions and expectations. The origins of this personality trait lie in Edith's memories of her emotionally deprived childhood. Her mother Rosa was too overwhelmed by her own disappointments in life to offer any emotional support to her young daughter, and she would behave cruelly toward her. Edith therefore learned at an early age how to suppress her own needs, since there appeared to be no possibility they would ever be met. Her kind and well-meaning father, at a loss to know how to deal with the tears of a small girl, would try to encourage her with the saying, "this is when character tells," a phrase that has stayed with Edith her whole life, and which she invokes (with some irony) whenever she is in an emotionally challenging situation. It means, in effect, one should grit one's teeth and endure, ignoring emotional pain in favor of a stoic attitude of resignation. It hardly seems like the recipe for a life lived in joy and emotional freedom.

Unfulfilled desires that are repressed, especially such powerful ones as the desire for comfort, security, and love, rarely disappear entirely in a person. They may find temporary underground hiding places, deep in the psyche but will eventually find a way of making their presence felt and dictating, to a certain extent, a person's behavior. Edith, crippled by her childhood deprivations and failing to make deep, loving connections with others in her adult life, finds some kind of salvation in the writing of romance novels, in which the desire for love can be expressed in all its instinctive ardor and its fulfillment guaranteed. In the novels Edith writes under the name of Vanessa Wilde, it is, she tells her agent Harold Webb, the "mouse-like unassuming girl who gets the hero, while the scornful temptress with whom he has had a stormy affair retreats baffled from the fray, never to return." Knowing herself to be that mouse-like girl, Edith boosts her own disappointed self by writing wish-fulfillment fantasies that, at one level at least, she knows are not true. As she wittily explains to her literary agent, using an analogy based on Aesop's fable of the tortoise and the hare, she writes for the "tortoise market." In real life, she says, the hare always wins the race with the tortoise, but the hares are so busy enjoying the fruits of their success that they do not bother to read books, which are left to the tortoises—losers in life but eternal victors in the world of the popular romance novel.

At another level, however, Edith does believe in what she writes. She may tell her agent that "The facts of life are too terrible to go into my kind of fiction," but in her letter to David at the end of the novel, when she is in a confessional mood and has no wish to lie to him or herself, she admits, in reference to her novels, "I believed every word I wrote." So it appears that Edith holds two contradictory beliefs in her mind: the romantic ideal is not attainable; or it is. She is at once realist and romantic. When she speaks to her agent, it is her intellect that comes to the fore, but when she writes to David, it is the heart that speaks, for the heart clings stubbornly to what it longs for, whatever the mind, with its habit of claiming a superior wisdom, may seek to tell it.

So what, in the real world, is a woman torn between realism and romanticism to do? How is

> " But although Edith is initially impressed by Mrs. Pusey, she eventually sees through the glittering façade and rejects the 'ultra-feminine' quality of her elderly acquaintance."

Edith, to use the jargon of the advertising world, to "position" herself as a woman in order to get what she wants and needs but in a way that preserves her emotional integrity? This is the question that occupies her mind during her two-week stay at the hotel. It arises in full force after her first encounter with the Puseys: "[W]hat behaviour most becomes a woman" is how she frames it, acknowledging that this is "the question around which she had written most of her novels . . . the question she had failed to answer and which she now saw to be of the most vital importance."

The reader has already learned, from Edith's conversation with Harold Webb, that she has little sympathy with the goals of feminism, in which women compete on equal terms with men. When Harold tells her how the market for romance novels is changing—"It's sex for the young woman executive now, the *Cosmopolitan* reader, the girl with the executive briefcase"—Edith replies that women prefer what she calls the "old myths," that the right man will miraculously appear just when all seems lost and will abandon everything to be with her.

Although, according to Edith, women may prefer such myths, there is only one character in the novel who could claim that the myth had come true for her, and that is Mrs. Pusey. This elderly but strong-willed and confident lady is an example of what Edith later calls the "ultra-feminine." At first, Edith is fascinated by her. Mrs. Pusey has completely accepted the old-fashioned contract between men and women and done very nicely for herself out of it. Edith observes that it is Mrs. Pusey's "femininity which has always provided her with life's chief delights." As Mrs. Pusey herself declares, "A woman should be able to make a man worship her," and it appears that her late husband easily succumbed to her feminine powers of enchantment. She frequently tells Edith that he loved her so much he gave her a blank check to spend on whatever she desired, and thanks to his apparently limitless Swiss bank account she is still able to live a luxurious life, even after his death.

But although Edith is initially impressed by Mrs. Pusey, she eventually sees through the glittering façade and rejects the "ultra-feminine" quality of her elderly acquaintance. She does so in no uncertain terms, dismissing such women as "complacent consumers of men with their complicated but unwritten rules of what is due to them. Treats. Indulgences. Privileges. . . . The cult of themselves. Such women strike me as dishonorable."

It is while Edith is considering such notions of the proper behavior for a woman—an issue she never satisfactorily resolves for herself—that she encounters Mr. Neville. It is here that Brookner quietly satirizes the stereotypes of contemporary romance novels. Edith meets Mr. Neville when she is having tea with the Puseys: "Startled, she looked up to see a tall man in a light grey suit smiling down at her." This might come from the pages of any pulp romance. The man is tall—of course—and he looks down at her—implying a position of strength and authority. As he hands Edith the notebook she inadvertently let slip, he says something to her ("Are you a writer?") that implies he has some secret knowledge, some secret insight into her, and this leaves poor Edith "in some confusion." Of course. But Mr. Neville will turn out to be as far from the ideal hero of pulp romance as could possibly be. Whereas all romantic heroes are expected to have muscular chests (prominently displayed on the cover of course, along with the long legs and spectacular cleavage of the heroine), what Edith most notices about Mr. Neville is his—*ankles*. As Edith tries to sleep that night, "the fine ankles, the unexpected evening pumps of the man in grey," are among the images that fill her mind. The next day, she observes him "crossing his elegant ankles," and it is not until they are formally introduced that she "register[s] his existence above ankle level and the profile usually presented to her." Ankles are what nineteenth-century Victorian gentlemen used to admire in women, a lady's trim ankle being considered a fine and alluring sight. Edith's first encounter with Mr. Neville may be the only example in literature in which the roles are comically reversed.

If real men whisk their beloved off to exotic and exciting destinations, men like Mr. Neville take them on chilly, desolate boat trips, such as the one that prompts Edith to reflect: "This banal and inappropriate excursion seemed to her almost perverse in its lack of attractions." She had been hoping for something better:

> But no, he had forced her on to this terrible boat, this almost deserted and pilotless vessel, from which there was no hope of rescue; she saw them drifting, their aimlessness raised to almost mythological status, into ever thicker mists, while real people, on the shore, went on with their real lives, indifferent to this ghost ship which seemed, to Edith, almost to have passed out of normal existence.

Mr. Neville is in fact a Mephistophelean figure, although even in that role he disappoints. A demonic tempter, such as the Satan who tempts Christ or the Mephistopheles who tempts Faust, usually offers his victim everything he desires if he will only agree to serve him. Mr. Neville, calculating businessman that he is, offers Edith exactly *half* of what she dearly wants: security and domesticity, but not love. Edith can only be thankful that she comes to her senses and rejects this chary Mephistopheles before it is too late.

Brookner uses much the same technique in satirizing Edith's lover David. He and Edith meet at a party, where they say almost nothing to each other. He is tall (obviously), and she looks up at him (of course), and they exchange nothing more than a silent glance. A few hours later, however, David pops over to her house, as she, apparently, knew he would. Not a single word is exchanged, a "long and hard look" being sufficient for their purpose, following which they go straight to bed together. Perhaps such things do happen in Vanessa Wilde's novels, but surely not in the life of Edith Hope.

David turns out to be a rather unorthodox romantic hero. There is no evidence that he is any great shakes in the chest department, but what he may lack in thoracic appeal, he surely makes up for only slightly lower down, for he is forever eating. Quickly noticing his remarkable appetite, Edith makes a habit of cooking "heroic fry-ups," which prompt him to reflect on what he calls "food fit for heroes." It appears that what a man requires in a woman is not a full and open heart but a full and open larder.

To her credit, Edith has no illusions about her lover. She knows, or suspects, that she is being used. While David probably regards their arrangement as perfect, for Edith, every encounter with him is tinged with a terrible sadness that he, being too busy eating, never notices.

By the end of the novel, Edith has learned something from her experiences. In the telegram she sends to David, she changes the message from

"Coming home," to "Returning." This is a more honest appraisal of her situation, since Edith's solitary existence, without husband or family, hardly fulfills her idea of what a home should be. The new wording suggests that she is now ready to look at her life less through the lens of romantic illusions and more with the eye of the realist. While not suppressing her romantic nature, she is prepared to see things the way they are, not the way she wants them to be.

Source: Bryan Aubrey, Critical Essay on *Hotel du Lac*, in *Novels for Students*, Thomson Gale, 2006.

Cheryl Alexander Malcolm

In the following essay excerpt, Malcolm notes differences between Hotel du Lac *and Brookner's previous novels, most notably the former's optimistic outcome.*

Brookner continues to explore the limits of free will in *Hotel du Lac*. But the outcome is far more optimistic. A subtle shift in Brookner's writing is first indicated in the novel's Swiss setting, which signifies a move away from London and families. Even in *Look at Me,* the adult protagonist regards herself in terms of her family and is frequently referred to as an orphan by other characters. Also, she remains in her family home although she knows she is wholly out of place in an apartment complex in which all its inhabitants are twice her age. *Hotel du Lac*'s Edith Hope is shown on her own in a Swiss hotel. Her anonymity should denote personal freedom. Her single suitcase should symbolize her lack of encumbering duties and the ease with which she can move on. In these respects, *Hotel du Lac* promises a new beginning for its protagonist, a beginning which, unlike that in Brookner's first three novels, is not centered on a male figure.

The title *Hotel du Lac* differs from the pattern set by Brookner's first three novels in that it refers to a place, rather than a theme concerning its protagonist. Nonetheless, *Hotel du Lac,* as much as its predecessors, concerns a single protagonist. The setting to which the title refers in fact reflects the condition of Edith Hope's life as much as it is a place for events to happen. From the start of the novel, as the narrative progresses from descriptions of the scenery to Edith Hope's self-observations, the protagonist and her surroundings become inextricably linked. The result is the introduction of suspense, as the elusiveness of the Swiss landscape in fog prepares us for mysteries surrounding this protagonist: "from the window all that could be seen was a receding area of grey. It was to be supposed

> **Edith Hope may be a romantic, but in the context of this novel it is a virtue that also makes good sense."**

that beyond the grey garden, which seemed to sprout nothing but the stiffish leaves of some unfamiliar plant, lay the vast grey lake, spreading like an anaesthethic towards the invisible further shore, and beyond that, in imagination only, yet verified by the brochure, the peak of the Dent d'Oche, on which snow might already be slightly and silently falling." The contrast between the grey dormancy of the lake and its "colour and incident" at other times will directly parallel the trouble with Edith Hope. For this protagonist, who dresses so impeccably and appears so very proper, does something so shocking that she is put on a flight to Switzerland by a friend who "was prepared to forgive her only on condition that she disappeared for a decent length of time and came back older, wiser, and properly apologetic." All expectations are that Edith Hope will not only return to London chastened, but moreover her old self again before "the unfortunate lapse which had led to this brief exile" and "that apparently dreadful thing" she had done. What comes across immediately in this passage is a gulf between others' perception of the "thing" that happened and the protagonist's. Another discrepancy is introduced between others' perception of Edith Hope's *normal* character and that which she reveals on this singular occasion. Chapter 1 closes with the head of the hotel staring with equal confusion at the protagonist's name in the hotel register. His thoughts, in the form of the notebook jottings of a detective, invite even further interest in the protagonist. Here he guesses from her name that Edith Hope is not easily definable or easily placed: "One new arrival. Hope, Edith Johanna. An unusual name for an English lady. Perhaps not entirely English. Perhaps not entirely a lady. Recommended, of course. But in this business one never knew."

Hotel du Lac, like the fog-covered lake for which its hotel is named, is a novel propelled by the unveiling of mysteries. The first is, what has the protagonist done to deserve social ostracization to such an extreme? The second is, what does this say about the protagonist's character? Other mysteries relating to the backgrounds, pasts, even ages of the other single women staying at the hotel contribute to an atmosphere of expectancy and anticipation for the reader. Otherwise, remarkably little happens in this novel. Its plot moves as little as the fog. But when it does, revelations are indeed startling. Almost every observation on the part of the protagonist, a romance novelist who studies people with a writer's eye, proves false. Similarly, any view we may have that this protagonist is the inspiration for the meek heroines of her romance novels is dashed. Twice offered marriage, she twice refuses. Why? Her name, after all, may be the clue. She is not "entirely a lady," but is the mistress of a man she writes to every day while she is a way, and to whom she will return in England. She is also "not entirely English," having been raised by a Viennese mother, aunt, and grandmother.

Protagonists of mixed background have featured in *The Debut* and *Providence* and will continue to figure prominently in Brookner's writing. Whether the protagonists' parentage is English and non-English and/or Christian and Jewish, feelings of being slightly out of place within one's family foreshadow these protagonists' unease in wider, adult social situations. The protagonist of *Hotel du Lac* is no exception. Although she has fame as a romance novelist and a face that people recognize from the covers of her books, she does not regard herself as a "wordly" sort of woman. She is a wearer of cardigans, who bears a "physical resemblance to Virginia Woolf." Others just might invite her to their table in the dining room of the Hotel du Lac, but it would never occur to her to do the same. Too content to be an observer of people and too self-conscious of her lack of levity to fit in with them, Edith Hope bears many of the character traits of Brookner's previous protagonists. What makes *Hotel du Lac* stand out from its predecessors is the incorporation of so many of their features in one text.

Stylistically, *Hotel du Lac* exhibits the circular pattern that Brookner has employed in earlier novels. It begins and ends with the protagonist's writing to her married lover, David. The first is a letter in which she gives a jocular account of her friend's driving her to the airport ("Penelope drove fast and kept her eyes grimly ahead, as if escorting a prisoner from the dock to a maximum security wing"), followed by an equally colorful description of the other guests in the hotel and ending with deep-felt expressions of her love. The second is a telegram that first reads, "Coming home," then is changed to the single word "Returning." At first glance, this circular pattern, which coincides with the protagonist's arrival in Switzerland and imminent return to England, might suggest a lack of progression or a dispiriting conclusion to the novel. But this is where *Hotel du Lac* dramatically differs from Brookner's earlier work. A closer look at the pieces of writing that frame the narrative shows marked differences that indicate a change in the protagonist's attitude and actions. The most striking difference is the change in length from many pages to a single word. The next is a difference in tone, from the letter's mask of joviality barely concealing deep sadness and anxiety to the telegram's resolute no-nonsense message. The other difference between these pieces of writing, and the most crucial, is that the telegram is actually sent, whereas the love letter never leaves Edith Hope's possession. If the letter at the start of the text shows Edith Hope to be a stoically passive person who allows herself to be put on a plane to a destiny she has not chosen and one where she spends her time silently observing the people around her, the telegram at the end of the text dispels this view altogether.

Hotel du Lac is basically about making choices. One occurs in the past, the other occurs in the present. The first is the reason for her being "exiled" to an out-of-season Swiss resort. The importance of this first choice is indicated by the many references to it that build anticipation by concealing more than they disclose. It is also shown in the devotion of an entire chapter to it. Whereas earlier there had been brief flashbacks concerning her lover, David, chapter 9 exclusively concerns the past as related by its omnipresent narrator. Beginning with the words "On the day of her wedding . . ." this chapter reveals how the protagonist decides, at the last instant, not to go through with a thoroughly respectable but passionless marriage. More than answering the mystery that has been steadily built around the protagonist's past, this earlier chance at marriage foreshadows a second one to come. What the reader cannot be sure of, however, is whether or not she will go through with it this time. Given events in the past, a proposal of marriage at the Hotel du Lac is given a momentousness that otherwise might not have been the case. After all, Edith Hope had been told by her married friends that "she had had her last chance" when she spurned Geoffrey.

One of Brookner's talents is to so subtly lure readers' interest in her protagonists through uncovering of mysteries that the many clues she scatters throughout the narrative can oftentimes go unnoticed. In retrospect, for example, the names of characters in *Hotel du Lac* virtually predict their future, in addition to revealing their innermost character. "Edith" is a fairly old-fashioned name, more usually given to women of an earlier generation than that of the protagonist. The implication is that she is somehow out of date. Her refusal to update her romance novels, in other words to reflect the social realities of sexually liberated career women, may make her appear prudish. Yet her refusal to cater to the tastes of "those multi-orgasmic girls with the executive briefcases" is rooted in her sense of justice. By perpetuating the maxim that "the meek will inherit the earth" (in her books "it is the mouse-like unassuming girl who gets the hero"), she is effectively putting the world aright. Extracts from her letters to her married lover, which interrupt the narrative, serve most of all to remind us that this is *not* a sexually inexperienced or repressed woman. Would the latter, after cancelling her wedding, have her married lover back to the house to help her finish the party champagne before making love, as Edith Hope does? It may seem old-fashioned to believe in the supremacy of romantic love over casual sex or marriages of convenience, but it increasingly makes sense coming from as unflinching a realist as this protagonist.

A quick look at the names of Edith Hope's three male love interests reveals some striking differences that help explain the choices she makes in their regard. The would-be husband whom she deserts in London is named "Geoffrey." The soft alliteration and assonance in this name should alert us to how he is flawed. "The totality of his mouse-like seemliness" strikes the protagonist when she sees him on the morning of their wedding. By leaving him standing on the steps of the registry office, she has spared herself (we are led to believe) seeing his "mouse-like seemliness" in bed. "Everyone [who] had said how good he had been to his mother . . . how lucky his wife would be . . . how lucky Edith was" did not suppose that this protagonist might want a husband who was at least as good a lover as he was a caregiver. True to her last name, "Hope," this protagonist aspires to more than that.

Edith Hope's second would-be husband is as flawed morally as the first is physically. Even Philip Neville's last name suggests there is something of the devil about him. And when he proposes to the protagonist, what comes to mind is the Faust legend. Like Mephistopheles, he comes not with a suitor's flowers, but proffering a new life. In a pragmatic tone and manner more suited to a business contract than affairs of the heart, he offers Edith Hope a marriage based on her natural virtue's being

corrupted. Asked how his "doctrine of selfishness" is to be shared, he explains:

> "I am proposing a partnership of the most enlightened kind. . . . If you wish to take a lover, that is your concern, so long as you arrange it in a civilized manner."
>
> "And if you . . ."
>
> "The same applies, of course. . . . Think, Edith. Have you not, at some time in your well-behaved life, desired vindication? Are you not tired of being polite to rude people? . . ."
>
> Edith bowed her head.
>
> ". . . You will find that you can behave as badly as you like. As badly as everybody else likes, too. That is the way of the world."

By repeatedly referring to this character as Mr. Neville, rather than just Philip, Brookner lends an air of authority to him that is confirmed seemingly by the protagonist's decision to accept his offer. Edith Hope changes her mind, however, when she finds him coming out of Jennifer Pusey's room the next morning. Mrs. Pusey's pampered life is in keeping with her kitten-like last name. The vulgar use of "pussy" to denote a woman's sex, especially in the context of "getting some" (i.e., sex), now makes the name "Pusey" appropriate for her daughter as well. In contrast to these characters' names, which have so many negative associations, the name of Edith's lover, David, has only positive ones.

Both associations with the name "Pusey" draw attention to the essential difference between these female characters and the protagonist. Whereas the former would seem to naturally draw adoration or sexual attraction, Edith Hope is the one who adores and gives herself over physically as an expression of her devotion. That David Simmonds may be unworthy occurs not only to the reader but also to her. In this, the depiction of love in *Hotel du Lac* is consistent with that in *The Debut, Providence,* and *Look at Me.* Inherent in each is the premise that love is no more rational than religious faith. Associations with the name "David" reinforce this view. In the Bible, David is the one chosen to be king. To explain this unlikely choice of a shepherd boy, we are told, "The Lord seeth not as man seeth; for man looketh on the outward appearance, but the Lord looketh on the heart." Since appearances repeatedly prove to be misleading, whether it is Edith Hope who is misjudged by others or she who misreads people's ages, occupations, social status, and character, trusting one's heart might after all be more advisable. This message at the end of *Hotel du Lac* sets it apart from Brookner's previous novels about single women in love. Edith Hope may be a romantic, but in the context of this novel it is a virtue that also makes good sense.

Source: Cheryl Alexander Malcolm, "Can't Buy Me Love," in *Understanding Anita Brookner*, University of South Carolina Press, 2002, pp. 53–61.

Sources

Alexander, Flora, *Contemporary Women Novelists*, Edward Arnold, 1989, p. 30.

Bayles, Martha, "Review of *Hotel du Lac*," in *The New Republic*, Vol. 192, No. 37, March 25, 1985, p. 38.

Brookner, Anita, *Hotel du Lac*, Dutton, 1986.

The Cambridge Guide to Women's Writing in English, edited by Lorna Sage, Cambridge University Press, 1999, p. 93.

Clemons, Walter, Review of *Hotel du Lac*, in *Newsweek*, Vol. 105, No. 87, February 25, 1885, p. 87.

Gerrard, Nicci, *Into the Mainstream: How Feminism Has Changed Women's Writing*, Pandora, 1989, pp. 111–12.

Jones, Robert, Review of *Hotel du Lac*, in *Commonweal*, September 20, 1985, pp. 502–03.

Kenyon, Olga, *Women Writers Talk: Interviews with 10 Women Writers*, Lennard Publishing, 1989, p. 13.

Mars-Jones, Adam, Review of *Hotel du Lac*, in *New York Review of Books*, Vol. 32, No. 17, January 31, 1985, pp. 17–19.

McRobbie, Angela, "Review of *Hotel du Lac*," in *New Statesman*, Vol. 108, No. 32, September 7, 1984, p. 34.

Review of *Hotel du Lac*, in the *New Yorker*, February 18, 1985, p. 121.

Showalter, Elaine, *A Literature of Their Own: British Women Novelists from Brontë to Lessing*, expanded edition, Princeton University Press, 1999, p. 323.

Tyler, Anne, "A Solitary Life," in *New York Times Book Review*, February 3, 1985, pp. 1, 31.

Wallace, Diana, "'Writing as Re-vision': Women's Writing in Britain, 1945 to the Present Day," in *An Introduction to Women's Writing: From the Middle Ages to the Present Day*, edited by Marion Shaw, Prentice-Hall, 1998, pp. 249, 255.

Waugh, Patricia, *Feminine Fictions: Revisiting the Postmodern*, Routledge, 1989, p. 126.

Further Reading

Haffenden, John, *Novelists in Interview*, Methuen, 1985, pp. 57–75.

In this interview, Brookner talks engagingly about her family background, her work as novelist and art historian, her love of nineteenth-century novelists such as Dickens and Trollope, Stendhal and Flaubert. On *Hotel du Lac*, she says that Mr. Neville is "really a very wicked man" and "Edith is desperate."

Malcolm, Cheryl Alexander, *Understanding Anita Brookner*, University of South Carolina Press, 2002, pp. 51–61.

Malcolm argues that the novel is basically about making choices and that Edith learns by the end to trust her heart.

Sadler, Lynn Veach, *Anita Brookner*, Twayne's English Authors Series, No. 473, Twayne, 1990, pp. 54–67.

Sadler argues that at the end of the novel, Edith remains essentially unchanged, still attached to her romantic view of the world. Her problem is the lack of suitable men; she is unable to see the flaws in David.

Skinner, John, *The Fictions of Anita Brookner: Illusions of Romance*, St. Martin's Press, 1992, pp. 66–83.

Skinner analyzes the allusions in *Hotel du Lac* to the world of popular romance. He argues that the novel exemplifies the ambivalent relationship between parody and the text being parodied; the relationship is not only of contrast but also of intimacy. The novel is typical of Brookner's fiction in that it presents romantic longing alongside detached analysis of such feelings.

Stetz, Margaret Diane, "Anita Brookner: Woman Writer as Reluctant Feminist," in *Writing the Woman Artist: Essays on Poetics, Politics, and Portraiture*, edited by Suzanne W. Jones, University of Pennsylvania Press, 1991, pp. 96–112.

Stetz argues that although Brookner has in interviews been dismissive of feminism, if definitions of feminism can be expanded to include the elements that recur in her fiction, such as the championing of literature written by and to women (Edith Hope in *Hotel du Lac*, for example), and the focusing of attention on the woman writer, Brookner might be considered a feminist, albeit a reluctant one.

Watson, Daphne, *Their Own Worst Enemies: Women Writers of Women's Fiction*, Pluto Press, 1995, pp. 37–55.

Watson compares Brookner's work with that of another British novelist, Barbara Pym, concluding that both writers are indebted to the Prince Charming myth. Their heroines embody a kind of hollowness, convinced that they need a man to release them from their humdrum lives.

The Hours

Michael Cunningham
1998

Michael Cunningham's Pulitzer-Prize winning novel *The Hours* opens with the suicide of Virginia Woolf, who was one of the most important writers of the twentieth century. She becomes a character in his book, as he weaves his depiction of her creation of her celebrated novel *Mrs. Dalloway* (1925) into the stories of two other women who are profoundly affected by her work. Cunningham traces a day in the three women's lives in which each becomes moved by an urge to create something of lasting significance to themselves and to others. Woolf composes her novel and prepares for a visit by her sister; Clarissa Vaughan and Laura Brown plan parties for friends and/or family.

During this process, the women experience moments of perfect harmony, which help them endure the losses that they inevitably must face. In this poignant exploration of the ironic tension between life and death, creativity and stagnation, Cunningham ultimately presents a life-affirming vision in his novel's celebration of hope and the endurance of the human spirit.

Author Biography

Michael Cunningham was born on November 6, 1952 in Cincinnati, Ohio, to Don and Dorothy Cunningham. Due to the father's career in advertising, the family was always on the move until Michael was ten years old, when they finally settled in

Michael Cunningham   AP/Wide World Photos

Pasadena, California. Cunningham's interest in literature began to develop when he was a teenager; he often read the works of his favorite authors, Virginia Woolf and T. S. Eliot.

After he graduated high school in 1972, Cunningham enrolled in Stanford University where he took literature courses instead of following his initial desire to study painting. Two years after receiving a bachelor of arts in English from Stanford, he received a Michener Fellowship to attend the master of fine arts (MFA) program at the University of Iowa Writers' Workshop. While attending, he had many of his stories published in periodicals such as *Atlantic Monthly*, *Paris Review*, and *Redbook*.

His first short story, "Cleaving," published in 1981, focused on the importance of family. In 1984, his first novel, *Golden States*, another exploration of the American family, was published without much critical attention. In an ironic twist of fate, Cunningham gained critical acclaim for his 1990 novel, *A Home at the End of the World*. With this novel, he attempted to prove to his partner, Ken Corbett, that his writing was not marketable. He submitted a chapter to the *New Yorker* expecting the magazine to reject it, but surprisingly, it was accepted and sparked much interest in the subsequent publication of the novel. His next novel, *Flesh and Blood*, published in 1995, also received

positive reviews from such publications as the *New York Times Book Review*.

As his reputation grew, Cunningham began to be noticed for his depiction of the unconventional post-nuclear family as well as his prose style that is often compared to that of his favorite author, Virginia Woolf. In 1998, Cunningham's novel, *The Hours* became his most successful work to date, earning the Pulitzer Prize and the PEN/Faulkner Award in 1999. The novel was made into a major motion picture in 2002.

As of 2005 Cunningham lives in Greenwich Village where he continues to write works that garner commercial and critical accolades, including the O. Henry Award, which he received in 1999 for his short story, "Mister Brother." He also teaches creative writing at Brooklyn College.

Plot Summary

Prologue

The prologue to *The Hours* focuses on Virginia Woolf in 1941, just as World War II has begun. "She walks purposely toward the river," feeling as if she has failed as a writer and noting the signs that her mental illness is returning. She gathers stones that she places in her pockets and wades out into the river. Suddenly, the current pulls her under. Back at their home, her husband Leonard finds the suicide letter she has written, telling him that she is certain she is losing her sanity and insisting that he has given her "the greatest possible happiness." Her body floats downstream and is caught on a piling. The specific time and place of this event is not identified in the novel, but the historical Virginia Woolf drowned herself in the River Ouse near her Sussex, England home on March 28, 1941.

Part I

The novel moves back and forth between three stories that focus on three different women: Virginia Woolf, Clarissa Vaughan, and Laura Brown. It begins in New York City at the end of the twentieth century with fifty-two-year-old Clarissa, who needs to buy flowers for the party she is giving for her best friend and former lover Richard in honor of his winning the prestigious Carrouthers Prize for poetry.

The narrator notes that Richard had given her the nickname Mrs. Dalloway when they were at college together, insisting that her own name was not appropriate for her. As she walks to get the flowers, she thinks about her relationship with

Richard, which began when she was eighteen. Clarissa buys the flowers and heads for Richard's apartment.

In Richmond, England in 1923, Virginia Woolf begins the novel, which will become *Mrs. Dalloway*, with her heroine determined to get flowers for her party that afternoon, just as Clarissa Vaughan does. Leonard, who has nursed her through her illnesses, "does not demand what she can't provide" and so is always gentle with her. He believes that she will be recognized as a great author and so does all he can to encourage her writing. She hopes that she will be able to persuade him to move back to London, but Leonard worries that the city will exhaust her. She feels this morning in a perfect creative state.

In her home in Los Angeles in 1949, Laura reads the beginning of *Mrs. Dalloway*, "trying to lose herself." She feels guilty for reading on her husband Dan's birthday, thinking that she should be downstairs fixing his breakfast. She senses that it will be difficult to believe in herself this day but determines that she will bake Dan a cake. She tells herself "she does not dislike her child, does not dislike her husband. She will rise and be cheerful."

Laura goes downstairs where Dan and her son Richie are happy to see her. After her husband leaves, she is alone with Richie, who, she feels, demands too much of her. She fights the urge to go back upstairs and read and tells Richie that he can help her bake the cake.

Clarissa passes a corner where she remembers that she and Richard had argued, about what she cannot remember. Soon after, they had stopped being lovers. She arrives at Richard's apartment and finds that he is having a bad morning. Richard is dying of AIDS, which has ravaged his mind as well as his body. He is not sure he has the will or the strength to accept his award, which he insists, he is getting because he has AIDS and not because of his literary talents. His last book, which includes a character based on Clarissa, was not well received. Clarissa tries to assure him that the award is well deserved and insists that she will help him get through the evening.

Virginia has had a successful morning writing, but she worries that her novel will not be good enough. She thinks that her heroine will die, possibly kill herself. She continually fears that the headaches that announce the onset of another period of mental instability will return. She determines to move back to London, better to die there "raving mad . . . than evaporate in Richmond."

Media Adaptations

- A celebrated film version of *The Hours* was produced in 2002 by Miramax and Paramount, directed by Stephen Daldry and starring Meryl Streep, Nicole Kidman, and Julianne Moore.

Laura and Richie begin to make the birthday cake. At this moment, Laura experiences an overwhelming sense of love for him and feels "she is precisely what she appears to be: a pregnant woman kneeling in a kitchen with her three-year-old son." When Richie makes a mistake, he crumbles, but a few kind words from her restore him. Laura wonders why he is so fragile and for a moment yearns to be free of him. Her feelings pass, however, and she returns to her earlier sense of tranquility as she finishes the cake and determines that "[s]he will not lose hope," that she can live happily.

Part II

As Virginia walks in Richmond, she plans what will happen to Clarissa and thinks that perhaps she will love a woman but will eventually "come to her senses, as young women do, and marry a suitable man." When she returns to the house, she has a disagreement with the cook and wonders why she always feels intimidated by her servants and cannot establish a good relationship with them.

In the apartment, Clarissa thinks about her relationship with Sally who has just left to have lunch with a film star. She determines that she is satisfied with her life, at least for this moment. Yet in the next, she feels "trivial" because the film star has not asked her to join them. Her thoughts wander back to 1965 to her past relationship with Richard and his other lover Louis and wonders what life would have been like if she had not left Richard, feeling a "sense of missed opportunity." She acknowledges her first kiss with Richard defined the most perfect moment of her life.

Laura is disappointed with the cake she has made, which is less than the perfect vision she had

had of it. She thinks of her husband's solid goodness and declares that she wants to be a good wife and mother. Kitty, her neighbor arrives, which gives Laura a pang of excitement. When she tells Laura that she may have a uterine tumor, Laura embraces her and the two share a brief kiss, which Richie observes. After Kitty leaves, Laura has the overwhelming desire to return to her book and the alternate world it offers. She turns instead to the cake and throws it in the trash, determined to make a better one.

Virginia's sister, Vanessa, and her children arrive for a visit. Vanessa's robust health is in stark contrast to Virginia's frailty. After the children find a dying bird, Virginia helps them create a death bed for it in the garden. As she thinks that she would like to lie down in the bird's place, she determines that Clarissa will live after all.

Clarissa plans to give Richard "the best party she can manage." As she prepares, Louis arrives, whom she has not seen in years. She tells him about Richard's ill health and they discuss his recent book and their relationships with Richard and each other when they all lived together in a beach house. Louis claims that he has fallen in love with one of his students and then suddenly begins to sob because he knows it is only an affair. Julia, Clarissa's teenaged daughter, arrives and soon after, Louis leaves, promising to come to the party. He wonders what would have happened if he had not broken off his relationship with Richard.

Part III

Laura drops her son off at a babysitter and drives to a hotel where she can be alone. She feels like a failure after making the second cake that did not meet her expectations. In the room, she thinks about committing suicide, noting the freedom it would afford her, but rejects the idea, insisting that she could not cause her family to suffer. She admits that at times "she loves life . . . hopelessly," yet she envisions Woolf's suicide and how easy it would be for her as well.

Virginia drinks tea with Vanessa, experiencing a perfect moment of happiness. She determines that someone else but not Clarissa will die. Behind her cook's back, she kisses Vanessa, which "feels like the most delicious and forbidden of pleasures." In a quick chapter, Julia arrives with her radical lesbian friend and Clarissa thinks about her relationship with her daughter. The next chapter reverts to Virginia at the end of the day after her sister and children have left.

Virginia again worries that her novel will not be any good and that the headache is returning. She sets out for London, which she feels will replenish her. As she waits for the train, Leonard finds her, and gently berates her for leaving without telling anyone where she was going.

A brief chapter follows, chronicling the meeting between Sally and the film star, ending with her back at the apartment where she and Clarissa experience a perfect moment of harmony together. In the next chapter, Laura picks up Richie who bursts out in tears when he sees her. On the way home, Richie expresses his love for her in a frantic tone, seemingly knowing what Laura has been thinking. She tells him that she loves him, which eases him.

Part IV

Clarissa arrives at Richard's apartment to help him get ready for the party. She finds it flooded with light and Richard, looking "insane and exalted" perched on the window sill. When he announces that he does not think he will be able to make it to the party, Clarissa, fearful that he will jump, insists that he does not have to go. Richard admits that he feels like a failure, tells Clarissa he loves her, leans further out the window, and falls five stories to the pavement. Clarissa runs down and stays with his body for a while, caressing his shoulder and thinking about how much she had loved him.

Dan blows out the candles on his birthday cake and claims that it is "perfect." Laura feels as if she is experiencing a perfect moment of happiness, looking at the scene in her dining room, and expresses hope for the future. But the moment soon passes.

Virginia thinks about returning to London, which Leonard has agreed to do. She decides that Clarissa will have loved a woman when she was young and will always remember a kiss that they shared. Virginia again determines that Clarissa will not die because she will be too in love with life. Another person, "a deranged poet, a visionary will be the one to die."

Laura prepares for bed where her husband is waiting for her. She sees the sleeping pills in the medicine cabinet and thinks how easy suicide would be, wondering if the moment she experienced earlier would be enough for her. She goes to bed, feeling detached and far away.

An elderly Laura arrives at Clarissa's apartment and the two discuss Richard, Laura's son. Clarissa has mixed feelings about Laura who eventually abandoned her family. They both claim that they wish they could have helped Richard more. Clarissa notes how ironic it is that Laura, who contemplated suicide, is still alive when the rest of her family has died. As she gazes at all of the food she has prepared for the party, Clarissa feels as if Richard is truly gone. She hopes that Richard will be remembered for his work but recognizes that "it's far more likely that his books will vanish along with almost everything else." Yet Clarissa feels comforted by thinking of the perfect moments people sometimes experience, which provide them with hope and the will to go on.

Characters

Vanessa Bell

Virginia Woolf's sister, Vanessa Bell, displays a robust healthiness that is in stark contrast to Virginia's own frailty. Vanessa provides the motive for Virginia's desire to create a perfect afternoon tea and gives her the guilty pleasure of a kiss behind the cook's back.

Dan Brown

Dan Brown, Laura's kind and gentle husband, has no idea how trapped Laura feels in her role as his wife and the mother of their son Richie.

Laura Brown

Laura Brown has become a traditional American housewife after World War II, a role that leaves her feeling "as if she is standing in the wings, about to go onstage and perform in a play for which she is not appropriately dressed, and for which she has not adequately rehearsed." She determines that she should be happy with a kind and loving husband and child but she continually feels empty and unfulfilled.

While she tries to become involved in the life of her family, as when she prepares a birthday party for her husband, her sense of desperation and inability to establish a separate identify for herself becomes so overwhelming that she considers suicide. Reading, especially *Mrs. Dalloway*, becomes her only solace. Eventually, she abandons her family in an effort to discover a true sense of self. This action has a great impact on her son Richard, who expresses his profound sense of loss in his poetry.

Richard Brown

Richard Brown, Clarissa's first love and now her best friend, displays a heightened sense of existence, needing "to live in a world peopled by extreme and commanding figures" and insisting on the best from himself and his friends. This spirit emerges in his poetry, which has won him great acclaim.

As a child, Richard displayed an extreme devotion to and need for his mother's love and attention. He was "transparently smitten" with his mother, "comic and tragic in his hopeless love." His recognition of his deteriorating mind and body as a result of the ravages of AIDS, along with his insistence that he has failed as an artist, prompts him to commit suicide.

Kitty

Kitty is Laura's attractive neighbor, who announces one day that she might have a uterine tumor. As Laura consoles her, the two share a kiss which suggests that Laura may have lesbian desires.

Sally

Sally, Clarissa's partner, represents "the stoic, the tortured, the subtly wise." She is patient with Clarissa, knowing the importance of her relationship with Richard, and loving, as when she brings Clarissa roses, which creates one of her perfect moments.

Clarissa Vaughan

Clarissa is a practical, yet romantic fifty-two year old who has devoted herself this day to providing a perfect moment for Richard, her best friend and former lover who is dying from AIDS. He has given her the nickname "Mrs. Dalloway," insisting that she was too special for an ordinary name such as "Vaughan." During the day, Clarissa reveals a thoughtful introspection as she reexamines the choices she has made in her life, expressing her doubts about her value as a friend, a mother, and a lover. Yet her generous spirit keeps her focused on her task.

After Richard dies, Clarissa displays courage and strength as she faces life without him. Cunningham ends the book on an affirmative note, with her insistence that the transitory moments of happiness that people experience are enough to help them endure and ultimately celebrate life.

Julia Vaughan

Julia Vaughan, Clarissa's headstrong and independent teenaged daughter, causes her mother a measure of regret who feels that Julia resents the fact that she has no father. Yet, Julia shows her generosity and devotion to her mother when she supports her after Richard's death.

Leonard Woolf

Leonard Woolf, Virginia's supportive husband, does all that he can to nurture his wife's creative talents and at the same time prevent her mental decline. In her suicide note, Virginia acknowledges his kindness and love for her when she declares, "*You have given me the greatest possible happiness.*"

Virginia Woolf

Cunningham includes factual biographical details in his fictional portrait of Virginia Woolf, one of the world's most celebrated writers. The historical person committed suicide in 1941 when she felt the return of the mental instability that had plagued her for years. In his novel, Cunningham depicts her as a physically as well as mentally fragile woman who is devoted to her husband but more so to her art which becomes all consuming for her to the point where she is willing to risk her health for it.

Cunningham's Virginia Woolf feels constricted by her life in Richmond, a suburb of London, where her life is carefully planned and overseen by Leonard, whose primary motive is to protect his wife's health. She insists that she needs the excitement and freedom of London to encourage her art. Losing herself in the act of creation becomes for her "the most profound satisfaction she knows." Yet when she begins to lose confidence in her ability to continue writing, under the threat of insanity, she determines that she will end her life, and so end her suffering, along with that of her husband.

Themes

Insanity

Both Virginia Woolf and Richard experience mental instability which eventually pushes them to suicide. Woolf feels her mind slipping at the beginning of the novel, when Cunningham describes her hearing voices and feeling the headache that always signals the decline of her sanity. Awareness of the instability of her mind and the probability that she will never be cured inspires her to accomplish as much as she can while she can think clearly and write well. Her condition also arouses the desire in her to move back to London even though she knows that the excitement of life there may exhaust her and so trigger a relapse into mental illness. The acknowledgment that she may not have much time encourages her to spend what she does

Topics for Further Study

- Some critics have found Cunningham's portrayal of Virginia Woolf to be unnecessarily bleak. Read a biography of Woolf and write an essay arguing whether or not Cunningham presented an accurate portrait of the writer.

- Write a poem or a short story that focuses on a life-affirming moment.

- Compare and contrast characters, plot, setting, and theme in *The Hours* and *Mrs. Dalloway* in a PowerPoint demonstration.

- All three women in the novel experience feelings for other women. Write an essay that discusses the issue of lesbianism in the novel and its effect on the lives of the three women.

have in the place that for her represents life. When she recognizes the symptoms returning, she cannot face the loss of her ability to write, the confinement she would have to endure, or the pain that Leonard would suffer, and so she decides to end her life.

Richard's insanity is brought on by the ravages of AIDS. Like Woolf, his mental state prompts him to take his own life because of his fears that he will never be able to write again. Yet Richard is also plagued by the sense that he has failed as a writer. He insists that he won the poetry prize because he has AIDS, not for the quality of his work. His desire to end his life stems from this sense of failure and the knowledge that now that he is terminally ill and in pain he can never become what he considers to be a true artist.

Past and Present

The past has a great impact on each character's life. Virginia's past frightens her, as she remembers the debilitating mental illness she has experienced. These fears inspire her creativity and eventually prompt her to take her own life. Clarissa's vision of the past is life-affirming. The most important moment in her life was the instant when she shared a kiss with Richard. That memory gave her the belief that love is possible and so are transcendental moments. Laura is not as influenced by the past, but her actions have a strong impact on Richard, her son, who has filled his poetry with vivid images of her. Her abandonment of him becomes the subject of much of his poetry and imbues it with power and artistry.

Style

Literary Allusions

A literary allusion is a reference in one work to other works of literature. Cunningham's allusions to the characters and themes in Woolf's novel *Mrs. Dalloway* give his own work a frame of reference with meaningful parallels if his reader already knows the literature and historical characters to which he refers, in this case the novel *Mrs. Dalloway* and the historical Virginia and Leonard Woolf. Clarissa's day parallels that of Mrs. Dalloway as she buys flowers for the party she is giving that evening. The lives of the three women are connected to Woolf's novel: Woolf is writing it; all are planning a party (Virginia for Vanessa, Clarissa for Richard, and Laura for Dan); all experience a significant kiss; all experience transcendental moments that involve a creative expression of themselves and a celebration of life; and all are faced with death, either their own or that of someone they love.

Cunningham also incorporates allusion to Doris Lessing's short story, "To Room Nineteen." When Laura checks into the hotel room that offers her a welcome respite from her suffocating life at home, she ends up in number nineteen, the same number of the room the main character in Lessing's short story visits regularly for the same reason—to escape from the demands of domesticity that have robbed her of her identity. Cunningham's version contains an important difference, however. While Lessing's character kills herself in this room, Laura contemplates suicide there but eventually finds the strength to leave it, as well as her restrictive world, to establish a true sense of self elsewhere. Cunningham's version then focuses on the effect that leaving the room has on Laura's son.

Historical Context

Mrs. Dalloway

In the Woolf section of *The Hours*, Cunningham notes that Virginia considered London to be the center of life. The city, in fact, had for the historical Virginia Woolf a mystical significance, one which she recreated in her celebrated novel, *Mrs. Dalloway* (1925). Cunningham reworked characters and themes from *Mrs. Dalloway* in *The Hours*, which was actually the working title of the earlier historical Woolf's novel.

Woolf's novel is set in London a couple years after World War I. It chronicles a June day in the life of Clarissa Dalloway, a fifty-two-year-old, upper-class Londoner who is planning a party for that evening. As she prepares for the event, she looks back wistfully over her life, noting the moments of lost possibilities and revealing her doubts about her choices and the significance of her life. When she hears the news that a shell-shocked now discharged soldier, Septimus Warren-Smith, who is developed in an important subplot in the novel, has committed suicide, she is prompted to reevaluate her sense of self and ultimately to reassert an affirmation of life.

Women's Roles in the United States in the 1940s

Laura Brown's limited choices in this decade, based on her gender, push her to consider suicide. During World War II, women were encouraged to enter the workplace where they enjoyed a measure of independence and responsibility. After the war, they were required to give up their jobs to the returning male troops. Hundreds of thousands of women were laid off and expected to resume their place in the home.

Training began at an early age to ensure that girls would conform to the feminine ideal of the perfect wife and mother. Women who tried to gain self-fulfillment through a career were criticized and deemed dangerous to the stability of the American family. They were pressed to find fulfillment exclusively through their support of a successful husband. Television shows such as *Ozzie and Harriet* and *Father Knows Best* and popular magazines such as *Good Housekeeping*, along with television and newspaper advertisements, all encouraged the image of woman-as-housewife throughout the 1950s.

The small number of women who did work outside the home often suffered discrimination and exploitation as they were relegated to low-paying clerical, service, or assembly-line positions. Women would have to wait until the 1960s and 1970s to gain meaningful social and economic advancement.

Meryl Streep as Clarissa Vaughan in the 2002 film version of The Hours   Paramount/Miramax/The Kobal Collection/Duhamel, Francois

AIDS

In 1978, cases of a virus, later identified as HIV (human immunodeficiency virus), which causes AIDS (acquired immune deficiency syndrome) appeared in the United States, Sweden, Tanzania, and Haiti. The U.S. public became aware of AIDS in the early 1980s, and it became a widely discussed matter when film star Rock Hudson died from an AIDS-related illness in 1985. By the beginning of the 1990s, the disease had spread rapidly, generating public fear since no treatment had been discovered. Most of the early cases were identified in homosexual populations and among intravenous (IV) drug users, but by the 1990s, cases were noted throughout the U.S. populace. Racial and ethnic minorities were hardest hit, representing approximately three-fourths of all new AIDS cases.

In the 1980s and 1990s, the incidences of AIDS increased rapidly. By 1994, there were an estimated 500,000 Americans infected with AIDS and the same number had died from the disease. Throughout the 1990s and into the early 2000s, approximately 40,000 people were infected each year and approximately 20,000 people died from

complications associated with the disease. The epidemic was worse in developing countries such as Africa where people have little access to medications that can help control the disease progression.

Critical Overview

The Hours has received overwhelmingly enthusiastic praise from readers and scholars alike. Many reviewers, such as Darlene E. Erickson in her essay on the novel for *Christianity and Literature*, applaud the novel's style. She comments that the "text is . . . rich and intricate" and that it is "refreshing" to discover a work "that is both beautiful and evocative—and a writer who takes the time to get it right, to say what he means with both clarity and originality."

Trudy Bush, in her review of the novel for *Christian Century*, claims that the novel is "[b]eautifully written." In her review of the book for *Lambda Book Report*, Sarah Van Arsdale concludes that *The Hours* is "engaging" and contains "gorgeous prose," which makes it "a fine example of how it's ultimately the writing, the crafting of prose, that makes or breaks a book. Here, the writing itself propels the three plots forward, bringing the reader along effortlessly."

Critics also admire Cunningham's reworking of the themes of Woolf's *Mrs. Dalloway*. Erickson writes, "One reads [*The Hours*] with growing awe at a mind that comprehends what T. S. Eliot called 'Tradition and the Individual Talent,'" concluding, "With his gracious homage to Woolf, Cunningham has reaffirmed what Eliot recognized long ago—namely, that all great texts build on those written before them." Bush claims, "The book performs the difficult feat of both lyrically echoing Woolf and being original" and admits that she was "struck by its connection to Woolf's novel and by the way writers are inspired by, react to and move beyond each other's work."

Michael Coffey in his article for *Publishers Weekly* concludes that Cunningham "skillfully interweaves three novellas" in his text. He adds, "The subtle interactions of these narratives, and each one's mirroring of scenes right out of *Mrs. Dalloway*, adds a dimensionality to *The Hours* that makes it much more than the sum of its parts." He claims that readers will be "mesmerized by Cunningham's attention to quotidian detail" and notes that he "deftly brings [the characters] all together."

Van Arsdale continues the praise for Cunningham's revisioning of Woolf's novel insisting that he breathes "new life into characters and a story created some 70 years ago." While Van Arsdale argues that "occasionally the set up . . . becomes too apparent, grabbing the attention from the writing," this fault, she claims is "offset by the brutal honesty here." She insists that the "emotional accuracy is so dead-on" and lauds "Cunningham's love and respect, not only for Woolf . . . but also for writing, for language, and for the daily, dogged work of honoring one's creative process."

Criticism

Wendy Perkins

Perkins is a professor of American and English literature and film. In this essay, Perkins focuses on the transitory, life-affirming moments experienced by the characters in the novel.

Virginia Woolf's works contain moments of perfect happiness, moments when life stands still,

when her characters experience a transcendent feeling of peace. These moments are always transitory since Woolf believed that people can never sustain a state of happiness for more than a short period of time. The two most famous examples of these moments in her work take place at or in preparation for a party. In *To the Lighthouse*, this moment occurs when Mrs. Ramsey sits down with her family and friends to share a superb dinner she has just organized. At one point she stops to recognize that she has created a transcendent moment for her guests and for herself, since her attempts to control the events in the lives of her family and friends have imbued them with her integrating vision of harmony, captured and crystallized in this moment.

Clarissa Dalloway in *Mrs. Dalloway* also experiences transcendent moments during a day when she is preparing a similar party for family and friends. The moments in these two works are ironically associated both with life and with death: Michael Cunningham, in his prize-winning novel *The Hours*, which was inspired by *Mrs. Dalloway*, enters into a dialogue with Virginia Woolf on the nature of these moments as he intricately weaves together the stories of three women who are connected by their responsiveness to the possibilities of a heightened sense of life.

The moments in the two novels by Woolf generate an affirmation of life that is amplified and, in Clarissa's case, precipitated by death: Mrs. Ramsey dies not long after her dinner party, and Clarissa learns of the tragic death of a poet during her party. These deaths help fix in time the moments that celebrate life and so infuse them with poignancy. Cunningham joins this dialogue on the interaction between life and death when he begins his novel with Woolf's suicide and immediately after, focuses on the influence her work has on two women: Clarissa Vaughan, whose best friend has given her the nickname "Mrs. Dalloway," and who follows a similar path to that of her namesake during the course of her day; and Laura Brown, whose reading of *Mrs. Dalloway* helps ease her struggle to function in a world in which she does not belong.

All three women in *The Hours* experience these life-sustaining moments through the act of creation. Clarissa begins her day getting ready for Richard's party. As she selects flowers in a shop, she feels an overwhelming sense of love on the beautiful June day in New York that "feels entirely serious to her, as if everything in the world is part of a vast, inscrutable intention," and full of life.

> All three women in *The Hours* experience these life-sustaining moments through the act of creation."

She transfers this love to the preparation of her party, to the creation of a moment that will provide the same harmony among those she loves as she fills "the rooms of her apartment with food and flowers, with people of wit and influence," all gathered together to celebrate Richard. Her desire is "to give Richard the best party she can manage. She will try to create something temporal, even trivial, but perfect in its way, her tribute, her gift."

Clarissa encounters another moment that day with Sally after she brings Clarissa roses, when the two "are both simply and entirely happy. They are present, right now," and they love each other; "At this moment, it is enough." Clarissa notes the importance of the experience when she thinks, "You try to hold the moment, just here, in the kitchen with the flowers. You try to inhabit it, to love it, because it's yours."

Virginia recognizes the creative spirit in planning gatherings for others when she notes, "There is true art in it, this command of tea and dinner tables." She finds it more strongly, though, through her writing, which in turn, inspires her readers. Her excitement in anticipation of the writing process compares to the anticipation one feels preparing for a party "full of wit and beauty" and "a spark of profound celebration, of life itself." Her perfect moment appears as she begins to write *Mrs. Dalloway* when she realizes that "there are infinite possibilities" in her ability to recognize, through her writing, "the animating mysteries of the world."

Laura Brown responds to the celebration of life in *Mrs. Dalloway*, understanding that she can "keep herself by gaining entry into a parallel world." Her home, usually a confining space, "feels more densely inhabited, more actual, because a character named Mrs. Dalloway is on her way to buy flowers." When she reads that Mrs. Dalloway loved "life; London; this moment of June" as she prepares for the party she is giving, Laura is inspired to create a perfect birthday celebration for her husband and son, which will provide them all with a sense of harmony. "She imagines making, out of the humblest materials, a cake with all the balance and authority of an urn or a house."

As she and Richie are making Dan's cake, Laura experiences another transcendent moment. Watching her son measure out the flour, she is suddenly struck with an overwhelming sense of love for him, "so strong, so unambiguous, it resembles appetite," and recognizes that "for a moment she is precisely what she appears to be," a loving wife and mother. The moment quickly passes, however, when the finished cake fails to match her expectations.

That evening, after she has baked another cake and prepares the party, "it seems she has succeeded suddenly, at the last minute, the way a painter might brush a final line of color onto a painting and save it from incoherence." Yet again, Cunningham reminds us of the elusive nature of happiness when, after the candles are blown out, Laura sees the moment passing: "Here it is, she thinks; there it goes. The page is about to turn."

Death, or the thought of death, encroaches on these moments. As Virginia writes her novel, she is plagued by the fear that she will descend into madness, the thought of which eventually drives her to suicide. Laura, whose moments of domestic harmony cannot be sustained in a place where she has lost her sense of self, contemplates suicide. Clarissa, who has put so much effort into planning the perfect moment for Richard, sees her vision dissipate with Richard's suicide. Yet, Cunningham illustrates the ironic power of death to reinvigorate the living: Virginia's fears inspire her to finish her work, which would provide life for others; Laura's suicidal thoughts eventually compel her to leave her family in order to save herself; and Richard's death causes Clarissa to reexamine her own and to ultimately find a sense of peace.

At the end of the novel, Clarissa recognizes, "There's just this for consolation: an hour here or there when our lives seem, against all odds and expectations, to burst open and give us everything we've ever imagined." Noting the temporal nature of these moments or this hour, inevitably followed by the tragedies of life, she concludes, "Still we cherish the city, the morning; we hope, more than anything, for more." As she spreads out the food for Laura, Sally, her daughter, and herself, she asks forgiveness of Richard, insisting that this was "a party for the not-yet-dead; for the relatively undamaged" and that is, "in fact, great good fortune."

What Do I Read Next?

- Virginia Woolf's novel *Mrs. Dalloway*, published in 1925, addresses similar themes involving life, death, and creativity.
- Cunningham's *Specimen Days*, published in 2005, focuses on another literary artist, Walt Whitman, as it weaves together different stories in a similar three-part structure.

- Woolf's *To the Lighthouse* (1927) also explores the creative urge and the role of women in society.

- *Congenial Spirits: The Selected Letters of Virginia Woolf* (2001) reveals the personal vision of the celebrated writer.

In her article on the novel for *Christianity and Literature*, Darlene E. Erickson writes that in *The Hours*, Cunningham has reaffirmed that "the questions [Woolf] asked about life remain urgent, and that, in spite of pain, sorrow, and death, the simplest gestures . . . can be, for one shining moment, enough." In his depiction of those shining moments, Cunningham celebrates the endurance of the human spirit and its continuing affirmation of life.

Source: Wendy Perkins, Critical Essay on *The Hours*, in *Novels for Students*, Thomson Gale, 2006.

Darlene E. Erickson

In the following review-essay, Erickson explores how Cunningham illustrates "the role that the body plays in the world of the mind, personality, and human action" in The Hours.

George Orwell probably had it right in "Politics and the English Language": our civilization *is* decadent, and our language shares in the general collapse. He also reminds us, however, that "If one gets rid of these [bad] habits, one can think more clearly, and to think clearly is the first step towards political regeneration." How refreshing it is, then, to find a contemporary novel that is both beautiful and evocative—and a writer who takes the time to get it right, to say what he means with both clarity and originality.

Michael Cunningham's *The Hours,* which has won both the Pulitzer Prize and the Pen/Faulkner Award, is such a novel. One reads it with growing awe at a mind that comprehends what T.S. Eliot called "Tradition and the Individual Talent." The text is so rich and intricate that it is possible only

to acquaint readers with the novel and to try to bring into focus at least one dimension of the book: Cunningham's subtle yet profound attention to the bodies of his characters and the role the body plays in the world of the mind, the personality, the soul, and the very actions of his characters. To a degree *biology is destiny* in ways far more complex than might at first be understood. Cunningham's *The Hours* is a tribute to his literary predecessors while at the same time a carefully crafted literary venture in its own right.

On a bright morning in June, a woman in her early fifties steps out into the streets of New York City, just at the end of the twentieth century, for "There are still the flowers to buy." She runs into old acquaintances and calls up significant recollections from her earlier life. She catches sight of a celebrity, although she really isn't sure who it is. She purchases the flowers, goes home, and proceeds to prepare for a party. Sound familiar? Cunningham is revisiting some of the essentials of Virginia Woolf's famous novel *Mrs. Dalloway,* just as she revisited the strategies of James Joyce after examining a portion of *Ulysses* that Eliot shared with Hogarth Press (the famous publishing venture begun in the Woolfs' dining room). Hogarth Press did not publish *Ulysses;* all of the printers they contacted were wary of the Joyce anomaly. Nonetheless, Woolf was impressed by Joyce's collage, his mosaic of a day in the life of Leopold Bloom and Stephen Dedalus and their unforgettable menagerie. Woolf worried about what she considered the "indecency" of Joyce's text, but she admired his innovative use of what would come to be called "stream of consciousness," his use of

Julianne Moore as Laura Brown in the 2002 film version of The Hours Paramount/Miramax/The Kobal Collection/Coote, Clive

simultaneity, the concept of the *Doppelgänger,* and the exploration of sanity and insanity—whether she was always willing to admit that admiration or not. Cunningham, however, is unabashedly frank about *his* connection to Woolf, quoting her diary entry for 30 August 1923 in the book's frontispiece:

> I have no time to describe my plans. I should say a good deal about the Hours & my discovery; how I dig out beautiful caves behind my characters; I think that gives exactly what I want; humanity, humour, depth. The idea is that the caves shall connect & each comes to daylight at the present moment.

The Hours was, after all, Woolf's working title for what became *Mrs. Dalloway.* Cunningham's novel by that name begins with a prologue set in 1941 featuring a woman in a heavy coat with a stone in her pocket. She is on her way to commit suicide. The references to "Leonard" and "Vanessa" and Woolf's own suicide note signed "V" dispel any doubt about the woman's true identity.

There are also differences between Cunningham's novel and *Mrs. Dalloway.* Cunningham's story is set in New York in the late 1990s; Woolf's takes place in London in the 1920s. The unknown

celebrity is a movie star in a trailer in one text, perhaps a queen or a prime minister in a car in the other. The main character in both novels is called "Clarissa," but in the later work "Mrs. Dalloway" is merely an assigned nickname. Writing for the *New York Times Book Review,* Michael Wood also points out that the chief difference between the two is that no one in the first novel can have read the second, whereas almost everyone in the second seems to have read the first. And there are many eerie consequences of this impression. The second novel begins to repeat some of the darker events of the first. It also repeats some of the language and metaphors. The *Doppelgänger* effect is all-pervasive. One of the characters from *The Hours* actually dies quoting from Woolf's suicide note. Another prefers reading and living in the world of Woolf's novel to her own real life. Most characters from the original have a shadow—or sometimes several shadows—in the world of the new novel. The intertwining is everywhere, again suggesting Eliot's "mythical method" of borrowing from the literature and literary structures of the past. Literature is indeed a part of our history, woven into our reality, and contemporary writers with modernist training have come to expect that.

Cunningham's *The Hours* has three separate but resonating story lines. The final intersection is what one critic describes as "such a thing of beauty and surprise that it must not be revealed" (Levine). This reviewer could not agree more. There is first the very plausible character of Mrs. Woolf herself, who is writing *Mrs. Dalloway* while living outside London in Richmond with her husband Leonard. Then there are the contemporary Clarissa, dubbed "Mrs. Dalloway" by her AIDS-stricken poet and friend, Richard, and last of all Mrs. Laura Brown, who is pregnant for the second time and caring for her small son on her husband's birthday. Laura lives in Los Angeles in 1949 and is mesmerized by Woolf's novel.

Woolf's story of her day in Richmond is told in seven episodes interspersed with eight episodes of Clarissa's New York day and seven episodes about Laura Brown in Los Angeles. After the brief prologue about Mrs. Woolf's suicide, the stories alternate in an intricate sequence of waves and rhythms, with each new episode echoing the preceding one and projecting the next while never forgetting the many connections to *Mrs. Dalloway*. If this all sounds painfully contrived, it simply is not. It is logical, eminently readable, satisfying, and oddly comforting.

Cunningham fulfills the reader's longing for the beautiful, for aesthetic perfection, by modeling after his mentor Woolf—and after her master, Joyce, and down through the ages unto his master, Homer. Cunningham writes with exquisite care, saying in a few pristine, well chosen words what others might say in forty. This clarity is sometimes breathtaking. These examples hang in the mind: a scattering of New York City pigeons have "feet the color of pencil erasers"; a pug "stares over its fawn-colored shoulder . . . with an expression of moist, wheezing bafflement"; a backyard pool appears as "liquid nets of sun wavering in the blue depths." When Clarissa gets into an old New York elevator and pushes the button for the fifth floor, "The elevator door sighs, and rattles shut. Nothing happens. Of course. It works only intermittently . . . Clarissa presses the button marked with a chipped white 'O' and after a nervous hesitation the door rattles open again." As Clarissa enters Richard's dark, overheated apartment, smelling of sage and juniper incense to cover the smells of illness, the narrator discloses that the apartment has, more than anything, an underwater aspect: "Clarissa walks through it as she would

> " In the small act of buying and arranging flowers, Cunningham has helped us grasp the importance of goodness, beauty, love, and art."

negotiate the hold of a sunken ship. It would not be entirely surprising if a small school of silver fish darted by in the half-light." Evocative of Woolf and *Mrs. Dalloway,* Cunningham writes that "the hallway of her building feels like an entrance to the realm of the dead. The urn sits in its niche and the brown-gazed floor tiles silently return, in muddied form, the elderly ocher light of the sconces." There is no denying Cunningham's devotion to precise language, which almost becomes poetry.

To return to my main point, however, about the role that the body plays in the world of the mind, personality, and human action, let me direct my examples to Cunningham at work describing his characters' bodies in ways that Woolf once described as "the upholstery of the soul," for we all have "upholstery" that serves to objectify our inner selves. We like to think of ourselves as "outside our bodies," looking on, but we are wrong: our bodies dictate not only our vision of ourselves but also the ways others view us—and ultimately the way we really are. So things like gender, age, body chemicals, beauty, physical infirmities, pain, illness, height, and sexual orientation cannot be relegated to the insubstantial.

With the subtle Cunningham-by-way-of-Woolf technique, the reader is allowed to look at some of the characters' bodies, both from the way they "see" themselves and the way others see them, to judge the impact of the body/soul relationship. "As Clarissa steps down from the vestibule," writes Cunningham, "her shoe makes gritty contact with the red-brown, mica-studded stone of the first stair. She is fifty-two, just fifty-two, and in almost unnaturally good health. She feels every bit as good as she did that day in Wellfleet, at the age of eighteen, stepping out through the glass doors into a day very much like this one." However, just as she straightens her shoulders while standing at the corner of Eighth Street and Fifth Avenue, waiting for the light:

> There she is, thinks Willie Bass, who passes her some mornings just about here. The old beauty, the old

hippie, hair still long and defiantly gray, out on her morning rounds in jeans and a man's cotton shirt, some sort of ethnic slippers (India? Central America?) on her feet. She still has a certain sexiness; a certain bohemian, good-witch sort of charm; and yet this morning she makes a tragic sight, standing so straight in her big shirt and exotic shoes, resisting the pull of gravity, a female mammoth already up to its knees in the tar, taking a rest between efforts, standing bulky and proud, almost nonchalant, pretending to contemplate the tender grasses waiting on the bank when it is beginning to know for certain that it will remain trapped and alone, after dark. When the jackals come out. She must have been spectacular twenty-five years ago; men must have died happy in her arms.

Willie's judgment is real, and even Clarissa understands that at some level. She fights her age and her body, but even she is clear about the fact that the "upholstery" has affected the reality. Later, "She stands looking at the books and at her reflection superimposed on the glass (she still looks all right, handsome now instead of pretty—when will the crepe and gauntness, the shriveled lips, of her old woman's face begin to emerge?)."

Cunningham then imagines Mrs. Woolf in the bathroom: "She does not look directly into the oval mirror that hangs above the basin. She is aware of her reflected movements in the glass, but does not permit herself to look. The mirror is dangerous; it sometimes shows her the dark manifestation of air that matches her body, takes her form but stands behind, watching her, with porcine eyes and wet, hushed breathing. She washes her face and does not look, certainly not this morning, not when the work is waiting for her."

Shortly thereafter her husband, Leonard, sees her and perceives what is at the same time the same yet different person:

> She stands tall, haggard, marvelous in her housecoat, the coffee steaming in her hand. He is still, at times, astonished by her. She may be the most intelligent woman in England, he thinks. Her books may be read for centuries. He believes this more ardently than does anyone else. And she is his wife. She is Virginia Stephen, pale and tall, startling as a Rembrandt or a Velasquez, appearing twenty years ago at her brother's rooms in Cambridge in a white dress, and she is Virginia Woolf, standing before him right now. She has aged dramatically, just this year, as if a layer of air has leaked out from under her skin. She's grown craggy and worn. She's begun to look as if she's carved from very porous, gray-white marble. She is still regal, still exquisitely formed, still possessed of her formidable lunar radiance, but she is suddenly no longer beautiful.

With glimpses of her own morning experience and of Clarissa's reflection in the glass, Mrs. Woolf

finds "her own face becoming more and more strongly reflected in the window glass as the streetlamps—pale lemon against ink-blue sky—light up all over Richmond." Virginia is plagued by what we loosely call mental illness. Her body is devastated by unruly chemicals that both feed and destroy her creativity. She cannot be productive when she is ill, yet her illness parallels her productivity. The paradox both alarms and intrigues her. She is mesmerized by her own illness and at the same time terrified by it. This dimension of her body is destroying her:

> She can feel the headache creeping up the back of her neck. She stiffens. No, it's the memory of the headache, it's her fear of the headache, both of them so vivid as to be at last briefly indistinguishable from an onset of the headache itself. She stands erect, waiting. It's all right. It's all right.

And later,

> She can feel the nearness of the old devil (what else to call it?) and she knows she will be utterly alone if and when the devil chooses to appear again. The devil is a headache; the devil is a voice inside a wall; the devil is a fin breaking through dark waves. . . . The devil sucks all the beauty from the world, all the hope, and what remains when the devil has finished is a realm of the living dead—joyless, suffocating.

The "devil" is part of her, however, perhaps even the part that makes her the writer she is. In 1993 Kay Redfield Jamison published a widely read text, *Touched with Fire: Manic Depressive Illness and the Artistic Temperament,* in which she pursues the thesis that there is a close association between bipolar disease and the artistic temperament. Jamison demonstrates with great care that the pattern of "habitual melancholy" and psychotic melancholia paired against periods of remarkable productivity and euphoria tends to parallel the creative mind. Her work on William Blake, Samuel Taylor Coleridge, Lord Byron, Percy Bysshe Shelley, John Keats, Robert Lowell, John Berryman, Theodore Roethke, Randall Jarrell, Ann Sexton, and, of course, Virginia Woolf makes fascinating reading. There is a good deal to support the biographical and scientific argument for a compelling association between the two temperaments, the artistic and the manic-depressive, and their relationship to the rhythms and cycles of the natural world. Cunningham uses that research along with the plethora of information about Woolf herself to create a memorable character, one who is capable of extraordinary leaps of creativity followed by months of listlessness and depression.

Another character is Richard, the brilliant poet and novelist who is dying of AIDS. Clarissa remembers her first vision of Richard when he was nineteen—"a firm-featured, hard-eyed, not-quite-beautiful dark-haired boy with an impossibly long and graceful, very pale neck." She remembers that "he was once avid and tall, sinewy, bright and pale as milk. He once strode through New York in an old military coat, talking excitedly, with the dark tangle of his hair tied impatiently away from his face by a length of blue ribbon he'd found." Now Richard sits alone in his squalid apartment:

> The shades are drawn and all six or seven lamps are lit, though their feeble output barely adds up to the illuminating power of one ordinary desk lamp. Richard, in the far corner, in his absurd flannel robe (an adult-size version of a child's robe, ink-blue, covered with rockets, and helmeted astronauts), is gaunt and majestic and as foolish as a drowned queen seated on her throne.

Clarissa goes to him and kisses the curve of his forehead, for she has always loved him. It is for him that her party will be given. She finds, however, that his body has betrayed him:

> Up close like this, she can smell his various humors. His pores exude not only his familiar sweat (which as always smelled good to her, starchy and fermented; sharp in the way of wine) but the smell of his medicines, a powdery, sweetish smell. He smells too of unfresh flannel. . . . and slightly, horribly (it is his only repellent smell), of the chair in which he spends his days. . . . The chair smells fetid and deeply damp, unclean; it smells of irreversible rot.

Richard too has his demons, his "visitors," his furies. "I think of them as coalescences of black fire," Cunningham writes; "I mean they're dark and bright at the same time. There was one that looked a bit like a black, electrified jellyfish. They were singing, just now, in foreign languages. I believe it may have been Greek. Archaic Greek." Clarissa wonders how this can happen to such a man. She thinks of his monumental ego and a kind of savantism, for Richard is an

> . . . opposite kind of egotist, driven by grandiosity rather than greed, and if he insists on a version of you that is funnier, stranger, more eccentric and profound than you suspect yourself to be—capable of doing more good and more harm in the world than you've ever imagined—it is impossible not to believe, at least in his presence and for a while after you've left him, that he alone sees through to your essence, weighs your true qualities.

Richard needs to live in a world peopled by commanding figures, a world of epic individuals, but his AIDS-ridden body is betraying him. When Clarissa takes one of his hands in hers, she is "surprised, even now, at how frail it is—how palpably it resembles a bundle of twigs." As he lifts his

ravaged head, "Clarissa turns her face sideways and receives Richard's kiss on her cheek. It is not a good idea to kiss him on the lips—a common cold would be a disaster for him." The novel's final view of Richard's body as described by Clarissa in the novel's climax is certainly most moving, but again one must leave something to the reader. Suffice to say that Richard's body, invaded by disease, is projected onto his mind, and the result is tragic in the epic manner that Richard might have claimed.

There is so much more about this rich novel that I have been unable to reveal. I can only invite you to read it for yourself, to discover the joy of intricacy, of great beauty, of verbal echoes, of painstaking choices. I have not told you that Clarissa is a lesbian with a loyal partner of eighteen years. I have not mentioned that she has a daughter who is being seduced by an older woman whom Clarissa cannot abide. I have not followed the story of Laura and her struggle with motherhood, insanity, jealousy, and responsibility. I have not spoken of Mrs. Woolf's wonderful day with her sister, Vanessa, and Vanessa's children. I have only suggested that each of Cunningham's characters has at least one shadow in *Mrs. Dalloway* and myriad connections with one another. I have not helped you understand the essence of "the hours": that one looks back at life "sometimes more than thirty years later to realize that it was happiness; that the entire experience lay in a kiss and a walk, the anticipation of dinner and a book. . . . That was the moment, right then. There has been no other." I have not helped you understand that there is holiness, sacredness, in beautiful acts well done. I have not helped you understand that no one is forever young or forever kind and generous. I have scarcely helped you to see how special each one of us really is. "For there she was" (Woolf 296). Is it necessary to have read *Mrs. Dalloway* to understand *The Hours?* Probably not, but that would be a wonderful idea.

To return to my premise, Cunningham has captured a world in a single day. In different years and different cities, in the lives of three women, he has found essential comparisons and profound resolution. The reader will find new meaning in Alfred Tennyson's words from "Ulysses": "I am a part of all that I have met." Finally, in the small act of buying and arranging flowers, Cunningham has helped us grasp the importance of goodness, beauty, love, and art. With his gracious homage to Woolf, Cunningham has reaffirmed what Eliot recognized long ago—namely, that all great texts build on those written before them. He has certainly reaffirmed that Woolf is of lasting significance, that the questions she asked about life remain urgent, and that, in spite

Nicole Kidman as Virginia Woolf in the 2002 film version of The Hours   Paramount/Miramax/The Kobal Collection/Coote, Clive

of pain, sorrow, and death, the simplest gestures—walking out the door on a lovely morning, setting a vase of roses on a table—can be, for one shining moment, enough. We are, after all, a part of one another, with only beautiful hours to share.

Source: Darlene E. Erickson, " 'The Upholstery of the Soul': Michael Cunningham's *The Hours*," in *Christianity and Literature*, Vol. 50, No. 4, Summer 2001, pp. 715–22.

Jonathan Dee

In the following essay excerpt, Dee provides an overview of The Hours *and an analysis of Cunningham's incorporation of Woolf and* Mrs. Dalloway *into the novel.*

Michael Cunningham's *The Hours,* published last fall to admiring reviews and winner of both the Pulitzer Prize and the PEN/Faulkner Award for the year's best work of fiction, bravely offers as its animating force that most unfashionable of love objects, a book. Not just any book, either, but *Mrs. Dalloway,* Virginia Woolf's slim, exacting treatment of one June day in the life of a group of Londoners, some of them related by friendship, some by birth, and some only by a kind of magical transfer of authorial sympathies as the characters pass one another on the street. Completed in 1925 (part of a six-year explosion of Woolf's genius that also saw the publication of *To the Lighthouse, A Room of One's Own,* and *The Waves*), *Mrs. Dalloway* is one of the peaks of Woolf's achievement, which is another way of saying that it is one of the signal achievements in all of Modernist literature; still, it takes an unusually ardent devotion to imagine, as Cunningham does, that Woolf's novel might enter the world as an instrument of fate, influencing lives for three-quarters of a century—even the lives of those who have never read it.

The Hours plaits together the stories of three women, each of them observed over the course of one June day in three radically different times and places: 1923 London, 1949 Los Angeles, and 1998 Greenwich Village. The present-day narrative is the dominant one, and it takes the form of a somewhat overdetermined contemporary replay of the very events of Woolf's novel. Cunningham's central figure is Clarissa Vaughan (same first name as Woolf's Mrs. Dalloway), whom we first see in the throes of preparation for an important party at her home that evening (same as Clarissa Dalloway). The coincidences pile up rapidly from there: Clarissa Vaughan's ignorance of them (in spite of the fact that she has even been nicknamed "Mrs. Dalloway" by a friend) is what saves these chapters from reading less like an act of homage than like a particularly highbrow episode of *The Twilight Zone.* Much more original and affecting is the novel's second, less emulative narrative strand, which concerns the tremulous existence of Laura Brown, a smart young housewife in suburban Los Angeles in the years of the post–World War II boom. Married to a doting war hero, mother of a three-year-old boy and with another child on the way, Laura is on a quiet course toward some sort of nervous breakdown, possibly even suicide; on the June day in question—her husband's birthday—she checks into a hotel room by herself and lies on the bed for two and a half hours reading *Mrs. Dalloway.* Never far from her mind is what she knows of the ultimate end of the woman who wrote the book she is holding; "How, Laura wonders, could someone who was able to write a sentence like that—who was able to feel everything contained in a sentence like that—come to kill herself? What in the world is wrong with people?"

The third character in *The Hours* is Virginia Woolf herself. She, too, is seen on an imaginary June day, eighteen years before her suicide by drowning (a scene that forms the book's prologue), a day on which she is struggling with the opening pages of a new novel—the novel that will become *Mrs. Dalloway* but whose working title is "The Hours." These chapters are narrated in the same psychologically intimate third-person style as are those chapters centered around the women who are entirely Cunningham's creation. And although there is no mistaking the fact that this narrative—indeed, the whole novel—is conceived by Cunningham as a sincere tribute to a predecessor whom he reveres, still it is remarkable to watch him demonstrate that there is no corner of Woolf's extraordinary consciousness that, for reasons of modesty, he might shy away from attempting to recreate. For the most part, the narrative sticks fondly to the quotidian arrangements of Woolf's day (washing her face in the bathroom, planning a lunch menu); but we are also made privy to the less penetrable mysteries of her creative process:

> It seems good enough; parts seem very good indeed. She has lavish hopes, of course—she wants this to

> **We are in Woolf's head when she engages the madness with which her difficult life was fired."**

be her best book. . . . But can a single day in the life of an ordinary women be made into enough for a novel? Virginia taps at her lips with her thumb.

We are in Woolf's head when she engages the madness with which her difficult life was fired: "she can feel the nearness of the old devil (what else to call it?), and she knows she will be utterly alone if and when the devil chooses to appear again." And, of course, in the prologue mentioned above, we are offered access to that consciousness even as it extinguishes itself, on the afternoon Woolf walks into the River Ouse with stones in her pockets.

The appropriation of genuine historical figures—people who actually lived—as characters in fiction is an act of imaginative boldness that, through simple attrition, readers of contemporary fiction have come to take entirely for granted. The past several years have seen a torrent of such novels, by Russell Banks (on John Brown), Pat Barker (Wilfred Owen and Siegfried Sassoon), Jay Parini (Walter Benjamin), Thomas Pynchon (Mason and Dixon), Susan Sontag (Lord Nelson), John Updike (James Buchanan), and a legion of lesser-known writers . . .

But whether or not it's true (and I think it's untrue) that the relationship between the real and the invented in the art of prose fiction hasn't changed significantly since Shakespeare's time, there's no debating that the practice of conscripting flesh-and-blood people into novels has become a veritable epidemic in the last twenty-five years or so. It is more than mere postmodern fashion, this appetite for the real among those whose traditional stock-in-trade is invention. It says something important—and, to those of us who care about making the case for the novel's continued vitality, something ominous—about the way in which fiction writers imagine their relation to the world.

What makes a novel a novel—what distinguishes it from other forms? More, surely than the question of invention: "invention" is a continuum, after all, and I know no fiction writer who would be so bold as to claim that no aspect of his or her characters had its origin in something observed in the real world. More, too, than its dependence upon language, or its use of story as a kind of tonality to be either relied upon or rebelled against, or its deployment of moving, speaking, acting human figures as the elements of art (all of which it has in common with movies and plays and television shows). If there is one thing the novel offers that no other form can approach, it is the opportunity to know those human figures *completely,* through the fiction writer's full uncompromised access to his or her characters' interior lives, as well as to the ways in which they define themselves through the observable phenomena of speech and action. In a novel, the dicrepancy, large or small, between what a person does and who that person is can be if not exactly erased then at least accounted for so fully as to provide a picture of human nature that we feel is sufficient in its totality. The satisfaction of knowing others—or even ourselves—in that kind of totality is a satisfaction with which our real lives most definitely do not provide us. And it is precisely this imaginary bridging of the gulf between the knowable and the unknowable about human motives that makes of fiction an alternative life: a life that transcends this one, and that brings us into closer contact with our natures than real life—that is to say, the life outside books—is capable of doing.

This idea, of course, is not new. "In daily life," E. M. Forster wrote in *Aspects of the Novel,* "we never understand each other, neither complete clairvoyance nor complete confessional exists. We know each other approximately, by external signs, and these serve well enough as a basis for society and even for intimacy. But people in a novel can be understood completely by the reader, if the novelist wishes; their inner as well as their outer life can be exposed. And this is why they often seem more definite than characters in history, or even our own friends; we have been told all about them that can be told; even if they are imperfect or unreal they do not contain any secrets, whereas our friends do and must, mutual secrecy being one of the condition of life upon this globe."

A more historically minded accounting can be found in Milan Kundera's 1986 manifesto *The Art of the Novel.* Centuries before the invention of the novel, Kundera says, in the work of the great storytellers like Boccaccio and Dante, "we can make out this conviction: It is through action that man steps forth from the repetitive universe of the everyday where each person resembles every other person; it is through action that he distinguishes himself from others and becomes an individual." Four hundred years later, in the work of proto-novelists such as

Cervantes and Diderot, Kundera finds a more complex portrait of existence starting to emerge: the unlucky hero of Diderot's *Jacques le Fataliste,* for instance, "though he was starting an amorous adventure, and instead he was setting forth toward his infirmity. He could never recognize himself in his action. Between the act and himself, a chasm opens. Man hopes to reveal his own image through his act, but that image bears no resemblance to him. The paradoxical nature of action is one of the novel's great discoveries. But if the self is not to be grasped through action, then where and how are we to grasp it?" Out of that last sentence's primary existential problem, the novel as we know it is continually reborn.

Source: Jonathan Dee, "The Reanimators: On the Art of Literary Graverobbing," in *Harper's Magazine*, June 1999, pp. 76–84.

Sources

Bush, Trudy, Review of *The Hours*, in *Christian Century*, September 22–29, 1999, p. 886.

Coffey, Michael, "Michael Cunningham: New Family Outings," in *Publishers Weekly*, November 2, 1998, pp. 53–55.

Cunningham, Michael, *The Hours*, Farrar, Straus, and Giroux, 2000.

Erickson, Darlene E., "'The Upholstery of the Soul': Michael Cunningham's *The Hours*," in *Christianity and Literature*, Vol. 50, No. 4, Summer 2001, pp. 715–22.

Van Arsdale, Sarah, "In Woolf's Clothing," in *Lamda Book Report*, January 1999, pp. 14–15.

Further Reading

Bell, Quentin, *Virginia Woolf: A Biography*, Harvest Books, 1974.
   Bell, Woolf's nephew, presents a comprehensive study of the author's life.

Bloom, Harold, ed., *Virginia Woolf's "Mrs. Dalloway": Bloom's Modern Critical Interpretations*, Chelsea House, 1988.
   This collection of essays examines the novel's major themes, style, and structure.

Iannone, Carol, "Woolf, Women, and *The Hours*," in *Commentary*, Vol. 115, No. 4, April 2003, pp. 50–53.
   Iannone critiques the film version of the novel and its feminist focus.

Schiff, James, "Rewriting Woolf's *Mrs. Dalloway*: Homage, Sexual Identity, and the Single-Day Novel by Cunningham, Lippincott, and Lanchester," in *Critique*, Vol. 45, No. 4, Summer 2004, pp. 363–82.
   Schiff examines three different contemporary novels that enter into a dialogue with Woolf's novel.

I Never Promised You a Rose Garden

Joanne Greenberg
1964

The autobiographical novel *I Never Promised You a Rose Garden*, published in 1964 by Joanne Greenberg using the pseudonym Hannah Green, recounts the experiences of a young girl who suffers from a mental illness. The novel draws from the author's own experiences in this story of Deborah Blau who struggles through childhood, fearful and sometimes even terrified by her circumstances. In an attempt to come to grips with a world she has trouble understanding, the protagonist creates an interior world of her own, one that includes various characters and an archaic language. As the young protagonist becomes more deeply entrapped in the world that she has created, the external reality begins to fade away.

The story opens as Deborah's parents are driving her to the mental hospital, where they hope their daughter will be quickly cured. Deborah's illness goes deeper than the family realizes, however, and Deborah ends up spending three years there. Readers observe the protagonist as she spends those three years fighting for her sanity. During that time, Deborah learns to trust her psychiatrist, through whom she re-establishes a healthy connection to the outer world. The title of this novel comes from the belief of the Deborah's psychiatrist that the journey from mental illness to health would not be an easy road to follow.

An immediate national bestseller, the novel was an unusual book for its time, revealing, as R. V. Cassill for the *New York Times* stated, "the internal warfare in a young psychotic." The book draws

Patient in a psychiatric hospital © Peter Turnley/Corbis

readers into the strangeness of Deborah's world and keeps them on edge as they root for the protagonist's success.

Author Biography

Joanne Greenberg was born in Brooklyn, New York, in 1932. Her early childhood was marred by the terror a child might well feel when talk of world war looms around her; but World War II turned out to cause some of the lesser fears that she faced. In her attempt to find peace in her personal world, young Joanne created an interior world of her own, one she developed so craftily it became both her sanctuary and her prison. By the age of thirty-two, Greenberg had fought her way out of that self-imposed, interior world and had the courage to write and have published an account of her battle. Her 1964 fictionalized autobiography about schizophrenia became a national bestseller, a book entitled *I Never Promised You a Rose Garden*, which she published under the pseudonym Hannah Green.

By the time Greenberg published *Rose Garden*, she had graduated from American University, with majors in anthropology and English. She had

also married Albert Greenberg, who encouraged her to write this book.

Greenberg went on to write a dozen novels, several collections of short stories, and many essays on a variety of topics. She was particularly interested in the subject of people who must cope with physical and mental deficits. For instance, while her husband was working with hearing-impaired clients, she became interested in the world of deaf people and the challenges they face. She learned sign language in order to communicate with deaf people. She also helped to set up a mental health clinic for the hearing-impaired. Later, Greenberg wrote a novel called *In This Sign* (1970), a story about the struggles a deaf couple face in raising a child who can hear.

One of Greenberg's subsequent novels, *Where the Road Goes* (1998), however, emphasizes another point of interest for the author. This novel tells the story of a grandmother who decides to reestablish her political activism of years gone by and to undertake a walk across the nation to raise awareness for environmental issues.

Besides her writing career, Greenberg taught at the Colorado School of Mines, an engineering school.

She started there as an anthropology professor, wanting to teach her students, as they began their mining careers and traveled all over the world, that they would have to understand not only the basic elements of the earth but also the characteristics of people of different cultures. Later in her career, Greenberg became a creative writing teacher. She also traveled around the nation, helping writers hone their skills at conferences and workshops. She even traveled as far as Japan, teaching U.S. soldiers there how to improve their writing.

Greenberg is the mother of two sons, and as of 2005 she lives in Colorado with her husband.

Media Adaptations

- *I Never Promised You a Rose Garden* was adapted as a film by Gavin Lambert and Lewis John Carlino in 1977 and starred Kathleen Quinlan as Deborah and Bibi Andersson as Dr. Fried. It was nominated for both an Oscar and a Golden Globe Award.

Plot Summary

Chapters 1–5

Greenberg's *I Never Promised You a Rose Garden* opens with the protagonist, Deborah Blau in the backseat as her parents, Esther and Jacob Blau, drive along country roads. Although the setting at first appears idyllic, with Esther even suggesting that the family is on a pleasure trip, there is mention of mounting tensions. The parents are concerned, for example, about leaving their daughter on her own when they stop at a diner for coffee. They are also concerned at night, when they leave their daughter in her separate motel room. Their anxiety rises again as they discuss the real reason for the trip, which is to take their daughter to a mental hospital.

When the focus of the story turns to Deborah, readers are told about the Kingdom of Yr, the imaginary world into which Deborah retreats. In this place, Deborah feels no tension. It is a neutral place, where her parents and her future do not faze her.

The next day, the family arrives at the mental hospital, a slightly rundown Victorian complex set in woods. The parents are disturbed by the bars on the windows and the disheveled patients who peer out of them. They rethink their reasons for bringing their daughter there. Both parents are torn between doing what might be right for their daughter and their guilt for bringing her to this place and for anything they might have done during Deborah's childhood to have caused the problems she now faces.

At the beginning of chapter two, the focus turns back to Deborah, describing her new environment, how she is constantly watched by nurses and attendants, and how she is watched in her in-side world by the guardians and rulers of the Kingdom of Yr. Meanwhile, Esther and Jacob decide to lie to their younger daughter, Suzy, about Deborah's sudden absence from the family. They also choose not to tell other members of the family.

Introduced next is Dr. Fried, a prominent psychologist who is world renowned for her effectiveness in communicating with mentally ill people. Fried reads Deborah's records and discovers that Deborah is very intelligent and suffers from schizophrenia.

In chapter three, readers observe the daily routine of hospital life. Deborah has met Carla, a fellow patient. Together they try to find out how long they will have to stay in the hospital. No one is able to answer their questions.

In her first session with Dr. Fried, Deborah discovers that she has opened up her true feelings, maybe for the first time in her life. Dr. Fried is honest with Deborah, supplying her with direct answers instead of attempting to soften things. She tells Deborah, for example, that yes, she does believe that Deborah belongs in the mental hospital because she is definitely sick. Dr. Fried also tells Deborah that she hopes one day to help her to see the world as a more beautiful place than the one Deborah sees at the present.

Dr. Fried announces in chapter four that she has received a letter from Deborah's parents and that they want to make a visit. Deborah tells the doctor she wants only her mother to visit, not her father. Deborah senses that the hospital is going to be good for her. She is concerned that her love for her father and his for her will weaken her if she sees him.

Esther Blau makes the visit to the hospital. Esther wants to know if her daughter will ever get better. Dr. Fried tells her that it will take a lot of patience. Then the doctor asks Esther for a family history. Esther describes her relationship with her own father and his relationship with Deborah, whom he adored but also placed a lot of pressure on because of her good looks and intelligence. Pop, as Esther calls her grandfather, had a lot of money and often supported Esther and Jacob when Jacob could not meet the family expenses. The support Pop gave came at a price. Pop was also domineering.

Esther then describes some of the symptoms that she noticed that made her realize that Deborah may not be well. Deborah hardly slept, for one thing. She also developed a tumor and had to have a very painful operation that seemed to affect her personality. At age ten, a school psychologist told Esther that the results of a test indicated that Deborah might be disturbed. At the end of the conversation, Dr. Fried suggests that Esther be completely honest with Deborah from now on.

Chapters 6–14

Chapter six begins with Dr. Fried asking Deborah to give an account of her life. Deborah replies that her mother has already done that. Dr. Fried assures her that Esther gave only one side of the story. In the process of telling her version, Deborah begins to give Dr. Fried a glimpse into her private world of Yr.

Later, Carla reappears and tells Deborah that the reason she went crazy was that her mother shot her and her brother, then shot herself. Her mother and brother died from their wounds. Carla could not adjust to their deaths, especially when her father remarried. Then the girls discuss various aspects of the hospital. They are in Ward B, which allows certain privileges, such as walking around the grounds of the hospital unescorted. There is another section, Ward D, where patients are under constant supervision. Patients there were considered in the worst state of their illnesses.

In her next session with Dr. Fried, Deborah relates how she was often taunted with anti-Semitic slurs by children her age. Dr. Fried, who is German, can relate to Deborah's anger. Deborah is impressed by Dr. Fried's empathy. However, when Deborah returns to her ward, her inner world rises against her for trusting Dr. Fried. In response to all the shouts of anger inside her head, Deborah uses a piece of tin to rip the skin on her arms. When her self-inflicted injury is discovered, Deborah is moved to Ward D.

Lee, a fellow patient who is introduced at the beginning of chapter seven, refers to herself as a psychotic and says that Deborah is a psychotic too. Deborah also meets the patient in the bed next to her, a woman who thinks she is the first wife of Edward VIII, king of England. Later, when Dr. Fried asks to see Deborah's wounds, she does not act shocked or condescending. Once again, Deborah is impressed with the doctor and tells her more about Yr. Because she has opened up once again, Deborah falls into a psychotic state once she is returned to her ward. She is wrapped into a cold, rubber sheet and strapped in for several hours until she is once again able to communicate.

It is next revealed that the patients know intuitively where the attendants' psychological weaknesses are and how they attack them. The attendant called Mr. Hobbs, for instance, always seems to be the target of these attacks, and patients believe that Mr. Hobbs is afraid of them because he himself is on the verge of going crazy.

Deborah is with Dr. Fried again at the beginning of chapter nine. She tells the doctor about some school experiences. She says that she could never understand why children, whom Deborah thought were friends, would come to her and suggest that Deborah had done mean things to them. Deborah claims that she has no recollection of ever doing anything wrong to them.

Dr. Fried notices Deborah's anger growing as she relates these stories. Dr. Fried believes this is a healthy sign. It is better for Deborah to be angry than to be apathetic. She anticipates, however, that the internal battle that Deborah will have to fight will be a major one.

Carla appears on Ward D. Deborah is surprised to see her there, wondering what Carla has done to have forced her to leave Ward B. Carla tells Deborah that she came up to Ward D so she could yell and scream and get all the anger out.

Later, Deborah overhears a conversation about Doris Rivera, a patient who was once in Ward D but was able to make her way out and is living outside the hospital. The thought of Doris gives everyone hope, although it also causes them to fear facing the outside world. When the fear becomes too great, all the patients start reacting strangely. Some get into physical fights, while others retreat so far into their own private worlds, they become unaware of the world around them. Deborah wakes up to find herself in the cold sheets again. Carla, too, is wrapped in the rubber sheets in the bed next to Deborah.

The story jumps back to Esther, who has become worried about her daughter because she has been transferred to Ward D. Esther asks for and receives an appointment with Dr. Fried, who tries to assure her that Deborah is in a natural process of her illness. But Dr. Fried cannot promise that Deborah will come out of this phase any better than she was. Esther leaves without being able to see her daughter.

Later in a session with Dr. Fried, Deborah tells the doctor that she has psychologically poisoned her sister Suzy. She talks about her jealousy and in the process exposes to the doctor how much Deborah dislikes herself. She also relates how she tried to kill her sister.

Chapter eleven begins with the news that Hobbs has committed suicide. It was not unexpected as far as the patients were concerned. They had often picked on Hobbs, sensing his refusal to accept his own insanity. At this point McPherson, another attendant, appears. Unlike Hobbs, McPherson is able to kid with the patients as well as laugh at himself. The patients tease but do not taunt him. They like and respect him. The patients and McPherson do not like Hobbs's replacement, Ellis, a conscientious objector and in the ward by default. He chose this work over going to prison. He is an angry person and is often mean to the patients. The patients continue to ridicule Ellis until McPherson approaches Deborah and asks her to lay off Ellis. McPherson, without outright telling her, suggests that Ellis is a mentally ill person himself. Ellis is not as lucky as Deborah, McPherson tells her. Ellis cannot afford the treatment that someone like Deborah can.

In the next session with Dr. Fried, the doctor encourages Deborah to go back into her history and relive some of the memories in an attempt to correct the errors that Deborah has stored. When Deborah returns to her ward, in chapter thirteen, she must pay the consequences of having opened up to Dr. Fried. She becomes lost in Yr and must be wrapped, once again, in cold sheets. As Deborah is returning to consciousness, she notices that one of the patients, Helene, is in a cold pack too. Ellis enters the room to take Helene's pulse. When she fights him, Ellis slaps her in the face several times. The next day when Deborah reports the abuse to a ward nurse, little is done about it. At Deborah's next meeting with Dr. Fried, Deborah repeats the details of the incident. Dr. Fried promises to bring this situation to the attention of the authorities.

In chapter fourteen, Esther and Jacob both visit Dr. Fried, who denies them a visit with their daughter. Deborah's sense of reality is shaky, Dr. Fried tells them, and Deborah's appearance would upset them. Deborah has lost all desire to groom herself. Jacob, however, insists that it is his right to see his daughter; so Dr. Fried relents.

On the way home, Esther and Jacob talk about their visit. They were both shocked by Deborah's appearance, not because of Deborah's unkempt hair but for the vacancy they saw in her eyes, as if she no longer had a presence in her body.

In their next meeting, Dr. Fried, whom Deborah now refers to by the nickname of Furii, talks to Deborah and coaxes out memories of her father. In the discussion the possibility is hinted that Deborah felt her father's sexual attraction for her. Upon exposing this feeling, Deborah cries, for the first time, in front of Dr. Fried. It is a release. Dr. Fried tells her that they are on the right path. She will help Deborah to reach the path of health. Once there, Deborah can decide if she wants to enter the world of health or remain in Yr.

At the end of this chapter, the patient Miss Coral appears. She is beloved among the patients. Despite her small 90-pound body, Miss Coral has been known to pick up and throw beds. She is an intelligent, well educated woman, who eventually tutors Deborah in Greek and Latin.

Chapters 15–23

During the next chapters, Deborah's education with Miss Coral continues. Carla's health is strengthened, and Carla returns to Ward B. As Carla leaves, Deborah realizes the depth of their friendship. Carla suggests that Deborah try to get permission to go down to Ward B, at least to visit her.

Esther, in the meantime, finally tells Suzy the truth about her sister. Suzy takes the news a lot easier than her parents had anticipated. She even mentions that she misses Deborah and wishes she would come home.

In her session with Dr. Fried, Deborah explains the Censor and talks about how it was developed to protect her from telling Yr's secrets. But then, the Censor became stronger, to the point that everything that Deborah said was controlled by the Censor. Dr. Fried tells Deborah that she is not a victim but rather a fighter. She can fight for her mental health.

Because Deborah has exposed yet another secret, she knows that she will be punished mentally. When she returns to the ward, she asks for the cold sheet. She suspects she will become wild as she fights her interior battles. Later, when she comes to, there are other patients in their own cold packs. They realize they have been in them longer than usual, maybe five or six hours instead of the normal three. Deborah's circulation is cut off, and she is in physical pain. Someone finally comes and lets her out.

Doris Rivera enters the scene in chapter seventeen. Doris was almost a mythical person to the patients. She was one of the few who made it out into the world. The patients used the thought of Doris as a symbol of hope. But she frightened them because the patients were fearful of getting well. But now, here she is, returned and defeated. Then a new fear breaks inside of the patients. If Doris could not make it, can any one?

During her next appointment, Deborah tells Dr. Fried about her experience in camp when she was a child. She had met Eugenia and had sensed that they had secrets in common, though they never came right out and talked about them. One day, Deborah found Eugenia standing naked in the bathhouse. Eugenia asked Deborah to beat her with a belt. She insisted that she needed the beating. Deborah could not do it and never had anything to do with Eugenia again.

Then Deborah finds that Carla has been returned to Ward D. When she first sees Carla, Deborah thinks Carla looks broken. Later, Carla tells Deborah that she has not given up. She just tried too much too fast. Then they both learn that Doris has made it again and has left the hospital.

Deborah learns that Dr. Fried is leaving to attend a symposium. She'll be gone for three months. Deborah decides that she will work harder, wanting to be healed before Dr. Fried leaves. She asks for and is granted permission to move to Ward B. At another session, Dr. Fried announces that Dr. Royson will take her place while she is gone. After Dr. Fried leaves, Deborah meets with Dr. Royson but does not like him. He invades Deborah's world of the Yr without asking permission, and Deborah withdraws in fright. She also feels abandoned by Dr. Fried.

In her fury and confusion, Deborah feels a volcano rising within her. She anticipates a great fire. In order to offset this internal fire, she thinks she needs to set an exterior one. She pilfers matches and old cigarette butts and burns herself repeatedly on the arms. Infection develops, but this does not stop her. She continues to inflict pain on her body.

Dr. Fried finally returns and is surprised that Deborah has slipped back into her sickness. She

helps Deborah understand what is happening inside of her. Deborah confides that she is worried about the volcano inside of her. Deborah hates herself for her situation. Dr. Fried tells her to try to comprehend that the degree of hate Deborah feels could be transformed into a like measure of love.

Finally, in Deborah's world, the volcano explodes. Deborah feels as if there has been a great collision. She tries to explain it to Dr. Fried, but her communication skills have all but left her. She finally is able to tell Dr. Fried that the power she feels inside of her is a mixture of fear and hatred, and she is worried about not being able to control them. As days pass, Deborah sinks deeper into her silent world. She hears others talking about her who are concerned that she is getting sicker. When Dr. Fried asks what Deborah thinks about that, Deborah states that she is tired of thinking. Dr. Fried is relentless until Deborah is finally able to say that she believes she is not sicker at all.

Slowly, Deborah regains her strength. She begins to distinguish colors and forms that appear new to her. She tells Dr. Fried that she thinks she will live. On Ward B, Deborah continues to get stronger. Carla is with her, and the two friends walk outside together, go to craft classes together, and talk to one another more than they ever have before.

Dr. Fried opens one of Deborah's deep secrets: Deborah's belief that she tried to kill her sister when Suzy was a baby. Dr. Fried proves to Deborah that she was too small to have picked the baby up and to have attempted to throw her out a window. She makes Deborah realize that this is an imagined memory that expresses Deborah's jealousy about the new baby's arrival. Deborah celebrates the lifting of the guilt she has felt all those years.

Chapters 24–29

Deborah makes great progress toward health. It does not happen quickly, but it is steady. She explores the community around her, going to a church and joining the choir. She often walks past the high school, yearning for her degree but unable to face going back to get it.

She returns home for short visits. During one, her sister, although happy to see her, is tired of all the attention that Deborah receives from their parents. Deborah learns that Suzy has passed up an opportunity to go out with her friends. She feels bad about having caused this imposition. Suzy lies about this not affecting her, which only makes matters worse. Deborah thinks about Yr and realizes that she is at the crossroads where she must choose one world or the other.

When Deborah returns to the hospital after this visit, a new patient, Carmen, is there. Deborah is attracted to Carmen and her honesty. Around this same time, Deborah and Carla decide to run outside the perimeter of the hospital grounds, which is against the rules. They are not gone long but the trip exhilarates them. Dr. Halle learns of their misconduct but decides not to punish them. Carmen's father comes a few days later and insists that his daughter is not sick and takes her home. Deborah reads in the newspaper a few days later that Carmen has committed suicide.

Deborah applies to live off the grounds and is granted permission. She rents a room from Mrs. King, who is new to the town and not afraid of the fact that Deborah is a mental patient. Deborah next wants to get a job, but she knows she must first have a high school diploma. She learns about the possibility of getting her G.E.D. and is finally enrolled in a tutoring program through which she can take specialized classes and pass exams without having to actually attend high school. She studies hard and eventually earns her degree with a high enough score that makes her eligible for college. But she still suffers. She fears she will never really fit into the world. This fear causes her to have another psychotic episode. She runs back to the hospital and suffers through it. When she comes out of it, she sees the looks on the faces of the patients. They do not like seeing that she has had to come back. The story ends, however, with Deborah asking for more books. She is still willing to fight.

Characters

Miss Coral Allen

Miss Coral is known among the patients and staff for her exceptional strength. She is an elderly woman who is small and rather frail. But when she has a fit of anger, she is capable of tossing beds. She knows a lot, and Deborah is attracted to her for that. Miss Coral teaches Deborah what she can remember of Greek and Latin.

Anterrabae

Anterrabae is the most powerful god who lives in Deborah's imaginary world, the Kingdom of Yr. He often directs her actions, thoughts, and communications.

Deborah Blau

Deborah Blau is the protagonist of this story, a fictional stand-in for the author herself. She is sixteen years old at the opening of the novel and is on her way to a mental hospital after having attempted suicide. She is never sure, as the novel progresses, how long she will have to stay in the hospital, as she watches patients come and go. But she has a feeling she belongs in the hospital. There, she can be honest about her feelings without fearing she will hurt anyone else's.

She is fortunate that a world famous psychiatrist works at this hospital, one who takes a great interest in her case. Dr. Fried respects Deborah's intelligence as well as her sickness, which she hopes to help Deborah to dismantle. Because of Dr. Fried's honesty, Deborah begins to allow the doctor into her interior world, one Deborah has created to protect herself from the outside world, which she fears.

With her keen intelligence, Deborah is able to explain what is going on inside her head as well as what is happening all around her. She understands the patients who are suffering through their own mental illnesses as well as the doctors, nurses, interns, and attendants who work in the wards. Because she is so intelligent she craves to learn, an activity that motivates her to get well.

Throughout the story, Deborah courageously attempts to open her interior world to the light and to examine it and all the reasons that she created it. She also fights to re-enter the world that at one time frightened her so much it sent her into her imaginary kingdom. As she disassembles her mysterious interior world, she recreates the other more rational exterior one, sometimes finding herself falling into the abyss that separates the two.

Esther Blau

Esther Blau, Deborah's mother, appears to be more in tune with Deborah's need for help than Deborah's father. However, Esther feels guilty, as she blames herself for Deborah's illness. Esther actively pursues answers to her questions, something that Jacob Blau, Deborah's father, does not do. Esther often writes to Dr. Fried, asking for explanations of Deborah's condition, but she is not much more honest with Deborah than Jacob is. Esther tries to dismiss Deborah's fears with easy fixes. She also attempts to solve Deborah's problems rather than teaching Deborah how to solve them herself. Because of Esther's attitude toward her daughter, Deborah seldom, if ever, confides in her mother.

Esther is deceitful when telling the rest of the family about Deborah's condition. She even lies to her husband and hides the doctor's reports, which concern Deborah's progress or lack of progress. Dr. Fried, at one point, tells Esther that if there is one thing she can do to help Deborah it is to be honest with her.

Esther's strength and her belief in her daughter give her the confidence to insist that Deborah stay in the hospital, despite common prejudices about mental hospitals and the early outwards signs that Deborah's mental health was declining.

While Deborah is still in the hospital, Esther examines her own life as she looks for causes of Deborah's illness. Esther realizes that throughout most of her marriage, she has placed Jacob second in importance to her own father. She understands that doing so may have caused Jacob to feel insecure. By the end of the novel, however, Esther seems little changed. When Deborah comes home for a visit, Esther still is less than honest with her daughter.

Jacob Blau

Jacob Blau, Deborah's father, loves his daughter but feels guilty that his love may have somehow crippled Deborah, making her vulnerable to mental illness. He is sad that she does not want to see him during her stay in the hospital, and he does not understand that Deborah does not want to see him because of her weakness for his love. If Jacob was part of Deborah's problem, it was not his love that caused it but rather his inability to face the truth. He could not look at his daughter's problems and accept them for what they were. He refused to hear her cries for help and had trouble accepting the fact that she really needed to stay in the hospital.

One other topic touched on only slightly deals with the possibility that Jacob was sexually attracted to his daughter. This possibility is obliquely examined in a therapy session Deborah has with Dr. Fried.

Suzy Blau

Suzy Blau, Deborah's younger sister, appears to be affected by her sister's illness. Even when Deborah is in the hospital, Deborah's presence looms over Suzy's life. When Deborah comes home to visit, Suzy explodes in a fit of anger because she must cater to her sister, whom, at this point, she hardly knows. She feels cheated of a life of her own and of her parents' attention.

Another aspect of Suzy's story is told through Deborah. When Suzy was born, Deborah was angered by her sister's sudden presence and imagined that she attempted to kill Suzy by throwing her out a bedroom window. This memory turns out to be only a figment of Deborah's imagination, which Deborah's mind turned into an actual event. Dr. Fried is finally able to get to the bottom of it, realizing that Deborah would have been too small to have lifted Suzy out of her crib, to have opened the window, and to have attempted to throw the baby out.

Suzy is jealous of the attention that her sister gets, but she still cares for her sister. Suzy mentions, upon being told that Deborah is having mental problems, that she misses her big sister.

Carmen

Deborah meets Carmen on Ward B. She likes Carmen and learns that Carmen is there because she has had to lie to her father all her life in order to please him. The pressure finally built up too much, and she was placed in the hospital for help. Carmen's father shows up one day and takes her out of the hospital before she is cured. Deborah later learns that Carmen has committed suicide.

The Censor

The Censor is one of the imaginary gods in Deborah's interior world. The Censor controls everything that Deborah says so she does not reveal the secrets of the Kingdom of Yr to the outside world.

The Collect

The Collect consists of various voices that emanate from Deborah's Kingdom of Yr. From time to time, the Collect criticize Deborah, often unmercifully. The Collect represents Deborah's own unflattering opinions of herself.

Ellis

After Hobbs's suicide, Ellis comes to work on Ward D. He is a conscientious objector and has taken this job as a way out of serving a prison sentence. He is very obvious about his dislike and discomfort around the patients. Deborah sees him beat one of the patients.

Eugenia

Eugenia is the young girl with whom Deborah makes friends at the summer camp she attended when she was a child. Deborah senses that she and Eugenia have something in common, probably the existence of secret worlds. One day, Deborah finds Eugenia standing naked in the bathroom. She asks Deborah to beat her with a belt. Deborah refuses and then never talks to Eugenia again.

Dr. Clara Fried

The character of Dr. Fried is based on a real psychiatrist from the 1950s, who actually helped the author of this story to find her way back to mental health. Dr. Fried is highly intuitive and quickly understands what Deborah needs in order to fight her way back to reality. Dr. Fried is honest with Deborah, never flinching at whatever Deborah tells her or what Deborah does. Because of this honest treatment, Deborah begins to trust Dr. Fried more and more and opens up her interior world to the doctor, who in turn helps Deborah to understand why she created that world in the first place. Eventually, Deborah gives Dr. Fried the nickname of Furii, a reference to fire, because once when Dr. Fried touched her, Deborah felt heat. She also used the nickname regarding Dr. Fried's keen insights.

Dr. Fried is attracted to Deborah because of her intelligence and her youth. She sees great potential in this young patient and decides to forego other teaching engagements and conferences in order to study Deborah. Dr. Fried becomes Deborah's ticket back into the world of health.

Furii

See Dr. Clara Fried

Dr. Halle

Dr. Halle becomes the administrator of Ward D. Deborah likes and trusts him because he does not belittle her in any way. She turns to him when she needs things, unafraid of approaching him. Dr. Halle learns to turn his head the other way when Deborah and Carla sneak off the premises.

Mr. Hobbs

Mr. Hobbs, an attendant on Ward D, is often rough and sometimes mean with the patients; they in turn taunt him and get into physical fights with him. Hobbs has a weakness, and the patients are clearly aware of it. That is why they pick on him. They see that he too is suffering from a mental illness. They suspect that he is mean to them to irritate them and make them appear crazier than he feels. In the end, Hobbs commits suicide. The patients' reaction is one of jealousy, noting that through his death, Hobbs has released himself from his problems.

Idat

Idat is a beautiful goddess who lives in the Kingdom of Yr. She is mentioned only briefly.

Mrs. King

It is into Mrs. King's house that Deborah moves as she receives her last treatments as an outpatient. Mrs. King trusts Deborah, despite her background, helping to build Deborah's self confidence in the outside world.

Lactamaeon

Lactamaeon is the most sarcastic of the imaginary gods in the Kingdom of Yr. He is the second most powerful voice and often taunts and ridicules Deborah.

McPherson

McPherson is the nicest of the attendants. He is not afraid of the patients on Ward D; therefore, the patients do not bother him. To a large extent, given the circumstances, he treats the patients as if he and they were equals. McPherson comes to Deborah and asks for her assistance in getting the other patients to stop picking on Hobbs.

Pop

Pop, Deborah's maternal grandfather, is a recent immigrant and a self-made man who creates a comfortable amount of wealth, which he shares with his family but not without strings attached. He rules his family rigidly. Deborah's mother, realizing how dependent she and her family are on her father's generosity, submits to his every wish.

Pop applies pressure on Deborah, the first of his grandchildren. She is born with blonde hair, a sure sign to Pop that she is his Americanized dream. Deborah must exhibit beauty and intelligence to show the world that Pop and his family are self-made aristocrats in their adopted country. He treats Deborah, on one hand, as a doll, making sure that she is dressed well. But, on the other hand, he constantly reminds her that she needs to excel. When Deborah shows signs of mental illness, Esther is most afraid to admit this to Pop, as if Esther has presented him with an imperfect granddaughter.

Doris Rivera

Doris Rivera became a model for the patients in the hospital because she was one of the few patients who made it to the outside world. Although she inspires hope, she also inspires fear. Deborah puts a lot of faith in the story of Doris but is shattered when Doris suddenly returns.

Dr. Royson

Dr. Royson replaces Dr. Fried when Dr. Fried must travel to attend a conference. He is nothing like Dr. Fried and his manner and treatment turn Deborah deeper into her sickness. He takes a more objective and distant stance and moves toward Deborah's illness too clinically. In response, Deborah injures herself. She feels abandoned by Dr. Fried and slips back into her world of mental illness, from which Dr. Royson is unable to release her.

Carla Stoneham

Carla Stoneham is one of the few patients with whom Deborah makes friends. They meet on the Ward B, but soon both of them end up in Ward D, for the mentally disturbed. Carla tells Deborah that she wanted to come to Ward D so she could scream her anger away. Carla also tells Deborah that she went crazy after her mother shot her. Her mother also shot Carla's brother and herself. Both the mother and brother died. The friendship with Carla is a sign that Deborah is getting better.

Themes

Fear

Fear is apparent in almost every scene of Greenberg's *I Never Promised You a Rose Garden*. There are less intense examples, such as with the protagonist's sister, Suzy, who fears the loss of love of her parents, and more intense instances, such as the massive and consuming fear that the protagonist must face in her battle against her illness.

Suzy's fears may cause her to feel at times somewhat insecure or maybe jealous of her sister, but these emotions affect her interpretation of her life and possibly create quirks in Suzy's personality. Deborah's fears, by contrast, are debilitating. They threaten her existence, leading her to hide in the shadows of her subconscious mind, which contorts reality to the point that Deborah has trouble functioning. Deborah's fears also drive her to drastic measures, to the point of causing herself physical harm. Her fears terrorize her and have the power to suggest to her that the best way to avoid them is for her to take her own life.

Fear also affects Deborah's parents. They fear they have made the wrong decision in sending Deborah to the mental hospital. They also worry that they have caused their daughter's illness. On a more superficial level, they fear what people

will say when the news of Deborah's condition is made public.

The story illustrates both the destruction that fear can cause as well as the strength that is required to diminish and control it. The author may intend to encourage others to face their own fears. Clearly, Greenberg wanted to present a picture of mental illness from the inside looking out, so readers might better understand that behind the faces of people who suffer from mental illness are minds struggling to free themselves from irrational and debilitating fear.

Mental Illness

Mental illness is often perplexing to mentally well-adjusted people. The science of psychiatry in the 1950s was young in some ways, and patients suffering from mental illnesses were often shut away from the view of healthy people. In focusing on the process of mental illness as well as the journey from illness to mental health, Greenberg sheds light on an otherwise dark subject. She provides a picture of people who exist sometimes behind their illnesses and at other times are so enmeshed by the symptoms of their illness that they lose contact with the real world. But even in some of the most severe cases of mental illness, Greenberg shows the intelligence, empathy, and intuitive understanding that mentally ill patients can have. This picture provides readers with a chance to view mentally ill patients differently than in the wild, harried images that Jacob, Deborah's father, for example, has of them. Through Deborah's story, Greenberg implies that mental illness is a coping strategy for some people, a way of managing their demons. She also makes clear that many patients engage actively in their own recovery and have a fighting chance to live normal lives.

Deceit

An important theme is delivered through Dr. Fried's treatment of Deborah: honesty builds trust in relationships and is essential in treating mental illness. Much of Deborah's confusion lies in the fact that she is intelligent enough to understand what is going on around her, but she often becomes disturbed when what she knows does not match what she is told. Doctors tell her, for instance, that her operation will not hurt, but Deborah experiences a lot of pain. Deborah's mother assures her that if Deborah is nice to her peers, the children will be nice to her. However, Deborah is rejected and taunted by her peers. Deborah's parents insist to Deborah and to other members of the

Topics For Further Study

- The protagonist Deborah Blau, in *I Never Promised You a Rose Garden*, receives her G.E.D. certificate in lieu of a high school diploma. Call your local community college and find out where people go and what they must do to attain a G.E.D. Then compile some research to find out how many people receive a G.E.D. in a given year. Interview one of the people who teach G.E.D. classes or one of the counselors at the community college in order to create a profile of people who earn a G.E.D. Present your findings to your class.

- Research the life of Frieda Fromm-Reichmann, the doctor who treated Joanne Greenberg and who is portrayed as Dr. Fried in Greenberg's novel. What was so special about her therapy? How did it differ from the more traditional therapies of her time?

- Study the passages in *I Never Promised You a Rose Garden* in which Deborah describes the various gods (or voices) that populate her Kingdom of Yr. From her descriptions, create images, in your choice of artistic medium, of what you think Anterrabae, the Censor, the Collect, or Lactamaeon may have looked like to Deborah.

- Deborah's relationship to her sister Suzy is less than ideal. As a child, Deborah desperately wanted Suzy to disappear. But despite Suzy's feelings of jealousy for all the attention that Deborah receives, she wishes that Deborah would come back home. Write a letter, pretending you are Suzy, in which you express your frustrations that are a result of Deborah's being sick. But let the undertone of the letter be that of a younger sister trying to get to know an older sister. So even though you express your disappointments and anger, also try to understand what Deborah is going through.

---

family that everything is good when Deborah does not feel good at all. Quite the contrary, she feels miserable, lost, and bewildered.

Being honest, Greenberg implies, has a healing effect; it creates congruity. Most of the adults around Deborah are deceitful, in one way or the other. Deborah is not able to find a way out of her confusion until she meets Dr. Fried. The honesty and trust in Deborah's relationship with Dr. Fried allows Deborah to expose her real feelings. Through Dr. Fried's complete honesty Deborah learns to trust the doctor and find her way to health.

Style

Chronicled Narration

I Never Promised You a Rose Garden is based on the author's real experiences. She chose to tell her story as if it were unfolding before the readers' eyes in a chronological order. In the beginning of the story, Deborah is being driven to the mental hospital. The following chapters chronicle her experiences as she adjusts to her new life. Her sessions with Dr. Fried follow a definite pattern, showing how Deborah at first is afraid to open to the doctor and later how she relies on Dr. Fried for her very life. By the end of the story, readers understand that the journey they have witnessed belongs to someone who has and continues to battle with mental illness.

This chronicled narration offers readers a predictable sequence through which to follow the details of the story. This might have seemed necessary because the protagonist weaves in and out of the outer reality around her. There are, for instance, times when the narrator becomes so fearful of her outer reality that she closes down her physical senses and thus loses touch with the outer world. She believes that she can protect herself by withdrawing. When the protagonist does this, she partially takes her readers along with her into the Kingdom of Yr, so they can understand her difficulties in communicating with the outer world. When her psychotic episodes are over, the narration returns to the chronicling of outer events.

Fictionalized Autobiography

The story of Greenberg's teenage struggle with mental illness could have been written as an autobiography. However, the privacy of the author and others involved in the story might have been at risk. Choosing the novel as the form for telling this story distanced the author from its protagonist and its subject matter. Greenberg published the novel under a pseudonym, Hannah Green, in the hope of keeping her own identity and that of her family's a secret. She assumed that if her authorship of the novel were known perhaps people in her own community would react negatively to her or to her children. Apparently for some years after its publication, her children only knew that she had published a book under another name. In time though the nature of that book and her authorship became known to them, and Greenberg had to admit that during her teen years she was mentally ill. Additionally, the novel as a form allows a writer more choices in creating a story in order to make a statement through art about life as it is experienced. The novelist writes fiction, which is to say holds a mirror up to real life, in order to convey certain truths about a subject, free to abandon or change the life experience in order to make her point. In this way, paradoxically, sometimes fiction can tell more of the truth of a subject than autobiography can.

Internal Conflict

The conflict in this novel is mostly internal. Although physical conflicts between patients and staff are presented as well as conflict between Esther and Jacob Blau, most conflict occurs within the protagonist herself. Her internal conflict drives the story. Also, Deborah sheds light on the internal conflicts of those around her, including not only the other patients but the hospital staff and her own family. In other words, despite the fact that much of this novel pertains to the inner reality of the protagonist, readers are not confined to Deborah's mind or her thoughts. The internal conflict affects the outer world, as Deborah must learn to deal with the people around her. Thus, internal conflict is shown to cause external conflict, too.

Historical Context

Schizophrenia

The German doctor Emil Kraepelin (1856–26) classified mental disorders in 1887. What would later be called schizophrenia, Dr. Kraepelin lumped together with several other mental disorders under the term "dementia praecox," which can be translated as "early dementia." In 1911, Swiss psychiatrist Eugen Bleuler (1857–1939) further distinguished several forms of schizophrenia and asserted that some were treatable. The word *schizophrenia* comes from a Greek word and means a split or shattered mind.

In 1959, Kurt Schneider listed the symptoms of schizophrenia, which include psychotic episodes during which a patient has trouble differentiating between real and imagined experiences; delusions, which cause false judgments; and disorganized speech and behaviors. These symptoms, according to Schneider, would often cause social dysfunction, withdrawal, and a loss of motivation, concentration, and emotional reaction.

Debate persisted on the cause of schizophrenia, whether it had a biological or behavioral origin. But in the early 2000s common psychiatric understanding of the illness tends to suggest a combination of the two factors, with an emphasis on genetic and biochemical causes. In the early 2000s, schizophrenia is treated with a combination of antipsychotic chemicals and therapy. Hospitalization, in the more serious cases, may still be required. Despite these efforts, there remains, according to a 2003 survey taken by the Center for Disease Control, a high suicide rate (10 percent) among people suffering with the illness. There is also concern that heavy use of drugs, especially hallucinogenic drugs, can trigger schizophrenia in people who are predisposed to the illness.

Mental Illness and Therapy in the United States

Mental illness is described as a disorder in the brain that causes a dysfunction in the way a person thinks, communicates, and experiences emotion. Although mental illness has been observed and recorded as far back as ancient times, there is still a lot of controversy about its causes and possible cures.

The first U.S. Surgeon General's report on mental illness (1997) found that mental illnesses account for more disabilities in the United States than other physical illnesses such as cancer and heart disease.

In 1904, in the United States, two people out of a thousand were in mental hospitals. Fifty years later, around the time of Greenberg's stay, that number had doubled to four in every thousand.

Compare
&
Contrast

- **Early Twentieth Century:** Clifford Beers spearheads the founding of the National Committee of Mental Hygiene, which eventually evolves into the National Mental Health Association.

  Mid-Twentieth Century: President Harry Truman signs the National Mental Health Act for research into mental illness. As a result, the National Institute of Mental Health is established.

  Today: President George W. Bush establishes the New Freedom Commission to conduct a comprehensive mental health service delivery system, which recommends mental health screening for all school children.

- **Early Twentieth Century:** Hospitals for the mentally ill become overcrowded. Added to the list of patients are soldiers returning home from World War I and, later, people suffering from the psychological effects of the Great Depression.

  Mid-Twentieth Century: In the United States alone, there are 560,000 people in mental hospitals.

This number will be the peak of mental hospital populations.

Today: Admittance to mental hospitals is low, but according to a 2005 statement from the National Mental Health Association, one-third of all homeless people suffer from a mental illness. Many of them are schizophrenics. Another report, this one from the Department of Justice (2001), claims that almost 300,000 people in prison are mentally ill.

- **Early Twentieth Century:** Electrical shock that induces convulsions, and lobotomy (a surgical procedure in which nerves connecting the frontal lobes to the thalamus are severed) are common practices in treating schizophrenia and other severe mental illnesses.

  Mid-Twentieth Century: The drugs lithium and thorazine are used in the treatment of schizophrenia and manic depression.

  Today: New lines of anti-psychotic and psychotropic drugs are used to control schizophrenia. Over 70 percent of patients using these drugs experience improvement.

Before the 1950s, although Sigmund Freud's work was becoming more accepted and his principles of psychoanalysis more practiced, most mentally ill people in the United States were treated with shock therapy or otherwise just kept locked in hospitals, away from the general public.

Beginning around the 1950s, however, psychiatry changed and became more influential. Around this time, behaviorists, such as B. F. Skinner (1904–90), for example, sought to prove that doctors could help their patients to improve their mental health by teaching them different, and more effective, behaviors.

Another breakthrough occurred in the 1950s when pharmaceuticals were introduced. The drug chlorpromazine was approved in 1954 and given to patients who were housed in state mental institutions. Chlorpromazine calmed mentally ill patients and helped them to live normal lives.

Chestnut Lodge Hospital

Chestnut Lodge Hospital, located in Rockville, Maryland, is the site of Greenberg's story. It was built in 1886 as a hotel but was later turned into a psychiatric facility. The hospital consisted of twenty buildings situated on more than twenty acres of land, which were dotted with 125 chestnut trees.

The hospital was run by the Bullard family, three generations of medical doctors, and was considered a pioneering facility in the treatment of long-term, mentally ill patients. In 1994, when Dexter Bullard retired, Chestnut Lodge was sold to a nonprofit organization. However, due to financial problems, the hospital was closed in 2001.

Frieda Fromm-Reichmann

Frieda Fromm-Reichmann was the actual psychiatrist upon whom Greenberg's Dr. Fried was based. Fromm-Reichmann's work, along with that of Harry Stack Sullivan, in the interpersonal school of psychiatry, was world renowned. Rather than using shock treatment, which was the more popular therapy of the time, Fromm-Reichmann believed that her patients could regain their mental health by talking through their experiences. She stated that she wanted to treat her patients as she herself would have wanted to be treated if she had suffered from mental disease.

Greenberg remained in therapy with Fromm-Reichmann from 1948 to 1955 and was supposedly going to collaborate with Fromm-Reichman in the writing of her story. Unfortunately, the psychiatrist died in 1957, with Greenberg's portion of the book written but not the part to be written by Fromm-Reichmann. Greenberg, then, apparently, decided to complete the book as a fictional autobiography.

Critical Overview

I Never Promised You a Rose Garden became a national bestseller when Greenberg published it in 1964 under the pseudonym Hannah Green. This narrative unlocked the doors to what was previously a mysterious interior—the inside of a psychiatric hospital and the inside of the mind of someone suffering from schizophrenia. The sixties were a decade of revolutionary ideas, and Greenberg's book fit right into the scene by throwing light on the then-obscure topic of mental illness and by providing a new perspective of psychological therapies.

R. V. Cassill, writing for the *New York Times*, praised Greenberg for showing "courage that is sometimes breathtaking in its concessions." Cassill continued: "the author makes a faultless series of discriminations between the justifications for living in an evil and complex reality and the justifications for retreating into the security of madness." Cassill's only complaint about this novel was that "it falls a little short of being fictionally convincing." Cassill explained that although the story was categorized as fiction, it does not quite fit the mold: "It is as if some wholly admirable, and yet specialized, nonfictional discipline has been dressed in the garments and mask of fiction." However, Cassill concluded that "[t]he reader is certainly not cheated by this imposition."

A critic for *The Times Literary Supplement* in the article entitled "Calling Mad Mad," also praised Greenberg's efforts: "Miss Green [Greenberg's pseudonym] is excellent when conveying relief and delight at the freedom from the propriety, freedom from lies, and most of all the freedom to call mad mad, crazy crazy. She is excellent too on the inventiveness of the insane." However, this critic also pointed out Greenberg's weaknesses, writing that some of her characters were not convincing, some of the plot predictable, and Dr. Fried, this critic found, is both "sometimes profound" and yet "sentimental." This writer stated that Greenberg "is rather better at describing the terror and imaginativeness of the schizophrenic than she is at the return to normality: her normality is perilously close to dullness."

Writing for the *Library Journal*, Miriam Ylvisaker found Greenberg's novel to be on the level of Ken Kesey's *One Flew over the Cuckoo's Nest* (1964). Ylvisaker then wrote that in *I Never Promised You a Rose Garden* "the hospital world and Deborah's fantasy world are strikingly portrayed, as is the girl's violent struggle between sickness and health, a struggle given added poignancy by youth, wit, and courage."

Criticism

Joyce Hart

Hart, a published writer on literary themes, examines the differences between the methods of Dr. Fried and Dr. Royson and their respective effects on the novel's protagonist, Deborah Blau.

Greenberg wrote *I Never Promised You a Rose Garden* as a fictionalized account of her three-year period in a mental hospital. She decided to fictionalize this story possibly to protect herself, her family, and the other patients with whom she shared the experience. This decision does not mean that the incidents that Greenberg relates are any less true, but it does raise curiosity concerning how Greenberg may have brought those elements together in order to tell her story.

For instance, what is Greenberg attempting to say when she juxtaposes the skills, intelligence, and therapy styles of Dr. Fried and Dr. Royson? These doctors are obviously opposed to one another in many ways. Deborah responds to Dr. Fried by trying hard to move toward health. But with Royson, Deborah fails miserably. Is it due to Deborah's feeling of abandonment because Dr. Fried has decided to travel away from the hospital? Or is Greenberg showing her readers how the difference in the doctors' approaches could make significant differences in a patient? Is Greenberg judging the two doctors, in other words, or is she merely describing them as they appeared to her in real life? Although the answers to these questions may never be fully understood, it might be interesting to lay out the ways Greenberg portrays these two people and to note the differences that Greenberg attributes to them.

Deborah meets Dr. Fried first, and her initial reactions to the doctor are mixed. The first is one of bemusement. She is surprised to find out that the "gray-haired, plump little woman" who answers the door at Deborah's first appointment is not a housekeeper but rather the doctor herself. But the bemusement fades shortly afterward and turns to anger, which is spawned by fear.

During her first session with Dr. Fried, Deborah is put off by one of the doctor's questions. Put off may not be the correct way of describing her response. Deborah's reaction is more like a recoiling, as if she has been confronted by a poisonous snake. This happens when Dr. Fried asks: "Is there anything you want to tell me?" This question seems to be direct and simple, but it throws Deborah off guard, so she becomes defensive. "All right," Deborah says, "you'll ask me questions and I'll answer them—you'll clear up my 'symptoms' and send me home . . . *and what will I have then?*" Upon seeing Deborah's reaction, Dr. Fried tries to assure the young patient. "If you did not really want to give them [the symptoms] up," Fried says to her, "you wouldn't tell me." Dr. Fried then adds, "You will not have to give up anything until you are ready, and then there will be something to take its place." Fried recognizes that her question has frightened Deborah, so Dr. Fried tries to calm the girl's fears, helping her to regain her equilibrium by reminding her that she is no victim in this doctor's office. Deborah, Dr. Fried reminds her, is the one in control.

This reassurance loosens Deborah up a bit. She exposes a little of herself to Dr. Fried, but unfortunately she does so by degrading herself, listing all the negative aspects of her personality or at least the depressing things others have told her about herself. But after offering this pessimistic description of herself, the narrator reveals that as Deborah sits there in Dr. Fried's office, she thinks "that she had perhaps spoken her true feelings for the first time." In other words, the narrator is telling the readers that Dr. Fried has made an impression on Deborah, one that has created trust between the patient and the doctor. This comment foreshadows, or hints, of what is to come. Without that trust, Deborah may have been lost forever in her mental nightmares.

> "Dr. Royson tried to open a path into Deborah's mind, not with a precise and intricate tool but rather with a pickax, an instrument that is more suited to killing his patient than to opening her mind to the light of a beautiful world."

Now the question is, how does Dr. Fried encourage this trust? Well, first she asks Deborah if she wants to share information about herself. Dr. Fried does not try to forcibly dislodge any of Deborah's secrets, which, as a therapist, Dr. Fried knows exist deep inside Deborah. Of course, Dr. Fried wants to expose Deborah's secrets, but she is a patient woman. She suggests to Deborah that she has an opportunity to talk about them if she wants. It is up to Deborah to decide if she wants to respond to the invitation. There is no pressure and no intrusion.

The other thing that Dr. Fried does to deserve Deborah's trust is to empower Deborah, something that no one else has ever done for her. This is not the false empowerment that she has received from her grandfather, who wanted to make Deborah the model example of their immigrant family. Neither is this the everything-is-fine attitude of Deborah's parents, who believe if they can convince Deborah to swallow their false assurances, she will be strong. Dr. Fried's offer is much more authentic and satisfying. She tells Deborah something that no one else has dared to. Deborah can remain sick, if that is what she chooses. Or she can get better. Either way, Dr. Fried will impose nothing on her that Deborah does not want.

There is another more significant ingredient that convinces Deborah to trust Dr. Fried. It is made known when Dr. Fried assures Deborah that she will not leave her stranded in a void should Deborah decide to give up her symptoms. In other words, Dr. Fried is committing herself to Deborah's cause, should Deborah choose the path to health. Deborah will not be stripped of everything she knows and left alone and vulnerable. Dr. Fried needs Deborah's trust so she can lead her to the place that is

What Do I Read Next?

- Greenberg has spent a large portion of her life helping others with physical and mental challenges. In her book *In This Sign* (1984), Greenberg follows the lives of deaf parents and the challenges they must face in raising a daughter who can hear.

- *Where the Road Goes*, Greenberg's 1998 publication, follows the journey of a grandmother who believes she must once again take a political stand by walking across the United States.

- John Neufeld's *Lisa, Bright and Dark* (1969) tells the story of a sixteen-year-old who suffers from a mental breakdown. Lisa's parents do not understand what is happening to their daughter, so Lisa turns to her friends for support.

- The novel *Go Ask Alice* (1971) by James Jennings, written in diary form, tell the story of a teenage girl who suffers from terrible mood swings that are exacerbated by drug use.

- The novel *Cut* (2000) by Patrick McCormick is about a teenage girl, whose guilty feelings resulting from her belief that she is responsible for her brother's illness send her into withdrawal. She ends up in a hospital, where she at first resists treatment but then slowly pulls herself back to health.

- *The Bell Jar* (1963) is an autobiographical novel that draws upon Sylvia Plath's own struggle with mental illness and her experience receiving shock treatment.

- *Girl, Interrupted* (1993) is an autobiographical account of a teenager's stay in a mental hospital. Susanna Kaysen is quick in mind and often funny as she tells her readers about her sometimes terrifying journey to health.

---

waiting for her should Deborah be willing to give up the patterns and thoughts that feed her illness.

Finally, there is Dr. Fried's honesty. When Deborah challenges Dr. Fried, saying that she is just like all the other doctors who have told her that she is faking her symptoms, Dr. Fried does not back down. On the contrary, Dr. Fried responds. "It seems to me that I said that you are very sick, indeed." Although no one wants to hear that they are mentally ill, it is obvious that Deborah is relaxed in hearing this, released from the need to pretend otherwise. Upon hearing these words from the doctor, the narrator responds that with these words came a light, which "shone back" through time, illuminating parts of Deborah's past, contrasting with the lies she had been told in attempts to hide the obvious.

In contrast with her first visit with Dr. Fried, there is little or no bemusement when Deborah first encounters Dr. Royson. Deborah notes how he sits stiffly in his chair. She attempts to make conversation with Royson, trying to ease the tension, but Dr. Royson's personality is as stiff as his posture.

He does not give in to Deborah's small talk, seemingly convinced that he must keep a professional distance. Contrary to Dr. Fried's style of inviting conversation, Deborah feels that each of Dr. Royson's questions are demands and that every time she offers an answer, Dr. Royson jumps on them as if they are prizes. She uses the word "pickax" to describe how she imagines his questions coming at her.

But more defeating than any other of Royson's misguided efforts is the mistake he makes when he reacts to an unfamiliar word that Deborah utters. "Oh, the Secret Language," Dr. Royson says. With this statement, especially in Deborah's mind, Royson has trespassed. He has attempted to move into Deborah's secret world without a hint of an invitation. All he offers in way of a defense for his transgression is: "Dr. Fried told me that you had a secret language." What Royson does not seem to realize is that not only is this not a valid ticket by which to invade Deborah's inner world, it is also a slap against Dr. Fried. Royson is implying that Dr. Fried is an accomplice in his invasion. So he alienates Deborah and turns her against Dr. Fried as well.

Deborah withdraws immediately. Although her health had progressed under Dr. Fried's care, Deborah decides she has nowhere to go except back into her illness. As she fades from reality again, she has one lingering thought for Dr. Royson. In all her sickness, she finds the strength to tell him: "[D]on't cut bangs with a hatchet." But Dr. Royson does not understand what she is saying. So Deborah rephrases it: "Don't do brain surgery with a pickax."

Clearly, Greenberg is suggesting that someone like Dr. Fried, through gentleness and honesty, is able to build a trusting relationship. This relationship ultimately leads Deborah (as it did Greenberg herself) to health. By contrast, stiff, oppositional Dr. Royson does nothing of the sort. His mistake is obvious. Dr. Royson tried to open a path into Deborah's mind, not with a precise and intricate tool but rather with a pickax, an instrument that is more suited to killing his patient than to opening her mind to the light of a beautiful new world.

Source: Joyce Hart, Critical Essay on *I Never Promised You a Rose Garden*, in *Novels for Students*, Thomson Gale, 2006.

Kary K. Wolfe
and Gary K. Wolfe

In the following essay, the authors discuss how I Never Promised You a Rose Garden *defined a genre of novels about mental illness, and then analyze the novel for "its specific relations to romance, and the reasons for its popularity."*

Movements and genres in popular literature, emerging as they do from a variety of media and often over an extended period of time, sometimes have the effect of "sneaking up" on scholars of the genre, of developing quietly over a period of years and then seeming to spring full-blown upon the consciousness of the reading public. Such was partially the case with science fiction, which grew almost unnoticed for decades before being "discovered" by critics during the last ten years or so. Such is also the case with the genre we propose to discuss today, a genre which has its roots in the literature of mental abnormality stretching back to classical times, but which has emerged as a genre in itself—drawing on the novel, memoirs, autobiography, and psychological case history—only during this century. Psychologists have long been aware of these works as a sub-genre of psychiatric literature, but it shall be the contention of this paper that such works have in recent years

> " One must wonder if in fact such works as *Rose Garden* are popularly read as novels *about* schizophrenia, or as vicarious schizophrenic experiences."

transcended in popularity and form the rather narrow scope of "professional literature" and become a profitable genre of popular writing (and to a lesser extent, of film and television). Such works not only enjoy an appeal that goes well beyond people professionally interested in psychology, but they also have evolved recognizable formulaic elements in structure and imagery. We propose to treat these works, then, not from the point of view of the psychologist so much as from the point of view of popular culture: specifically, what are their characteristics and what might be the reason for their popularity?

Robert Coles, in his introduction to Barbara Field Benzinger's *The Prison of My Mind*, remarks that the book "shares a tradition that goes centuries back" and even cites Augustine's *Confessions* as a precursor. While this statement is undoubtedly true in the broadest sense, and while the list of autobiographical accounts of mental illness include such illustrious figures as Strindberg, Nijinsky, Boswell, de Maupassant, Arthur Symons, and others, a more immediate source for works such as Benziger's can be found in the works of "muckraking" novelists, reporters, and autobiographers. Perhaps the most significant of these, and perhaps the seminal work in this genre in the twentieth century, is Clifford Beers' *A Mind that Found Itself* (1908), both a moving account of a severe manic-depressive's years of illness and recovery and powerful indictment of the treatment of mental patients at the beginning of this century. The muckraking theme is a recurrent one in later works as well, and what is probably this genre's first major best-seller, Mary Jane Ward's 1946 *The Snake Pit*, is less concerned with the structure of mental illness or the process of therapy than with the nightmarish conditions of the asylum itself. More recently, a similarly social-minded concern with the manipulative aspects of mental treatment is expressed in Ken Kesey's *One Flew Over the Cuckoo's Nest* (1962) and Elliott Baker's *A Fine Madness* (1964), and in such related non-fiction studies as Thomas Szasz's *The Myth of Mental Illness* and Phyllis Chesler's *Women and Madness* (which curiously demostrates little awareness of this genre, whose major figures are all women).

The Snake Pit was not the first novel in the 1940's to deal with mental illness and recovery; it had been preceded by several years by Millen Brand's *The Outward Room* (1941), and it came at a time of extensive interest in psychological topics in the popular media, especially films (more about which in a moment). But it established as no other book had the market potential of this subject, and for the next twenty years the genre developed steadily, with narratives told not only from the patient's point of view, but from the doctor's as well. In 1955, Max Lerner could write, "One of the byproducts of the post-Freudian age has been the emergence of a new genre of American writing—the work of the writing psychoanalyst or psychiatrist, who applies his insights to the problems of the day or tells of some of his adventures with his patients." Lerner was writing in the introduction to Robert Lindner's *The Fifty Minute Hour,* itself one of the more successful collections of case histories published during the 1950's. It was followed in 1957 by a similar collection, Joseph Anthony's *The Invisible Curtain,* as well as Corbett Thigpen and Hervey Cleckley's *The Three Faces of Eve* the same year. In 1962 appeared *Lisa and David,* the best-known of Theodore Isaac Rubin's series of novelized case histories.

None of these works from the therapist's viewpoint ever achieved the resounding success of a 1964 novel told from the patient's viewpoint, however. Joanne Greenberg's *I Never Promised You a Rose Garden,* published under the pseudonym "Hannah Green," remains the most famous and influential book in this genre, with sales of nearly four million copies in its first decade of publication. Its success is almost certainly a key factor in the present growth and popularity of the genre. Following *I Never Promised You a Rose Garden,* booksellers began to set up displays of popular psychology paperbacks; publishers began to re-issue earlier works, citing similarities to the Greenberg book in an effort to increase sales, and in some cases even changing the titles in order to point up similarities: Margaret Wiley Emmett's *Satan Have Pity,* originally published in 1962, was reissued in paperback in 1971 under the title *I Love the Person You Were Meant to Be.* Characteristic paperback blurbs would read "A book to equal *I Never Promised You a Rose Garden*" (*Autobiography of a Schizophrenic Girl*); "Not since *INPYRG* [which we shall hence-forth abbreviate thus for Convenience]" (*I Love the Person You Were Meant to Be*); "A novel in the poignant tradition of *INPYRG*" (*Lisa, Bright and Dark*); "As haunting as *INPYRG*" (*The Eye of Childhood*); "A novel with the poignancy of *INPYRG*" (*The Better Part*); or "A novel for those who enjoyed *INPYRG*" (*Crown of Flowers*). "I Never Promised You a Rose Garden," bizarrely, even became the title of a country and western song in 1971 that had nothing to do with mental illness. The genre, at least as far as the marketing departments of publishers were concerned, was established—and highly lucrative.

The sudden flowering of sales of these books also brought renewed attention to such writers as Mary Jane Ward, Lucy Freeman, and Vera Randal, each of whom has published more than one book in the genre since the late forties, with Freeman at least (whose first book, *Fight Against Fears,* appeared in 1951), making a successful career out of such writing. Writers with more serious literary ambitions also found the genre attractive during this period. J. R. Salamanca's *Lilith* (1961) enjoyed some critical success, as did the Robert Rossen film later adapted from it. Both Ken Kesey's *One Flew Over the Cuckoo's Nest* (1962) and Sylvia Plath's *The Bell Jar* (1963) gained wide audiences and critical attention, and both have become "cult" books of a sort, reflecting as they do the values of the counterculture and the women's movement, respectively.

At the same time, the genre has grown in popularity in the movies and on television. Psychiatry in general, and amnesia in particular, became a common theme in films of the forties, most notably in such films as Hitchcock's *Spell-bound* (1945) and the film adaptation of *The Snake Pit* (with a screenplay co-authored by Millen Brand, 1949), but also in films from other popular genres, such as *Pride of the Marines* (1945). The fifties followed with film adaptations of William Gibson's *The Cobweb* (1955), Jim Piersall's *Fear Strikes Out* (1957), and Robert Lindner's *Rebel Without a Cause* (1955), the latter, as Gene and Barbara Stanford have observed, turning a psychopathic case study into "the cultural hero of the fifties." *The Three Faces of Eve* won an Academy Award for Joanne Woodward in 1957, and *David and Lisa,* an adaptation of Rubin's *Lisa and David,* brought director Frank Perry to prominence in 1962. This is not to mention the flood of psychological horror stories following Hitchcock's *Psycho* (1960), Robert Aldrich's *Whatever*

Happened to Baby Jane (1962), and Samuel Fuller's *Shock Corridor* (1963).

Television also entered the arena briefly in the early sixties, with two series, *The Eleventh Hour* and *The Psychiatrist,* dealing on a weekly basis with mental problems. Mental illness remains a frequent theme on such programs as *Marcus Welby, M.D.* and *Medical Center,* and John Neufeld's *Lisa Bright and Dark* recently appeared as a tv-movie. As far back as 1955, Max Lerner castigated television and motion picture exploitation of mental illness in terms that are still applicable today:

> They have usually taken the cheap-and-easy way of starting with some highly dramatic event and, with psychiatric help, working back to infancy and mother-fixation. Although the psychiatric play or movie is still young it is already so threadbare as to be vulnerable to caricature. The trouble with most of them is that they start with a prefabricated drama rather than with a given personality. It takes honesty to avoid the temptation of this kind of synthetic pattern, where everything is untangled neatly and tied together again just as neatly.

Before proceeding to a fuller discussion of the popularity of this genre, and to a more detailed analysis of *I Never Promised You a Rose Garden* as an example of the genre, it is necessary to outline briefly just what it is that justifies lumping all these works together, beyond a common concern with psychology. The more familiar genres of popular writing—westerns, detective stories, gothics, and the like—may be characterized and identified by a number of structural and conventional elements involving style, atmosphere, setting, and characterization, as well as plot. Largely through the cross-influence of writers within the genre, certain formulae are evolved, and popular writers who most successfully make use of these formulae become, in John Cawelti's sense of the term, *auteurs.* In our psychological narratives, such cross-influence seems relatively sparse, and while easily discernible formulae may not yet have completely evolved, there are noteworthy recurrent elements. We shall attempt to characterize the genre in terms of these elements, specifically in regard to imagery and metaphor, structure, point of view, and characterization.

Our first area of concern is imagery and metaphor, and in some ways this is the most important. A striking feature of many of these narratives is their organization of a deliberate metaphoric pattern, guided or controlled by one or two central metaphors that set the tone and attitude for the entire work. Many of these controlling metaphors are evident in the titles of the works: *The*

Snake Pit, The Prison of My Mind, Labyrinth of Silence, Halfway Through the Tunnel, The Invisible Curtain, The Bell Jar. Most of these are simple metaphors of madness, although some, like the snake pit, serve the dual function of representing both the patient's state of mind and the horrors of the mental hospital itself. The central importance of the controlling metaphor in these works stems in part from the fact that many of the works tend to be autobiographical, and, as James Olney writes in his study of metaphor in autobiography, "By their metaphors shall you know them." In other words, the power of metaphor becomes the central link between the experience of the reader and the experience described by the author in an autobiographical work. On the most basic level, it represents an attempt at communicating the incommunicable; Frank Conroy writes of the anonymous author of *Autobiography of a Schizophrenic Girl* that she "attempted to re-create through metaphor . . . sensations in the mind of the presumably sane reader that were in her mind while she was insane." Another reason for the importance of such metaphor is the significance of metaphor and metaphoric language in the structure of many psychoses. The personal mythology of Deborah in *I Never Promised You a Rose Garden* is guarded from the outside world by an artificial language based on metaphors; an exchange with Deborah's doctor in therapy illustrates the complexity of this metaphoric structure:

> "There must be some words," the doctor said. "Try to find them, and let us share them together."
>
> "It's a metaphor—you wouldn't understand it."
>
> "Perhaps you could explain it then."
>
> "There is a word—it means Locked Eyes, but it implies more."
>
> "What more?"
>
> "It's the word for sarcophagus." It meant that at certain times her vision reached only as far as the cover of her sarcophagus; that to herself, as to the dead, the world was the size of her own coffin.

Metaphors, then, often represent not only an attempt to communicate the emotional quality of the illness, but to some extent its structure as well. It is not surprising that the most common metaphors are metaphors of darkness and confusion: fog, mazes, labyrinths, tunnels, pits, water, caverns, fire and ice.

Many of these metaphors suggest the classical journey to the underworld, and indeed this is a useful analogue to the structure of many of these works. The pit, among the most common of metaphors, is readily analogous to the pit of Hell, as the less common but occasional mountain metaphor is analogous to Purgatory. Most of the narratives involve some sort of chaotic, metaphoric journey within the hospital, from ward to ward and in some cases from hospital to hospital, with certain wards representing relative health and others representing the "forgotten," the hopeless cases whose screaming isolation seems like nothing so much as the condition of the damned in the lower circles of Dante's Hell. Janet Frame, in *Faces in the Water* (1961), gives evidence of the extreme importance of particular wards to patients in these stories:

> What is Ward Seven but a subaqueous condition of the mind which gave the fearful shapes drowned there a rhythmic distortion of peace; and what if, upon ny getting up from my bed, the perspective was suddenly altered, or I was led into a trap where a fire burning in the walls had dried up the water and destroyed the peace by exposing in harsh daylight the submerged shapes in all their terror?

The ward becomes like the unconscious mind itself, hiding "fearful shapes" in a labyrinthine distortion of space and perspective. This distortion of perspective is also mentioned by Mary Jane Ward in *The Snake Pit:*

> The nurse led her to a door she had never seen before. Naturally. The door was not there before. Just as the washroom was at one end of the corridor one day and at the other end the next day. Entirely new doors were created in order to insure perpetual confusion.

Labyrinthine chaos such as that described in these passages, followed by emergence into some sort of an ordered universe, seems to be the central dramatic movement of many of these narratives: a movement from disorder to order, or at least the promise of order. The movement is highly—and literally—cathartic, and as we shall see later, this catharsis may be a strong reason for the popularity of this genre.

A third element worth noting in these narratives, along with metaphor and structure, is point of view. The autobiographical element again becomes important here, for in most of the narratives we find that the point of view is confined narrowly to the narrating patient or doctor, with perhaps an occasional shift back and forth, but almost never shifting to the point of view of another patient. Within these limits, point of view might further be categorized fourfold: (1) the patient, describing her or his own illness and internal conflicts (*I Never Promised You a Rose Garden; The Prison of My Mind*); (2) the patient, describing hospital conditions and the outward appearance and character of other patients (*Faces in the Water; The Snake Pit*); (3) the therapist, describing a particular case history (*The Fifty-Minute Hour; My Language Is Me*); and (4) the therapist or doctor, describing a number of patients and/or conditions in a hospital (*Labyrinth of Silence; Savage Sleep*). In addition to these most common points of view, a few narratives may be told from the perspective of someone outside the therapist-patient relationship, usually a relative (*In a Darkness; This Stranger, My Son*), and some may contain more than one perspective on the same case, such as Mary Barnes and Joseph Berke's *Two Accounts of a Journey Through Madness* or Marguerite Sechehaye's interpretation appended to the narrative of *Autobiography of a Schizophrenic Girl*. But the prevalence of the four major points of view, with their concentration on the process of therapy or the conditions of therapy and with their clearly defined narrative scope, offers some evidence for the didactic nature of this kind of narrative—and this didacticism may be yet another reason for the genre's popularity.

Finally, there is the element of characterization, and in this area the genre begins more to resemble conventional characteristics of other genres of popular fiction. As we have already noted parenthetically, the vast majority of these narratives concern women, and most of the autobiographical narratives are written by women as well. Furthermore, it seems evident that the majority of readers are women. Much is done, then, toward the development of identification with the central character or characters, who are usually presented as highly intelligent, witty, articulate (within the bounds of their illness), and yet vulnerable and perhaps above all, passive. The narrator's wit is a distinguishing mark of the style in *The Snake Pit* and Sylvia Plath's *The Bell Jar;* it is described as a psychotic defense in *I Never Promised You a Rose Garden.* Yet the protagonists of each of these novels, as well as many others, hardly could be called protagonists in the real sense at all: they simply don't make much happen. They tend to be presented as passive victims, buffered about by family, friends, other patients, doctors, nurses, orderlies, strangers, society in general, and their own internal disturbance. Furthermore, they tend to be creative, usually as artists (*Two Accounts of a Journey through Madness; I Never Promised You a Rose Garden*) or writers (*The Snake Pit*). This dual aspect of the central character—the creative, intelligent woman victimized by roles she is forced into—probably accounts for a large measure of the popularity enjoyed at least by *The Bell Jar* among feminists.

What villains there are in these narratives tend to be unwittingly played by family and friends who mean well but simply "don't understand." Usually, however, the only major figure to recur in a number of the books is a variation on the wise old person, the wizard or wise woman of fairy tales. This role is generally occupied by the therapist, who often represents the first benevolent authority figure the patient encounters during the illness. Advocates of the women's movement may rightly question the frequency with which this figure is a strong male character, but not infrequently the figure is a woman therapist—such as Dr. Fried in *I Never Promised You a Rose Garden.*

Having surveyed thus all too briefly the genre in terms of imagery, structure, point of view, and characterization, we should look back over these elements and try to see what in them, if anything, might account for the growing popularity of this kind of writing. Max Lerner contends that much of this popularity may derive from certain similarities to the detective story, with the process of unravelling the past even more ingenious than in most mysteries, because all we have to begin with is a victim who, with the aid of the doctor, must discover not only who the villains are but indeed if any "crime" was committed at all. Frank Conroy, writing of *Autobiography of a Schizophrenic Girl,* describes the book in terms of another genre: to him the book is "clearly a triumph of faith. . . . As a human document Renee's book is without doubt inspirational." Gene and Barbara Stanford offer yet another explanation:

> Part of the fascination seems to be the sense of strangeness and horror that some of the books convey. In our modern world, where fierce beasts and uninhabited continents have all been conquered, the frontiers of the mind are about the only places where adventures are still possible. This interest in the strange world that lies beyond the borders of the rational mind may partially account for experimentation with drugs as well as for an interest in mental illness.

This "adventure into the unknown" aspect of the books, we might add, also would seem to relate their popularity to the resurgence of interest in witchcraft and occultism, and to the popularity of fantasy and science fiction, particularly the artificial cosmologies of such writers as H. P. Lovecraft or J. R. R. Tolkien.

Certainly all these factors are involved in the popularity of these books, but we might also find clues to popularity from the characteristics we have already mentioned. In terms of structure and imagery in particular, and characterization to a lesser

extent, we might regard these works as a variety of romance, which uses the interior landscapes of real mental illness in much the same way that the interior landscapes of the poetic imagination have functioned in romances from the Middle Ages to the present. We may use the term "romance" in a fairly broad sense here, since we are speaking primarily of the manner in which these works are received by a popular audience rather than the manner in which they are deliberately conceived by their authors. We have already noted how these narratives are often structured as a journey into a kind of inferno or wasteland in search of a mysterious goat or boon; this quest element certainly calls to mind heroic romance of the Arthurian sort, and indeed Erich Neumann has already demonstrated at some length the manner in which such quest romances can represent, in Jungian terms, the evolution of consciousness from the unconscious—a process which is often reconstructed in therapy with psychotics.

On another level, these journeys also represent a consciously educational process of self-discovery, and this factor, coupled with the frequently youthful or adolescent protagonists, suggests thematic relationships with the *bildungs-roman* of Romantic narrative art. Still a third literary relation, mentioned above, may be found in fantasy and science fiction, whose artificial systems and fantastic imagery are echoed in the detailed fantasies of many psychotics.

Finally, yet another variety of romance that is of perhaps even greater interest than the others in explaining the current popular appeal of the genre is the Gothic romance. We have already noted the passive "victim" aspect of many of the heroines, and this is certainly an element shared with the popular "modern Gothics" that grace newstands with endless cover paintings of ladies in nightgowns fleeing dimly lit mansions. But many of our protagonists also share the dark obsessions and compulsions of a Heathcliff, thus partaking of the Gothic villain as well as the Gothic heroine and becoming romantic figures in themselves. Janet Frame demonstrates awareness of this aspect of popular psychological fiction in *Faces in the Water:*

> There is an aspect of madness which is seldom mentioned in fiction because it would damage the romantic popular idea of the insane as a person whose speech appeals as immediately poetic; but it is seldom the easy Opheliana recited like the pages of a seed catalog or the outpourings of Crazy Janes who provide, in fiction, and outlet for poetic abandon. Few of the people who roamed the dayroom would have qualified as acceptable heroines, in popular taste; few were charmingly uninhibited eccentrics.

But even Frame's own prosaic narrator is capable of wildly "poetic" outpourings and images. Add this aspect of the protagonist to the presence of the very real "ghosts" and "demons" of mental illness and the labyrinthine settings of huge, shadowy institutions—a modern equivalent of the Gothic castle—and the narratives seem even closer to the more familiar Gothic romance.

To illustrate these various points in a more unified manner, we should now like to examine in greater detail one of these works, analyzing it for the characteristics of the genre, its specific relations to romance, and the reasons for its popularity. The work we have chosen is one which by its huge popular success and influence has become virtually the archetype of the genre, Joanne Greenberg's *I Never Promised You a Rose Garden.* Published in 1964 under the name "Hannah Green," the novel is a fictionalized account of Joanne Greenberg's own illness and her therapy at Chestnut Lodge under Dr. Frieda Fromm-Reichmann. While the novel was generally received well critically as a didactic work concerning mental illness, many reviewers had reservations about its value as fiction. Frank Haskel, writing in *Saturday Review,* complained that "the two-steps-forward, one-step-backward progression of Deborah's surfacing to life lacks that tightness which fiction requires." R.V. Cassill, while generally lauding the book in his *New York Times Book Review* review, observed that it is not wholly "fictionally convincing" and that "it is as if some wholly admirable, and yet specialized, nonfictional discipline has been dressed in the garments and mask of fiction." The *Times Literary Supplement* reviewer noted what is probably the book's chief defect as a novel by pointing out that the "real" world to which Deborah must return is never made nearly as convincing or attractive as her fantasy world: "her normality is perilously close to dullness." And Brigid Brophy in *The New Statesman* declared flatly that "should it turn out to be a work of fiction, its value would vanish overnight." It soon became publicly known that the novel is *not* entirely fiction, of course, and in the years following these initial reviews, as the book phenomenally grew in popularity, relatively little attention was paid to it as anything other than a highly readable case history. And yet there is much evidence, both from the novel itself and from Greenberg's other works, that the book is an attempt at a coherent novel and not merely fictionalized autobiography.

In *Rose Garden,* Greenberg has tried to portray the often chaotic imagery of schizophrenia and the often uneven process of therapy, and to impose upon these realities of her own experience the order and structure of a unified narrative. This is not to suggest that she has deliberately misrepresented either her illness or her therapy for the sake of novelistic expediency; rather it is to suggest that the aesthetic elements of the book exist on two principle levels. For example, the imagery of mountains, which serves a number of complex functions in the context of Deborah's own schizophrenic world, is introduced into the narrative late enough so that it can also function in aesthetic terms as an image of the struggle toward sanity, toward resolution of conflict: "All Deborah heard were the sounds of her own gasps of exhaustion as she climbed an Everest that was to everyone else an easy and a level plain." Similarly, the imagery of the underworld ("the Pit"), which seems to appear more or less at random within the context of the illness, is for the sake of the narrative organized into the more familiar aesthetic pattern of the underworld journey: descent, chaos, and purifying ascent. The danger of this kind of dual use of imagery, of course, is that it tends to lead the reader to confuse the structure of the novel with the structure of therapy, and the pattern of aesthetic imagery with the pattern of schizophrenia. Such confusion is furthered by the commonplace belief that there is some sort of *de facto* relationship between insanity and art, and one must wonder if in fact such works as *Rose Garden* are popularly read as novels *about* schizophrenia, or as vicarious schizophrenic experiences; the word "seductive" appears prominently twice on the cover blurb of *Rose Garden.* But this question is merely another way of asking the reason for the popularity of these books, and perhaps it can be in part answered by looking at the four key aspects of *Rose Garden* itself: characterization, structure, style and imagery, and rhetoric.

The central element in characterization, as we have already noted for the genre as a whole, is the nature of the protagonist herself. The protagonist in *Rose Garden* is 16-year-old Deborah Blau, a plain but highly intelligent and witty girl whose psychosis involves an elaborately imagined, almost Blakean universe called Yr, with its own pantheon of gods, its own language, and its own landscapes. During the course of the novel, Deborah moves in both the real world and this world of her own creating. But the "real world" in this novel is the world of the mental hospital and its surroundings, a world that is in its own way as artificial as the one Deborah has created. The arbitrary and sometimes hostile nature of this reality is what provides the book's title; in warning Deborah that reality is not necessarily more rewarding than the world of Yr, and in arguing that Deborah's choice must be based on deeper criteria than mere comfort, the therapist Dr. Fried says, "I never promised you a rose garden. I never promised you perfect justice . . .". And in making this statement, Dr. Fried herself is reminded of her days in Nazi Germany, as if to underline to the reader the point that "reality" is not necessarily morally superior to the world of the psychotic. In fact, it is this real world, the "outside," represented initially in the novel by the almost mythic figure of Doris Rivera, a patient who has apparently successfully "gone outside," this is the mystery. The artificial worlds of the hospital and the psychosis itself are clearly delineated; the world outside is presented only slightly near the end of the novel.

Deborah must somehow learn to function in all three worlds: her own mind, the hospital, and finally the outside. Each world has a different landscape, a different set of rules, even a different language, and in each world the character of Deborah is developed along certain lines congruent with the fictional reality of that world. And in each world, she must pass from a stage of passivity to one of self-determination and control. Put another way, Deborah must undergo a process of education on three levels: first mastering the workings of her own mind, then mastering the fairly simple rules of life with the other patients in the hospital, and finally mastering the more complex rules of life on the outside. This multifaceted educational process, together with Deborah's adolescence and her relative innocence in each situation, suggests the kind of education undergone by the adolescent protagonists of the *bildungsroman*. It is also, of course, a stylized version of the process of socialization in the development of any personality, and it may be for this reason that it is easy to identify with Deborah's problems, stated as they are in such bizarre terms.

Deborah is also appealing because she is essentially an heroic figure, and her Kingdom of Yr is an heroic, even mythopoeic, world. In that world, she initially seems to identify with Anterrabae, "the falling god," who is later revealed to be her own version of Milton's Satan, with all its associations of heroic defiance, eternal punishment, and the underworld. She must endure the derision and hostility of the Collect, "the massed images of all the teachers and relatives and schoolmates standing eternally in secret judgment and giving their endless curses." She is often referred to her gods as

"Bird-One," with its suggestion of Icarus, of pride and freedom. Finally, she must declare her self-mastery by renouncing all her gods and the Kingdom of Yr itself—an act which dramatically parallels the myth which gave rise to Anterrabae in the first place, and which in itself represents a kind of Promethean defiance. Deborah renounces her own security in favor of knowledge of the world and freedom; such an ideal is not uncommon in Romantic poetry and fiction.

Another reason for Deborah's success as a popular heroine is her appeal to our own fantasies of irresponsibility. Almost anything she does is excusable in the context of the fiction, and as such she represents, however perversely, a kind of absolute behavioral freedom. She doesn't necessarily get away with all her actions, but she isn't entirely responsible for them either, and it is likely that this freedom is, on a rather basic level, an example of the sort of wish-fulfillment that characterizes much popular literature. The freedom has its limits, however, and these limits seem at least in part defined by the necessity of maintaining reader sympathy. None of the violence on Deborah's part is directed at anyone other than herself, and the general absence of sexual motives and experience from her story—even though it seems likely that such experiences would comprise a significant element of her psyche—give her the aspect of the "innocent." Not even her most repulsive actions, such as her continued self-mutilation, are sufficient to remove our sympathies from her, and in this respect she is not unlike many other adolescent heroines in popular fiction.

The structure of the novel also may be a contributing factor to its popularity, for despite all its images of doom and confusion, *Rose Garden* is essentially comedic. There is from the outset a feeling of imminent resolution and hope; like the traditional fairy tale, elements of horror may be introduced as long as there is no overall feeling of despair. Part of this may be due to the journey motif; the suggestion of a journey naturally implies that the journey will have an end, and in the case of Deborah, this end is relative sanity (the alternative end, death, is only suggested slightly in the novel in brief references to her earlier suicide attempt). *Rose Garden* begins literally with a journey—the trip to the mental hospital—and continues with Deborah's movement from ward to ward and finally back out into the world. This movement, though not effortless, seems inevitable, and its inevitability is reinforced by the time sequence of the book. Deborah is in the hospital for three years, and in each of these years, springtime represents a progression towards sanity. The first spring arrives when Deborah first secures her relationship with Dr. Fried by learning that she is of value to the doctor: "'If I can teach you something, it may mean that I can count at least somewhere.'" The second spring is characterized by Deborah and her friend and co-patient Carla declaring their friendship and running away from the hospital in a show of self-assertion and fun, prompting the doctor in charge to comment, "'I'm kind of proud of you.'" The third spring, coming at the conclusion of the book, includes Deborah's successful passing of the high school equivalency exams—an act which symbolically certifies both her maturity and her sanity. The three episodes taken together constitute Deborah's learning about the value of her person to others, then asserting that value, and finally proving it with the socially accepted measure of the high school exams. She finally emerges from her private world and prepares to leave the hospital in springtime, just as she had entered it, three years earlier, in the autumn. The three years become metaphorically compressed into one cycle of the seasons, and the inevitability of this cycle—the inevitability of spring—lends to the novel an overall tone of hope.

Yet another source of popularity may be the book's imagery. The idea of the "secret garden"—the private respite from the world that is known only to the child—has long been popular in children's and adolescent literature, and it is not unlikely that Deborah's Kingdom of Yr is just such a garden to many readers. Though on a more intense level, it is not unlike Frances Hodgson Burnett's secret garden in her book of that title, or C. S. Lewis's Narnia. Its landscape is a wildly romantic, exciting one of fire and ice, and its language bears resemblance, though on a much more complex level, to the "secret codes" popular among children. In other words, Yr, though the myth of a psychotic mind, is still a myth, and as such bears strong attraction for the imagination. Thus, as we have mentioned earlier, some of the attraction that readers feel for the novel may be akin to the attractions of Blake, or Lewis, or Tolkien.

Finally, and probably most importantly to the novel's professional audience, there is the didactic element. *Rose Garden* has been used as a supplementary text in many university psychology courses because of its accurate dramatization of facts about psychosis and therapy. Karl Menninger wrote of the book, "'I'm sure it will have a good effect on lots of people who don't realize that this sort of exploration can be done and this sort of effect achieved.'" Robert Cotes reacts in a similar manner: "If I were upset, in despair, worried about whether there will be many days left, I would be grateful to people like Clifford Beers or Hannah Green or Barbara Benzinger." It appears, then, that the book is widely read as an object lesson in mental illness, and that for many its value as fiction is secondary to its value as case history. And it seems likely that a didactic motive was one of the major reasons the book was written in the first place; a number of novelistic decisions seem to be made on didactic (i.e., what will teach most effectively) rather than aesthetic (i.e., what will work best as fiction) grounds. We learn a great deal more about Deborah's psychosis than we do about her actual personality, for example. Such didacticism may occasionally weaken the novel as fiction, but it probably adds to its popularity.

Rose Garden, then, brings together in a single book many of the elements that have gone into the making of a popular narrative genre. And in terms of the popular audience, it is the book most responsible for the present ascendance of that genre. Part autobiography, part fiction, part educational tract, it is in many ways one of the most significant popular books of the last twenty years. It and the other books in its genre may represent the most broad-based connection yet established between practicing psychology and popular culture. As such, it is worth studying, and the genre is one whose development is worth watching, not only for what it may tell us about how popular genres evolve, but also for what it may tell us about changing attitudes of a mass audience toward issues in psychology and mental health.

Source: Gary K. Wolfe, "Metaphors of Madness: Popular Psychological Narratives," in *Journal of Popular Culture,* Spring 1976, pp. 895–907.

Sources

"Calling Mad Mad," in *Times Literary Supplement,* No. 3259, August 13, 1964, p. 721.

Cassill, R. V., "A Locked Ward, A Desperate Search for Reality," in *New York Times,* May 3, 1964, p. BR36.

Green, Hannah, pseudo. *I Never Promised You a Rose Garden,* Signet, 1964.

Ylvisaker, Miriam, Review of *I Never Promised You a Rose Garden,* in *Library Journal,* Vol. 89, No. 4, February 15, 1964, p. 881.

Further Reading

Amador, Xavier, *I Am Not Sick I Don't Need Help!*, Vida Press, 2000.

In a clear, concise manner, Amador addresses this book to the friends and family of people with mental illness. He helps them to understand the pressures, fears, and anxieties of someone who is suffering and how to help him or her.

Beam, Alex, *Gracefully Insane: The Rise and Fall of America's Premier Mental Hospital*, Public Affairs, 2001.

New England's McLean Hospital has been known as the country club of mental institutions, with its tennis courts, golf course, and riding stables. Beam interviewed patients as well as hospital staff in preparation for drawing this portrait of the hospital.

Green, Michael Foster, *Schizophrenia Revealed: From Neurons to Social Interactions*, Norton, 2003.

In this quite accessible book, Green offers his readers an up-to-date account of current definitions of schizophrenia, its symptoms, and contemporary attempts to understand and treat the illness.

Porter, Roy, *Madness: A Brief History*, Oxford University Press, 2003.

A readable history of mental illnesses from the Greeks who were known to drill holes in skulls to find a source of madness to present-day controversies concerning psychiatry. Porter discusses techniques to help cure and definitions that help explain madness.

Wagner, Pamela Spiro, and Carolyn Spiro, *Divided Minds: Twin Sisters and Their Journey through Schizophrenia*, St. Martin's Press, 2005.

Sisters, one a gifted poet, the other a psychiatrist, offer their stories of what it was like growing up as twins and watching themselves drift apart as schizophrenia affected the poet-sister. Each sister offers her version of the experience, along with her frustrations, fears, and insights.

Kaddish for a Child Not Born

Imre Kertész

1990

Kaddish for a Child Not Born by Imre Kertész is the third book in a series of four novels which examine the life of a man who survives the Nazi concentration camps of World War II. *Kaddish* focuses on this man in his middle age as he reflects upon his childhood, his failed marriage, and his survival thus far. His wife leaves him because he refuses to father a child. She realizes that he does not want to live but she very much does. The narrator uses his writing to keep himself going. The story is in the form of a monologue by this man, and the novel has no chapter divisions or other breaks.

Kaddish was published in Hungary in 1990, twenty-five years after the first novel of the four appeared. It was first translated into English in 1997 by Christopher C. Wilson and Katharina M. Wilson. A new translation by Tim Wilkinson (retitled *Kaddish for an Unborn Child*) was released in 2004. Although Kertész's first novel *Fateless* (1975; English translation, 1992 and 2004) was initially coldly received in Hungary, his literary talent was gradually acknowledged. He was relatively unknown, even in Hungary, when he was awarded the prestigious Nobel Prize for Literature in 2002.

Author Biography

Imre Kertész was born November 9, 1929 in Budapest, Hungary. In 1944, when Kertész was only fifteen years old he was sent with 7,000 other

Hungarian Jews to Auschwitz, the Nazi concentration camp in Poland. He was later transferred to Buchenwald, Germany. Kertész was liberated from the Buchenwald concentration camp in 1945.

Kertész returned to Hungary and worked as a journalist for the Budapest newspaper *Világosság*. Although he had joined the Communist Party, Kertész found, in practice, that he did not agree with many of its tenets. He was fired from the newspaper in 1951 after it adopted the Communist Party line to be in compliance with the Communist government of Hungary. Kertész was in the military for two years before he decided to support himself exclusively by writing and working as a literary translator. He specialized in translating German authors, especially Friedrich Nietzsche, Hugo von Hofmannsthal, Sigmund Freud, Ludwig Wittgenstein, and others. These writers had considerable influence on Kertész, and many are mentioned by name in *Kaddish for a Child Not Born* (originally published in 1990 in Hungarian as *Kaddis a meg nem született gyermekért*).

Kertész, like many other writers who were not favored by the ruling Communist Party, made most of his money from writing translations. For more than forty years, Hungry was occupied by the Soviet Union and had a communist form of government. In this political environment Kertész lived and wrote, believing for many years that his writing would not be read.

Fateless, Kertész's first novel, was published in 1975 after seeking publication for ten years. It was first translated into English in 1992; a new translation was published in 2004. This novel draws on Kertész's experiences at Auschwitz and Buchenwald as a fifteen-year-old boy. *Fateless* is generally considered to be the first in a series of four novels. The second novel, *Fiasco*, published in 1988, has as of 2005 not been translated into English. The third novel, *Kaddish for a Child Not Born*, was published in Hungarian in 1990 and translated into English in 1997; a subsequent translation (retitled *Kaddish for an Unborn Child*) was released in 2004. Kertész's fourth novel is *Liquidation* (2003). Although not labeled by the author as a tetralogy, these four titles share the same main character and follow him from youth to death.

As of 2005 Kertész lives and works in Budapest and spends part of the year in Germany where his books have a strong following. He became known to the world when he won the Nobel Prize for Literature in 2002. Kertész has also won the 1995 Brandenburg Literary Prize, the 1997 Leipzig Book Prize, and the 2000 Welt Prize.

Imre Kertész © Nicolas Guerin/Azimuts Production/Azimuts Production/Corbis

Plot Summary

Kaddish for a Child Not Born opens with an emphatic "No!" The narrator is responding to an as-yet unknown question while on a walk with a philosopher. He thinks about how "life itself demands explanations from us," and we end up "explaining ourselves to death." He would rather not talk, but he finds the urge irresistible. The narrator and philosopher are staying at a resort near the Central Mountains in Hungary. The narrator explains, "if I didn't work I would have to exist, and if I existed, I don't know what I would be forced to do then." But he does not want to socialize with his fellow intellectuals at the resort. His meeting in the woods with Dr. Oblath, a professor of philosophy, is by chance.

In thinking about the question, the narrator claims "with this 'no' I destroyed everything, demolished everything, above all, my ill-fated, short-lived marriage." Dr. Oblath has asked the narrator if he has a child. Although the answer is a simple "no," the underlying decision is complex and at the heart of the story to be told. Dr. Oblath expresses that he and his wife do not have a child, and it has only recently occurred to him to regret their lack of offspring. For the rest of their walk the narrator and Dr. Oblath talk about the state of the world and other large topics, to which the narrator privately assigns little value. He finally admits to himself that he stays to walk and talk with Dr. Oblath to avoid his own emptiness.

This emptiness catches up with him at night, when he is alone in his room. There is a thunderstorm and his mind, mirroring the explosive weather, goes back over the question of children: "'Were you to be a dark-eyed girl? With pale spots of scattered freckles around your little nose? Or a stubborn boy? With cheerful, hard eyes like blue-grey pebbles?'" Many years pass before he is able to capture his thoughts about his unborn children and what they mean on paper, "[his] life in the context of the potentiality of [their] existence."

The narrator thinks of his career as a literary translator and writer, which draws him to thoughts about his ex-wife. She questioned him about his motives: "'if you don't want to be successful, then why do you bother to write at all?'" He acknowledges that his ex-wife is more insightful than he originally acknowledged. Now when they meet each other she seems to feel guilty and nostalgic. He bears her no ill will because all she wants is to live fully, which she could not do while married to him.

The narrator slips back to thinking about his writing, pondering how he used it to engage in a dialogue with God, but now God is dead so the dialogue needs be with other people and with oneself.

He recalls how as a child he was sent one summer to visit relatives in the country. He thinks of these relatives as "real Jews," those who observe rituals and rites of their religion, Judaism. While there, the narrator opens a bedroom door and sees his aunt as "*a bald woman in a red gown in front of a mirror.*" The narrator, as a child, is disgusted and mortified; this image comes to signify real Jewishness for him.

When the war engulfs Hungary, the narrator finds himself, a secular Jew, being grouped with people like his relatives, and he suddenly sees himself as "*a bald woman in a red gown in front of a mirror.*" The narrator then explains how he has come to terms with his Jewishness. One time while waiting for his future wife at a café he overhears two beautiful young women talk about men. One tells the other that she could not have sex with a Jew, which enrages the narrator.

His future wife then arrives. She has read his work and wants to talk to him about it. He remembers their love when it was young and is pained. He

finally settles on wanting to remember because "memory is knowledge." His thoughts about memory and knowledge trail into ones about the war, the Holocaust, and being a survivor. He makes no fuss over being a survivor, although he finds himself writing compulsively, inexplicably. He makes a living from his writing although he does not feel he has to because he could have chosen some other profession. Ultimately he feels there is a very serious connection between his writing and survival. His writing does not offer solutions, just occupation and possible escape. He considers his writing to be a form of grave digging, a grave begun at the concentration camps: "the pen is my spade." He sees his fate is not so much about choosing childlessness as about just never having children. Earlier in life, when thinking about his unborn children, the narrator saw his "life in the context of the potentiality of [their] existence." Now he sees their "*nonexistence in the context of the necessary and fundamental liquidation of [his own] existence.*"

He remembers again the party at which he met his wife. Someone got the idea to name where they were during the war. When someone says "Auschwitz" (just ahead of the narrator), the host declares that that response is "unbeatable," as if this were a contest grimly won. The partygoers then begin to discuss a popular book which contained this sentence: "Auschwitz cannot be explained." The narrator is appalled at how easily the intelligent people at this party accept the value of this sentence. He voices his opinion and at this point his future wife notices him and comes to speak to him afterward.

He says that now he rarely voices his opinions, although they have not changed. He does not go to the resort to exchange opinions with intellectuals. When he is not at the resort, he is in his apartment in Józsefváros, a district near the heart of Budapest. It is the same place where he lived as a child. He thinks unhappily upon his childhood.

The narrator then returns to the statement: "Auschwitz cannot be explained." He accuses the book's author of telling people to be silent about Auschwitz, act as if it never existed. The narrator states that rather "what could not be explained is that no Auschwitz ever existed." He then philosophizes that Auschwitz has been waiting to happen for a long time, that the explanation of Auschwitz can be found only in individual lives—and that people are ruled by common criminals. Alluding to Adolf Hitler, he states that even when "demonic," a great man is still a great man and such a man was needed for "our disgusting affairs." The narrator then declares that rulers do not interest him, but saints do because they are irrational.

He tells a story about an emaciated man called the Professor who was with him on a carriage transport for sick prisoners. The narrator was ill, and there was very little food. The Professor got the narrator's portion and then they were separated. The narrator knew that while he would likely die without that food, the Professor's chances of survival would have been greatly increased with the extra food. But the Professor found the sick boy and gave him his food. When he sees the surprise on the narrator's face, he replies with "recognizable disgust on his moribund face: 'Well, what did you expect . . . ?'"

The narrator then writes about failure, concluding that "failure alone remains as the one single accomplishable experience." Life and writing both are strife; writing is about life and doomed to failure as soon as the writing begins. The narrator wonders why he works—except that he must. He recalls a conversation with his ex-wife about the Professor. He tells her what the Professor did is about freedom, rather than survival (which is what would be natural). She disagrees, saying that what the Professor did is natural.

The narrator thinks about women and relationships. He would like to believe that his personal freedom is required to keep himself enthusiastic about his work but actually it is the struggle for that freedom. Both freedom and happiness seem to stunt his work. Thinking upon unhappiness, he realizes his situation: he requires a continuous source of pain to maintain his ability to work. Having realized it, he is able to dismiss it as having any power over himself. Following this analysis, in his next relationship with a woman the narrator avows that they can remain together only so long as love is not a part of their union. But then he meets his future wife. He is living in a rented room while his friends have bought houses at the price of their mental and physical health; however, he willingly chooses his more transient lifestyle.

The narrator remembers how, when his camp was liberated, he came upon a German soldier cleaning a bathroom sink and smiling at him. The experience was disorienting, this reversal of their situations. After liberation, the narrator continued to live at the camp for some time, and he feels that he is continuing that experience by being a renter. But this so-called freedom is complicated by the sense that "the Germans may return at any time." Therefore he is not living, only surviving.

He clings fiercely to his few possessions, but otherwise he keeps himself free of being controlled by possessions. He rents and is not concerned with maintaining the property. He rents furnished apartments and never thinks to rearrange or replace the furniture. Once in a while he buys a book; otherwise, he despises clutter.

He has long suffered from a sense of alienation. The narrator feels that if he could only understand all of himself—his physical bodily functions as well as his mind and soul—all in one tremendous moment, then he would not feel alienated. He is searching for salvation beyond any religion or creed. The narrator lives the life of a renter so that he can be "ripe for change." When he was younger, he decided that his life was not an arbitrary set of occurrences. All of his experiences are tools of recognition. He and his ex-wife were fated to meet and marry; his failed marriage showed him his path of self-destruction.

When he first met his ex-wife, she asked him if he still suffered for his Jewishness. The narrator does not answer her immediately, but he knows his Jewish identity to be a sin he carries with him, although it is not a sin he committed. She wants to talk about the story of his she read: a Christian man learns he qualifies as a Jew by law and is carted off to the ghetto, the cattle train, and beyond. He finds salvation and freedom from his bigotry regarding the Jews in his new identity: "by being excluded from one community one does not automatically become a member of another." His future ex-wife is fascinated with the idea that "*one can make a decision concerning one's Jewishness.*" She experiences the same liberated feeling and credits the narrator's writing with teaching her how to live.

He learns then that she was born after Auschwitz but feels that she has always lived with the stigma of being Jewish. Her parents were both at Auschwitz and there her mother contracted an unidentified illness. She died at a relatively young age. Her mother's illness and death drove his ex-wife to become a doctor. After her mother's death, her aunt came to live with her and her father. His future ex-wife avoided all talk about Jewish matters, throwing herself into her school work. On the one occasion that she did voice an opinion, she was shamed into silence by her aunt.

After they are married, they overhear an anti-Semitic sentiment being sung by drunks in the street. The narrator disregards it but his wife is brought to tears, afraid that there will never be an end to the curse of their Jewishness. She wonders what it is that makes her Jewish since she is not religious and knows nothing of the culture. The narrator tells her "the one singular fact that made her a Jew was this and nothing else: that she had *not* been to Auschwitz." Their marriage is already deteriorating at this time. The narrator and his wife talk of a novel he will write about the struggle for happiness. His wife is excited about it, seeing this work as a testament to their marriage. The narrator belatedly understands that it is a mistake to let her get so close to his writing. At the same time, he enjoys her attention. But he has *always had a secret life* and that *has always been the real one*."

One night his wife asks him to father her child. He answers, "No." What if the child did not want to be a Jew? The narrator is content to live out the life he has been dealt but cannot bear the thought that his child would not be content with the same life. He recalls seeing a family board a streetcar in which he was riding, a mother, father, and three girls. The sulky middle child was jealous of the attention her weeping younger sister got from their mother; the eldest tried to comfort her sister but was shaken off; and the father finally quiets the youngest child. The narrator is horrified by their miserable, exhausted faces.

He then clearly states that he will not have a child because he "could never be another person's father, fate, god . . . It should never happen to another child, what happened to me: my childhood." Thus he begins to explain his childhood to his wife. He recalls an old, repeating dream of visiting his grandparents. In the dream, they are weak. He brings them a ham but it is not very big and they are hungry. Death is near for them. The dream dissipates but the narrator has other memories of his grandparents, all of them dark with age, antique.

Then the narrator remembers the boarding school he attended from age five to ten. His father would take him to school every Monday morning. One rainy Monday morning as an adult, he revisited that building and the memories there: the building is derelict, converted to tenements. A plaque has been installed to commemorate his old director, the Diri. At the boarding school the students were all assigned an individual number. The narrator's was 1 because he was the youngest student. He remembers the dining hall meals fondly; he remembers always being hungry. The prayer before meal was carefully scripted to be appropriate for both Jews and Christians. He attended the boarding school following his parents' divorce. The reason they gave him for their divorce was that they "*didn't understand each other*," which was very

confusing to a five-year-old boy: "It was like a death sentence, I had to accept it."

As an adult he recognizes his boarding school as an echo of other institutions. The authority of his director was the result of organized fear and not any kind of earned respect. Even the teachers feared him. The narrator recalls a scandal that occurred one year when a senior student and a new kitchen girl locked themselves in a closet overnight. A teacher known as "Pudge" discovered the student missing and made a very public scene of trying to get him and the girl out of the closet. The senior was expelled which the narrator thinks of as a public castration that all of the other students cooperated with by way of their silent acceptance.

He also remembers the "Saturday *rapports*." The students lined up in front of the faculty, including the Diri, and heard the weekly verdict of their behavior and scholarship. He likens it to divine judgment. Just a few years later, the Diri was sent to the crematorium—which end, he believes, is "the fruit of the successful education I received at his hands, of the *culture* in which he believed and for which he prepared us pedagogically."

His father took over his education at the age of ten. The narrator has long tried in vain to understand his father and their relationship. His father lectured him repeatedly; the narrator knew what he was going to say. He pitied his father, and perhaps loved him, though he does not believe his love was sufficient. His pity led to loneliness because it undermined his father's authority. "Auschwitz . . . struck me later as simply an elaboration of those virtues in which I have been indoctrinated since childhood." He concludes that it all began with his childhood: the breaking of his spirit and his own impulse toward survival. He tells his wife: "Auschwitz . . . appears to me in the image of a father" and "if the observation is that God is an exalted father, then God, too, is revealed to me in the image of Auschwitz."

One night the narrator's wife comes home and tells him that she wants to live and cannot save him from himself or his past and so they must separate. She has found another man, a Gentile. After his marriage and indeed throughout his life, the narrator knows that "my work saved me, albeit it saved me for the sake of destruction."

At the end of the novel, the narrator remembers how, during the years when he visited the resort, he agreed to meet his ex-wife as usual at a café. She arrives with two children, a girl and a boy—her children from her second marriage. The narrator is swept with emotion and offers this conclusion to his book-length mourner's kaddish:

> with the baggage of this life in my raised hands I may go and in the dark stream of the fast-flowing black warmth / I may drown / Lord God / let me drown / forever, / Amen.

Characters

Boy

The boy is the son of the narrator's ex-wife, from her second marriage. He and his sister appear at the end of the novel, and he is described by the narrator as "stubborn . . . [w]ith hard eyes like grayish blue pebbles."

The Diri

The Diri is the director of the boarding school that the narrator attends from age five to ten. He is a short man with a large belly, yellowish-white mustache, and long white hair. His students call him the Plug behind his back. The Diri controls the school with strict authority and fear. He is rarely seen by the students except during the occasional outburst of misbehavior and at Saturday afternoon *rapports*. The Diri is ultimately killed in the Nazi concentration camp gas chambers during the Holocaust.

Ex-Wife

The narrator meets the woman who becomes his wife at a party where she is impressed with his opinions and with his writing. She is ten years younger than he is, and he describes her as "a beautiful Jewess" with shiny, thick hair. Born after Auschwitz, she has only experienced the Holocaust as history. She is very troubled by her Jewishness which she feels was forced upon her since she is not religious and does not take part in Jewish culture. This issue is especially troubling to her because anti-Semitism is still rampant in Europe after the end of World War II.

She and the narrator are lovers first. Even early in their marriage they are happy together, and she hopes to inspire and influence the narrator's writing as well as his own healing from the Holocaust. The narrator realizes belatedly that he and his writing thrive on pain. He does not want to heal and this fact drives the couple apart. She wishes to live and for her that means marriage and children. She meets a Gentile, falls in love, and leaves the narrator for this other man.

The narrator's ex-wife is a dermatologist. She chose to go into medicine after her mother died young from a mysterious and incurable illness that she contracted while at Auschwitz. After the narrator and his wife divorce, they continue to meet in cafés where she writes him prescriptions for drugs that keep him relaxed and happy. This ongoing relationship gives the impression that theirs was not a bitter divorce. At the end of the novel, she brings her children from her second marriage, a girl and a boy, to meet her ex-husband in a café.

Father

The narrator's parents are divorced by the time he is five years old and his mother disappears permanently from his life at that point. He attends a boarding school from age five until he is ten years old. After he turns ten, his father takes over his education. During this time the narrator discovers how different he and his father are and how complicated their relationship is. He does not believe in or accept his father's authority and pities him that he cannot truly exert the authority he assumes he has. The narrator believes that he loves his father but also feels that his love is not sufficient.

Girl

The girl is the daughter of the narrator's ex-wife, from her second marriage. She and her brother appear at the end of the novel and she is described by the narrator as "dark-eyed . . . with pale dots of scattered freckles around her . . . nose."

Narrator

The narrator of *Kaddish for a Child Not Born* is a middle-aged Hungarian Jew who has survived the Holocaust. Survival has cost him a normal life. He is nihilistic (believes life is senseless and useless) and keeps to himself and his writing. His writing is his way of not existing in the real world, of digging the grave that was begun for him in Auschwitz. He cherishes this writing-as-grave-digging as his life work, grim as it is.

Over the course of the novel, he recalls his unhappy childhood: his parents' divorce, and his five years in a boarding school. His father assumes authority over the child traditionally given to adults and parents, but the narrator sees through this facade of power, anticipates his father's lectures, and generally pities the man. His mother is never mentioned.

At fourteen the narrator is sent to Auschwitz and later to Buchenwald concentration camps. A year later, when Buchenwald is liberated by the Allies, he returns to Józsefváros, a district near the heart of Budapest where he grew up. He works as a literary translator and writer but is not an insider to the preferred circles of the Hungarian literature scene. He rents a pre-fab apartment and owns very few possessions, mostly books. He is married for a short time but his wife leaves him after he reveals to her that he will not father a child for her. His childhood and the Holocaust predispose him against having children. The narrator says that he cannot be god to another human being.

Dr. Oblath

Dr. Oblath, a professor of philosophy, stays at the same resort as the narrator, near the Central Mountains. At the beginning of the novel they meet by chance in the woods. The narrator describes him as "a man bursting with inappropriate vitality" with "a face resembling soft dough, kneaded and already risen."

Dr. Oblath regrets that he and his wife do not have children. Dr. Oblath then asks the narrator if he has a child. This seemingly simple question is the catalyst for the stream-of-consciousness monologue (a rambling story that emerges from the natural sequence of thoughts in the narrator) that makes up *Kaddish for a Child Not Born.*

Professor

During the winter he is imprisoned the narrator meets the Professor, a skinny man, starving from inadequate nutrition and suffering from hard labor, on a carriage transport for the sick. The Professor makes sure the narrator, who is ill and lying down, receives his portion rather than keeping it for himself. This small action saves the narrator's life and probably further jeopardizes the Professor's survival. The narrator regards his action as irrational since human nature drives one toward survival, and the Professor's behavior is counter to his own survival. What is even more significant is the Professor's disgust at the narrator's amazement. When he sees the look on the narrator's face, he says "Well, what did you expect . . . ?" For the Professor, civility and compassion are more essential for survival than his body's need for food.

Wife

See Ex-Wife

Themes

Children and Childhood

A central theme of *Kaddish for a Child Not Born* is how childhood experience shapes adult experience. The narrator remembers his childhood as being bleak and unhappy, full of authoritarian personalities. His parents divorced when he was very young and he spent five years in a strict boarding school. As a teenager he experienced the horrors of a concentration camp. Although he survived, he is forever marked by it. He will not and cannot live a "normal" life with children, a wife, and a house full of *things*.

The Western idea of childhood is that it is a time of innocence. The thought of children being killed in the Holocaust is terrible to dwell upon, but their survival in some ways is worse because they are freighted to carry what they have seen and heard with them for the rest of their lives. The personal burden of the Holocaust is heavy but can never be set aside. The narrator's own feelings that his childhood innocence was betrayed—by "*a bald woman in a red gown in front of a mirror*," by the Diri, by his father—make him adamant that he will not willfully bring a child into this world.

His wife leaves him, remarries, and has two children, a girl and a boy. At the end of the novel, he meets these children and is struck with physical manifestation of all that he has feared, dreaded. Overwhelmed, he prays that he will drown.

Religion

Kertész, like his narrator in *Kaddish*, was born to a Jewish family but he is not religious. As is often the case in countries outside the United States, "Jewish" is an ethnicity of which the Jewish religion is one aspect. It is therefore possible and not unusual to be a secular Jew. The Holocaust still had a profound impact on the mentality and spirituality of these secular Jews, as is readily apparent in Kertész's novel. The narrator identifies himself early in the book as secular (in contrast to his religious country relatives), but he frequently refers to God colloquially and even declares once that God is now dead. The narrator immerses himself instead in his writing, relying on that for his salvation.

Despite not being religious, Kertész has structured and named the book after the mourner's kaddish, a Jewish prayer for the dead. This long prayer is recited in a certain tone, without music or any other embellishment. In this novel, the narrator offers up his life as a kaddish for the children he would not have. A kaddish, in more general terms, is a prayer celebrating the greatness of God, of which the mourner's kaddish is by far the most common.

Topics for Further Study

- Research online the lives of three people who survived the Holocaust; pick them randomly. How are their stories similar? How are they different? Did they spend time in a concentration camp? Did they lose loved ones in the Holocaust? What was life like for them after the war? Prepare a presentation about Holocaust survivors, focusing on these three. The websites http://www.yadvashem.org/ and http://www.holocaustsurvivors.org/ may be helpful.

- Kertész could not publish for many years because of state controls on the media. Research the history of banned books in the United States. Why were books banned? Give titles of famous books that have been banned and state the reasons given for their banning. Prepare a report about banned books, focusing on the history behind and content of a specific book.

- Since World War II, people have sought to prevent genocides through international law. But as of 2005 genocide still occurs around the world. Research another time and place where genocide occurred, such as Rwanda (1994) or Yugoslavia (1991–2001). Write a short story from the point of view of someone who lived during the genocide you researched, using the information you gathered.

- Hungarian (or Magyar) cuisine features paprika, sweet peppers, onions, and sour cream, and it can be very spicy. Some dishes known in the United States are adaptations of original Hungarian recipes, such as goulash, paprikash, and strudel. Look up some authentic recipes in cookbooks or online. As a class, have a potluck consisting of different Hungarian dishes and desserts. Alternately, have a Hungarian food night with your family and try out an appetizer, a main dish, and a dessert. Write a short review of how this cuisine compares to what you normally eat.

- Nazi extermination of Jews during World War II is an extreme example of anti-Semitic behavior. Research the ways in which anti-Semitism continues in the early 2000s, especially in the United States. Gather news reports as well as scholarly studies and prepare a visual display about modern anti-Semitism.

Survival

This novel is about the nature of survival, of living through and beyond a horrible experience. It is about the legacy that such survival brings to those who continue to live. The narrator first survived his childhood, an unhappy time that he recalls vividly: five years at the boarding school; being sent to visit religious country relatives; being educated by his father. He learned at the boarding school how to survive institutional authoritarianism, which is not only a matter of physical survival. His childhood, such as it was, ended abruptly when he was sent away to a concentration camp at the age of fifteen. After a year in the camps, he emerged. Ironically, becoming ill may have improved his chances for survival because he was sent to the camp hospital where he received better care than well prisoners received.

The narrator, like Kertész himself, is a survivor of the Holocaust and specifically, Auschwitz, the largest of the Nazi concentration camps. Although he was not and still is not religious, the narrator believes, as a result of the atrocities that were committed during the war, that God is dead. He uses his writing as a kind of religion, a lifestyle, a way to sustain himself after the Holocaust.

He also survived a short-lived marriage, belatedly discovering that he was not suited to happiness (and other people were not suited to unhappiness). As a way of coping with his trauma and loss, he lives a transient life, renting furnished apartments and owning nothing more than books. He fears "the Germans may return at any time." Having known what the Nazis could do, he lives in perpetual fear that they can return and make him suffer all over again.

Writing as a Coping Strategy

The narrator of the story uses writing as a coping strategy after surviving Auschwitz. He reflects upon how he learned over the course of his life that he seeks pain with his writing. Ultimately, he sees his writing as a way of digging his own grave, the one begun for him at the camps. He says, "the pen is my spade." In this way, in writing he appropriates the role of sadistic others who made him suffer and sought to kill him.

Writing also helps him avoid living directly in the real world. Writing insulates him from experience; he faces the page instead of the immediate experience. Although he makes money with his writing, he is not concerned with success because it is an ongoing process of self-examination and this is more important to him than material comforts. Writing is how he continues to survive. Without it he would be lost.

It cannot be ignored that the narrator's writing affects his ex-wife, who is drawn to him after reading a story of his that helps her come to terms with her Jewish identity.

Style

Stream of Consciousness

Kertész uses stream of consciousness to tell the story in his novel. This form requires that the inner thoughts of the speaker, in the order in which they occur naturally to the speaker, form the sequence in which the plot is revealed. This technique permits the narrator of the novel to move from topic to topic as he explores his thoughts, memories, and feelings about his childhood, his imprisonment at Auschwitz, his failed marriage, and his subsequent life and career, without the constraint of chronological order. It permits him to tie together seemingly unrelated topics which are linked meaningfully in his own thoughts. The narrator loops and curves through the past, avoiding an objective timeline of his life, filling in details as events arise in memory.

Stories told in stream of consciousness follow the subjective associations of the character, the way his mind moves from one thought to another. It is appropriate then that *Kaddish for a Child Not Born* has no chapter breaks and is comprised of seventeen long paragraphs. Most action is conveyed indirectly through reflection and memory, and the novel is engaging not because of what happens but because of the way the character remembers and now thinks about what happened.

Irony

The kaddish is a prayer recited over the dead body or at the burial site. Ironically, in this case, Kertész wrote a mourner's kaddish, or prayer, about a child who is not only *not* dead, but was never born and does not exist. The narrator in this novel is mourning something he never had, but he remains committed to not bringing a child into the world.

It is also ironic that the traditional mourner's kaddish itself never mentions death or the dead. The Jewish prayer for the dead is about the greatness of God, which is believed to be a comfort to mourners. Kertész and his narrator are secular Jews so perhaps they are not comforted by this prayer. But it is a prominent text in the Jewish experience of the Holocaust, (known as *Shoah* in Hebrew), because of the 6 million Jews who were killed.

Historical Context

The Holocaust

During World War II, Nazis in Germany sought to create a "pure" race of humans, which they called the Aryan race. The Nazis engaged in systematic extermination of groups of people considered by the Third Reich to be impure, such as Jews, Roman Catholics, gypsies (or Roma), homosexuals, the disabled, and anyone who disagreed with their politics. This extermination of an estimated 11 to 26 million people is called the Holocaust. European Jewry was practically erased, with at least 6 million Jews killed by the end of the war. This catastrophe is called *Shoah* in Hebrew. Anti-Semitism, or hatred of Jewish people, was intensified in Germany before the war by the Nazi propaganda machine, which convinced many people that Jews, along with many others, were the cause of economic depression and other social problems and that they should be removed from society.

Nazi soldiers collected these so-called undesirable people in concentration camps between 1933 and 1945 where they were forced to work and were methodically exterminated. After experimenting

Compare & Contrast

- **1960s:** The Hungarian government, recovering from the Revolution of 1956, enacted policies to engender a more liberal society and a healthier economy.

  Today: Hungary joins the European Union on May 1, 2004.

- **1960s:** Race riots erupt across the United States, including Los Angeles in 1966 and Detroit in 1967.

  Today: Racial tension is still evident in the United States but civil rights of all individuals, regardless of race, ethnicity, religion, or medical condition are protected under the law.

- **1960s:** The Berlin Wall is built in 1961 as the cold war escalates. The wall separates Soviet-occupied East Berlin from West Berlin.

  Today: The cold war ends in 1991 with the dissolution of the U.S.S.R. Relations between the United States and Russia improve in the following decade.

- **1960s:** Almost twenty years after its founding, Israel fights Egypt, Syria, Jordan, and Iraq in the Six-Day War (June 5–10, 1967). During this war, Israel captures several territories, including the West Bank and the Gaza Strip.

  Today: The West Bank, a territory on the Jordan River, and the Gaza Strip, a territory on the coast of the Red Sea, are hotly contested by resident Palestinians who disagree with Israel's occupation of their ancestral land.

---

with different methods of mass extermination, Nazis settled on the gas chamber as the most efficient. Conditions in the camps were harsh. Many died from illness and malnutrition. Those who survived, lived on bereft of many of their friends and family.

Life after the Holocaust was difficult for those who survived. Many lost their faith, committed suicide, or were otherwise unable to resume normal lives. Millions of people were displaced, feeling unwelcome or unable to return to their former homes. Many Jews left Europe and moved to Palestine or elsewhere in the world.

Post-War Hungary

Hungary was occupied by the Soviet army at the end of World War II. Budapest was almost completely destroyed during the seizure and occupation. The Hungarian Communist Party took over the government after it lost the 1945 election. This communist government, headed by prime minister Mátyás Rákosi, saw the execution and imprisonment of tens of thousands of dissidents. Education and literacy programs were expanded to include the poor, but these efforts served as a conduit for communist propaganda. In this environment, people were not free to express themselves, and many artists and writers either left the country or suppressed their work.

The economy and standard of living suffered under communist rule, making this government eventually unpopular. Rákosi was replaced as prime minister in 1953 after Joseph Stalin died. The new prime minister, Imre Nagy, undid a lot of Rákosi's work. Prisoners were released, public debate was encouraged, and the media were freed from state control.

On October 23, 1956, students in Budapest demanded an end to the Soviet occupation. During the next two weeks, protests grew violent, and the Soviets fought to maintain their hold on Hungary. Approximately 20,000 people died during this uprising. Nagy was removed from power and executed two years later. Hungarians were not successful in throwing off Soviet control, and not until the late 1980s did the Hungarian government begin to embrace democratic policies. The Soviets finally agreed to withdraw, and in May 1990 Hungary held its first free election.

Artillery in a street in Budapest, Hungary, during World War II   © Yevgeny Khaldei/Corbis

Critical Overview

Kaddish for a Child Not Born has not received as much critical attention as Imre Kertész's first book, *Fateless*. English-language reviewers generally regard *Kaddish* and Kertész's subsequent novel *Liquidation* (2004) as experimental in form and less accessible. M. Anna Falbo wrote in *Library Journal* just after *Kaddish* was published that Kertész's novel is "rambling but always compelling." She described the author's intent as an "exploration of identity and the will to survive." Three years after publication Robert Murray Davis, writing for *World Literature Today*, described the book as very dense, but he still appreciated the work and recommended reading the slim novel in a single evening. Examination of the author's work increased considerably after the announcement that Kertész was awarded the 2002 Nobel Prize for Literature. But Tim Wilkinson, writing in *The Hungarian Quarterly*, severely criticized the original English translation (Vintage Press released a new translation, retitled *Kaddish for an Unborn Child* by Wilkinson in 2004) as awkward and incomplete. For example, the original translators Christopher C. Wilson and Katharina M. Wilson left out the opening poem, Paul Célan's "Death Fugue"

even though it is referred to throughout the novel. Gary Adelman gave a comprehensive examination of Kertész's writings in the *New England Review*. He pointed out (as have others) that Kertész himself is very jovial and unlike the semi-autobiographical narrator of his novels. Writing for *The New Leader*, Alvin H. Rosenfeld stated that Kertész's work stands out from the body of Holocaust literature as "thoughtful and challenging." John Banville, reviewing *Kaddish* and *Liquidation* for *Nation*, was less praiseworthy, however, commenting that "*Fatelessness* is such a powerful and coolly horrifying work that, for all their fine qualities, its successors may seem hardly more than variations on a theme."

Criticism

Carol Ullmann

Ullmann is a freelance writer and editor. In the following essay, Ullmann explores the theme of survival in Kertész's novel.

Imre Kertész's *Kaddish for a Child Not Born* is a novel about survival after the Holocaust, written by a man who lived through Auschwitz, the worst of the Nazi death camps during World War II. In the novel, the narrator refuses to have children after the war ends, which ruins his short-lived marriage. In contemplating his past, the narrator realizes that he cannot bring a child into a world that could produce an Auschwitz, to do to a child what was done to him.

The survival of children is fundamental to the survival of the species; after all, the human race would not survive if individuals did not reproduce. On a smaller scale, those who live through devastation can be called survivors even if they are too scarred, mentally or physically, to reproduce themselves. These individuals may find other means of leaving a legacy, if only in their stories of struggle. Kertész's narrator survives; he lives through his writing, and his writing—this novel—concerns his survival, his existence. He explains that "if I didn't work I would have to exist, and if I existed, I don't know what I would be forced to do then." The narrator does not want to exist. He writes to escape living.

His survival is not just a matter of emerging from the death camp alive. He feels his unhappy childhood prepared him to face Auschwitz, prepared him for the impulse to survive. "Auschwitz . . . struck me later as simply an elaboration of those virtues in which I have been indoctrinated since childhood." His struggles began as a child when his parents divorced. Their reason for parting ("*We didn't understand each other*") was completely baffling to their son. Moreover, he had no choice about what happened and had to just accept it. After the parents' divorce, the boy was sent to a strict boarding school which taught him how some institutions operate on fear tactics; this schooling was good preparation for his year in the concentration camps. After boarding school, the boy was taken under his father's tutelage. This education proved more difficult to endure than the boarding school since the narrator had to face his complicated relationship with his father. He quickly lost faith in his father's authority and began to pity the man instead. His father seemed like a stunted god. The experience of the boarding school and his education by his father showed him how slight authority could be as well as how the loss of the presence of authority could leave one feeling lonely. Without his father, he had no protection against the wide world. Both the camp and his image of deity took on paternal characteristics: "Auschwitz . . . appears to [him] in the image of a father." Moreover, if the paternal God is

> " A common response to survival of a catastrophe is shame at being the one who lived while others died."

omniscient, then He was also apparent in Auschwitz.

Unlike other Holocaust survivors, the narrator of *Kaddish for a Child Not Born* does not have a crisis of faith: he is not religious and has no faith to lose. He and his immediate family are secular Jews, completely assimilated into the non-Jewish city life of Budapest. But unlike his ex-wife, the narrator does not detest his Jewishness. He cherishes it because it brought him the experience of Auschwitz. It offers some explanation for what happened to him, "*a bald woman in a red gown in front of a mirror.*"

In part, the narrator owes his physical and psychological survival to a character in the novel referred to as the Professor. Through an accidental meeting, the Professor helped and protected the narrator when he had no one else to rely on. The Professor made sure the narrator got his food portion at a time when food was scarce and the narrator was too sick to fend for himself. The Professor's action was irrational from the narrator's point of view because the Professor himself needed the food just as much as the narrator; however, the Professor's actions express his humanity and his compassion. Then, too, the Professor's action was not carefully planned—his response to the narrator's surprise is disgust—he is surprised that the narrator expected him to behave in any other fashion. The Professor's extraordinary kindness leaves the narrator with an "irrational" concept he cannot fully grasp, although his ex-wife is perfectly comfortable with it and considers the Professor's behavior to be normal.

The narrator's ex-wife, who was born after the Holocaust, has a dramatically different outlook on life. She is driven to become a medical doctor after her mother's early death and thereafter dedicates her life to helping others. At the same time, she rejects her Jewish identity because she does not want to carry the stigma that goes with being a Jew in post–World War II Europe. But she is not afraid to bring a child into this world. She is not troubled that she may be subjecting her progeny to the same

What Do I Read Next?

- *Fateless* (1975) by Imre Kertész tells the story of a teenage boy who survives a year at Auschwitz and Buchenwald. This is the most accessible of Kertész's novels.

- *Anne Frank: Diary of a Young Girl* (1947) by Anne Frank is the true story of a Jewish Dutch girl. She was in hiding with her family in Amsterdam during the Nazi occupation. She was given a diary for her thirteenth birthday and in it she recorded the events of her life from June 12, 1942 until August 1, 1944. Her family was eventually betrayed and sent to concentration camps. Her father was the only one to survive, and when he returned to Amsterdam and found her diary, he worked hard to have it published.

- *Night* (1958) by Elie Wiesel is a semi-autobiographical novel about the author's experiences at Birkenau, Auschwitz, and Buchenwald. Like Kertész's character in *Fateless*, Wiesel's narrator is only a teenager; however, unlike Kertész's character, Wiesel's is religious and must struggle to reconcile his faith with the realities of the Holocaust.

- *Selected Poems and Prose of Paul Célan* (2001) by Paul Célan and translated by John Felstiner offers a selection of this Holocaust survivor's prolific work. Célan was profoundly shaped by his Holocaust experience and the loss of his parents. His poem "Death Fugue" about Auschwitz is quoted at the beginning of *Kaddish for an Unborn Child* (2004), in the newest translation as well as in the original Hungarian edition.

- *"A Problem from Hell": America and the Age of Genocide* (2003) by Samantha Power is about the three years, 1993–1996, that Power spent in Bosnia and Srebrenica, observing the war and genocide. She learned while she was there that the U.S. leadership has a history of not intervening when genocide is being carried out and she argues for this policy to change in order to save lives.

---

pain and prejudice she has experienced. Of course it would be unreasonable to assume that anyone could live without a little anguish. Does survival through suffering make life sweeter? It does not appear so from the narrator's perspective.

The narrator feels no elation, no triumph at having survived the Holocaust. To him, Auschwitz was inevitable, a grotesque expression of human hatred that was a long time in coming. It was a place where god-like powers over life and death were exerted over believer and unbeliever alike. The horrible assault of the Holocaust on the human psyche was such that many people lost their faith, unable to believe in a God who would let such terrible things happen. Kertész has been known to express his gratitude for experiencing Auschwitz. Stefan Theil, interviewing Kertész for *Newsweek International*, expressed his surprise and Kertész responded:

> I experienced my most radical moments of happiness in the concentration camp. You cannot imagine what

it's like to be allowed to lie in the camp's hospital, or to have a 10-minute break from indescribable labor. To be very close to death is also a kind of happiness. Just surviving becomes the greatest freedom of all.

A common response to survival of a catastrophe is shame at being the one who lived while others died. There is often no satisfying explanation for why one person was stronger or luckier. The narrator of *Kaddish for a Child Not Born* expresses this feeling: "I am as much or as little an accomplice to my staying alive as I was to my birth. All right, I admit, there is a tiny bit more shame in staying alive." He strives through his writing to be worthy of life.

What is perhaps most interesting about the narrator's feelings in *Kaddish for a Child Not Born* concerning his survival of the Holocaust is that those feeling change drastically through the course of Kertész's four novels. In his first novel, *Fateless* (1975) the teenaged narrator "emerges from the camps with a mental clarity that promises a successful rehabilitation," as Gary Adelman observes in his very readable essay about Kertész's novels published in the *New England Review*. In the second book *Fiasco* (1988), the narrator is a little older and embittered by the cold, silent reception of his book about surviving Auschwitz. By the third novel, his bitterness has blossomed into a lifetime of disappointment, isolation, and neuroses. The narrator's clarity and chance for recovery have transformed completely into nihilism. In Kertész's fourth book, *Liquidation* (2003), the narrator has committed suicide and a friend of his looks back on the man's life while he is finally settling the writer's estate.

A once bright young man, the narrator survives terrible catastrophe only to live a half-life for the remainder of his days. He *is* a survivor, if only because he has not (yet) succumbed to suicide; he has not done the work for his tormentors. Although he does not choose to live a conventional life with wife and children, grandchildren, houses and furniture, he has dedicated himself to the arduous task of examining the meaning of his life and therefore his survival. He has given generations the gift of his writing, which, like a child, lives beyond its maker. Unlike a child, his writing attests to his survival long after he dies and perhaps help others come to terms with their own endurance in cataclysmic times.

Source: Carol Ullmann, Critical Essay on *Kaddish for a Child Not Born*, in *Novels for Students*, Thomson Gale, 2006.

Ivan Sanders

In the following essay, Sanders explores why Kertész was not a well-known writer in Hungary until he won the Nobel Prize.

To non-Hungarians or non-East Europeans, the title of this essay may seem odd. Why the emphasis on Imre Kertész's Hungarianness? Isn't it natural, self-evident, that someone who has won the ultimate literary prize as a Hungarian writer should have a Hungarian identity? In reality the situation is more complicated. When the announcement was made in Stockholm that the Hungarian Imre Kertész won the Nobel Prize in literature, the general response was: Who is this man? The question was not at all unreasonable. In the U.S. only two of his books had been published, in small editions by a rather obscure university press. What is much more strange and ironic is that the same question was asked by many people in

> **It should be stressed that Kertész's preoccupation with Hungary's "Jewish question" makes many Hungarians uncomfortable on the left as well as the right."**

Hungary, too, upon receiving the news. Though not a complete unknown, Imre Kertész, until October 10, 2002, the day his Prize was announced, was not exactly a household word either, in spite of the fact that he was 74 years old at the time and his literary career began decades ago. A number of reasons have been offered by Hungarian critics and writers for this lack of familiarity in a country that otherwise prides itself in being a nation of readers and book lovers, and where—despite, or because of, the vicissitudes of history—literature, indeed the written word, has a very special place in the culture.

One explanation given is Kertész's subject matter. In almost all of his works Kertész is preoccupied, some would say obsessed, with the Holocaust, as a historical event, as the defining experience of his life, and as a defining moment in European culture. It is argued that since the Hungarian people have never come to terms with their own role in the deportation of hundreds of thousands of their fellow citizens, they weren't too receptive to works that thirty, forty, fifty years after the fact still insist on the primacy of the event in modern European history, indeed in the history of modernity.

Actually, plenty of books about the Holocaust have been published in Hungary—reminiscences, memoirs, fiction—in the immediate postwar years and again in the sixties and seventies. There was no shortage of "*lager* literature," as the genre was then called. Generally speaking, these books could also be classified as anti-Fascist literature. And as such, they were praised and popularized during the Communist era. The problem with Imre Kertész's first and best-known novel, *Sorstalanság* (*Fateless*), was that it didn't fit into this category. When first published in Hungary in 1975, after a long wrangle with a state publisher, it was greeted with puzzlement, incomprehension, indifference. The reception can be compared to the way Tadeusz Borowski's Auschwitz stories were received in postwar Poland—stories which in spirit, if not in execution, are the closest thing we have to a novel like *Fateless.* In Poland there was even hostility and indignation when the stories, published later in English under the title *This Way For the Gas, Ladies and Gentlemen,* first appeared. Borowski was accused of amorality, nihilism and decadence. According to Czeslaw Milosz, Communist critics and ideologues had a clear idea of how a writer about the concentration camp should have proceeded: "1) the prisoners should have banded together in secret organizations; 2) the leaders in these organizations should have been Communists; 3) all the Russian prisoners appearing on the pages of the book should have distinguished themselves by their moral strength and heroic behavior; 4) the prisoners should have been differentiated according to their political outlook." In many examples of anti-Fascist literature, this is just what happens.

The hero of Kertész's second important novel, *A kudarc* (Fiasco) is a middle-aged novelist whose narrative about a young boy's experiences in Auschwitz and other concentration camps was returned by the publisher, its style, its approach to an otherwise "horrifying and stirring" subject having been judged odd, inappropriate, offensive even. This part of the novel clearly reflects Kertész's own difficulties in getting *Fateless* published in the Hungary of the 1970's. What Hungarian publishers at the time didn't like was that György Köves, the fourteen-year-old hero of Kertész's novel, throughout his ordeal assumes nothing. He doesn't anticipate, judge or rebel. In anti-Fascist literature, of course, this doesn't happen. The boy's compliance and passivity was then seen by many as shocking evidence of a victim's self-denigration, his identification with the aggressor's view of him. Only years later did readers and critics realize, after revisiting the novel following the fall of communism, that what they boy discovers for himself in the camps is the "banality of evil," to use Hanna Arendt's famous phrase, and his "normal" reaction to the process of dehumanization is a confirmation of this banality. Imre Kertész and his hero reject humanist clichés; they are past humanism, even past Borowski, the "disappointed lover" of humanism. "Imre Kertész's basilisk eyes see that the model of our world is the concentration camp," wrote a Hungarian commentator in an appreciation of Kertész's achievement.

Another reason given for Kertész's relative obscurity even in his own country is that in terms of form and style he writes rather traditional narratives, whereas his better-known contemporaries, Péter Nádas and Péter Esterházy, have produced linguistically more innovative, structurally unconventional postmodern fiction. For example, a recent survey of contemporary Hungarian literature by Ernö Kulcsár Szabó, who was among the first literary historians in Hungary to introduce and apply the new critical vocabulary in the early 90's, doesn't even mention Kertész in his book, implying that he is not part of the canon. In reality, a great deal can be said and, surely, a great deal will be said and written about Kertész's literary language as an apt vehicle for his ideas.

Fateless conveys entirely convincingly the point of view and sensibility of its "innocent" first-person narrator, although the language used is clearly not that of a fourteen-year-old—it's far too precise and fastidious and subtly ironic for that. Yet, remarkably enough, this language does not seem jarring.

The third and most sensitive reason offered to explain why Imre Kertész was not usually thought of as a writer of the first rank in Hungary is that he is of Jewish origin. For many in Hungary, and not only on the extreme right, it is surely a bittersweet vindication, a great irony, that when the Swedish Academy for the first time since the Prize in Literature was instituted decides to bestow the Nobel on a Hungarian writer, he should be a Jew. Never mind that this writer writes only in Hungarian, that he has lived all his life in Hungary and that his subject matter, too, is Hungarian—the Holocaust as experienced by someone born, raised, acculturated in Hungary. Gáspár Miklós Tamás, a brilliant if erratic essayist, philosopher, political commentator, gave this provocative title to his homage to Kertész in a Hungarian daily: "Nobel Prize Won by Hungarian Writer Imre Kertész, a Jew." Someone on the far right sanctimoniously attacked him for this, calling him a Nazi and a racist. Let it be said that one can almost sympathize with the Hungarian right's frustration over the fact that when liberals say something that is, shall we say, politically incorrect, it is all right, but when they do it, it's anti-Semitism. The fact is that Hungary is such a small country, its culture and intelligentsia so inbred, that everyone keeps track of who is who and what. It so happens that three out of four Hungarian writers, whose books are regularly translated and who have an international reputation, are Jewish born, and the fourth, Péter Esterházy, is the scion of the most famous Hungarian aristocratic families. Not exactly a representative sample of the Hungarian population. The normal response—the only response—to this fact has to be: So what? The obsession with origins is, as we all know, unhealthy, dangerous, counterproductive and, in the final analysis, irrelevant. István Csurka, the leader of the far right Hungarian Truth and Life Party, and a writer himself, published in his newspaper a list of writers featured at the Frankfurt Book Fair in 1999 (Hungarian literature was the focal point of the Fair that year), and he italicized the names of all the writers and translators who to him were not truly Hungarian, in most cases because they were Jewish. There were quite a few italicized names on that list. Writers and intellectuals in European capitals were appalled. This didn't stop a columnist of the same newspaper from referring to the now Nobel laureate Imre Kertész as "a writer living in Hungary," and another from ending his article with the following sentence: "I can't wait to see who will be the first Hungarian writer to win the Nobel Prize."

Of course in Kertész's case, his Jewishness—if only because of the subject matter of his novels and the way he treats that subject—is not irrelevant. And his Nobel Prize *is* a challenge to Hungarian society and culture. It forces them to rethink certain values, standards, rankings; it forces literary historians to reconsider the Hungarian literary canon. It is a big job. Or as the previously mentioned G. M. Tamás put it in his tribute to Kertész: "it is a painful, onerous duty, toilsome work, a rude awakening. Yet it's wonderful that Imre Kertész has won the Nobel Prize. We can be happy, we can be ashamed—Hungary is incomprehensible, fantastic, baffling, an enigma! If Imre Kertész lives and writes, then perhaps we, too, can live. For us it's easier."

It should be stressed that Kertész's preoccupation with Hungary's "Jewish question" makes many Hungarians uncomfortable on the left as well as the right. Moderately conservative intellectuals are right to point out that leftist liberals, former Communists—before the announcement from Stockholm—had not been quick to embrace him and his work. When it came to Holocaust literature, many leftists, including Jewish leftists of course, took their cue from Georg Lukács and held up the Spanish-French writer Jorge Semprun as their example, citing a line spoken by one of the characters in his novel, *Le grande voyage:* "I don't want to die a Jewish death."

It should also be stressed that Kertész's attitude toward his own Jewishness is complex and problematic. In a recent essay he has this to say about the subject:

> If I say I am a Jewish writer, I don't necessarily mean that I myself am Jewish for what kind of a Jew is one who did not have a religious upbringing, speaks no Hebrew, is not very familiar with the basic texts of Jewish culture, and live not in Israel but in Europe? What I can say about myself, however, is that I am a chronicler of an anachronistic condition, that of the assimilated Jew, the bearer and recorder of this condition, and a harbinger of its inevitable demise. In this respect, the *Endlösung* has a crucial role: no one whose Jewish identity is based primarily, perhaps exclusively, on Auschwitz can really be called a Jew. He is Isaac Deutscher's "non-Jewish Jew," the rootless European variety, who cannot develop a normal relationship with a Jewish condition that has been forced upon him. He has a role to play, perhaps an important one, in European culture (if there is still such a thing), but he can have no part whatsoever in post-Auschwitz Jewish history or in the Jewish revival (if there is, or will be, such a thing, I must again add).

"I am one who is persecuted as a Jew, but I am not a Jew," Kertész wrote in his diary as recently as the early 1990s.

There are those in Hungary, mostly politicians and journalists on the right not well disposed toward Kertész, who keep reminding their audiences that it was the Germans who had been pushing Kertész's candidacy for the prize. There is no doubt that Germany is the country where Imre Kertész has the largest readership, and where critics have responded to his books most perceptively and sensitively. It has been suggested, cynically perhaps, that the reason why *Fateless* made such a deep impression on German readers is that here is one Holocaust novel that is not concerned with German culpability—here German officers are not portrayed as monsters; they are not any better or worse than other characters in the book. Kertész's aim in the novel was to depict a concentration camp universe, one that had engulfed all of Europe. So, in a sense, present-day Germans could be relieved of their guilt when reading the book. (Some feel that, more recently, praise was heaped on Roman Polanski's film *The Pianist,* especially in Europe, for similar reasons. As Michael Oren put it in *The New Republic,* *The Pianist* "conflates the Jew's identity as victim with the Jew's role as savior; [it] reduces Europe's guilt to a specific evil and purifies it. Here, at last, is the film Europe has been waiting for: the one that gets it off the hook.") As for Kertész, he doesn't exonerate anyone; and his conclusion about the meaning of Auschwitz is more devastating than that of many other artists. In his Nobel lecture he made it clear that

> I have never tried to see the complex of problems referred to as the Holocaust merely as the insolvable conflict between Germans and Jews. I never believed that it was the latest chapter in the history of Jewish suffering, which followed logically from their earlier trials and tribulations. I never saw it as a one-time aberration, a large-scale pogrom, a precondition for the creation of Israel. What I discovered in Auschwitz is the human condition, the end point of a great adventure, where the European traveler arrived after his two-thousand-year-old moral and cultural history.... The real problem with Auschwitz is that it happened, and this cannot be altered—not with the best, or worst, will in the world. This gravest of situations was characterized most accurately by the Hungarian Catholic poet János Pilinszky when he called it a "scandal." What he meant by it, clearly, is that Auschwitz occurred in a Christian cultural environment, so for those with a metaphysical turn of mind it can never be overcome.

This last thought, in the interpretation of the extreme right in Hungary, means that Christianity brought about the Holocaust.

Many in Hungary expected, or hoped, that (though he certainly wasn't their candidate for it) once Kertész was awarded the Nobel Prize, he would behave like a good Hungarian, an ambassador of goodwill, and sing the praises of his native country wherever he went. But Imre Kertész, though he stated a number of times, that his prize was a recognition of the achievements of Hungarian literature and a tribute to the Hungarian language, did not and does not see himself as a cultural ambassador, and is unwilling to assume a public role that would inhibit him in any way and keep him from voicing his opinion. So in interviews and public statements he did say there was open anti-Semitism in Hungary, reminiscent in some ways of the 1930s—though he also made it clear that he was referring to the extreme right, to István Csurka's party and his publication, the coarseness and hatefulness of whose tone, the incendiary nature of whose rhetoric, he added, cannot be compared to the tenor of the West European populist right, or of the moderately conservative camp in Hungary. But such public statements by the new Nobel laureate—in the foreign media yet—were deemed unforgivable. More than ever Kertész was branded un-Hungarian, a hater of all things Hungarian, and his work as an alien phenomenon in Hungarian culture.

In a way, the right has a hard time with Kertész. Even before his Nobel, they couldn't dismiss or discredit him, as they do other city-bred, urban writers, as a left-leaning cosmopolite, for Kertész is second to none in his abhorrence of Communism. The tormented hero of his novel *Kaddish for a Child Not Born* is an Auschwitz survivor who in postwar Hungary, in the new political order, feels even more alienated. The ugliness of the housing project where he lives—the concrete slab of a building protrudes from an old Budapest neighborhood like an "oversized false limb"—becomes emblematic of the ugliness of "existing socialism." Indeed, Kertész sees his own unhappy life journey as one taking him from one totalitarian system to another.

> Socialism for me was the *petite madeleine* that, dipped into Proust's tea, evoked in him the flavor of bygone years. For reasons having to do with the language I spoke, I decided, after the suppression of the 1956 revolt, to remain in Hungary. Thus I was able to observe, not as a child this time but as an adult, how a dictatorship functions. I saw how an entire nation could be made to deny its ideals, and watched the early, cautious moves toward accommodation. I understood that hope is an instrument of evil, and the Kantian categorical imperative—ethics in general—is but the pliable handmaiden of self-preservation.

Elsewhere he talks about how during the darkest years of Stalinism he, along with many other fellow citizens, was intent on survival and, ironically, didn't have the luxury, the freedom, to succumb to despair, as did fellow writers and Auschwitz survivors in he West, some of whom—Primo Levi, Paul Celan, Jean Amery—ultimately took their own lives. And about the conditions under which he wrote *Fateless* Kertész has said: "The nausea and depression to which I awoke each morning [in the sixties] led me at once into the world I intended to describe. I had to discover that I had placed a man groaning under the logic of one type of totalitarianism in another totalitarian system."

Under communism Imre Kertész held himself aloof from public life; he published little, wasn't an active presence on the Hungarian literary scene, and really came into his own only after the fall of communism. Yet a writer for the moderately conservative journal *Heti Válasz* (Weekly Response) has recently taken him to task for not raising his voice against the atrocities committed by the Communists in the 1950s, while expecting Hungarians to do serious soul-searching about their country's role in the catastrophe of the Hungarian Jews in the forties. It is true that Kertész wasn't a dissident intellectual openly opposed to the Kádár regime. But chances are, his acts would be belittled today even if he were. Just as the acts of former dissidents and members of the democratic opposition are belittled by many Hungarians on the right. Since many of those dissidents came from leftist homes and are of Jewish origin, they are seen today by rightists as not such great heroes, but as people who—arrests and harassments notwithstanding—were tolerated by the regime as gadflies simply because—and this is always implied or at least insinuated—they remained close to those in power. These are the necessary distortions of nationalists who find it difficult to accept that "rootless cosmopolites" openly defied the Communist dictatorships, while they, the "true Hungarians," lay low or blended into the silent majority.

There is no question that Imre Kertész is an assimilated Hungarian Jew who is ambivalent about his Hungarian identity. Unlike many of his contemporaries, he decided not to leave Hungary in 1956 "for reasons having to do with the language I spoke." He knew already then that he wanted to be a writer and felt he was too old (he was 26) to change languages. It is also true—as indicated earlier—that Kertész is equally ambivalent about his Jewishness. He has grappled with his "Jewish problem" all his life, and it emerges powerfully in his autobiographically inspired fiction. For example, the hero of *Kaddish* recalls a childhood visit to religious relatives in the country.

> Yes, there it was that I lived among Jews for the first time, real genuine Jews, I mean, not Jews like we were—city Jews, Budapest Jews, that is to say, not Jews at all, but of course not Christians either; we were the kind of non-Jewish Jews who still observe the holy days, long fasts, or at least, definitely, until lunch. No, indeed the village relatives (I no longer remember how we were related, why should I, anyway, they have dug their graves a long, long time ago in the air where the smoke from their remains dissipated), *they* were real Jews: prayer in the morning, prayer in the evening, prayer before food, prayer on the wine . . . other than that, they were fine people, though unbearably boring for a little boy from Budapest.

And George Köves, the hero of *Fateless* and Kertész's alter-ego, realizes in the camps that he has nothing in common with fellow Jews, especially the religious, for whom he is no Jew because he speaks not a word of Yiddish, while feeling odd about his Hungarian identity, too, since Hungarians do not want him either. *Fateless* may be seen as an existentialist novel in which an absurd universe appears in the guise of a totalitarian system that strips one of his self and imposes a role, a fate. "Why can't you see that if there is such a thing as fate, then there is no freedom," the boy tells a journalist after his return

from the camps. "If, on the other hand . . . there is freedom, then there is no fate."

The narrator of *Kaddish for a Child Not Born* remembers his father and the director of the boarding school where he was sent after his parents' divorce as stern and tyrannical authority figures. Indeed, he sees the tyrannies of the modern world, authoritarian rules that led to Auschwitz, in terms of forbidding fathers. "The two terms Auschwitz and father resonate the same echoes in me," he says. He refers repeatedly to another childhood memory. He visited observant relatives in the country. One morning he accidentally opened the bedroom door and saw not his sheitel-wearing aunt but "a bald woman in a red gown in front of a mirror." He was shocked, appalled, and the image stayed with him—in the narrative it becomes a potent, many-layered symbol of Jewish vulnerability and shame.

Kaddish is one long howl of negation, but as in Kertész's other novels of despair something strange, almost incomprehensible, happens that negates the negation. The narrator remembers a fellow inmate in Auschwitz, a "skeleton" everybody called Professor, who one day, upon seeing how very weak the narrator was, gave him his ration, though by doing this he lessened his own chances of survival. Under the circumstances, the narrator says, this act made no sense whatsoever. At the end of his recitation, the man without hope wants to be swept away by the "filthy flow of memories," he wants to drown in their "black warmth"—yet he lives on.

In his Nobel lecture, this is what Kertész said about his own family:

> I was born in Budapest, in a Jewish family, whose maternal branch hailed from the Transylvanian city of Kolozsvár (Cluj) and the paternal side from the southwestern corner of the Lake Balaton region. My grandparents still lit the Sabbath candles every Friday night, but they changed their name to a Hungarian one, and it was natural for them to consider Judaism their religion and Hungary their homeland. My maternal grandparents perished in the Holocaust; my paternal grandparents' lives were destroyed by Mátyás Rákosi's Communist rule, when Budapest's Jewish old age home was relocated to the northern border region of the country.

Curiously enough, he says nothing about his parents in this brief family history. In light of his novels (which, we must remember, are novels and not memoirs; novels which nevertheless turn the material of his life into serious fiction)—in light of his fiction, then, the omission is not that surprising. Kertész did have a difficult pre-Auschwitz childhood, a difficult relationship with his parents, who, like George Köves's parents, were divorced. It is interesting to note that in the works of a number of Hungarian Jewish writers (George Konrád, Péter Nádas, István Vas, György Moldova and others), in novels and memoirs, the young narrators, who are also frequently the authors' alter egos, are for one reason or another disappointed in, or estranged from, their own assimilated, more or less deracinated, alienated or absent fathers, and turn for love and attention to their traditionalist Jewish grandfathers and grandmothers, and are fascinated and strengthened by their unswerving faith.

It may be said that Imre Kertész writes grim novels, yet the grimness is tempered by satire and irony. Behind a prose that often seems self-consciously formal and mannered, there are glimmers of subtle humor. Kertész does believe that evil can be confronted with a smile, even a grin. Significantly enough, while he considers Steven Spielberg's *Schindler's List* cinematic kitsch, he has found Roberto Benigni's *Life Is Beautiful* a Holocaust parable after his own heart.

In spite of his life experiences, Imre Kertész has remained in his daily life a warm, affable, unpretentious man, with the grace and wit of a Central European intellectual, and the wry, bracing, irreverent sense of humor of a denizen of Budapest. He is of that milieu and his mental habits reflects that milieu. And best of all, even as a famous writer, and now a Nobel laureate, he doesn't take himself too seriously. When reminded in an interview that his works until now had not been part of the Hungarian literary canon and weren't required reading in secondary schools, Kertész replied that he hoped that they wouldn't be required readings in the future either, because he remembered that as a schoolboy there was nothing he hated more than having to write a school essay on a book he'd read, even if he liked the book very much. And when asked to comment on the controversy surrounding the building of a Holocaust memorial in Berlin, and the possibility of a similar controversy in Hungary, Kertész said he doesn't believe in a forced consensus on issues on which there is very little agreement. And to illustrate, he recounted an anecdote from the 60s—the Communist era, that is. It would not be inappropriate to conclude by repeating this anecdote, if only to suggest that Kertész is, in an important sense, heir to a tradition of Eastern European Jewish humor, a particularly and characteristically Hungarian variety. According to the anecdote, Mr. Gruen—the proverbial Mr. Gruen of Budapest jokes—goes over to a uniformed young man standing next to a monument to Soviet heroes

and asks him why he was posted there. "I must make sure that the monument is not vandalized or desecrated," the young man says. "For example, I have to stop anyone from, say, urinating on the statue." "What an idea," says Gruen, "who would want to urinate on a monument to Soviet heroes?" "I would," replies the guard, "if I weren't on duty."

Source: Ivan Sanders, "The Hungarian Identity of Nobel-Laureate Imre Kertész," in *The Treatment of the Holocaust in Hungary and Romania During the Post-Communist Era*, edited by Randolph L. Braham, The Rosenthal Institute for Holocaust Studies, 2004, pp. 189–200.

Péter Nádas

In the following essay, Nádas describes the weight of Auschwitz and the Holocaust and how it overshadows literary contemplation of Kertész's work.

Imre Kertész's literary work, for the greater part, has always been obscured by his subject, and it will take a goodly lapse of time yet for that not to obscure it. The monstrous attempt at the total disfranchisement, dispossession and destruction of European Jewry is not the sort of story or subject that can be dealt with on a Tuesday and set aside on the Wednesday. The statute of limitations does not apply. It cannot be refashioned in hindsight, in line with the wishes of family histories, so as to be forgotten, along with other historical crimes regarded as pardonable. The collective attempt at the total disfranchisement, organised dispossession and systematic destruction of European Jewry was a consequence of the conscious intellectual efforts and coordinated mental conditioning of several European generations. Not even remotely can it be considered an operational hitch of either European or Hungarian history. There is no absolution for it, ecclesiastic or secular, nor will there be. And even if someone does not bear personal responsibility in this connection, that is not to say that he does not bear an enduring historical responsibility.

Over the past fifty-eight years, the reality of Auschwitz has become a universal touchstone for an ethical approach, for political thinking, and for legislation. It cannot be avoided even by nationalists and fascists, those who would have the greatest interest in doing so. They are obliged to dissociate themselves from the very thing they would wish to do all over again. Ethnic cleansing, mass murder and genocide no longer figure amongst legitimate national fantasies. The historical experience of Auschwitz acts as a high threshold against which every one of us, every day of the week, can individually measure off the degree and efficacy of his

Survivors of Nazi concentration camp, Dachau, Germany AP/Wide World Photos

own personal ignorance, or the trustworthiness of his own good faith. Anyone not contemplating Auschwitz cannot contemplate God. No one can contemplate the human dragon's brood and leave out Auschwitz. Neither state institutions nor churches, neither families nor private individuals may step over this high threshold of the collective conscious. Neither those born yesterday, nor those born today.

They may, at best, not intentionally step over into the adjoining room. Even then, however, they must reckon with the consequences of their isolation.

Without Auschwitz the human image limned by European culture cannot be drawn. We see it in the Mona Lisa's coolly ethereal smile; its corpses stick out from beneath the Isenheim Altar. God is not dead. But masks, make-up, painted images, finery and shrouds are no longer of assistance to man. The several millennia-old divine image of self-veneration and self-pity really and truly vanished definitively in the corpse-burning pits of Majdanek and Sobibor, the ovens of Auschwitz and Ravensbrück, and in the goods yards of Szeged, Nyíregyháza, Debrecen, Miskolc, Pécs, Zalaegerszeg and Mohács. Christianity does not have some other, more ideal reality, a history that is separable from Auschwitz. There can no longer be a Christian theology without Auschwitz.

Oddly, Imre Kertész's literary work is obscured not only by his subject, but that enormous subject also obscures what might be called his more intimate subjects.

His subjects are internested like some ghastly Chinese puzzle.

He recognised Auschwitz as the most profound, essential reality of European culture by looking back from the continuity of dictatorships to the one and only, beautiful Auschwitz of his own childhood. It is the great structural insight of his literary work that Auschwitz cannot be seen when viewed from Auschwitz, but from the standpoint of the continuity of dictatorships it can be looked back on as if it were a treasured memory. In a dictatorship every content of consciousness is distorted from the start. It is a painful insight to see continuity where others wish, at best, to see only a short-circuit in civilisation, the inexplicable workings of evil, or a product of chance. This conception of historical reality, of the human endowment and condition, permits no sentimental illusions either in looking back or in looking ahead to the future. Neither has it any reference with the aid of which one might place a comforting equals sign between Red and Brown dictatorships and, ala Ernst Nolte, excuse the criminal acts of one with the criminal acts of the other. What has

> " Oddly, Imre Kertész's literary work is obscured not only by his subject, but that enormous subject also obscures what might be called his more intimate subjects."

happened today can also happen tomorrow. In the pause for thought whilst the execution squad reloads, Kertész identifies the connection, designates the points of intersection of dictatorships. He makes it clear how the Chinese puzzles of European history and human nature nest within one another.

This language, this culture, this state of order—none of this is accidental or arbitrary.

Just one—albeit indisputably a substantial—part of Imre Kertész's literary work that is obscured by his subjects is comprised of philosophical analysis. That might, in principle, have been carried out in any of the world's languages.

It is intriguing nevertheless that he has chosen to carry it out in the material of a language whose concepts have barely been scratched hitherto by any spadework of philosophical scrutiny. In a language which, at best, recognises the philosophical interpretations of other languages, but has no self-sufficient philosophy of its own. In his literary language Kertész has turned this drawback, a near-general absence of analysed and fixed conceptual substance, into an advantage. He has fashioned the surfaces of a dispassionate way of viewing things from the material of the Hungarian language. In hindsight, it can now be seen that the malleable sentence structure of Hungarian gives the language the ability to adopt a dispassionate view. In the pause of a feeling charged by two commonplaces, with a barely flinching gaze, Kertész's sentences take note of painful reality. He has thereby created a new quality for the Hungarian language's sense of reality.

Source: Péter Nádas, "Imre Kertész's Work and His Subject," in *Hungarian Quarterly*, Vol. 43, No. 168, Winter 2002.

Tim Wilkinson

In the following review, Wilkinson analyzes the 1997 American translation of Kaddish for a Child Not Born, *finding omissions by the translators and numerous problems with the translated text.*

Translating is so very much a matter of individual choices and style that it is hard to comment on another's work without appearing to nit-pick. The style Imre Kertész adopts in *Kaddish for the Unborn Child* depends crucially for its effect on its weaving together of a densely poetic web of allusions and associations. It is very clearly constructed as a stream-of-consciousness text that runs together numerous strands of memory, of both personal and wider cultural significance, in setting out the reasons why the narrator chooses not to father a child. Sustaining that delicate web in the target language (English) must be a prime task for any translator who hopes to pass on an idea of its magic in the Hungarian. Even quite small disruptions or distortions are jarring. The problems with the American translation, for me, start with the title: *Kaddish for a Child Not Born* (Nortwestern University Press, 1997) sounds and is awkward, a signal of more awkwardnesses (and worse) to come. Besides the lumpy prose, the text is so riddled with errors that one is forced to conclude that the translators were unequipped for the task—a sadly all too common event with the miserably few Hungarian works that get published in the UK or America (a long-running average of one or two titles per year).

For some inexplicable reason, the quotation from Paul Celan's 'Death Fugue' used as a motto at the front of the Hungarian text is omitted. This is not a trivial slip, as the whole poem is the direct source of some of the most striking imagery in the text (the page references are to the American edition): not just what is in the epigraph— ". . .more darkly now stroke your strings then as smoke you will rise into air / then a grave you will have in the clouds there one lies unconfined" (p.16), but also lines such as "he whistles his Jews out, in earth has them dig for a grave" (reference omitted on p. 20, 27, 66); "death is a Master from Germany his eyes are blue / he strikes you with leaden bullets his aim is true" (lamely rendered, on p. 45, as "Death is a blue-eyed German maistro and magister, he may come at any time, wherever he may find you, he'll take aim and he never misses"); "your golden hair Margarete / your ashen hair Shulamith" (p. 57). Kertész himself has remarked that "the Paul Celan motto was only added to *Kaddish* at a later stage, when I noticed that my sentences were quite involuntarily following the poem's rhythm of thought. Earlier on I had often read the text in the original German, because it is virtually untranslatable, and then I found that the images and metaphors of my own text were returning, time and time again, to Celan's Fugue."

That is not the only puzzling omission, incidentally. At the very least, the translators seem to be bul[c]mics of sorts, as well as having no comprehension of what air-raid precautions might be, for on page 16 we get: "No, indeed, the village relatives (I no longer remember how we were related, why should I, anyway, they have dug their graves a long, long time ago in the air where the smoke from their remains dissipated), they were real Jews: prayer in the morning, prayer in the evening, prayer before food, prayer with the wine . . . other than that, they were fine people, though unbearably boring, of course, for a little boy from Budapest. I believe the war had already started then, but as everything was still quiet and beautiful here, we merely practised darkening the windows; . . ." (Try: ". . . no, the 'auntie' and 'uncle' (I no longer recall exactly how we were related, but then why would I recall, they long ago dug their graves in the air into which they were sent up in smoke) were real Jews, with prayers in the morning, prayers in the evening, prayers before meals, prayers over the wine, but otherwise decent people, even if unbearably dull, of course, for a young boy from Pest, their food dripping with grease, goose, cholent, and suety raisin slices of flódni. I think war had already broken out, but everything was still nice and quiet here in our country, they were still only conducting blackout drills, . . ."). More food aversion on pages 20–21: "I don't want to remember, in this respect, not even in the sense of the famous *. . .* dipping ladyfingers into premixed spiced tea instead of the famous *. . .*. Although, of course, I do want to remember . . ." What the hell is that supposed to mean? Someone freaking out? You might be forgiven for not noticing that this is a straightforward reference to Proust, because the actual Hungarian text runs more like: ". . . I don't want to remember, to dunk ladyfingers, as it were, in my cup of Garzon scented tea-bag mixture, instead of the madeleine cakes that are unknown, even as unobtainable articles, in this benighted part of the world, though of course I want to remember . . ."

The Shulamith referred to above is misprinted as "Julamith," by the way. Nor does "a stardust melody" (p. 20) have quite the signification of 'Stardust Melody.' It is equally irritating, if not downright puzzling, to find (on p. 25) "Hauthausen . . .

Hain Street" (did the printer runs out of m's?). Similarly, on page 30, one might just about work out what is meant by ". . . he is the demon, who takes all our demonlike qualities upon his shoulders, like an Antichrist shouldering his iron cross, and doesn't insultingly escape our claws to prematurely hang himself like Stravrozin." But might it not help if this were set into proper English? ". . . he is the devil who will carry all of our own devilishness on his shoulders, like an Anti-Christ bearing the Iron Cross, and will not insolently slip through our fingers to string himself up before the time, as Stavrogin did." More seriously, back on page 25, is the word "Kistavesa," which any reader would be forgiven for not recognising is actually 'Kistarcsa,' one of several notorious places on the outskirts of Budapest that Eichmann's SS Sonderkommando (and their willing Hungarian helpers) set up as a transit camp for deporting the Jews to Auschwitz in 1944.

That leads straight to egregious mistranslations. Does it matter that the Hungarian word which in English means 'beech wood' is translated (p. 1) as "oak forest or glade"? One tree is pretty much like another, after all. Well, try the German for beech wood: 'Buchenwald . . .' (And the tree motif is picked up later, with an oblique reference to a line from one of Horace's Odes, quoted by both Schopenhauer and Nietzsche: "Why do you torture your poor reason for insight into the riddle of eternity? Why do we simply not lie down under the high plantane? or here under this pine tree?"). A similar failure of cultural bearings on the translators' part means you will probably miss the allusion to Arnold Schönberg's composition in ". . . the last soma Jisroel of the Warsaw captive . . ." (p. 20). But most hilarious of all is (p. 80): "His Most Honorable Highness the Governor, dressed in a hat as large as the sea and a mysterious fringed uniform." Anyone might guess that this refers to Miklós Horthy, Hungary's head of state from 1920 to 1944: "His Serene Highness the Regent, in his admiral's cap and that arcane uniform with the tasselled epaulets" Yes, the translators have read the Hungarian word for 'admiral'—tengernagy—literally as 'sea-big.'

It gets no better when it's a question of figures that one might hope were common knowledge, even in America. On page 12, for instance, we get "I only do this as really simply a precautionary measure, as if I were, or rather, had been, a cautious, promiscuous person moving in AIDS-affiliated circles." How does a "circle" of people affiliate to AIDS? Is it a club? Try: ". . . I adopt that pose merely as a prophylactic, as if I were a wary libertine moving around in an AIDS-infected milieu . . ."

What you're getting, dear reader, is bunkum, and not even the most astute amongst you could guess that the work of a deserved Nobel laureate was behind the original on which this travesty is based (p. 82): "Scandal . . . was the term they used to describe these inevitable, always unexpected, and, one could say, rain falls. You must imagine these . . . in the manner of when a drunk gentleman, after controlling himself for a while, finally gives in to temptation and falls down with a sigh, relaxing . . ." The Hungarian text shows that this puzzling association of rainfall with scandal is just a figment of the translators' imagination: "Scandal . . . that's what they called these irresistible, always unexpected plunges into licentiousness, so to say, which you should imagine, I said to my wife, as somewhat like an inebriated gentleman, who, having kept a strict hold on himself for a good while, suddenly yields to temptation and falls down flat on the ground in relief . . ."

Source: Tim Wilkinson, "Kaddish for a Stillborn Child?" in *Hungarian Quarterly*, Vol. 43, No. 168, Winter 2002.

Sources

Adelman, Gary, "Getting Started with Imre Kertész," in *New England Review*, Vol. 25, No. 1–2, Winter-Spring 2004, pp. 261–78.

Banville, John, "Beyond Good and Evil," in *Nation*, Vol. 280, No. 4, January 31, 2005, p. 29.

Davis, Robert Murray, Review of *Kaddish for a Child Not Born*, in *World Literature Today*, Vol. 74, No. 1, Winter 2000, p. 205.

Falbo, M. Anne, Review of *Kaddish for a Child Not Born*, in *Library Journal*, Vol. 122, No. 10, June 1, 1997, p. 149.

Kertész, Imre, *Kaddish for a Child Not Born*, translated by Christopher C. Wilson and Katharina M. Wilson, Northwestern University Press, 1997.

Rosenfeld, Alvin H., "The Auschwitz Disease," in *New Leader*, Vol. 87, No. 6, November-December 2004, pp. 30–31.

Theil, Stefan, "The Last Word: Imre Kertész, A Voice of Conscience," in *Newsweek International*, December 30, 2002, p. 96.

Wilkinson, Tim, "Kaddish for a Stillborn Child?" in *Hungarian Quarterly*, Vol. 43, No. 168, Winter 2002, pp. 41–43.

Further Reading

Bauer, Yehuda, and Nili Keren, *History of the Holocaust*, Franklin Watts, 2002.

   This book is accessible to high school students and gives a thorough account of Jewish history, culminating with detailed information about how and why the Holocaust occurred.

Dalos, György, Günther Grass, and Imre Kertész, "Parallel Lives," in *Hungarian Quarterly*, Vol. 45, No. 175, Autumn 2004, pp. 34–47.

   In the following interview, Grass and Kertész compare the differences and similarities in their lives.

Siegal, Aranka, *Upon the Head of the Goat: A Childhood in Hungary, 1939–1944*, Puffin, 1994.

   This book is a memoir of a Hungarian girl who was sent to a concentration camp and survived to tell her story.

Spiró, György, "In Art Only the Radical Exists," in *Hungarian Quarterly*, Vol. 43, No. 168, Winter 2002, pp. 29–37.

   In this article, Spiró writes about his old friend Kertész, offering a more personal and friendly account of the author's life and career.

Middlemarch

George Eliot

1872

Subtitled *A Study of Provincial Life*, George Eliot's novel *Middlemarch*, published in eight books or installments between 1871 and 1872, is also a study in human nature; a portrait of several memorable characters, the first of whom is Dorothea Brooke; and a historical reflection from the vantage point of the early 1870s on the three years culminating in the passage of the first Reform Bill in 1832. By the time she was writing this novel, Eliot was already a well-established and highly respected author. In her editorial work at the *Westminster Review* and through George Henry Lewes and their London circle of intellectuals, Eliot was exposed to the leading scientific, medical, and psychological thinking of her day. This novel reflects that exposure and demonstrates the breadth of her reading in English and other languages. Each chapter begins with an epigram (a concise, often satirical poem or witty expression) that is related to the text, sometimes ironically. Some of the epigraphs are attributed to other writers and were taken from a wide range of sources, while the unsigned ones were written by the author herself.

Author Biography

George Eliot was the pseudonym of Mary Ann Evans (later Marian Evans and in the last year of her life Marian Cross), who was born on November 22, 1819, in Arbury, Warwickshire, the daughter of Robert Evans, an estate manager. Her

George Eliot Hulton/Archive/Getty Images

excellent education was first shaped by Christian teachings and then by her conversion to Evangelicalism. In her schooling at Coventry, Evans lost her provincial accent and learned to speak English perfectly in a well-modulated voice. She learned French and German and was adept at playing the piano. Influenced by the German school of thought called Higher Criticism, she came in her twenties to regard sacred texts as historical documents rather than divinely revealed truth. Though she stopped going to church, she remained committed to the values of duty and love, and her writings, which are didactic, provide many positive portraits of clergymen and Dissenters.

After her mother died in 1836, Evans became the mistress of the family home and cared for her widowed father. In addition to housekeeping duties, she pursued her education rigorously, reading widely and furthering her study of foreign languages. In the early 1840s, she and her father relocated to a home outside Coventry, and there she met freethinkers Charles and Caroline Bray. The Brays contributed to Evans's shift from traditional religious thinking, which assumes sacred texts are divinely inspired, to a more radical position, in which she viewed such texts as humanly wrought fictions holding psychological and moral truths, a position to which her father strongly objected. In 1846,

Evans published an English translation from the German of David Strauss's *Life of Jesus*; at the same time, she submerged herself in the work of Spinoza and published essays on various other subjects. After her father died, she traveled with the Brays to Europe, returning thereafter to live in London.

In 1850, she met John Chapman (1821–94), publisher and editor of the *Westminster Review*. Evans began contributing to this journal and in 1851 boarded temporarily in the home of Chapman and his wife. Evans was infatuated with the handsome, philandering Chapman, and subsequently, as assistant editor of the *Westminster Review* she became enamored with the scholarly Herbert Spencer (1820–1903), who throughout the coming decades published books on biology, sociology, and evolutionary theory. In 1854, Evans published a translation of Ludwig Andreas Feuerbach's *Essence of Christianity*. During this time she began to use the pseudonym George Eliot (and it is conventional to use this name when referring to her).

In 1854, Eliot began a long-term intimate union with George Henry Lewes (1817–78), an exceptional thinker with a wide variety of scholarly interests, who was estranged from his wife Agnes yet unable to obtain a divorce at the time he met Eliot. Lewes lived for the rest of his life with Eliot, and his influence on her work cannot be overstated. Among his many works, Lewes published a highly respected *Life of Goethe* (1853), which he and Eliot researched together in Weimar. Lewes was a constant support to Eliot, and though the irregularity of their relationship caused her initial social discomfort, the couple's London circle gradually accepted them. Indeed, Eliot preferred in social circumstances to be called Mrs. Lewes.

During the next twenty-two years, Eliot produced some of the greatest of all nineteenth-century English fiction. Her most highly respected novels are *Scenes of Clerical Life* (1858), *Adam Bede* (1859), *The Mill on the Floss* (1860), *Silas Marner: The Weaver of Raveloe* (1861), *Romola* (1863), *Felix Holt, The Radical* (1866), *Middlemarch* (1872–73); and *Daniel Deronda* (1876). *Middlemarch* is arguably the finest of all these works.

By the time she published *Daniel Deronda*, Eliot had reached the highpoint of her stellar career and was acknowledged to be the greatest living English novelist. Two years later, Lewes died. In 1880, Eliot married John Walter Cross, her financial advisor whom she had met in 1869 while in Rome. She died in London of heart failure seven months later on December 22.

Plot Summary

Prelude

In the Prelude to *Middlemarch*, Eliot tells a story about Saint Teresa of Avila (1515–82), a Spanish mystic and founder of religious communities. In the story, the child Teresa and her little brother leave their village in search of martyrdom, but their uncles intercept them and turn them back. This story introduces one central idea in the novel: young people may envision lofty goals that later circumstances or forces beyond their control prevent them from reaching. Eliot writes: "Many Theresas have been born who found for themselves no epic life . . . perhaps only a life of mistakes, the offspring of a certain spiritual grandeur ill-matched with the meanness of opportunity." Eliot explores this conjunction between character and context. The Prelude introduces the "foundress of nothing" who cries after "an unattained goodness," her high intentions thwarted by immediate obstacles. The suggestion is that the would-be saint of this novel is Dorothea Brooke, since Book I focuses on her.

Book I: Miss Brooke

Like its title, this installment, the first of eight books in the novel, focuses on nineteen-year-old Dorothea Brooke, who aspires to improve the world and ponders how to begin. She and her younger sister, Celia, orphaned a few years earlier, live with their bachelor uncle and guardian, Mr. Brooke, at his home Tipton Grange. In the first chapter, the sisters examine their mother's jewelry, Celia eager to wear it, Dorothea having no interest in adornment. This scene introduces the theme of inheritance and how differently people react to it.

The solicitous baronet, Sir James Chettem, courts Dorothea, trying to win her favor by showing interest in her cottage plans. Myopic in more than a physical sense, Dorothea incorrectly assumes he is interested in Celia. At dinner with their uncle, Sir James is contrasted with Edward Casaubon, rector of Lowick. In this nearly fifty-year-old bookworm, Dorothea mistakenly sees a man on a grand mission, the writing of a philosophical history, a "Key to All Mythologies"; by contrast, Celia sees a mole-dotted, spoon-scraping old man. Mistaken in his own way, Casaubon upon hearing Dorothea's lovely voice imagines the older Brooke sister to be the perfect candidate to be a reader to relieve his tired eyes and a nurse to ease him in his declining years. He proposes, she accepts, and Mr. Brooke admits not being able to make sense of young women.

Media Adaptations

- *Middlemarch* was adapted in 1994 as a film by Random House and PBS in a co-production with WGBH Boston and BBC Lionheart Television, starring Juliet Aubrey and Douglas Hodge. As of 2005, the DVD is available from Netflix.

Mr. Brooke, Dorothea, and Celia visit Lowick. Dorothea is pleased with the old house but disappointed when she hears the tenant farmers are doing quite well. She regrets that "there was nothing for her to do in Lowick," a conclusion truer than she knows, since once married she finds she is also unable to assist Casaubon in fulfilling his goal. One part of their conflictive relationship, over the eighteen months they are married, pertains to the clash between her expectation that he will indeed write the book and his habit of using research to avoid writing and to insulate himself from others.

On this first visit to Lowick, Will Ladislaw, the grandson of Casaubon's aunt Julia, is introduced. Will, a youthful lover of the arts, is also attracted to Dorothea's voice, which for him associates her with the Aeolian harp, a romantic symbol of creative inspiration. Casaubon faults Ladislaw for not working diligently in a serious career.

The wedding trip is planned for Rome. Casaubon intends to bury himself in Vatican manuscripts while Dorothea sees the sights.

A dinner party at the Grange introduces other major characters. Nicholas Bulstrode, the banker who will be disgraced, pontificates that coquetry comes from the devil; his example is his niece Rosamond Vincy, who is a contrast to the unadorned Dorothea. Tertius Lydgate, the recently arrived doctor, is rumored to be connected to a titled Northumberland family.

By the time Mr. and Mrs. Casaubon are in Rome, Lydgate is fascinated by Rosamond Vincy. For him, being with Rosamond is like "reclining in a paradise with sweet laughs for bird-notes, and blue eyes for a heaven." Rosamond sets her sights on Lydgate because she thinks the doctor can lift her up and out of provincial Middlemarch society. Committed to the practice of medicine in this small town but also a cultivated man who likes nice things, Lydgate is seduced by her because he mistakes her refined manners for docility and her musical training as balm for him after a long day of work. Ironically, the worldly and sexually experienced Lydgate is more mistaken than the inexperienced, provincial Rosamond.

Fred Vincy and Mary Garth are related by marriage to Peter Featherstone: their aunts were Featherstone's two wives, now both deceased. The twelfth chapter in Book I, which is set at Stone Court, introduces Mary Garth, who attends her sickly and cantankerous uncle Featherstone. It also describes the first meeting between Rosamond and Lydgate, during which, significantly, he hands her a whip. In marriage, Rosamond will take charge of Lydgate. Mary Garth is contrasted with Rosamond and Featherstone's sister, Mrs. Waule.

Book II: Old and Young

Money matters affect most characters in this novel. Fred Vincy, in debt for £160 and having talked Caleb Garth into co-signing on the loan, asks Bulstrode for a letter confirming to Featherstone that Fred has not tried to borrow money against the prospect of an inheritance from his uncle. Featherstone gives Fred £100, but Fred misuses that money in a horse deal with Bambridge, and the Garths, with considerable personal hardship, are forced to pay the debt.

Lydgate, now twenty-seven, is assumed to be above the common physician. Orphaned and apprenticed early, with an education in Paris financed by his uncle Sir Godwin, Lydgate aspires to scientific discovery but is hampered by what the narrator calls "spots of commonness," which lie in his prejudices, his tastes in furniture and women, and in his proud assumption "that he was better born than other country surgeons." His past involvement with an actress in Paris who kills her husband foreshadows (or predicts) Rosamond's true character and the ultimate effect on him of his marriage to her.

Reverend Tyke is elected to the newly salaried position of chaplain to the hospital over Reverend Farebrother, who has been serving in that capacity without pay for years. Lydgate breaks the tie between the two by arriving late and casting his vote last. People take the election outcome to confirm the doctor's involvement with Mr. Bulstrode who has urged Tyke's election.

In Rome alone in a museum Mrs. Casaubon accidentally meets Will. She urges her husband to write and realizes that he will not accept her help and that he is full of his own difficulty regarding his book idea.

Book III: Waiting for Death

While at the horse fair, Fred contracts typhoid, and Lydgate treats him in the Vincy home, where the doctor frequently meets Rosamond and soon becomes engaged to her.

Back at Lowick, Mrs. Casaubon sees the house now as shrunken and dark, this new view caused by her honeymoon insights regarding her husband. Casaubon has a fainting spell, and Lydgate tells him to shorten his hours of study. At the end of Book III, Mary sits up with Featherstone one night during which he directs her to burn one of two wills. She refuses to do so without a witness. By morning he is dead.

Book IV: Three Love Problems

This book opens with Featherstone's staged funeral at Lowick. Mr. and Mrs. Casaubon, Mrs. Cadwallader, Sir James, and Celia watch the funeral from inside the rectory. Mr. Brooke joins them, apparently having arrived at Lowick in the company of Will Ladislaw who remains outside. Will's presence in Middlemarch is news to Mrs. Casaubon who, given Casaubon's frail health, directed her uncle to write Ladislaw and urge him not to come to Lowick. Actually, Mr. Brooke has done so, but he saw no problem at the same time in inviting Will to visit Tipton Grange. In his brief bid for a seat in Parliament, Mr. Brooke will enlist Will to serve as editor of the *Pioneer*, a local paper Mr. Brooke has secretly purchased.

The two Featherstone wills are read the next day. The first leaves £10,000 to Fred and the land to Joshua Rigg; it is superseded by the second will, which leaves both the money and the land to Rigg. Mary realizes that in not complying with Featherstone's direction to burn the second will, she has played a part in disinheriting Fred; this action on Mary's part identifies one of the three love problems referred to in the title of this book.

The second problem pertains to Rosamond Vincy's relentless pursuit of economic gain through attachment to an up-and-coming bachelor. She perceives Lydgate to be just the right choice, given he has aristocratic relatives and in her opinion seems to have a promising career. In this choice, she ironically overlooks the far more prosperous local, Ned Plymdale, who is initially interested in her and stands to inherit his father's manufacturing company. Lydgate misconstrues Rosamond to be submissive when in fact she has more drive to pursue her ambitions than he will prove to have for his.

The third love problem is suggested in the contrast between how Mrs. Casaubon is totally eclipsed by her jealous, mean-spirited husband and how validated and appreciated she feels by Will Ladislaw, who takes her seriously and listens to her ideas. Will meets Dorothea at Lowick while Casaubon is out and meets her again at Tipton. She discovers how Will has been affected by the disinheritance of his grandmother Julia and suggests to Casaubon that as a corrective her husband arrange for her to share her inheritance with Will. This altruistic initiative causes Casaubon to suspect Will has manipulated Dorothea for his own gain. This interpretation causes Casaubon to secretly draft a codicil (or modification) for his will: he leaves his estate to Dorothea; however, if she marries Ladislaw she forfeits her claim to this inheritance. It also causes Casaubon to write a harsh letter to Will insisting that his local work as editor constitutes an embarrassment and he should leave the area. Will writes back that his work is respectable and his choices are his own.

John Raffles shows up at Stone Court, intent on getting money from Rigg, his stepson whom he abused as a child. While at Stone Court, Raffles finds a letter signed by his former employer, Bulstrode, whom he sees as another possible source for money. This action introduces the plot concerning Bulstrode and his past involvement with a coastal pawnshop which has illegal dealings. Bulstrode worked in the place as an accountant, even after he realized it handled stolen goods. When the pawnbroker Dunkirk died, Bulstrode married his widow. When she died, Bulstrode paid off Raffles to remain silent regarding the location of the widow's daughter, Sarah, who by this time had married and had a son. Bulstrode justified his taking possession of the widow's estate with his intention to move elsewhere and henceforth use the money legally. That choice brought him to Middlemarch nearly thirty years earlier. Thus, Bulstrode, Rigg, and Raffles are all connected to the same business, originally run by Will Ladislaw's grandparents.

Book V: The Dead Hand

Lydgate tells Casaubon that his heart trouble may cause sudden death, and, separately, Mrs. Casaubon learns that her husband's condition is serious. At the same time, Lydgate introduces Mrs. Casaubon to his hopes for a new fever hospital and discusses people's objections to his accepting financial contributions from Bulstrode. Townspeople have mixed views of Lydgate, especially since he recommends certain new medical procedures. For example, he thinks autopsy is a logical way to determine the cause of death, and he also believes doctors should be paid for their services and time instead of being compensated only by the profits they make from selling drugs.

Medical reform is part of the spirit for reform that infuses other areas of English life in the late 1820s and early 1830s. In the Houses of Parliament located in London, a Reform Bill is being debated that would redraw voting districts according to current population distribution and extend the franchise further into the Anglican male upper middle class. Mr. Brooke seeks election on a Whig (liberal), pro-reform platform and alludes vaguely to "machine-breaking and general distress." This reference pertains to workers' attacks on machinery in mills and factories that threatened to ruin the cottage industries. These attacks began about 1811 and continued through the 1820s. Regarding Mr. Brooke's bid for election, local people are suspicious: they know his tenants pay high rents and the Tipton cottages are in dire need of repair. Moreover, Brooke's assistant and advocate, Will Ladislaw, who admittedly writes well and argues passionately for poor people's rights, is an outsider to this provincial town. His curious manners cause people to wonder about him: after all, he likes to sprawl on Lydgate's carpet, enjoys children, and is kind to Reverend Farebrother's idiosyncratic maiden aunt, Henrietta Noble.

Casaubon presses his wife to promise to finish his book after he dies, but understandably she hesitates. The following day after breakfast, he takes a walk in the garden, sits down, and dies. Mrs. Casaubon discovers his body, realizes she has arrived too late to reassure him, and is swamped with guilt. However, when Dorothea learns about the codicil, she sees everything differently. She reacts to the codicil as "a violent shock of repulsion from her departed husband, who had had hidden thoughts, perhaps perverting everything she said and did."

Mr. Brooke attempts to give a speech, is egged and mocked, and withdraws from the race, claiming heart problems. Soon he goes to Europe, supposedly for a rest. Fifteen months after Featherstone's death, Rigg Featherstone sells Stone Court to Bulstrode, who hires Mr. Garth to oversee the estate. While Mr. Garth is with Bulstrode, they are approached by John Raffles, who creates a compromising scene for Bulstrode. In fact, Raffles appears three times in

Middlemarch, intent on blackmailing Bulstrode. Readers learn later that after this first appearance, Raffles happens to meet Bambridge at a horse fair and tells him about Bulstrode's sullied past.

Book VI: The Widow and the Wife

Mrs. Casaubon spends three months at Freshitt Hall with Celia and Sir James. People in town learn about the codicil. Will visits Mrs. Casaubon and reports his intention to go to London and study law. They part abruptly upon the arrival of Sir James. As it turns out, Ladislaw remains in Middlemarch another two months. Mrs. Casaubon gives Reverend Farebrother the living at Lowick, a promotion which considerably increases Farebrother's income. The good cleric resolves to keep the position of vicar at the poor parish of St. Botolph as he becomes rector of the affluent Lowick parish.

Mr. Garth, now working on the estates of Lowick, Freshitt Hall, and Tipton Grange, decides to apprentice Fred Vincy, who has graduated from college. Fred asks Reverend Farebrother to speak to Mary Garth on his behalf. She confesses her love for Fred, which dashes Farebrother's unexpressed hopes of marrying her himself.

Captain Lydgate, Sir Godwin's third son and a particularly objectionable cousin in Tertius Lydgate's eyes, visits Rosamond and encourages her to go riding with him. Lydgate tells her not to go because she is pregnant, but she goes anyway and thus apparently contributes to the premature birth and death of her first child. Lydgate realizes the limits of his marriage to this woman who subverts his best resolutions and does not even follow his medical recommendation where her own unborn baby is concerned.

Through the Farebrother family, Fred learns about the codicil and takes that information to Rosamond who in turn tells Will Ladislaw. Brothrop Trumball holds an estate auction during which Will is embarrassed that people know about the codicil. He thinks it is "tantamount to an accusation against him as a fellow with low designs." Raffles has returned and recognizes Will Ladislaw at the auction. Then Raffles informs Bulstrode about Ladislaw's relationship to the banker's first wife.

To assuage his guilt, Bulstrode offers Will £500 a year. Will realizes that Bulstrode's money came from a illegal dealings and that the banker knew of Will's mother but intentionally failed to contact her regarding her claim on the estate. Will refuses Bulstrode's money, insisting that to accept would be dishonorable; Will wants "no stain" to contaminate his birth or connections. After they separate, Bulstrode weeps "like a woman."

Mrs. Casaubon learns that two months after his supposed departure from Middlemarch, Ladislaw is still in town and spending time with Lydgate's wife, Rosamond. She meets Will accidentally at the Grange and misconstrues his words to mean that he is now leaving because he is in love with Rosamond. As they part, Mrs. Casaubon realizes it is actually she whom Will loves, but Will leaves without figuring out that she returns his devotion.

Book VII: Two Temptations

Rosamond and Tertius have lived beyond their means since they were married and now the bills are due. They are threatened with losing their house and belongings. Lydgate hopes to get the soon-to-be married Ned Plymdale to rent the house and buy its furnishings. Rosamond rigidly opposes this humiliation and secretly interferes to prevent his plan. Lydgate is mastered by her, effectively paralyzed by her obstinate will. While he considers asking Sir Godwin for a loan, Rosamond secretly writes Lydgate's uncle. Three weeks later, Sir Godwin writes angrily to Lydgate with a refusal, criticizing him for apparently delegating to his wife a business matter a man should handle on his own behalf. Desperate, Lydgate experiments with opium and gambling. Farebrother tries to extend himself to Lydgate but is rebuffed.

The first temptation in Book VII concerns Mr. Farebrother who considers looking the other way as Fred engages in some unwise behavior which may cost him Mary's regard. But Farebrother resists this temptation: he interrupts Fred at the billiard hall to remind him of his duty and there discovers Lydgate engaged uncharacteristically in gambling. Fred calls the doctor away from a game he is losing, and Farebrother urges Fred to exercise self-control. Thus, Fred befriends Lydgate as Farebrother is befriending Fred.

As a last resort, Lydgate asks Bulstrode for a loan of £1000 and in their conversation learns that the hostile Bulstrode may be moving away and plans to withdraw his support from the hospital. The banker assures the doctor that Mrs. Casaubon is willing to take over the role of hospital patron.

Terrified of disgrace, Bulstrode tries to placate and remove Raffles. At the same time, the banker prepares for failure in that attempt by planning to leave Middlemarch to live at a "less scorching distance." He asks Caleb Garth to identify a potential tenant for Stone Court, and Garth thinks immediately of Fred Vincy. Then Garth runs into Raffles, who is ill, and takes him to Stone Court. En route, Raffles tells Garth about Bulstrode's past. Later, Lydgate is called to attend Raffles, who is suffering from delirium tremens, and directs Bulstrode to give him opium through the night, but not alcohol. Separately, Bulstrode appears to have a change of heart and gives the doctor a loan of £1,000. That night Bulstrode leaves Raffles in the care of the housekeeper. She asks about giving Raffles brandy, and Bulstrode gives her the key to the liquor cabinet. This action identifies the second temptation of Book VII: Bulstrode so wants Raffles dead that he deliberately ignores the doctor's orders. In the morning, Raffles dies.

The care of Raffles on his deathbed is fraught with irony. It turns out that the care actually given was standard treatment at the time. Lydgate prescribes a new approach to Raffles's condition, which if followed might also have resulted in death. Nonetheless, the fact that the officiating doctor's orders were not followed implicates Bulstrode in the reader's eyes. While the refusal to follow doctor's orders in the case is not discovered by the townspeople, their knowledge that Lydgate was involved in Raffles's care and subsequently has money to pay his creditors implicates both Bulstrode and the doctor in what appears to them to be a wrongful death.

Having heard it at a horse fair, Bambridge repeats Raffles's story about Bulstrode, and Middlemarch buzzes with questions about Bulstrode's role in Raffles's death. Bambridge also distributes information about Will's disinheritance. Gossip energizes the town: inference become fact and suggestion becomes evidence.

At a town meeting to discuss another matter, Bulstrode is confronted directly by Mr. Hawley, who officiated at Raffles's burial. Bulstrode is asked to leave and is visibly shaken as he does so, on the arm of Lydgate, whose aid further incriminates the doctor in the eyes of those present. Mrs. Casaubon returns from a trip to Yorkshire to learn of Bulstrode's disgrace and the accusations against Lydgate; she immediately takes up the doctor's cause.

Book VIII: Sunset and Sunrise

Lydgate realizes that the townspeople think he has taken Bulstrode's money as a bribe. He rides out of town to consider the matter. The scandal reaches Rosamond and Mrs. Bulstrode. Rosamond is faulted now for having married an interloper. After a poor reception from Mrs. Hackbutt and Mrs. Plymdale, Harriet Bulstrode goes to her brother, Mr. Vincy, and learns of the talk about her husband

and Lydgate. She goes home and puts on plain clothing and combs her hair simply off her face; her new appearance constitutes the outward sign of her resignation to a life of humiliation. She remains loyal to her husband in the face of his disgrace. By contrast, Rosamond hears the scandal about Lydgate and goes home assuming the worst of her husband.

Lydgate visits Mrs. Casaubon who expresses her faith in him and offers help. She gives him £1,000 to pay back Bulstrode and resolves to visit Rosamond and speak to her on Lydgate's behalf. In the meantime, Rosamond has urged Will to return to Middlemarch for a visit, and when Mrs. Casaubon enters the Lydgate home, she discovers them together in what appears to be an intimate conversation and leaves abruptly. Once Mrs. Casaubon is gone, Will explains to Rosamond that he is in love with Dorothea. After a soul-searching night at Lowick during which Dorothea fears Will is attached to Rosamond, Mrs. Casaubon resolutely returns to the Lydgate home to affirm her faith in the doctor. In this conversation, Rosamond opens up to the generous Dorothea and reassures her of Will's love.

Mr. Brooke announces Dorothea and Will are going to marry. When Sir James says it is wrong of her to do so, Reverend Cadwallader replies it is easy to label as wrong what one does not like in others. Mrs. Bulstrode arranges for Fred to have the tenancy at Stone Court.

The last chapter in Book VIII sums up the "after-years" of these characters. Fred Vincy and Mary Garth, who marry and prosper, have three sons. Rosamond and Tertius relocate to London and the Continent and his practice among the rich flourishes. He writes an essay on gout. But Lydgate dies prematurely of diphtheria; his "hair never became white." Rosamond and their four children are well provided for by a life insurance policy and by her second marriage to a wealthy physician. Dorothea and Will have two children. Their firstborn, a son, inherits Mr. Brooke's estate. They live in London but visit Middlemarch twice a year. Will goes into politics, ultimately gaining a seat in the House of Commons.

Characters

Arthur Brooke

Mr. Brooke, a bachelor of sixty and owner of Tipton Grange, is a justice of the peace. In this capacity, he sentences poor people, without consideration or mercy, who poach illegally because they are starving. In family matters, he is well meaning, though ineffectual. Mr. Brooke is the guardian of his orphaned nieces, Dorothea and Celia Brooke.

Mr. Brooke is said "to have contracted a too rambling habit of mind"; indeed, his speech is vacuous, filled with phrases which in their recommendation of moderation betray his lack of information and refusal to take a position. He faults Mr. Casaubon for not expressing ideas, but Mr. Brooke himself rarely hits upon one. Still, his claim that scholarship can take one "too far" is valid regarding Casaubon.

Mr. Brooke aspires briefly to a seat in the House of Commons. With reform opinions in the wind, he purports to run on a liberal platform, but locals recognize how stingy he is regarding tenants on his own property and how he endlessly postpones making improvements. Self-deluding and dim-witted, Mr. Brooke believes he has more astute insights than he is capable of expressing. When he is mocked by a crowd and pelted with eggs, he retires from the campaign, claiming a heart condition, and flees to Europe supposedly for a rest.

Celia Brooke

Dorothea Brooke's younger sister, seventeen-year-old Celia Brooke does not share her sister's idealism or interest in cottage plans and, while her own narrow and conventional interests preclude concern for local poverty, pretty and docile Celia sees quite clearly Dorothea's blind spots. Celia's nickname for her sister is Dodo.

Dorothea assumes every man who visits the Grange may be interested in Celia, and of the sisters local cottagers prefer the "amiable and innocent-looking" Celia. Sir James Chettam, who owns the adjacent property, initially seeks to marry Dorothea, but as soon as she becomes engaged to Casaubon, Sir James transfers his devotion to Celia, whom he marries. Celia and Sir James have a son, Arthur, named after Mr. Brooke. Celia's devotion to this child eclipses any potential in her for interest in the larger world.

Miss Dorothea Brooke

Given the prefix Miss because she is the older sister, Dorothea Brooke at nineteen is classically beautiful yet myopic. Her exceptional good looks are accentuated by the simplicity of her dress, and her sincere manner of expression by her lovely voice. Idealistic, ardent, devoted to good works, and selfless, Dorothea seeks to accomplish some practical good in the parish of Tipton. Yet the narrator immediately forecasts disaster or martyrdom for her, in part because Dorothea lacks her sister Celia's common sense. The narrator explains the nature of Dorothea's vision: "She was blind . . . to many things obvious to others—likely to tread in the wrong places, as Celia had warned her; yet her blindness to whatever did not lie in her own pure purpose carried her safely by the side of precipices where vision would have been perilous with fear."

Dorothea is "regarded as an heiress." If she married and had a son, he would inherit Mr. Brooke's estate, a legacy of £3,000 per year. Sir James Chettam, who owns the adjacent property, seeks her hand in marriage, a plan that makes more than financial sense since the good-hearted, cooperative Sir James is eager to carry out Dorothea's cottage plans for his tenants. Inexplicably, Dorothea finds irritating his quick accommodation of her and chooses instead the learned Mr. Casaubon, twenty-seven years her senior, who quietly boasts about a monumental work he is supposedly writing. Latching onto the idea that she can assist in this great work, Dorothea jumps decidedly into the wrong place by marrying Casaubon.

After her first husband dies, Mrs. Casaubon marries his second cousin, Will Ladislaw, and together they have two children. Their firstborn, a son, inherits Mr. Brooke's estate.

Nicholas Bulstrode

Middlemarch banker and self-righteous moralizer, the outsider Nicholas Bulstrode is a manipulative, greedy, and self-deluding man. Called "a Pharisee" by some, Bulstrode buys Stone Court to signal his financial eminence and contributes to the new hospital, assuming he will have a say in how it is staffed. For thirty years, local people have endured his superciliousness, ignorant of Bulstrode's shady past.

When he was young, Bulstrode worked as an accountant for a corrupt pawnbroker named Dunkirk and married that man's widow. When she died, Bulstrode maneuvered with the help of John Raffles so that the woman's daughter Sarah, mother of Will Ladislaw, would not be contacted. This action caused Bulstrode to inherit his wife's estate, and with her money, he relocated to Middlemarch, intent on using the funds in legitimate ways (convincing himself that doing so would exonerate him from any wrong doing in preventing the estate from going to its rightful heir).

Guilt-stricken Bulstrode is willing to pay to silence the blackmailer Raffles, and when the truth of Will Ladislaw's claim on the estate is made known, Bulstrode attempts to assuage Will by offering him £500 a year. When Raffles's claims and townspeople's questions regarding Bulstrode's role in Raffles's death surface, Bulstrode is publicly disgraced and professionally ruined. One important point in the Bulstrode plot is that legally the banker might not have been found guilty in a court of law; however, public opinion turns against him, and this social verdict forces him out of Middlemarch.

Elinor Cadwallader

Mrs. Cadwallader, the wife of Rector Cadwallader, is an effective purveyor of neighborhood gossip and enjoys matchmaking, especially on behalf of her friend Sir James Chettam, who at the outset of the novel is a most attractive, eligible bachelor. Mrs. Cadwallader makes memorable remarks, particularly regarding Mr. Casaubon. She quips, for example, regarding his blood: "Somebody put a drop under a magnifying-glass, and it was all semicolons and parentheses." Mrs. Cadwallader informs Sir James before he proposes to Dorothea that she has already accepted Casaubon and thus saves him some embarrassment. Regarding the news of that upcoming nuptial, Mrs. Cadwallader says, "I wish her joy of her hair shirt." Then she directs Sir James's attention to Celia, whom she claims he has already won.

Rector Humphrey Cadwallader

Large, easy-going Rector Cadwallader is an affable sort of man who takes others at face value and whose chief pleasure is fishing. He does not share his wife's desire to meddle and often works to neutralize her reactions to others. Mrs. Cadwallader objects to her husband's accepting nature: "Humphrey finds everybody charming. . . . He will even speak well of the bishop, though I tell him it is unnatural in a beneficed clergyman." The narrator remarks that he "always saw the joke of any satire against himself." Kindly Humphrey Cadwallader illustrates an all-too-rare live-and-let-live attitude, which provides him with distance and understanding regarding Middlemarch politics and gossip.

Rector Edward Casaubon

Reverend Casaubon, who is past the age of forty-five, lives in the rectory at Lowick and buries himself in the study of religious history. He describes himself as "liv[ing] too much with the dead." Hours of reading are ruining his eyesight, and when he first hears Dorothea speak, he attends more to her pleasant voice than to what she says, because he needs someone to read to him. His purported goal, to reconstruct the world as it once was with the hope of isolating a single principle or truth operating in it (which he intends to entitle the "Key to All Mythologies") inexplicably appeals to Dorothea, a person naturally committed to making practical improvements in the world of the here and now.

Metaphors associated with Mr. Casaubon suggest that he is dried up, that as Mrs. Cadwallader says, he is "a great bladder for dried peas to rattle in!" To marry Casaubon is tantamount to going into the convent. In fact, during courtship with Dorothea, Casaubon "abandon[s] himself to the stream of feeling" and finds it to be "an exceedingly shallow rill." The suggestion appears to be that his marriage to Dorothea is unconsummated.

Moreover, Dorothea's assumption that she can assist him in accomplishing his great work effectively paralyzes Casaubon in his already advanced case of writer's block. He interprets her urging as criticism. Finally, in his rejection of Will Ladislaw and his suspicions of Will's intentions regarding Dorothea, Casaubon proves the degree to which he is undone by the "inward sores" of jealousy, suspicion, self-doubt, and fear of failure.

Mr. Casaubon is married to Dorothea for eighteen months and dies of heart failure, leaving her a widow at twenty-one.

Sir James Chettam

Sir James Chettam, handsome, genial bachelor and baronet, owns Freshitt Hall and the property adjacent to Tipton Grange and is initially a suitor to Dorothea Brooke. He says "exactly" to Dorothea, thus coming across to her as having no mind of his own. In truth, Sir James is willing to take up Dorothea's ideas for improvement and make them a reality. But she buys into Mr. Casaubon's purported ambition instead, seeing in it an avenue for her own aspirations.

Sir James marries Celia Brooke, and they have a son, Arthur. Sir James continues to be protective of Dorothea, and when the codicil to Casaubon's will becomes known to him, he resents the inference that Dorothea is not above reproach regarding Will Ladislaw. While committed to his station and to social appearances and in all a rather conventional man, Sir James is nonetheless good-hearted, and his family loyalty and generosity are constant.

Dodo

See Dorothea Brooke

Reverend Camden Farebrother

Often wearing a threadbare suit, the Reverend Farebrother, about forty, makes £400 a year as vicar of St. Botolph parish. With this money, he supports his widowed mother, Mrs. Farebrother; his aunt, Miss Henrietta Noble; and his unmarried sister, Winifred Farebrother. As his name might indicate, he is fair in his dealings, even when being so is at the expense of his own desires or interests. For example, though he is attached to Mary Garth, he speaks to her on behalf of Fred Vincy, who also wants to marry her. Reverend Farebrother has served at the hospital without pay for many years; however, when the position becomes salaried, Bulstrode wants Tyke to have it. Lydgate among others votes with Bulstrode for Tyke, and yet Farebrother, utterly free of malice, remains the doctor's friend.

Farebrother has only one vice: he gambles. He is good at cards and billiards and uses his skill to supplement his meager income. After Casaubon dies, however, Dorothea gives the living at Lowick to Reverend Farebrother, which substantially increases his income. He remains vicar of St. Botolph as he becomes vicar of Lowick, but his family moves into the much larger vicarage at Lowick, and with this double income he is financially quite comfortable. Now he can easily afford to give up his gambling.

Joshua Rigg Featherstone

See Joshua Rigg

Peter Featherstone

Peter Featherstone is the elderly, wealthy owner of Stone Court. As he lies dying, his siblings and their spouses gather, eager to learn what part of his estate they have inherited. Featherstone's deceased first wife was Mary Garth's aunt; his second wife, now also dead, was Mrs. Vincy's sister. Thus, by marriage, Featherstone is connected to the Garths and the Vincys.

Featherstone's blood relatives, whom the narrator calls "Christian Carnivora," resent and fear these marital connections and hope he decides to leave his estate to them. In one will, Featherstone leaves £10,000 to Fred Vincy; in a subsequent will, he leaves his entire estate to Joshua Rigg, apparently his illegitimate son; in both wills he leaves virtually nothing to his blood relatives.

Caleb Garth

Caleb Garth is an overseer or estate manager, who works hard to support his wife and five children. Mr. Garth is soft-hearted and kindly, even indulgent. He acquiesces to his wife in most things but is absolutely rigid when he decides to help someone despite her wishes to the contrary. His particular pleasure is to ride across an estate, identifying and correcting problems in the buildings, irrigation system, and fencing. He loves his work. A slow speaker and a man who does not engage in gossip, Mr. Garth proves the fine quality of his character by his actions.

Mr. Garth's income increases when he is hired by Sir James to oversee both Tipton and Freshitt estates. Then Bulstrode hires him to take care of Stone Court. However, after Raffles reveals incriminating information about Bulstrode, Mr. Garth refuses to work for the banker. Mr. Garth takes Fred Vincy on as an apprentice and assists in arranging for Fred to rent Stone Court, much against his wife's desires.

Mary Garth

Shrewd and satiric at the age of twenty-two, Mary Garth is the daughter of Mr. and Mrs. Caleb Garth. One of five children and the oldest girl, Mary is required to work outside the family home in order to contribute to the family income. At first, she attends her uncle, the bedridden Peter Featherstone, and next she helps out in the Farebrother household.

Mary Garth is exceptionally perceptive and free of egoism. Of ordinary appearance but with an interesting face, she is astute about human nature and foibles. The narrator says, "Rembrandt would have painted her with pleasure." Mary has candor and "truth-telling fairness." She is not inclined to self-deluding illusions, and her humor allows her to laugh at herself.

From early childhood, Mary Garth and Fred Vincy have been loyal friends. She is devoted to him but refuses to express it until he makes something of himself in the world. Eventually, they marry and live at Stone Court. Later in life Mary and Fred both become published authors.

Will Ladislaw

Grandson of Casaubon's maternal aunt Julia, Will Ladislaw is repeatedly contrasted to his second cousin. He is young, has light curls, and a bright face. While Casaubon is associated with tombs (perhaps a pun on tomes), vaults, and dimly lit corridors, Will is associated with sunlight and open air. In contrast to Casaubon who buries himself in study, Will calls himself "Pegasus" and thinks "every form of prescribed work 'harness.'"

Casaubon blames him for not finding work, for following the arts instead of finding some serious purpose. When Will becomes editor of the *Pioneer*, he discovers his natural talent for communicating ideas and arguing for reform. This work in Middlemarch leads Will to consider studying law in London and perhaps becoming a politician.

Will's maternal and paternal antecedents experienced disinheritance. Thus he has been disinherited on both sides of his family. His father was the son of Casaubon's aunt Julia and her husband, a Polish teacher. Casaubon's mother's family disinherited Julia because she married this foreigner. Now that Julia and Will's father are dead, Will has some claim to Casaubon's estate. When Dorothea learns this connection, she recommends to her husband that Will share her inheritance, an idea that prompts the suspicious Casaubon to accuse Will of manipulating Dorothea. Casaubon writes a codicil, or modification, to his will that stipulates Dorothea will forfeit her inheritance as his widow if she marries Will.

Will's mother, Sarah Dunkirk, was the daughter of a seashore pawnbroker and his wife. Sarah ran away from home to pursue a life on the stage. After the pawnbroker Dunkirk died, the widow became Bulstrode's first wife. After Sarah's mother died, Bulstrode withheld information concerning Sarah's whereabouts in order to take possession of his wife's estate. Thus, Sarah's son, Will, was disinherited through Bulstrode's circumvention. Ladislaw's first name points to this family pattern regarding inheritance.

Dr. Tertius Lydgate.

In his late twenties when he appears in Middlemarch, proud, naïve Tertius Lydgate is an idealistic doctor who arrives in this provincial town with new ideas and a lack of tact that causes him unwittingly to alienate and antagonize the more conventional local doctors. The narrator states that Lydgate shines with an "unreflecting egotism . . . called commonness." He envisions discovering the fundamental tissue in all life forms, aspires to establishing a fever hospital with enlightened treatment, and assumes despite his habit of spending beyond his means that his bills will be met. Though he has no initial intention of marrying, he becomes infatuated with the ambitious, materialistic, and completely egoistic Rosamond Vincy and is eventually derailed by her obstinacy and selfishness. He is drawn off course in the current of others' willfulness and pays dearly for his passivity.

John Raffles

The blackmailer, alcoholic John Raffles, age sixty, shows up first in Middlemarch to claim money from Joshua Riggs, his stepson whom he abused as a child, and on a second occasion to get money from Mr. Bulstrode, his former employer, of whom he knows entirely too much for Bulstrode's comfort. The florid, whiskered Raffles is a presumptuous opportunist, who uses what he knows to get money from those who would wish him silent and residing at a great distance. Raffles dies from alcohol poisoning under circumstances that implicate Mr. Bulstrode and Dr. Lydgate, who attends the drunkard in his final illness. When news of Raffles is announced by the horse dealer Mr. Bambridge, gossip about the banker's past and questions concerning the manner of Raffles's death ignite across Middlemarch. Raffles's appearance in Middlemarch contributes directly to the downfall of Nicholas Bulstrode.

Joshua Rigg

The illegitimate son of Peter Featherstone and also the stepson of John Raffles, cool and composed Joshua Rigg is unknown in Middlemarch when he appears for the reading of Featherstone's will, and its contents are apparently no surprise to him. According to Mrs. Cadwallader, Joshua is "frog-faced" with his prominent eyes and slicked-back hair. In accordance with the second will, Joshua Rigg, henceforth to be called Rigg Featherstone, inherits Stone Court and all property attached to it. His goal is to acquire money, so he sells Stone Court quickly and moves to a seashore town where he wants to establish himself as a moneylender and pawnbroker.

Fred Vincy

The brother of Rosamond and son of Lucy and Walter Vincy, Fred Vincy is a young man in leisurely search of a career who along the way falls into the typical traps set by unscrupulous horse dealers and gamblers. Fred has a long-term devotion to Mary Garth, and though she argues against it, he is under his father's edict to go to college and become a clergyman. Fred is disappointed in his hopes of inheriting a sizeable sum from Peter Featherstone, and this turn of events drives him to complete his education. Fortunately, an accident causes him to help Mr. Garth and that incident leads the overseer to take Fred on as an apprentice. Eventually, Fred takes on the tenancy of Stone Court and marries Mary Garth.

Rosamond Vincy

Sister of Fred and daughter of Lucy and Walter Vincy, Rosamond Vincy is a product of a typical nineteenth-century finishing school for girls. She has acquired the social graces, refined dress, and proper pronunciation designed to help her snare a suitable husband, which means someone who can improve her middle-class standard of living. She is ashamed of her mother's lack of breeding and indifferent to her father's demands. Headstrong, self-centered, and vain, Rosamond does exactly what is necessary to get what she wants. She lights on Dr. Lydgate as her ticket up and then out of Middlemarch, assumes his distant wealthy uncle will provide for him, and moves as smoothly and as inconspicuously as a spider toward entrapping him. She marries Lydgate, and their combined appetite for nice things drives them into debt and then threatens them with bankruptcy. She pursues her flirtation with her husband's cousin, Captain Lydgate, at the risk of her pregnancy, and after an episode out riding, gives birth prematurely and the baby dies. Next she flirts with Will Ladislaw. In her one selfless act, she tells Dorothea that Will loves her.

Eventually, Rosamond and Tertius relocate to a seashore town, and they have four children. After he dies at age fifty, Rosamond marries an older, wealthy man who leaves her with a comfortable inheritance.

Themes

Marriage

Middlemarch intertwines three courtship and marriage plots. The courtships of two couples, Dorothea and Casaubon and Rosamond and Lydgate, illustrate how the illusions, impressions, and expectations reached during courtship are shattered by the day-to-day familiarity and difficulties of married life. The initial misconceptions these characters have regarding their partners lead them to project onto their partners the qualities they seek in marriage. Dorothea wants entry into the world of male knowledge, and she sees Casaubon's book project as a worthy cause to serve in her hunger for action that will improve the world. Casaubon seeks a nurse, secretary, and reader, all menial jobs he believes Dorothea can handle. Rosamond seeks wealth and prestige through aristocratic alliance and believes that Lydgate offers the means by which she can be lifted out of the embarrassingly unrefined society of her family and social circle. Lydgate thinks Rosamond's physical charms and musical skills will create a perfect haven in which he can rest after a long day of medical practice and scientific research. In his eyes, Rosamond's submissive manner indicates that she is a woman who knows the man is boss in marriage and will rely on his good judgment. Once married, each person learns much more about the partner and sees that person more accurately. Sadly, for these couples, that subsequent clearer vision proves the marriage union cannot fulfill initial expectations.

In each case, others see quite easily the early signals the infatuated person fails to recognize. One illustration occurs in the first exchange of letters between Casaubon and Dorothea. His marriage proposal, which consists in his affirming her "fitness" to supply his needs, shows in every convoluted sentence his solipsistic concern for his own welfare. But Dorothea, eager to hear what she longs for, reads this letter as a confirmation of her hopes. Her direct and far more concise response begins: "I am very grateful to you for loving me," which in fact he never said he did, and he is unable to do. Another irony here is that he is a scholarly author, but she at nineteen writes far better. At the news of this sudden engagement, the less ambitious but in some ways more perceptive Celia responds with "shame mingled with a sense of the ludicrous."

While Dorothea and Casaubon have a cerebral and probably unconsummated union, sexual chemistry colors the courtship and early marriage of Rosamond and Lydgate. Regarding this self-deluding intoxication, the narrator comments: "Young love-making—that gossamer web! Even the points it clings to . . . are scarcely perceptible." The educated and sexually experienced Lydgate should know better, but even he "fell to spinning that web from his inward self," and Rosamond "too was spinning industriously." Still, Mr. Vincy cautions Rosamond that Lydgate does not have the potential of a good income, and the connection to his uncle cannot be depended upon to compensate for it. Older women in Rosamond's circle recognize Ned Plymdale, a local man from a manufacturing family, as far more financially well placed. But Rosamond's desire to move up and out of Middlemarch blinds her to the reasonableness of marrying Ned. Mr. Brooke says of marriage, "It *is* a noose, you know," but these two couples do not hear him.

The third couple stands in contrast to the first two because the plain and sturdy Mary Garth has long understood she is not the center of the

Topics for Further Study

- Select a footnote in the Norton Critical Edition of *Middlemarch* on an historical person or event and conduct further research on this subject. Then write an essay on the passage in the novel which the footnote helps to elucidate, explaining how your research increases your understanding of the passage and its relevance to the novel as a whole.

- Read about the Renaissance thinker Isaac Casaubon (1559–1614) and his cosmology (theory of the universe), then write a compare and contrast paper on him and Edward Casaubon. Conclude your paper by theorizing about how this comparison gives a reader fuller understanding of Edward Casaubon's research topic and his character.

- Consult books on the history of fashion and photo histories that contain pictures of people in Victorian dress. Use photocopies of some of these photographs to create a poster. Choose pictures that may approximate what Eliot's characters wear in certain scenes: for example, a morning dress worn by a middle-class woman at home, riding outfits for a woman and for a man, mourning attire for a formal funeral, a servant's dress, and the dress of a parish priest and rector. Make a presentation to your class on fashion during the Victorian period, contrasting it with dress in the early 2000s. Include discussion of how clothing styles influence behavior.

- Read about medical developments in England between 1830 and 1870. You may want to begin by checking relevant footnotes in the Norton Critical Edition, for example, on the stethoscope, blood letting, and fever treatments, in order to narrow your research. Next, write a paper which attempts to assess Dr. Lydgate's training and expertise in light of your research.

- Do some research on grave robbers and the nineteenth-century practice of autopsy and on the practice of autopsy in the early 2000s. Write a contrast paper explaining why autopsy was a crime in the early nineteenth century but is used to solve crimes in the early 2000s.

---

universe. She believes "things were not likely to be arranged for her peculiar satisfaction." Moreover, Mary sees "life very much as a comedy in which she had a . . . generous resolution not to act the mean or treacherous part." She is loyal to Fred Vincy because he alone has from childhood been kind to her, but she holds off courtship with the self-awareness that she needs a partner who is as independent and hard-working as her father. She does not want a person who enters the clergy as a last resort or hangs on the promise of inheritance and wastes his talents and money in the meantime. In short, she awaits Fred's maturation. Thus, Eliot maps out the kind of pitfalls that lie ahead of the idealistic, the self-seeking, and the infatuated when it comes to selecting a mate. In Mary Garth, Eliot dramatizes how self-awareness, common sense, and lack of egoism all help a person find the partner and choose the time that portend a happy marriage.

Inheritance

Matters of inheritance constitute an important part of *Middlemarch*, a novel that repeatedly illustrates how land and money transfer upon death from one man to another. Patriarchy, male privilege and power, and paternity, all perpetuate this centuries old pattern. In each story behind the double disinheritance of Will Ladislaw, a woman is cut off from inheritance. Sarah Dunkirk Ladislaw, daughter of the widow Dunkirk who was Bulstrode's first wife, was Will's mother. In the legal transmission of the Dunkirk estate, Sarah's son Will would be the rightful heir. Bulstrode, however, kept the daughter's whereabouts and the existence of her son a secret, and by this maneuver he gained control of the Dunkirk estate. In the second story, Casaubon's aunt Julia ran away from her family, married, and had a son, Will's father. Because she married without family approval, her father disinherited her. This fact explains why Casaubon takes the initiative to pay for Will's education and perhaps justifies Casaubon's disappointment that Will did not take up some more respectable area of study than the arts. In Dorothea's view, Aunt Julia was unjustly disinherited and that action unfairly revoked Will's right of primogeniture (the law under which the eldest son in the most direct line of descent inherits the estate).

In the case of Peter Featherstone, because he remained childless in both his marriages, his relatives logically assume he is dying without a direct heir. In this situation they know he could designate blood relatives and relatives by marriage as inheritors. He chooses in both versions of his will to place his estate away from his siblings. In the first will, he gives some of the estate to his illegitimate son, Joshua Rigg, and a large sum of money to his second wife's nephew, Fred Vincy. In the superseding will, Featherstone designates most of the estate to Rigg.

The early scene in which Dorothea and Celia divide their deceased mother's jewels initiates the novel's exploration of female rights to inheritance, which are established by law only in lieu of a male heir. Rosamond Vincy has attended Miss Lemon's finishing school and been raised with tastes above her class in the expectation that she will marry a wealthy man. Marrying up in this way is believed to be her only way of achieving financial security because Fred will inherit their father's inconsequential estate. Rosamond is conditioned to use her physical beauty, her etiquette, and her musical training to attract an appropriate suitor. She does not think beyond this system, but she has not been encouraged to do so, and she has a face and figure she can market.

But what of a middle-class ordinary woman who does not marry, for example, Reverend Farebrother's elder sister, Winifred? This woman is dependent first on her father and, when he dies, on her brother (or any other male relative) for support. In this case, indeed, Farebrother supports his widowed mother; his maiden aunt, Henrietta Noble; and his spinster sister. Without his provision for them, these women would be what was called redundant (meaning without male support). In addition, money available for education in middle-class families was spent on behalf of the sons' professional advancement. For example, the Garths save money for the formal education or apprenticeship of their sons while the home-schooled Mary must work and offset the family's expenses. Similarly, Mr. and Mrs. Vincy send Fred to college, in hopes that he will enter the clergy and thus secure a permanent income, but Rosamond only goes to a finishing school. Her social refinement and charm will secure a husband who can provide for her.

Style

Epigraph and Allusion

Each chapter in *Middlemarch* begins with an epigraph that has relevance, sometimes ironic, to surrounding text. For example, the epigraph that heads chapter X is a quotation from Thomas Fuller: "He had caught a great cold, had he no other clothes to wear than the skin of a bear not yet killed." This statement points humorously to Casaubon's vulnerability to criticism; he is so filled with suspicion and self-doubt he needs to use the prospect of writing a great work to compensate for his inadequacies. Thus, he uses the promise, writing a definitive work to bolster his self-image. He also holds himself above others by talking about a work he in fact will never write. The enormous demands of this magnum opus (or great achievement) are a screen or defense mechanism that insulates him from experiencing life directly and from being intimate with fellow human beings. Casaubon reads without overview, gets lost in details, and thus avoids writing the book. Will labels the problem this way: "the . . . long incubation producing no chick." Fear reinforces procrastination: Casaubon privately believes critics would be harsh if they reviewed even his research. He senses a scholarly "chilling ideal audience which crowd[s] his laborious uncreative hours." Even Mr. Brooke can spot some trouble. When he asks Casaubon how he organizes his documents, Casaubon replies: "In pigeon-holes partly," to which Brooke replies, "Ah, pigeon-holes will not do." The unstated question that apparently confounds Casaubon is how does one organize a vast, comprehensive study; craft an outline; and then write. (Sad to say, the question Casaubon does not consider is whether his medieval study has any relevance for readers in the 1830s; according to Will Ladislaw it does not.)

Allusions (references to other works of literature or to historical persons or events) create a cultural framework within which the text gains meaning. For example, chapter LXVI begins with a quotation from William Shakespeare's *Measure for Measure*: "'Tis one thing to be tempted, Escalus, / Another thing to fall.'" Readers familiar with this play recognize the puritanical magistrate Angelo justifying himself for having sentenced to death the young Claudio for impregnating his fiancée. The irony is that Angelo, who boasts here never to have sinned, will shortly be undone by Claudio's beautiful sister, the nun Isabela. Sexually attractcd to the pure Isabela, Angelo offers her a corrupt bargain: if she agrees to have sex with him, he will release her brother. He is willing to make a serious exception to the law in order to engage in illicit sex with this virgin. Angelo's hypocrisy, then, provides a clue for how readers should assess Bulstrode's hypocrisy. The banker has been the self-appointed, self-righteous judge of his neighbors on small matters when he is himself guilty of much more serious wrongdoing.

Other allusions in the novel refer to historical persons and events. Some of these references serve to locate the action in the three years prior to the passage of the first Reform Bill. For example, to place Mr. Brooke's bid for election in the wider political framework of the time, Eliot writes: "By the time that Lord John Russell's measure was being debated in the House of Commons, there was a new political animation in Middlemarch." Lord John Russell (1792–1878) was prime minister and a sponsor of the Reform Bill, which was debated in Parliament in 1831 and passed the following year. Mr. Brooke wants people to think he is progressive, but actually he tries to say only enough of what townspeople want to hear in order to win their votes. In his upbringing and his current lifestyle, Mr. Brooke is a Tory (conservative) at heart. While he says he is for reform, he does not see the contradiction in wishing "somebody had a pocket-borough to give . . . Ladislaw." In other words, while he speaks publicly in support of a bill that would eliminate pocket-boroughs, privately he thinks they are useful for placing certain men in office. Eliot contrasts the self-serving landed Mr. Brooke with the aristocrat yet socially minded reformer, Lord Russell.

Point of View

Eliot uses limited omniscient point of view in *Middlemarch*, which means the narrator uses the third person and reveals the thoughts of some but not all the characters in the novel. The action of the novel is presented through the shifting points of view. By controlling the point of view, the narrator can provide or withhold information, often for purposes of characterization. For example, in the scene in which Dorothea goes to the Lydgate home to convey her faith in the doctor to his wife, the reader sees with Dorothea's poor eyesight that Rosamond and Will are sitting close together in intimate conversation. Even the maid does not know Mrs. Lydgate is at home and so has not announced Dorothea's entrance. Dorothea leaves with the faulty impression that Will is attached to Rosamond. Next, the reader learns the truth, as Eliot keeps the third person point of view located in the Lydgate home and Will confesses that no other woman exists for him besides Dorothea. Then the reader is allowed to observe the mistaken Dorothea as she ponders during a wakeful night. She decides that, despite her apparent loss of Will's love, it is right for her to return the next day to complete her original purpose, affirming her confidence in Lydgate. This decision expresses Dorothea's belief that doing good in order to ease another's distress is more important than withdrawing in despair over one's own private loss. During the conversation that ensues the next morning, Rosamond rises reflexively to Dorothea's generous action by informing Dorothea of Will's devotion. Thus the handling of point of view distinguishes Dorothea from those who recoil in discouragement or broadcast their neighbors' shortenings based on negative perceptions or gossip. In contrast to them, Dorothea acts kindly despite her negative impressions of the situation. The boon in this action is that it elicits reciprocal kindness, in this case from the habitually unkind Rosamond.

Point of view is also used to dramatize people's inner struggles. For example, the scene in which Featherstone's wills are read shows the listeners' reactions. The detached Mary Garth "could see all complexions changing subtly," except for Joshua Rigg, who sits in "unaltered calm." However, when the second will is read, which designates the whole estate to Rigg, Mary turns away. She cannot look at Fred. Mary provides a reliable or neutral view of the participants because she does not listen in blind self-interest. While not involved directly in the assignment of wealth, Mary is able to observe the comic selfishness of others. However, when she realizes that by not burning the second will she in effect helped disinherit Fred, her view of the scene is no longer detached. Now, she is self-conscious and fears Fred's distress. She avoids looking at his face. As Mary averts her eyes, the reader learns more about Mary's feelings. Yes, she wants Fred to develop himself and, in her opinion, gaining an inheritance might prevent that. Yet she would not knowingly stand in the way of his receiving one. She faces the irony that in doing the right thing by refusing Featherstone his request, she inadvertently blocked a huge inheritance for Fred. Thus, in the handling of point of view, the scene shifts from focusing on outward expressions of the self-seeking relatives to the inner, quite selfless struggle of the well-intentioned Mary Garth.

It is easy to label the point of view in a given work, but it is often unwise to assume it is only handled one way throughout the text. Point of view is the author's chosen camera lens. In directing this lens, the author chooses frame by frame what information is delivered in the text and what information is not. The lens of point of view contributes substantially to the meaning the reader sees in the work as a whole.

Meaning of Names

Some names in *Middlemarch* seem to have extra meaning. First, Lowick is the name of Casaubon's parish and house. Given the darkness in his house, "his Lowick library," and the catacombs in which he wanders "taper in hand," it seems a very low wick indeed and only faintly illumines both his location and his thinking. Second, Celia calls her sister Dodo. A dodo is an extinct, flightless bird or a stupid person. Celia may intend only the diminutive of her sister's full name, but this nickname implies negative aspects of Dorothea's personality. She is flightless so long as she is tied to Casaubon, and one could also say she is stupid in marrying him in the face of her eagerness to draw up cottage plans in order to directly improve tenants' lives. Dorothea is wholeheartedly committed to doing good, to helping others, and this impulse is antithetical to Casaubon's meanspirited nature and self-protective choices. So the nickname directs readers' attention to limitations in Dorothea she is slow to recognize. A third example may be found in the last name of Tertius Lydgate. "Lid" and "gate" are two mechanisms of enclosure, so his last name is composed of words that suggest obstruction, confinement, and limit. These may be cues that foretell the defeat of his aspirations.

Descriptions of characters are often metaphoric in this novel. For example, Will Ladislaw describes himself as an unfettered "Pegasus." Will thus compares himself to a mythological creature, the flying horse. This figure underscores the difference between Will and Casaubon, who studies mythology in subterranean vaults. Will's similarity to the fanciful air-bound creature is apparently positive; in fact, Mr. Brooke describes Will this way: "he is trying his wings. He is just the sort of young fellow to rise." So here the winged creature is interpreted to be one who will succeed.

Historical Context

Reform

Eliot deliberately locates the action of this novel in the three years that culminated with the passage of the Reform Bill of 1832. Following the American and French Revolutions, demands for political reform increased in England. There was a growing belief in the rights of all Englishmen to participate in government, whether they were property holders or not. Anglican clergy and landowners were the two groups staunchly opposed to this development. Against weakened Tory (conservative) opposition and rising agitation outside Parliament, the first of three nineteenth-century reform bills was passed in 1832. The Reform Act eliminated so-called rotten boroughs (voting districts that had far fewer residents than others yet had equal political representation), redrew voting districts in light of current population distribution, and extended the franchise further into the property-owning middle class. With the passage of this act the aristocracy's political monopoly was broken forever, and about half of all land-owning, middle-class Anglican men received the right to vote.

Writing in the early 1870s with the clarity of hindsight regarding a time forty years earlier, Eliot knew how medical science evolved during the middle decades of the nineteenth century. Her novel touches on several issues and discoveries that were important during those years. First, as a result of land enclosures, populations suddenly increased in mill and factory towns as rural, landless workers sought urban employment. Slums developed in major cities that were ill equipped to handle this influx of people. Many writers, both scientific and literary, described the actual conditions faced by thousands. For example, Friedrich Engels (1820–95) presented eyewitness accounts of London and Manchester in *The Condition of the Working Class* (1845), and Charles Dickens (1812–70) in *Bleak House* (1852–53) described a London slum and the cholera and typhoid fevers that spread through it. So it is not surprising that Dr. Lydgate comes from Paris and London particularly aware of urban crowding and epidemics. That he believes in autopsy as a valid procedure for determining cause of

Compare & Contrast

- **1832:** Doctors are not paid for their time and their services. Rather, their income derives from the profits they obtain through selling drugs.

  Today: Doctors charge for their time, their services, and their medical opinions. Patients obtain medicine with a doctor's prescription from a licensed pharmacy. In addition, in the United States, pharmaceutical companies advertise directly to consumers, and their sales representatives canvass doctors' offices, distributing free samples of new drugs to be given out to patients.

- **1832:** A candidate with no credentials other than money and influence may run successfully for election to the House of Commons.

  Today: In Britain, as in many democracies in the world, the most important factor in the success of a candidate is his party affiliation. A candidate for the House of Commons stands little chance of being elected unless he is adopted by one of the three major parties, Labour, Conservative, or Liberal Democrat.

- **1832:** Many middle-class, educated young men enter the clergy, seeking a sinecure (a permanent, respectable job requiring little work and providing a steady income).

  Today: The Church of England finds it increasingly difficult to recruit suitable candidates for the clergy. A similar problem is faced by the Catholic Church in the United States, and many churches share priests. There is a debate among Catholics in the United States about the ordination of women.

---

death makes sense, too. Particularly in the first half of the century, doctors performed illegal autopsies on corpses sometimes procured by grave robbers. This double crime existed because doctors wanted to learn about the human body but were prevented by law from dissecting it. But Middlemarchers are suspicious of a man who cannot identify the physical problem and treat it in order to prevent death and then wants permission to cut apart the body in hopes of identifying what he should have known in the first place.

Estate law was another area of reform, and the issue of primogeniture was debated throughout most of the century. The longstanding right of the first-born male to inherit the estate protected land from being subdivided among siblings and also assured familial continuity in membership of the House of Lords. The succession of certain titled individuals perpetuated aristocratic dominance by concentrating wealth in one descendent, and it prevented large land tracts from subdivision. One change came in the passage in 1870 of the Married Woman's Property Act, which provided that a married woman retained control of property she brought into marriage. Despite this small gain for women's rights, throughout the century the vast majority of women were, in terms of wealth, satellites of males to whom they were attached by blood or law, and this relationship determined their financial circumstances.

Critical Overview

Middlemarch appeared in eight books or volumes between December 1871 and December 1872. In 2000, W. W. Norton published a second edition of its Norton Critical Edition of the novel.

In her journal for January 1, 1873, Eliot reported on the initial response to *Middlemarch*: "No former book of mine has been received with more enthusiasm." Indeed, the *Saturday Review*, for December 7, 1872, stated: "as a didactic novel it has scarcely been equaled." It also pointed out: "The quarrel with humanity in *Middlemarch* is its selfishness." By contrast to this widespread human failing, it stated that "Dorothea is so noble and striking a character—her charm grow[s] upon us as the story advances." Once the complete novel

English country house   © Bettmann/Corbis

had been published, Sidney Colvin, writing for *Fortnightly Review* on January 19, 1873, called *Middlemarch* "the chief English book of the immediate present" and "the ripest" of all Eliot's novels to date. Colvin further stated that the novel shows a "powerful knowledge of human nature" and demonstrates its author's "studies in science and physiology."

Henry James agreed and disagreed. In his March 1873 review, which appeared originally in *Galaxy*, James argued that the characterization was uneven. He acknowledged that Mr. Brooke, along with the Garth and Farebrother families, among others, were deftly handled, but James found the portrait of Will Ladislaw to be "a failure." James also wrote that the subject of the novel as defined by "the eloquent preface" is "a young girl framed for a larger moral life," yet after Casaubon dies, the entire plot having to do with Dorothea centers on whether she will marry Ladislaw. Thus, in James's view, the high ideal of taking action to improve the world dissipates disappointingly in a somewhat conventional marriage plot.

Regarding the Norton Critical Edition 2000 second edition of *Middlemarch*, the *Contemporary Review* praised its "wealth of additional material" but singled out as "[p]erhaps most valuable" the

explanatory notes that allow a reader to understand many references in the text itself.

Criticism

Melodie Monahan

Monahan has a Ph.D. in English and operates an editing service, The Inkwell Works. In the following essay, Monahan explores how Eliot's parable of the pier glass explains the limitation of characters' points of view and implies those limitations can be surpassed.

George Eliot's *Middlemarch* has as its title the name of a fictional town in the English Midlands; the novel presents a picture of provincial life during a little less than three years, from September 30, 1829, to May 1832. This broad subject is narrowed by Eliot's focus on characters whose romantic and professional lives are interconnected. Four courtships (two of which involve the main character, Dorothea Brooke) are dramatized, along with the professional struggles of the newcomer Dr. Lydgate and the sudden disgrace of the well-established banker, Nicholas Bulstrode. These plots show various angles on several themes, chief among which perhaps is the way that egoism (self-interest or an inflated sense of self-importance) affects characters' actions. Given the limited omniscient point of view, readers see the action through the characters' subjective perceptions, their thoughts, their interpretations, and their interests, and they also see through the lens of the narrator (the voice in the text that relates the story as distinct from George Eliot the author). The narrator frequently stops relating the story in order to analyze it by pointing out discrepancies and contradicting evidence and by contrasting characters' views of particular events. In this way, the narrator shows repeatedly how subjective human understanding is and how likely that understanding is to be limited by self-interest or personal motive. Characters are distinguished by their different interpretations and by their actions, which express their motives and beliefs. In the world of this novel, it may be safe to say that most people act out of self-interest, but some individuals are able to see beyond themselves and act on behalf of others. Individual gestures of kindness, especially those which require some form of personal sacrifice, constitute for Eliot true heroic acts; however small or seemingly inconsequential, these moral actions in incremental degrees improve the world this novel depicts.

Egoism is the belief that self-interest determines a person's actions. The idea here is that people value themselves (and their own drives and goals) over others, and self-interest determines how they interpret their circumstances and choose to act. Of the main characters, the highly egoistic are Rosamond Vincy, Edward Casaubon, and Nicholas Bulstrode, and to a lesser extent Tertius Lydgate. By contrast, those who are able to see beyond personal desire and act on behalf of others, even when it requires personal sacrifice or going against public opinion, are Dorothea Brooke, Reverend Farebrother, Mary Garth, and Caleb Garth, along with the minor characters Humphrey Cadwallader and Henrietta Noble.

In the key passage about the pier glass, Eliot employs a scientific illustration as an analogy (or comparison) in order to explain how the egoist sees the world. The narrator describes something empirical (that can be tested through material means) in order to explain something psychological (in this case, how self-interest affects interpretation). This passage appears at the beginning of Chapter XXVII:

Your pier-glass or extensive surface of polished steel . . . will be minutely and multitudinously scratched

> **The pier glass illustration suggests that a person who wants to see beyond the blind spots of egoism can learn about the world by testing immediate impressions against impartial empirical evidence."**

in all directions; but place now against it a lighted candle . . . and lo! the scratches will seem to arrange themselves in a fine series of concentric circles round that little sun. It is demonstrable that the scratches are going everywhere impartially, and it is only your candle which produces the flattering illusion of a concentric arrangement. . . . These things are a parable. The scratches are events, and the candle is the egoism of any person.

The surface patina of a rubbed pier glass (a large mirror on a wall, often placed between two windows) or polished steel is covered with tiny scratches that go in every direction. When a lighted candle is brought close to the surface, its scratches appear to take on a concentric organization because only concentric scratches catch the light. The illusion of concentricity exists despite the "demonstrable" fact that the scratches go "everywhere impartially." The narrator then explains the analogy: "The scratches are events, and the candle is the egoism of any person." This scientific illustration is meant to explain how an inflated sense of self-importance causes a person to see events as having a flattering order and meaning, whereas in fact that order is superimposed by his own wishes or interests. The character that most engages in this self-serving distortion is Rosamond Vincy, daughter of an indulgent mother and graduate of a typical female finishing school, who has been conditioned to believe her physical beauty and social refinement are sufficient to garner her a rich husband and speedy transit to a class above that of her birth family.

The pier glass illustration suggests that a person who wants to see beyond the blind spots of egoism can learn about the world by testing immediate impressions against impartial empirical evidence. The reliance on empirical evidence is in line with Victorian thought of Eliot's own day, a time in which scientists and enthusiastic amateurs engaged in scientific experimentation and data collecting.

What Do I Read Next?

- Readers who enjoy *Middlemarch* may find Eliot's *Mill on the Floss* (1860) also interesting, especially regarding insights on the schooling of children according to gender rather than ability and the way fashion in clothing affects female behavior. This novel also deals with bankruptcy and the ways in which a love relationship can sabotage aspirations.

- Charlotte Brontë's romantic novel *Jane Eyre* (1847) traces the education and professional development of a young woman without family or financial support.

- Tim Dolin's 2005 biography *George Eliot*, part of Oxford University's Authors in Context series, studies Eliot's life within its larger social and intellectual context. The final chapter of this book comments on television adaptations of *Middlemarch*.

- For a contrast to *Middlemarch* in so many ways, readers may enjoy the American study of small town life provided in Sherwood Anderson's brief novel, *Winesburg, Ohio* (1919).

That Mr. Farebrother, for example, shows his personal collection of insects and other found objects to a visitor to his home and is interested in Dr. Lydgate's formal experiments reflects a quite widespread, middle-class interest in the empirical world. Moreover, Mr. Farebrother's decision to seek information from Mary Garth about her feelings for Fred Vincy before Mr. Farebrother expresses his own interest in her shows how a person can act considerately in the wider realm despite personal longing. The conceited and willful Rosamond assumes she is a star and all else orbits her. When contrary evidence presents itself (for example, Lydgate's inability to pay his debts), Rosamond disregards it, relying on tears and deliberate manipulation to pursue her social-climbing aspirations.

Similar self-delusion can confound even a person trained in objective analysis. For example, during courtship the infatuated Dr. Lydgate misreads the nature and intention of Rosamond Vincy: Lydgate's ability for "inspection of macerated muscle or of eyes presented in a dish . . . and other incidents of scientific inquiry" is not sufficient to correct the distortions generated by sexual attraction and "poetic love." Lydgate is charmed by Rosamond's demure manner, her sweet voice, and her taste for fine things. He assumes these attributes will soothe him after a long day of work, and he completely misconstrues as love for him her statement rejecting her father's objection to their engagement. If he could see more objectively, he would recognize as ominous her admission that she never gives up anything she decides to do. But he thinks he is superior and she submissive; thus, he misconstrues her obstinacy as devotion to him.

In contrast to these egoistic characters, some characters are more able to see from others' perspectives and are good to others as a result. Their altruism (the unselfish regard for and commitment to the welfare of others) affects their interpretation of events and their behavior. The leading person in this group is Dorothea Brooke, whom the Prelude suggests is one of "[m]any Theresas," saintly women who try "to shape their thought and deed in noble agreement." Dorothea explains the belief behind her kind actions this way:

> [B]y desiring what is perfectly good, even when we don't quite know what it is and cannot do what we would, we are part of the divine power against evil—widening the skirts of light and making the struggle with darkness narrower.

Dorothea acts on this belief as soon as she understands what to do. For example, she overrides her great disappointment in the apparent romantic involvement of Will Ladislaw with Mrs. Rosamond Lydgate in order to affirm her confidence and trust in Dr. Lydgate. Dorothea is quick to defend Lydgate, and when Sir James Chettem and Mr. Brooke urge her to remain uninvolved, Dorothea responds: "What do we live for, if it is not to make life less difficult for each other?" When Lydgate benefits from her generosity he concludes that Dorothea has "a heart large enough for the Virgin Mary," and he calls her "a fountain of friendship towards men." Dorothea is willing to put her money and her faith in Lydgate, despite the townspeople's belief that his risk of bankruptcy comprised his ethics in dealings with Bulstrode and in the treatment of Raffles. Given what happens to both the doctor and the banker, the townspeople may be understood as more correct than Dorothea.

Readers may ask what is the sum of Dorothea's achievement or in the larger scheme of things what effect does her kind action have. The answer near at hand is given in the scene in which Mr. Farebrother acts altruistically toward Fred Vincy. The narrator explains that such "a fine act . . . produces a sort of regenerating shudder through the frame, and makes one feel ready to begin a new life." Rosamond is permanently affected by Dorothea's kindness: Rosamond "never uttered a word in depreciation of Dorothea, keeping in religious remembrance the generosity which had come to her aid in the sharpest crisis of her life." Thus, Eliot might assert, the tiny increments of good assist in the slow evolution of human community. However, whether those increments are sufficient to identify a latter-day saint, the novel does not explicitly affirm.

Art that depicts human kindness can serve the high moral purpose of "enlarg[ing] men's sympathies," Eliot explained in a letter to Charles Bray. The small acts of characters in a fiction serve to direct attention to the importance of seeing beyond egoism to the world as it is and making efforts to do good in that world. Eliot put her faith in gradual amelioration (slow improvement), and *Middlemarch*, while it dramatizes the narrow field of human egoism and altruism, brings its readership to contemplate the wider ways in which the enlightenment of the incremental good mitigates, however imperceptibly, the darkness of self-interest.

Source: Melodie Monahan, Critical Essay on *Middlemarch*, in *Novels for Students*, Thomson Gale, 2006.

Sources

Colvin, Sidney, Review of *Middlemarch*, in *Middlemarch*, Norton Critical Edition, Norton, 2000, pp. 575–78; originally published in *Fortnightly Review*, January 19, 1873, pp. 142–47.

Eliot, George, Journals, in *Middlemarch*, Norton Critical Edition, Norton, 2000, p. 535; originally published in *George Eliot's Life as Related in Her Letters and Journals*, Vol. 3, edited by J. W. Cross, Blackwood, 1885, pp. 191–92.

———, Letter to Charles Bray, dated July 5, 1859, in *Middlemarch*, Norton Critical Edition, Norton, 2000, p. 526; originally published in *The George Eliot Letters*, Vol. 3., edited by Gordon S. Haight, Yale University Press, 1954–1955, pp. 110–11.

———, *Middlemarch*, Norton Critical Edition, Norton, 2000.

James, Henry, "George Eliot's *Middlemarch*," in *Middlemarch*, Norton Critical Edition, Norton, 2000, pp. 578–81; originally published in *Galaxy*, March 1873, pp. 424–28.

Review of *Middlemarch*, in *Middlemarch*, Norton Critical Edition, Norton, 2000, pp. 573–75; originally published in *Saturday Review*, December 7, 1872, pp. 733–34.

Review of the Norton Critical Edition of *Middlemarch*, in *Contemporary Review*, Vol. 277, No. 1617, October 2000, p. 255.

Further Reading

Beer, Gillian, *Darwin's Plots: Evolutionary Narrative in Darwin, George Eliot, and Nineteenth-Century Fiction*, Cambridge University Press, 2000.

This synthesis of nineteenth-century intellectual thought and art traces the effects of Darwin's evolutionary narrative on diverse texts, both fictional and scientific. Chapter 5 is specifically on *Middlemarch*.

Cox, Gary W., Randall Calvert, and Thrainn Eggertsson, *The Efficient Secret: The Cabinet and the Development of Political Parties in Victorian England*, Cambridge University Press, 2005.

This analysis of institutional changes in parliamentary government in nineteenth-century England concentrates on the period between the first and third Reform Acts. It is an overview of the political and historical context in which these changes occurred.

Holcombe, Lee, *Wives and Property: Reform of the Married Women's Property Law in Nineteenth-Century England*, University of Toronto Press, 1982.

This important history of English common law focuses on the evolution of nineteenth-century women's legal rights over their own property.

Shaw, Harry, *Narrating Reality*, Cornell University Press, 2005.

This book examines works by George Eliot and others, providing a close analysis of the role of the narrator in realist fiction.

Midnight's Children

Salman Rushdie

1981

When it was published in 1981, *Midnight's Children* won the Booker Prize, Great Britain's equivalent of the U.S. Pulitzer Prize; in 1993, the novel was awarded the "Booker of Bookers," a honor accorded to the best novel to be published in the competition's first twenty-five years. The book follows the life of Saleem Sinai, who is born at the very moment in 1947 when India gained its independence from British colonial rule. The infant Saleem is switched at birth with a child from a rich family and as a result leads a life of luxury until the mistake is discovered. Like the other children born that night, whom he dubs "the children of midnight," he finds himself to have mystical powers; despite the advantages conferred on him, Saleem's life takes him down paths of struggle and ruin before he is able to find peace.

Midnight's Children, roughly based on the early life of its author, Salman Rushdie, is considered a masterful blend of fiction, politics, and magic. Critics credit it with making the worldwide literary audience aware of the changes that India underwent throughout the twentieth century. With his masterful control of the English language and his ability to render even the most minute events in full, vivid details, Rushdie takes readers on an imaginative trip that makes them see his native country in a way that they never did before.

Author Biography

Salman Rushdie was born in Bombay, India, on June 19, 1947, just two months before the protagonist of *Midnight's Children*, whose birth coincides with the moment India receives its independence. He attended school in Bombay and in Rugby, England. At Cambridge, he joined the Cambridge Footlights theater company. After graduation, he lived with his family, which had moved to Pakistan in 1964, then he returned to England and worked for an advertising agency. In 1975 he published his first novel, *Grimus*, about a Native American who receives the gift of immortality. In 1976, he married Clarissa Luward, the first of four marriages.

Midnight's Children was published in 1981 and was an instant literary success, garnering the prestigious Booker Prize for Fiction, the James Tait Black Memorial Prize (for fiction), an Arts Council Writers' Award and the English-Speaking Union Award. The book established Rushdie's international reputation. His next book, *Shame*, published in 1983, won the Prix du Meilleur Livre Étranger and was a finalist for the Booker Prize. He then published *The Jaguar Smiles*, a non-fiction account of his 1986 travels in Nicaragua.

In 1988 Rushdie published the book that put his picture on newscasts worldwide and made him a household name beyond the literary world. His fourth novel, *The Satanic Verses*, contained a section parodying the prophet Mohammed, offending millions of Muslims worldwide. On February 14, 1989, the government of Iran, led by the Ayatollah Ruholla Khomeini, ordered a fatwa, or decree of death against Rushdie. The Iranian government lifted the fatwa in 1998, but extremist Muslim groups continued to call for his death. Rushdie has lived in constant fear of assassination, and as a result has had only a handful of public appearances since 1989: one notable appearance took place in 1999, when he joined the rock group U2 onstage to sing their song "The Ground Beneath Her Feet," which was inspired by a novel Rushdie published that year. After the fatwa was lifted, however, his public appearances became more frequent.

Rushdie's first marriage ended in 1987, and he was remarried the following year to author Marianne Wiggins, but that marriage ended soon after the fatwa was imposed. He was married to Elizabeth West from 1997 to 2004. In 2004 he married model/actress Padma Lakshmi. He has a son from his first marriage and a daughter from his second.

Rushdie continues to publish frequently. His most notable novel since *The Satanic Verses* was *The Moor's Last Sigh*, published in 1994. His two books of essays, *Imaginary Homelands: Essays and Criticism 1981–1991* and *Step Across This Line:*

Salman Rushdie   Getty Images

Collected Non-fiction 1992–2002, are considered virtuoso performances. His ninth novel is 2005's *Shalimar the Clown*, about the assassination of a U.S. antiterrorism expert by his Kashmiri chauffeur.

Plot Summary

Book One

Midnight's Children is the first-person narrative of Saleem Sinai, an obscure thirty-year-old pickle factory worker who writes the fantastic story of his life each night, reading it aloud each night and having it commented on by a doting woman named Padma. He starts his story by describing how his grandfather came to the Kashmir region of India in 1915 after receiving his medical degree from Oxford and how he was approached by a wealthy landowner to examine his daughter. He was not allowed to look at her, though, and during each examination for months could only view her through a hole in a sheet that was held up by attendants. Aadam Aziz, Saleem's grandfather, fell in love with his grandmother, Naseem Ghani, by viewing her in parts.

After their marriage, the couple is in Amritsar on April 13, 1919, when British troops massacre

Media Adaptations

- *Midnight's Children* was adapted for the London stage in 2003. Based on a five-hour script that Rushdie wrote for the BBC which was never filmed, the West End production was staged by the Royal Shakespeare Company, with financial assistance from the University of Michigan and Columbia University. After its London run, it played in Ann Arbor, Michigan, then at Harlem's Apollo Theater in New York for twelve performances in 2003.

hundreds of Indian nationalists. Doctor Aziz avoids being killed in a confrontation when, sneezing, he bends over as the troops fire.

The narrative jumps to 1942, when Aadam and Naseem have grown children, three girls and two boys, and live in Agra. Aadam becomes optimistic about India's coming freedom in advance of the arrival of Mian Abdullah, a social activist known as the Hummingbird. The poet Nadir Khan, dating Aziz's daughter Emerald, is one of the Hummingbird's confidantes: when Abdullah is assassinated, Khan comes to the Aziz house and is hidden in the basement for three years. During his confinement, he and Mumtaz Aziz fall in love and are married. Emerald, feeling jilted, tells the army officer, Major Zulfikar, that Khan is hidden in the house. Zulfikar falls in love with Emerald and marries her; Khan runs away; Mumtaz becomes attracted to a leather merchant, Ahmed Sinai, and marries him, changing her first name to Amina.

Ahmed and Amina move to Delhi: though she does not love him, she does want to have children. Ahmed's business is threatened when he finds out that local criminals demand protection money from businessmen, including him. As tensions between Muslims and Hindus intensify, an angry mob chases a street vendor, Lifafa Das, and, standing between him and the mob, Amina makes a very public announcement that she is pregnant. Ahmed and some other businessmen arrange to make payments to the gangsters, but when they leave a suitcase containing the payment money at a deserted fort, a monkey

steals it: that night, Ahmed's warehouse burns down. After Ahmed collects the insurance money, the family moves to Bombay.

In June 1947 they move into the Methwold estate, an historic site being sold by its owner, a descendent of one of the first British in India, who is leaving as independence approaches. When the baby is born, at the stroke of midnight on August 15, the midwife, Mary Pereira, exchanges the Sinai child with the child of Vanita. Vanita is married to the street musician Wee Willie Winkie and dies soon after childbirth. The child whom the Sinais take home is celebrated as a symbol of Indian independence: his picture is on the front page of the paper, and prime minister sends a letter addressed to him. The other baby falls into obscurity.

Book Two

Saleem's father, Ahmed Sinai, invests his money in a factory designed to create the parts needed for sea walls, but the government freezes all his assets, leaving him weak, an invalid. His wife Amina proves lucky at betting on horses and secretly amasses a fortune, which she uses to hire lawyers to have the accounts unfrozen. When the accounts are freed, the father loses his money by investing with a man who dies, leaving no record of the investments. Saleem's childhood is tough, given the financial strife and the fact that other children pick on him because of his odd looks.

When Saleem is nine, his father hits him on the ear, and he develops the ability to communicate telepathically, to put himself in the minds of other people. When he enters the head of a neighbor child, Evie Burns, she becomes upset, and he learns that other people know when he is reading their thoughts. This discovery leads him to create a network connecting all of the Children of Midnight, the ones who, like him, were born on August 15, 1947 (1001 were born then; only 581 have survived to the age of nine). They all have special powers, ranging from a boy who can walk through mirrors to a girl whose dazzling beauty blinds anyone who looks at her. Saleem uses his ability to find out that his mother is meeting privately with her first husband, Nadir Khan. Through the group he calls the Midnight's Children's Conference, he telepathically contacts Shiva, the child with whom he was switched at birth, who believes that he, not Saleem, should be the conference leader, advocating violence and control.

Saleem is injured at school; a blood type test reveals that neither of the people he thinks are his parents actually are. He is sent to live with his uncle Hanif and aunt Pia, who are in the film business. Saleem finds out that the financier of their films, Homi Catrack, is having an affair with the wife of a navy officer, and he sends an anonymous letter to the officer, who then shoots Catrack and his wife; Uncle Hanif, without financing, kills himself. Saleem's whole family gathers for forty days of mourning. Saleem is then taken to Pakistan, where his telekinetic powers are too weak to contact the Children. Living with his uncle General Zulfikar, he is involved in the military plans for a coup.

When he returns to Bombay, Saleem's father arranges an operation to fix the boy's draining sinuses, and as a result Saleem develops an extraordinarily keen sense of smell but loses his telekinetic power. His 15-year-old sister becomes a popular singer in Pakistani radio. Saleem confesses love for her, and she is repulsed, refusing to ever see him again. War breaks out between India and Pakistan: Indian bombs kill Saleem's grandmother, his aunts Pia and Emerald, and his parents.

Book Three

Saleem wanders around Pakistan with amnesia. He joins the army and leads his patrol up the Padma river, away from the war, and the other men are slaughtered deep in the jungle. He comes across Parvati-the-witch, one of the Midnight's Children, who recognizes him from the image that he projected, and he is taken under the care of her and Picture Singh, a snake charmer. They hide him from the Indian army then help sneak him back into India to the family of his uncle Mustapha, where he stays for 420 days, mourning the dead. He then returns to the Magician's Slums, to Picture Singh and Parvati, and becomes a Communist. He marries Parvati and finds out that Shiva, the child with whom he was switched at birth, is a war hero who has fathered hundreds of children. Saleem cannot have children with Parvati because he keeps thinking of his sister, but she gives birth to Shiva's son. Government forces, led by Shiva, attack the ghetto, and Parvati is killed. The remaining children of midnight are sterilized by the government.

Saleem accompanies Picture Singh to Bombay. There, Picture challenges another man at a nightclub for the title of greatest snake charmer in the world, and he wins in a long competition. Saleem smells chutney, which reminds him of his childhood: he goes to the factory where it is made and finds the factory is run by Mary Pereira, his old nanny. She hires him, and he works in the factory by days and tells his story to Padma by nights.

Characters

Mian Abdullah

The founder of the Free Islam Convocation, Mian Abdullah is assassinated by government agents in Agra in 1942.

Aadam Aziz

Aadam Aziz is Saleem's grandfather. The story starts by telling how, as a young doctor, Aadam Aziz met Saleem's grandmother. He lives an unhappy life with her. He is briefly involved in politics in Amritsar in 1919, helping people who are being suppressed by British troops and nearly being shot for it, and again in Agra in 1942, when he is friends with the Rani of Cooch Naheen, who is involved in subversive politics. Aadam dies in 1964 after returning to Kashmir to find a religious icon, a strand of the Prophet Mohammed's hair.

Hanif Aziz

Hanif Aziz, one of Saleem's uncles, becomes a celebrated film director and marries Pia, a famous actress. While Saleem is living with them, he sends an anonymous letter that gets their financier, Homi Catrack, shot by a jealous husband; deprived of income, Hanif commits suicide.

Mumtaz Aziz

See Amina Sinai

Mustapha Aziz

Mustapha Aziz is one of Saleem's uncles, a brother of his mother. After most of the family members have been killed when India bombs Pakistan, Saleem goes to Mustapha's house and lives there for forty days of mourning, even though his uncle and his aunt want him to leave.

Naseem Aziz

Naseem Aziz, the narrator's grandmother, is the daughter of a wealthy landowner who brings the single young doctor, Aadam Aziz, to examine her. Her father only allows Aadam to view her through a sheet with a hole in it, and so he falls in love with her a little at a time.

After they are married, Naseem turns into a hard, bitter woman. She is domineering, ruling the lives of her daughters when she sees them. It is at this time in her life that she gains the nickname Reverend Mother, indicating that she is as domineering as a nun. She also develops a verbal tic, adding the phrase "whatsisname" into the middle of sentences at random.

Late in life she convinces Saleem's Aunt Pia to go to Pakistan with her and open a gas station.

Brass Monkey
See Jamila Sinai

Evelyn Lilith Burns
A tough girl from the United States who lives in Saleem's neighborhood when he is a boy, Evelyn Lilith Burns, also called Evie, is a leader of the children until one day when, first learning about his telepathic power, he enters her thoughts and finds out that other people are aware of him when he is there. The experience is disorienting to Evie, who is more aloof after it.

Evie's personality is patterned after that of a cowgirl. She has an air rifle and goes around the neighborhood shooting cats with it. One day, Saleem's sister, the Brass Monkey, who is sympathetic to the cats, waits for her and fights her. Soon after that, Evie's father sends her home to the United States.

Homi Catrack
Homi Catrack is a financier of films in Bombay. He has an affair with the wife of navy officer Commander Subarmati. Saleem sends a note to the commander, tipping him off. The commander shoots his wife and her lover, triggering a scandal that fills the news in 1958.

Joseph D'Costa
Joseph D'Costa betrays his girlfriend Mary Pereira and her sister Alice, which leads Mary to change the Sinai baby with Wee Willie Winkie's. For years after his death, Mary sees the ghost of Joseph periodically around Methwold's estate, a constant reminder of her guilt.

Lifafa Das
When Saleem's parents are newlyweds in Delhi, Lifafa Das walks the streets with a box for showing photos. One day an angry mob sets on him, accusing him of being a child molester because he is a Hindu in a Muslim part of town; to save him, Amina announces to the crowd that she is pregnant.

Ghani
The father of Saleem Sinai's grandmother, Ghani is a wealthy land owner who calls the doctor frequently to examine his daughter, clearly promoting a romance between Aadam Aziz and his daughter, Naseem. Ghani brags about the expensive European artwork that decorates his house, even though he is blind.

Naseem Ghani
See Naseem Aziz

The Hummingbird
See Mian Abdullah

Sonny Ibrihim
Sonny Ibrihim is Saleem's childhood friend.

Nadir Khan
Nadir Kahn is an anti-British poet who dates Saleem's aunt Emerald and then, while hidden from British troops under the Aziz house, falls in love with her sister Mumtaz and marries her. Their marriage is a secret, since he cannot come out from hiding in the basement of the Aziz house. Emerald, whom he dated first, betrays his hiding place to the police, forcing him to run away, and Mumtaz is left still a virgin after two years of marriage. Kahn shows up later in the story, meeting Amina Sinai (the name that Mumtaz has been going by) at the Pioneer Café, but Saleem lets his mother know that she is being watched, and she breaks off their relationship.

Ilse Lubin
A college friend of Aadam Aziz who comes to visit him while he is courting Naseem Ghani, Ilse Lubin goes for a ride on the lake with the boatman Tai and mysteriously ends up drowned. A brief suicide note ("I didn't mean it") is later found.

William Methwold
A descendant of the William Methwold who was one of the original British occupiers of India, this William Methwold sells his estate to several people, including Saleem Sinai's parents, in order to leave before Indian independence in 1947.

Padma
Padma is the narrator's confidante, the person to whom he tells the story of his life. Her name means "The One Who Possesses Dung." Throughout the novel, Saleem tells the story that he is writing to Padma, who is uneducated and illiterate. She listens and comments critically, telling him what parts she likes and what parts she finds impossible.

In the end, Padma convinces Saleem that he should be married, if only for the sake of his son, Aadam. The novel ends with Saleem marrying Padma.

Parvati-the-witch

Parvati-the-witch is one of Midnight's Children. Saleem runs into her in Pakistan, while he is suffering amnesia, and she helps him remember who he is. She helps smuggle him back into India and then marries him. Saleem cannot have children with her because every time he touches her he thinks of his love for his sister, Jamila. Parvati becomes pregnant by Shiva instead and has a son whom Saleem raises as his own after she dies in a government raid against the Magician's Ghetto.

Mary Pereira

A midwife at Dr. Narlikar's nursing home in 1947, Mary Pereira loses her boyfriend to her sister: bitter about love, she exchanges the Sinai baby with Wee Willie Winkie's baby when they are born. Filled with regret soon after, she arranges to become the Sinais' nurse and thus is the person primarily responsible for Saleem's upbringing.

Rani of Cooch Naheen

In Agra, the Rani of Cooch Naheen is a supporter of the Free Islam Convocation and sponsor of Mian Abdullah.

Reverend Mother

See Naseem Aziz

Shiva

The true son of Ahmed and Amina Sinai, Shiva was switched with a poor family's baby at birth. He is known for his powerful, bulbous knees. When he is a boy, Shiva is a tough-talking street urchin, a bully. When he finds out about the Midnight's Children's Conference, he claims to be co-leader. Saleem fears him and tries to keep him out of the telekinetic conference.

As an adult, Shiva becomes a celebrated army hero in the India-Pakistan war. He enters into hundreds of affairs with women and leaves them when they become pregnant, leaving hundreds of children when he dies. The one woman about whom he is concerned, though, is Parvati-the-witch: he leads the attack on the Ghetto of the Magicians, where Saleem is living with Parvati. She dies in the attack. Soon after, there is a regime change, and Shiva is court-martialed as a traitor. Saleem tells a story of his being shot while in military prison by a woman who had his child, but later he says that the story was a lie.

Aadam Sinai

Aadam Sinai is the son to whom Parvati gives birth. Her natural father is Shiva, but Saleem raises the boy as his own, and the story ends with his trying to be a father to the boy.

Ahmed Sinai

The father of Saleem Sinai, Ahmed Sinai married Mumtaz Aziz after her first husband left her, and he encouraged her to change her name to Amina. Over the years, his fortune goes up and down: he is a wealthy merchant, then is ruined by a fire, then has insurance money to invest, then his holdings are frozen by the government, then they are unfrozen. In the end, he operates a successful towel manufacturing plant in Pakistan. He dies when India invades Pakistan in 1965.

Amina Sinai

Originally named Mumtaz, Amina Sinai, the narrator's mother, first marries Nadir Kahn, a revolutionary poet. He is wanted by the government for involvement with revolutionaries, and their marriage takes place in secret while he is hiding in her family's basement. After Kahn goes into hiding, Amina marries Ahmed Sinai and changes her first name. She has a run of good luck betting on horses when her husband's bank account is frozen and is able to pay for lawyers with the money she earns from gambling, in order to have his money released. She dies in 1965, during the bombing of Pakistan by Indian forces.

Saleem Sinai

Saleem Sinai, the narrator of *Midnight's Children*, tells a story that begins decades before his birth, with details about his grandparents' courtship and his parents' lives before he is born. Regarding the details of his own life what he narrates is so fantastic that Padma, the person who listens to his life story night after night, often refuses to believe him.

Saleem is born at the stroke of midnight on August 15, 1947, the very moment at which Great Britain granted India, its former colony, its independence. Minutes after his birth to a poor street singer and his unfortunate wife, who dies during childbirth, he is switched with the son of a wealthy merchant family, and they raise him. He is an ugly child with a large, constantly congested nose. When Saleem is young, a blow from his father triggers telepathic ability in him, which eventually lets him bring all of the children born on that night in August into mental contact with each other. He finds out that his rival, Shiva, who was born at approximately the same time, wants to control the Midnight's Children, to use the special powers they all have to rule the country. After an operation to fix his sinuses, Saleem loses his telepathic ability.

When his parents learn after a blood test that Saleem is not their real child, they send him to Pakistan to live with relatives. He is there when India invades Pakistan. Most of his family is destroyed, and Saleem, having lost his memory, travels the countryside as a conscript in the army, going deep into territories that are sparsely inhabited. He regains his memory when Parvati-the-witch, one of the children who was connected to him telepathically, recognizes him. Parvati is part of a traveling magic show, and she helps him sneak back into India. She is killed, and Saleem is left to raise Aadam, the child fathered by his rival Shiva.

In the end, Saleem works at the pickle factory run by his old nurse. It is a job for which he is particularly well suited because he has an extraordinarily keen sense of smell. Padma, an uneducated worker who has listened to his stories throughout the book, tells Saleem that a man his age, 31, should be married, and so he marries her.

Jamila Singer

Saleem's younger sister, Jamila Singer starts life known as Brass Monkey, a plucky, tomboyish girl. After Saleem is found not to be her biological brother, she deals with his exile out of the country by turning to the Catholic religion.

In her teens, living in Pakistan, Jamila is found to have a beautiful singing voice; a friend of the family puts her on the radio, and she becomes a national sensation and a symbol of Pakistani pride. She is never seen in public, and nobody knows that she is actually Indian. Saleem falls in love with her, but she refuses to see him and sends him away.

After the India-Pakistan war, she is thought to be dead, but Saleem is certain that she has gone to live in a convent.

Tai

Tai, the boatman on Lake Dal, becomes a foil for Aadam Aziz when he moves to the Kashmiri region. He mocks the doctor for being too self-important. Tai becomes increasingly eccentric and stops bathing. When the doctor's college friend Ilse visits, she is last seen in Tai's boat before she drowns. Tai is rumored to have died in 1947 while protesting the struggle for Kashmir between India and Pakistan.

Vanita

Wife of Wee Willie Winkie and the real mother of Saleem Sinai, Vanita has a baby just as India is granted independence, but her baby is exchanged with the Sinai baby in the crib. Vanita dies soon after the baby is born.

Wee Willie Winkie

The actual father of Saleem Sinai, Wee Willie Winkie loses his own child when it is switched with the Sinai child soon after the babies are born. Wee Willie Winkie is a traveling singer who happens to be around the Methwold estate in August 1947. After he loses the child's mother in childbirth, he stays around Bombay for a while, a ruined alcoholic, singing on the streets with his ruined voice.

Major Zulfikar

Investigating the assassination of Mian Abdullah in Agra in 1942, Major Zulfikar falls in love with Saleem's aunt Emerald and marries her.

Themes

Identity

Saleem Sinai, the protagonist of *Midnight's Children*, examines the thirty years of his life covered by this novel (and the thirty-six years that preceded it) in order to understand who he is. Throughout the story, he is torn by conflicting evidence that his is either a special, magical existence or quite an ordinary one. He is born to common parents, so poor that he finds out at one point that the man who is his natural father would have broken the legs of the boy he thought was his son, in order to make him a more effective beggar. For the first ten years of his life, though, neither Saleem nor his family knows of his humble roots, and so he is raised as the son in an educated and wealthy family. Because he was born at midnight on the day of Indian independence, he grows up knowing that his birth was marked with honors, by a newspaper article and a letter from the prime minister. He comes to find that he has supernatural powers, which he uses to communicate with the other children born on the same day he was, finding that they are all gifted, but not as gifted as he is, except for Shiva, the child with whom he was switched at birth. He sees himself in them, especially in Shiva. He understands his powers through their powers, and he lacks the personal attributes which Shiva, whom he understands to be his opposite, has, particularly aggression.

Saleem's later years are humbling, which helps him understand the life of a poor anonymous peasant such as the one to whom he was born. In the bombing of Pakistan that kills off most of the members of his family at the end of Book Two, he loses his memory. Thereafter he uses the name

Topics for Further Study

- Saleem Sinai's life is influenced by the fact that he was born at the date and hour of Indian independence. Find out the most significant fact concerning the date on which you were born, and make a chart of events from your life that could possibly have been influenced by it.

- When Saleem's sister becomes a pop music icon in Pakistan, her fans do not know her true identity. Choose another country, and determine what your persona would be if you were to become a pop singer there.

- This novel starts in Kashmir, a region that in the early 2000s was still involved in territorial disputes between India, Pakistan, and China. Research the history of the Kashmir valley and propose what you think would be a fair solution to the political uncertainty of the region.

- Near the end of his story, Saleem Sinai befriends Picture Singh, a famous snake charmer. Give a report to your class on the science and the superstition of snake charming.

- How many different ways are there to make pickles? What are the variables? What changes in the formula will create what changes in the outcome? Examine some recipes or, if you can, talk to someone at a pickle factory to find out how challenging Saleem's work is.

- Watch one of India's famous musical films and discuss which elements of the film style resemble techniques that Rushdie used in writing *Midnight's Children*.

"Buddha": though the name implies religious insight, he achieves nothing in this guise other than leading his fellow soldiers to their deaths. He lives in a ghetto among carnival workers, adapting a Marxist philosophy, but in the end the homes of the poor are simply bulldozed by the rich. The novel ends with Saleem's finding a balance in his life, an identity that is both anonymous and singular: he works in a pickle factory as a humble laborer, but there, with his extraordinary sense of smell, he is able to create the greatest pickles and chutney ever known.

Post Colonialism

The fact that Saleem Sinai's life begins just as the era of Britain's colonial control of India ends links the life of the novel's protagonist to India's post-colonial growth. As the novel's narrator, looking back over the events of his life, Saleem proclaims himself to be dying of the same problem that can be seen of any country that has been thrust abruptly from immaturity to maturity: he is, he says, "falling apart." At first, newly independent India is strong and thrives, enjoying inherited wealth the way that a child like Saleem, born into a prosperous family, might enjoy a secure sense of privilege. Like Saleem's Midnight Children's Conference, though, there are always underground organizations, and these alliances produce someone like Shiva who competes for control and pushes a violent agenda. Saleem's fortunes totter back and forth, just as the nation's do, depending at times on chance, coincidence, and the willingness of those around him to ignore his illegitimacy, as the people of India prove willing to accept the illegitimate military rule that imposes martial law. When India invades Pakistan, Saleem's life is changed forever by the loss of his family, and India's identity is changed by its brutal suppression of the county that was its twin. In the end, Saleem reaches a state of peace but only by accepting his own lingering frailty, a sign that Rushdie finds India to be continuously vulnerable.

Absurdity

Many aspects of Saleem's life as presented in this novel do not make much sense. Some of these, such as the magical powers enjoyed by the children of midnight, can be read as symbols of the inherent promise of the generation born into a free country. In other cases, though, Rushdie gives details that do not easily correspond to any larger message. These details, which are notable but not necessarily meaningful, help to heighten the reader's sense of the absurdity of Saleem Sinai's world.

Saleem's looks, for instance, are presented as a mockery of the traditional epic hero. His nose is his most prominent feature, so large that people remember him years after having last encountered him. His nose looks unheroic and, worse, it is always runny. In his childhood, Saleem has his hair pulled out by its roots and he loses a finger in a slammed door. All of these traits combine to make him look miserably grotesque. It is absurd to expect readers to identify with Saleem.

There are many instances in the novel in which Rushdie makes the case that life in post-colonial India is absurd, from the power of Saleem's archrival to crush enemies with his mighty knees to the cowgirl persona of young Evie Burns to the national fascination with the trial of Commander Subarmati to the fact that Padma, who is the only person who cares about Saleem in the end, has a name that means "Dung Princess." There are elements in this book that indicate a higher significance, but there are also cases in which the notable elements are here to indicate that, even at its most grotesque, the world of this novel is a strange place full of wonders.

Fatalism

After all of the events that affect Saleem's life, and all of the ways in which he affects the course of India's development, the story ends on a note of fatalism. Throughout the book, Saleem returns repeatedly to the fact that his life seems to be significant: he was born at the moment of independence, he has the power of telepathy, he can smell the very emotions that surround him. As late in the book as the start of the Indo-Pakistan war of 1965, he muses that the whole battle was probably waged just to destroy his family. Rushdie does not present the exaggerated elements in the book as having sprung from Saleem's imagination, and yet it is hardly likely that all of India's development would center on the life of one boy.

By the end of the book, Saleem realizes the simple notion that life goes on. He does not want to affect the outcome of the world any more; he just wants to make really good pickles. Though the book starts at a moment of promise, it ends with a mood of realism: Saleem has a son and a new wife to live for, but by the last page he has given up the expectation that he alone will be able to affect drastic changes.

Style

Foil

Rushdie ends the first book of *Midnight's Children* with the revelation that the man who has been telling the tale, known as Saleem Sinai, is in fact the child of other parents, and that the child the Sinai family had was raised by paupers. Because of their connection by birth, Saleem and the other child, Shiva, are set up to function as foils to each other. A foil is a character whose physical and psychological attributes are opposite of another character with whom he is paired; each of the paired characters highlights the qualities of the other.

It is true that Saleem and Shiva are physical opposites: Shiva is strong and handsome, while Saleem is weak and ugly. It is also true that they are temperamental opposites, as Saleem freely admits when he discusses his fear of Shiva's violent nature. Rushdie even brings their lives together at various times, having them vie for leadership of the Midnight Children's Council that Saleem calls together and bringing Shiva into the story when Saleem is unable to impregnate his wife, Parvati. Still, their paths only cross several times: hundreds of pages of the novel go by without Shiva being mentioned. If he were a more conventional foil, Shiva would be a more constant presence, giving readers a gauge by which to measure how Saleem grows and changes.

Method of Narration

Some novels are written in third person, in which the narrator tells the story using "he" and "she," or in first person, in which the narrator relates the story using "I" and "me." *Midnight's Children* is told in first person. Saleem tells his own story. Readers are told at the start of the second chapter and reminded repeatedly that this story is being written by a sick man and commented on by a critical woman named Padma. The nature of Saleem's relationship with Padma is gradually revealed. Rushdie's handling of the telling of the story creates suspense, making readers wonder about the circumstances of its telling until the end of the last chapter.

Episodic Plot

Although readers know that Saleem Sinai is going to survive the events of the novel, they cannot anticipate other aspects of the story's outcome. The plot of *Midnight's Children* does not rise and resolve the way readers may expect; instead, separate episodes are strung together, a series of incidents with no particular logical arrangement. There is no way that a reader could guess, while reading the first half of the book, that Picture Singh would play an important role at the end or that someone such as Sonny Ibrihim, often mentioned in the early chapters, would disappear from the narrative altogether. While some plots weave events into a complicated situation that must be resolved for the plots to reach a conclusion, this novel's plot consists of dozens of episodes that have little in common beyond the fact that they all happen within one individual's life.

Historical Context

Indian Independence

European interest in India as a source for materials and labor goes back to the 1490s, when Portugal won exclusive rights to the lucrative markets and continued through control gained by the Dutch East India Company, which broke the Portuguese monopoly in the beginning of the seventeenth century. The East India Company, an unofficial arm of the British government, impinged on the Dutch, fighting a series of battles for control of different areas of India, eventually consolidating control in the 1750s. The country was under British control for the next two centuries.

After the formation of the Indian National Congress in 1885, protests against British rule became increasingly common. Nationalistic parties were distracted, however, by the rise of ethnic and religious groups within the country, such as the Muslim League, formed in 1906. In-fighting between Muslims and Hindus diverted attention from the general protest against the British.

After World War I, Mohandas K. Gandhi (1869–1948), an Indian nationalist and spiritual leader who preached non-violent protest, launched a movement to resist Britain, based on non-cooperation and the refusal to buy British goods. The British jailed Gandhi from 1922 to 1924, but he went on to revive the independence movement, successfully leading the people of India in civil disobedience. He convinced Indians to refuse to pay British taxes, particularly the tax on salt, and, to call attention to the plight of his people, he fasted to near starvation.

Weakened by World War II, Britain determined that it could no longer fight to control India and agreed to give up control. The British government arranged to relinquish all command over the area at midnight on August 15, 1947: the very moment that the narrator of *Midnight's Children* was born. At that time, the territory was partitioned between India to the west and a new country, Pakistan, to the east, with the region of Kashmir left open for dispute. Also freed from British rule at that time were Burma (later called Myanmar) and Ceylon (later called Sri Lanka).

Indo-Pakistani War

The partition of India and Pakistan was followed by massive riots in both countries, resulting in millions of deaths. The exact details concerning the countries defined by the British upon their departure were considered matters of dispute. On October 20, 1962, India was attacked along its long border with China in the Himalayas, losing the border territory in a battle that lasted roughly a month (the border territory remained in dispute into the early 2000s). Pakistani military leaders took this defeat as a sign that India was weak. They also believed that there was massive dissatisfaction in the Kashmir territory against Indian rule. On August 5, 1965, Pakistan sent an estimated 30,000 troops into Kashmir, encouraging the Kashmiri people to rise up for independence from India. Indian forces of equal strength entered Kashmir August 15. In September, when Pakistani forces attacked the town of Ackhnur, India attacked directly against Pakistan, beginning a quick and bloody conflict, though no formal declaration of war was ever issued. By September 22, the United Nations arranged a ceasefire, which both sides signed.

Six years later, in 1971, the two countries were at war again. The conflict came about because Pakistan had been created in two distinct territories: East Pakistan, which was mixed ethnically and included Punjabis, Sindhis, Pathans, Balochis, Mohajirs, and more, and West Pakistan, which was mostly Bengali. In 1970, in the first general elections since Independence, a Bengali leader, Sheikh Mujibur Rehman, led his party to victory in national elections; rather than give in to democratic rule the country leaders declared a state of emergency and jailed the sheikh. Months of bloody riots led to a plan to give the Bengalis a separate land in East Pakistan. Eight to ten million refugees fled over the border into India. Realizing a crisis, Indian Prime Minister Indira Gandhi (1917–84) declared war in December 1971.

Though the Pakistani military counted on a conflict with India ending in a stalemate as the 1965 conflict had, they were quickly and decisively defeated. The Indian Army chief, General Sam Maneckshaw, drove into Pakistan and secured the

Compare & Contrast

- **1950s:** Newly freed from colonial rule, India has a poor but promising economy. Indian businessmen, taking control of their own country, pattern their methods after those of the Europeans.

  1980s: After decades of misgovernment, India's economy is considered weak, making a country of 683 million people one of the world's poorest nations.

  Today: The Indian economy is growing at an impressive rate, as globalization makes it possible for jobs from anywhere in the world to be outsourced to workers in India.

- **1950s:** Tensions are high between the Hindu majority of India and the Muslim majority of Pakistan, leading to a succession of treaties that finally gives way to all-out war in 1965.

  1980s: Having tested a nuclear device in 1974, India is a member of the small group of global nuclear powers. Pakistan proposes a non-nuclear treaty with India but is later found to be conducting research into building nuclear bombs.

  Today: As recently as 2002, India and Pakistan have come to the verge of nuclear war.

- **1950s:** The Indian film industry, in business since the turn of the century, gains international attention as prestigious directors such as Satyajit Ray and Ritwik Ghatak present their works at the prestigious Cannes Film Festival.

  1980s: Concentrated in Bombay, the film industry, nicknamed "Bollywood," becomes a commercial powerhouse.

  Today: Bollywood films are viewed worldwide. India produces more films than any other country.

- **1950s:** Begging in the streets of a large city like Bombay or New Delhi is a full-time profession for thousands if not millions.

  1980s: The hoards of beggars that descend on tourists in India are legendary and are a standard part of travel books.

  Today: Laws are enacted to curtail begging in the streets.

---

country in a matter of weeks. Sheikh Mujibar was established as prime minister of the new country, Bangladesh, formerly East Pakistan.

Indira Gandhi

Indira Gandhi (1917–1984), the prime minister of India while this novel was being written in the 1970s, was not, as Rushdie mentions, related to the freedom leader Mohandas K. Gandhi. She was the daughter of Jawaharlal Nehru, who had been a disciple of Gandhi and became the first prime minister when India gained its independence. She grew up in a household surrounded by the most powerful figures in Indian politics and married Feroze Gandhi, a politician who died in 1960. In 1964, Indira Gandhi was elected to Parliament, and in 1966, when the prime minister died suddenly of a heart attack, she was nominated as a candidate whom the power brokers could easily control. After her election, she became fiercely independent, ruling the country from 1966 to 1977, and again from 1980 to 1984.

Gandhi was immensely popular with the Indian people immediately following the 1971 victory over Pakistan, but social conditions soon changed that. By 1973 there were demonstrations across the country against India's terrible economic situation. In June 1975 India's high court found Gandhi guilty of campaign irregularities and ordered her to resign her position. Instead, Gandhi declared a state of emergency: the constitution was suspended, the press was suppressed, and political opponents were jailed. Confident that she had successfully suppressed the opposition, she called for elections in 1977, but her party ended up losing badly. In 1980, though, she was reelected. She was assassinated in 1984 by her bodyguards, and her son, Rajiv Gandhi (1944–91), was sworn in as the new prime minister.

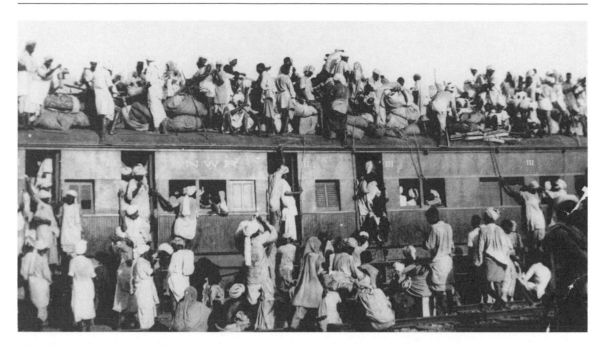

Hundreds of Muslim refugees crowd atop a train leaving New Delhi for Pakistan on the day when British India was divided up into officially Muslim Pakistan and mostly Hindu India, September, 1947

AP/Wide World Photos

Critical Overview

Salman Rushdie's second novel after *Grimus*, *Midnight's Children* brought Rushdie international acclaim. It won Britain's prestigious Booker Prize and praise from practically every reviewer who wrote about it. Phyllis Birnbaum, for instance, noted in the March 1981 *Saturday Review* that "Rushdie pleases the senses and the heart." Charles R. Larson, in the May 23, 1981, issue of *The New Republic*, called the book "a dark and complex allegory": "The narrative conveys vindictiveness and pathos," Larson wrote, "humor and pain, and Rushdie's language and imagery are brilliant."

Almost as soon as it was published, reviewers began seeing in the book great significance, for India as well as for the author. *Midnight's Children* was examined with a close eye and appreciation for its achievement. For example, V. S. Pritchett, himself an acclaimed novelist, began a multi-page review in the *New Yorker* by noting that with this novel "India has produced a glittering novelist—one with startling imaginative and intellectual resources, a master of perpetual storytelling." Pritchett ended his review by noting that "as a tour de force, [Saleem Sinai's] fantasy is irresistible." Father David Toolan gave his perspective as a

Jesuit reading about Rushdie's India, referring to it as a "Chaplinesque novel" and commenting that "In remythologizing disenchanted Bombay—and so much else—without domesticating the energy there one whit, Rushdie somehow worked the same metamorphosis on my New York, and indeed on any Western city."

Criticism

David Kelly

Kelly is an instructor of creative writing and literature in the Chicago area. In this essay, Kelly examines the ways in which the novel can be seen as too rich with possible symbolism to be understood, identifying the central symbolic structure.

Into his sprawling, dense novel *Midnight's Children*, Salman Rushdie packs hundreds of ideas that do not serve any clear purpose in advancing the narrative. There are details that are not only unnecessary but are distracting, little loose ends that do not make any real sense. When a writer does that, it is an open invitation to readers and critics to inquire into the significance of what the author has included. Not all elements must serve the story,

What Do I Read Next?

- The fantastic elements of this novel remind many critics of Günter Grass's novel *The Tin Drum*, published in 1959, which tells the story of the build up to the Nazi era in Germany through the eyes of a little boy who wills himself to never grow up.

- *Midnight's Children* is frequently compared to *One Hundred Years of Solitude* published by Columbian novelist Gabriel García Márquez in 1967. Márquez spins incredible tales into the history of a fictional South American town, Macondo, in what is considered the finest example of the "magical realism" category into which many critics fit Rushdie's novel.

- Rohinton Mistry, an Indian author, wrote *A Fine Balance* (1995), which is set in the India of Indira Gandhi during the declared state of emergency of 1974 and 1975 and covers crackdowns on journalists and political opponents, forced

sterilization, and many other subjects touched on in Rushdie's novel. It is available from Vintage International.

- The works of Sadaat Hasan Manto, a respected Urdu writer, often focus on the partition of India on August 15, 1947. His story "A Question of Honor" is representative of his work and his worldview. It is available in *Kingdom's End and Other Stories*, published in 1987 by Verso Press.

- Taslima Nasreen wrote the novel *Homecoming—Phera*, about a woman who is forced to emigrate from her homeland of Mymensingha at the time of the partition and returns, years later, to find many changes in her country. It was published in 2005 by Srishti.

- Rushdie's *Shalimar the Clown* concerns a U.S. counterterrorism expert who is assassinated by his chauffer. Random House published the novel in 2005.

---

and no one even asks that all elements be connected logically, but they all must have some reason for existing. It could well be that the reason some things seem unconnected in *Midnight's Children* is precisely to keep the story unfocused: starting, as it does, at such a significant time as the very moment of India's independence, the life of the novel's narrator, Saleem Sinai, is bound to have some allegorical meaning, and the allegory just might be that free India has no focus. If this were the case, though, then any sort of nonsense could happen in the novel, to be justified with the excuse that any sort of nonsense could happen in India. Works have been written based on theories of chaos, but Rushdie's prose is just too precise, his characters too intricately connected, and his sense of the society too acute, for one to believe that he is going for nothing more than proof that life in postcolonial India was weird.

The novel does clearly want to walk a balance between sense and nonsense. The protagonist, for

instance, is about as far from a dashing leading man as Rushdie could make him. Saleem is a thirty-one-year-old castrated employee in a pickle factory, ugly to the point of gruesome, with no companion except for a woman who cannot read the story that he is writing about his life and who mocks him, apparently finding him more ridiculous than he does himself, which is saying a lot. Much about his life is absurd, but not all of it, and as his story unravels readers are struck by just how much sense there actually is among all of the trivia. His life is not just capricious, but it follows a cyclical pattern, with Saleem's fortune going from good to bad, then good to bad, then bad, then good, *ad infinitum* (a process the book captures deliberately in its reference to the children's game Snakes and Ladders).

As with many novels, *Midnight's Children* presents its readers with differing degrees of significance. What makes this a particularly difficult book to understand is that there are so many specifics mentioned that readers are constantly trying to find where each detail fits in the larger scheme of things. Is a detail mentioned for local color and mood, such as the ghost of Joseph D'-Costa, haunting his old girlfriend, Saleem's nanny, with no apparent connection to the plot? Is it told for emotional significance, a personal sort of symbolism, such as the spittoon that Saleem carries around with him for years after the destruction of his family? Or maybe, as in the case of his sister Jamila's popular singing career in Pakistan, it could be social satire. Most of the details of the novel can fit into one of these categories, or they can be connected to the book's main stream of symbolism, the duality between Saleem and his archrival, Shiva.

It would be difficult to argue that the relationship between Saleem and Shiva lacks symbolic significance. They are both the true Children of Midnight, born at the same exact time on August 15, 1947: the other 999 referred to as Midnight's Children in the novel are actually born in the minutes and hours following the stroke of twelve. The novel seems built around this conceit, making it both the story of a boy, Saleem, whose destiny is the destiny of free India, but also the story of two children whose lives are forever, inexorably linked, having had their fates inverted, a device with literary echoes of *The Prince and the Pauper* and *A Tale of Two Cities*. However, the parallel between Saleem and Shiva is obscured by the fact that Shiva hardly appears in the book. He is a vague presence during childhood; he appears as a menacing presence in Saleem's psychic connection to the other survivors who constitute Saleem's Midnight's Children's Conference when they are all nine; and then he is gone from the story for another twenty years, only coming face-to-face with Saleem at the end of the book.

Putting Shiva in the background does not erase his symbolic significance, but it does make it harder for readers to consider this book as a story of two people. It is the story of one, with the other existing only to highlight his personality. Shiva, in fact, might not even truly exist: his exploits are so unreal, so shadowy, that it is easy to read him as a figment of Saleem's imagination. Of course, the same could be said about most of the fantastic journey that Saleem dictates to Padma throughout this novel, but many other characters and incidents have enough details to make them plausible, even if they rely on magic or coincidence or other supernatural factors. Shiva, by contrast, shows up only when Saleem's psyche seems to need him.

"Nose and knees" is one of the book's refrains, characterizing the relationship between Saleem and

> For the most part, Rushdie makes it difficult for readers to tell what facts, among the thousands related by Saleem, are important: which are the author's imagination running rampant, and which result from an over-imaginative narrator."

Shiva as if it covers the whole world. And so it does, if one looks at the two elements simplistically. If Saleem's nose is meant to signify intellect and Shiva's knees are meant to be violent force—interpretations that not only fit their personalities, but also work crudely with one's understanding of the Indian and Pakistani natural characteristics—then, yes, all of nature might be fitted into one category or the other. But these two basic meanings do not capture it all.

For one thing, Shiva's knees are a weak symbol at best. They are supposed to represent physical strength and military prowess: Rushdie relates several times, particularly in the meeting between the two main characters on the battlefield, how Shiva's mighty knees make him something to be feared. Knees, though, are not really effective military weapons. The act of crushing one's opponent in the knees, which is supposed to make Shiva fearsome in this book, is actually more awkward than intimidating. Readers are left to imagine how one would become a world-class slayer with powerful knees, but it only takes a little imagination to see that the conceit is stretched mighty thin. On the other hand, even if the knees are not as powerful as Saleem says in his narration, they do carry with them a lingering hint of defeat: knees are more often associated with supplication, with kneeling in surrender or with paying homage, than they are with destruction.

The nose is just as imperfect a symbol, but the novel at least puts more effort into making it work, starting with the nose of Saleem's grandfather, which, in the first chapter, spews gems, and carrying on through several different meanings attached to Saleem's own nose. For the first years of his life, it is just plain ugly, a large and runny feature in the middle of a face that is marred with birthmarks, and then when he is a schoolboy, he is further disfigured by premature baldness. Rushdie seems determined to make his protagonist almost painfully hideous: this could be fit into the "Saleem-as-India" symbolism scheme, but it could also be a way of marking the book's protagonist as outstanding, unique.

When Saleem is nine, however, his nose becomes the source of his own super power, a match to Shiva's strong knees. It is somehow connected to his telepathic powers, which appear when he has a pajama tie that he has shoved into it yanked out abruptly and disappear after his sinuses have been drained. The connection is never made clear—the narrator accepts this as just one of those things that is bound to happen—leaving readers to determine whether the book is trying to say something symbolically. The situation is rich with possibilities, from Freudian psychology (the telepathy kicks in just after he sees his mother naked; it ends with an operation as feared as Saleem's later forced castration) to political intrigue (while it is working, his nose makes it possible for him and Shiva to vie for control of an army of talented, neglected children).

In the end, though, it is just a segment of Saleem's life, giving way to a different exaggerated power: an ability to smell things well beyond the power of ordinary noses. For the rest of the Saleem's life, he is said to be able to smell, not just people's particular scents, but moods and attitudes as well. When this ability develops, the parallel between Saleem and Shiva is broken. They cease to be two near-twins with matching powers; Saleem's power is still related to his nose, but it is not the power invested in him as a child of midnight. His ability to sniff things out certainly does make him a suitable protagonist for an epic, symbolizing the ability of a good observer to know the story behind what he sees, but it is not the interlocking power that was once the compliment to Shiva's knees.

Midnight's Children is a story that takes its own time, sprawling across the Indian subcontinent, over decades. For the most part, Rushdie makes it difficult for readers to tell what facts, among the thousands related by Saleem, are important: which result from the author's imagination running rampant, and which result from an overimaginative narrator. The only sure thing is that he has taken special care to force the central relationship, between the two boys born at midnight, to be meaningful, even when it might not be obviously so. Readers who find themselves lost need to bear in mind that, whether it is intrinsically important to the story or not, anything to do with knees or noses

will be connected to the world of the novel in a way that gives it power. A hundred years from now, literary critics will still look for signs in this book: Rushdie starts the hunt out by confirming only two.

Source: David Kelly, Critical Essay on *Midnight's Children*, in *Novels for Students*, Thomson Gale, 2006.

Sources

Birnbaum, Phyllis, Review of *Midnight's Children*, in *Saturday Review*, March 1981, p. 72.

Larson, Charles R., Review of *Midnight's Children*, in *The New Republic*, Vol. 184, May 23, 1981, p. 40.

Pritchett, V. S., "Two Novels," in the *New Yorker*, July 27, 1981, pp. 84–86.

Toolan, David, Review of *Midnight's Children*, in *Commonweal*, December 4, 1981, p. 699.

Further Reading

Barnaby, Edward, "Airbrushed History: Photography, Realism, and Rushdie's *Midnight's Children*," in *Mosaic*, March 2005, pp. 1–16.

> The author makes the point that this novel, rather than being a work of "magical realism," is actually based on a series of imaginary photographs.

Booker, M. Keith, "Salman Rushdie: The Development of a Literary Reputation," in *Critical Essays on Salman Rushdie*, edited by M. Keith Booker, G. K. Hall, 1999, pp. 1–15.

> Booker takes a close look at this novel's critical role in making Rushdie the literary giant he was at the end of the twentieth century.

Goonetilleke, D. C. R. A., *Salman Rushdie*, St. Martin's Press, 1998.

> In the *Midnight's Children* chapter of this installment of St. Martin's *Modern Writers* series, Goonetilleke examines how Rushdie, already a good writer, blossomed by turning to his homeland as his subject matter.

Hassumani, Sabrina, "*Midnight's Children*," in *Salman Rushdie: A Postmodern Reading of His Major Works*, Fairleigh Dickinson University Press, 2002, pp. 31–46.

> As the title of Hassumani's book implies, this interpretation uses postmodernism to give some understanding to the novel, even though some critics find such a style of interpretation incomplete.

Heffernan, Teresa, "Apocalyptic Narratives: The Nation in Salman Rushdie's *Midnight's Children*," in *Twentieth Century Literature*, Vol. 26, No. 4, Winter 2000, pp. 470–91.

> Heffernan argues against the idea that this novel is nationalistic, instead making the point that it does just the opposite, that Rushdie rejects the idea of the modern nation.

Kortenaar, Neil Ten, "Women," in *Self, Nation, Text in Salman Rushdie's "Midnight's Children,"* McGill-Queen's University Press, 2004, pp. 109–27.

A subject too frequently overlooked is the ways that Rushdie uses women in this novel, from Indira Gandhi to Parvati to Evie Burns to Padma. Kortenaar considers them as a group.

————, "Salman Rushdie's Magic Realism and Return of Inescapable Romance," in *University of Toronto Quarterly*, Summer 2002, pp. 765–85.

This article examines the concept of magical realism in this novel and the various interpretations of it that apply.

Paradise of the Blind

Duong Thu Huong

1988

Paradise of the Blind, by Vietnamese novelist Duong Thu Huong, was first published in Vietnam in 1988 and translated into English in 1993. It was the first novel from Vietnam ever published in the United States and gave American readers authentic insight into the poverty and political corruption that characterized Vietnam under the communist government from the 1950s to the 1980s. Although to most Americans the name Vietnam conjures up images of the Vietnam War, the novel does not concern itself with what the Vietnamese call the American War. It begins in Russia in the 1980s, as Hang, a young Vietnamese woman, travels to Moscow to visit her uncle. As she travels, she recalls incidents from her childhood and adolescence in Hanoi and also tells of life in her mother's village during the communists' disastrous land reform program that took place in the mid-1950s. The novel, which was banned in Vietnam, is essentially the story of three women from two generations whose family is torn apart by a brother who insists on placing communist ideology above family loyalty. The exotic setting and descriptions of the lives of ordinary Vietnamese people in rural and urban areas, combined with the story of young Hang's struggle to forge her own path in life, make for a compelling story.

Author Biography

Duong Thu Huong was born in 1947, in Thai Binh, Vietnam, the daughter of Duong Dinh Chau, a North

Vietnamese military officer who fought in the communist guerilla army against the French in the 1950s. Duong Thu Huong's mother was Ngo Thuy Cham, a primary schoolteacher. Duong grew up in poverty and as a child often went hungry. She attended an arts college in Hanoi, studying music, dance, and painting. At this time she had no particular interest in literature and no desire to be a writer.

In 1968, during the Vietnam War (1959–75), Duong volunteered to lead a Communist Youth Brigade, an arts troupe that sang and put on theatrical performances for the North Vietnamese troops. She served in this capacity for the next seven years, until the end of the war in 1975, when she traveled south to Saigon. While she was in Saigon she read some of the world's great novelists, including Honoré de Balzac, Gustave Flaubert, and Leo Tolstoy.

Returning to Hanoi, Duong became a screenwriter at a film studio but soon became disillusioned with life in the communist state. She started to write political pamphlets and protested against censorship, for which she was fired from her job. In 1979, however, Duong was one of the first women to volunteer for battle when China invaded Vietnam. But her disillusionment with government corruption and repression increased in the 1980s, and she began to express her feelings and frustrations first by writing short stories and then through the medium of the novel.

Her first novel was *Beyond Illusions* (1987). It sold 60,000 copies and made her a well-known literary figure in Vietnam. *Paradise of the Blind* followed in 1988 (English translation, 1993), which was also a big seller in Vietnam. The novel was shortlisted for the Prix Fémina Étranger, 1992, and translations of it made Duong an internationally famous writer. However, the novel aroused the disapproval of the Vietnamese authorities, and Duong was expelled from the Communist Party in 1989. In the same year, her third novel, *Fragments of Lost Life*, appeared, which, like the first two, chronicled the disillusionment of ordinary Vietnamese with their political system.

In April 1991, Duong was arrested and imprisoned without trial for seven months for allegedly trying to smuggle secret documents out of the country. The document was in fact a manuscript of one of her own novels. A campaign by Amnesty International and others helped gain her release in November, 1991.

In 1994, Duong was allowed to travel to France, where she was awarded the Chevalier de

Duong Thu Huong © Aubert Dominique/Corbis Sygma

l'Ordre des Arts et des Lettres. She could have sought political asylum in France, but chose instead to return to Vietnam. Her passport was subsequently confiscated.

Duong's other novels are *Novel without a Name* (1990; English translation, 1994), *Memories of a Pure Spring* (1997; English translation, 2000), and *No Man's Land: A Novel* (2005). Her fame as a writer has helped her to avoid further imprisonment, but she has still faced harassment by the authorities, such as being followed by government agents and having her telephone tapped. As of 2005, she remains determined to continue writing, whatever the personal cost.

Plot Summary

Chapters 1–3

Paradise of the Blind begins in the 1980s. Hang, a young Vietnamese woman receives a telegram telling her to visit her uncle, who is very ill, in Moscow. Hang works in a textile factory in Russia, thousands of miles from Moscow. The account of her train journey to Moscow is then interspersed with her reminiscences of her childhood and adolescence in Vietnam and the earlier history of her family.

Que, Hang's mother, lives alone in a village after the death of her parents. When she is twenty she marries Ton, a schoolteacher. They are happy together for nearly two years, until Que's brother Chinh returns, in about 1956. He has been fighting with the communists, who now run the country. Chinh forbids Que to speak to Ton because his family are landlords and are therefore enemies of the peasantry. They belong to what Chinh calls the exploiting class, who must be denounced and punished. Such denunciations are carried out in front of all the villagers. All the landowners are denounced, and their land is confiscated, which includes Que's sister-in-law Tam and her grandmother Nhieu. However, Hang's father escapes. Que is left alone; Chinh will not even let her talk to Tam. Distressed, Que disappears from the village for six months, during which Chinh also leaves.

Some years later, the land reforms, which have been a failure, are rescinded. The Special Section for the Rectification of Errors arrives in the village, and at public gatherings the villagers vent their grievances over the injustices they suffered. Que is a target for vengeance, because Chinh is her brother, but Tam protects her.

On the train ride to Moscow, Hang recalls a visit she made with a friend to Kiev and then returns to the family story. Her mother could no longer live in the village and leaves for Hanoi, where she lives in a working-class slum and makes a living as a street vendor. Ten years later, Hang is born. She grows up miserable and lonely, knowing nothing about her father, since her mother refuses to answer her questions.

When Hang is nine, Uncle Chinh returns. It is ten years since he and his sister have seen each other. Que invites her neighbors to meet him, and they are all impressed that he is responsible for ideological education in a northern province. Chinh reproaches Que for being a street vendor, since he thinks such people are members of the bourgeoisie who are enemies of the revolution. He says he will get her a job in a factory, even though she does not want one. The real reason for Chinh's visit is that he wants his share of the money from the sale of their parents' house. Que takes Hang to the village to get the money.

Chapters 4–6

Finally, Hang's mother tells her the story of her father. Ton flees the village and finds shelter at the home of the parents of a former student of his. They ask him to leave quickly, however, because

it is dangerous for them to harbor strangers. Ton takes a three-day trip up the river in a sampan. Eventually he arrives in a Muong minority region, where he settles down and marries again, becoming the son-in-law of the village vice president. He teaches the village children, and his wife bears him two sons. After six years, a traveling salesman stops at the village, and it transpires that he knows Hang's mother. Ton visits her in Hanoi, and that is when Hang is conceived.

Hang next recalls a visit she and her mother made to Aunt Tam, who has become rich. It is the first time Hang has met her aunt, and Tam tells the story of how she survived after she was evicted from her house. During the Rectification of Errors, her house was restored to her as well as her five acres of rice paddy fields. She tells of what happened to Ton. After visiting Que, he returned to the Muong village and his wife, but she refused him permission to visit Que again and to care for his child. Feeling shamed, Ton drowned himself in a river. Tam has not forgiven Chinh for his persecution of her brother.

Back in the present, Hang recalls a quarrel with her roommates in Russia over a lost sewing machine, before returning to her childhood memories. She recalls how, as she and her mother are about to return to Hanoi, Aunt Tam showers her with love and gives her gold earrings. It is an unsuitable gift for a nine-year-old and it makes Hang feel uncomfortable.

When they are back in Hanoi, Uncle Chinh visits and tells Que that he has found her a job as a clerk in the office of a factory. But she refuses to accept it. After Chinh leaves, Que is depressed but is comforted by her neighbor, Neighbor Vi. During Tet, the national holiday celebrating the Lunar New Year, Aunt Tam arrives, bringing huge provisions as a gift for Hang. She also gives Hang money.

A year or so passes, and Que and Hang visit Uncle Chinh and his wife and two young sons. They believe Chinh has recently been very sick, but he denies it, although he is clearly undernourished.

Que discovers a new purpose in life by sending gifts to her two young nephews, even though she is robbed of everything she has at her vendor's stall. At Tet, she takes more gifts for the boys, but Hang does not enjoy the visit and decides she will never visit her uncle again. Meanwhile, Aunt Tam showers gifts on Hang, who is now a teenager.

Chapters 7–9

Hang remembers when Aunt Tam stayed at their house, looking after Hang as she studied for her college entrance exams. Because Aunt Tam is looking after Hang, Hang's mother becomes indifferent to her. Hang tries to win back her love, while Que seeks acceptance from Uncle Chinh's family. Hang goes to stay with her aunt for a week, where she enjoys the feasts that Aunt Tam prepares. At one banquet, almost the entire village is invited, including Duong, the village vice president, who is hated for his high-handed behavior. Aunt Tam criticizes him to his face about an incident in which a man was arrested without a warrant. She says the man's only crime was that he insulted Duong and the Party secretary. Aunt Tam then tells stories about wise and foolish leaders in Vietnamese history, which everyone enjoys except Duong. Embarrassed by Aunt Tam's taunting of him, he makes an early departure.

Hang reveals that this is not her first trip to Moscow to see her uncle, who visits Moscow on government business. She saw him there a year ago and discovered that he makes money by trading on the black market.

Chapters 10–12

Ten days after the banquet, Hang returns to live with her mother and also to attend the university. She is happy for a while, but then Chinh falls ill with diabetes. He needs American medicine, and Que makes sacrifices in order to provide it. As a result, she and Hang do not have enough to eat. Hang wants to sell one of the rings that Aunt Tam gave her, but her mother will not let her. Aunt Tam finds out about the situation and demands her gifts back. She refuses to allow her money to be used to help Chinh, whom she regards as a mortal enemy of her family. After this, Hang's relationship with her mother deteriorates, and during a quarrel her mother throws her out of the house. For a while Hang stays at a dormitory in her high school while she continues her college education, supported by Aunt Tam. But then her mother is hit by a car, and her leg is amputated. Hang visits her in the hospital and they are reconciled. Hang discontinues her studies and takes a job in Russia, so she can support her mother.

Back in the present, Hang arrives in Moscow. Uncle Chinh is no longer in the hospital but is staying at the apartment of Mr. Khoa, a Vietnamese graduate student. She finds Chinh alone in Khoa's room. It turns out that he works for Khoa and two other Vietnamese students, cooking and housekeeping for them. When the men return, they do not treat him well. When he is not there they speak mockingly about him, and the one Hang calls the Bohemian picks an argument with him over his practice of enforcing Communist Party orthodoxy.

The next morning, the Bohemian gives Hang money to cover shipping expenses for Chinh's black market trading.

Hang returns to the Russian province where she lives in a dormitory for textile workers. She finds a telegram asking her to return home because Aunt Tam is dying. She returns to Moscow where the Bohemian helps her to get an exit visa and also buys her a plane ticket. She returns briefly to her mother's house before going to the village where Aunt Tam lives. Aunt Tam has managed to hang on to life, waiting for Hang to come. She gives Hang a key to a trunk that holds the jewelry she bought for her and map of the garden to show where Hang's inheritance is buried. After Aunt Tam dies, Hang arranges for three memorial ceremonies, but she decides to disobey her aunt's instructions to live in her house. She cannot live in the past and must strive to fulfill her own dreams.

Characters

Bich

Bich is a peasant whom Chinh puts jointly in charge of land reform in Que's village. He is wholly unsuited to the position. Before being elevated by Chinh, Bich was a good-for-nothing who wandered from village to village. He was discharged from the French Colonial Army for drunkenness. Bich is handsome but lazy, although he knows how to flatter the village elders. After Chinh promotes him, he becomes for a while a respected figure in the village, mouthing the revolutionary slogans that he has picked up. But he brings no wisdom, only injustice, to the position he occupies, and after the Rectification of Errors he leaves the village and lives in obscurity.

The Bohemian

The Bohemian is the nickname Hang gives to a Vietnamese student whom she meets in Moscow at the apartment of Khoa. He is handsome and charming and reminds Hang of a character called Yen Thanh the Bohemian in a film she saw. She also remembers that he was one of the students who used to tease her at the university. The Bohemian berates Chinh regarding the corruption of the Communist Party, and he shows great kindness to Hang, giving her money, helping to secure her an exit visa, and paying for her air fare to Vietnam. She knows him too briefly to become romantically involved with him; with his kindness and "his confident, youthful smile" he seems to represent the possibility of love and happiness that is out of Hang's reach.

Aunt Chinh

Aunt Chinh is Uncle Chinh's wife. Like her husband, she is a Communist Party official and teaches in a school run by the Communist Youth League. Hang hears through friends that she is neurotic and a bully, often losing her temper with her students for no reason. She has little education herself, having completed only two courses designed "for workers and peasants," yet because she serves the party loyally for many years, she becomes dean of the philosophy department at the school.

Uncle Chinh

Uncle Chinh is Que's brother and Hang's uncle. Chinh is one year younger than Que. When he is young he joins the Viet Bac, the anti-French resistance movement, in the north. Later he joins the Liberation Army that drives the French out of Vietnam. After the war, Chinh becomes an official in the Communist Party and returns to his village to supervise land reform. He shows himself to be a narrow-minded, selfish man who cannot see beyond the ideology he has adopted. He behaves cruelly to his sister, banning her from even speaking to her husband and also telling her not to mix with former landowners, including her sister-in-law, because this will reflect badly on his career prospects in the party. Chinh's real goal is to rise to power in the communist hierarchy, but he never becomes much more than a party hack. Later, Chinh marries, has two children, and becomes a cadre responsible for ideological education in the northern province of Quang Ninh. He still seeks to control his sister, trying to persuade her to accept a job in a factory. Her occupation as a street trader, which in his eyes makes her a member of the despised bourgeoisie, is an embarrassment to him and a hindrance to his career. Although Que always defends her brother and tries to please him, neighbor Vi speaks the unpalatable truth: "God, he's a real little tyrant, that brother of yours." Hang also knows the truth about her uncle, and she dislikes him. When she finds out about the illicit black market trading he engages in on his official party trips to Moscow trips and how he manipulated her into visiting by pretending to be ill, she feels ashamed to be associated with him. In Moscow, Chinh is reduced to doing domestic work for a group of Vietnamese students, who have nothing but contempt for him. When Hang first sees her uncle there, he cuts a ridiculous figure, wearing an apron and a pair of women's house slippers.

Madame Dua

Madame Dua is an old woman who is a servant at Aunt Tam's house. She is also a distant relative of Hang and Tam. Although Madame Dua was born into a rich family, she fell on hard times, and Aunt Tam took her in when she found her begging on the street.

Duong

Duong is the vice president of Aunt Tam's village. All the villagers dislike him because he abuses his power. He has people arrested for criticizing him, and he takes a plot of farmland from a widow, leaving her with nothing. The woman later gets her revenge on him, killing him with one blow of a hammer.

Mr. Hai

Mr. Hai is one of the Vietnamese students in Moscow who employ Chinh as domestic help.

Hang

Hang, the daughter of Ton and Que, is the narrator of the story. She is raised by her mother in poverty in Hanoi, and as a child she does not know who her father was, since her mother refuses to tell her. She grows up lonely and miserable, finally learning the story of her father when she is nearly ten. At about the same time she meets her uncle Chinh for the first time. Hang is a sensitive, reflective child, who does not know her place in society. To her, life seems aimless and without purpose. Adding to Hang's confusion is the fact that she is caught up in a difficult family situation that is not of her making. Her Aunt Tam showers her with love and gifts, after which her relationship with her mother, who cannot afford such things, becomes distant. Hang is highly intelligent and does well at school. She passes her college entrance exams, and her aunt ensures that she is able to attend college. But Hang discontinues her studies when her mother loses a leg in a street accident. Hang takes a job in Russia, working in a textile factory, so she can send money back to her mother. She also twice visits her Uncle Chinh, although she resents his attempts to manipulate her into helping his black market activities.

As a young woman Hang must decide how she is going to shape her life. She does not want to play the traditional subservient role allocated to women in Vietnamese culture, which she sees embodied in her mother. Nor does she want to follow the instructions of her late Aunt Tam, and she decides not to live in the house she inherited from her aunt.

She wants to forge her own destiny rather than live in the past. At the end of the novel, she plans to return to university and has dreams of foreign travel.

Mr. Khoa

Mr. Khoa is a second-year Vietnamese graduate student in biology at Lomonosov University in Moscow. His apartment is where Chinh works, and where the other Vietnamese students live. Khoa has a reputation for inviting prostitutes to visit his room.

The Man in Train

The Man in the Train, who is distinguished by his pug nose and silver-capped teeth, is Hang's traveling companion on the train journey to Moscow. He is a kind, older man, and is very protective of Hang. He chases off two aggressive young men when they board the train and start to bother Hang, and he holds her hand as they make their way through the train station on their arrival in Moscow.

Nan

Nan is a huge peasant woman afflicted with the vice of gluttony. Before his death, her husband used to beat her for selling part of their rice supplies so she could buy snacks and sweets. She also used to go around the village pilfering. When Chinh unaccountably puts Nan in charge, along with Bich, of land reform in the village, she abuses the authority given her. She chooses to live in Aunt Tam's confiscated house, sharing it with Bich, but she does not take good care of it. After the Rectification of Errors, Nan ends up living on the edge of the village. According to Tam, "[s]he's just a sack of meat and filthy rags."

Nhieu

Nhieu is Hang's grandmother. During the land reform, she is denounced and is forced to kneel in front of the entire village. In the second denunciation session, she is forced, with Hang's Aunt Tam, to squat in a deep pit. As a result of this humiliation, she falls ill and dies.

Que

Que is Chinh's sister and the mother of Hang. Because of the hostility generated by her brother, Que leaves her native village and moves to Hanoi, where she raises Hang in a slum, scraping together a living as a street vendor. Her husband is dead. To Hang, her mother's life seems wasted, since she has no one to live for, and her life is filled with sorrow. Que's life is dominated by her brother, who

behaves cruelly toward her while pretending to act in her best interests. Que manages to resist Chinh's attempt to get her to work in a factory, but in spite of his selfish behavior she remains emotionally attached to him, since he is the only close family member who is still living. Que resents the efforts of Aunt Tam, her late husband's sister, to win Hang's love, and for a while there is an emotional distance between Que and her daughter. Que finds new purpose in life by trying to win acceptance from Chinh and his family by lavishing gifts on her two young nephews. She even dresses like her sister-in-law in order to win favor. When Chinh is ill with diabetes, Que goes hungry so that she can send money to Chinh for his medicine. After Que is hit by a car and loses a leg, she and Hang are reconciled, but this does not last long. After a quarrel, Que asks her daughter to leave the house, although later, after Hang returns from Russia, they are reconciled once more. They experience estrangement once again when Hang remains in Aunt Tam's village for over three months after her aunt's death instead of returning to her mother in Hanoi, a decision that angers Que.

Aunt Tam

Aunt Tam is Hang's aunt, the sister of Ton. She is an educated, proud, aloof, strong-willed, resolute woman. The humiliation of being denounced in front of the entire village, and also having her property confiscated, does not break her spirit. Aunt Tam has great strength, both physical and mental, and she works hard for many years, enduring many hardships, to build up her wealth after her property is restored to her. She never marries, and she harbors a deep and lasting hatred of Chinh, whom she blames for the death of her brother. Tam is a traditionalist; she likes to observe all the ancient rituals and regards the bonds of family as sacred. For this reason she mourns deeply for her dead brother and lavishes love and gifts on Hang, because Hang is her closest blood relative. She adopts Hang as a surrogate daughter, while at the same time disliking and ultimately hating Que, Hang's mother and the sister of the hated Chinh. Tam blames Que for the fact that Hang goes to Russia to work in order to support her mother. When she dies, Tam leaves her house to Hang, assuming she will live in it to preserve the family tradition and the altar of her ancestors.

Thu

Thu is Hang's playmate when she is little. Thu is a mean little girl who lies shamelessly. One day, the two of them go out to play without the knowledge of Thu's mother. Later, when they are caught, Thu blames Hang, who gets yelled at by Thu's mother.

Ton

Ton, Que's husband, was an educated man who was a schoolteacher. According to his sister, Tam, he could read French fluently by the age of twelve. Ton married Que, but within a year or so of their marriage, Ton was denounced by Chinh merely because his family hired farm labor. Ton could not bear the shame of being denounced in front of the entire village, and he fled. He traveled far and made a new home for himself in a Muong minority region, where he married again, becoming the son-in-law of the village vice president. After six years, he visited Que in Hanoi, and they conceived Hang. But Ton's wife would not allow him to visit Que again. Once more feeling shamed, Ton drowned himself in a river.

Tu

Tu is the younger son of Uncle and Aunt Chinh. He is three years old when Hang first meets him.

Tuan

Tuan is the son of Uncle and Aunt Chinh. He is seven years old when Hang first meets him.

Madame Vera

Madame Vera is the caretaker of the dormitory where Hang lives in Russia. She is an old Russian war widow. She can be nasty sometimes, Hang says, but she is kind and affectionate to Hang, lending her one of her hand-made shawls to keep her warm on the trip to Moscow.

Neighbor Vi

Neighbor Vi is the neighbor of Que and Hang in Hanoi. She is the only person Que can really call a friend. She is a matronly kind of woman, full of common sense and good advice.

Themes

Failure of Communism

What sets in motion the multiple individual tragedies of the novel is the attempt by the victorious communists to impose the principles of Marxism on their society. According to Marxism, in every society there is a struggle between the exploiters, the landowners or factory owners (the bourgeoisie), and the exploited, the peasants and the working classes. The so-called land reform that the communists enact in the novel is a catastrophic failure and causes great injustice, "sowing only chaos and misery in its wake," as far as Que's village is concerned. In the village, anyone who owns even a tiny amount of land is declared to be an enemy of the peasantry, even though these small landowners have never exploited anyone. Nonetheless, their property is arbitrarily seized on the orders of Que's brother, Chinh, who thinks only in terms of rigid Marxist theory of class struggle. It is Chinh's adherence to this theory that creates and perpetuates injustice in his own family. Putting ideology above family, he denounces Ton, his own brother-in-law, for the simple reason that Ton's family hired farm labor and, therefore, belong to the exploiting class. Chinh's ideological zeal leads to Ton's exile and death; Que's unhappiness; the lifetime enmity of Ton's sister, Tam; and Hang's loneliness as she grows up without a father.

In addition to applying Marxist theories in a rigid, uniform manner regardless of local conditions or common sense, the Communist Party depicted in the novel is also corrupt. Chinh and his Party hacks use official visits to Russia to make money by trading luxury goods on the black market. The hypocrisy of this is apparent in Moscow when Chinh, who must be well aware of what is going on, hectors his colleagues, telling them they "must behave in an absolutely exemplary manner while you are in this brother country." Not only this, Chinh enriches himself with the perks available to government officials. He owns a new Japanese television set and refuses to sell it even to help raise money for his sister Que, who has just had her leg amputated.

There is also the corruption of Duong, the vice president of Aunt Tam's village, who seizes land to which he has no right. The most savage indictment of hypocrisy of the communist rulers comes from the student Hang refers to as the Bohemian, who harangues Chinh in Khoa's Moscow apartment: "They decreed their thousands of rules, their innumerable edicts, each one more draconian than the last. But, in the shadows, they paddled around in the mud, without faith or law." The Bohemian asserts that what all the Party officials really sought was not the good of the country but power and perks for themselves. Indeed, this is the thread that runs through Chinh's life. For example, he claims to be concerned with his sister's welfare, but the

Topics for Further Study

- Some of the most memorable passages in the novel occur when Hang describes the effect on her of certain landscapes, including her first sight of snow falling in Russia, and her impressions of Along Bay that immediately follow (chapter 5). Write a paragraph describing the effect on you of a particularly striking scene in nature that you had not seen before. How did it make you feel? Why was it so memorable?

- As she grows up, Hang rejects many things in her culture and forms her own values. Describe how you have developed your own moral values. How do you decide what you believe in? To what extent has American culture (as found in television, books, movies and music, etc.) influenced or changed your values? In what ways do your values differ from those of your parents? What experiences have been most influential in the formation of your own value system?

- Research single-parent families in the United States. How many children grow up in single-parent families? Is the head of the household usually the mother or the father? Is the number of such families increasing, when compared to twenty years ago? If it is, why is this so? What are some of the challenges faced by children growing up in single-parent families? What challenges do the parents face?

- Since the Vietnam war ended, over half a million Vietnamese people have immigrated to the United States. What were the political and economic reasons that led them to leave their native country? What has their experience been in the United States? Where have they mostly settled? What professions have they entered? How have they adapted to American culture?

---

real reason he gets her a job in a factory is that he thinks having a street vendor for a sister is harming his own chances of advancement in the Party. It is ironic that Chinh lectures his sister about putting the interests of her own class above her self-interests, when he himself, under the guise of ideological purity, does the opposite.

Loneliness, Love, and the Bonds of Family

The devastation brought about by the land reform, which results in the persecution and eventual death of Hang's father Ton, is that Hang grows up with deep feelings of loneliness, and two families are permanently divided. Mocked by her neighbors for being the fatherless child, Hang looks back on her childhood, seeing it "like a ball kicked across the road, aimless, without any purpose." She lacks any sense of self-worth, a consequence of growing up without a name, not knowing who her father was. She compares herself to "an anonymous weed [that] grows between the cracks of a wall" and also feels a long-lasting sense of humiliation and injustice about her life. One night she dreams she is being beaten, and this feeling of senseless oppression stays with her as she matures. She feels shame at having to associate with her uncle, who has been the cause of such distress to the family. When she visits him in Moscow she refers to her life as "this slow torture, this bottomless sadness." When she is twenty she refers to the "dark circles of misery" she sees under her eyes when she looks in the mirror, and she sees the same unhappiness in an entire generation of young Vietnamese, who see no future for themselves in their society.

The child takes its cue from its mother, and Que's life has been similarly devastated by the loss of her husband. For years, she has nothing to live for, and no one to love. Hang senses this, realizing that her mother's beauty and youth had faded early, "From sorrow. For nothing. For no one." There is a deep sadness about Que's existence as a widow who ekes out a living on the margins of society. She attempts to overcome the loss of her husband by doing everything she can to win acceptance from her brother's family, showering gifts on her young nephews and serving Chinh's needs as best she can. This is how she finds meaning in her life, by clinging onto the bonds of family, even though Chinh has not behaved well towards her and is in fact the direct cause of much of her misery.

Aunt Tam lives a lonely life as well and is in perpetual mourning for her lost brother. She carries a sense of injustice around her all her days, with terrible consequences for her peace of mind. As Hang observes of her aunt, "This past had poisoned life for her, taking with it all joy, all warmth, all maternal feeling, all the happiness the world might have offered her." The love that Aunt Tam bestows on Hang, like Que's service of her brother, is an assertion of the primacy of blood ties. "She's a drop of his blood," Tam says of Hang when she first meets her. Aunt Tam takes into her house her distant relative, Madame Dua because "a single drop of our own blood, even a hundred times diluted, is worth more than swamp water."

The desperate need of both women to preserve the bonds of family is to be expected in a culture which places such importance on respect and reverence for ancestors. Indeed, ancestors are worshiped and prayed to in times of crisis. When Que is alone as a young woman, she burns incense and prays to the ancestors, imploring them to protect her, and Aunt Tam maintains an altar to the ancestors in the center of her living room.

Style

Imagery

Although Hang regards life as hard and depressing, disfigured by human greed and stupidity, she still manages to cling to hope. This view of life is conveyed by a key image that occurs in chapter 7, that of purple Japanese duckweed growing in ponds. When she is a young girl, the beauty of the purple flower makes a big impression on Hang, and years later, whenever she travels in the Vietnamese countryside, she always contemplates the beauty of these flowers, contrasting them with the ugliness of the murky pools in which they grow and the squalor of the surroundings: "At the center of these stifling landscapes, on a green carpet of weed, those purple flowers always glistened, radiant in the middle of the filth." The duckweed therefore becomes a symbol of hope and beauty emerging from the misery of life. A similar image occurs in chapter 2, where Hang refers to life as "this flower plucked from a swamp."

Setting and Atmosphere

The narrator creates a reflective, often sad atmosphere through her poetic descriptions of the landscapes she remembers, both in Vietnam and Russia. She emphasizes the emotional effects these landscapes had on her. One example occurs in chapter 5, when she describes the first snowfall she ever witnessed, in Russia. The beauty of it "pierced my soul like sorrow." This thought prompts her to recall a moment when she was a girl and her mother had taken her to visit a beach; the beauty of the scene at dawn was so extreme it was painful to Hang, perhaps because it was such a contrast to the reality of her impoverished and insecure life.

Particularly evocative are the descriptions of the slum in Hanoi where Hang grew up. She recreates the sights, smells, sounds of her childhood in all their sensory details: the brick hut in which she lived, with its leaky roof; the sounds of the street vendors as they set up their stalls in the morning and their characteristics cries as they hawk their wares; the voice of the crippled man who always sings the same mournful song; the sounds and smells of many families cooking. There are numerous descriptions of food in the novel; food is important to Hang because in her childhood she sometimes goes hungry, and even at the best of times her diet lacks variety. On occasions, too, her mother gets sick because of lack of adequate food. Therefore, as Hang grows up she always notices and records in great detail occasions when food is present in abundance and variety, such as the feasts put on by Aunt Tam. Such occasions, suggesting the resilience and goodness of life, act as a counterweight to the adversity that in general characterizes the lives of the Vietnamese people.

Historical Context

Vietnam from the 1950s to the 1980s

Vietnam was under the control of the French from the late nineteenth century until the 1950s. In 1945, communists and Vietnamese nationalists combined under the leadership of Ho Chi Minh (originally Nguyen That Thanh, 1890–1969), who made a declaration of Vietnam's independence. The French opposed independence, and in 1946, a long guerilla war began. It ended when the French, whose war effort had been heavily financed by the

Compare & Contrast

- **1950s:** The communists, known as the Viet Minh, fight in Vietnam to throw off French rule. The French do not believe that as a great colonial power they can be vanquished by ill-equipped Vietnamese guerillas. For years the pattern is that the French hold the cities while the Viet Minh grow stronger in the countryside, where they have overwhelming popular support. In 1954, the French are defeated in a decisive battle at the small town of Dien Bien Phu.

  1980s: In the early 1980s, the independent, united republic of Vietnam is at a low level of development. The war involving Vietnamese forces in Cambodia has a negative effect on the economy. In the late-1980s, the Vietnamese government begins to take steps toward a free market economy.

  Today: Vietnam remains a one-party communist state. However, in the early 2000s, the government has promoted economic liberalization and structural reforms designed to modernize the economy and produce more industries that can compete in the international market. The economy shows continual growth, increasing by 7 percent from 2000 to 2004, although 28.9 percent of the population still live below the official poverty line.

- **1950s:** Global politics is dominated by the cold war between the two superpowers, the United States and the Soviet Union. The United States pursues a policy known as "containment," in which it seeks to limit communist expansion around the globe. This policy is understood to be the reason why the United States becomes involved in the struggle in Vietnam, supporting South Vietnam against the Soviet-backed North Vietnam.

  1980s: In the late 1980s, following the economic and political reforms of Soviet president Mikhail Gorbachev, the cold war begins to come to a close. The nations of Eastern Europe throw off over forty years of communist rule. In 1989, the Berlin Wall that has divided the city of Berlin into Western and Eastern (communist) sectors, comes down, and East and West Germany are unified within a year.

  Today: The cold war is a relic of the past. The Soviet Union no longer exists, and Russia is no longer a communist state. Many formerly communist Eastern European nations are now members of NATO, the Western defense alliance. The Czech Republic, Hungary, and Poland join NATO in 1999 followed in 2005 by Bulgaria, Romania, Slovakia, Slovenia (which was part of the former Yugoslavia), and three states formerly under Soviet control, Estonia, Latvia, and Lithuania. The focus of NATO shifts from defending the West against communism to fighting international terrorism.

- **1950s:** The United States begins its involvement in Vietnam by financially supporting the French as they battle the communist guerilla army under Ho Chi Minh. After the French are defeated and Vietnam is divided, the goal of the United States is to establish a stable, non-communist South Vietnam.

  1980s: The United States maintains its long-standing trade embargo against Vietnam. It also continues to press Vietnam for information and cooperation regarding the fate of American servicemen listed as prisoners of war (POW) or missing in action (MIA) during the Vietnam War. Vietnam begins economic reforms leading to a market economy and withdraws its forces from Cambodia. Both actions help to end Vietnam's isolation in the international community.

  Today: In 2005, Vietnamese prime minister Phan Van Khai meets with President George W. Bush at the White House. He is the first head of Vietnam's communist government to visit the United States. The United States is Vietnam's biggest trading partner, and Vietnam applies to join the World Trade Organization. In July 2005, Vietnam celebrates ten years of relations with the United States at a series of events in Washington, D.C. The United States and Vietnam resumed full diplomatic relations in 1995.

United States, were defeated at Dien Bien Phu in 1954. This was the end of French colonialism in Indochina. In a cease-fire agreement at Geneva concluded in July, 1954, Vietnam was divided along the 17th parallel. North Vietnam became a communist state, supported by the Soviet Union, and South Vietnam by a non-communist, U.S.-backed government. This division was meant to be a temporary arrangement until an election could be held in 1956 that would unite the country. But the election never took place, and the 17th parallel became a firm political boundary between two separate nations.

During 1953, even before the final defeat of the French, and continuing until 1956, the North Vietnamese government undertook its land reform campaign, the effects of which on a small village are described in *Paradise of the Blind*. Privately owned land was redistributed to over 1,500,000 peasants. According to Nina McPherson, in her introduction to the Penguin edition of *Paradise of the Blind*, tens of thousands of villagers were arrested and nearly 100,000 "landlord" farmers were sent to forced labor camps by courts often run by illiterate peasants (as is the case in Que's village, in which Bich and Nan, two good-for-nothings, preside over the proceedings).

Recognizing that the land reform movement had been a mistake and had caused widespread social unrest, the North Vietnamese began a campaign to undo it, which was called "Rectification of Errors." People were sent home from labor camps and allowed to reclaim their land. (This is the campaign described in the novel in which Aunt Tam is restored her house and land.)

Following their success against the French, the North Vietnamese began a guerilla campaign to reunite North and South Vietnam. The United States provided financial support to the South Vietnamese and then, starting in 1961, military support. In 1964, the Gulf of Tonkin resolution authorized the administration of President Lyndon Johnson (1908–73) to greatly expand American forces in South Vietnam, following an alleged attack on U.S. ships in the Gulf of Tonkin by North Vietnamese forces. The United States had committed over half a million troops to Vietnam by 1969 but could not defeat the communist guerillas known as the Viet Cong. A cease-fire agreement was signed in 1973, and American forces withdrew. But in 1975, North Vietnamese forces captured the South Vietnamese capital of Saigon. The country was formally unified in 1976 as the Socialist Republic of Vietnam.

The Vietnamese government announced a five-year plan to rebuild the war-torn economy, which met with only limited success. In 1978, Vietnam invaded Cambodia, which resulted in a Western economic blockade, and the following year there were border clashes with China. During this period Vietnam was heavily dependent on foreign aid, and imports were three times the value of exports. In 1982, the International Monetary Fund reported that Vietnam needed radical economic restructuring if it was to be able to meet its debts.

In the mid-1980s, a wave of change began to sweep over communist societies throughout the world, stimulated by President Mikhail Gorbachev's policy in the Soviet Union of *perestroika* (openness) and economic reform. Vietnam had close ties with the Soviet Union and since it was continuing to face economic difficulties, exacerbated by cuts in Soviet aid, it too found itself changing course. In 1986, the Vietnamese government adopted a policy of "renovation" which included free market reforms and cultural liberalization.

Vietnamese Literature in the 1970s and 1980s

According to Maurice M. Durand and Nguyen Tran Huan, in *An Introduction to Vietnamese Literature*, Vietnamese novels written in the 1970s fell into three main categories: first, the romantic novel, including works based in myth and history; second (in communist North Vietnam), socialist realism that concerned itself with "the achievements of the Party and the anti-Imperialist struggle"; and third, the scholarly type of novel, that concerned itself with preserving Vietnam's cultural heritage. Durand and Huan single out Khai Hung and Nhat Linh as the outstanding Vietnamese novelists of the twentieth century, although they also comment that no Vietnamese author of world class appeared during this period.

In the 1980s, Vietnamese literature began to change, stimulated by the period of "renovation" that began in 1986, in which the government became more tolerant of free expression among writers and artists. The Communist Party even encouraged writers to become social critics. This invitation resulted in a wave of fiction, drama, and films that satirized clumsy, incompetent government bureaucracies and exposed official corruption. This new work was quite different from the novel of socialist realism, in which working-class heroes were presented as perfect examples of revolutionary ideology in action. The new literature presented life in Vietnamese society more realistically, rather than as that life was supposed to be according to communist propaganda. Writers who made names for themselves in this period included Huong and Ngugen Huy Thiep.

But the new freedom of expression had its limits. As Greg Lockhart reports in his introduction to *The General Retires and Other Stories*, by Ngugen Huy Thiep, in 1988, the editor of a prominent literary magazine was fired, probably because he published a story by Thiep that questioned the moral character of an eighteenth-century Vietnamese hero who defeated an invading Chinese army. Lockhart further notes that in 1990, alarmed by the pace of change in the Soviet Union and Eastern Europe, the Vietnamese government began once more to restrict freedom of expression for writers. The work of the new renovation writers became suddenly hard to find in Vietnamese bookstores and their names disappeared from public view.

Critical Overview

Paradise of the Blind was a huge success in Vietnam when first published in 1988. Forty thousand copies were sold before the authorities banned the novel for its critical attitude toward the communist government and its revelations of the disillusionment felt by ordinary Vietnamese with the system under which they lived.

In 1993, as the first novel by a Vietnamese writer to be published in the United States, *Paradise of the Blind* received respectful and enthusiastic reviews. For a *New Yorker* reviewer, Duong "fashions a vivid portrait that details unfamiliar vistas of Vietnamese life as finely as it evokes the dilemmas of adolescence." In similar vein, *Publishers Weekly* noted: "Contrasts between young, old, urban and rural, help to convey the full variety of Vietnamese lifestyles."

Several reviewers commented on the strong characterization of the two female characters, Que and Aunt Tam. Jonathan Mirsky, in the *New York Review of Books*, thought the novel was the best Vietnamese novel he had read "mainly because of its portrait of the heroine's Aunt Tam." This judgment was supported by Xueping Zhong, in *Belles Lettres: A Review of Books by Women*, who commented on the strength and self-reliance of the two women. But Zhong also saw two sides to this resilience in the face of tragedy: "The novel, however, also conveys a strong sense of ambivalence toward the two women's willingness to endure

Group of female Vietnamese prisoners of war, Qui Nhon, Vietnam, 1969 AP/Wide World Photos

hardship. The desire to preserve family lineage gives the two women strength, yet also debilitates them." Peggie Partello, in *Library Journal*, also commented on the author's depiction of women, writing that "we feel the pain of women living in a male-dominated society where they are on equal footing only with servants."

Criticism

Bryan Aubrey

Aubrey holds a Ph.D. in English and has published many articles on twentieth century literature. In this essay, he discusses the novel as a coming-of-age story.

Paradise of the Blind is a bildungsroman, a coming-of-age story. Although it is set in a society that is probably unfamiliar to American readers, the story of a young girl growing up in an impoverished single-parent family, pulled in different directions by various family ties and obligations, feeling lonely and out of place, disillusioned with society and longing to get away so she can forge her own destiny and realize her own dreams, will be recognized by many a young American.

What Do I Read Next?

- Duong's *Memories of a Pure Spring*, translated by Phan Huy Duong and Nina McPherson (2000), is set in Vietnam after the American war. It chronicles the disillusionment experienced by a composer, Hung, and his wife Suong, a singer, with the political system whose victory they helped to bring about. Hung was formerly enthusiastic about the revolutionary ideology, but he sees his former wartime comrades installed in high-ranking bureaucratic positions which they use to further their own material interests. When Hung is falsely accused of trying to flee Vietnam in a boat, he is "re-educated" in a prison, after which the authorities make it almost impossible for him to earn a living.

- In *Vietnam, Now* (2003), veteran journalist David Lamb returns to Vietnam for the first time since he reported on the Vietnam War in the 1960s and 1970s. His book is a readable, subjective account, rather than a scholarly analysis, of Vietnam as it in the early 2000s. He describes the places he visits and the people he meets and gives historical information about the country.

- *Love after War: Contemporary Fiction from Vietnam* (2003) edited by Wayne Karlin and Ho Anh Thai, is a wide-ranging collection of fifty short stories by contemporary Vietnamese writers. Particularly interesting are the sixteen stories grouped under the heading, "Love in a Time of Renovation," dating from the 1980s to the early 2000s, in which writers examine the failings of the communist system and also of the consumer society created by the free market reforms of the late-1980s, which appears to have undermined traditional Vietnamese cultural ideals.

- *The Sorrow of War* (1994), by Bao Ninh, is a novel about the Vietnam War by a Vietnamese writer who fought on the side of the communists. Reviewers have described it as fierce and emotionally gripping although sometimes hard to follow. The protagonist is the soldier Kien, who looks back just after the war has ended and relives some of his experiences, interspersing his account with childhood memories, dreams, and scenes from his postwar life.

- *Understanding Vietnam* (1995), by Neil l. Jamieson, provides a portrait of twentieth-century Vietnam. Against the background of traditional Vietnamese culture, Jamieson, who lived and worked for many years in Vietnam, discusses modern Vietnamese history and Western involvement in the country, from the coming of the French in 1858 through the Vietnam War and its aftermath. He allows the Vietnamese to speak for themselves through poetry, fiction, essays, newspaper editorials, and reports of interviews and personal experiences.

- *The Sacred Willow: Four Generations in the Life of a Vietnamese Family* (2000) by Duong Van Mai Elliott, is a family saga that gives an intimate portrait of the history of twentieth-century Vietnam. Elliott is a Vietnamese woman who studied in the United States and married an American in 1964. The couple moved to Saigon, then the capital of South Vietnam. Elliott was not a communist and at first supported the U.S. intervention, but by 1969, she was advocating American withdrawal. She describes the traditional values of her culture and explains the divisions created in her family by the political turmoil: her eldest sister was a convinced communist, while one of her brothers was imprisoned by the Viet Cong.

Hang, a highly sensitive, reflective, intelligent girl, has few role models to emulate as she grows up. Like many teenage girls, she refuses to contemplate a life that resembles the one lived by her mother. Even when she is only nine years old, she shudders at the thought that in ten years time, she might be living a life similar to that of her mother. Her mother accepts the traditional role accorded to women in Vietnamese society, of being subservient to men. She never seeks to question it, and she never really thinks for herself. According to Hang, her mother lived by "proverbs and duties." Her aim is simply to endure misfortune, believing that unhappiness makes a woman selfless and compassionate, and she hopes her daughter grows up to display the same selflessness. During Hang's early childhood, the natural love between mother and daughter prevails, but as Hang grows older a distance springs up between them. Hang loses respect for her mother because of the way Que always seeks the approval of Chinh, even after all the grief he has caused her. Hang thinks her mother is putting herself in a humiliating position, since she is acutely aware of how Chinh has divided the family. Aunt Tam will not let her (or Que) forget it.

As the disillusionment between mother and daughter grows, their relationship takes on a rhythm of bitter quarrels followed by increasingly temporary reconciliations. However, Hang does make one huge sacrifice for her mother. After Que loses her leg in a street accident, Hang abandons the college career at which she excels and takes a soul-destroying job at a textile factory in Russia so that she can send money back to her mother. At no point does Hang give any insight into how hard it was for her to make this decision, and not once does she complain about it. She probably regards it as simply doing her filial duty. But this act of loyalty and self-sacrifice cannot save their relationship for long, and their slow estrangement continues. The final communication between them comes after Tam's death, when Hang notifies her mother that she intends to remain at Aunt Tam's house for over three months, until the last memorial ceremony is completed. Que is furious and replies that Hang can stay there three years if she wants to. Hang chooses not to respond: "Life had taught me the value of silence." This is a symbolic moment showing that Hang has now permanently left her mother's orbit. The gap between them is too great, and Hang has decided that she must live life in her own way, which is not the way of her mother.

Aunt Tam presents another possible role model for Hang. She is a formidable, independent, wealthy woman who has succeeded by sheer hard work, and she lavishes her love on Hang as her closest surviving blood relative. Hang is therefore pulled in two different directions, by mother and by aunt, a struggle made more acute by the fact that Que and Tam are at loggerheads over Que's loyalty to her brother Chinh, whom Tam regards as a murderer.

Hang's relationship with Aunt Tam is a complex one. As a young girl of nearly ten, she cannot understand how she could possibly be so important

> **"Although she is only in her early twenties, Hang has no illusions about life. Her own life has been hard, and she has observed with a keen eye and ear the sufferings of others."**

to her aunt. Later, she comes to feel a genuine love for her, but it is not a simple feeling:

> No one was closer to me; yet no one could have been stranger. It was through her that I knew the tenderness of this world, and through her too that I was linked to the chains of my past, to the pain of existence.

Hang eventually throws off these chains of the past. As a young woman, she becomes the voice of a new generation that believes in change and modernity, while in their different ways her mother and her aunt represent stability and tradition.

Hang is never comfortable with the traditional family rituals that her mother is so careful to observe. As a young girl she feels awkward at family gatherings; all the rules of etiquette she is instructed to follow make her feel on edge. A few years later, at Aunt Tam's house, the traditional, elaborate celebrations of Tet, the Lunar New Year, bore her, seeming to be no more than "an extravagant, postponed form of regret, a yearning for their lost paradise."

It is Aunt Tam who preeminently represents tradition to Hang. On Hang's very first visit to her aunt, when she is nine, Aunt Tam tells her she should pray to the ancestors and to the spirit of her father. She instructs Hang to remember and fulfill her duties in this regard, to which Hang dutifully assents. But in her heart Hang cares nothing for these old rituals. Many years later, at Aunt Tam's funeral, as she follows the custom of carrying a cane and walking backward to the grave, she comments, "I was indifferent to the sacred in all this, and I still don't believe in the cults and rites. But the affection between two human beings is something that I will always hold sacred." This shows that Hang has developed her own values and has adopted a humanist approach to life. The most important thing for her is not the human relationship with the divine or the supernatural—transcendental concepts that mean nothing to her—but people's relations with each other.

It is after Aunt Tam's death that Hang makes her most decisive break with everything that her aunt represents. She knows that she cannot live her life in Aunt Tam's house, honoring the ancestors as her aunt wanted her to do. That would mean "a life deprived of youth and love, a victory born of the renunciation of existence." Thus Hang rejects the past in favor of the future. She must make her own way, based on her own talents and her own values, and it will be different from the way trodden by her mother and her aunt, who have been the two most significant people in her life. Hang's way will also be very different from the corrupt, selfish values embodied in Uncle Chinh, the third major figure in her life, which fill her with contempt.

Although she is only in her early twenties, Hang has no illusions about life. Her own life has been hard, and she has observed with a keen eye and ear the sufferings of others. She has already become a social critic and knows that her experience is representative of an entire generation of young Vietnamese. When she is in Russia she thinks of the faces of her friends, the people of her generation: "faces gnawed with worry, shattered faces, twisted, ravaged, sooty, frantic faces." Facing the future means facing pain. And yet Hang does not lose the capacity to savor the beauty of life, which she refers to as "this strange muddle, this flower plucked from a swamp." She also knows that hope, however many times it is crushed, must always be reinvented, for life must go on.

This resilience, the persistence of hope in the face of all the things that would destroy it, characterizes Hang's attitude after the death of her aunt. Her strongest desire is to return to university and resume her studies. This might strike an American reader as an unexceptional desire, but it is a rather significant decision for a young Vietnamese woman in the 1980s. Hang is aware that her Aunt Tam was an educated woman and that that was part of the reason—together with Tam's aloof personality—why she was unable to attract a husband. In this traditional, male-dominated society, it appears that an educated woman is not perceived by men as desirable. But Hang does not seem concerned by this; the desire for romance and marriage is not what motivates her. Indeed, other than Uncle Chinh, men play a small role in her life, and she has no model on which to base a successful relationship. There are only two occasions when she briefly accepts male friendship, from the man on the train and from the Bohemian, both of whom treat her in a fatherly, protective way. Hang, the fatherless young woman, recognizes in the protective look of the man on the train something for which she has

yearned all her life. But he is soon gone, causing her to express the somber, pessimistic view of life she has developed: "No happiness can hold; every life, every dream, has its unraveling." Thus does Hang arm herself for the world she must now enter as an adult. Depending on no one but herself, she clutches the flower of hope, knowing that in this world, such a flower is a precarious but necessary thing.

Source: Bryan Aubrey, Critical Essay on *Paradise of the Blind*, in *Novels for Students*, Thomson Gale, 2006.

Pamela S. Saur

In the following essay, Saur examines the portrayal of daily life in Paradise of the Blind *and how Huong "depicts both the beauty and oppression of life permeated by culture and ideology."*

Paradise of the Blind (1991), by Duong Thu Huong, was the first novel from Vietnam published in the United States. Through a first-person account of a young woman named Han, the reader learns much about contemporary Vietnamese culture, which is still steeped in ancient tradition as well as shaped by recent history. The book presents the characters' appreciation of life, dedication to work, political ideology, and family obligations. The novel also includes the protagonist's ambivalence and mixed emotions. The title, which labels the Vietnamese homeland a "paradise" and at the same time calls its unquestioning traditional residents "blind," captures this ambivalence. Alongside much suffering and struggle, the novel abounds with cherished moments filled with beauty or pleasure, whether a moment of love, a taste of traditional food, a vision of nature's beauty or the sound of music. The narrator recalls her reaction to one such moment, "[. . .] this was life, this strange muddle, this flower plucked from a swamp." Han expresses affection and admiration for the land and people, but she also adds negative comments, as in this description of her homeland: "A place where young women bend like slaves at their husbands' feet. A place where a man whips his wife with a flail if she dares lend a few baskets of grain or a few bricks to relatives in need. A strip of land somewhere in my country, in the 1980s [. . .]."

Paradise of the Blind depicts daily life in a third world economy, whose people often display extraordinary perseverance and a powerful work ethic. Han's aunt, for example, survives and eventually prospers after being evicted by communist land reformers and left with no buffalo, cow, or wagon. Forced to sleep outdoors, protected by a knife under her neck, she sells her two dresses for food, labors to turn a few acres of barren wasteland

Three generations of Vietnamese women   © Catherine Karnow/Corbis

into a rice paddy, and even invents a machine to grind duckweed into flour. The novel demonstrates the devastating effects of imposing Marxist economic concepts on a primitive rural economy. Han comments, "No one understands why my grandma Nhieu had suddenly become an 'enemy of the people,' 'a member of the reactionary class of exploiters,' just because she had inherited a few acres of rice paddy."

Strong ideals surrounding family bonds, no doubt reflecting Confucian principles, are dominant in the book. They result in conflict between Han and two powerful women, her mother and her aunt. Han recalls her mother's words, "To live with dignity, the important thing is never to despair. You give up once, and everything gives way. They say ginger root becomes stringy, but pungent with age. Unhappiness forges a woman, makes her selfless, compassionate." Han thinks, "My mother had lived like this, according to proverbs and duties." She admires her selflessness.

As a young girl, Han becomes painfully aware of weighty family bonds when she and her mother visit their ancestral village. She recalls her thoughts

on meeting her Aunt Tan, her father's sister. "I knew she was my blood, my link to my father. This was the love that had been buried, impossible to imagine. I stood very still, letting her touch me, caress me." The woman is ecstatic, even reverent, at meeting the little girl. She says, "She's a drop of his blood, my niece." Aunt Tan sets a fine table in honor of Han, and proclaims, offering a toast, "Today, because you have brought the child back to this house, I have prepared offerings to the ancestors." Han recalls, "I had never imagined that I could have such importance to others." She continues, "I felt as if I were drinking to some solemn, merciless vow, some sacred, primitive rite." Of her aunt's passionate traditionalism, Han says, "She was a lost replica of my father. The past had poisoned life for her, taking with it all joy, all warmth, all maternal feeling, all the happiness the world might have offered." Her aunt tells her that all her hard-earned wealth will be left to her. For years, she sends the girl food and gifts, including jewelry inappropriate to her age, and requires her to write and tell about her studies. Aunt Tan's extreme self-sacrifice and ardor over her as a representative of her father seem unnatural and sinister to Han, "like throwing flower petals on an abandoned grave."

> Strong ideals surrounding family bonds, no doubt reflecting Confucian principles, are dominant in the book. They result in conflict between Han and two powerful women, her mother and her aunt."

As Han's life unfolds, her aunt continues to show her extraordinary devotion, while her own mother becomes more distant. Out of pride, Han's mother refuses to sell the jewelry given her daughter by Aunt Tan, despite Han's entreaties, and nearly starves herself and her daughter. Meanwhile, she also finds a reason of her own for extreme self-sacrifice: familial objects representing her bloodline in the form of Uncle Chinh's two children. Han recalls, "I realized she had a mission now, a new source of happiness: to serve the needs of my little cousins. How intoxicating it can be, self-sacrifice."

When her aunt is dying, Han dutifully travels to her village. Although she has mixed feelings about the "ceremonies and superstitions" prevailing there, she respectfully performs the funeral rites asked of her. She doubts the sacredness of the ceremonies, yet adds, "But the affection between two human beings is something I will always hold sacred." As the book concludes, Han says, "Forgive me, my aunt: I am going to sell this house and leave all this behind. We can honor the wishes of the dead with a few flowers on a grave somewhere. I can't squander my life tending these faded flowers, these shadows, the legacy of past crimes." The young woman has performed her last duties as an ancient symbol and is ready to turn to other roles befitting her rebirth as a modern young adult. *The Paradise of the Blind* depicts both the beauty and oppression of life permeated by culture and ideology and shows in its hopeful ending that it is possible for determined individuals to resist and transcend these powerful forces.

Source: Pamela S. Saur, "Huong's *Paradise of the Blind*," in *Explicator*, Vol. 60, No. 4, Summer 2002, pp. 239–41.

Harriet Blodgett

In the following essay excerpt, Blodgett identifies "an intricate embroidery of thematic images" in the text of Paradise of the Blind.

Structured as a bildungsroman, *Paradise of the Blind* is the densely textured first-person narrative of a young North Vietnamese woman's growth into personal freedom in the 1980s. We first meet Hang, the intelligent narrator, in her early twenties, as an exported worker in a Russian textile factory after she has left university to support her recently crippled mother because she is the docile and dutiful daughter trained to self-sacrifice. Even though her mother threw her out, Hang remains filial. Besides her personal reminiscences of growing up, we learn the harrowing past history of her family via her account of the stupidities and agonies caused by the land-reform program of the 1950s, before her birth. We finally resume her story as she moves from the present into a more promising, self-aware future.

The novel's title has a double resonance, for it refers both to the deluded state of those who believe in the communist paradise on earth and to the bliss of youthful ignorance. Hence Hang's reflections, as the book is nearing its conclusion, on "my own paradise, etched into the final evening of my childhood . . . the magical, unique paradise of childhood." Both are fools' paradises, of course, the first encompassing those who will not face reality, whereas the second takes in those who cannot face it because they do not yet know it. The humanistic theme of the book is the need to engage reality, not indulge in illusions; only those who face the truth of reality are free. Duong reminds us how much harder this universal task may be for a female in a staunchly patriarchal world. Not only does traditionalist Vietnamese culture encourage nostalgic illusions about the past; it especially precludes thinking for oneself if one is a woman. Nevertheless, to refuse tradition is prerequisite for Hang's freedom.

In this tightly woven, ever-symmetrical novel, two women, mother and aunt, each with a significant brother, control the direction of Hang's life by commanding her loyalty and affection. For her family, the personal is the political. Hang's father Ton, a country schoolteacher, was forced to flee the village when Uncle Chinh, a Communist Party cadre and the brother of Hang's mother-to-be, Que, denounced him and his sister, Aunt Tam, as small landowners; after a brief return to his wife, he committed suicide. (Like many feminist novelists, Duong dispenses with the father in order to strengthen maternal influence.) Ton's mother dies from the strain of events, his sister becomes a farm laborer until the eventual restoration of family property, and his wife Que is driven off to become a food vendor in a Hanoi slum. Uncle Chinh controls Hang's immediate life through his tight and abusive hold on Hang's mother's loyalties, one that not only affects the course of Hang's life but even threatens it. Mother Que channels their slender resources into providing food for Chinh's family because he has two sons, almost starving her own daughter to do so, for in a patriarchy, sons, like brothers, are more important than daughters. (The use of food to make thematic points proves characteristic of this novel.) Traditionalist Que's persistent blind devotion to her morally bankrupt, preying brother, simply because he is her younger sibling, for whom she feels a maternal responsibility, alienates the equally traditionalist Aunt Tam, who is devoted to the continuance of the blood line and hates Chinh for destroying her brother Ton. By cultivating Hang as her father's heir, Aunt Tam divides Hang from her mother and almost from her (Hang's) own self.

Hang must free herself from the demands made upon her by both paternal aunt and maternal uncle. Although much of the book is flashback, two significant parallel events in present time advance her toward freedom. While still convalescing from illness, Hang makes a physically exhausting trip to Moscow when called upon to visit her presumably dying uncle Chinh, only to find that she is actually summoned to help him with his black-market deals. This proves to be the proverbial straw that breaks the camel's back, and, already detesting him, she divests herself of all responsibility for him thereafter. Hang next returns to Vietnam to visit her actually dying aunt. However, she refuses Aunt Tam's legacy, which would tie her to the ancestral estate, the more attractive good and a renunciation much harder to make. Although Tam's deathbed wish is that Hang stay in the ancestral house and honor her ancestors, the price, Hang reflects, is "a life deprived of youth and love, a victory born of the renunciation of existence." Even if she were to become wealthy and honored, instead of remaining bound to the past with its legacy of wrongdoings and restrictions, she determines to sell the place and depart for a distant port. It has taken all her growing-up years to accomplish this freedom, which leaves her, at the end of the book, dreaming of return to university, convinced that "we can honor the wishes of the dead with a few flowers on a grave somewhere. I can't squander my life tending . . . shadows, the legacy of past crimes."

It is a familiar outcome. A young woman opting for the life of the mind in place of her conventional duties and her cultural norms has been a common story since the early days of the contemporary women's movement. When Margaret Drabble's academic Rosamund Stacey, with a promising career before her in *The Millstone* (1965), for

> " This threat to female autonomy through mothers' gendering their daughters to passivity and subjection is also a familiar feminist theme."

example, refused to take on a mate even though she had a child (Drabble, 188–91), and Angela Carter's Marianne in *Heroes and Villains* (1969), standing on the seashore, chose the lighthouse of the mind over the fleshly woman bound to time (Carter, 138–39), they were but anticipating a trend whose variable might be the particular cultural expectations of the setting depicted but whose premise would always be the right to individual self-development. Even closer in type is Maxine Hong Kingston's book *The Woman Warrior* (1976), tracing a girl's determination to grow into a free and powerful individual; she must therefore struggle to free herself from the misogyny of her Chinese heritage and her ties to her mother while simultaneously retaining her attachment to what she values in both her mother and her Chinese past. Nor is the need for self-determination limited to the young in feminist fiction. Ramatoulaye in the Senegalese author Mariama Bâ's *So Long a Letter* (1979; Eng. 1981), having known "thirty years of silence, thirty years of harassment" (57–58), discovers and articulates her selfhood only in middle-aged widowhood when she progresses from being no more than a wife—legally defined in relation to a man according to a rigid traditional code of behavior—to a free and opinionated individual, self-defined.

Hang's grandfather's home is described early on as "a traditional house, solidly built, but dimly lit and sinister," and when Hang is welcomed by her aunt as the family heir, she feels "as if I were drinking to some solemn, merciless vow, some sacred, primitive rite." Valuable in the loyalty it requires of family members (as Duong acknowledges), cultural traditionalism also is unenlightened and threatens oppression for women because it subjects them to patriarchal devaluation and rule. When Hang moves under Aunt Tam's aegis, she submits to the authority of "the glory of the Tran family, my father and grandfather," not any female glory. If Aunt Tam will support Hang's university education, it is not for Tam's sake but because her grandfather and father were learned men, and "You must study conscientiously so you will never dishonor their memory." But there is a female tradition too, valorized through mother-daughter relations. Que teaches Hang to practice self-abnegation, especially toward family—or know guilt:

> "They say ginger root becomes stringy, but pungent with age. Unhappiness forges a woman, makes her selfless, compassionate."

> My mother had lived like this, according to proverbs and duties. She wanted me to show the same selflessness. And what had I done? My uncle, her younger brotherly—her only brother—had asked for my help. He was sick, and here I was, preparing to abandon him.

This threat to female autonomy through mothers' gendering their daughters to passivity and subjection is also a familiar feminist theme. Fay Weldon even begins her *Female Friends* (1974) with a warning against maternal indoctrination in self-subordination: "Understand, and forgive. It is what my mother taught me to do, poor patient gentle Christian soul, and the discipline she herself practiced, and the reason she died in poverty, alone and neglected. The soles of her poor slippers, which I took out from under the bed and threw away so as not to shame her in front of the undertaker, were quite worn through by dutiful shuffling" (Weldon, 5). Even more resentful of the costs of such training, the late Japanese author Fumiko Enchi shows the potential ugliness of maternal indoctrination in self-sacrifice in *The Waiting Years* (Eng. 1971), when respectable fifteen-year-old Suga is sold unawares into service as a concubine, to help out following the decline in the family's fortunes (she thinks she goes as a maid): "The one thing she dreaded above all was a reprimand [from her master], being resolved all her days to observe her mother's solemn injunction that she look after her master well and never disobey his wishes whatever might happen."

The excessive sense of importance it gives Que to serve Chinh's sons with gifts of food and money shows Hang "how intoxicating it can be" to engage in self-sacrifice—and hence how doubly dangerous and blinding. A rift grows between mother and daughter during Hang's teen years as the mother seeks only recognition from Chinh's family by what she can do for them, even stealing Hang's gift jewelry to do so, buying their love as Aunt Tam does Hang's, while the daughter wants only her mother's love. Though Chinh may trample on her with his commands, insults, and rudeness, the mother's simple perspective remains, "He's my brother. You can't deny blood ties." If Hang recognizes the flaws in her mother's perspective, "In spite of everything she

stood for, everything I was trying to escape, she was still my mother. . . . I loved her." Duong is credible about the resiliency of filial love when a mother is all that the growing child has ever had.

Even while young, Hang is entrusted with the author's perception that peasant women have long been trapped in traditions which exact extremely hard work and great suffering from them, and are handed down from mother to daughter—the daughter, so to speak, following in the mother's footsteps. Hang's encounter at nine years of age with a woman vending barley sugar—one detail in an extensive pattern of food imagery—is worth reproducing in full, because it shows how dexterously the novel's overall imagery is selected.

> As she trudged past us, a straw hat hiding her face, I stared at her blackened, dusty feet.

> "Mother, when you were little, was there always someone like this?"

> "Mmh. She's dead now. This one is her daughter."

> I was mesmerized by her huge, splayed feet. They were scored with tiny cracks, encrusted with gray patches of dead skin. Decades before her, another woman, just like her, had crisscrossed the same village, plodded along with the same feet.

Here, Hang is en route to meet Aunt Tam, her blood link to a father, for the first time; meeting her, two pages later, she is struck by how Tam's feet are elegant and thin but is also "fascinated by the thick calluses and cracks that scored the skin of her feet. Horrible, deep, ugly furrows separated the soles of her feet into flaky layers. Time and backbreaking work in the fields had ravaged them." The task for Hang is to refuse to follow in her birth mother's self-sacrificing steps of devotion to her brother or her foster mother Aunt Tam's bitterness based on loyalty to her wronged family and brother. The description of the barley sugar woman thus concludes with Tam "too frightened to speak. . . . I didn't dare ask [my mother] if, in another ten years, I would live her life, this life. The thought made me shiver."

Music also serves Duong in constructing her patterns of themes. The progress of Hang's loss of innocence, growing up into increasingly disillusioned female maturity, with disappointments, poverty, and confused loyalties, is punctuated by a refrain that emphasizes how time brings sorrow rather than joy. The slum where Hang and her mother live includes also a crippled man who sings of the universal passage of the seasons: "Hail autumn and its procession of dead leaves." We are reminded of that burden of time passing as Hang struggles to understand how her mother can accept the humiliations meted out to her by Chinh and his family: "Why did she love people who enslaved her? The cripple had started to howl again, his chant a sinister echo amid the joy and the bustle of those festival days." Yet a more elaborate use of music tied to Hang's maturing perceptions not only shows how Duong's images typically are intertwined (in this case, music with flowers), but also indicates that the overall perspective of the book is positive. A visit to Kiev with a girlfriend subjects Hang, in the friend's absence, to the foiled attempt of the friend's uncle to rape her. Safety for women is ever precarious; we have already witnessed the attempted rape that Aunt Tam bravely fended off in her field-laborer days. After Hang's escape from bodily harm when her friend chances to return, as Hang listens to records she thinks about the woman singing, who must herself have suffered, "must have known this weariness, this despair. Like us, she must have had to reinvent hope and a yearning for life." More important, Hang reflects, "The music had come from that bastard's room. So this was life, this strange muddle, this flower plucked from a swamp." In the present, as she is traveling to Moscow at Chinh's behest, she chances to hear the music again on radio and understands even more "why the voice had enchanted me. Like a call, it beckoned me to a kind of love—to revolt, the most essential force in human existence. . . . If only my mother could feel this revolt." Hang's strengthening sense of self-love induces her exaggeration about human motivation; evidently, she herself has begun to see the possibility of revolting. Faith in the possibility of good coming out of evil, a flower from a swamp, is, moreover, very much Duong's perspective in this novel, with the proviso that one grant the reality of the evil.

That perspective is elsewhere made concrete through Hang's fascination with purple duckweed flowers. For the naïve child, these are only beautiful anticipations: "Purple flowers [that] bloomed out of this blanket of green, just as the face of a loving woman blooms into mysterious, laughing promise." But when she is older, they are seen against the reality that nourishes them and thus become at once "both the purest balm and the most overpowering poison." For they are testimonials to beauty flourishing over corruption and destruction, floating on murky, rotting ponds surrounded by miserable hovels: "At the center of these stifling landscapes, on a green carpet of weed, those purple flowers always glistened, radiant in the middle of the filth: the atrocious ornament of a life snuffed out." The task is to admire the beauty and retain faith in life as possibility without ignoring the realities that menace them.

It has taken time for Hang to reach so mature and equable a perspective. Hitherto she had thought of beauty only as an essential source of esthetic delight, until it helped occasion her disillusionment with life. This we learn through juxtapositions of ideas and images. Hang first tells us how sensitive she is to natural beauty, whether the painfully transitory green beauty of Along Bay—"an exquisite green that would only exist once, in one place in the universe"—or the universal beauty of snow in Russia—"light sparked off . . . in blinding shards, frail and luminous as a childhood dream"—for "Beauty knows no frontiers, seduces without discrimination. The snow spilled onto the earth as if the sky had welled over with flowers." Such beauty gives her a sense of something perfect, as a part of life. She then, without transition, recounts an ugly incident with a sewing machine. One of Hang's roommates in her Russian apartment, when she cannot find her sewing machine, accuses her mates of stealing it. Although the machine is soon found where its forgetful owner had hidden it, the discovery comes only after recriminations that crush the girl's sense of self-worth and of importance to her comrades. That Hang herself really sees the accusing girl "for the first time," though she has lived with her for two years, is a revelation to Hang of her own blindness. More, for Hang, the incident proves epiphanic, since she comprehends fully "perhaps for the first time" that every life is subject to the experience of deep disillusionment such as the girl has had, and "the values we have honored and cherished reveal themselves in all their poverty and vulgarity." For Hang personally, however, what the incident proves on the pulses is the discrepancy between the human real and the natural ideal. For "the storm, this torrent of pure beauty, continued to flood the earth. Outside my window, a sense of perfection still permeated the air. But I felt lost."

The most encompassing imagery of the book involves not nature but food, so sustained and frequent that the published translation includes after the text a supplementary eight-page glossary of Vietnamese food and related cultural terms. Two whole pages in sequence in the text are even given to descriptions of food; elsewhere too, there are menus, recipes, cooking instructions, extensive food rituals provided, in addition to the many descriptions of food throughout. In her introduction, the translator Nina McPherson points out the Vietnamese "reverence" for food; she remarks that in predominantly rural cultures like Vietnam, food is often a powerful form of human expression, a currency that, like money, is used to quantify one's love, respect, or hatred for another person, and certainly there are plentiful examples of such human interactions in the book. However, so much emphasis on food is not a characteristic of Duong's style, as her other novels set in Vietnam show; the food imagery here is a device for the statement and embellishment of themes. This is not so unusual. Women writers worldwide have found food imagery a powerful thematic resource for both short and long writings. The Mexican author Laura Esquivel's novel *Like Water for Chocolate* (1989), for example, exploits such imagery to the point of providing recipes, as does the Indian writer Arundhati Roy in *The God of Small Things* (1997). The Ghanaian Ama Ata Aidoo's *Our Sister Killjoy* (1977) makes food the central image for the African heroine's experience of European temptations; the Egyptian Neamat El-Biheiri's "Dreaming of Dishes" makes food a testimonial to female self-denial. Even Virginia Woolf (a frequent user of food imagery, as I have shown elsewhere) contrasts the dining resources of male and female universities to enhance her attack on gender inequities in *A Room of One's Own* (1929).

Duong has many uses for food. It serves her, for one thing, to concretize status. Thus, Chinh, whose values in time do not prevail, ultimately sinks so low as a party cadre that he becomes a cook/servant to wealthier Vietnamese studying in Russia. He is even subjected to retributive justice in becoming a diabetic on a restricted diet. That the days of unchallenged communist control which put him in power are over is thus graphically clear. More important, Duong gives food special meaning by using it to show the hold of particular traditional rituals. Most significantly, this occurs when Hang, invited to Aunt Tam's for an elaborate celebration of Hang's secondary-school graduation, observes in great detail how blood pudding is made by a father and his sons. This particular ritual is obviously chosen because blood ties as established in this patriarchy are such a central thematic issue. Although the ritual is described dispassionately, it is also made ugly from the outset when Hang hears the squealing of the pig waiting to be butchered, until "a sharp screeching, a few rasping grunts, and then it was all over." After three consecutive pages of description of the ritual, Hang has an epiphanic moment: "It was that evening that I felt for the first time the emptiness here, silence, and loneliness of the countryside. Everywhere, an indescribable backwardness hung in the air, immaterial yet terrifyingly present: It would be like this for eternity. This backwardness seeped into the stillness here, like the brackish waters of the past: . . . a sluggish, liquid sweetness . . . ready at any moment to

drown those unable to rise to its surface." The association with destructive sweetness is to recur. Suffice it to say now that Hang follows up her perceptions of backwardness with a perception of her aunt and how "I finally understood" that, through her, she is "linked to the chains of my past, to the pain of existence." That way happiness does not lie. But since it is her aunt who is to fund her at university, Hang represses the fact.

Important also is that Duong gives Hang a nostalgic attraction to the time-honored foods of her country, because if she is drawn to their smells, textures, and tastes, it will be difficult for her to pull herself away from her native land and traditions. And being what one ingests, food readily symbolizes personal values, thus is the perfect concretion for the issues the book raises. Hang's mother and aunt, who represent the opposing loyalties threatening Hang's being, are emphasized as sources of food, hence values: the aunt through her copious gifts of food to Hang; the mother through the food that she sells as a street vendor to support herself and her child, or, equally as important, the food she gives to her brother Chinh's boys—"my two little drops of Do blood"—instead of her own child, so that, as Hang perceives, "At bottom she was just like Aunt Tam." We have food as necessity and food as luxury; we also have bribery by each of the sisters-in-law for personal gratification: Que to become more important to Chinh as much as to honor her blood, and Tam to secure the heritage of the house she has painstakingly rebuilt. The lavish banquets and generous gifts of food (and some money and jewelry) that mark Aunt Tam's relations with Hang do carry the price that she forever remember Chinh's injustice to her father and his house and disassociate herself from her mother's support of Chinh, hence from her mother as well. When relations between her mother and Aunt Tam are reaching a breaking point, Que, in a symbolic gesture of recognizing her antagonist as such, refuses to eat any of Tam's food.

Significantly, food is shown not only as a necessity but, thematically more important, as a pleasure, a means to make life agreeable through gratifying the senses. Like beauty, it is seductive. It can serve as the immediate bit of paradise that lets one forget ugly realities. The corollary, food as cover-up, is forced upon our attention in the description of the Hanoi working-class slum where Hang and Que live, with its street vendors who "hawk their homemade snacks: sticky rice, fried dumplings, steamed rice cakes, spring rolls, snail and crab soups, and other delicacies. . . . The aroma of onions, crispy dumplings, and red chilies fried in oil filled the air, their fragrances overpowering the stench of the garbage, the open sewers, the walls reeking of rancid urine." The point is made early and repeated later through juxtaposition in another description of the slum, where "food stalls sprung up selling dog-meat dishes, grilled sausage, dried squid and fish, beef marinated in vinegar and red-hot chilies. The street reeled with these tantalizing aromas. Drunks lurched and staggered, relieving themselves against the walls. The buildings were streaked with streams of rancid urine. On hot days, the stench was overpowering." As with the flower in the swamp, the attractive and appealing must be known to have its baser side. However, it is also to be comprehended as what life is: a mix neither base nor ideal.

Sweetness, like the purple duckweed flowers, may also be both balm or delight and threat. Hang's youth is clouded by the stigma of her lack of a father in a very, patriarchal world. When young Hang cries bitterly over not knowing even his name, her mother buys her two sticks of barley sugar to comfort her. Because the fidelity to blood required by Aunt Tam is a threat in its destructive sweetness, when nine-year-old Hang is first brought to the ancestral home, Tam has her drink wine to the ancestors with the prayer "May these deceased souls taste this sweetness," and Hang feels "a dense sugary perfume . . . intoxicating" in it. Such sweetened gratification of the senses may be tolerable for children; it becomes reprehensible for adults. Food is probably most important to *Paradise of the Blind* as a medium for the transmission of themes, because it connotes the immediate gratification of the senses. But it is blindness to live only for that. In the days of land reforms, Chinh sets up two ignorant peasants, Bich and Nan, to run the village. Cleverly tied to the story, they anticipate something of the personal conflicts to come, although they also serve for a general statement. They differ in the focus of their immorality. The man Bich is a lazy and filthy-minded drunk, corrupt in spirit (hence a parallel to Chinh); even more pertinent here, the woman Nan, who has a lone daughter, is a glutton, an abuser of her bodily appetites who cannot stop eating (hence a parallel to Aunt Tam and Que with their food excesses). "When she squatted down in front of a food vendor, she forgot everything"; "incapable of controlling her sweet tooth" and obsessed with food, she destroys her family and her inheritance. The two are Duong's indictment of a nation that debased itself body and soul during the time of land reform and

must guard against such corruption again. Fortunately, Hang learns to beware of immediate gratification. She brings home a refrigerator from Russia for her mother but goes on to divest herself of Aunt Tam's legacy. At the outset she had a vision of "a past to which each of us is linked, inextricably, by the ties of blood and race," but in the event it proves possible to extricate oneself by recognizing the link rather as shackles.

What Frank Stewart has said about the short story "Pantomime" by another important Vietnamese woman writer, Phan Thi Vang Anh, is wonderfully applicable to Duong as well, even though the details may differ: this story can be read as indicative of current societal problems, but its central theme can also be understood as a "universal" clash of values between generations "complicated by" Vietnam's past. Duong's *Paradise of the Blind* likewise reaches across national borders to depict a universal problem without losing its contextual national identity as the site for this particular version of the problem. Nor, although it has analogies to other feminist fictions, does it lose its originality. Undoubtedly, one learns from *Paradise of the Blind* about the horrors of land reform and about the customs and mores of Vietnam, including its contemporary materialistic corruption and predatory officials. But the novel is just as significant as a quietly emphatic feminist statement about a universal situation: the need for women to choose to control their lives in order to develop their individual potential instead of settling for traditional norms or easy gratification—at least if they are young intellectuals such as Hang. The text is an intricate embroidery of thematic images, and much of the success of the book lies in the concreteness and shapeliness with which its tale of female maturation into freedom of mind is told.

Duong's *Novel Without a Name* is a eulogy for lost innocence whose soldier protagonist Quan laments, "There is no way back to the source, to the place where the pure, clear water once gushed forth." *Memories of a Pure Spring,* as its title suggests, concurs by contrasting the debasements of the present with the beauty and promise of the past. *Paradise of the Blind,* however, devotes itself rather to the need for a woman to grow up avoiding illusions of paradise and, less despairingly, accepts a world that is necessarily neither ideally perfect nor completely corrupt. Its universal themes succeed because they are sustained by credible particulars.

Source: Harriet Blodgett, "The Feminist Artistry of *Paradise of the Blind,*" in *World Literature Today,* Summer-Autumn 2001, pp. 31–39.

Sources

Duong Thu Huong, *Paradise of the Blind*, translated by Phan Huy Duong and Nina McPherson, Penguin, 1994.

Durand, Maurice M., and Nguyen Tran Huan, *An Introduction to Vietnamese Literature*, Columbia University Press, 1985, p. 179.

Lockhart, Greg, "Introduction," in Ngugen Huy Thiep, *The General Retires and Other Stories*, Oxford University Press, 1992, pp. 1–12.

McPherson, Nina, "Translator's Note," in Duong Thu Huong, *Paradise of the Blind*, translated by Phan Huy Duong and Nina McPherson, Penguin, 1994, p. 7.

Mirsky, Jonathan, "No Trumpets, No Drums," in *New York Review of Books*, September 21, 1995, p. 60.

Partello, Peggie, Review of *Paradise of the Blind*, in *Library Journal*, February 15, 1993, p. 190.

Review of *Paradise of the Blind*, in the *New Yorker*, June 7, 1993, p. 113.

Review of *Paradise of the Blind*, in *Publishers Weekly*, Vol. 240, No. 3, January 18, 1993, p. 451.

Xueping Zhong, Review of *Paradise of the Blind*, in *Belles Lettres: A Review of Books by Women*, Spring 1994, Vol. 9, No. 3, p. 64.

Further Reading

Duffy, Dan, "Tara Incognita?" in *The Nation*, Vol. 256, No. 14, April 12, 1993, pp. 491–94.

This is a review of *Paradise of the Blind* in which Duffy describes Duong as "a social panoramist who writes with a tight focus on individual consciousness and personal relations." He also discusses Duong's work in the broader context of other contemporary Vietnamese writers and the oppressive political atmosphere in which they write.

Eads, Brian, "She Dares to Live Free," in *Reader's Digest*, October 1998, pp. 159–64.

Eads traveled to Hanoi to interview Duong, and they met in a hotel room, despite the fact that Eads did not have permission from the government to speak to her, which is required of foreign journalists. The article tells the story of her life and pays tribute to the courage she has shown in standing up to the repressive government in Vietnam.

Hy V. Luong, *Revolution in the Village: Tradition and Transformation in North Vietnam, 1925–1988*, University of Hawaii Press, 1992.

This is a detailed, sympathetic account of the land reform movement as it affected North Vietnamese villages in the time span covered by the novel.

Stephenson, Heather, "Out of the Kitchen and Traveling On: New Fiction by Asian Women," in *New England Review*, Vol. 16, No. 1, Winter 1994, pp. 169–75.

In this review, Stephenson praises Duong's realistic portrayal of life in Vietnam. The novel conveys a "deep, disturbing sense of pain and injustice"; it is a "devastating indictment of conditions in contemporary Vietnam."

The Razor's Edge

W. Somerset Maugham
1944

The Razor's Edge, by British novelist W. Somerset Maugham, was published in London and New York in 1944. Maugham was seventy years old when the book was published, and it was to be the last of his major novels. He was one of the most popular writers of the day, and *The Razor's Edge* was an immediate success on both sides of the Atlantic. More than one million copies were sold within a few years.

The novel spans a period of twenty-four years, from 1919 to 1943, and takes place in many different locations, including Chicago, Paris, London and India. It is a novel of ideas and of character. The main characters are upper-middle-class Americans, although Maugham, in his own person as the writer Somerset Maugham, is the narrator. The principal character is Larry Darrell, a former World War I aviator who is haunted by the fact that his friend was killed in the war saving Larry's life. Seeking an answer to the question of why evil exists in the world, Larry sets out on a quest that takes him to India, where he studies with a guru and gains mystical illumination. Larry's spiritual approach to life is contrasted with the materialism of the other characters, such as Gray Maturin, who becomes a wealthy stockbroker, and Elliot Templeton, a worldly, superficial man who spends most of his time socializing at upper-class parties.

In his depiction of a young man who rejects the dominant values of American culture and looks to the East for spiritual inspiration, Maugham anticipated the work of the Beat writers of the 1950s and the values of the counterculture of the 1960s.

W. Somerset Maugham AP/Wide World Photos

Author Biography

Playwright, short story writer, and novelist William Somerset Maugham was one of Britain's finest twentieth-century writers. He was born in the British Embassy in Paris on January 25, 1874. His father, a lawyer who was serving in the British Embassy, died when Maugham was ten; his mother, who had a keen interest in art and literature, died when Maugham was eight. After his father's death, Maugham was sent to live with his uncle in England.

Maugham was educated at King's School, in Canterbury, and then attended medical school at St. Thomas's Hospital in London, from which he received an M.D. degree in 1897. But Maugham never intended to practice medicine. Instead, he wanted to be a writer, and he wrote constantly. His first novel was *Liza of Lambeth* (1897), which was based on his medical experience. This was followed within a few years by two more novels and Maugham's first collection of short stories: *Orientations: Short Stories* (1899).

Maugham had long held ambitions to be a playwright, and in 1907 his play, *Lady Frederick*, ran for over year at the Royal Court Theatre in London. Over the next quarter of a century, Maugham was an extremely popular dramatist. He had twenty-nine plays produced, including

The Circle (1921), *Our Betters* (1923) and *The Constant Wife* (1926).

In 1911, Maugham began writing what is usually considered his finest novel, *Of Human Bondage* (1915). His literary activities were temporarily interrupted by World War I; from 1914 to 1915 he served with a British ambulance unit and with military intelligence in Geneva. In 1916, he visited the South Sea Islands where he collected material for *The Moon and Sixpence* (1919), a novel based on the life of the artist Paul Gauguin. The following year, he was again in war service, this time as chief agent in Russia for the British and American secret services. In the same year, Maugham married Syrie Wellcome, with whom he had already had a daughter, Liza, in 1915. The marriage was not a happy one and the Maughams were divorced in 1927.

In the 1920s, Maugham traveled throughout the world and yet still found time to continue his literary output. He forged a reputation as a short-story writer with the publication of *The Casuarina Tree: Six Stories* (1926) and *Ashenden* (1928). The stories in the latter collection were based on Maugham's experience in the wartime secret service.

In 1930, Maugham published one of his finest novels, *Cakes and Ale*. He was then one of the most widely read authors in the English-speaking world, and he continued to publish novels during the 1930s, including *The Narrow Corner* (1932) and *Christmas Holiday* (1939). Another novel, *The Razor's Edge*, was published in 1944. It was in part based on a trip Maugham made to India in 1936. Maugham's last novel was *Catalina* (1948). Maugham died on December 16, 1965, at his villa in France, at the age of ninety-one.

Plot Summary

Chapter 1

The Razor's Edge begins in 1919. The narrator, Somerset Maugham, is invited to a lunch in Chicago given by his friend Elliot Templeton. He meets Mrs. Louisa Bradley, her daughter Isabel and Isabel's fiancé Larry. The next day at a dinner party Maugham meets a friend of Larry's, Gray Maturin, who is also in love with Isabel. Gray's rich father has offered Larry, who does not have a job, a promising position in his company. But Larry is still suffering from the shock of seeing his best friend killed during World War I. He has no ambition or desire to work, and he turns the job offer down. Instead, he says he intends to go to Paris and loaf around for two years. Disappointed, Isabel says she will wait for him.

Chapter 2

In the fall of the following year, Maugham meets Larry in Paris, and Elliot, Mrs. Bradley and Isabel meet him in the spring. Larry shows no interest in returning to Chicago. He tells Isabel he spends his days reading. He reads French and Latin literature, and is teaching himself Greek. He loves acquiring knowledge. He asks Isabel to marry him straightaway, but she refuses because he does not have enough money. They break off the engagement but remain friends, and Isabel remains in love with him. Isabel is puzzled by Larry's attitude, but Maugham explains to her his theory that Larry is searching for God.

Chapter 3

Larry goes to work in a coal mine near Lens, in northern France, where he gets to know his co-worker, a Pole named Kosti. Kosti is an uncouth man, but he is educated and knows a lot about mystical religion, and this arouses Larry's interest. In the spring, Kosti and Larry leave the mine and wander across Belgium and into Germany, where they find work on a farm. They stay there through the summer, but Larry decides to leaves after Becker's daughter-in-law Ellie, whom he does not even like, crawls into his bed one night. He makes his way to Bonn, where he remains for a year.

Meanwhile, Isabel marries Gray Maturin, and they settle down in Chicago. Within three years she gives birth to two daughters. Gray prospers and becomes a partner in the family business. He and Isabel are wealthy and happy. Then in October 1929, the New York stock market crashes. Gray's father Henry dies of a heart attack and Gray is destroyed financially. He cannot find another job and his health breaks down. With no other option available, he and his family go to live on their plantation in South Carolina.

Chapter 4

Elliot, who remains wealthy in spite of the stock market crash, takes pity on the Maturin family and installs them in his apartment in Paris. A little while later, Maugham meets Larry by chance in Paris, and Larry calls on Gray and Isabel. He tells them he has just returned from five years in India, two of which he spent in an ashram, studying with a holy man. Two days later, Larry cures Gray of a bad headache by the use of auto-suggestion, while Isabel admits to Maugham that she is still in love with Larry.

Media Adaptations

- *The Razor's Edge* was made into a movie by Twentieth Century Fox in 1946, directed by Edmund Goulding, with Tyrone Power playing Larry.

- Another film version of *The Razor's Edge* was made by Columbia/Tristar Studios in 1984, with Bill Murray as Larry.

Chapter 5

Isabel persuades Maugham to take them on a tour of the rougher areas of Paris. In a café they meet a drunken American named Sophie MacDonald, who is an old friend of Isabel's. Sophie has never gotten over the loss of her husband and baby in a car crash. She became promiscuous and took to drink. Some while later, Larry, who has known Sophie since she was fourteen, decides he wants to save her from the degradation of her life. He proposes marriage, and she accepts. Isabel is distraught at this news, but Maugham advises her to befriend Sophie in order to keep Larry in her life. Isabel agrees to do so, but she is not at home when Sophie arrives at her apartment for the shopping expedition they had planned. Isabel has left instructions for a bottle of Polish vodka to be left on a tray in the vacant apartment. Sophie is duly tempted and goes back to her former dissolute lifestyle. Her marriage to Larry never takes place.

Meanwhile, Elliott's health is failing, and he is desperately disappointed not to have received an invitation to a grand party given by Princess Novemali. Maugham manages by a trick to get him an invitation, and Elliott dies happy.

Chapter 6

Maugham meets Larry by chance at a play performance. Larry talks about his life in Germany, and how he spent some months in a monastery in Alsace. But he was not satisfied with the answers given to his spiritual questions by the monks. He returned to Paris and then traveled to Spain, where he lived in Seville with a girl. Then he traveled to India. He was fascinated by Indian spirituality and made his way to the holy city of Benares and later to a place called Madura. He absorbed the Vedantic philosophy of reincarnation and liberation. Eventually he became a disciple of the renowned saint, Shri Ganesha. When he had been at the guru's ashram for two years, he had a mystical experience one morning at sunrise. Larry then decided to return to Europe. He tells Maugham that he now intends to return to America, get a job as a car mechanic and live with calmness and compassion. Eventually he plans to settle in New York, where there are lots of libraries, and become a taxi driver.

Chapter 7

Six months later, Sophie MacDonald has her throat cut and is thrown into the river in Toulon. Maugham is asked by the police to identify the body. Larry is there also. He informs Maugham that he has got rid of all his money and has booked his passage on a ship leaving for America from Marseille. Gray and Isabel are also returning to America. Using Isabel's capital, Gray is getting back into business as vice-president of an oil company in Dallas, Texas. Maugham does not see Larry, Isabel or Gray again, but he assumes that the Maturins are happily settled in Dallas and that Larry is pursuing exactly the life that pleases him.

Characters

Paul Barton

Paul Barton is a young American whom Elliot Templeton helped make his way in the world. But when Barton became successful he snubbed Elliot, and Elliot hates him for it.

Becker

Becker is the German farmer who offers Larry and Kosti employment.

Ellie Becker

Ellie Becker is the daughter-in-law of Becker. She is a widow; her husband was killed during World War I. She initiates a bizarre nighttime sexual encounter with Larry, in which Larry thinks she is Frau Becker.

Frau Becker

Frau Becker is the wife of Becker. She is uneducated and is jealous of Ellie. Frau Becker takes an amorous interest in Larry.

Gregory Brabazon

Gregory Brabazon is one of the most successful decorators in London. Elliot engages him to decorate the house of his sister Louisa in Chicago.

Mrs. Louisa Bradley

Mrs. Louisa Bradley is Elliot Templeton's widowed sister and Isabel's mother. She opposes Isabel's plan to marry Larry when Larry refuses to take the job Henry Maturin offers him. Some years later, she becomes ill with diabetes and dies in 1930, soon after the stock market crash.

Larry Darrell

Larry Darrell is an orphan who grew up in Marvin, Illinois. During World War I, he was an aviator, and he saw his best friend killed saving his life. This experience profoundly affected him and altered his personality. Before the war, he was a normal boy, but, now that he has returned, he has no ambition and does not want to get a job. Instead, he prefers to loaf around Paris for two years, reading and studying for long periods. This costs him his engagement to Isabel, since she will not marry him unless he returns to America and secures their future. But Larry is interested not in money but in philosophical questions. He wants to be able to answer the ultimate questions about the nature and purpose of life. He leaves Paris and goes to work in a coal mine, making friends with a Pole, Kosti, who stimulates his interest in mystical religion. Larry and Kosti then work on a farm in Germany before Larry leaves for Bonn. After this, he stays in a monastery in Alsace for three months, studies science in Paris, has an affair with Suzanne Rouvier, and then lives with a Spanish girl in Seville. He then travels to India where he spends five years (from 1925 to 1930), two of them in the ashram of Shri Ganesha. Larry studies Vedanta and has a moment of mystical illumination. Returning to Paris, he meets up again with Sophie, whom he has known since childhood. He wants to marry her in order to save her from her unsavory lifestyle, but his plan is thwarted by Isabel's devious plan. Finally, Larry returns to America, planning to become a mechanic and eventually a taxi driver in New York. He has acquired spiritual wisdom and wants only to be of service to others.

Shri Ganesha

Shri Ganesha is the renowned Hindu holy man whom Larry adopts as his guru. Shri Ganesha radiates peace, goodness, and selflessness.

Kosti

Kosti is a Pole who works in a coal mine in France. Larry works with him and shares a room with him. Kosti is a rough-and-ready former Polish cavalry officer. He cheats at cards, but he is also an educated man who talks to Larry about mysticism. Kosti travels with Larry to Germany, where they find work on a farm.

Sophie MacDonald

Sophie MacDonald went to the same school as Isabel, and she also knew Larry when they were both in their teens. Larry says that she was a modest, idealistic girl who wrote poetry. After the war, she began to write about the misery of the poor and the exploitation of the working classes. Isabel thinks that as a young girl Sophie was in love with Larry, but Larry disagrees. Sophie marries Bob Macdonald and has a baby, but both husband and child are killed in a car accident. Sophie cannot get over the shock of her loss. She takes to drink and becomes promiscuous. But when Larry returns from India and meets her again, he wants to save her. She gives up drink, and they agree to marry, but Isabel, jealous of Sophie and unwilling to let go of Larry, sabotages the relationship by tempting Sophie with vodka. Sophie falls into the trap and returns to her dissolute lifestyle. She is murdered in Toulon in 1934, and her body is thrown into a river.

Gray Maturin

Gray Maturin is a big, powerful man, a friend of Larry's. He is in love with Isabel and marries her some time after Larry and Isabel break off their engagement. Gray joins his father's stockbrokerage firm, and during the 1920s he becomes very wealthy. He and Isabel have two daughters, and the family is happy. Gray is a good husband and father. But in 1929, the stock market crashes, and Gray's finances are wiped out. His health suffers, and he has frequent headaches. He cannot find another job. Gray gradually recovers after Elliott provides him and his family with an apartment in Paris. Eventually, Gray gets a job as a vice-president of an oil company and returns to America to live in Dallas.

Henry Maturin

Henry Maturin is a rich man who owns the best brokerage house in Chicago. He is a ruthless businessman, but he is very fond of his son, Gray, whom he invites to join the brokerage firm. Henry Maturin dies of a heart attack when he hears that he has been ruined by the stock market crash in 1929.

Isabel Maturin

Isabel Maturin is Louisa Bradley's daughter and Elliot Templeton's niece. She expects to marry Larry but is willing to allow him to spend two years in Paris before they set a date. She is shocked when Larry says he has no intention of returning to America. He wants to marry Isabel straightaway in Paris, but she refuses because she thinks his income is too small for them to live on. She has been raised to expect a certain standard of living and is not prepared to adjust, even for love. She expects Larry to change his mind and agree to return to America and find a job. She has always in the past been able to control him, or so she believes. But Larry shows an independence of mind that is beyond Isabel's power to influence. She marries Gray Maturin instead and has two daughters. They are wealthy and happy until the stock market crash, after which Elliott's generosity and a legacy from her mother help to ease her situation. Despite her marriage, Isabel never ceases to be in love with Larry. Possessive and selfish, she is horrified when she discovers that Larry is about to marry Sophie, and hatches a plot to ensure that Sophie gives in to her alcohol addiction and that the marriage does not take place. Eventually, Isabel and Gray move back from Paris to America, settling in Dallas, Texas.

W. Somerset Maugham

Somerset Maugham appears as himself in the novel. He is the narrator, who meets the different characters as the years go by and tells their story. He comes across as tolerant, diplomatic, and modest. Maugham is largely passive, but he does play a part in the action when he filches a party invitation that the dying Elliot Templeton desperately wants to receive, and sends it to him.

Dr. Bob Nelson

Dr. Nelson is a doctor from Marvin, Illinois. He is Larry's guardian, but the two men are not close, and Dr. Nelson has little influence on Larry's decisions.

Suzanne Rouvier

Suzanne Rouvier is a friend of Maugham. As a young woman, she kept the company of artists in Paris and was both model and mistress to several. She also had an affair with Larry, who was kind to her when she was recovering from typhoid and took her and her daughter on a holiday in the country. Soon after this, Suzanne began an arrangement with an affluent businessman from Lille, who now keeps her in an apartment in Paris.

She is thoughtful and considerate to him and marries him after his wife dies. Having taken up painting herself, she arranges an exhibition of her paintings. She is content with her life.

Elliott Templeton

Elliott Templeton is Isabel's uncle. A wealthy man and a snob, Elliott was not born rich but was successful as an art dealer. He assiduously cultivates social relationships with the high-born and loves the aristocratic social world of London and Paris. He tries to introduce Larry into Parisian society but Larry is not interested, to Elliott's disgust. Elliott becomes even more rich in the 1920s because he follows Henry Maturin's investment advice. In 1926, however, at the age of sixty-five, he becomes disillusioned with the changing Paris social scene and buys a house in Antibes on the Riviera, where he entertains lavishly. In 1929, acting on a tip from his friends at the Vatican (he is a Catholic convert), he sells his stocks before the financial crash. In gratitude, he builds a church on a tract of marshland that had been reclaimed by Mussolini. For what is seen as his piety, the Vatican awards him a courtesy title of count, which greatly flatters his sense of his own importance and good breeding. When he becomes old and sick, he no longer receives social invitations and this leaves him lonely and bitter. But he is cheered up just before his death when he receives an invitation— thanks to Maugham's ruse which he knows nothing of—to a particularly desirable fancy-dress party. When Elliott dies, he insists on being buried in the costume of a Renaissance count whom he claims as his ancestor. For all his snobbery and superficiality, Elliott is a kind-hearted man, helpful and obliging, as well as courteous and amiable.

Themes

Materialism versus Spirituality

The main character, Larry, is an embodiment of the spiritual approach to life as it is found in the Hindu religion. He is contrasted with the characters who embody American materialism. From the beginning, Larry is more interested in pursuing intellectual and spiritual knowledge for its own sake than in becoming part of the great American industrial money-making machine. He turns down a job with Henry Maturin's company, choosing instead to go to Paris, where he spends most of his time reading and studying. He wants to become enlightened; he has no interest in money. The Maturins, on the other hand, are

the embodiment of American prosperity. They are hard-nosed businessmen who know how to make money. It would never occur to either to them that the real purpose of life might be something other than the acquisition of wealth. The difference between these two approaches is the difference between East and West. Larry explains this toward the end of the novel, in his long conversation with Maugham: "They [Indians] think that we with our countless inventions, with our factories and machines and all they produce, have sought happiness in material things, but that happiness rests not in them, but in spiritual things."

After studying with his Indian guru for two years, Larry realizes that spiritual knowledge consists of the realization that the essence of the individual, the Atman, is one with Brahman, the all-pervading eternal spirit, the nature of which is bliss and joy. This is not just a matter of intellectual understanding, but of direct experience. When a person has this knowledge and experience, he is no longer attached to the things of the world, leaving him free to live, as Larry puts it, "With calmness, forbearance, compassion, selflessness, and continence." The needs of the small ego no longer drive his actions.

When Maugham the narrator meets Larry after the latter's return from India, he talks to Isabel about this aura of detachment that Larry possesses. He says that even though Larry is easy to get on with, "one's conscious of a sort of detachment in him, as though he weren't giving all of himself, but withheld in some hidden part of his soul something." Isabel agrees, saying that sometimes, just when Larry seems to be just like everybody else, "you have the feeling that he's escaped you like a smoke ring that you try to catch in your hands."

The fact that Larry does not cling to possessions, or to people, or to his own emotions, is a marked contrast to Isabel. She is both materialistic and possessive. The reason she decides not to marry Larry is because he refuses to provide her with the material luxuries that she thinks is appropriate to her station in life. Isabel is a woman who likes to be in control. One of the reasons she loved Larry in the first place was because she felt that she could control him. Later she discovered this was not the case. But even when she marries Gray, she cannot let go of her obsessive attachment to Larry, which causes her to scheme against Sophie when Sophie and Larry become engaged to marry.

The other character who is contrasted with the world-negating Larry is the worldly Elliot Templeton. As an arch-snob, he is excessively concerned with social position. He loves the trappings of

Topics for Further Study

- Larry Darrell is changed by his experiences during World War I. Today, psychological trauma caused by war is called post-traumatic stress disorder. Research the history of this term. What are the causes and symptoms of post-traumatic stress disorder and how is the disorder treated?

- When Larry stays for several months at a monastery, what does he find unsatisfactory about Christianity, and why does he eventually prefer Vedanta?

- What role does Suzanne Rouvier play in the novel? Is she an essential character, or would the novel be just as effective without her? How does she compare with Isabel and Sophie?

- Write a short story in which the central character is changed by some important, possibly traumatic, event. How does the incident change the way the character sees the world, or make him think deeply about his priorities in life? If such an event has happened to you, write the story based on your own experience.

---

wealth, such as fine art and furniture in fine houses, and lavish parties in Paris where the rich and high-born rub shoulders with one another. Whereas Larry wants to discover the deepest truths about life, Elliot lives only for its superficialities. He is fascinated by trivia rather than truth. Larry searches for reality, but Elliot is satisfied with appearances, which for him are the reality.

The Problem of Evil

In chapter 6, when Maugham reports his conversation with Larry in a Parisian café, Larry tells him that it was the question of why evil exits in the world that propelled him on his long spiritual quest. This was after he had experienced the carnage of World War I, in which his friend had been killed saving Larry's life. Larry's Polish friend Kosti believes that "evil is as direct a manifestation of the divine as good," an idea that horrifies Larry. The Christian explanation he receives from the monks at the monastery in Alsace does not satisfy Larry either. When he asks why God created evil, the monks reply that it was so that man could conquer wickedness and resist temptation, accepting those things as trials sent by God to purify them and make them eventually worthy of His presence. Larry finds a partial answer to his question in the Hindu belief in reincarnation, which he describes as "at once an explanation and a justification of the evil of the world." According to this view, there is no such thing as injustice or innocent suffering; the

evils that afflict humans are simply the consequences of sins committed in past lives.

But this does not answer the question of how the process begins in the first place. Larry mentions the philosophy of Ramakrishna, that good and evil are both components of "the sport of God," and neither can exist without the other. Larry says he rejects this idea, but what he proposes in its place is in fact very similar:

> The Chinese craftsman who makes a vase in what they call eggshell porcelain can give it a lovely shape, ornament it with a beautiful design, stain it in a ravishing color, and give it a perfect glaze, but from its very nature he can't make it anything but fragile. If you drop it on the floor it will break into a dozen fragments. Isn't it possible in the same way that the values we cherish in the world can only exist in combination with evil?

Style

Structure and Narrative Technique

The structure of the novel is quite complex. It covers a period of twenty-four years, from 1919 to 1943, and is set in a number of different locations, mainly Chicago, Paris and the French Riviera, but with some action set in Alsace and Toulon, France; London, England; Seville, Spain; India, and Germany. The thread that holds the structure together is the meetings that Maugham the narrator has with the

Compare & Contrast

- **1919:** In the aftermath of World War I, the Treaty of Versailles is signed. Austria and Hungary are separated; Yugoslavia is created out of Serbia and neighboring states; Poland and Czechoslovakia become independent nations. Germany is forced to pay war reparations.

  1944: The world is again at war. The tide has turned in favor of Britain, the United States and France in their struggle against Germany, Italy, and Japan. June 6, 1944, is D-Day, when the allied powers land at Normandy to free Europe from Nazi tyranny.

  Today: Europe is no longer the scene of major wars. Former enemies are now members of NATO and the European Union.

- **1919:** The United States, which suffered less economically than the major European powers during World War I, is poised for a period of huge economic expansion, known as the Roaring Twenties.

  1944: World War II has brought the U.S. economy out of the Depression of the 1930s. The war creates jobs, and industry serves the needs of war; instead of making cars and consumer items, factories produce tanks, munitions, and airplanes. In 1944, the United States builds more than 96,000 planes.

  Today: The U.S. economy continues to recover from the impact of the recession of 2000 and the terrorist attacks of September 11, 2001, although some analysts are concerned about slow job growth, outsourcing of U.S. jobs abroad, and rising levels of debt.

- **1919:** India is ruled by Britain but there is restlessness in the country and a desire for independence. Britain promises full self-government in stages.

  1944: World War II stalls the negotiations for independence, and Indian troops fight for Britain in the British army. However, India receives its independence in 1947.

  Today: With a population of more than one billion people, India is the world's largest democracy.

characters over the years, in which they tell him their stories. This means that the action does not always unfold in a linear sequence, but often makes use of flashbacks, as one character or another tells Maugham what has happened in the years since they last met. The flashback technique is most noticeable in chapter 6, when Maugham meets Larry in 1933, and Larry relates the events in his life from 1922, when he left the German farm, to 1930 (or possibly 1932), when he returned to Europe from India. The earlier part of Larry's story of his travels—his work in the coal mine in Lens and on the German farm—has already been told in correct chronological sequence in chapter 4.

Another part of the story that is told out of chronological sequence is the life story of Suzanne Rouvier in chapter 4. Most of this chapter is set in 1932, but after Suzanne's early history is related there is a section set in 1924, which describes Suzanne's affair with Larry.

Central to the novel's structure are the five conversations Maugham the narrator has when he is alone with Isabel. These occur in chapter 1 (set in 1919), chapter 2 (1921), chapters 4 and 5 (1932), and chapter 7 (1934). Maugham uses these conversations to progressively reveal Isabel's character, culminating in her admission that she selfishly manipulated Sophie to thwart her former friend's marriage to Larry.

Historical Context

Stock Market Crash of 1929

In the 1920s, America was increasingly prosperous. Spurred by the massive growth in the automobile industry, the Gross National Product increased by 59 percent. Personal income rose by an average of 38 percent. Consumer goods such as washing machines, refrigerators and radios became commonplace. The rapid development of industrialization and technology, and the rise in wages, made many people (like Henry and Gray Maturin in the novel) believe there was no limit to the production of wealth, and that the economy would continue to grow for the foreseeable future. Seeing stock prices constantly rising, ordinary people began to invest in the stock market, thinking they could become rich almost overnight. Many families invested their entire life savings in the stock market, sometimes taking money out of safer investments like treasury bonds. A common practice was buying "on margin," which meant buying on credit. A person would make an investment, and then wait until the price rose in order to pay for it, and make a profit too.

Caught up in the prevailing financial optimism, banks also began to speculate on the market with their investments. In spite of some warnings, there was a collective illusion that stock prices would continue to rise. But for years the economy had been over-producing, and when in 1929, the rich began to reduce their investments and their spending on luxury items, consumers of more modest means did not have the purchasing power to maintain demand. As a result, stock prices began to fall, and investors began to sell. A rush to sell became a stampede. On October 24, 1929, thirteen million shares were sold; the following Tuesday, October 29, more than sixteen million shares were sold, and the value of stocks dropped $14 billion. The day became known as Black Tuesday. Public confidence in the market and the U.S. economy was destroyed, and many people were left bankrupt. The selling continued for another two weeks, until November 13, by which time all the gains made over the previous two and a half years were wiped out.

Although the crash caused immense distress for thousands, a myth developed, fueled by the popular press, that ruined investors committed suicide by jumping from high windows in New York, but this was not the case. Nor was there an increase in the suicide rate across the country. (In the novel, Henry Maturin dies of a heart attack, not suicide, following the disastrous news; but in the 1984 film version, he commits suicide.)

The stock market gradually recovered over the next year as buyers returned and prices rose. By the spring of 1930, about half the losses had been recovered. President Herbert Hoover declared that the crisis was over, but he turned out to be completely

wrong. Hindered by a sluggish economy, the stock market plunged again in June 1930, and went on falling until it hit rock bottom in July 1932. By this time the United States had entered the Great Depression. Thousands of banks failed, unemployment reached eight million—in the novel, Guy Maturin cannot find another job—and many people lost their homes because their mortgages were foreclosed.

Critical Overview

The Razor's Edge had a mixed reception when first published in 1944. Joseph Warren Beach in *The New York Times* called it a "novel of ideas." He appreciated the skillfulness of Maugham's storytelling technique, commenting that "The story is carried forward with Maugham's usual deftness and ingenuity of manipulation." Cyril Connolly, in a positive review in *New Statesman and Nation*, called the novel "powerful propaganda for the new faith . . . the Vedanta of the West." He noted that an interest in mysticism and the spirituality of the East was not a new thing for Maugham, who despite being a worldly writer was also "fascinated by those who renounce the world." For Connolly, the best-drawn character was Elliott Templeton, whose career through the social world of London and Paris "Maugham paints with lingering tenderness, right down to the wonderful death scene which is a kind of farewell offering to his old corrupt world of Paris and the Riviera." Connolly admired the descriptions of India and also argued that Maugham succeeded in his hardest task, which was to convey the nature of mystical experience. But he thought the novel would have been more effective had Maugham not given Larry any specific religious system to embrace. Kate O'Brien in *Spectator* also praised the novel but thought that the depiction of Larry was a weak element. Maugham used "Larry too easily throughout, as a beautiful symbol, and never attempt[ed] to hack down to the bones of the man himself."

Over the last fifty years, the novel has generally been accorded a high place in Maugham's work, although critics have also argued that the novel is flawed. Much of the criticism centers on the character of Larry. John Whitehead's comment in *Maugham: A Reappraisal* is typical of later verdicts (and differs from Connolly's view). Whitehead argues that Maugham was unable "to convince the reader that Larry underwent any real religious

Brian Doyle-Murray as Piedmont and Bill Murray as Larry Darrell in the 1984 film version of The Razor's Edge The Kobal Collection.
Reproduced by permission

experience in India or had any true potential for saintliness."

Criticism

Bryan Aubrey

Aubrey holds a Ph.D. in English and has published many articles on twentieth century literature. In this essay, Aubrey discusses Larry Darrell's enlightenment and his desire for celibacy, which contrasts with the needs and attitudes of Isabel and Sophie.

Unanimity among literary critics is a rare phenomenon, but in the case of *The Razor's Edge*, there is near universal agreement that the flaw in the novel is the characterization of Larry Darrell. Robert Lorin Calder, for example, argues that Larry is the weakest of the main characters. In contrast to the fully realized Elliott Templeton, Larry "remains on the level of the ideal—a symbol or abstract representation of the potential of the spirit."

Similarly, M. K. Naik argues that Maugham failed to evoke the real nature of a spiritual quest. But the development of spiritual values

> cannot come about, in an ordinary man, without severe struggle and trial. . . . The actual picture of the change in Larry gives one the impression that the process has been over simplified. Larry has hardly to face any struggle in his progress to salvation, either from enemies within or from without.

There is no arguing with these verdicts, which have been echoed by other critics. Larry simply seems too good to be true. Although he tells Maugham that he finally gained the illumination he sought in India, and the narrative strives to give the impression that Larry has been on a long spiritual quest, the truth is that he does not seem much different in the end than he was in the beginning. He was never greatly attached to things or to people—witness his lack of interest in making money and the ease with which he renounces Isabel—so the spiritual development that he later describes does not have much impact on the reader.

However, it would be a pity if this flaw in the novel, serious though it is, should be allowed to obscure or diminish its philosophical depth. Maugham was brave enough to tackle a large and important theme: what is the ultimate truth of life, and by what values are we to live? Larry's pursuit of enlightenment is at the heart of these questions, and Maugham the narrator remarks (in the first section of chapter 6) that had it not been for the conversation he had with Larry about his spiritual experiences, he would not have thought it worthwhile to write the book.

Maugham had long had an interest in Indian religion, and in 1936 he traveled to India with the intention of meeting scholars, writers, artists, religious teachers, and devotees. He was particularly inspired by his meeting with one of India's most revered saints, who became the subject of Maugham's essay, "The Saint." The man's name was Ramana Maharshi, and he lived in an ashram (hermitage) at the foot of the holy mountain Arunchala, a few hours' journey by car from Madras. Soon after he arrived, Maugham sat in a hall with the Maharshi's devotees as the holy man meditated. At this time, he writes, "A little shiver seemed to pass through those present. The silence was intense and impressive. You felt that something strange was taking place that made you inclined to hold your breath." Ramana Maharshi became the model for Larry's spiritual teacher, Shri Ganesha, in *The Razor's Edge*. Indeed, when Larry sits silently with Maugham in a café after Sophie's death and says,

What Do I Read Next?

- Maugham's short story "The Fall of Edward Barnard" (in *The Trembling of a Leaf: Little Stories of the South Sea Islands*, 1921) has remarkable parallels to the plot and themes of *The Razor's Edge*, especially the clash of Eastern and Western cultures. Two young men from Chicago are in love with the same woman, Isabel. One of them, Edward, travels to Tahiti. He is expected to return in two years and marry Isabel, but he discovers a new set of values in Tahiti and does not return.

- *A Passage to India* (1924), by E. M. Forster, is set in India when that country was governed by Britain. The novel deals with the difficult relations between the English and the Indians. Like *The Razor's Edge*, it discusses Indian religion but in a less explicit, more allusive way.

- *Siddhartha* (1922), by Herman Hesse, is about a young man's search for enlightenment in ancient India. It contains descriptions of mystical philosophy and experience that are similar to but more convincingly presented than those of Larry in *The Razor's Edge*.

- *Shankara's Crest-Jewel of Discrimination* (first English edition published in 1947), translated by Swami Prabhavananda and Christopher Isherwood, is a short explanation by Shankara (686–718 A.D.) of the Vedantic philosophy that Larry Darrell adopts in *The Razor's Edge*. There is also an informative introduction. Isherwood was one of a group of expatriate English writers in California who were deeply involved with Vedanta. It has been suggested that Isherwood was the model for Larry, although both Maugham and Isherwood scoffed at the idea.

"Shri Ganesha used to say that silence also is conversation," Maugham the author is quoting the exact words Ramana Maharshi said to him on his visit, when Maugham was unwell and could not think of a question to ask the guru.

The crucial incident in Ramana Maharshi's life came when he was sixteen years old. Up until that point, he had been a normal boy who enjoyed all the usual pastimes of one his age. Then suddenly one day he feared that he was going to die. In order to overcome this fear of death he decided to examine exactly what it means to die. What is it that dies? He concluded that the body dies but the essence of the Self is immortal, and this is truly who he is. He is not his body, his senses, his individual mind, or his ego. Over the years, Ramana Maharshi's experience of the absolute, unchanging, infinite consciousness deepened, and he attracted visitors and disciples from all over India. Maugham writes in "The Saint":

> When men asked how it was possible to attain this blessed state, he told each one to ask himself, "Who am I?" He sought to impress upon the aspirant that he was not the body which he temporarily inhabited, but the Self which was eternal.

It is this truth that Larry Darrell grasps, not only as an intellectual theory but as a direct experience, and this is what makes him radically different from the other characters. It is what makes him so detached from worldly life. He can be *in* the world—and act in the world for the good of others—but not *of* it. The fact that Larry's ultimate goal is to become a taxi driver in New York nicely conveys this point. A man who can maintain a state of detached equanimity even amidst the honking horns, screeching tires, and scurrying pedestrians of Manhattan has surely passed some kind of spiritual threshold. In this respect Larry is in direct contrast to Elliot Templeton. Elliott's sense of identity is so bound up with his social position that when he becomes old and sick and does not get any party invitations he mopes around and sulks like a child. He is at the mercy of how others regard him. In spiritual terms, he is ignorant of the real nature of the Self. Maugham underlines this point with gentle humor when he has Elliott stipulate that he is to be embalmed and buried dressed in the costume of the Count de Lauria, whom he claims as an ancestor. For Elliott, clothes are the man. Even in death, he retains his attachment to appearances rather than reality.

> Larry's desire for celibacy, which he believes promotes spiritual freedom, is one of the main points of contrast between him and two of the female characters in the novel: Isabel and Sophie."

Larry's spiritual realization also has consequences for that most urgent of human instincts: sexual desire. Larry tells Maugham after his return from India that he intends to live a celibate life, and does not believe this will be difficult: "I am in the fortunate position that sexual indulgence with me has been a pleasure rather than a need." This statement is borne out by the manner of Larry's sexual encounters in the novel. Even before his spiritual illumination in India, he is not as driven as many men are by the need for sexual fulfillment. Two of the women he makes love to—Ellie, the daughter-in-law of the German farmer, and Suzanne Rouvier—take the initiative themselves, and his attitude seems to be that he can take it or leave it. Some critics have suggested that Larry is a latent homosexual, or bisexual, but there is no support for this in the text. According to Isabel, when she and Larry were engaged, Larry's desire for her was perfectly normal. Her certainty that, at the age of thirty-two, Larry is still a virgin stems from her belief in his innocence, not his homosexuality. The simple explanation is that intensity of sexual desire varies naturally in people, and Larry, a man of very refined sensibilities, finds that his greatest pleasures come from knowledge and spiritual awakening, rather than from sexual indulgence.

Larry's desire for celibacy, which he believes promotes spiritual freedom, is one of the main points of contrast between him and two of the female characters in the novel: Isabel and Sophie. Isabel admits to Maugham that she is a very sensual woman, and for her, sex serves the needs of her possessive personality. If Larry is a man who can let go of his attachments, Isabel is a woman who must cling on to hers. She tells Maugham that it is through sex that a woman keeps a man, and she adds, "it's not the first time she goes to bed with him that counts, it's the second. If she holds him then she holds him for good." Some might call this love; others might call it sexual enslavement. But Isabel is the one who is enslaved. This is conveyed in remarkably harsh language when Maugham the narrator tells of his car journey back to Paris in which Isabel is in the back seat and Larry in the front, while Gray drives. Larry's arm is stretched out across the seat, and Maugham catches sight of how Isabel's eyes are fixed on his "sinewy wrist with its little golden hairs and on that long, delicate but powerful hand." He is shocked by the expression on her face:

> It was a mask of lust. I should never have believed that her beautiful features could assume an expression of such unbridled sensuality. It was animal rather than human. The beauty was stripped from her face; the look upon it made her hideous and frightening. It horribly suggested the [b——] in heat and I felt rather sick.

It is because of sexual desire that Isabel cannot let go of Larry, even though she is married to Gray and has two children. Her slavery to passion warps her personality and later makes her behave in a devious and malicious way toward Sophie.

Sophie is another character who falls victim to uncontrolled sexuality. However, she is very different from Isabel. Isabel has no spiritual inclinations; she is a conventional woman who takes the world as she finds it and lives as someone of her class is expected to live. Sophie on the other hand has a more sensitive, questing nature, and in that respect she is more like Larry. As a girl she was idealistic; she read a lot and wrote poetry. She felt the misery of the poor and wanted to be a social worker, to sacrifice herself in service to others. Larry says she had "a lovely purity and a strange loftiness of soul." But when life treated her so cruelly, taking her husband and baby, she was too weak to recover and sank into a life of promiscuous sex and alcohol addiction.

Sophie's weakness reveals Larry's strength. Larry, for all his sweetness, is a tough, independently-minded man. He has the strength to defy conventional expectations and pursue the life to which he is called. The moral seems to be that those who wish to serve must first make themselves strong, otherwise they will not be able to endure the inevitable buffets of the world. Larry's strength lies in his spiritual nature and the use he makes of it. Through his illumination in India and his consequent decision to become celibate, he escapes the snares of sexuality that warp Isabel and contribute to Sophie's destruction. With his awareness of the absolute, eternal consciousness of Brahman, and his desire to live a saintly

Crowds of panicked stock traders fill the sidewalks outside the New York Stock Exchange on the day of the market crash © Bettmann/Corbis

life, helpful to others, Larry needs nothing more for his happiness.

Source: Bryan Aubrey, Critical Essay on *The Razor's Edge*, in *Novels for Students*, Thomson Gale, 2006.

Nicky-Guninder Kaur Singh

In the following essay, Singh explores how Hindu mysticism and Oriental spirituality "are absolutely central to the text" of The Razor's Edge.

Even the slightest acquaintance with W. Somerset Maugham's stories, novels, and critical writings, shows his literary expertise. But Maugham would never strike one as a philosopher. Indeed he never claimed to be one. In a letter to Klaus W. Jonas he wrote, "I have little patience with the novelists who preach or philosophise. I think it much better to leave philosophy to the philosophers and social reform to the social reformer." This letter which forms the preface to *The World of Somerset Maugham,* draws a clear line of demarcation between literature and philosophy. The theme reappears in other writings of his. For instance, in *A Writer's Notebook* Maugham praises Santayana for his gifts of imagery and metaphor, and regrets his turning towards philosophy. "It was a loss to American Literature when Santayana decided to become a philosopher rather than a novelist." Did Maugham really believe that there was such a gap between the literary and philosophical enterprises? If we look closely at his own works there seems to be an interplay of the two. *The Razor's Edge* is not simply art for art's sake: it raises profound questions about personal identity and moral philosophy, and it elucidates them in light of Hindu metaphysics. We discover in this novel ancient values and modern concerns coming together imaginatively and artistically; indeed, Maugham's fictional creation brings us to a fascinating conjecture, a point in human history where the radically different ideas of East and West intersect.

The following verse from the Katha Upanisad forms the epigraph to *The Razor's Edge.*

> uttisthata jâgrata prâpya varân nibodhata:
> ksurasya dhârâ nisitâ duratyaya; durgam pathas tat
>   kavayo vadanti (I.3.14)

> The sharp edge of a razor is difficult to pass over;
> thus the wise say the path to Salvation is hard.

This verse clearly is the source of the title of the novel, which was published in 1943. Though he did travel to India in 1936 and spent time in the country, sometimes even as a guest of Mâhârâjâhs, it is difficult to say how far Maugham was influenced by the Indian milieu. Some Eastern influence has been traced in his writings, and his personal library

> "
> Maugham's fictional
> creation brings us to a
> fascinating conjecture, a
> point in human history where
> the radically different ideas of
> East and West intersect."

contained many classics from the East. In *Points of View* Maugham himself acknowledges his familiarity with Indian philosophical texts such as Sir Charles Eliot's *Hinduism and Buddhism*; Radhakrishnan's *History of Indian Philosophy* and his translation of the Upanisads; Krshnaswamy Iyer's *Vedanta or the Science of Reality;* Professor Barnett's *Brahma-Knowledge,* and Sankara's *Vivekachudamani.* Maugham's acquaintance with Hindu philosophy was not just through books but also through direct encounter with Hindu sages. One chapter in *Points of View* is devoted to his meeting with a Hindu Mâhârishi in Tiruvannmalai near Madras and is rich in Hindu philosophical concepts describing the sage's extraordinary personality. Clearly it was not shooting tigers or seeing the Tâj Mahal or the caves of Ajanta but Indian philosophy embodied in the Swami—the "saint in the flesh" as he called him—that impressed Maugham most during his trip to India, though the exotic sensual aspect of the East is the first to strike the Western reader of Maugham's works.

Several of Maugham's works have an Asian setting, but its significance should not be exaggerated, because it is by no means the most important and meaningful contribution of the East to his imagination. Klaus W. Jonas has identified the novels, the plays, the travel books, and several volumes of the short stories that are set in the East. In "Maugham and the East" Jonas even attempts to show a synchronization between the publication of the "exotic" writings and the events of the author's own life. His thesis is that "Maugham is primarily concerned with the depiction of the European in a strange, exotic environment and with the effect which remote outposts, tropical climate and the native population exercise upon him." Jonas attends to the geographical and social environment but as for the literary and philosophical environment of the "exotic" East in Maugham's writing, Jonas offers no in depth

study. Even critics who acknowledge the Eastern mystical element in Maugham's literary output are generally inclined to reject it as an aberration. To quote Joseph Warren Beach:

> Those of us who are not much taken by the notion of sainthood *in vacuo*, nor easily impressed by selflessness except where it is shown working in a *medium*, are not likely to hail this oriental model of spirituality.... And it does not help much for Maugham to have put himself into the story as one of the characters by way of offering his own type of humane hedonism as an alternative to Hindu mysticism.

In similar vein a review in *The Catholic World* hastily dismisses *The Razor's Edge:* "it is a novel of manners with a dash of mysticism thrown in, for what purpose it is hard to say."

We cannot fully appreciate the value of this novel if we regard its Hindu mysticism and Oriental spirituality as side issues. They are absolutely central to the text which is, in fact, constructed upon the fundamental Hindu experience of liberation. *The Razor's Edge* (which was published after *Of Human Bondage* and *Cakes and Ale*) is about a young American who has a close encounter with death while serving as a pilot during the First World War. The war over, he gives up his life of material and emotional comfort to search for his real self. In this essay, I will not argue whether or not Maugham made any serious study of Hindu philosophy or any of its central texts such as the Katha Upanisad, but I do suggest that we read Maugham's novel as a modern, Western appropriation of the classical Sanskrit text. Besides Maugham's title and overture, which is a direct citation from the Katha Upanisad, the theme of the novel bears an exact parallel with a key event in the life of a Katha Upanisad protagonist, namely, young Naciketas' journey into the realm of Yama. During his encounter with the Hindu God of death, Naciketas opts for a knowledge of the self over a life of luxury, love and money. Larry, the lad from Marvin, Illinois and Naciketas, the Brahmin boy, make identical passages: both give up the pleasant mode for a realization of their true self, and both go on to experience the co-presence of immanence and transcendence. This striking connection between the two literary pieces compels me to re-read Maugham's *The Razor's Edge* as a fictional hermeneutics of the classical Indian text.

At the very outset, Maugham expresses his reservations about *The Razor's Edge*'s genre:

> If I call it a novel it is only because I don't know what else to call it. I have a little story to tell and I end neither with a death nor a marriage.

Why would an author view his novel as a "little story"? What we find here is a remarkably subtle emulation of the literary format of the Upanisad. Belonging to the Taittiriya school of the Yajur Veda, Katha Upanisad is one the most philosophically powerful and sophisticated of the Upanisads. Yet, ironically, it is known as *katha,* literally, a little story. But simplicity must not be mistaken for insignificance. From ancient times and across cultures, the pure story-form has conveyed the most profound and absolute meaning. Maugham, who spoke with disparagement about complicated and convoluted dialectics, may have been drawn to the simple narrative of the Katha Upanisad. Furthermore, like all Upanisads, the Katha maintains the dialogue form which is conducive to explanations and narrations. *The Razor's Edge* is also set up as a dialogue between the author and his characters. The novelist is right inside his own novel, on the same plane as his fictional characters, and conversing with them. He is not a distant, omniscient, *author*itarian voice but rather an immanent figure in his own work—just as Yama appears in his realm. In so far as both stories are told in the form of dialogue—and neither ends with death or marriage!—there is an implicit stylistic link between the ancient Indian scripture and Maugham's own imaginative creation.

At the beginning of his novel Maugham expresses his apprehension that he may not be able to understand the "Other:"

> It is very difficult to know people, and I don't think one can ever really know any but one's own countrymen. For men and women are not only themselves; they are also the region in which they were born, the city apartment or the farm in which they learnt to walk, the games they played as children, the old wives' tales they overheard, the food they ate, the schools they attended, the sports they followed, the poets they read, and the God they believed in. It is all these things that have made them what they are, and these are the things you can't come to know by hearsay, you can only know them if you have lived them. You can only know them if you are them.

Maugham poses the problem of the hermeneutic process: can we ever know others without being them? *A Writer's Notebook* also offers a sobering picture of cross-cultural understanding: "The student of a country other than his own can hope to know comparatively few of its inhabitants, nor with the difference of language and of culture will he even after many years become intimate with them. Even with the English and American . . . there can be no real understanding." Profound issues raised by literary critics, linguists and anthropologists are couched here in simple idiom. From food to sports to stories to the belief in God, each is an important ingredient in the constitution of a people's culture—how then can we comprehend without sharing and partaking in *their* physical and ideological world? Can we ever hope to understand *another* who is culturally apart from us? Although the American-English encounter forms the subject in the above passage, I see here the widely travelled Englishman tacitly articulating his apprehension about understanding the distant Eastern culture. Maugham even criticizes Henry James for not being able to create an Englishman through and through after living in the country for forty years. By emphasising the distance between the two coasts of the Atlantic, he is preparing the reader for the even greater gulf between the West and India.

In both the Katha Upanisad and *The Razor's Edge,* an encounter with death sets the plot in motion. Critical of his father's empty rituals, young Naciketas is sent off to the House of Death. The ancient story begins with his father Vajasravasa, a Brahmin priest, offering old and feeble cows as sacrifice. Naciketas is hurt by the formalism and hypocrisy of the action and proposes that he himself may be presented as an offering. He keeps persisting in his request. The third time the father is enraged and says: "Unto Yama I give thee." The obedient Naciketas takes his father's words literally and goes to the abode of Yama. The god of death is absent for three days and nights. Upon his return, he offers three gifts to compensate for the delay and discomfort he had caused the Brahmin's son. As the first gift Naciketas asks for an appeasement of his father's anger; as the second, a description of the fire sacrifice which is the path to heaven; and as the third, knowledge about what happens after death. While the first two boons are granted immediately, Yama pleads with Naciketas not to press for the third request.

In Maugham's novel, Death visits Larry's close friend during World War I. Patsy was a twenty-two year old aviator who was going to marry an Irish girl after the war. But his plane crashed, shattering his hopes and dreams. Seeing his friend die at such a close proximity, Larry's comfortable world is changed. His fiancée cannot understand and wonders what happened to the fellow who was quite normal before the war: "One of the nice things about him was his enormous zest for life. He was so scatter brained and gay, it was wonderful to be with him; he was so sweet and ridiculous. What can have happened to change him so much?"

None of his friends realize the magnitude of Larry's close experience with death in the war. While they go on with their everyday life styles, Larry withdraws inwardly, to an inner cosmos. He is found reading William James' *Principles of Psychology* with the deepest concentration for hours in the library. His life begins to revolve around the fundamental question:

> I want to know whether I have an immortal soul or whether when I die it's the end.

His passionate quest seems to be but an English translation of Naciketas':

> yeyam prete vicikitsâ manusye 'stity eke nâyam
>   astîti caike;
> etat vidyâm anusistas tvayâham, varânâm esa varas
>   trtîyah

This is Naicketas' ardent request for his third boon, instruction from Yama concerning what happens after death—"there is this doubt in regard to a man who has departed, some holding that he is and some that he is not" (I.1.20). A passion for knowledge dominates Naciketas' and Larry's existence.

While an encounter with death is the cause of transformation in both characters, in neither instance is it feared. Nor is death a phenomenon that is gruesome in itself. Lord Yama's pleasant nature and hospitality echo in the Western novel. It is to make up for his absence at his home for three days that the God of death offers Naciketas the three boons. He makes obeisance to the boy and apologizes for making him stay in his house without food for three nights (I.1.9). Similarly, Elliott Templeton (the socialite uncle of Larry's fiancée), even while he is dying, insists on making a courteous and elegant reply to Princess Novemali's dinner invitation. At a most tragicomic juncture in the novel, Elliott sends his "regrets" from his deathbed: he could not make it to the Princess's party, which indeed he had desperately wanted to attend, "owing to a previous engagement with his Blessed Lord."

This r.s.v.p. illustrates an extension of the social world that Elliott lived in and expresses the same values that are upheld in the house of Yama where the Brahmin boy should have been properly greeted and fed. That societal intercourse and propriety carry on after death is envisioned in both the Eastern and Western texts.

In both narrations, the encounter with death is a significant moment which sets the central protagonist at a very complex juncture: it makes both Naciketas and Larry come face to face with the choice between the life of the pleasant and the life of the good. The distinction between *sreyas* (that which is good) and *preyas* (that which is pleasant) clearly outlined in the Katha Upanisad is central to Hindu philosophy.

> Both the good and the pleasant approach a person. The wise, pondering over them, discriminates. The wise chooses the good in preference to the pleasant. The simple-minded, for the sake of worldly well-being, prefers the pleasant. (I.2.2)

In lieu of the third boon, Yama offers Naciketas sons and grandsons, cattle, elephants, gold, horses, vast expanses of land and life of as many years as he would choose. Yama places every imaginable pleasure before Naciketas.

> Whatever desires are hard to attain in this world of mortals, ask for all those desires at thy will. Here are noble maidens with chariots and musical instruments, the like of them cannot be won by men. Be served by these whom I give to thee. O Naciketas, (pray) ask not about death. (I.1.25)

But Naciketas rejects the transient pleasures of the world. "Let thine be the chariots, thine the dance and song," he says to Yama. Opting for *sreyas,* Naciketas persists in his search for immutable and permanent knowledge.

The antithetical modes of the good (*sreyas*) and the pleasant (*preyas*) also face Larry, and like Naciketas, he chooses the "good." Maugham's twentieth century version of Yama's pleasant offerings entail stock-gambling materialism, a house on the Riviera with Savonnerie carpets, lavish entertainment, a routine where husband and wife do not dine by themselves for three months, luncheons at Claridges, gluttonous dinners at the Ritz. . . . The pleasant life-styles—of Isabel with a stable marriage and lovely children and butlers and diamond rings and sable coats or that of Gray Maturin (whom Isabel eventually marries) with high stocks and great economic security or that of Elliott Templeton (Isabel's uncle) with invitations from society's highest échelons as his greatest wish and who is always found hobnobbing with princes, dukes, and counts in the most extravagant clothes over expensive wines and meals—are all rejected by Larry in favour of loafing around and discovering something more permanent. Maugham's twentieth century images of the pleasant life with its manifold frivolties are all found in Yama's presentation: "sons and grandsons that shall live a hundred years, cattle in plenty, elephants, gold and horses. Choose vast expanses of land and life for thyself as many years as your wish" (I.1.23). In spite of all the changes, in spite of all the technological advances, the same economic power, aesthetic delights, and ideals of marriage and progeny mark the world of *preyas*—be it the one offered to Naciketas or Larry.

And the choice for *sreyas* leads both the Indian and American protagonists to the highest form of knowledge. This knowledge is not an abstract cognition of facts and concepts, but rather an experience, an experience that is simultaneously one of immanence and transcendence. The Katha Upanisad and Maugham's imaginative hermeneutic process bring to light the presence of the Universal Reality within the individual self. Ironically, with death as the point of departure, Naciketas and Larry make a voyage towards infinity and eternity. In the two instances, Lord Yama and Shri Ganesha (whom Larry meets with in India) are the vehicles which lead them onward in their journey. These two figures play the role of the Gurû, that is one who restrains (*ru*) darkness (*gu*), leading their disciples from the road of ignorance (*avidyâ*) to illumination (*vidyâ*).

Lord Yama informs Naciketas that the self is made up of five layers. He uses the parable of the chariot to explain that the individual is made up of the body, senses, mind, intellect, and bliss:

âtmânam rathinam viddhi, sariram ratham eva tu: buddhim tu sârdhim viddhi, manah pragraham eva ca (I.3.3)

Know the Self as the lord of the chariot and the
  body as, verily, the chariot, know the intellect
    as the
charioteer and the mind as, verily, the reins.

In this seemingly simple parable, the complex nature of the person is drawn. The chariot with its sensitive horses represents the psycho-physical vehicle in which the transcendent owner rides: the physical self is the external carriage and subject to the conditions of mortality; the horses are the senses (indrayâni hayân âhur, I.3.4) which are held by the reins (mind); these reins remain at a critical point for they can either control or be dragged away by the team of the senses; the charioteer (intellect) ultimately holds the reins in the hands but again the pull of the horses could exert an influence on the driver's role. With proper guidance, the senses like the horses, can take one to the proper goal. The owner or âtmâ mahân, however, remains beyond—sitting blissfully in the back seat. This subtle self constitutes the inner reality of each individual. Verses reminiscent of those in the Bhagavad Gita resound in the Katha Upanisad to describe the immutablity of this intrinsic self: it is unborn, eternal, abiding and primeval, not slain when the body is slain. Lord Yama depicts the owner of the chariot in great poetic beauty: "anor aniyân mahato mahiyân, âtmâsay jantor nihito guhâyâm—smaller than the small, greater than the great, the self is set in the heart of every creature" (I.2.20.). Both sides

of the scale "large and small" have been utilized to portray the utter transcendence of the self: by being "greater than the great and smaller than the smallest," all qualities and quantities are annihilated; by being infinite and infinitesimal at once, all categorizations of space, time, gender are transcended. It is this totally formless self that abides constantly within the cave-like heart (guhâyâm).

Thus does Lord Yama explain the self to Naciketas, and what we discover in turn is the paradoxical co-presence of transcendence and immanence. But are they not mutually exclusive? How can the Infinite formless reside within an individual form? How can the singular reality be manifest in multiplicity and plurality? If the transcendent becomes immanent can it really be transcendent? Maugham is attempting to explain this incomprehensible Upanisadic worldview to the Western reader. Having given up the world of pleasure, including his lovely fiancée, and a prospective stable married life along with all economic guaranties promised by his wealthy friend Gary Maturin, Larry lands in India. What Somerset Maugham records in *Points of View* as his own wish is also true of Larry in *The Razor's Edge:* he does not go to India "to shoot tigers or buy or sell anything, but only to learn." As soon as he gets off at the port in Bombay, Larry meets with one of the Ramakrishna Swamis who asks him to spend time in India for "The East has more to teach the West than the West conceives." Actually they had travelled together from Alexandria and Larry gets his first introduction to Hinduism through him at the Elephanta Caves, in front of the famous *trimurti* with the three manfestations of Ultimate Reality—Creator, Preserver, Destroyer. It is at the suggestion of this saffron-robed Swami friend that Larry goes to see Sri Ganesha. "He will give you what you are looking for," Larry is told.

Larry then recounts his insight to the narrator in the form of a conversation at a café in Paris several years later. That the transcendent is immanent within the self forms the theme of their dialogue. Five points from the Katha Upanisad come to the fore: the self has a transcendent core; the individual self is but the absolute transcendent; the transcendent is immanent in the myriad of forms; nowhere and in no way is the transcendent exhausted in its immanence; and that to recognize the transcendent as immanent, an inward journey into the self has to be made which results in the experience of transcendence.

The first point is that the material, sensual, mental, intellectual, and the transcendent âtman combine together to make up the individual self. Translating the âtman as soul, Larry explains that "it is distinct from the body and its senses, distinct from the mind and its intelligence." Perhaps Larry's translation of âtman as soul may not be the best for it may bring to mind the Christian conception. Yet, we clearly find him approaching the self not simply as a synthesis of (dualized) body and mind— an antithesis which has dominated Western philosophy. For Larry the self is rather that integral unity of body, senses, mind, intellect, and the "subtle self" that we find in the chariot image from the Katha Upanisad. One also notices Larry explaining the âtman through the terminology of the Gita: "It is uncreated; it has existed from eternity." Lord Krsna's words stressing the transcendent nature of the core of the self seem to have entered his own vocabulary.

A second aspect that emerges is that the individual self is the Absolute Self. A basic identity is established between persons existing in particular form and body and the Universal Reality that keeps expanding, always growing, and is without any spatial or temporal or causal limitations. The owner of the chariot is the Owner and Enjoyer *par excellence.* As the Katha Upanisad unfolds, Lord Yama explains this self through many lovely similes: "agnir yathaiko bhuvanam pravisto rûpam rûpam prati rûpo babhûva—it is like the fire which is one but entering this world becomes varied in shape according to the object it burns;" "vayur yathaiko bhuvanam pravisto rûpam rûpum prati rûpo babhûva—it is like the air which is one but entering this world becomes varied in shape according to the object it enters" (II.2.9). Thus the fire in one form is not any different from Fire Itself, nor the air in a vessel any different from the Air outside. Can we claim that the fire in a log of wood is not Fire or that the fire in a piece of coal is not Fire?

Maugham, of course, does not argue for cases as fire or air but uses instead the supreme example of his human protagonist. For Larry, his own self "is not part of the Absolute, for the Absolute, being infinite, can have no parts; rather, it is the Absolute itself." He explains to his European companion the Absolute in terms of the Upanisadic conception of Brahman:

> It's nowhere and everywhere. All things imply and dependupon it. It's not a person, it's not a thing, it's not a cause. It has no qualities. It transcends permanence and change: whole and part, finite and infinite. It is eternal because its completeness and perfection are unrelated to time. It is truth and freedom.

Although the term "It" may connote, for some; an impersonal relationship, Maugham's deliberate choice of the word reveals a remarkable intuition of Hindu metaphysics. The Radhakrishnan translation which he relied on had referred to âtman in the masculine form. Maugham's usage of the neuter, far from being impersonal, actually reveals a more personal and a more sensitive translation. It is a fine appropriation of the idea of Brahman for it substantiates the formless and infinite characteristics of the Ultimate. True to the Sanskrit "Brahman" (etymologically the root *brh* refers to constant expansion and bursting forth), Larry's usage of the term "Absolute" signifies pure dynamism and energy which cannot be confined to space, temporality, causality, or gender; "It" is sheer Transcendence. But this sheer Trancendence, the total Absolute, *is* everything particular, it is all the manifold forms of relations and relativities. Like Yama, Larry resorts to literary devices to explain a phenomenon that goes beyond normal language. He uses the analogy of "the drop of water that has arisen from the sea and in a shower has fallen into a puddle, then drifts into a brook, finds its way into a stream, after that into a river, passing through mountain gorges and wide plains, winding this way and that, obstructed by rocks and fallen trees, till at last it reaches the boundless sea from which it rose." Can the drop of water in some tiny puddle be any different from the ocean Itself? The self in a particular form is not a part, nor a division, nor a fracture or fraction of the all-pervasive and absolute Reality, but rather That Reality Itself.

Larry underscores his thesis once again in the novel. This time it is in the context of his meeting with the Swami whose presence is a benediction and makes him very happy:

> I felt that at last I had found what I wanted. The weeks, the months passed with unimaginable rapidity. I proposed to stay either till he died, and he told us that he did not intend very much longer to inhabit his perishable body, or till I received illumination the state when you have at last burst the bonds of ignorance, and know with a certainty there is no disputing that you and the Absolute are one.

The final goal for Larry is to know without any doubts or uncertainties that he and the Absolute are one. This knowledge constitutes an immediate and exhaustive illumination. No ontological, epistemological, teleological or moral proofs are required to attest the identity. This insight is the highest goal set forth in the Upanisads. The path of ignorance (*avidyâ* in Upanisadic terminology) comes to an end with the recognition of the identity between the individual and the Absolute Self.

This intimacy between the two discloses yet another central Upanisadic relationship: the Transcendent is immanent. It is placed within all. During his conversation with Naciketas, Lord Yama describes the âtman as thumb-sized (there are two references to angustha-mâtrah, II.1.12 and II.3.17) and even uses the simile of a dwarf that is seated in the centre of the body (*madhye vâmanam âsînam,* II.2.3). It seems to me that the smallness is emphasized to convey the *âtman* as a substrate that inheres in everything. Such images are essential to portray that the infinite and illimitable vastness can be within the finite. Earlier too we found Lord Yama comparing the âtman with the basic elements of fire and air, a comparison that further reveals the âtman as the basic *ing*redient of the cosmos.

Lord Yama's instruction to Naciketas that the Transcendent is immanent receives an experiential exegesis in *The Razor's Edge.* When Larry reaches the temple in Madura he sees it packed with men, women, and children. He witnesses them making obeisance at one shrine or another and he hears them calling one another, quarrelling with one another. In Larry's words, "There was an ungodly row, and yet in some mysterious way God seemed to be near and living." In Madura, God, who seems so distant in the Judeo-Christian image of Him as Almighty Father, is suddenly felt by the young American to be present in the hustle and bustle of everyday life. It is as though the Hindu temple gravitationally pulled the Transcendent into its vicinity, making It reside within its own precincts.

There are two other moments when Larry strongly voices his perception of the Transcendent as immanent. While discussing the notion of personal gods, Larry emphatically states,

I believe that God is within me or nowhere.

Clearly Larry believes the Transcendent exists within his very own self; the idea of worship to an external deity—outside of himself—is outrightly rejected. According to him, "the need to worship is no more than the survival of an old remembrance of cruel gods that had to be propitiated." Through his awareness of the Transcendent residing within himself, Larry becomes conscious of the identity between the individual self and the Ultimate Self.

After the rapturous experience in the mountains in India, Larry once more expresses the Transcendent as immanent.

I felt in myself an energy that cried out to be expended. It was not for me to leave the world and retire to a cloister, but to live in the world and love the objects of the world, not indeed for themselves, but for the Infinite that is in them.

Here Larry is giving vent to the joy that he experienced on the dawn of his birthday when he was ravished by the beauty of the mountains with their deep jungle, the mist entangled in the treetops, the lake below him, the sun shining like burnished steel. "I'd never known such exaltation and such a transcendent joy," he utters. This heightened experience fills him with an infinite energy which he wants to expend in loving the objects of the world—and as he says—loving them "not indeed for themselves, but for the *Infinite* that is *in* them." In the moment of his exalted consciousness, Larry discerned the Infinite *in* the objects around him. Instead of seeing the ephemeral and delicate mist he has seen the eternal and transcendent reality. Yama's idea of the transcendent fire being immanent in the varied forms is palpably felt by Larry.

However, the immanence of the self does not exhaust its transcendence and the Transcendent transcendent remains. This fourth insight gained by Larry is a central element of the Katha Upanisad. Is the owner of the chariot limited to his or her chariot? Surely there may be many more under one's regard. Throughout the Upanisad it is maintained that while the *âtman* permeates all, there is still evermore beyond.

As the fire which is one entering the world
     becomes varied in form according to the object
So also the One Self within all beings becomes
     varied according to whatever it enters and also
     exists outside them all. (II.2.9)

The concept of transcendence is important throughout Hindu philosophy and we see it celebrated as early as in the Rg Veda. The Hymn of Creation (Rg Veda 10.90) provides a beautiful depiction of the entire cosmos being generated out of the sacrifice of the Cosmic Man. This Primeval Man (*Purusa*) is huge, as huge as the imagination can possibly conceive (thousand-headed, thousand-eyed, thousand-footed),—yet he still extends beyond! Thus immanent though the *âtman* may be, it still retains its extension and infinity.

That the infinite Reality cannot be encapsuled within any form or all forms as such is also illustrated in *The Razor's Edge.* We may recall Larry emphatically stating that the self "is not part of the Absolute, for the Absolute, being infinite, can have no parts, but the Absolute itself." The self thus does not get limited and confined to any particular format. In fact, in this connection, Larry makes a very perceptive point about Hindu art. If there is but the Transcendent Reality, why, then, the 330 million gods and goddesses?

The Absolute is in Isvar, the creator and ruler of the world, and it is in the humble fetish before which the peasant in his sun-baked field places the offering of a flower. The multitudinous gods of India are but expedients to lead to the realization that the self is one with the supreme self.

According to Larry, the Hindu imagination has evolved the millions of manifestations of the Transcendent Reality to explain that the intrinsic self is the All. Although he does not explicitly say so, Larry strongly implies that the plurality of forms and images in Hindu art only goes to show that there is no one image in which the Transcendent is immanent. No single image can contain the Transcendent.

The final point that emerges is, in fact, the most essential one, and it permeates both the Katha Upanisad and *The Razor's Edge*. The protagonists learn that the path to recognizing the transcendence that is immanent within requires an inward journey to be made, and it leads to the experience of transcendence itself. Knowledge in the Hindu worldview is not simply knowledge for knowledge's sake; the Katha Upanisad raises the issue of how this knowledge is attained and how it performs a soteriological function. It discloses that the knowledge of the self comes only with a moral way of life, and leads to ultimate liberation and immortality. Lord Yama's comments expressing the intricate relationship amongst the epistemological, ethical, and soteriological dimensions seem to be highlighted by Maugham in a fictional context thousands of years later.

Knowledge of the self does not come in a flash; it is a gradual process, requiring years of moral discipline. To quote Lord Yama:

> This self cannot be attained by instruction, nor by intellectual power, nor even through much hearing. It is to be attained only by the one whom the self chooses. To such a one the self reveals Its own nature. (I.2.23)

The knowledge regarding the deep-seated inner self cannot be gained through outward methods. Therefore all usual intellectual talents, methods of instruction, and external techniques of listening are of no avail. This illumination is self revelatory— an individual is, so to say, chosen for the enlightenment. And who is chosen?

> Not he who has not desisted from evil ways, not he who is not tranquil, not he who has not a concentrated mind, not even he whose mind is not composed can reach this (self) through right knowledge. (I.2.24)

The criterion is the morally cleansed person. Only by being physically and mentally serene does one prepare oneself for the ultimate enlightenment. The serenity is attained after many years of discipline.

An unethical life style with evil habits has to be discarded; a mental equilibrium with a tranquil psyche acquired. The epistemological and ethical dimensions fuse together in Hindu philosophy as the former is impossible without the latter: only a morally superior person is fit to receive the higher type of knowledge. By not accepting all the wonderful material pleasures offered by Lord Yama, Naciketas has shown his high ethical standards. Yama is very happy with his pupil and only then goes on to instruct him. In the *Laws of Manu* we find a division of Hindu life into four equal stages (*âsramas*) with the first quarter being devoted to learning which means that the pupil actually lives in the Guru's home, developing ethical, mental, and intellectual virtues. Similarly, we find an episode in the Chândogya Upanisad where Lord Indra ends up spending 101 years with Prajâpati prior to attaining knowledge of the Self. By stressing the combination of praxis and intellectual advancement, these examples from Hindu scripture elucidate the fusion of ethics and epistemology. The individual is a total unit and therefore knowledge of the intrinsic self cannot be acquired without bringing the body, senses, mind, and intellect into a harmonious whole.

Since the knowledge of the self pertains to the metaphysical reality, it cannot be informed by a physical or objective vision.

> The Self, though hidden in all beings, does not shine forth but can be seen by those subtle seers through their sharp and subtle intelligence. (I.3.13)

One needs to go beyond the regular intellect and reason, and reach the most subtle and refined insight in order to perceive the hidden self. Not with eyes that focus ahead on the phenomena but with eyes that turn inwards (termed âvrtta-caksuh by Lord Yama) can the eternal self be seen. Indeed, for a transcendent goal, a transcendental approach has to be taken.

> The self is without sound, without touch and without form, undecaying, is likewise, without taste, eternal, without smell, without beginning, without end, beyond the great, abiding. By discerning that, one is freed from the face of death. (I.3.15)

The method of yoga is emphasized by Yama as an epistemological technique. From the root *yuj*, meaning to yoke, Yoga brings to mind the image of the horses controlled by the reins and held firmly by the charioteer. By yoking the senses singlemindedly, one discerns the inner self—the self without sound, smell, touch, form, the self without a beginning or an end, and one attains that very transcendence. The disclosure of transcendence takes place when the senses are withdrawn from the external world and retreat into the ground of one's being. By going into the very "is-ness" of the phenomenal self, the transcendent self shines forth. Thereafter the individual does not see himself or herself confined to his or her individuality; but rather as a transcendent being, partaking of the infinity and eternity of the Transcendent Itself. Knowledge in this Upanisadic framework is not knowledge of something; knowledge is experiencing the spaceless, timeless, causeless, genderless Reality. The subject and object of knowledge are but one, and the knowledge into essence leads to the experience of ultimate liberation and joy. Epistemological insight (*darsan*) leads to spiritual salvation. As Lord Yama says, "by discerning that, one is freed from the face of death."

Soteriological freedom from the cycle of birth and death is the natural accompaniment of knowledge. By recognizing transcendence, one becomes transcendent and is no longer subject to rebirth. The unity of the self extends into the unity of the cosmos; the myriad phenomena become a unified entity. In Lord Yama's poetically charged words:

> yad eveha tad amutra, yad amutra tad anviha
> mrtyos sa mrtyum âpnoti ya iha nâneva pasyati
>   (II.1.10)
>
> Whatever is here, that is there; what is there, that
>   too is here
> Whoever perceives manyness here goes from death
>   to death.

By recognizing the unity of all, by recognizing that the here and the hereafter are one, Naciketas triumphs over death. The god of death tells the pupil that there is after all no death! The problem of death resolves itself in eternal and transcendent life. All opposites and contradictions dissolve. This world is to be celebrated, every moment to be lived to its utmost, nothing to be feared, nothing to be craved; for, "Whatever is there, that is here." Why look for something else somewhere else? The Transcendent is but here—immanent in all. The Katha Upanisad ends on a triumphant note. Having attained knowledge and the entire technique of yoga enunciated by the God of Death himself, young Naciketas is set free from passion and death; his particular example manifests the opportunity of salvation for everybody.

> Thus Naciketas, having gained this knowledge declared by Death and the whole rule of Yoga, attained Brahman and became freed from passion and from death. And so may any other who knows this in regard to the self. (II.3.18)

Larry spends several years in India before he has the revelatory experience. He stays in the ashram for two years during which he meditates, reads a lot, and listens to Sri Ganesha, that is, when the Swami chooses to talk. By reading, meditating, and listening to the words of wisdom, he develops his inner faculties. Living in the ashram goes together with learning in the ashram. He is not attending a formal institution of education that merely imparts instruction. What he learns is the method of Yoga that is simpy defined by Yama as "the steady control of the senses—tâm yogam iti manyante sthirâm indriya-dhâranâm" (II.3.11). Larry becomes quite skillful at the yogic techniques, for on his return to America he is able to help Gray out of his acute migraine headaches. Where all medical inventions including "aspirin" and advanced "American prescriptions" fail, Yama's age-old advice works. By making him concentrate on a coin, Larry impels the unconscious of the suffering and contorting Gray to take over and heal himself immediately.

Only after having lived in the ashram for two years, does Larry get an insight into the Transcendent Reality. On the morning of his birthday, Larry goes up in the mountains and perceives the ravishing beauty of the scene. This is how he describes his experience: "a knowledge more than human possessed me, so that everything that had been confused was clear and everything that had perplexed me was explained." The physical beauty fills him with a metaphysical insight, and all that was confusing and perplexing becomes suddenly elucidated. The formless self is seen through the âvrttacaksuh (inner eye). He does not learn about the facts of the flora and fauna or about the minerals or the atoms in the water that would delight any botanist or geologist. The knowledge pertaining to transcendence is gained through his inner eye and cannot quite be verbalized in any ordinary words. Perhaps Larry "sees" the Reality through the channel of the heart, mind, intellect—just as Naciketas is instructed by Yama to do. For the result, it seems to me, is exactly the one articulated by Lord Yama:

> hrdâ manîsa manasâbhiklpto ya etad vidur amrtâs te
> bhavanti (II.3.9)
>
> They who apprehend Reality by heart, by thought,
> by mind, become immortal.

Literally, the Sanskrit term *amrtâ* denotes immortality (*a* + *mrtâ*); but it has also come to signify the experience of intense joy—a joy of such intensity that perhaps no mortal can feel it! Larry experiences *amrtâ* in both these senses, for while he feels totally liberated from any mortal confinements he also feels a transcendent joy. "No words can tell the ecstasy of my bliss," he exclaims. Death is no longer feared by him. While continuing to explain his ineffable experience he says, "I was so happy that it was pain and I struggled to release myself from it, for I felt that if it lasted a moment longer I should die; and yet it was such rapture that I was ready to die rather than forgo it." Through the rapture of his epistemological disclosure Larry overcomes death. In mortal frame he becomes Immortal (amrtâ).

The epistemological-soteriological nexus—central to the Katha Upanisad—finds another interesting point of exegesis in Maugham's novel. As Larry recalls his noetic experience, "I had a strange sensation, a tingling that arose in my feet and travelled up to my head, and I felt as though I were suddenly released from my body and as pure spirit partook of the loveliness I had never conceived." This ascending process recounted by Larry is marked out by Lord Yama as the path to immortality:

> A hundred and one are the arteries of the heart; one of them leads up to the crown of the head. Going upward through that, one becomes immortal; the others serve for going in various other directions. (II.3.16)

The Upanisadic point of view is that if a person has lived an ethical life and found the self within, then, at the time of death, the intrinsic self goes up through the crown of the head, merging with the Transcendent one. Freed from the cycle of birth and death, never again will it return to this world in any embodied form. By depicting the sensation going from Larry's feet to his head, and by stressing his "release," Maugham reflects this Upanisadic verse; Larry has discerned his real self, he has been freed forever from the cycle of life and death.

In Lord Yama's teaching, the path and the objective are the same: freedom is attained by becoming free from everyday constraints. "When all the knots that fetter the heart are cut asunder, then a mortal becomes immortal" (II.3.15). Here immortality is understood as a harmonious mode of being. Immortality is not achieved after death but is a state that can be accomplished in our world. Larry as we know is quite free from attachment, and the freedom of the immortal state is reflected in his exterior. Very often we hear the narrator describe in an impressed tone how "Larry appeared as unconscious of the time as of the surroundings," Or, "Although he spoke of serious things he spoke of them quite naturally. . . ." The peace and calm that surround Larry and radiate from his person enable one to understand Lord Yama's statement: "When the five senses knowledge together with the mind cease [from their normal activities] and the

intellect itself does not stir, that, they say, is the highest state" (II.3.10). The psychological mastery of Larry over himself affects his appearance. The physical change is conspicuous after his return from India and the narrator wonders—making the reader wonder even more—as to what it signifies.

> He was a year younger than Gray, they were both in their early thirties, but whereas Gray looked ten years more than his age, Larry looked ten years less. Gray's movements, owing to his great bulk, were deliberate and rather heavy; but Larry's were light and easy. His manner was boyish, gay, and debonair, but with it had a serenity that I was peculiarly conscious of and that I did not recollect in the lad I had known before . . . in Larry . . . there was a singular detachment. . . . I don't know whether to call it awareness or a sensiblity or a force, that remained strangely aloof.

Maugham uses Larry's transformation to portray the contrast between the two life styles: on the one hand, the decadent and material life of Gray Maturin which leads to his deteriorated health; on the other, the ethical discipline which leads Larry to his intellectual-spiritual progress. Indeed Lord Yama's ethical ideal is concretized in Larry's "natural," "serene," "detached," "aloof" presence and expression.

Untouched by the murkiness and slipperiness of the material world, Larry remains free. The freedom from passions (*rajas*) that Naciketas attained (mentioned in the final verse of the Katha Upanisad) is also attained by Maugham's hero. No sexual, economic, professional or social ambitions entangle Larry.

> He is without ambition and he has no desire for fame; to become anything of a public figure would be deeply distasteful to him; and so it may be that he is satisfied to lead his chosen life and be no more than just himself.

Being "just himself" is the most vital mode of existence. Unlike the rest of his friends, who not knowing themselves try to be something other than themselves, Larry is very much at home with himself. As a result, his body, his senses, his mind, and his intellect do not waver or fluctuate tempestuously. His is a handsome, well harnessed chariot: the horses are not going wildly out of control, the reins are held strongly by the driving mind and his essential self seems to revel fully in freedom like that of an owner resting—aloof—in some deeply hidden chamber of the carriage.

Interestingly enough, Naciketas' victory over death is also given a modern twist by Maugham. In a culture which is continuously battling against death, trying desperately to find some new method that fights against the inevitability of death in the medical, cosmetic, dietary, athletic arenas, Larry's success is depicted in his remaining youthful. In Maugham's words, "He has plenty of time, for the years have left no mark on him and to all intents and purposes he is still a young man." A twentieth century approach to immortality?

The story that begins with death, ends with life. When asked about what he would do when he returned to America, Larry simply replies, "Live." When asked again to qualify his response, Larry answers, "With calmness, forbearance, compassion, selflessness, and continence." Maugham's hero seems to have absorbed the very virtues put forth to the Brahmin boy by Lord Yama in the Indus Valley. After having experienced the singular unity, Larry transcends all either-or categorizations. No longer is the subject in quest of an object; he realizes that the Ultimate objective was his subjective self. "Whatever is here, that is there and whatever is there, that too is here." No wonder, then, that Larry decides to return to America. Perhaps America and India do not seem to be two different and distant continents anymore. He intends to put the ancient Indian virtues into practice in the metropolis of the modern world, New York City. Upon his return, Larry looks forward to driving a taxi. A modern version of the chariot, the taxi is for Larry "an equivalent to the staff and the begging-bowl of the wandering mendicant."

Playing the role of Hermes, then, the go-between of gods and men, Maugham translates, analyzes, and elucidates the ancient Sanskrit text for the modern English-speaking reader. Just as Hermes tried to convey the message of the distant gods to the mortals, Maugham takes up the task of explicating and articulating the complex theme of transcendence and immanence present in the classical Hindu text for his Western contemporaries. Now Maugham, a self-claimed agnostic, had no intention of delivering sacred messages from the gods but he was certainly fascinated by the Hindu conception of the Transcendent. He says, "I have sometimes gone back, beyond Mohammed, Jesus and Buddha, beyond the gods of Greece, Jehovah and Baal, to the Brahma of the Upanishads. That spirit, if spirit it may be called, self-created and independent of all other existence though all that exists, exists in it, the sole source of life in all that lives, has at least a grandeur that satisfies the imagination." He expresses this fascination for the Upanisadic notion of the Transcendent in *The Summing Up* which was published in 1938. Maugham must have spent the next few years performing Hermes' task—grappling with this five thousand year old concept and rendering it imaginatively in *The Razor's*

Edge which came out in 1943. As Gadamer who has given new directions for the study of the hermeneutic enterprise would say, Maugham creates "a dialogue with the past." In Maugham's own words the Gadamerian dialogue is simply paying homage to the past. In *The Summing Up* he wrote:

> I have little sense of reverence. There is a great deal too much of it in the world. It is claimed for many objects that do not deserve it. It is often no more than the conventional homage we pay to things in which we are not willing to take an active interest. The best homage we can pay to the great figures of the past, Dante, Titian, Shakespeare, Spinoza, is to treat them not with reverence, but with the familiarity we should exercise if they were our contemporaries. Thus we pay them the highest compliment we can; our familiarity acknowledges that they are alive for us.

Maugham has attempted to bring the temporally and spatially distant text to life for us; in a very simple and delightful manner, he has attempted to familiarize the Western reader with the Katha Upanisad. And as far as I can see, Maugham's hermeneutic procedure, his "paying homage," is quite accurate, valuable, and enjoyable.

The horizon of the ancient Hindu scripture is fused with Maugham's twentieth century horizon. Throughout the novel we discover contemporary images, references, and vocabulary from Maugham's own culture bringing out the import of the ancient and distant text. By appropriating the classical text to his own concrete historical situation, Maugham sets up a dynamic encounter between the traditional text and modern reader. He accomplishes the imperative enjoined by Gadamer:

> Every encounter with tradition that takes place within historical consciousness involves the experience of the tension between the text and the present. The hermeneutic task consists in not covering up this tension by attempting a naive assimilation but consciously bringing it out.

We remember that at the very outset of the book Maugham clearly makes us aware of the Other. He distinctly notes his apprehension about understanding *another* culture. *The Razor's Edge* is not a naive assimilation; during the course of the novel, the reader is again and again made conscious of the chasm between the East and the West. Even his protagonist Larry, who lives in India and absorbs so many of its ideals and values, admits that he cannot quite believe in the theory of reincarnation with the same fervour as the Indians themselves. "I don't think it's possible for us Occidentals to believe in it as implicitly as these Orientals do. It's in their blood and bones. With us it can only be an opinion. I neither believe in it nor disbelieve in it."

Moreover, Maugham clearly realizes that Larry's experience of the Absolute in the Indian scenario is not something easily understandable. At the end of the novel he admits, "I am of the earth, earthy; I can only admire the radiance of such a rare creature. I cannot step into his shoes and enter into his innermost heart as I sometimes think I can do with persons more nearly allied to the common run of men." Very often a poignant contrast between the two milieus is brought out humorously. For instance, when Larry mentions to the narrator that "Shri Ganesha used to say that silence also is conversation," the English gentleman quickly retorts, "That suggests a jolly social gathering of intellectual dons at the University of Cambridge." One way or the other, gravely or humorously, Maugham is constantly juxtaposing the Indian context of the Katha Upanisad to that of the Occidental context of the author and reader, thereby accurately highlighting for his reader the wide historical and cultural gulf.

Simultaneously, however, *The Razor's Edge* is very valuable in breaking the fear of the "foreign," "the other," "the alien"; it paves a path for co-operation of East and West. The novel opens up avenues for readers that a religious text may close. Scripture, another's scripture especially, may be "too reverential," too daunting to enter into. Maugham's fiction creates a sense of familiarity. The modern reader can identify with Larry's nausea at the material world and with his quest for something higher and deeper. The identification with the protagonist creates an attitude of open-mindedness and cordiality disclosing the efficacy of the traditional Hindu text. Indeed, Maugham's artistic interpretation enables the Western audience to absorb the "unfamiliar" worldview of the Katha Upanisad into their personal worldview. Maugham in his fictional recreation succeeds in making the ancient Sanskrit text come "alive for us."

Maugham's success in doing so may be attributed to the conversational mode of the novel. The Hindu philosophical concepts are analysed informally in a Parisian café—during a conversation between Larry and the narrator. The primacy of conversation as a hermeneutical method has been underscored by Gadamer. According to Gradamer, when interpretation is performed in spoken language, "it does not mean that it is transposed into a foreign medium; rather, being transformed into spoken language represents the restoration of the original communication of meaning." Thus the comprehension of ancient and distant philosophical issues becomes fluid and meaningful for the present

through Maugham's dialogical style. Although some readers may object to the narrator's questions and his plea to Larry for clarifications as a clumsy didactic device on Maugham's part, the conversation between Larry and his European companion does make the intricacies of Hindu philosophy vibrant and lively. Such a use of conversation is fully vindicated by Gadamer as a creative and legitimate process of interpretation: "When it is interpreted, written tradition is brought back out of the alienation in which it finds itself and into the living present of conversation, which is always fundamentally realized in question and answer."

Of course, there is the added element of enjoyment in reading *The Razor's Edge*; instead of a translation and exegesis that would come across or underneath or between the verses, Maugham's artistic rendering of the Katha Upanisad creates an aesthetic delight. There is a stylistic play in interpreting the ancient story by means of another story, making the readings and re-readings very provocative. Devoid of any dull x=y equations, *The Razor's Edge* provides tantalizing glimpses into the Katha Upanisad; without narrowing any possibilities, it stimulates the reader's imagination to discover the tacit connections between the classical Hindu text and the modern Western novel. Wolfgang Iser has rightly emphasized the importance of the reader's imagination in a literary text: the moment the imagination is put out of action, "we feel we have somehow been cheated." In Maugham's artistic hermeneutic process, the reader continuously faces the task of mediating between the ancient and modern texts, of working out the interplay between the philosophical and literary dimensions. Searching for the Transcendence of the Katha Upanisad immanent in Maugham's *The Razor's Edge* ends up being a very engaging and envigorating process.

Source: Nicky-Guninder Kaur Singh, "Crossing the Razor's Edge: Somerset Maugham and Hindu Philosophy," in *Durham University Journal*, Vol. LXXXVII, No. 2, July 1995, pp. 329–42.

Archie K. Loss

In the following essay excerpt, Loss discusses ways in which The Razor's Edge *departs from Maugham's earlier novels including its focus on Americans and its detailing of a broader range of characters.*

The Razor's Edge, Maugham's last major contribution to the novel, appeared in 1944, toward the end of World War II, and was written for the most part while its author was living in the United States during that conflict. His residency on these shores

Mound of tailings showing the location of coal mines in Lens, which were closed in 1985
© Setboun/Corbis

was appropriate to its subject, since most of the characters in *The Razor's Edge* are Americans, but in theme and in form the novel carries on where the earlier novels left off: the character who emerges by its final chapters as most central to its theme, Larry Darrell, is in many ways an extension or amplification of the personal qualities we have already noted in Charles Strickland and Edward Driffield, and the novel in which he figures depends more heavily than either *The Moon and Sixpence* or *Cakes and Ale* upon the narrator-as-novelist as a connecting force, giving sequence and form to the narrative, which, in this case, is of greater length than that of those previous novels. *The Razor's Edge* has its own peculiar qualities, however, which give it a special place in the Maugham canon of long fiction.

One unusual aspect of the novel I have already mentioned: it deals almost exclusively with Americans. In the opening chapter of the book, the narrator—who is in fact given Maugham's name—comments on the difficulties this decision posed: "It is very difficult to know people and I don't think one can ever really know any but one's own countrymen. For men and women are not only themselves; they are also the region in which they were born, the city apartment or the farm in which they

learnt to walk, the games they played as children, the old wives' tales they overheard, the food they ate, the schools they attended, the sports they followed, the poets they read, and the God they believed in." Because "you can only know them if you *are* them," it is difficult to give such characters credibility in a book. It is to Maugham's credit that he handles his American characters so well. It is true, of course, that by the time he wrote *The Razor's Edge* he had the benefit of having traveled in this country many times for many years. He also had the benefit of having many personal friends who were American. In addition, his work had an immense popularity here, reflected in the generous sales of this particular work, which became an immediate bestseller.

The Americans with whom he deals in this novel are a special sort; they are all well-educated and well-to-do, and most of them at least have leanings toward England or the Continent. Elliott Templeton, in some ways the most interesting of them all, has spent most of his life in England or in Europe, and Larry Darrell spends at least part of his life there. The Bradleys have lived all over the world in the course of the diplomatic career of the late Mr. Bradley, and Mrs. Bradley has an extensive European acquaintance. In other words, they

" Maugham's characters in *The Razor's Edge* remain for the most part consistent to their nationality; however special, they are representative American types. . . ."

are all fairly cosmopolitan, and much of the novel in fact does not take place in the United States, but in France and in England. Nonetheless, given the special sort of Americans they are, Maugham's characters in *The Razor's Edge* remain for the most part consistent to their nationality; however special, they are representative American types, later versions of the innocents abroad from the fiction of Mark Twain and Henry James.

A second aspect of the novel that sets it apart from those already discussed in this book is that it does not concentrate upon the lives and fates of two or three characters. Rather, it tells the story of a sizable group of characters over a long period of time, never concentrating for very long on any one character. *Of Human Bondage,* for all its length and number of minor characters, remains in memory principally the story of two: Philip and Mildred. *The Moon and Sixpence* concentrates upon three characters: Charles Strickland, Blanche Stroeve, and her husband Dirk. *Cakes and Ale* has a somewhat broader canvas, but focuses principally upon Rosie and Edward Driffield; the narrator Ashenden is an important third principal, but Alroy Kear is important only in the frame. In *The Razor's Edge* one follows the lives of eight characters over a period of approximately twenty years; five of those eight receive more emphasis than the other three, and one, Larry Darrell, comes by the end of the novel to seem most important of all. In effect, here is a chronicle novel, albeit a short one, in which the stories of the various characters are tied together by the device of the author-narrator.

In writing about Chekhov's approach to drama in *The Summing Up,* Maugham remarks on the difficulty of writing a play like *The Cherry Orchard,* which does not focus upon a few individuals, but rather upon a group. In recognition of this difficulty, the narrator of *The Razor's Edge* begins with the comment, "I have never begun a novel with more misgiving. If I call it a novel it is only because I don't know what else to call it. I have little story to tell and I end neither with a death nor a marriage." Although the novel that follows this admonition has more form and substance than this statement implies, it remains a good question whether the device works or not. Before considering that question seriously, however, one needs to look at what happens in the novel itself.

The character who prompts the whole effort, and whose life stands in marked contrast with the lives of the other characters, is Larry Darrell. When he is first encountered in the novel he has just returned from World War I, in which he served as a flier. This experience contributes greatly to his decision not to become part of the materialistic society in which he lives. He rejects the offer of a good job with the Maturin Company and also rejects the notion of going to college as an undergraduate. "I don't mind if I make mistakes," he tells the narrator at one point. "It may be that in one of the blind alleys I may find something to my purpose."

Larry's goals turn out to be largely ascetic. As he goes to live in France, Germany, and elsewhere in Europe, and then later in India, it becomes clear that his is a spiritual quest—a search for the meaning of life—which he feels he must conduct at his own pace, in his own way, earning his living as he can. With each step that brings him closer to the unattainable state of spiritual perfection, he moves further away from the ties that bind him to the other characters in the novel. Toward the narrator, however, he remains to the last fairly open, recognizing in him a stance, not ascetic, yet similar to his own. The artist, like the philosopher, remains apart from others; this is perhaps the ultimate tie between Larry and the author-narrator.

Given Larry's nature, it is not strange that he should find such satisfaction in Eastern philosophy. Chapter 6 of the novel, which has the form of a long digression, gives us a detailed view of Larry's spiritual development. In it, one sees how Larry moves from the Christian experience to the Hindu, much in the manner of so many young Americans of a later generation, the 1960s. For Larry, the stumbling block to Christianity is the old, unanswerable question, "If an all-good and all-powerful God created the world, why did he create evil?" Neither Larry nor the monks he lives with in Germany can answer that question, and the failure to do so leads him to proceed further with his spiritual quest. In India, through study with a guru, Larry, to the extent that he can, comes to terms with the absolute by adapting an ancient philosophy to his present needs. Setting as his goal self-perfection—with its concomitant ideals of self-abnegation and sexual abstinence—he plans to return to the United States, support himself by manual labor or by driving a taxi, and continue his studies.

Larry is the ultimate idealist in a world filled with people who have either lost their ideals or have adopted strictly materialistic ones. Even the narrator, sympathetic as he is to Larry's quest, feels in the end the distance between them: "I am of the earth, earthy; I can only admire the radiance of such a rare creature, I cannot step into his shoes and enter into his inmost heart as I sometimes think I can do with persons more nearly allied to the common run of men." As Larry melts into the common mass of Americans at the end of the novel, one can only guess, with the narrator, what will become of him in the future.

Isabel Bradley—whose love for Larry ends in frustration—is not able to share his ascetic ideals. She moves from the point early in the novel at which she is willing to let Larry go off for a few years to make up his mind about things, to the point later at which she comes to the painful recognition that he is forever lost to her. She knows by then that she has no chance to realize the love she has felt for him for so long. Given the nature of her character, such a realization is inevitable.

Born into a family of wealth and prominence, brought up in various parts of the world as her father's diplomatic posts dictated, Isabel is scarcely in a position to appreciate the ascetic way of life. She has aristocratic features characteristic of her family, a great sense of joie de vivre, and a liveliness and intelligence that speaks more for sociability and conversational ability than for intense intellectual interests. From the first she feels a rapport with the narrator that corresponds to what Larry feels, though she and Maugham seem more like personal cronies than intellectual allies; she reveals herself to him freely, discussing her feelings about both Larry and Gray Maturin. She loves Larry very much, but she is not willing to accommodate her standards to his. She cannot understand why he wants to live in Europe and spend all of his time reading. "We're the greatest, the most powerful people in the world," she says of her fellow countrymen. "We're going forward by leaps and bounds. We've got everything. It's your duty to take part in the development of your country." It seems inevitable that, her love for Larry notwithstanding, Isabel should become the wife of Gray Maturin, who is spiritually Larry's opposite. In the end, after the vicissitudes of the stock-market crash of 1929 and its aftermath, she, Gray, and their children settle in Dallas, where the narrator imagines them leading a charmed, decidedly upper-middle-class life. In the end, Isabel has been unable to have only one thing that she has most wanted—to marry Larry.

Gray Maturin, in contrast with Larry, is, as the narrator puts it toward the end of the book, "the quintessence of the Regular Guy." In almost every way different from Larry, he represents Isabel's philosophical choice; the pragmatic entrepreneur who feels as she does that America is the most exciting place in the world to be. Gray is the man of action, in contrast with the more contemplative Larry; he is tall and muscular, in contrast with Larry's slighter, more wiry, build; Gray is ultimately at one with the world he lives in, with all its weaknesses and faults. His only goals are to be married to Isabel, to have a family, and to make a fortune. For Gray, who is not so much anti-intellectual as nonintellectual, to be is to do; for Larry, to be is to think. Gray's type was best defined in American fiction by Sinclair Lewis, in such novels of the twenties as *Babbitt* and *Arrowsmith*. In Maugham's Gray Maturin we almost feel that one of Lewis's characters has been filtered through a different artistic consciousness.

Gray's only moment of serious weakness in the book comes after the crash and the failure of his father's business. Like his father, Gray defines himself largely in terms of that business, and, until he is able to build a similar place for himself once again, he suffers from a sense of failure and also from intense migraines that incapacitate him for days. In spite of his weaknesses and inadequacies, Gray is a character with whom we can feel some sympathy. He and Isabel—the most materialistic of the characters—represent one approach to reality in a novel that shows various approaches, some valid, some not.

Philosophical positions aside, of all the characters in *The Razor's Edge,* Elliott Templeton has the most flavor. Elliott is also the most Europeanized of the American group. Originally of the Southern aristocracy, he has lived in France and England since shortly after the turn of the century, when he arrived bearing letters of introduction to some of the best people. He is a social butterfly and a snob, but he has gotten to know everyone "worth knowing." The narrator, hard-pressed to account for Elliott's snobbishness given his equally strong intelligence and taste, ascribes it ultimately to a form of romanticism: "I can only guess that to be on terms of intimate familiarity with these gentlemen of ancient lineage, to be the faithful retainer of their ladies gave him a sensation of triumph that never palled. . . . In the company of such as these he felt that he lived in a spacious and gallant past."

It is similar feelings that prompt Elliott to convert to Roman Catholicism and to dedicate part of his considerable fortune—which weathers the crash because he has converted it to gold—to the construction of small chapels in imitation of those of the Romanesque period. Elliott is by turns foolish and wise, but he is always shrewd about money. His death scene—which becomes tied, like his whole life, to a social event—is one of the most memorable scenes of the book.

Maugham knew the type of character Elliott represents well, having encountered it many times in many places. If with other characters in the novel Maugham seems to be working from literary prototypes, in Elliott's case he is dealing with a closely observed type. Missing only from the development of Elliott's character is the logical fact of his homosexuality; one must read between the lines for that, but it certainly can be felt. At no time in his fiction does Maugham openly present a homosexual character, but with Elliott he comes very close.

The other characters in *The Razor's Edge* are given briefer treatment; they are the minor figures in the canvas, though they play at times crucial roles. Especially important among these are Sophie MacDonald and Suzanne Rouvier, the only nonAmerican character in the book to have any great significance.

Sophie and Suzanne form an interesting contrast; the one is a woman who destroys herself, the other a woman who finds a new life for herself in her mature years. In Maugham's work the women most favorably portrayed are always those, like Rosie Driffield in *Cakes and Ale,* who take a realistic view of themselves and their chances; in *The Razor's Edge* Isabel falls into this category, and so does Suzanne. Suzanne makes the best of what might have turned out a bad bargain; Sophie (partly as a result of the workings of fate) makes the worst of what might have been at least a satisfactory one. Together, their stories form a complement to the longer, more complicated one of Isabel and her involvement with Larry and Gray, though, even so, it is difficult to justify the amount of detail we are given about Suzanne, who otherwise plays little part in the book.

Maugham dealt with the themes important to *The Razor's Edge* in one of his early short stories, "The Fall of Edward Barnard," published in the same collection as the celebrated "Rain." In this story, two young men are in love with the same woman, but she favors one over the other. The favorite—Edward Barnard—has moved to Tahiti as representative of an American business firm; the one not favored—Bateman Hunter—is in business in Chicago with his father, who, like Gray Maturin's father in *The Razor's Edge,* owns an imposing home on the lake.

The object of Edward's and Hunter's affections in this story is Isabel Longstaffe, a product of Chicago who combines American aggressiveness with European refinement. This Isabel is a neoaristocrat for whom Louis XV furnishings (compare the description of the furnishings of the Bradley house in *The Razor's Edge*) are an appropriate backdrop. Bateman has learned that Edward never plans to return from Tahiti to marry Isabel, and much of the story has to do with his recounting the reasons why.

Edward, it seems, has succumbed to the influence of the Tahitian environment and begun to consider his philosophical position, his attitude toward life. Like Larry Darrell, he has begun to read simply for the sake of reading, and he now rejects the whole idea of material success that took him to Tahiti in the first place. "I haven't failed," Edward tells Bateman. "I've succeeded. You can't think with what zest I look forward to life, how full it seems to me and how significant." Edward surrenders to his friend all rights to Isabel, and, at the end of the story, Bateman and Isabel look forward to their life together, with all its material success, in what they feel is the greatest country in the world.

Edward's fall is clearly fortunate, both for him and also, ironically enough, for Bateman. As in *The Razor's Edge,* this short story presents us with two ways of life, one more idealistic than the other. In "The Fall of Edward Barnard" the alternatives are less equal in their attractiveness than they are in *The Razor's Edge.* Mixed with the desire for greater self-knowledges on Edward's part is a certain euphoria that comes (as for Strickland in the later pages of *The Moon and Sixpence*) from the tropical environment, but thematically, as well as in certain of its details, this early short story represents Maugham's first run-through of the materials of his novel of more than twenty years later. It also serves to highlight some of the major themes of the novel.

In *The Razor's Edge,* Maugham never makes completely clear whether it is Larry's way that should prevail or the way of Isabel and Gray. Part of the problem is that—as with Charles Strickland in *The Moon and Sixpence*—Maugham never quite succeeds in bringing Larry Darrell to life.

As a character on a philosophical quest, Larry lacks credibility. As a result, the novel in which he figures becomes to some extent a novel without a hero.

It is true that Maugham has the narrator say that the whole purpose of the novel is to tell Larry's story, and that chapter 6, with the detailed account of Larry's spiritual development, is the most important in the book. It is also true that in one of the key scenes of the novel (and also, incidentally, one of the least credible) it is Larry, the ascetic, who teaches Gray, the materialist, how to overcome the terrible pain of migraine by the application of principles of yoga that Larry has learned in India. This overly explicit example of the triumph of mind over matter is intended to illustrate the spiritual theme associated with Larry; it overstates that theme at the same time that it shows its significance to the book.

In contrast, Isabel—though she is never able to have Larry as her own—has everything else with Gray, including a good sexual life, and the narrator, who is, he says, "of the earth, earthy," is perpetually noting the gown by Molyneux, the luncheon at a certain restaurant, and the other trappings of materialistic success that are so important to Isabel's and Gray's way of life. Furthermore, when mind does triumph over matter in Gray's cure, the result is that Gray is able to earn even more money than before. This application of the principles of yoga does not seem to make much difference to the spiritual progress of the world. On the whole, viewed in terms of actions and consequences in the novel, the more materialistic characters—not only Isabel and Gray, but also Elliott Templeton and Suzanne Rouvier (whose real significance to the book may lie in her having this quality)—fare very well, even in comparison with Larry, and the narrator at times seems strongly to share their view.

John Brophy has noted that Maugham's attitude toward his characters can be described as that of a clinician. He notes their condition, remarks on whether it is stable or growing worse, and then moves on to the next character or story. Such an attitude comes across clearly in the pages of *The Razor's Edge*, where one feels that ultimately, despite gestures in the direction of Larry, the narrator does not wish to pass judgment in his favor, merely to indicate the direction his life has taken. Despite his sympathy for Larry and despite the amount of space devoted to his story, one ends by feeling that Maugham wishes to suspend his judgment and let the reader decide.

Source: Archie K. Loss, "Innocents Abroad: *The Razor's Edge*," in *W. Somerset Maugham*, Ungar Publishing, 1987, pp. 58–71.

Forrest D. Burt

In the following excerpt from the conclusion to his W. Somerset Maugham, *Burt discusses how Maugham "cultivates the special relationship that he has established with his readers" in* The Razor's Edge.

Puzzlement in Fiction

Factors beyond the text—such as Maugham's celebrity status, image as a British gentleman, secret agent during World War I, tasteful craftsman of fiction, and a model of the effective use of the queen's English—undoubtedly influenced the reception of each of his later works. In *The Razor's Edge,* Maugham's pattern continues. He approaches the readers as equals—respected members of the audience and as fellow travelers on adventures of life, one in whom he confides. He begins: "I have never begun a novel with more misgiving. If I call it a novel it is only because I don't know what else to call it." Thus, his growing number of readers knew immediately that they had yet another treat ahead of them.

In *The Razor's Edge,* the last novel in the tradition of *The Moon and Sixpence* and *Cakes and Ale,* the Ashenden narrator/character is named Mr. Maugham. Visiting in Chicago, he is contacted by a friend of many years, Mr. Elliott Templeton (a close parallel to Alroy Kear), and invited to dinner. That evening Maugham meets Isabel, Elliott's niece, Isabel's mother, Gray (who will eventually marry Isabel despite her preference for Larry), Sophie, a friend of the family, and most noteworthy, Larry Darrell, Isabel's fiancé, who has just returned from the war. With Elliott, Mr. Maugham will have a relationship very much like that between Mr. Ashenden and Alroy Kear. Larry is the character about whom Mr. Maugham has a sense of puzzlement—similar to that between Willie Ashenden and Rosie and between the narrator and Charles Strickland. And the relationship between Isabel and Mr. Maugham is warm and open, yet flirtatious at times and at others quite critical. This relationship Mr. Maugham no doubt had with a few women in his life—perhaps most notably with Barbara Back, wife of Ivor Back, the prominent London surgeon, and with the novelist G. B. Stern.

Mr. Maugham is at first impressed and later quite puzzled by Larry. Then he learns that Larry has put off his marriage to Isabel, feeling that he must go to Paris and to the East in search of the meaning and purpose of life—to find God. Still later he learns that Larry had a friend in the war who lost his life saving Larry from certain death. This and his natural goodness and sensitive nature lead Larry on a quest for meaning and answers.

Maugham cultivates the special relationship that he has established with his readers. He takes unusual liberties in developing this highly structured work—which on the surface may seem quite casual (moving back and forth in time, using the flashback technique, a narrator who is a world traveler)—all a plausible harmony. In a sense the reader is a fellow traveler with Maugham.

Typical of the personas of earlier works, the Mr. Maugham narrator shows a fascination with an exceptional individual such as Larry gradually becomes. Although modern readers no doubt identify with Mr. Maugham's attraction to such a saintly individual, they most likely relate even more strongly to Mr. Maugham's inability to reach the same lofty heights as Larry does. These dimensions of the novel and of reader participation were present in other novels, of course—notably in *Cakes and Ale*. Here, though, readers experience the emotions and attitudes from a greater distance, have less of a sense of what Larry's life and values meant than, for instance, Strickland's or Driffield's. Mr. Maugham's answer to his lack of understanding comes at the end of the novel: "I am of the earth, earthy; I can only admire the radiance of such a rare creature, I cannot step into his shoes and enter into his inmost heart as I sometimes think I can do with persons more nearly allied to the common run of men." In contrast to Larry, Mr. Maugham, the English gentleman, sees life through the eyes of moderation, pragmatism, objectivity.

The novel follows the common Maughamian pattern of concealment: concealing information—about Larry's quest, his adventures, his findings, etc.—and revelation: revealing the emotions and attitudes of the narrator, Isabel, Larry, Sophie, and Elliott. And there are close parallels here to *Cakes and Ale* and *The Moon and Sixpence:* Larry to Rosie and Strickland; Mr. Maugham to Willie Ashenden; Elliott Templeton to Alroy Kear, etc.

Mr. Maugham presents the novel in a deceptively casual manner—admitting misgivings for even calling it a novel, etc. But beneath this surface informality the reader finds a highly structured, intricately worked-out system of individuals, use of time, events, etc. We know of the date of the opening, reference is made to the publication of *The Moon and Sixpence,* ages are given of characters, dates of events—such as the stock market crash, etc.—that give the novel historic credibility.

But beyond this craftfulness there is a shift in concern from plot to character—as was true in *Cakes and Ale.* That is, the novel concerns Larry—about whom we learn very little. At the beginning of chapter 6, in the heart of the novel, Mr. Maugham states: "I feel it right to warn the reader that he can very well skip this chapter without losing the thread of the story as I have to tell, since for the most part it is nothing more than the account of a conversation that I had with Larry." He adds ironically that if it had not been for this conversation he would not have written the book. Here the Mr. Maugham narrator/author (as the two are fusing at this point) teases the reader, enticing him or her to read further. Also here Mr. Maugham is shifting the focus on character, that of Larry. As in countless other Maugham novels the involvement is an intensely dramatic one. And what the reader comes away with is, like the Persian rug, in direct proportion to what he or she has put into it; it is an experience in which there is no intrinsic meaning.

Source: Forrest D. Burt, "Conclusion," in *W. Somerset Maugham*, Twayne Publishers, 1985, pp. 134–42.

Sources

Beach, Joseph Warren, "Maugham Considers Mystics," in *W. Somerset Maugham: The Critical Heritage*, edited by Anthony Curtis and John Whitehead, Routledge & Kegan Paul, 1987, pp. 353–54; originally published in *New York Times*, April 23, 1944.

Calder, Robert Lorin, *W. Somerset Maugham and the Quest for Freedom*, Doubleday, 1973, pp. 224–53.

Connolly, Cyril, "The Art of Being Good," in *W. Somerset Maugham: The Critical Heritage*, edited by Anthony Curtis and John Whitehead, Routledge & Kegan Paul, 1987, pp. 358–61; originally published in *New Statesman and Nation*, August 26, 1944.

Maugham, W. Somerset, *The Razor's Edge*, reprint ed., Penguin Twentieth-Century Classics series, Penguin Books, 1992.

———, "The Saint," in *Points of View*, Heinemann, 1958, pp. 56–93.

Naik, M. K., *W. Somerset Maugham*, University of Oklahoma Press, 1966, p. 95.

O'Brien, Kate, Review of *The Razor's Edge*, in *W. Somerset Maugham: The Critical Heritage*, edited by Anthony Curtis and John Whitehead, Routledge & Kegan Paul, 1987, pp. 356–57; originally published in *Spectator*, July 21, 1944.

Whitehead, John, *Maugham: A Reappraisal*, Vision and Barnes & Noble, 1987, pp. 175–83.

Further Reading

Brander, L., *Somerset Maugham: A Guide*, Barnes & Noble, 1963, pp. 182–88.

This is mainly a discussion of characters. Brander also has high praise for the final discussion between the narrator Maugham and Larry, which some critics have found unconvincing.

Burt, Forrest D., *W. Somerset Maugham*, Twayne's English Authors Series, No. 399, Twayne, 1985, pp. 137–39.

In this survey of Maugham's life and work, Burt comments on the complexity of the novel's structure, ably handled by Maugham behind a casual veneer, and the shift in Maugham's concern from plot to character.

Curtis, Anthony, "Introduction," in *The Razor's Edge*, Penguin, 1992, pp. vii–xxiv.

Curtis has written several books on Maugham, and this is an authoritative introduction to the novel, covering circumstances of composition, parallels with earlier works, possible origins of the characters in real people known to Maugham, and the novel's critical reception.

Holden, Philip, *Orienting Masculinity, Orienting Nation: W. Somerset Maugham's Exotic Fiction*, Greenwood Press, 1996, pp. 131–45.

Holden discusses how in the novel masculinity is defined by work and femininity is defined by sexual desire. The male characters are largely free of desire. He then examines how India functions as a metaphor of transcendence and the release from desire.

The Stone Diaries

Carol Shields

1993

The Stone Diaries by Carol Shields is the story of an ordinary woman's life, told in an unusual combination of shifting first- and third-person points of view. Daisy Goodwill Flett is both the narrator and the subject of her life's story, which spans and reflects the changing social and family scenes in North America during the twentieth century. A work of fiction, The Stone Diaries presents itself as a mix of autobiography, biography, and historical memoir and contains as well a compilation of papers and family photos which purport to belong to or be relevant to the protagonist. To read this novel is to feel on some level as though one is compiling a report from various sources regarding the protagonist, Daisy Goodwill Flett. The 1993 novel was exceedingly well received in Canada, the United States, and Great Britain, and established Shields as one of the twentieth century's finest novelists writing in English.

Author Biography

Carol Shields was born June 2, 1935, in Oak Park, Illinois, to middle-class parents, her father the owner of a candy store, her mother a teacher. Interested in writing during her teen years, Shields attended Hanover College in Indiana and spent a semester abroad at Exeter University in England where she met her future husband, Don Shields. The couple was married in 1957, settled in Ottawa, Ontario, Canada, and eventually had five children.

Carol Shields © Jerry Bauer. Reproduced by permission

By the time Shields was thirty-three, she aspired to obtaining a master's degree. She graduated from Ottawa University in 1975. Thereafter, she began working, at first editing part time from home and also writing short stories. Material she had found while conducting research for her master's essay provided Shields with a plot for her first novel, *Small Ceremonies*, which was published in 1976. Next, she wrote *The Box Garden* and *Happenstance*, works that some criticized for being too domestic but which nonetheless identified Shields's chosen subject, women at home with their families.

With an established readership in Canada, Shields gained both U.S. and British recognition with her 1987 publication of the novel *Mary Swann*. But far and away more successful was her 1994 novel, *The Stone Diaries*, which won awards in Great Britain and in North America. In the United States the novel won the 1995 Pulitzer Prize.

Following the 1997 publication of *Larry's Party*, the first Shields novel with a male protagonist, the author was diagnosed with breast cancer. She retired from her two-decade-long tenure at the University of Manitoba, and she and her husband moved to British Columbia. While receiving treatment there, Shields wrote and published in 2002 her last novel *Unless*. Shields died at the age of sixty-eight on July 16, 2003, at home in Victoria.

Plot Summary

Epigraph and Genealogy

The Stone Diaries begins with an epigraph, which is identified as a quotation from a poem, "The Grandmother Cycle" by Judith Downing, published in *Converse Quarterly* in Autumn, no year given. Judith Downing is a granddaughter of Daisy Goodwill Flett. The quotation, which appears on the page before the genealogy, stresses the failure of communication to convey exactly what is intended; yet it affirms the value of the individual who attempts to communicate. Despite the discrepancy between intention and statement or action, a person's life is still important, the quotation asserts, and "could be called a monument." This epigraph, which claims to be a quotation from a published poem written by a real person, initiates the pretense maintained throughout that the text is a factual record and not fiction. Moreover, the point that the life lived is a person's true monument counteracts the effect of the stone monument Cuyler Goodwill erects over the grave of his first wife, Mercy Stone Goodwill. Ironically, that stone monument hides altogether the grave marker which records the dates of Mercy's brief life and thus the monument eclipses the facts of the life it seeks to memorialize.

The genealogy includes four generations of the Goodwill and Flett families. The span of years encompasses just about all of the twentieth century. Daisy is born in 1905 and her death sometime in the 1990s is later than all the other years listed. Her life spans the century; the stages of her life parallel the periods or stages of that century, and she is the link between the present of the 1990s and the previous generations, now dead.

Chapter One: Birth, 1905

In July 1905, at age thirty, Mercy Stone Goodwill dies in the process of giving birth to a daughter. Mercy begins labor while fixing a Malvern pudding for her husband, Cuyler Goodwill, who does not eat with interest but who appreciates Mercy's homemaking skills. Unlike her husband, Mercy loves food. The narrator says: "Eating was as close to heaven as my mother ever came." Obese and uninformed, Mercy is unaware that she is pregnant and does not know what is happening to her when her water breaks and labor begins. The narrator projects what would happen that day if it were like other days: Cuyler would come home at 5 p.m., wash up, and come to the table at 5:30 p.m. But on this particular day, while Mercy ponders how to cool the pudding, her labor pains begin. The narrator describes Mercy's months of indigestion, her menstrual periods of which there have been only two, her sexual relations with Cuyler, and her chronic illness (pregnancy).

Next door, menopausal Clarentine Flett hangs out the wash, and the narrator tells about how she has become estranged from her stingy husband, Magnus, and isolated in their house. She realizes she is "no longer willing" to be Magnus's wife. Clarentine has heard Cuyler pronounce his love for Mercy. The narrator describes Cuyler as a short, slight man who is dwarfed by his morbidly obese wife. Now, as Clarentine considers her neglected garden, she thinks about inviting Mercy to tea.

The neighborhood peddler, Abram Skutari, comes across the yard and grabs Clarentine, urging her to come quickly to help Mercy, just as Cuyler is walking home from work along the dusty road. From Abram's shocking view of Mercy, the narrator slides into a history of Cuyler. He grew up in an ugly run-down house in nearby Stonewall, where his parents did not care about him. He worked in the dolomitic limestone quarry from age fourteen to twenty-six, and then one day he visited the local orphanage and met Mercy Stone, the housekeeper there, age twenty-eight, who called to have a doorsill repaired. He fell in love with her, admiring her gentle housekeeping, her softness. He took coffee and bread from her as payment for repairing the sill. When Cuyler and Mercy married in 1903 they moved to nearby Tyndall where he took a job in a new quarry. He revels in their sex life and her "lavish body."

Abram Skutari, Dr. Horton Spears, Clarentine Flett, and Cuyler Goodwill are present when Mercy gives birth at 6 p.m. and then dies of eclampsia (convulsions during labor). The baby is "the uninvited guest" at the scene. The witnesses to this birth and death "are borne up by an ancient shelf of limestone."

Chapter Two: Childhood, 1916

This chapter begins with description of the bachelor Barker Flett, Wesley College professor of biology, age thirty-three, and how his female students admire him. Unaware that they find his hand gestures erotic, he describes for his students the sex organs of flowers: pistil, stigma, ovary, stamen. World War I has begun, and most male students have enlisted, but not Barker Flett. He supports his mother and a child others assume to be his niece, age eleven. Now the narrator presents teachers' views and information gained by the dentist and observations from the church congregation, all different perspectives chiming in on Barker and his family. Barker suspects "love is no more than a

diminutive for self-injury." He was happiest alone at age twenty-two in the summer of 1905 when he was writing his dissertation on the western lady's-slipper, a flower he loves, but that was before his mother left his father and moved in with him, bringing a baby with her.

That fall 1905, Mrs. Flett arrived with a baby she had named Daisy, having left no note for Cuyler and traveled fifty-three minutes by train to Winnipeg. The narrator shifts here, and a group of letters are presented which date from the years between 1905 and 1916. Barker wrote his father about money, and Clarentine wrote Cuyler about Daisy's development and about her allergies and asthma, and she thanked Cuyler for the money he regularly sent her. The Fletts heard of and read about the Goodwill Tower, which Cuyler built to honor Mercy's memory. In 1916, Clarentine dies; Barker's response to a condolence from Cuyler reports that Barker intends to move to Ottawa, and being a bachelor living alone he cannot continue to provide for or live alone with a female child, to whom he is not related.

Cuyler felt Mercy's simple grave was "pitifully inadequate" and began piling unusual stones around the flat marker. He used balance and gravity to hold them in place. As he worked he wondered why Mercy did not tell him she was pregnant (the answer is she did not know). He would wake at night, "his head soaked with the sweat of memory." He thought of it as a betrayal. In the time of the composition of this text, the narrator, Daisy, looks back and wonders if his sense of Mercy's withdrawal caused Cuyler to be incapable of loving her.

Barker has suppressed sexual feelings for the child Daisy as they live together in 1916 in Winnipeg. Now, as if writing history, the narrator describes how churches are built, and Winnipeg is fast becoming a stone city. Young people take summer train trips to Tyndall to see the Goodwill Tower. They peer down into it, but they cannot see the grave marker. Cuyler is interviewed by journalists. He reports that "a person starts a piece of work and the work takes over." The grief over his wife's death has dimmed as have his memories of her. Cuyler receives a letter from Barker raising questions about Daisy's future, and at the same time Cuyler gets a job offer from the Indiana Limestone Company in Bloomington. Barker moves to Ottawa. Cuyler takes Daisy on a train to Bloomington, talking to her nonstop all the way: "Her father's words came toward her like a blizzard of dots."

Chapter Three: Marriage, 1927

This chapter opens with quotations from the social page of the local newspaper, reporting a luncheon, a tea, a kitchen shower, and white dinner held locally for bride-elect, Daisy Goodwill, and groom-to-be, Harold A. Hoad. The couple is to marry in June. Cuyler gives long-winded speeches on Bloomington's "white Salem stone." He uses patronizing, artificial, and ornate language. His longest speech engulfed Daisy on their three-day trip from Winnipeg to Bloomington. On that journey, Daisy was queasy and dreamed of her home in Winnipeg, of Aunt Clarentine and Uncle Barker. In this way, even as a child, she realized "the absent are always present."

Historical information about Canada and emigration to Montreal leads into the life of Magnus Flett, born 1862, who traveled to Canada as a boy, married there, and had three sons. Some time after his wife Clarentine left him, he decided to return to the Orkney Islands where he was born. Having spent forty-six years in Canada, he took a train to Montreal and from there a ship to Liverpool, an eight-day Atlantic crossing. He took along only a few possessions, one of which was a photo of the Ladies Rhythm and Movement Club. He believed this photo proved that Clarentine was happy during her marriage to him. He had gone repeatedly to Winnipeg to see her but had lost his nerve each time. In her absence, he had discovered Clarentine's romantic novels and read them; he especially liked *Jane Eyre*, a novel he in time wholly committed to memory. Over the years he practiced romantic statements and whispered his wife's name, Clarentine.

A week before the wedding, Daisy has lunch with her future mother-in-law. A few days before the wedding, she has a final fitting with her bridesmaids, Fraidy and Beans. The father of the groom, Arthur Hoad, committed suicide when Harold was seven years old. Mrs. Hoad explained to Harold and his brother Lons that Arthur knew he was going blind and did not want to be a burden to her. Her statement is unconfirmed; there is no letter, no doctor's report. Later, Harold heard rumors about financial problems and a "woman 'friend'" in Bedford.

Suffering (he thinks) from "congenital cynicism," Harold wants to know the details, but he is daunted by his mother's fictions: his father's suicide morphed into "a sacrificial act"; Lons was "'artistic'" not "mildly retarded." In truth, Mrs. Hoad's "creative explanations had the effect of making Harold feel perpetually drunk." According to Bloomington society, he is "[a] first-class example of America's young manhood." Daisy sees a less attractive side to him. Rich and handsome, Harold is also a cheat and a drunk.

Barker Flett has heart pangs after Daisy's letter arrives, in which she announces her impending marriage. He does not want to admit feeling sexual about her. Now forty-three, he remains a bachelor, by others "thought to have frosty reservations" about intimacy. Detached from the real world, Barker can list varieties of lady's-slippers but knows nothing about the foxtrot or Charles Lindbergh. As wedding gifts, he sends Daisy $10,000, the proceeds from the sale of his mother's flower shop, and a book on Canadian wild flowers. Her father gives her a stone elf he carved himself. This gift is crude and embarrassing. Cuyler's gift of speech is as exhausted as is his artistic ability.

Before the wedding Daisy and Harold walk in a garden. He strikes delphinium with his cane, knocking off the blooms. She tells him to stop and he does. He wants to be checked by her. She is twenty-two and marrying because it is time, and she believes she can change him. He is drunk during the wedding ceremony and continues drinking on the train to Montreal. They are both seasick crossing the Atlantic. Still drunk, Harold rents a car "black as a hearse" and drives them from Paris to the Alpine town of Corps. In a hotel room, Harold gets onto a windowsill and throws coins to children in the street; Daisy closes her eyes and tries to sleep. When she opens her eyes he is no longer in the window. He has fallen to his death, his body hitting the pavement with "a crashing sound like a melon splitting."

Contained within this chapter are a group of photographs much like those that might appear at the center of an autobiography or memoir. These photographs purport to be of some of the characters in this novel; however, they are actually photographs of the author's own family and thus suggest that the novel may be autobiographical of Shields's life. There is no photograph said to be of Daisy. Other photographs do not concur with the text description of the characters. Photographs of two different women both bear the name of Clarentine Flett. The discrepancies these photographs present speak to the inability of the record to be accurate or complete.

Chapter Four: Love, 1936

The narrator states at the outset that "real troubles . . . tend to settle on the misalignment between men and women." The narrator states that men are "honored by the stories that [erupt] in their lives" while women go "all gray and silent beneath the weight of theirs." For years following Harold Hoad's death, Daisy Goodwill Hoad is defined by Bloomington society in terms of various interpretations of the spectacular story of his death, her actual personality and feelings quite eclipsed by it.

Cuyler Goodwill goes to Italy in search of stone cutters and comes home with a bride, Maria, age twenty-eight, who speaks Italian only and whom no one other than Cuyler understands. With his new wife, Cuyler is suddenly silent, his "tongue . . . stilled." Daisy decides to take a trip to Canada. She goes to Ottawa and meets Barker Flett. He is fifty-four; she is thirty-one.

Magnus Flett went from Montreal to Liverpool in the summer 1927, the same summer as Daisy and Harold made their transatlantic voyage. Magnus vomited overboard his painful memories, landed light as a boy, and headed north by foot. He arrived at Stromness, his home, and believed life could now be sweet and he would live forever.

Barker wrote Daisy every other month for twenty-two years. During that time, he lived detached from passion and secured by exactitude and classification, sublimating his libido by obsessing about "the pockets within pockets" of his flowers. His letters survive; her responses, which were so girlish they disappointed him, do not. Now as Daisy approaches Ottawa, she realizes she cannot go home to Bloomington to live in Cuyler and Maria's house. She seeks Barker as a "refuge."

Daisy and Barker marry on August 17, 1936. In his sexual relationship with Daisy, Barker realizes that "[t]here is a part of the human self that is unclassifiable." Next are presented various views on the unexpected marriage. The chapter concludes by stating that Daisy's "own thoughts on her marriage are not recorded." Mrs. Flett has come to think it would be embarrassing for others to read a journal of her private thoughts. This concluding paragraph is one of many instances in which the novel suggests that no matter how much information is given and deduced and manufactured about an individual, the individual is never fully revealed or known by others.

Chapter Five: Motherhood, 1947

This chapter opens at dinnertime in the Flett Ottawa household. Barker is nearly sixty-five and soon to retire. He and Daisy have three children, Alice, now nine; Warren, seven, and Joan, five. The children are presented individually. Alice learns separately about sex and is disgusted; Warren likes

being told he was born "[i]n the early days of the war" and is reassured when his mother says she is too old to have another child. The "other child," Joan, has secrets, an imaginative life.

Mrs. Flett's niece, Beverly, presents her views of the children. Cousin Beverly is the daughter of Barker's brother Andrew. A letter from Beverly's mother, Frances, is included here. Cuyler and Maria sell their Bloomington house and move to a country home, in the back garden of which Cuyler sets about to build a miniature pyramid, twenty-seven square yards at the base. He plans a time capsule to be hidden inside and asks the Flett children to send him items to include in it; they send a stamp, a maple leaf, and a news headline from 1947 announcing the upcoming marriage of Princess Elizabeth and Prince Philip. Cuyler adds the gold ring of Mercy Goodwill, which had been destined to go to Daisy. Cuyler feels like he has "lost his way in life."

The narrative repeats and shifts into a distant third-person voice. For example, though she has already been introduced, readers are told again Maria is Cuyler's "second wife" and "Fraidy Hoyt and Daisy Goodwill Flett went to school together back in Indiana." The headings "Mrs. Flett's Old School Friend" and "Mrs. Flett's Intimate Relations with her Husband" make the text sound like someone quite detached from Daisy is tabulating information about her life. Several times readers learn that Barker goes off on business trips. Daisy tries to follow the marital advice offered in *Good Housekeeping, McCalls*, and *The Canadian Home Companion*. Barker likes to have sex before he leaves and upon his return. But Mrs. Flett does not know how to demonstrate "ardor and surrender." Again, the accident that killed Clarentine Flett is described, but this time the boy on the bike is named, Valdi Goodmansen.

Daisy expects Barker back from the dedication of the Clarentine Flett Horticultural Conservatory and thinks about her own mother and how she has nothing from her. Barker feels cut off as he approaches retirement; Daisy feels "the loss . . . of any connection in the world." She has "gusts of grief." She suffers even now from "orphanhood" and is "anointed by loneliness." The chapter concludes with information under the heading, "Mrs. Flett's House and Garden," which includes a description of the Ottawa house interior and Mrs. Flett's "dearest child," her paradise of a garden.

Chapter Six: Work: 1955–1964

This chapter consists only of letters, presented here as though drawn from Mrs. Flett's personal and business files. Events occurring in this period are thus presented indirectly to the reader by references made in the correspondence. Obviously, the first-person point of view shifts from one letter writer to the next. As with her twenty-two-year-long correspondence with Uncle Barker, the letters Daisy receives are kept, but the letters she writes are lost. Thus, readers of the novel only learn about Daisy's life through inferences they draw from letters written to her and not through her own words.

The first letter presented, dated April 25, 1955, is from solicitor W. W. Kleinhardt, who refers to Mrs. Flett's "late husband." In this indirect way, readers learn that Barker Flett has died. The next letter is from Barker himself, written April 6, 1955, in which he sums up Daisy's financial circumstances, lectures her on his collection of lady's slippers, and closes with a description of how she embraced him on the day when he experienced his "first terrible headache." He mourns "the waste of words that passed" between them. The third letter, from the *Recorder* editor Jay W. Dudley, contains an invitation to Mrs. Flett to attend a memorial ceremony for her husband and comments in passing that the annual tulip festival will not be covered by Mr. Flett this year. Letters from Dudley and from readers of the column by Mrs. Green Thumb trace Mrs. Flett's successful work in writing for publication on gardening and horticultural events. Beverly Flett, unmarried and pregnant, offers to come to Ottawa and work for Mrs. Flett. Fraidy writes on May 29, 1955, to extend her condolences to Daisy regarding her father's death. Readers of Mrs. Flett's newspaper column write with questions and appreciation for her expertise. Subsequent letters from Jay Dudley imply his increasing admiration of her work and suggest that he is becoming sexually involved with her. Letters from Alice tell about her college experience. Both Fraidy and Beans write regarding an April 1956 trip to Chicago the three friends take during which Mrs. Flett visits the Chicago Horticultural Conservatory in order to write a review of it for the *Recorder*. The professional snare involving Pinky Fulham begins to unfold in these letters, as he writes the column while Mrs. Flett is in Chicago. A letter from a *Recorder* reader confirms that Mrs. Flett knows more than "Pinky What's-his-name."

In their abbreviation of years, the letters provide a sense of how things change over time. Beverly's daughter Victoria is born, and Alice resents her bedroom being used for the baby, but a year later Alice writes that she cannot wait to see Vicky again. Also, the budding relationship

between Mrs. Flett and Jay Dudley, a widower of three years when he meets Daisy, jumps ahead, along with Alice's marriage and her move to England, the birth of Alice's baby Ben Junior, and Daisy's loss of her job when Pinky Fulham takes over the column. Letters from Fraidy and Alice that conclude the chapter comment that Mrs. Flett has not been writing back. Though they "[h]ope all is well," the suggestion is that it is not. Mrs. Flett, a successful writer, stops writing letters when she loses her job at the *Recorder*. The point may be that work provides professional identity; others see the worker as a person in her own right. But when a person loses her job, it is as though her whole identity is erased.

Chapter Seven: Sorrow, 1965

This chapter begins in the third person: "1965 was the year Mrs. Flett fell into a profound depression." At age sixty, Daisy was full of resignation, which "hardened into silence, then leapt to . . . blaming estrangement." After this introduction, the rest of the chapter consists of people's theories about Mrs. Flett's depression. These interpretations demonstrate how differently others view a person and how disparate views can each contain valid points. Like the letters of the previous chapter, the theories here are written in first-person point of view; they come from Alice, Fraidy, Cousin Beverly, Warren, Joan, Jay Dudley, Beans, Cora-Mae Milltown (Cuyler Goodwill's Bloomington housemaid), Skoot Skutari (grandson of Abram Skutari), and finally from Mrs. Flett herself.

Alice's theory is the self changes, that it is not carved in stone. She recalls coming back to her old bedroom after completing her first year at college and suddenly feeling compelled to repair a crack in the ceiling. Next, Alice decided "to grow kind." She burned her old diaries and began to modify her personality. Now she offers "a diagram" of the family before and after her father's death. She notes that while her father was alive the nuclear family was traditional and habitual and that her mother "was part of that mid-century squadron of women who believed in centerpieces." After Barker died, her mother was "a different person, a person who worked." "It was as though she had veered, accidentally, into her own life" as a writer on horticulture. Then Cousin Beverly arrived. In 1954, the Fletts were an ordinary family: a father and breadwinner, a stay-at-home mother, and three children; by the end of 1955, the household contained one working parent, an unwed mother, and three teenagers. In the chaos of that second stage, her mother seemed happy. Nine years later, Mrs. Flett lost her job. At fifty-nine, she is out of work and feels so stunned by the sudden change, "she's like some great department store of sadness with its displays of rejection and inattention." Alice comes back from England to check on her mother and finds her unable to "get over this."

Fraidy's theory begins by discounting Alice's. Fraidy has known Daisy since they were girls in Bloomington. Alice is married to a professor and has written a book on Chekhov, and, according to Fraidy, is way too focused on work. While Alice thinks "We are our work!" Fraidy maintains that work is not the self. Fraidy says the work ethic was too strong in the Flett family, that it buried them in "fairy dust," which leads "to the unpacking of lies and fictions . . . scraps of inbred history." Fraidy assigns the depression to sexual frustration, to Daisy's life with "plodding Barker" followed by "a brief flutter with an editor," in sum, a lifetime of erotic experience equal to "about one and half bean sprouts." Fraidy goes to Ottawa to see if she can relieve Daisy's depression. She thinks a candid conversation between friends may help. Confessing to some fifty-four sexual partners, Fraidy wants to speak about the "sexual spasm" and "the realm of the ecstatic." But the visit is a disaster: Daisy cannot be coaxed from her dark bedroom.

Beverly theorizes that the children got Daisy down. Warren thinks his mother mourns "the squandering of herself"; he thinks, "Something, someone, cut off her head, yanked out her tongue." Warren thinks his mother is on the edge and about to fall off. Joan thinks her mother cannot let go of the injustice of her column being given to Pinky Fulham, that her mother relishes hating him. Jay Dudley admits feeling guilty about Daisy's depression; he admits to realizing she had "a more permanent arrangement in mind" and yet he knew all along that being married once was enough for him. His wording, that "it seemed best to put a little distance between us," suggests that giving Daisy's column to Pinky was Dudley's way of removing Daisy from his professional and personal life. Beans, here referred to formally as Labina Anthony Greene Dukes, a woman who has been married three times and knows what disappointment is, thinks women are "breakable." Reflecting much of her own disappointment in love relationships, Labina concludes: "It's . . . like a thousand little disappointments raining down on top of each other. After a while it gets to seem like a flood, and the first thing you know you're drowning."

Looking back to 1916, Cora-Mae Milltown speaks of being in the Bloomington house working as a maid when Cuyler Goodwill arrived with eleven-year-old Daisy, "this washrag of a girl," a "poor motherless thing." Cora-Mae realizes she is all Daisy has by way of a mother, so she takes particular care of the child. Back then, with Daisy just a little girl, Cora-Mae looked into Daisy's future and could not imagine she would be able to find happiness. She imagined Daisy headed for "the blackest night." Looking back to 1905, Skoot Skutari tells the story of his grandfather Abram who was permanently changed by witnessing the birth of Daisy, by receiving the "final glance" of Mercy Goodwill, and by his blessing of the ignored baby. Abram remembered how he stood with the doctor and how "[t]heir tears mingled." Abram grieved for that baby, "so alone in the world," and for its sadness. Finally, the "nut case" Mrs. Flett herself presents a theory: "sorrowing . . . has limits." "[I]n the thin bony box of her head," Mrs. Flett knows "her immense unhappiness is doomed to irrelevance." Mrs. Flett assumes life will resume in the details of polishing jars and licking stamps.

Chapter Eight: Ease, 1977

Victoria Louise Flett, twenty-two, is a student at the University of Toronto. She is touched by how women scrutinize genealogical records at the library. Her great-aunt Daisy lives in Florida, preoccupied with thoughts of two dead fathers, Cuyler Goodwill and Magnus Flett. Daisy moved to Florida and bought a condo near her friends, Fraidy and Beans. Victoria spends her vacations there. At seventy-two, Daisy has an easy life, is in good health, and has money enough in her savings. The Ottawa house was sold in 1967; Victoria's mother Beverly died in 1973. Cuyler Goodwill's earlier death in 1955 is described, how he was working in his back yard when he had a heart attack and fell to the ground. Maria, his wife, was shopping and taking her time walking home. He lay on the grass, his mind slipping away. He thought in his final moments of his parents, "now firmly erased," and of his first wife, whose name he struggled to recall.

In Florida, Great-aunt Daisy ponders how much of life is spent being old. She moves along, "[n]umbly." Victoria talks Daisy into taking a trip to the Orkney Islands. Victoria and her instructor (later her husband) Lewis Ray plan to conduct research on local fossils. Remarkably, Magnus Flett is still alive at age 115. Mr. Sinclair, the hotel owner, drives Mrs. Flett around and out one day to the site where Victoria and Lewis are excavating. There, at God's Gate, a rock arch at the shore, Mrs. Flett feels happiness. They are so tiny against the immensity of the rock, like insects. Lewis and Victoria seek traces of life in the stone, of "Life turned to stone."

Mrs. Flett visits Magnus Flett, who has made a reputation for himself by living into such great old age and by being able over the years to recite from memory much of *Jane Eyre*. On this meeting, however, the "barely breathing cadaver" can only recite part of the novel's first sentence. He cannot respond when Daisy asks about Clarentine, his wife. He mouths the word, "Clarentine" and "Daisy" but not in recognition. She touches his covers from which rises the "scent of decomposition."

Chapter Nine: Illness and Decline, 1985

With a heart attack, broken knees, and cancer in one kidney, Daisy Goodwill Flett lives now in "the wide-open arena of pain, surrounded by row on row of spectators." She drifts between sleep and waking "[i]n the pleat of consciousness." In the hospital, Mrs. Flett is visited by Reverend Rick. She feels insulated by the medicine, disoriented, unable to communicate, floating in a peripheral reality interrupted moment to moment by hospital activity. Her room is decked with flowers and an inflated giraffe from Warren and his third wife, Peggy. At 5 p.m., Alice telephones from England. Alice speaks in a soothing, reassuring tone, trying to encourage her mother. To Warren in New York, she uses another voice, emphatic, pessimistic.

The children feel guilty about not being there, but they have their reasons: Alice cannot come until the end of her teaching semester; Warren's new baby daughter has Down's syndrome and she and his wife need his presence; Joan's four teenage girls and unfaithful husband cannot be left unsupervised; Victoria, now with twins in Toronto, writes every other day but a visit is not possible. The family is so scattered, Mrs. Flett has trouble picturing them grouped together in one place. Her local friends, called collectively The Flowers, visit her every two to three days. They laugh at death. They pose the toast: "here's to another year and let's hope it's above ground." The secret Mrs. Flett cherishes is that someone in Admissions left off her married name from her identification bracelet, which now reads Daisy Goodwill. This point leads into a series of labels people assign to Mrs. Flett: "a fighter"; "a sweetheart"; "a real lady . . . of the old-fashioned school." All of Mrs. Flett's possessions are in one metal hospital drawer; she laments: "So much shrinkage."

Reverend Rick visits Mrs. Flett in a convalescent home. He confides in her his desire to tell his mother he is gay. Mrs. Flett says his mother knows and he should not mention it. As her mind goes, she sees there is a lot of humor even in old age and "[v]anity refuses to die." She has pictures of herself in her head; in all of them, she is alone, without a witness. She repeats herself, "[t]o keep the weight of her memories evenly distributed." Sitting with her mother, Alice realizes, "the moment of death occurs while we're still alive."

Chapter Ten: Death

This chapter contains various summaries of Daisy Goodwill Flett's life, such as an obituary, a poem, statements people make during a funeral and reception, a list of physical problems in chronological order, her bridal lingerie list, books she read, a recipe, a list of addresses in chronological order of places in which she once resided, and a final comment about the flowers at the funeral, no daisies included. The children comment on their mother's personal belongings and discover that Daisy was married before she married their father. They assume incorrectly she was too broken up over Hoad's death to talk to them about it. They remark that they were unable to talk to her about death, and they agree that their "genes are pure granite."

Characters

Beans

See Labina Anthony Greene Dukes Kavanaugh

Alice Flett Downing

Oldest child of Barker and Daisy Flett, Alice Flett marries Ben Downing and moves to England, where the couple has three children, Benjamin, Judy, and Rachel. Later, the marriage falters and Alice and Ben separate. Alice takes Daisy's maiden name, Goodwill, as her last name after the divorce is final.

Jay W. Dudley

Jay W. Dudley is editor of the Ottawa *Recorder*, which publishes a column, "Mr. Green Thumb," written by Barker Flett. After Barker dies, the column is renamed, "Mrs. Green Thumb," and is written by Daisy Flett. Jay Dudley becomes socially and sexually involved with the widowed Daisy Flett and then abruptly ends the relationship. He replaces her as author of the "Green Thumb" column with a full-time employee, James (called Pinky) Fulham, claiming company policy in doing so. The suspicion is he uses this opportunity to distance himself from Daisy Flett. The sudden loss of this relationship and her work puts Daisy into a long-term depression.

Barker T. Flett

The oldest son of Magnus and Clarentine Flett, Barker Flett was born in 1883. He earns a master's degree in science and becomes a professor of biology at Wesley College in Winnipeg, Manitoba. His students wonder at his remaining a bachelor, suspecting him to be "one of those men who feel toward women both a delicate sensibility and a deep hostility." When his parents separate, Barker Flett supports both his mother and the child, Daisy Goodwill, whom Clarentine Flett rears to age eleven. After years of separation between Barker and Daisy while she lives with her father in Bloomington, Indiana, and Barker works in the Department of Agriculture at Ottawa, the couple reunites and marries suddenly in 1936. They have three children, Alice, Warren, and Joan. In the spring 1955, Barker Flett dies of a malignant brain tumor.

Beverly Flett

Daughter of Barker Flett's brother Andrew, a Baptist minister, and his wife Frances, Beverly Flett joins the WRENS during World War II and is stationed in England. Back home in Saskatchewan, Canada, she is impregnated by a married man. To keep secret her pregnancy, she moves to Ottawa and into the home of the recently widowed Daisy Flett. Beverly gives birth in 1955 to a daughter, whom she names Victoria Louise. Beverly Flett dies of pancreatic cancer in 1973.

Clarentine Flett

Unhappily married twenty-five years to Magnus Flett and mother of three sons, Clarentine Flett at age forty-five is the neighbor of Mercy Goodwill in Tyndall, Manitoba. Inclined to depression, she is described as "a woman whose desires stand at the bottom of a cracked pitcher, waiting." Mrs. Flett is present when Mercy dies in the process of giving birth to a daughter. Clarentine leaves her husband and takes the newborn, whom she names Daisy, to live with her son, Barker, in Winnipeg. Clarentine Flett has a successful life there selling flowers and caring for the young child. She dies of complications resulting from an accident in which she is hit by a bicyclist.

Daisy Goodwill Flett

Daisy Goodwill Flett, born in 1905 in Tyndall, Manitoba, narrates part of this novel, a work that is presented as both an autobiography and biography of her life. Describing herself as a newborn "out of reach" of "that filament of matter we struggle to catch hold of at birth," Daisy is as disconnected from her mother as Mercy Stone Goodwill, an orphan herself, was from hers.

Raised by Clarentine Flett and Barker Flett until age eleven and then by her widowed father, Cuyler Goodwill, Daisy obtains a bachelor's degree in Liberal Arts from Long College for Women in 1926. In 1927, she marries Harold Arthur Hoad, who dies on their honeymoon, and then in 1936, at age thirty-one, Daisy marries the fifty-four-year-old Barker Flett. They have three children, Alice, Warren, and Joan. The third-person narrator refers to Daisy variously according to the stages of her life: Daisy, Mrs. Flett, Great-aunt Daisy, and Grandma Flett. Daisy Goodwill Flett dies sometime in the 1990s.

Magnus Flett

Born in the Orkney Islands in 1862 and immigrated to Canada as a boy, stingy Magnus Flett prefers a plain house and plain food. His control of the household money to the point of denying his wife Clarentine the fee for a dentist appointment drives her away from their home in Tyndall, Manitoba, to Winnipeg to live with their oldest son Barker. Left alone, Magnus rehearses romantic words and rereads *Jane Eyre* in hopes that if his wife returns to him he will be able to communicate his love for her. In time, Magnus returns to his native Orkney Islands and dies there at the ancient age of 115.

Victoria Louise Flett

Born out of wedlock in 1955, Victoria Louise Flett is the daughter of Beverly Flett, Barker and Daisy's niece, who comes to live and raise her daughter in the Ottawa household of the widowed Daisy Flett. Victoria becomes a student at the University of Toronto where she studies paleobotany under instructor Lewis Ray, whom she eventually marries. Victoria spends her vacations with her great-aunt Daisy in Sarasota, Florida, and as a result of the niece's initiative Daisy visits the Orkney Islands and meets for the first and only time her father-in-law, Magnus Flett. Living in Toronto, Victoria and her husband have twins, Sophie and Hugh.

Warren Flett

The only son of Barker and Daisy Flett, Warren Flett is born in 1940, "[i]n the early days of the war." As a young man he studies music at the University of Rochester in Rochester, New York, and when his mother goes through a period of depression he assesses the situation with a distanced academic attitude. Warren, who is a musicologist in the Lower Manhattan public schools, marries three times. With his third wife, Peggy Ambrose, he has a Down's syndrome child, Emma, whose immediate needs prevent him from visiting his ailing mother in 1985. Nonetheless, Warren and Peggy do visit the elderly Daisy before she dies.

The Flowers

The bridge group, The Flowers, consists of four elderly women who play cards together at the retirement home: Lily, Myrtle, Glad (short for Gladys, not gladiola), and Daisy. These women enjoy a game every day, joking about age and mortality and showing off their exclusive friendship to other, more isolated residents. Though the remaining three women visit Daisy in the hospital, they are unable to travel the considerable distance to visit her in the convalescent home. The loss of their friendship heightens the ailing Daisy's sense of alienation and isolation.

Fraidy
See Elfreda Hoyt

James Fulham

James Fulham, whose nickname is Pinky, is a full-time writer for the Ottawa *Recorder*, and with some knowledge of plants, he aspires to taking over Mrs. Flett's column. Eventually he is given the column and thus is the immediate cause for Daisy's losing her job with the paper. According to editor Jay Dudley, it is a simple case of the rights that full-time employees have over part-time workers, but for Daisy it signifies loss of self-worth and a personal rejection by Dudley. James Fulham is killed when a vending machine overturns and crushes him.

Cuyler Goodwill

Born November 26, 1876, Cuyler Goodwill grows up in Stonewall and when he is married lives nearby in Tyndall, Manitoba. An only child raised in a dirty house that faced the lime kiln of Stonewall, Cuyler left school at fourteen to work in the quarry and add his wage to the family's "jam pot." He has no schooling but a naturalist's love of stone. More than anything else, though, he adores his obese wife, Mercy Stone Goodwill, "[b]ody and soul." When his wife dies unexpectedly in childbirth, he takes the fact that she did not mention her pregnancy as signifying a betrayal or withdrawal, though in truth she did not know herself that she was pregnant. In the pangs of grief, Cuyler builds

a stone tower over Mercy's grave in tribute to her memory and as an expression of his undying love. Later, he takes a job in Bloomington, Indiana, where Daisy goes to school and marries. Here, the diminutive but long-winded Cuyler rises in the quarry business and is described as having a "silver tongue" because he gives long speeches. On a trip to Italy he meets Maria, whom he takes as his second wife. Cuyler Goodwill dies in 1955.

Maria Goodwill

The second wife of Cuyler Goodwill is Italian by birth and knows very little English when she relocates to Bloomington to live with her husband. While Cuyler maintains that he understands her, most people do not. After Cuyler's death, Maria takes a small amount of money from the estate and relocates without telling anyone her whereabouts. She perhaps goes back to Italy or she may begin a relationship with an older man in Bloomington. Ultimately, what happens to her remains a mystery.

Mercy Stone Goodwill

Obsessed with food and obese, Mercy Stone Goodwill, who was raised in the Stonewall Orphans Home where all the orphans have the last name of Stone, grows into womanhood adept at cooking and housekeeping. She marries the diminutive stonemason, Cuyler Goodwill, and then dies in childbirth at age thirty. Without blood relatives, Mercy "stands apart from any coherent history." An illegitimate child left at the home, Mercy Stone Goodwill may be Ukrainian or Icelandic.

Mrs. Arthur Hoad

Mrs. Arthur Hoad, mother of Harold Hoad and widow of Arthur Hoad, a suicide, appears first in the novel at lunch with Daisy Goodwill, her future daughter-in-law. Mrs. Hoad takes this prenuptial opportunity to tell Daisy how she should speak, eat, and act when she is married. She also gives her information about Harold's bowel movements and what she can do to keep them regular. Mrs. Hoad is an expert on keeping up appearances, and she creates acceptable stories to mask the hurtful embarrassments in her life, namely her husband's financial difficulties and infidelity, her one son's cruelty and alcoholism, and her other son's retardation.

Harold Arthur Hoad

Harold Arthur Hoad, Daisy's first husband, dies on the couple's honeymoon. His father, Arthur Hoad, shot himself in the East First Street stone castle where the important quarry owner lived with his wife and two sons, Harold, age seven at the time, and Lons.

Harold's mother explains the suicide as a result of her husband's knowledge that he was going blind and his wish not to become a burden to her. Traumatized by his father's death and frustrated by his mother's inability to speak the truth, Harold is cruel and alcoholic. He comes to his own wedding drunk and engages in a drunken binge on the honeymoon trip which prevents sexual intercourse and results in his accidental death in a fall from a hotel window. His mother manufactures a story regarding his death, interpreting the fact that the suddenly widowed Daisy remains a virgin as proof of her frigidity which, Mrs. Hoad concludes, drove Harold to drink.

Elfreda Hoyt

Daisy's college friend and bridesmaid, Elfreda Hoyt, fondly referred to as Fraidy, is worldly, sexually experienced, and good humored. She has been to France and can explain what a bidet is, and she has seen a nude male in life drawing class. As a young woman Fraidy swears in 1920s style, for example, spelling out the common swear word "*h-e*-double toothpicks." Though she remains unmarried, Fraidy keeps track of her sexual encounters in a little journal. She visits Daisy after Barker Flett dies and tries to cheer her up. In the 1970s, Fraidy becomes senile.

Labina Anthony Greene Dukes Kavanaugh

Daisy's college friend and bridesmaid, Labina Anthony, fondly referred to as Beans, marries Dick Greene one month after Daisy marries Harold Hoad. Not as close a friend of Daisy as Fraidy is, the supercilious Beans distances herself from others by giving everything a pious or cliché interpretation. In all, she marries three times; she dies suddenly in the 1970s.

Cora-Mae Milltown

Maid to Cuyler and Daisy Goodwill in their Bloomington house, Cora-Mae gives her notice when Maria arrives, since the new Mrs. Goodwill does all the work around the house herself, even answering the door in her apron and with her hair tied up in a scarf.

Old Jew

See Abram Gozhdë Skutari

Pinky

See James Fulham

Lewis Ray

Instructor and future husband of Victoria Louise Flett, Lewis Ray is a post-doctoral student at the University of Toronto. Together with Victoria and her great-aunt Daisy Flett, he travels to the Orkney Islands to do research on fossils along the rugged coastline. After they are married, Lewis and Victoria have twins and live in Toronto.

Reverend Rick

Reverend Rick, a chaplain, visits Daisy Flett during her final illness. Instead of comforting her, he takes her politeness and motherliness as an invitation to confide in her that he is gay. He is troubled that he cannot discuss this subject with his own mother. Daisy tells him that his mother already knows and that he should not bring up the subject with her. He says he "'can't go on living a lie,'" to which Daisy responds, "'Why not? . . . Most people do.'"

Abram Gozhdë Skutari

Born in Prizren, Albania, the son of a rabbi, the Sephardic Abram Gozhdë Skutari, age thirty-four, is a peddler in Tyndall where Clarentine Flett refer to him as "the old Jew." Abram is present at the birth of Daisy Goodwill and receives Mercy Goodwill's "final glance." He signs the birth certificate, and the fact that he is able to write is a surprise to the other witnesses. In later years, he becomes the millionaire founder and owner of a nationwide chain of retail stores that sells whatever Eaton's mail order catalogue does not, including bicycles. Abram's grandson, Skoot Skutari, compiles a history of the family that goes back to the fifteenth century. Ironically, Abram, whom Clarentine Flett so looks down upon, has a distinguished lineage and becomes an exceptional success in business. The bicycle involved in the accident that causes the death of Clarentine was sold by his company.

Joan Flett Taylor

Joan Flett is the youngest of Daisy's children. She lives in Portland, Oregon, with four teenage daughters and her unfaithful husband, Ross Taylor.

Themes

Autobiography and Biography

The complex nature of autobiography and biography is a central subject in *The Stone Diaries*. Autobiography, a first-person account of one's own life, and biography, a third-person account of someone else's life, are both the form and content of this novel. The novel examines whether it is possible for such an account either about oneself or another

Topics for Further Study

- Visit a local quarry or rock store and purchase a sample of limestone and a fossil. Do some research on these materials. Bring them to class and make a presentation in which you explain what geological connection may exist between them.

- Read *Spoon River Anthology* (1916) by Edgar Lee Masters. Select one of the grave marker poems in this collection and imagine the life story of the speaker. (You may have to do some research on the period during which the speaker is said to have lived.) Then using first-person point of view, write the speaker's autobiography.

- Research the materials used in the construction of the Empire State Building. Write an essay in which you connect what you learn to Cuyler Goodwill's 1927 speech on the anticipated growth in the limestone mining industry and the development of buildings and monuments in New York City and Washington, D.C.

- Browse through library copies of women's magazines published between 1947 and 1955. Then write a paper on how they portrayed wives and mothers and how their views anticipated or contradicted comparable images promoted in women's magazines in the early 2000s.

- Make a genealogy of your family, using the one provided in *The Stone Diaries* as a model. Interview relatives to learn the names and dates of your ancestors. Use a poster to write your genealogy and write a story based on an interview session you conducted or on a story a relative told you about an ancestor.

- Read *The Diary of Anne Frank* and write a paper on how the diary was treated after it was found by Anne Frank's father at the end of World War II. In your paper describe how the text of the diary was changed before it was published.

---

person to be in any sense a complete and accurate picture of an entire life or of an evolving person's character. The novel suggests that the text is always less than the whole story, always less than the sum of a whole personality or psyche as a person changes over time. Regarding the summary of Cuyler Goodwill's early years, for example, the narrator says: "The recounting of a life is a cheat . . . our own stories are obscenely distorted." However one writes the story, the story itself is an abridgement of the total life experience. It cannot contain everything and it is not the life itself, but rather a text about the life. Life itself slips away moment by moment, much experience fading from awareness even as it is lived.

That sense of losing track of experience, of one's things, oneself, is countered by an act of the imagination which in the writing of the life story conjures, retrieves, and creates in order to fill in the blanks left by missing information. For example, the narrator describes a time when the child Daisy is ill and lies for weeks in her darkened Winnipeg bedroom. The child realizes that life goes on outside the house even though she does not participate in it. Sequestered in a sick room, the child is "erased from the record of her own existence." In order to counteract this sense of leaving no mark or not existing in the world, the narrator states the following about Daisy: "She understood that if she was going to hold on to her life at all, she would have to rescue it by a primary act of imagination, supplementing, modifying, summing up the necessary connections . . . getting the details wrong occasionally." In other words, reflecting on one's experience and on one's own self is essentially a form of story-making, of writing fiction. The person selects and edits life experience, emphasizing some parts, omitting other parts. Even all of the remembered parts are not included. Elsewhere the narrator states: "There are chapters in every life which are seldom read, and certainly not aloud." For various reasons the storyteller censures some material. Thus, in this fictional work, a novel, autobiography and biography are subjects discussed in order to show the way in which these forms of writing reinvent the life that is their subject.

Genealogy

The novel begins with a genealogy of four generations in the Goodwill and Flett families. This information pinpoints each character in relationship to all others and in relationship to the twentieth century. The book, which appears to be a composite of letters, different theories, family photographs, and other documents connected to Daisy Goodwill Flett's life, pretends to present a family history. The combined information from disparate parts, though, does not make a whole, any more than genealogical research brings forth a complete record of a family's past. The genealogy and the varied texts included in the novel invite readers to think about the elusive essence of ordinary lives and the incomplete record those lives may leave behind. In this respect, the narrator pieces together the found parts in the hopes of making sense, if not providing a complete picture. Proof that the effort fails lies in the discrepancy between parts. For example, different theories or interpretations are presented side-by-side, showing the various ways in which the subject can be viewed and how these views in a sense change the subject. Similarly, discrepancies exist between the photographs (for example, two photographs are identified as being of Clarentine Flett and yet close examination reveals they are of different women) and between photographs and the texts which describe them (for example, Cuyler Goodwill is said to be shorter than his first wife, Mercy, yet the photograph shows him to be taller; the outfits portrayed in the Ladies Rhythm and Movement Club photograph do not match in-text description of them).

Geological Record

Stone is at the center of this novel, both literally and metaphorically. Limestone itself is a central subject. Stonemasons, quarries, the stone industry through the twentieth century, the development of cities filled with stone buildings, sculpture and architecture in stone, and research into fossils, all are subjects explored in the book. Female softness and interest in flowers, Clarentine Flett and Daisy Goodwill Flett's interest in gardens, and Barker Flett's fascination with lady's slippers, all represent the other end of the continuum in which through ages of decomposition organic life becomes inorganic limestone. Cuyler Goodwill explains in his lecture how certain geological factors converged to produce limestone. The geological record is the

"written" history of the physical world; organisms live, in death their bodies decompose, in time the sediment of their matter becomes stone, in some of the stone, fossil marks of organic material can be found. Workers mine the stone, carve it, erect monuments and buildings of it, and then in time these creations erode, as the Goodwill Tower over Mercy's grave is vandalized and the pyramid Cuyler attempts in his backyard rounds and eventually falls apart. Add to this literal focus on stone, the fact that the orphans in Stonewall all have the same last name, Stone, and Daisy Flett's children say they have "genes of pure granite." The book is a layering of texts, composite "diaries" much about stone and family members descended from a woman named Stone.

Communication

The epigraph at the beginning of the novel states the discrepancy between what one says and what one intends to say. Indeed, talk fills this novel and often the talk is not aligned with the truth or with the intended meaning. The novel is self-consciously focused on how language use marks an individual's development and that person's place in society or in a given time. For example, Cuyler Goodwill is much characterized by his use of language. Born "bereft of language" and reared among people who were not expressive, Cuyler was at the outset reticent and reserved. After he married, though, he believed "the stone in his throat became dislodged" during sexual relations with his beloved first wife, Mercy. Daisy theorizes that Cuyler's language was influenced by his study of the King James Version of the Bible after Mercy died. From this text, she believes, he appropriated his "archaic formal locutions." In addition, as Cuyler was repeatedly interviewed by journalists regarding the Goodwill Tower, his "tongue learned . . . evasion . . . fiction and distraction" and his "voice . . . became the place where he lived." In Bloomington, he gives long-winded speeches and is known to have a "silver tongue." His speeches keep people at a distance, prevent intimacy. Years later, he marries a woman who speaks only "a dithyrambic mixture of Italian and English that [Cuyler] alone . . . seemed able to understand."

By contrast to Cuyler Goodwill who is fluent and verbose, Magnus Flett is described as taciturn and noncommunicative. He came to believe his wife Clarentine left him because he failed to speak his love for her. In the years of her absence, Magnus practiced saying his wife's name tenderly, practiced romantic phrases he learned from reading the novels she left behind in their Tyndall house. On his deathbed, Magnus could quote some of the first sentence from *Jane Eyre* because by his old age he had memorized much of that novel. In his use of language Magnus Flett illustrates how imitative speech patterns are. A similar point is illustrated in the slang expressions Beans and Fraidy use as young women. Speech patterns are also a matter of fashion. No character illustrates this point more completely than Mrs. Hoad, who coaches Daisy Goodwill on how her future daughter-in-law should speak ("we invite people to dinner, not for dinner") and whose "creative explanations" made her son Harold stumble "under the unreality of her fantasies."

Daisy Goodwill Flett speaks for herself as a first-person narrator and is spoken of by a third-person narrator. Others express their theories about her, and documents such as letters she receives, newspaper articles, obituary statements, and lists convey information about her. However, letters she wrote over the years do not survive. En route to Ottawa, she lost her journal, and after that she gave up writing her thoughts. In her final decline, her mind drifts between dreams with certain phrases rattling in her brain. In these and other ways, the novel comments on the effects and limitations of language, differences in fluency and levels of inhibition, which facilitate or hamper communication. While the novel is a portrait of one woman's life, it also explores, paradoxically, the ways in which language obstructs such a portrait from conveying the whole person that is its subject.

Style

Title

The title of a novel is a sign pointing toward its central subject. In this case, the title suggests diaries made of stone or diaries written by a person or family named Stone. From the pyramids to grave markers, stones provide the solid pages of recorded events, and characters here descended from Mercy Stone leave their reports and interpretations regarding her daughter, Daisy. Mercy Stone Goodwill leaves no record of her own. The only surviving text of her life is the flat marker on her grave, and that marker is completely obscured by the Goodwill Tower built of limestone, which her husband, Cuyler Goodwill, erects over it. Finally, in terms of geology, the earth's crust holds the incomplete record of the millennia of life and death on its surface, as the research performed by Lewis

Ray and Victoria Louise Flett on the Orkney Islands points out.

Shifting Tense and Point of View

In this novel the tense shifts continuously from past to present and back again to past. In some passages the text reads like social history, describing how Winnipeg or Bloomington was built during the twentieth century; in other passages it zooms in with the immediacy of present tense, filling in and amplifying a long-past moment and bringing it alive as drama in the here-and-now. Similarly, the point of view shifts. First person provides immediacy and personal insight, while third person can provide an overview for which distance is required. Sometimes the perspective abruptly shifts, even in one sentence. For example, the following sentence, which describes how the eleven-year-old Daisy was sequestered during a long illness, shifts from first to third person: "The long days of isolation, of silence, the torment of boredom—all these pressed down on me, on young Daisy Goodwill and emptied her out." The point here may be that in autobiography the narrator is both the speaker and the subject. The narrator exists in the present tense of the text, telling the story of Daisy's life; Daisy, the subject of the story, is conjured forth in past moments that are dramatized. Thus, the past exists in the present as memory exists in present thought. It is not the past itself, but present conceptualization of it. Similarly, a life story is not the life itself, but a way of imagining that life as it was. This sense of how the past permeates the present is relevant to the writing of history in general, whether it is the personal history of one's own life or of a selected other person or the history of a city, say Winnipeg, or a decade, say the 1950s. In this seamless shifting of tense and point of view, Shields provides a sense of how fluid and incomplete any conceptualization or story of the past is. Memory writes a story based on past experience and information that survives in all kinds of records of it, and in thinking about what has happened people come to better understand who they are and how they have changed over the years. This dynamic interaction between past and present is at the core of any writing of autobiography or of any history.

Sensory Description

Vividness is achieved by rendering detail through the use of the five physical senses. Sensory description is specific and concrete; it conveys a clear picture of its subject. For example, Mercy Goodwill loves Malvern pudding, both the pudding and its name: she "thrills to see the dish . . . oozing juices . . . she loves the words too and feels them dissolve on her tongue like a sugary wafer." Effective use of simile (the comparison of two different things using "like" or "as") conveys meaning through fresh combinations. Mercy's first labor pain is described as "a squeezing like an accordion held sideways." The echoing loss of her mother at birth fills Daisy with "gusts of grief." In her final illness, in the mental state between sleeping and waking described as "the pleat of consciousness," Daisy Goodwill Flett marches "straight into the machinery of invention," her mind filled with "[c]ertain phrases, remembered and invented." Sensory descriptions use the five physical senses to convey what may be hard to describe otherwise. The apt image or the unusual comparison helps convey what often may seem indescribable.

Literary Allusion

The most important literary allusion (reference to another work of literature) in *The Stone Diaries* is the many references to Charlotte Brontë's *Jane Eyre* (1847), another autobiographical novel. *Jane Eyre* is written in first-person point of view and tells the story of an orphan between the ages of ten and twenty from the perspective of that girl now a woman of thirty. The intelligent, honest Jane Eyre proves to be an exceptionally capable person who rises, with a good dose of luck, above social, familial, and educational obstacles to create a place for herself, complete with work and family. Brontë's *Jane Eyre* presents a literary point of departure, a work of comparison and contrast to the present work. *The Stone Diaries* is another story of the foundling, but it follows the trajectory of that life all the way into old age, whereas Brontë's novel concludes at the high point with its protagonist married ten years and raising the couple's son. The effectiveness of the literary allusion depends on the knowledge shared by the author and the reader. The well-chosen allusion informs the work in which it is mentioned by creating a frame of reference and by shedding light on that work through various parallels, echoes, and differences.

Historical Context

The Twentieth Century

Published in 1993, *The Stone Diaries* mentions historical events and social changes that span the whole of the twentieth century. The novel begins with Mercy Goodwill's at-home labor and delivery of her baby, during which Mercy, who did not even know she was pregnant, dies of eclampsia. Houses in this village do not have electricity or telephones; Abram Skutari runs for the neighbor, Mrs. Flett, and then runs for Dr. Spears. The doctor comes to the house, and husband and neighborhood witnesses sign the birth certificate. In a remote village such as Tyndall, Manitoba, in 1905, childbirth at home was the norm. It would be commonplace to enlist the help of a neighbor woman who had already given birth and considered unusually fortunate for a physician to be in attendance.

In the early 1900s household conveniences were rare: when Mr. Flett buys a Labrador zinc-lined ice chest, he shocks his wife and impresses the neighbors who have virtually no way to keep food cool. Transportation was by horse and wagon for short distances and by train for longer trips, such as the fifty-eight kilometers from Tyndall to Winnipeg. The train trip in 1905 took fifty-three minutes; in 2005, by car the trip might take just about the same length of time. But in 1905 the train crossed open farmland, stopping at many little villages along the way, whereas in the early 2000s people from Tyndall drive through the suburban greater metropolitan area in order to reach the city limits of Winnipeg.

In Bloomington in 1927, Cuyler Goodwill gives a speech in which he forecasts a boom era for the building industry. He takes as proof of future prosperity the fact that Charles A. Lindbergh Jr. (1902–1974) has just completed the first solo nonstop transatlantic flight. Cuyler also describes how much stone is being shipped to Washington, D.C., and New York City, and he anticipates the construction of the Empire State Building in New York City, which in fact began in 1930. Industry owners and upper management enjoyed great wealth in the years just prior to the Great Depression (1929–1939), and the stone mansions on East First Street in Bloomington reflect that affluence among successful industrial owners and company heads.

In the late 1940s and early 1950s, the post–World War II era, middle-class women were encouraged to marry and be stay-at-home mothers. They read magazines about housekeeping, about how to meet their husband's every need and wish, and about parenting techniques. The 1947 description of Daisy Goodwill Flett preparing dinner and urging her three children to wash up quickly since their father will be home soon from work reflects an era which idealized the nuclear family with the father as the breadwinner and the mother at home teaching the children good table manners and proper social behavior. This era was also known as the Baby Boom period, since family size at an average of four

Compare & Contrast

- **1930s:** Construction of the Empire State Building is underway in 1930. The art deco building is made of Indiana limestone and at 1,250 feet in height is famous for being the tallest building in the world.

  Today: The Taipei 101 building in Taipei, Taiwan, is completed in 2003 and at 1,671 feet is the tallest building in the world.

- **1930s:** For long distances, travel by train is the common method. On May 20 and 21, 1927, Charles Lindbergh Jr. makes the first nonstop solo transatlantic flight; however, transatlantic travel continues to be by ocean liner.

  Today: Attacks involving airplanes destroy the World Trade Center Towers in New York. Film footage of the plane crashes contributes to a sharp reduction in people flying on U.S. airlines.

Reduction in flight travel threatens the viability of some U.S. airline companies.

- **1930s:** Born May 28, 1934 in Corbeil, Ontario, the Dionne quintuplets become celebrities. The Ontario government makes them wards of the state, removes them from their parents, and operates a theme park, Quintland, where the identical sisters are on display twice a day to thousands of tourists. Their doctor, Allan Roy Dafoe, becomes famous and rich. In the novel, Daisy Goodwill sees the quintuplets on display.

  Today: In 1965, the quintuplets publish their bitter autobiography, *We Were Five*, and in the late 1990s, the three surviving Dionne sisters who are poor sue the Canadian government for compensation for exploiting them as children and profiting from them. The sisters are awarded $2.7 million.

---

children was large by comparison to later decades of the twentieth century.

As in earlier decades, a husband's death often required the wife to go to work to provide income for the household and dependent children. Women at mid-century increasingly achieved college educations and through the 1950s and 1960s, greater numbers assumed they would have professional lives concurrently with rearing their children. At the same time, though, an unmarried woman was often considered unfortunate in love or someone to be pitied. Even more acute, the unwed mother was an embarrassment to her family and friends. In many cases an unmarried pregnant woman was obliged to leave her hometown, gestate and give birth elsewhere, and commonly expected to give up her baby for adoption. Beverly Flett's situation illustrates these assumptions and her choice to keep her baby anticipates the subsequent shift to more common acceptance of the unwed mother raising her child herself.

Increasingly through the 1970s and 1980s, adult children moved great distances from their parents' homes, pursuing professional lives of their own.

In the mobile culture, these long distances caused separated family members to rely on occasional flights home and frequent long-distance telephone calls to remain in touch with aging parents. Alice telephones from England to Florida to check on her ailing mother; when she has time off from work, she hops on a transatlantic flight to visit her. Left without extended family members to care for them on a day-to-day basis, aging parents retired to Florida or other warm-climate locations, lived first in condos and then as their needs increased frequently moved into assisted care institutions. They died often times among strangers in hospitals and convalescent care centers, with children perhaps reaching their deathbeds in time to say good-bye. *The Stone Diaries* dramatizes all of these social patterns.

Critical Overview

Shortly upon its publication in 1993, *The Stone Diaries* began to receive high praise and win awards. That year it was nominated for the National

Typical nuclear family, circa 1950s © Bettmann/Corbis. Reproduced by permission

Book Critics Circle Award and the Booker Prize; it won the first of these two in 1994. Also in 1993, *Publishers Weekly* listed it as one of the year's best books and the *New York Times Book Review* identified it as a "Notable Book." In the August 20, 1993, *New Statesman & Society*, in an excellent review of the work, Kathryn Hughes described the novel as "a sharp-as-tacks investigation into the limits of the autobiographical form." While Hughes pointed out that "[w]hole tracts of [Daisy's] life . . . appear to have been emptied of meaning," it is precisely "into those voids and gaps that Shields inserts her

narrative, filling up the ruptures in Daisy's interior life with an account of the strange double-headed family (no mother, two fathers) that produced her." Hughes explained that "Shields holds fast to the conceit that this is no novel, but rather a documentary account of an ordinary Canadian woman's life of the type that became so central to recuperative feminist history in the 1970s." Finally, Hughes pointed out the "wonderful prose" that is both "abundant and particular." In December 1993 a review in *Publishers Weekly* stressed that "Stone is the unifying image here: it affects the geography of Daisy's life, and ultimately her vision of herself"; this review praised the novel for its "succinct, clear and graceful" prose style.

Alice Joyce, writing for *Booklist* on February 1, 1994, described the novel's subject as "the commonplace but never mundane life of Daisy Goodwill." Joyce praised the "finely crafted fiction" as "[a]ltogether satisfying" because it "reveal[s] the transformation of an unremarkable life into a reflecting pool of change." In the same month, Allyson F. McGill wrote a review of the novel for *Belles Lettres: A Review of Books by Women*. McGill explained how Daisy Goodwill Flett's life is "extraordinary" even though it "follows the familiar trajectory," that for example in her brief marriage to Harold Hoad, Daisy's quite typical life is "touched by the grotesque." Noting the shifting point of view, McGill states: "By writing her life in the third person [Daisy] becomes her own observer, knowing that the outer person and the inner self often diverge." McGill also noted that Victorian-bred Daisy Goodwill, who lives through the feminist era of the 1960s and 1970s, at times cannot speak for herself, "the spirit within unable to find true expression in the conventions allowed to her."

The novel won the Pulitzer Prize in 1995 and positive critical attention continued. For example, Louisa Ermelino, in the June 1995 publication of *People Weekly* recommended the novel as an "absorbing, subtly comic, beautifully crafted narrative that teaches, entertains and moves to tears." In 1998, Karen Bell, writing for *Performing Arts & Entertainment in Canada*, praised Shields's twenty-two-year writing career. Bell explained that the prolific writer used "a disciplined approach," writing an hour a day once her five children were all in school. In all the work, Bell saw the main subject to be "Love, friendship, families and memories . . . rendered tenderly and with considerable understanding."

Criticism

Melodie Monahan

Monahan has a Ph.D. in English and operates an editing service, The Inkwell Works. In the following essay, Monahan explores the limitations and contradictions implicit in autobiography as it is handled in The Stone Diaries.

Carol Shields's *The Stone Diaries* (1993) is a work of fiction which maintains throughout the conceit (an ingenious and fanciful idea) that it is an autobiography augmented by a compilation of other kinds of documents (biography, letters, photographs, and background historical information), all intended to accurately record the life of a real person, Daisy Goodwill Flett. In large part the novel accomplishes its aim of being one thing (fiction) yet appearing to be something else (autobiography), and in this double function the novel examines the limitations and contradictions implicit in autobiography while it also engages in telling the story of Daisy's life. While it follows Daisy through her more than eighty years, including perspectives and theories from those around her, the novel also demonstrates how its subject disappears behind a text that intends to define her. In its effort to draw a portrait of her, the text also draws attention to those aspects omitted from that portrait. Writing autobiography is a creative act that produces a work of fiction. No matter how complete the record of a life is, an autobiography is, the narrator explains, merely "an assemblage of dark voids and unbridgeable gaps." Events are obscured with passing years and writing about them is a process of recreating them: Daisy "understood that if she was going to hold on to her life at all, she would have to rescue it by a primary act of imagination, supplementing, modifying, summoning up the necessary connections, conjuring." In this way the novel is an examination of the limits of autobiography as a form in which to catch the whole of a life as it is lived. To show how this works, Shields articulates some parts of the story while deliberately omitting or being self-contradictory about other parts. It is as though to show Daisy, the narrator must also demonstrate how she cannot be seen. This essay examines parts of the novel which illustrate how Daisy Goodwill Flett is hidden by the very record intended to expose her.

The day the baby is born is vividly portrayed. There are those moments in that hot kitchen as Mercy Stone Goodwill prepares a Malvern pudding for her husband, Cuyler, and the scene next door in which Clarentine Flett pauses as she hangs out her wash to think about her life, her marriage, and her garden that needs attention. But from the absolute beginning, from the moment of birth, the baby itself is not seen. The baby whose advent causes Mercy to die is wrapped in a towel and laid on the kitchen table, virtually ignored. Abram Skutari describes the scene this way: "[n]o one [paid] attention to [the baby]. It was as though it wasn't there. As though it was a lump of dough left by mistake."

When eleven-year-old Daisy Goodwill is sick with measles, she is wrapped, even smothered, in

> **Thus the person behind the subject of the story is covered up by the story. The story fabricates a version of her, which in effect hides the actual person she is.**

feather pillows and comforters to which she is allergic while the world goes on as it always has outside her darkened bedroom windows. She feels during those weeks as though she is eclipsed from life itself, left out, blotted out. At eleven, Daisy realizes that she can be "erased from the record of her own existence" and that "if she was going to hold on to her life at all, she would have to rescue it by a primary act of imagination . . . getting the details wrong . . . exaggerating or lying outright, inventing." The life itself can be totally eclipsed, just as a little girl smothered in a down comforter is lost from sight; writing the life into text is a creative act which requires imagination and filling in what one does not know or cannot substantiate.

News of Daisy Goodwill's 1927 marriage to Harold A. Hoad is presented indirectly to the reader via announcements rendered in social page journalism of an engagement luncheon, tea, kitchen shower, and white dinner honoring the bride-elect. Readers hear Cuyler Goodwill's long speech at the wedding reception, learn later that the groom showed up at the church drunk and remained intoxicated as the couple traveled afterward to Montreal. The facts of seasickness on the transatlantic journey and intoxication during the drive to an alpine village are given. At the moment Harold balances on the hotel room windowsill and then falls to his death, Daisy has her eyes closed, and she sneezes, still allergic to feather pillows. Daisy's first wedding is presented on the periphery of the event, the text routed around the subject rather than dwelling directly on it. Missing are the obvious subjects of how Daisy feels during the ceremony, descriptions of her dress, the church and her father's giving her away; these key parts of the wedding are suppressed.

In the aftermath of Harold's honeymoon death, Daisy becomes known to others in terms of the story they tell about her. That is, people see the story of his sudden death on their honeymoon rather than seeing her. The narrator explains that "[t]he real troubles in this world tend to settle on the misalignment between men and women." That "misalignment" is seen, at least in part, in the different ways in which the sexes cope with the story. The narrator explains: "Men, it seemed to me in those days, were uniquely honored by the stories that erupted in their lives, whereas women were more likely to be smothered by theirs." Men "strut" around in their adventures, wearing them like medals, but "women [go] all gray and silent beneath the weight of theirs." In a sense this misalignment results, perhaps especially in the late 1920s, from men being known by their public lives, while the stories that are the stuff of rumor and gossip regarding women blot out their often more commonplace domestic lives. Thus, Daisy herself is subsumed by the extraordinary story of Harold's death; she is gobbled up by the gossipy version that paints her as a young widow with a broken heart. No matter what she does, the narrator explains, "wherever she goes, her story marches ahead of her. . . . and cancels her true self." Thus the person behind the subject of the story is covered up by the story. The story fabricates a version of her, which in effect hides the actual person she is.

Daisy Goodwill leaves her father's Bloomington home after his remarriage not so much because she wants to go somewhere as that she no longer feels she can stay where she is. Motherless from birth, bereft of her surrogate mother Clarentine Flett from the age of eleven, Daisy finds refuge in Ottawa, in another father figure, Barker Flett, who is twenty-two years her senior and age fifty-four at the time he marries her in 1936. About their marriage, the text includes "The Things People Had to Say About the Flett-Goodwill Liaison" (the prime minister's view, Barker's housekeeper's opinion, Fraidy's thoughts, along with Mrs. Hoad's disgust), but Daisy's "own thoughts on her marriage are not recorded." Her two decades of letters to Barker do not survive; no photographs of Daisy survive. In the photographs included in the novel, none of them is said be of Daisy herself. While readers follow her life, her own words and her own image are pointedly omitted from it.

The description of Mrs. Flett preparing dinner for the family in 1947 hangs like a scrim over the true nature of the woman Daisy Goodwill Flett. Her apron, the jellied veal loaf, the stereotypical urging of children to wash quickly because their father will be home in "three shakes," all suggest the extent to which Daisy has taken on a superimposed role.

What Do I Read Next?

- Shields's three volumes of short stories (*Various Miracles*, *The Orange Fish*, and *Dressing Up for the Carnival*) are collected in *The Collected Stories of Carol Shields*, which was published by Random House of Canada in 2004. The collection also contains Shields's last and hitherto unpublished story, "Seque."

- In her biography *Jane Austen*, published by Penguin Group in 2005, Shields uses her own appreciation of family life and its dynamics as she describes the early nineteenth-century novelist, Jane Austen, in her domestic scenes at Steventon and Bath, England. She also explores Austen's intense relationship with her sister, Cassandra, and Austen's broken marital engagement. The biography is perhaps most important because it explores how great fiction is created.

- Shields's novel, *Unless*, which was published by Harper in 2003, tells the story of Reta Winters, forty-four, an author of light fiction and a nominee for important prizes, as her successful life crumbles in the face of her oldest daughter's decision to drop out of college and become a street person and panhandler. The novel explores the nature of goodness as it tracks the family response to this daughter's choices.

- Ian McEwan's popular novel, *Atonement*, which was published by Doubleday in 2002, is set in England, on one day in 1935 and a subsequent day during the retreat from Dunkirk, early in World War II. Written in prose similar to that of Henry James and concerned with an accusation that ruins two lives and a subsequent question about whether it was justified, this novel explores the way in which past events can be reexamined and reinterpreted years later.

- Alice McDermott's *Child of My Heart*, published in 2002 by Farrar, Straus, and Giroux, is set on Long Island one summer in the 1960s. The story pertains to fifteen-year-old Theresa and her visiting cousin Daisy, about their fantasies and emerging sexual awareness.

- Elizabeth Forsythe Hailey's novel, *A Woman of Independent Means*, which first appeared from Viking in 1978 and was reissued by Penguin Group in 1998, has certain similarities to *The Stone Diaries*. The life of Hailey's protagonist Bess Steed Garner extends from the early 1900s to the 1960s, and it is told by a compilation of documents, letters, newspaper articles, telegrams, and announcements. Bess has the money and determination to survive through a less than perfect marriage and difficulties with children, and she defies a society which expects her to conform to its standards.

As a wife and mother of three, Mrs. Flett relies on women's magazines for her parenting style, for recipes and centerpiece ideas, even for directions on how to demonstrate "a rise in ardor" during intimate relations with her husband. Even in her sexual expression, she acts on cue, expecting sexual intercourse with her husband, before he leaves for a trip ("a sort of vaccination" for him, she thinks) and upon his arrival home. For these moments she prepares as if donning a costume, appropriately by getting herself "bathed, powdered, diaphragmed, and softly nightgowned." She is confused by the magazine directions, how ardor and surrender are communicated by the loving wife by a single gesture of the body. Daisy's "brain, heart, and pelvis" struggle to imagine what such a gesture might be. As Barker rocks "back and forth above her," Daisy thinks of a movie. Spontaneity is absent; emotion is checked. "The debris of her married life rains down around her."

After Barker dies, readers view Daisy's life through a shuffling of letters, legal, friendly, consoling, directive. The letters allow Shields to snap from one prose style to another, from one way of seeing the subject to another. Readers learn about Daisy's depression through theories regarding its

Businesswoman on cell phone at work © JLP/Sylvia
Torres/Corbis

cause given by an array of other characters. When
at last Daisy's own theory is given, there is the
small prediction "sleeping inside her" that she will
recover and that "her immense unhappiness is
doomed to irrelevance anyway." The letters responding to Daisy's newspaper column comment
on her writing style, her ability to personify plants,
use metaphor, make a story while providing information; in all of this, readers of the novel only
"hear" about what she has to say, but they do not
read it directly in her own words.

Total eclipse slowly arrives through scenes in
her Florida retirement, final illness, and decline. Her
parents, long since dead, are "firmly erased." As she
thinks about her situation she feels a generalized
shrinkage, of things "lacking in weight"; she remarks
to herself that "[n]o one told her so much of life was
spent being old." It is as if she is already disappear-
ing into the dust that death makes of the body, and
the "real and the illusory whirl about her in smooth-
dipping waltz time." Her vision in the Orkney Islands of that "barely breathing cadaver," Magnus
Flett, gives the outward forecast of the dying process
of which in the final chapter the text presents in
Daisy as an inward journey of rattling thoughts.

Throughout the novel, it is as though Shields
shows readers that in autobiography, in the text that
is the record of a life, the human being occupies

the white space around the words, fills the place no
one sees, inhabits the shadow of what is said to be
the person. To put into words is to grab the grains
of time and try to hold on to oneself and others
caught in them. No matter how much it intends to
define and convey, though, the text is at once sieve
and lens, filtering some parts, distorting others.

Source: Melodie Monahan, Critical Essay on *The Stone
Diaries*, in *Novels for Students*, Thomson Gale, 2006.

Carol Shields with Elgy Gillespie

*In the following interview conducted just be-
fore the U.S. publication of* The Stone Diaries,
*Shields discusses her background, her thematic
concerns, and her audience.*

When her latest work is described by the seemingly innocent phrase "a novel with an appeal to
women," Carol Shields seems to shudder deli-
cately. And yet, the appraisal is contained in an
overwhelmingly favorable review of Shields's *The
Stone Diaries* in a review written by none other
than Anita Brookner in a recent issue of the *Spectator.* And the phrase arrives knit to the flattering
qualifier, "but of an altogether superior kind." Still,
a faint distress registers somewhere within the outwardly placid Shields.

"No," she says slowly and carefully, shaking
her small round head with its acorn-shaped blonde
bob and still wincing at what she appears to view
as the "women" put-down. She does not, she
believes, write for women first, last or always. The
reality of her writing life is instead somewhat more
complicated. Shields is willing to consider the possibilities calmly, and from more than one angle.
Her voice is light and uninflected; her manner is
sweetly conciliatory.

Already thriving in literary Britain and Canada,
Shields is poised now to reach new American readers with the March publication by Viking of *The
Stone Diaries* (Fiction Forecasts, Dec. 13, 1993), her
fictional life story of heroine Daisy Goodwill, as well
as with the first American publication of *Happenstance,* a pair of linked novellas, in paperback by
Penguin. In short, this writer shouldn't worry. The
winner of major awards, from the prestigious
Governor-General of Canada Prize to a Booker Prize
nomination for *The Stone Diaries,* Shields has drawn
a devoted international following.

We are sitting in her kitchen inside a converted
warehouse building near Berkeley, Calif., where her
husband Don holds a yearlong visiting professorship
in techno-engineering at the university. The old

cinderblock walls have been artfully renovated; sculptural, vast and white, they leave hardly any room for the kitchen. But in what room there is, *PW* and Shields hunch over coffee—very strong and black—and wine, decent and drinkable. Clearly, Shields attends to human needs; despite her frequent absences from her home in Winnipeg and her annual travels to France, she knows how to make the most challenging rented space into a cozy ersatz kitchen.

Kitchens come up quite a bit in *The Stone Diaries,* perhaps partly because in 1905 Daisy Goodwill is born in one—in a rural Canadian kitchen, in fact, where her mother has spent a good deal of time concocting a special pudding before Daisy makes her surprise entry into the world. The mother is fat, so much so that the pregnancy has gone unnoticed, and, like Tom in Shields's *The Republic of Love* (Viking, 1992), she is a changeling. Daisy, motherless, gradually finds a new home and family for herself, and the 20th century seems to flow softly around her slow life in a Canadian border town. Then she moves south to Indiana, back again to Canada and on to motherhood of her own; at length, the novel tails the elderly Daisy to her residence in a Florida rest home. We follow her from astonished first cry to gloomily overripe old age via widowhood and breakdown. She somehow muddles through, a Canadian Candide.

Details of successive eras abound in the novel. Conveniences for keeping food cool, like ice chests, and other kitchen innovations, like Mixmasters, occupy Daisy's homes and her life, which coincides generously with the century. The novel is also replete with unexpected quasi-documentary elements, including the character's own amusing album-style "family photos," although none are provided depicting Daisy herself. Shields embellishes the story with love letters, clips, ads, botanical ramblings and diaries.

To enrich the effect of Daisy's womanly evolution, the author read old newspapers and 1902 Eton mailorder catalogues in the library, adding a "Ladies Rhythm and Movement Club" photo from the South Manitoba Folk Museum, a photo found at a Paris postcard fair, a snap located by her London editor Christopher Potter and photos of her own children, who look disarmingly like her. "But I don't want you to think I spent a lifetime in the library," she protests, denying any scholarly ambitions and protesting that she was reared on The Bobbsey Twins, The Five Little Peppers and Tales of the Limberlost.

Written in a poetic manner (Shields began her writing life as a poet), the novel deals—despite some demurrals from the author—with the business

> **A serious, intelligent champion of romantic love and marriage who never insults her readers, Shields believes in the possibility of happiness."**

of being a woman. Much of Shields's fiction does. And her women—usually in their 30s or 40s, and like their creator, mothers, take in a broad range of experience. A serious, intelligent champion of romantic love and marriage who never insults her readers—either by condoning and-they-all-lived-happily-ever-after fairy tales or by impugning testosterone—Shields believes in the possibility of happiness. Her themes are not just love, courtship and marriage, but also children and the nature of male and female sensuality, compared and contrasted. These are indeed subjects of some interest to women, though also, one guesses, to men.

"Oh, I think there's some truth in that," she concedes warily about the relevance of the "women" category to her work and her readers, when asked again. But in fact, her male characters are just as fully realized as the female. There are set pieces in both *The Republic of Love* and *Swann* (Viking, 1989)—when deejay Tom endures memorably, hilariously bad sex in *Republic,* or when elderly reporter Cruzzi passes through a fit of rage against his wife—when Shields's kindness toward men is unfashionably apparent. Clearly she feels sympathy for them and for what she reckons as their newfound vulnerability.

"I hope men will be interested in what it's like to be a woman," she says, referring to likely readers of her work. She adds, "I mean, men have to be a little bit curious [about that] nowadays." She has watched some battling of the sexes from her quiet campus office at the University of Manitoba in Winnipeg, where she teaches literature, and concludes, "I mean, if men weren't curious about it all, they'd be a bit foolish. They do want to know what it's like [to be a woman] nowadays, don't they?"

Even if they don't, without a doubt women do. "When you think about what women read," Shields observes, "you're actually thinking about nearly all the novels that were ever written. Because over

70% of readers are women anyway. So maybe I'm fooling myself by thinking my readership is balanced." Do men attend her readings? "Sure." Her hunch: "[They are] husbands buying books for their wives." She remembers the man who once came up to her after a reading to tell her that he would have bought her book—if only it hadn't come out too late for his wife's birthday.

"Men have changed, because they've had to change," Shields asserts. Her male voices may ring persuasively to the ear, but she believes she is fairhanded. Like Daisy Goodwill's men in *Diaries,* one of whom falls out of a window on his honeymoon, Shields's men are sometimes confused but never utterly wicked. She attributes her mostly generous and thoughtful gallery of men—from Tom in *Republic* to Frederic in *Swann*—to a fond and loving father, brother, husband and son in her life.

Born in Oak Park, Ill., to a candy manufacturer and his wife, Shields left to study at Hanover College in Indiana, then earned a master of arts in literature at Ottawa University, where she met her future husband. She has lived in Winnipeg for 16 years.

However, she has also spent long periods living with her family in the French Jura while her husband was at work there; hence the French interludes that appear in her short stories. "I feel I belong to all three places, in a sense," Shields says, meaning Canada, France and America. "But I find this which-country-reads-me-and why stuff so difficult to deal with. Novels are individualistic; they don't break down along nationalist lines." In purely personal terms, she feels considerable loyalty to Canada, having lived there since she was 22. And in her books, Shields's affection for the country is plain; she may mock it gently, yet she cherishes it, too.

How did her career as a writer begin? "My writing life was a case of very slow and late evolution," Shields modestly explains. Not until her 40th birthday in 1977 did the letter arrive from McGraw-Hill accepting *Small Ceremonies,* her first novel. Why not sooner? "I had all these kids." For years she had written poetry and stories fitfully at dawn while the children slept, and she had no agent. "In those days," Shields says, "you didn't need one in Canada."

Her habits have changed. The five younger Shieldses are now in their 20s and 30s. The parents have downsized their Winnipeg house accordingly, take plenty of sabbaticals and travel abroad as they like. Shields's American agent is Virginia Barber; in Canada, she is represented by Bella Pomer. When at home, she writes daily at her office, and she is currently at work on a play (plot as yet undisclosed). Her last two did well at home, and *Thirteen Hands*—about a women's bridge team—was twice taken up and performed by amateur American repertory companies. Shields's acknowledged influences include Mavis Gallant, and she counts Alice Munro and Newfoundland writer Joan Clark as literary confidantes.

These days, she is happily computerized—and, she says, just barely edited. Her Macintosh Classic can be heard upstairs, where her husband Don is making pinging noises with it. But the computer entered her life with an odd result, initially: when she first changed over in the middle of writing *Republic,* she found that digital fluidity made her unbearably verbose.

"Luckily, that novel was edited by Mindy Warher at Viking in New York. It was the first time any novel I'd written was drastically cut. Mindy was wonderful; she cut two huge chunks and about a thousand smaller ones. Yes, I felt a tiny bit of pain. But at the same time, she had a kind of genius for making me think it had really been my idea to do the cuts." Shields attributes her growing American success to Warner's astuteness, and she's been careful not to let her keyboard run away with her again. "I get a parentheses tic easily, so they all get taken out now."

Happy though she is with Warher, she claims, "I was quite the literary slut. I have a promiscuous history with editors and went through four before *Swann.*" Her first novels were published in Canada by McGraw-Hill Ryerson, "but they kind of got out of the novel business after *Happenstance* [1980], my third. So I went to Macmillan Canada for the fourth [*A Fairly Conventional Woman,* 1982]. But that didn't work out in any way—they just didn't seem to have much faith in the book."

Realizing that she'd have to move, Shields chose the Canadian house, Stoddart Publishing. "I had a really good editor, Ed Carson. He worked hard with me and for me. People call him one of the best editors in Canada. So I stayed with Ed for *Swann* and *Various Miracles* [Stoddard, 1985; Penguin 1989]. But Ed was an ambitious young man, so when he moved to Random House, I moved with him." She's still with Random in Canada, while in England she is published by the Fourth Estate imprint, also the publisher of Annie Proulx.

Like Brenda Pulaski, the housewife heroine of *Happenstance,* Shields learned she was an artist only when she reached the cusp of middle age. The discovery came slowly. Only now, in her 50s, does she feel that she has committed herself to writing. "There was a time," she concedes, "when I shrugged off my writing in embarrassment."

Her readers seem as committed to her work as she does. Many write to her, receiving postcards in reply. "That's much the best kind of review," Shields remarks of this mail. "I dash off several postcards a day. That connectedness is an important part of my life."

From three slim poetry collections, Shields has graduated in less than 20 years to a 30,000-copy first printing at home in Canada, and she has an upcoming tour for Viking of American cities. She is no longer That Other Canadian Novelist.

Source: Elgy Gillespie, "Carol Shields: Life in America, Canada and France Has Influenced Her Booker-Nominated Fiction," in *Publishers Weekly*, Vol. 241, No. 9, February 28, 1994, pp. 61–62.

Gail Pool

In the following essay, Pool explores the characters and viewpoints in Happenstance *and* The Stone Diaries.

You would expect that good books from a country as close to us (in every sense) as Canada would quickly find American covers. Apparently not. It has taken more than a decade for the first U.S. edition of Carol Shields' *Happenstance* to appear, and I suspect we might not have it even now if her latest work, *The Stone Diaries,* had not been short-listed for last year's Booker Prize. Whatever their literary merit, awards are good promotion even for finalists, encouraging publishers to furnish early and out-of-print work. In Shields' case this is all to the good, and I hope we will soon see her earlier novels, *Small Ceremonies* and *The Box Garden.* Her work should be read in its entirety, that entirety hangs together so well.

Shields staked out her fictional territory early in her novel-writing life, and has explored it inventively ever since. Her realm of interest is the chronicling of lives, our efforts to find stories that give them shape and meaning. Underlying her own chronicling of people chronicling lives is the point that no one ever really knows enough. Shields' characters may be professional biographers or ordinary folk trying to make sense of their lives; all confront a picture that is inevitably incomplete. Beyond the mysteries of life (the role of fate or choice), we each have a particular perspective that determines what we see and miss, an individual framework that leads to readings that are sometimes comically, some-

> " Daisy's narrative constantly raises the question of veracity. She cannot know what happened at her birth or past her death, though she relates both."

times poignantly wrong. Nor do we readily enter other perspectives: in Shields' world, people misconstrue each other regularly, even if—perhaps especially if—they sleep together nightly.

With her eye on perspective, Shields plays nicely with viewpoints, shifting not only within books but even between them. In *Small Ceremonies,* the central character is biographer Judith Gill; in *The Box Garden,* the protagonist is Judith's sister. The setup offers great potential to enrich both books, but shields uses it only modestly here, as if trying it out.

In her next two novels, though, she works this construction ingeniously. *Happenstance,* which first appeared in 1980, follows historian Jack Bowman's lift over five days when his wife Brenda, a quiltmaker, is away at a handicrafts exhibit; *A Fairly Conventional Woman,* published in 1982, examines the same five days, focusing on Brenda. Together the novels create a vital portrait of a marriage, as the subtitle of this new edition suggests, it is a marriage "in transition." Fittingly, in this volume, the two are bound together but open from opposite sides of the books, each upside down to the other.

Jack's story takes place in Chicago, where Shields, now a Winnipeg resident, was born and raised. The Bowmans' suburb is comfortable, a world that applies equally well to Jack. At 43, he has a secure, unpressured research position. Married twenty years, he has two healthy if adolescent children. He meets his good friend Bernie Koltz weekly to discuss such topics as entropy or the death of God. As he sees it, he owes his good fortune to "happenstance," which has "made him into a man without serious impairment or unspeakable losses."

But during Brenda's absence, comfort disappears amidst a slew of comically depicted disasters: Bernie turns up, announcing his wife has left him;

a neighbor, an amateur actor, is trashed in a review and attempts suicide; Jack's son has stopped eating; in the background, housekeeping degenerates, the kitchen overflows with gnawed bones, dirty glasses, wadded-up napkins.

Worst of all, Jack confronts a crisis. He learns that a book on the same subject as the one he is writing will soon appear; he may have to drop his project. If truth be told, it would be a relief. Only in chapter six after three years, he can barely face the boring text. "I'm a man who has lost his faith," he says dramatically, posing a bit for this crisis much as he has posed at writing his book.

A philosophizing fellow, Jack has trouble grounding himself in everyday reality. By contrast, there is nowhere else that Brenda lives. So we realize as, during her five days at the conference, she remembers her unmarried mother and missed father, and reflects on her years as a housewife and her recent quilting success.

For Brenda, these are heady days. A woman who hasn't traveled alone, she calls room service for the first time in her life. She wins honorable mention for her quilt, is interviewed by a reporter, meets feminists at the conference, is shaken to find her hotel roommate having sex, gets horribly drunk and sick, meets a man for whom she feels an affinity, not everything is wonderful, but everything is new.

Shrewdly depicting the same moments as seen by each spouse, Shields reveals different visions of the past as well as different views of the present. In Jack's story, the comedy depends partly on Brenda's forth-coming, continuing presence, which he never doubts. In Brenda's, though her love for Jack is clear, we find her reflecting on her anger, wondering if it means her life has been a mistake. Ruminating guiltily about taking over the guest room for her work, she realizes she deserves it: she is more serious about her work than Jack is about his. This, in view of their history, seems to me the most startling realization of all, one that Jack has yet to come to, though it lies just ahead.

Sheilds is expert at combining satire and sympathy. Alongside the gaps in Jack and Brenda's comprehension of each other lies the substance of all they share. Canny and unsentimental, this double chronicle captures not just this couple but men's and women's lives and marriage in our time.

If *Happenstance* is ingeniously constructed, it is nonetheless straightforward compared to *The Stone Diaries,* an intricate novel and complex commentary on living and telling lives. Simply described, it is the autobiography of Daisy Goodwill Flett, from her birth in Tyndall, Manitoba, in 1905. to her death in Florida in the nineties. It is very much a woman's story.

Starting with her birth and advancing approximately by decades, Daisy describes how her mother Mercy Stone died when she herself was born; how a neighbor, Clarentine Flett, cared for her and, in the midst of change of life, changed her life, abandoning her husband, Magnus, and taking Daisy to her son Barker in Winnipeg; how at Clarentine's death, Daisy's father, a stone worker, took her to Bloomington, Indiana, where he flourished in business; how she married a handsome alcoholic who fell out a window on their honeymoon; how, feeling swamped by her "tragic" story as orphan and widow, she went to Canada at 31, to visit—and marry—Barker Flett; how she lived as housewife and mother for twenty years, thrived in widowhood writing a gardening column, fell into depression when she was fired; how she moved to Florida and made a comfortable life. The final chapters, unsparing and grimly funny, chronicle her decline and death.

Throughout, Daisy generally refers to herself in the third person, perhaps because she has stationed herself as an observer, perhaps because she fells an absence in herself, an absence of self. Her detailed chronicle includes stories and descriptions alongside commentary about life, men and women, autobiography in general and the one is writing.

Shields plays intriguingly here with invention and truth. The novel has not only a family tree, easily conceived of as pure invention, but also family photographs, which are sure to give a reader pause: pictures of whom? Daisy's narrative constantly raises the question of veracity. She cannot know what happened at her birth or past her death, though she relates both. And all her wonderful stories—including the ones about events she could never have witnessed.

Consider one of my favorite tales (unfortunately, condensed here): the laconic Magnus Flett, abandoned by Clarentine, misses her intensely. He doesn't understand why she left. Discovering her stash of novels, her reads them; he especially likes *Jane Eyre*.

It astonished him, how these books were stuffed full of people. Each one was like a little world, populated and furnished. And the way those book people ! . . . Some of the phrases were like poetry, nothing like the way folks really spoke, but nevertheless he pronounced them aloud to himself and committed them to memory, so that if by chance his wife should decide to come home and take up her place once more, he would be ready.

Magnus practices: "O beautiful eyes, O treasured countenance, O fairest of skin."

But Clarentine never comes home. Magnus returns to his homeland, the Orkneys. Years later, Daisy, who never met her father-in-law, visits the Orkneys and discovers he is still alive. At 115, he is famous as the oldest man in the British Isles. But he is still more famous as the man who could recite *Jane Eyre* by heart.

Now I find this story both moving and hilarious. But what is true here? The "facts" are few. Magnus did, for example, return to the Orkneys. It is interesting to imagine the various routes by which Daisy might have arrived at her tale.

Daisy doesn't hide the fact that her autobiography abounds in distortions and inventions. She warns us often. "The recounting of a life is a cheat," she observes. Daisy, she says,

> is not always reliable when it comes to the details of her life; much of what she has to say is speculative, exaggerated, wildly unlikely. . . . Daisy Goodwill's perspective is off. Furthermore, she imposes the voice of the future on the events of the past, causing all manner of wavy distortion. She takes great jumps in time, leaving out important matters. . . . Still, hers is the only account there is, written on air, written with imagination's invisible ink.

Daisy knows the power of storytelling: it way by this "primary act of imagination" that she determined to hold onto her life. She is also aware of different perspectives: she records with humor varied explanations of her breakdown, from her new-generation daughter's theory that it was the loss of her job to her friend's assertion that it was sex. And she is aware of her own perspective: her abiding sense of motherlessness and abandonment, the feeling of being "erased from the record of her own existence" (no picture of Daisy appears among her photographs) have influenced the story she tells. So we construct our life stories, the book suggests, seeing or inventing what we need, filling in the picture we cannot truthfully complete.

Tue or invented, a distinct person emerges from these pages, her story is a quietly riveting chronicle of an ordinary life. valiant and tedious. If we finish *Happenstance* feeling "yes, this is a marriage," we finish *The Stone Diaries* feeling "Yes, this is a life."

Source: Gail Pool, *"The Stone Diaries,"* in *Women's Review of Books*, Vol. 11, No. 8, May 1994, p. 20.

Sources

Bell, Karen, "Carol Shields: all these years later, still digging," in *Performing Arts & Entertainment in Canada*, Vol. 31, No. 3, Winter 1998, pp. 4–6.

Ermelino, Louisa, Review of *The Stone Diaries*, in *People Weekly*, Vol. 43, No. 25, June 26, 1995, p. 32.

Hughes, Kathryn, Review of *The Stone Diaries*, in *New Statesman & Society*, Vol. 6, August 20, 1993, p. 40.

Joyce, Alice, Review of *The Stone Diaries*, in *Booklist*, Vol. 90, No. 11, February 1, 1994, p. 995.

McGill, Allyson F., Review of *The Stone Diaries*, in *Belles Lettres: A Review of Books by Women*, Vol. 10, No. 1, Fall 1994, pp. 32–33.

Shields, Carol, *The Stone Diaries*, Vintage Books, 1993.

Review of *The Stone Diaries*, in *Publishers Weekly*, Vol. 240, No. 50, December 13, 1993, pp. 60–61.

Further Reading

Great Events, 1900–2001, Salem Press, 2002.
This illustrated, eight-volume set gives descriptions of well over one thousand major events in the twentieth century, including national and world politics, civil unrest, disasters, and important scientific and medical discoveries.

Kinnear, Mary, *A Female Economy: Women's Work in a Prairie Province, 1870–1970*, McGill-Queen's University Press, 1999.
One hundred years of women's work in Manitoba since the province's admission into the Confederation in 1870 are presented here largely through women's own views.

Osmand, Donald, ed., *The Orkney Book*, Birlinn Limited, 2003.
This book presents an overview of the sixty-seven islands that make up the Orkneys, which lie north of the Scottish mainland. These islands, half of which are inhabited in the early 2000s, have been occupied since 3500 B.C. and boast the highest concentration of prehistoric monuments.

Robertson, Brian C., *Forced Labor: What's Wrong with Balancing Work and Family*, Spence Publishing Company, 2002.
The premise of this book is that the 1960s shift in attention from home to work was caused by certain ideologies, governmental policies, and corporate pressures, and these converged to cause parents to think a family could not exist on only one income.

Staebler, Edna, *Edna Staebler's Diaries*, Wilfrid Laurier University Press, 2005.
Excerpts from the diaries describe this Canadian writer's life and professional development. Staebler kept a diary from age sixteen to well into her nineties, years which span most of the twentieth century.

The Ugly American

William J. Lederer

Eugene Burdick

1958

The Ugly American, by William J. Lederer and Eugene Burdick, was published in 1958. Set for the most part in the fictional Southeast Asian country of Sarkhan, with excursions to Cambodia, Vietnam, Hong Kong, and Burma, the novel takes place in the 1950s, during the cold war, when the United States and the Soviet Union struggled for supremacy across the globe. Sarkhan is presented as a country of about 18 to 20 million people with a rather shaky government that fears a possible coup attempt by the communists, who are powerful and well-organized. Sarkhan tries to stay independent of the two superpowers and as a result receives aid from both. But too often, as the authors make clear in this fictional story that they claim is based on fact, U.S. aid does not meet the needs of the local people. Moreover, the American diplomats who serve in Sarkhan and throughout Southeast Asia do not for the most part have any knowledge of the country's language or culture, so they are not effective in winning the people to their side. By contrast, Russian diplomats are well trained. The authors fear that unless the United States adopts a different strategy and trains its foreign service personnel better, it may end up losing the cold war.

The Ugly American was a bestseller and had an impact on the politics of the day, being read reportedly by President Dwight Eisenhower and many U.S. senators. It helped to create an atmosphere in which the United States reaffirmed and reshaped its commitment to defending freedom against communism. This new commitment was

Marlon Brando as Ambassador Harrison Carter MacWhite (with Arthur Hill as Grainger in the background) in the 1963 film version of The Ugly American   Universal/The Kobal Collection

apparent during the presidency of John F. Kennedy, from 1961 to 1963. Kennedy fostered new methods of fighting communism in South Vietnam, developed the U.S. Special Forces, and founded the Peace Corps.

Author Biography

William J. Lederer was born on March 31, 1912, in New York City, the son of William Julius and Paula (Franken) Lederer. He attended the United States Naval Academy, from which he graduated with a bachelor of science degree in 1936. Lederer's main career was in the U.S. Navy, from 1930 to 1958. He retired as captain. During wartime he served in Asia and with the Atlantic Fleet. From 1950 to 1958 he was special assistant to the commander-in-chief, Pacific.

After Lederer retired from the navy, he went into journalism, becoming Far East correspondent for *Reader's Digest*, from 1958 to 1963. He was author-in-residence at Harvard University, 1966–1967.

Lederer has written many books, including novels, short stories, and nonfiction on a variety of topics, during his long career. His best known work is *The Ugly American* (1958; with Burdick). His other novels include *Sarkhan* (1965; with Burdick) and *I, Giorghos* (1984). *Ensign O'Toole and Me* (1957) is a humorous look at life in the navy; *A Nation of Sheep* (1961) discusses how the United States could be more successful in its foreign aid projects. *The Mirages of Marriage* (1968; with Don D. Jackson) is an analysis of marriage in the United States. Other works include *The Last Cruise* (1950), *All the Ships at Sea* (1950), *Timothy's Song* (1965), *The Story of Pink Jade* (1966), *Our Own*

Worst Enemy (1968; published in England in 1969 as *The Anguished American*), and *A Happy Book of Christmas Stories* (1981).

Lederer married Ethel Victoria Hackett in 1940. They were divorced in 1965. In the same year, Lederer married Corinne Edwards Lewis. They divorced in 1976. Lederer has three sons.

Eugene (Leonard) Burdick was born in Sheldon, Iowa, on December 12, 1918. He was the son of Jack Dale, a painter, and Marie (Ellerbroek) Burdick.

Burdick gained a bachelor of arts degree from Stanford University in 1942. During World War II, he served in the U.S. Navy and became lieutenant commander. He was awarded the Navy/Marine Corps Cross. After the war he studied in England and received a Ph.D. from Magdalen College, Oxford University, in 1950.

Burdick became assistant professor and then professor of political theory at the University of California, Berkeley, from 1950 to 1965. In addition to his scholarly writings, which included a book on voting behavior, Burdick wrote novels. His first was *The Ninth Wave* (1956), about a California politician who exploits fear and hatred. This work was followed in 1958 by *The Ugly American*, which he co-wrote with William J. Lederer. The book became a bestseller. Burdick wrote several more novels: *Fail-Safe* (1962; with Harvey Wheeler) is about the accidental triggering of a nuclear war; *The 480*, about the selection of a Republican presidential candidate, followed in 1964. In 1965, Burdick collaborated again with Lederer on another novel set in southeast Asia, *Sarkhan* (1965), which was published as *The Deceptive American* in 1977. Burdick's final work was the novel *Nina's Book* (1965).

Burdick married Carol Warren in 1942; the couple had three children. Burdick died on July 26, 1965.

Plot Summary

Chapters 1–4

The Ugly American begins in the fictional Southeast Asian country of Sarkhan, in the office of U.S. ambassador Louis Sears. Sears is upset because a hostile cartoon of him has appeared in the local newspaper.

Meanwhile an American named John Colvin is recovering in the hospital after being beaten up. Colvin has been trying to help the Sarkhanese learn how to use milk and its by-products, and he set up a milk-distribution center outside the capital city, Haidho. But he is betrayed by an old friend named Deong who has turned communist. Deong tells a group of Sarkhanese women that Colvin is trying to put a drug in the milk that would enable him to take advantage of Sarkhanese girls. Colvin denies it, but the women beat him. He is left unconscious on the steps of the U.S. Embassy.

The ambassador complains about the cartoon to Prince Ngong, the head of the Sarkhanese government. Ngong fears that a large U.S. loan may be in jeopardy and instructs the newspaper to print a flattering cartoon and editorial about Sears.

The second story introduces Ambassador Sears's Russian counterpart, Louis Krupitzyn. Unlike Sears, Krupitzyn has had long preparation for his position. He can read and write Sarkhanese and understands Sarkhanese culture. He is also cunning. During a famine, the Americans send 14,000 tons of rice. However, Krupitzyn arranges for every bag of American rice to have stenciled on it in Sarkhanese that it is a gift from Russia. The Americans protest, but the Sarkhanese continue to believe the Russians were their benefactors.

The next character to be introduced is Father Finian, a Catholic priest from Boston who has been assigned to Burma. A fierce anti-communist, Finian recruits nine local Catholics who also want to fight communism. They publish a small anti-communist newspaper and then trick a Russian expert by secretly recording and then broadcasting disparaging things he has said about the local peasants. It then becomes clear to the local people that the Russians do not have their best interests at heart.

Chapters 4–10

Joe Bing, a flamboyant American public relations officer in the Southeast Asian city of Serkya, gives a presentation in Washington about employment opportunities abroad. He paints a rosy picture of luxury travel, an excellent salary, low expenses, with no need to learn a foreign language. A young American, Marie McIntosh, is recruited. She writes home about the pleasant and luxurious life she now lives in Sarkhan.

Sears makes another diplomatic blunder over a rumor that the United States is about to evict the Sarkhanese Air Force from land lent to them. But Sears soon gets what he wants when he is recalled to the United States to take up a federal judgeship. The new ambassador is Gilbert MacWhite, a professional foreign-service officer. Unlike Sears, MacWhite learns the local language. MacWhite is eager to combat communist influence, but he makes the mistake of trusting his old Chinese servants, Donald and Roger. Li Pang, a visitor and friend of MacWhite, interrogates Donald and tricks him into revealing that he has been passing information to the communists. MacWhite tries to learn from his mistake by traveling in the Philippines and Vietnam so he can understand how to combat communism. In the Philippines, he hears about Colonel Hillandale, an American who embraces local culture and is known as "The Ragtime Kid" because of his love for jazz and his ability to play the harmonica.

Chapters 11–15

Major James Wolchek of the U.S. Army visits Major Monet, a Frenchman, in Hanoi, Vietnam. The French are losing the battle against communist insurgents; at Dien Bien Phu, French forces are encircled. Monet invites Wolchek to parachute with French troops into the besieged fortress as a foreign observer, but before they can do this Dien Bien Phu falls to the communists. In subsequent skirmishes with the enemy, Monet and his legionnaires are defeated again and again. Wolchek explains to Monet and MacWhite that the communists are winning because they are practicing a new kind of warfare. As the communists press their assault on Hanoi, Wolchek and Monet are slightly wounded. MacWhite acquires a pamphlet by Chinese leader Mao Tse-tung that explains his concept of guerilla warfare. Monet uses these new tactics and wins a skirmish with the communists. But then the French evacuate Hanoi and a communist army enters the city.

In Cambodia, Tom Knox, an American, helps the local people improve their chicken and egg yield and is greeted with enthusiasm by villagers wherever he goes. At a conference that appraises the results of U.S. aid to Cambodia, Tom makes practical proposals for further increasing chicken and egg yield, but he is overruled because the Americans want to develop mechanized farms. When French government diplomats and a wealthy Cambodian landowner provide Tom with a series of luxury trips, he forgets all about his good idea.

In Sarkhan, Colonel Hillandale attends a dinner party given by the Philippine ambassador. Hillandale entertains everyone by giving palm readings, which is a respected practice in the country. He is given an opportunity to read the palm of the king, but the appointment is sabotaged by the hostility and incompetence of George Swift,

Media Adaptations

- *The Ugly American* was made into a film in 1962, produced and directed by George Englund and starring Marlon Brando as Ambassador Gilbert MacWhite. For his work on the film, Englund was nominated for a Golden Globe award.

MacWhite's deputy. The king is insulted, and MacWhite gets Swift transferred.

Chapters 16–18

In Hong Kong, a meeting of the Special Armament section of the Asia conference is discussing the prospect of placing U.S. nuclear weapons on Asian soil. The Asians become suspicious when the Americans refuse to discuss classified material about the safety of the weapons. Solomon Asch, leader of the American delegation, feels let down by Captain Boning, one of his negotiators, who gives the impression he is deliberately holding back information. As a result, the Asians decide to oppose the installation of nuclear weapons on their soil.

In Vietnam, Homer Atkins, a retired engineer, meets with Vietnamese, French, and U.S. officials. He has been asked to give advice on building dams and military roads, but he tells the Vietnamese that they should start with smaller projects they can do for themselves, such as building brick factories and a model canning plant. MacWhite is impressed by Atkins and invites him to Sarkhan, where Atkins teams up with a local man named Jeepo to design a water pump. They go into business together, hiring workers who manufacture the pumps and then sell them.

Chapters 19–21

Atkins's wife Emma notices that all the old people in the village of Chang 'Dong have badly bent backs. She realizes this pervasive condition is due to the short-handled brooms they use for sweeping, so she invents a long-handled broom using sturdy reeds as a handle. The local people soon learn to make their own long-handled brooms.

Jonathan Brown, a tough U.S. senator, visits Vietnam to find out for himself what use is made of U.S. aid. He wants to meet local people, but the U.S. Embassy staff tries to control the information he has access to. On a visit to an ammunition depot, Brown questions a Vietnamese man, but Dr. Barre, the interpreter, alters the man's answer in a way that he thinks will please the senator. The same thing happens when Brown visits Hanoi and tries to find out what the real military situation is there. As he goes home to the United States he realizes that he has talked only to military men and government officials, although later on the Senate floor he claims that he understands the situation in Vietnam because he has been there.

MacWhite is rebuked by the secretary of state for his testimony to a Senate committee about the situation in Southeast Asia. MacWhite replies that he fears the Russians will win the cold war unless the Americans act in the real interests of the countries whose friendship they need, not in the interest of propaganda. He makes many practical suggestions, all of which are rejected. He resigns as ambassador, and the State Department decides to replace him with Joe Bing.

The Ugly American ends with a "Factual Epilogue" in which the authors explain that although their stories are fiction, they are based on fact.

Characters

Apache

Apache is a Vietnamese man who fights for the French. He is captured by the communists who cut out his vocal cords.

Solomon Asch

Solomon Asch is the head of the American delegation to the Special Armament section of the Asia Conference. He is a tough and experienced negotiator.

Emma Atkins

Emma Atkins, the wife of Homer Atkins, is a simple, straightforward woman who in her own way is as physically ugly as her husband. But also, like her husband, she has a creative and inventive mind and, in fact, supplies him with some of his best ideas. She also develops her own ideas, managing to invent a long-handled broom that the old people in Sarkhan can use in place of

their short-handled brooms, which are too hard on their backs.

Homer Atkins

Homer Atkins, the "ugly American" of the book's title, is ugly in physical appearance, not in character. A tough, blunt-spoken man, he is a highly successful retired engineer who is worth $3 million. The U.S. government consults him about building dams and military roads in Southeast Asia, but he insists that what is really needed are things that the local people can manufacture and use for themselves. His advice is ignored, but Ambassador MacWhite is impressed by him and invites him to Sarkhan. In that country, Atkins, in collaboration with a Sarkhanese man named Jeepo, invents a water pump that proves to be an immense labor-saving device for the local people. Atkins sets himself up in business with Jeepo and twelve local workers, and his enterprise is a big success.

Dr. Hans Barre

Dr. Hans Barre is a naturalized American citizen who specializes in Oriental languages. He is on temporary duty at the U.S. Embassy in Vietnam and acts as interpreter during the visit of Senator Brown.

Joe Bing

Joe Bing, an American information officer living in Burma, is a gregarious, sociable man who is very popular amongst other Americans and Westerners, but he is also the kind of American disliked by Asians, since he is loud and ostentatious in his manner and does not mix with the local people. Asians are not invited to his diplomatic parties, at which there is always plenty of alcohol. He appears to think that representing the United States abroad is more about having a good time than in promoting U.S. national interests. When Gilbert MacWhite resigns as ambassador to Sarkhan, Bing is nominated by the State Department to take his place.

Captain Boning

Captain Boning is a Navy officer who takes part in the negotiations in Hong Kong about the placing of U.S. nuclear weapons on Asian soil. During the time of the conference, Boning has an affair with a local Chinese woman who is also a communist agent, and he spends most of his nights with her. Thus he is not alert during the conference sessions, and he gives hesitant answers to questions from the Asian delegates, which makes them think that the Americans are hiding something.

Senator Jonathan Brown

Senator Jonathan Brown, a tough and experienced U.S. senator, started his career as a corrupt man who granted favors to corporations in exchange for financial contributions to his campaign. But once in the Senate he changed his ways and became a man of integrity. As a member of the Senate Foreign Affairs Committee, he visits many countries in Southeast Asia to see for himself what is being done with U.S. aid. But in Vietnam his desire to meet and talk to the local people is thwarted by the plans of the embassy staff, who ensure that he talks only to military and government officials. The result is that he never does find out the real situation, but he fails to realize this.

John Colvin

John Colvin is an American who was an Office of Strategic Services (OSS) agent in Sarkhan during World War II. After the war he ran his family's business in Wisconsin, buying bulk milk and drying it into powder. In 1952, he returns to Sarkhan because he hears that the country is leaning towards communism, and he is convinced the situation is being handled badly. He tries to help the local people by selling them milk made from powder. But he runs afoul of a former friend of his named Deong, who has turned communist. Deong tricks some local women into believing that Colvin is trying to put an aphrodisiac in the milk so that he can seduce local girls. The women beat him up, almost killing him. Colvin returns to the United States but later goes back to Sarkhan and succeeds in his milk enterprise.

Jim Davis

Jim Davis, a black man from Los Angeles, is serving in the French Foreign Legion in Vietnam. He is captured by the Vietnamese, who gouge out one of his eyes.

Deong

Deong is a Sarkhanese communist who betrays his old friend John Colvin.

Donald

Donald is an old Chinese servant who has given many years of loyal service to the U.S. Embassy in Sarkhan. He does not read or write and knows almost no English. Ambassador MacWhite trusts Donald completely. However, it transpires that Donald is not quite what he appears. Through interrogation, Li Pang discovers that Donald has been passing along information from the embassy to the communists.

Father Finian

Father Finian is a Catholic priest from Boston who is assigned to Burma. A Jesuit, Father Finian has a fine intellect and is a scholar, but he is also tough-minded and practical, and he relishes the challenge of combating communism in Burma. He regards communism as an evil ideology. Father Finian makes a point of learning the local language and eating the local food, even though at first he finds it very hard to digest. He recruits nine local men who are also anticommunist Catholics and asks them what strategy they want to pursue. He does not make the mistake of imposing his own views but encourages the men to make their own decisions. Eventually, Father Finian establishes a four-year college in Burma, at which the curriculum includes study of the writings of both communist and Western leaders.

Ambassador Arthur Alexander Gray

Arthur Alexander Gray is the U.S. ambassador to Vietnam. When Senator Jonathan Brown visits, Gray makes extensive preparations with his staff to ensure that the senator only has access to the information the embassy thinks he ought to have.

Colonel Edwin B. Hillandale

Edwin B. Hillandale, a U.S. Air Force colonel, was sent to Manila, in the Philippines, in 1952. He is extremely popular with the local people because he embraces their culture. His love of jazz and his skill with the harmonica earn him the nickname The Ragtime Kid. He is not so popular, however, with the officials at the U.S. Embassy in the Philippines. But Ambassador MacWhite recognizes Hillandale's worth and invites him to Sarkhan. Hillandale's knowledge of palmistry, which is valued in the local culture, stands him in good stead at a dinner party given by the Philippine ambassador.

Thomas Elmer Knox

Thomas Elmer Knox, an American farmer from Iowa who lives for a while in Cambodia, knows more Cambodians than any other Westerner, and he loves Cambodian food. In Iowa, he raises chickens, and he is full of ideas about how the local people can improve the quality of their chickens and increase the chickens' egg yield. But when he puts his ideas to American and Cambodian agricultural experts, as well as some French officials, he gets nowhere. The officials are only interested in developing canals and mechanized farms. Tom is angry at their refusal to listen to him, but after some high-level diplomats and businessmen treat him to luxury trips to Paris, Indonesia, and India, he forgets all about his good ideas for Cambodia.

Louis Krupitzyn

Louis Krupitzyn is the Russian ambassador to Sarkhan. Unlike his American counterpart, Ambassador Sears, Krupitzyn is well prepared for his position. He began his diplomatic career in 1935 and has been stationed in the United States and China. When he becomes ambassador to Sarkhan he learns the language, immerses himself in the local culture, and attends lectures on Buddhist religion and practice. He outwits the Americans when he tricks the Sarkhanese into believing that a shipment of U.S. rice, sent to relieve a famine, in fact came from Russia.

Jeepo

Jeepo is a Sarkhanese man who has a talent for working with machinery. He gets on well with Homer Atkins, and the two of them develop a water pump for raising water economically and efficiently. They try various versions of the pump, and it is Jeepo who points out their shortcomings to Atkins. He is not intimidated by working with an American, and the two men argue as equals. It is Jeepo who comes up with the final version of the water pump, solving a problem that had eluded Atkins.

Ruth Jyoti

Ruth Jyoti, editor and publisher of one of the best independent newspapers in Southeast Asia, is invited to the United States, and at a dinner for the press in San Francisco she gives a talk on how and why Americans in Asia are not effective.

Marie MacIntosh

Marie MacIntosh, a twenty-eight-year-old American, is impressed by a talk given by Joe Bing and applies for a position in government service in Sarkhan. She writes back to her friends about her new, rather luxurious and easy life.

Ambassador Gilbert MacWhite

Gilbert MacWhite replaces Louis Sears as U.S. ambassador to Sarkhan in 1954. Quite unlike his predecessor, MacWhite is a professional foreign service officer, and he has a long diplomatic career already behind him, even though he is only in his mid-forties. MacWhite has read the communist writings of Karl Marx and Lenin and is a recognized expert on Soviet theory and practice. He learns Sarkhanese and reads books about Sarkhanese history and politics. He is courageous, efficient, and imaginative, and has an ability to recognize and learn from his mistakes, an ability his predecessor conspicuously lacked. He travels extensively in Southeast Asia because he is determined to learn everything he can about how to defeat communism. He has good judgment and invites some of the best American talent, such as Homer Atkins and Colonel Hillandale, to visit Sarkhan and put their ideas into practice. When he is well established in his job, he writes to the U.S. secretary of state asking permission to make some urgent and practical changes in the U.S. diplomatic mission to Sarkhan. He is turned down, and as a result he resigns as ambassador.

Bob Maile

Bob Maile is an official in the United States Information Service (USIS) stationed in Setkya, a city in Southeast Asia. According to Ruth Jyoti, Maile has done more than anyone else to raise U.S. prestige in the area. He mixes easily with the local people and everyone trusts him. He even sends his children to an Asian school, which is very unusual for an American.

Major Monet

Major Monet is a French soldier in Hanoi, in charge of a company of French foreign legion. He comes from a long line of soldiers in his family, and he understands the art of war, at least in its traditional form. But his legionnaires keep losing their skirmishes with the communists. It is left to Major Wolchek to point out to Monet that he needs to study the works of Mao Tse-tung, since Mao describes a new kind of warfare. As a proud Frenchman, Monet is reluctant at first, but he later realizes the value in Wolchek's advice.

Prince Ngong

Prince Ngong is a distinguished Sarkhanese poet and drama critic and member of the government. He tells the Sarkhanese cabinet that they must do something to remedy the offense that Ambassador Sears has taken from a hostile cartoon in one of the local newspapers.

Li Pang

Li Pang, a businessman and soldier, is a representative of Chiang Kai-shek, the Chinese nationalist leader. He is also an old friend of Ambassador MacWhite. While visiting MacWhite, Li Pang interrogates Donald, the old Chinese servant, and finds that he has been passing on information to the communists.

Roger

Roger is one of the two old Chinese servants at the U.S. Embassy in Sarkhan.

Ambassador Louis Sears

Louis Sears is the U.S. ambassador to Sarkhan. Known as "Lucky" because of the good fortune he enjoyed during his long political career, he is a former U.S. senator. He is only in Sarkhan for two years while he waits for a vacancy to arise for a federal judgeship. While he is ambassador, Sears does not bother to learn the Sarkhanese language, nor does he make any attempt to mingle with the Sarkhanese people, so he has little idea of what is really going on in the country. He spends too much of his time attending cocktail parties and talking to other diplomats. Sears is presented as an example of all that is wrong with U.S. diplomacy in Southeast Asia. The Russians regard him as so incompetent that they are eager for him to remain in his position, since his presence helps them so much. Sears eventually gets his judgeship and is replaced as ambassador by Gilbert MacWhite.

U Maung Swe

U Maung Swe is the best known journalist in Burma. In 1954, at dinner in honor of Ambassador MacWhite, U Maung Swe explains in detail why U.S. prestige in Southeast Asia is low.

George Swift

George Swift is the deputy chief of mission at the U.S. Embassy in Sarkhan. He is responsible for sabotaging Colonel Hillandale's appointment to read the palm of the king of Sarkhan. Hillandale is so angry he punches him, and Ambassador MacWhite, sensing that Swift has no understanding of the local culture, arranges for him to be transferred.

Major James Wolchek

Major James Wolchek, whose nickname is "Tex" because he comes from Texas, is a combat veteran of World War II and the Korean War. He was wounded in both wars. In 1954, he is assigned as a foreign observer to the French foreign legion in Hanoi, Vietnam, where he meets Major Monet. After the French suffer a series of defeats at the hands of the communists, Tex realizes that their failure results from their fighting war by the old rules, while the communists follow the new rules

of war written by Mao Tse-tung. Tex explains Mao's battle tactics, and, as a result, Monet and the legionnaires finally win an encounter with the communists, during which Tex is slightly wounded.

Themes

American Arrogance and Failure in Southeast Asia

The purpose of the novel is to point out the ways in which the United States is failing in its attempt to defeat communism in Southeast Asia and to explain the alternative methods that must be adopted in order to succeed. In brief, the United States is in danger of losing the cold war in this part of the world because it relies on a complacent political and bureaucratic establishment that fails to understand the local culture and relies on large-scale foreign aid programs that do not address the real needs of the people. Each story in the book illustrates some aspect of this or related themes, showing an American who is either part of the problem or part of the solution.

First among those who put U.S. enterprise at risk is Ambassador Sears. Sears has no training for his position, which is handed to him by the leader of the Democratic Party merely out of political loyalty. Sears knows nothing about the country to which he is assigned and makes little attempt to find out. He spends his time at social events, entertaining visiting American politicians and military men, and never meets any of the local people. He also forbids any of his staff to go into the local villages. In spite of the fact that he is despised by the locals and outwitted by the Russians, he believes that his relations with the Sarkhanese "couldn't be better." He has no grasp of the seriousness of the communist threat in Sarkhan, and there is an unconscious irony in his letter to the U.S. State Department in which he dismisses the prospect of a communist takeover: "I get around at one hell of a lot of social functions, and official dinners out here, and I've never met a native Communist yet."

Similarly Joe Bing, the information officer, thinks the situation is positive. Americans in the region regard him as a charming man who knows everyone in Setkya, but he is viewed very differently by the locals. Ruth Jyoti says of him that far from knowing everyone, he acknowledges only those who are "European, Caucasian, western-educated, and decently dressed." Her description of him suggests the image of the "ugly American" that

Topics for Further Study

- What was the Gulf of Tonkin incident in 1964, and how did it lead to the Vietnam War? What are the lessons to be derived from the Vietnam War? In what ways does the early 2000s conflict in Iraq resemble the Vietnam War and in what ways does it not? Give a classroom presentation in which you compare and contrast the Vietnam War and the conflict in Iraq.

- As of 2005, what is the U.S. mission in the world, given that the cold war is over? Does the United States have a right to expect other countries to adopt democracy? Is democracy always the best form of government? Explain your position with examples.

- In terms of an enemy that threatens the United States, what is the difference between international terrorism by a group such as Al Qaeda, and Soviet communism? How does the fight against terrorism resemble the fight against communism, and how does it differ? What is the best way to defeat international terrorism?

- Research the cold war and discuss the various reasons that have been advanced to explain the fact that the United States won and the Soviet Union lost. What were the roles played by President Ronald Reagan and Soviet president Mikhail Gorbachev? Write a compare and contrast paper on Reagan and Gorbachev.

- Select any international problem and write a short story, in the style of *The Ugly American*, illustrating two different ways, one foolish and counter-productive and the other wise and effective, in which the problem might be approached or solved. The problem can be anything from global warming to nuclear proliferation or the AIDS epidemic.

---

since the book's publication has come to symbolize the worst aspects of American behavior abroad: "He drives a big red convertible, which he slews around corners and over sidewalks. And he's got exactly the kind of loud silly laugh that every Asian is embarrassed to hear."

When Bing gives a lecture in Washington, D.C., he reveals a flaw in American recruiting strategies for foreign service. He emphasizes the easiness of the life—the perks of free housing and the availability of servants—not the challenges. Americans are not even required to learn the language of the country to which they are sent. Bing's statement reveals his ethnocentric view of the world: "Translators are a dime a dozen overseas. And besides, it's better to make the Asians learn English. Helps them too." The result of all this is that the Americans attract only mediocre people into foreign service.

Since few Americans bother to learn the local language most Americans end up staying in the cities, talking to others just like them—American and European diplomats, and cultured, English-speaking members of the Asian elite. This language insulation contrasts with the Russian diplomats, who all learn to speak the local language and understand the culture. The Russians go out to the countryside and the villages and work hard to get the local people on their side. They are better at propaganda and "dirty tricks" than the Americans, as is shown when they convince the Sarkhanese that the rice delivered from the United States was in fact from Russia.

How to Win the Cold War in Southeast Asia

The success of the communists and the failure of the bureaucratic Americans is countered by those American characters who understand and respect the local people and their culture. Father Finian, for example, is the inspiration behind a small-scale black propaganda campaign in Burma, in which he helps a group of local men to publish a fake communist newspaper that undermines support for the communists. The key element in Father Finian's strategy is that he allows the local men themselves to decide what they want to do. He does not impose his views on them; he merely guides their discussions. "It is your country, your souls, your lives," he says. "I will do what we agree upon." Thus the authors criticize the prevailing attitude of Americans that they, rather than the people who actually live there, know what is best for southeast Asia.

Just as Father Finian knows how to combat communist propaganda, Major "Tex" Wolchek is an American who understands the military demands of the struggle. Unlike the French and their American supporters, Tex realizes that the war in Indochina is a new kind of conflict that demands knowledge of guerilla warfare, as explained in the writings of Mao Tse-tung. It is no longer enough to rely on the old concepts of war as the French are trying to do. But when Tex and Ambassador MacWhite explain this to a meeting of French and American generals in Hanoi, they are met with ridicule. The words of a French general sum up the sense of cultural superiority and snobbishness that characterize the West's attitude to the region:

> If you are suggesting . . . that the nation which produced Napoleon now has to go to a primitive Chinese for military instruction, I can tell you that you are not only making a mistake, you're being insulting.

Another American, Colonel Hillandale, shows the importance of understanding and respecting the local culture. When Hillandale was stationed in the Philippines he "embraced everything Filipino": the food and drink, the music, the people, and he also learned the language. When he is assigned to Sarkhan he walks the streets of Haidho and takes note of what he sees. He observes that well-qualified astrologers and palmists occupy elegant buildings, and he deduces from this the importance of such practices in the Sarkhanese culture. Had he been one of those Americans who never ventured further than the cocktail-party circuit, he might never have made this key observation. Since he has made a hobby of palmistry, he uses this knowledge to win influential local friends. Hillandale's opposite is George Swift, a diplomat at the U.S. Embassy, who expresses what in the book is typical American cultural arrogance in dismissing something foreign that he does not understand. "A vaudeville stunt," he says of palm reading, to which Ambassador MacWhite, who is thoroughly aware of what is really required of Americans in Southeast Asia replies, "[N]othing is fake if people believe in it. Your business is not to judge whether or not things are fakes, but who believes them and why and what it means."

Other Americans, such as John Colvin and Homer and Emma Atkins, develop strategies for helping the local population with agricultural and technological projects at the grass-roots level. Like Tex, Homer Atkins comes up against the obduracy of U.S. officialdom. They seek him out as an adviser on foreign aid projects, but what they have on their minds are big technological projects such as dams, highways, and irrigation systems. These are of immediate benefit only to local politicians who use them as a means to gain wealth and power. Atkins is more aware of what the people really need, and he uses his skill, ingenuity, and perseverance to bring his idea to fruition. He respects the local people and works with them as equals, showing none of the underlying assumptions of racial superiority shown by many other Americans, such as the technical adviser to the U.S. Embassy who tells Atkins that "for white men to work with their hands, and especially in the countryside, lower[s] the reputation of all white men."

Style

Parables

The Ugly American is an unusual novel in that there is only a loose connection between all the different episodes. The only semblance of a unified plot is in Ambassador Gilbert MacWhite's gradual accumulation of the knowledge about how to win the struggle against communism. Each story serves as a parable, illustrating either the folly of U.S. behavior and policy or a positive alternative. According to M. H. Abrams, a parable is "a short narrative presented so as to stress the tacit but detailed analogy between its component parts and a thesis or lesson that the narrator is trying to bring home to us." Thus in the first story, of "Lucky" Lou Sears, every detail contributes to the theme of the book: Americans in foreign service are not performing their jobs in a way that is likely to bring any success, but they are mostly unaware of this fact. In the third story, "Nine Friends," about Father Finian, every detail contributes to the opposite effect: Father Finian is one of the few men who knows how to act effectively and decisively in American interests. There are no subtle nuances in this black and white approach to story-telling. The meaning of each parable is crystal clear.

Historical Context

The Cold War in the 1950s

During the 1950s, and continuing until the late 1980s, global politics was dominated by the struggle between the West (the United States and its Western European allies) and the communist Soviet Union, its Eastern European allies, and China. This struggle was described as a cold war because it did not lead to direct armed conflict between the two superpowers. Instead, much of the contest was played out in the Third World, in Africa, the Middle East, and Asia. The United States would give economic and military support to emerging nations in these regions as a reward for any government that adopted an anti-communist stance. The Soviet Union lent support to Third-World communist parties and to communist insurgencies, which they described as wars of liberation against the retreating Western colonial powers. The Soviets denounced as imperialism any U.S. attempt to influence public opinion or government in such countries. The United States denounced Soviet aggression and claimed that the Soviets were bent on world domination.

In 1950, cold war rivalry focused on Korea, where Russian-backed North Korea invaded South Korea. The United States entered the war with United Nations support and engaged Chinese forces. After a truce in 1951 and an armistice in 1953, the United States regarded Vietnam as the next Asian country that had to be defended against communism, and it channeled huge military aid to the French, who were already battling Vietnamese communist forces. After the French defeat in 1954 (described so vividly in *The Ugly American*), the United States tried to halt any further communist advance by creating a viable South Vietnam state. It also sought stability by founding the Southeast Asia Treaty Organization (SEATO), which in fact included only two Southeast Asian states, Thailand and the Philippines, in addition to Britain, France, New Zealand, Australia, Pakistan, and the United States. SEATO was designed to prevent the invasion of any nation in Southeast Asia by a foreign power. But as Lea Williams points out in *Southeast Asia: A History*, SEATO ignored the reality of communist advance, which was not by direct invasion but by agitation from within and by guerilla warfare; it was very unlikely that traditional methods such as full-scale invasion would take place. Williams criticizes the limitations of U.S. diplomatic and military thinking at the time that produced such an ineffective treaty as SEATO: "Generals are inclined to be prepared for the last, rather than the next war; and SEATO was proof that diplomats, as exemplified by John Foster Dulles [U.S. secretary of state], can be equally hypnotized by history." This is essentially the same point made by Burdick and Lederer in their story of the French and U.S. generals who expect to be able to win a war in Indochina using outdated tactics.

The shock of the French defeat in Vietnam in 1954 was taken by the United States as a warning of what the future might hold if it did not exert all its influence in the region. The so-called domino theory which dictated U.S. policy in Southeast Asia held that if one nation went communist the others would soon follow, one by one, like falling dominoes. The theory reflected what was perceived as the reality of the global power game, that smaller nations would be unable to avoid being drawn into the orbit of one or other of the two superpowers. If the United States did not win control, the Soviets would.

The Strategic Importance of Southeast Asia

Southeast Asia was considered to be of great strategic importance for both sides in the cold war, from both an ideological point of view and because the region was rich in natural resources. Writing in 1953, political scientist Amry Vandenbosch, declared:

> Control of the oil, rubber, tin, rice, and other commodities of the region would give the Communist bloc a very great advantage and the loss of these strategic materials would constitute a severe blow to the West.

In 1958, the year *The Ugly American* was published, Southeast Asia consisted of nine independent states: Thailand, Burma, Malaya, North Vietnam, South Vietnam, Cambodia, Laos, Indonesia, and the Philippines. Singapore and Borneo were still British colonies, and Timor was a Portuguese colony. In the global struggle between the West and communism, North Vietnam committed itself to Russia and China, while Thailand, the Philippines, and South Vietnam sided with the United States and accepted U.S. military aid. The remaining four nations sought to remain independent, not wanting to commit to either side, and accepted only nonmilitary aid. (This is the position of the Sarkhanese government in *The Ugly American*, whose main goal is to maintain its independence.) These neutral nations were courted by both the West and by the communists, and they accepted aid from both sides.

Compare
&
Contrast

- **1950s:** In 1957, the Russians launch Sputnik 1, the first space satellite, thus inaugurating the space age. This event prompts fears in the United States that the Soviet Union may be leading in military technology and may be able to launch ballistic missiles from Europe that could reach the United States. The Sputnik launch leads directly to the creation of the National Aeronautics and Space Administration (NASA) in 1958. The following decade is dominated by the so-called space race between the two superpowers.

  Today: In 2004, President George W. Bush announces a new vision for the nation's space exploration program. The president commits the United States to a long-term human and robotic program to explore the solar system, starting with a return to the Moon that will ultimately enable future exploration of Mars and other destinations. The return to the Moon is planned for as early as 2015 and no later than 2020.

- **1950s:** The cold war between the United States and the communist Soviet Union dominates global politics. Fear of communist conspiracies in the United States leads to the McCarthy era, named for the role played by Senator Joe McCarthy (R-Wis.). McCarthy uses unscrupulous and demagogic methods to expose alleged communists and their sympathizers, but his methods are so extreme that he is discredited. He is censured by the Senate in 1954.

  Today: The cold war is over, and communism survives in only a few states in the world (Vietnam, Cuba, North Korea). Instead of communism, the greatest perceived danger to the United States and the West is international terrorism. Just as during the cold war, politicians did not want to be perceived by voters as being "soft on communism," so today, politicians like to win votes by presenting themselves as tough on terrorism and their opponents as weak.

- **1950s:** The United States begins its involvement in Vietnam by sending military aid to the French in their struggle with the communists. After the French defeat, U.S. efforts in the region focus on establishing a stable noncommunist government in South Vietnam that will be friendly to U.S. interests.

  Today: The Vietnam War, which ended in U.S. defeat, still casts a shadow over the national psyche and national politics. In the presidential election of 2004, Democratic candidate Senator John Kerry relies heavily on his experience as a decorated Vietnam War veteran, while his record in Vietnam is challenged in television advertisements by a conservative group of Vietnam veterans.

The criticisms of U.S. attitudes and policies in Southeast Asia made in *The Ugly American* were not uncommon at the time. For example, in *Southeast Asia and the World Today*, which was published a few months before *The Ugly American*, Claude A. Buss, professor of history at Stanford University, made a number of similar points when he reviewed relations between Southeast Asian countries and the United States. Buss reported that many people in these countries reacted with skepticism to U.S. military aid and also had reservations about economic aid, which was perceived as serving American self-interest. Buss also reported that regarding foreigners who worked in their countries, Asians regarded the Americans as mediocre; they were people who viewed their overseas posting "as an interesting experience or a good deal—as an excellent opportunity to see the world at government expense and to collect cheap, unusual souvenirs." Buss further states, in another passage that might have come directly from *The Ugly American*, "Asians decried the waste, the rusting machines, and the useless projects which they also helped pay for. . . . They wished that programs had been more tailored for their own needs and desires."

Marlon Brando as Ambassador Harrison Carter MacWhite in the 1963 film version of The Ugly American   Universal/The Kobal Collection

Critical Overview

The Ugly American was an immediate success with the American public. It was on the bestseller list for seventy-eight weeks and went on to sell four million copies. The message of the novel seemed to strike a ready chord amongst Americans who feared that their country was not pursuing the wisest policies abroad and that the Soviet Union might be winning a decisive advantage in the cold war.

Critical reaction, however, was mixed. Robert Trumbull, in the *New York Times Book Review,* praised the "sharp characterizations, frequently humorous incident and perceptive descriptions" in the book. He offered the opinion that it may act as a "source of insight into the actual, day-by-day by-play of [the] present titanic political struggle for Asia that will engage future historians—unless, of course, the Communists win, and suppress all such books." In contrast to Trumbull, Robert Hatch in *The Nation*, commented sharply on the book's "easy, surface characterizations," but he had some appreciation for it nonetheless: "[A]t once slick and angry; [the authors] have an awkward way of advocating decency and generosity, to say nothing of intelligence, not for their own sake but because that is the way to beat the Russian game."

In *Yale Review*, Edward W. Mill commented that his experience as an American diplomat abroad led him to believe that there was much truth in the critique of U.S. policy offered in *The Ugly American*. He acknowledged the need for more effective training for overseas service but suggested that for such a policy change to be made, there would need to be much more support and understanding of the issue by the American people, Congress, and the nation's colleges and universities. Mill concluded: "If the American people want to be represented by the MacWhites and the Hillandales instead of 'Lucky Lou' and the Joe Bings, they will have to make their wishes clear."

The Ugly American had a pronounced influence on the politics of the day. It was reportedly read by President Eisenhower, who then ordered an investigation of the U.S. foreign aid program. In 1959, then-Senator John F. Kennedy, who was preparing to run for president, and three other unnamed men prominent in public life, sent a copy of the book to every U.S. senator. It was not well received by all. In September, 1959, Senator William Fulbright denounced the book on the Senate floor. He claimed that there were many successful American aid projects in Southeast Asia and complained that "in the world of Lederer and Burdick, almost everything is reduced to idiot simplicity" (quoted in John Hellman's *American Myth and the Legacy of Vietnam*). The following year Vice President Nixon referred to *The Ugly American* in a speech at the University of San Francisco. He acknowledged that while some of the charges in the book might be partially correct, the real lesson to be absorbed was the need to understand the strategy of world communism.

One result of the popularity of the book was that the title became part of the American language. The "ugly American" was soon in common usage and referred to a certain type of arrogant American who when abroad did not understand or respect the culture he was in and saw everything through ethnocentric eyes.

Criticism

Bryan Aubrey

Aubrey holds a Ph.D. in English and has published many articles on twentieth century literature. In this essay, he discusses the novel in the context of the cold war, the Vietnam war, and the nature of the U.S. national identity and character.

Central to *The Ugly American* is the historical reality of the cold war. Behind all the individual stories lies the larger picture of a global struggle between two superpowers who embrace competing ideologies and compete ruthlessly for influence and control over smaller countries not only in Southeast Asia but all over the world. Given the fact that both superpowers have the capacity to destroy each other several times over through the use of nuclear weapons, the future of human civilization may depend on the outcome of the struggle.

Since the novel is so rooted in a particular period of history, it is impossible for readers in the early 2000s to respond to it in the same way that the original readers did, in the 1950s. In the early twenty-first century, the outcome of the cold war, far from being in doubt, is known, and that long struggle has receded into the pages of history. In fact, young people of college age in the early 2000s can have little or no direct memory of the cold war, since it wound down during the late-1980s and finally ended with the break-up of the Soviet Union in 1991. Since the United States and its allies won the cold war, and communism has completely lost the worldwide appeal it held for so many people from the 1950s to the 1980s, it is apparent from the perspective of the early 2000s that many of the fears expressed by Burdick and Lederer did not come to pass. The Soviets did not outwit or outlast the Americans. American ideas, the clarion call of freedom and democracy, proved to be more durable than the collectivist ideas of Marx and Lenin.

Tragically, however, that is only part of the story. Some of the fears expressed by the authors in *The Ugly American* did indeed come true. The United States did not learn its lessons quickly enough to avoid the catastrophe of the Vietnam War, in which over 58,000 Americans were killed

> The preeminent example of the ideal American character in action is Homer Atkins. Although he is the "ugly American" of the title, his rough outward appearance does not reflect the inner core of the man."

from 1964 to 1973, and the nation lost a war for the first time in its history.

In connection with Vietnam, *The Ugly American* seems prescient indeed, as the two chapters, "The Iron of War" and "The Lessons of War" demonstrate. The French, as they battle the communist insurgency, believe that their well-trained army, equipped with all the most modern weapons of war, will surely triumph over a ragged band of poorly equipped communists. They continue to believe this, according to *The Ugly American*, even when the evidence proves them wrong, again and again. When the French finally capitulate and withdraw from Hanoi, Major Monet, who has been enlightened by his discussions with Major "Tex" Wolchek and Gilbert MacWhite, expresses the truth as he watches the final French military parade: "No one bothered to tell the tankers that their tanks couldn't operate in endless mud. And those recoilless rifles never found an enemy disposition big enough to warrant shooting at it with them."

Less than a decade later, the United States made the same mistake as the French, thinking that a huge army—U.S. troop numbers in Vietnam reached 543,000 in 1969—with the most sophisticated military equipment in the world would defeat an enemy that possessed almost nothing in comparison. The shock of that defeat in Vietnam continued to reverberate in the national psyche for over thirty years.

But *The Ugly American* is about more than history and the cold war and the forewarnings about Vietnam. Behind the swirl of political events in Southeast Asia, the authors ground their work in a larger issue, the nature of the U.S. national identity and character. They are very careful to draw a distinction between the real American character and the distortions of it that occur when Americans get caught abroad in the twin traps of bureaucracy and shallow conventional wisdom. When Ambassador MacWhite visits the Philippines, for example, he meets the head of the government, Ramon Magsaysay, who makes the following observation:

> [A]verage Americans, in their natural state . . . are the best ambassadors a country can have. . . . They are not suspicious, they are eager to share their skills, they are generous. But something happens to Americans when they go abroad.

Magsaysay, who, incidentally, was a real historical figure, believes that many Americans abroad are "second-raters" who get carried away by their luxurious style of living and all the cocktail parties they attend. They lose the natural good qualities that are otherwise such a prominent feature of the national character.

The Burmese journalist U Maung Swe expresses the same idea. At a dinner party in Rangoon, he remarks that the Americans he knew in the United States "were wonderfully friendly, unassuming, and interested in the world." He trusted and respected them. But he continues:

> The Americans I meet in my country are not the same as the ones I knew in the United States. A mysterious change seems to come over Americans when they go to a foreign land. They live pretentiously. They're loud and ostentatious. Perhaps they're frightened and defensive; or maybe they're not properly trained and make mistakes out of ignorance.

The characters in the book who accomplish something of value are presented as examples of the true American character, as opposed to the distortion of that character that seems to occur in the foreign service. These "real Americans" are all practical men, not intellectuals. They are adventurous, creative, and ingenious. They are brave, they relish a challenge, and they are hardworking. They are also open and friendly, and not prejudiced. They speak their minds, and a rough exterior often hides a gentle heart. They are always willing to use their talents and knowledge in service of others not because they are especially religious or saintly, but because they are naturally warm and good-hearted, and they like to share what they know.

An example is John Colvin, the man who tries to help the Sarkhanese with his milk and cattle scheme and is betrayed by his former friend turned communist, Deong. Colvin is a tough, confident, battle-hardened World War II veteran. Back home in Wisconsin, he is a successful small-businessman who runs the family milk business. When he hears that Sarkhan is in danger of going communist, he feels a sense of personal responsibility to the Sarkhanese people, whom he had learned to love during his adventures there in World War II. So he

What Do I Read Next?

- In *Sarkhan* (1965; published as *The Deceptive American* in 1977) Burdick and Lederer return to the fictional landscape of *The Ugly American*. The novel is about the attempts of two Americans, one a businessman and the other a professor, to prevent a communist takeover of the country. As in *The Ugly American*, the authors are critical of the U.S. government, and the characterization exhibits the same black and white quality of the earlier novel. But unlike *The Ugly American*, *Sarkhan* is a suspense novel that builds to a thrilling climax.

- *The Quiet American* (1955), by British novelist Graham Greene, takes place in Saigon, Vietnam, during the later stages of the French war in Indochina in the 1950s. The "quiet American" is Alden Pyle, who works for an American aid mission in Saigon but is also involved through the Central Intelligence Agency with espionage and terrorism. The novel offers insight into the early U.S. involvement in Vietnam. Greene's apparent anti-American stance meant that the novel was not initially popular in the United States, but Greene's warnings about American policies proved prescient.

- Dennis Bloodworth's *An Eye for the Dragon: Southeast Asia Observed, 1954–1970* (1970) is a lively journalistic account of Southeast Asia by a veteran Far Eastern correspondent. Bloodworth's purpose is to describe historical and contemporary events in a way that reveals the beliefs, customs, prejudices, and patterns of thought in the people of Southeast Asia. He also describes the love-hate relationship between these countries and the West.

- Eric F. Goldman's *The Crucial Decade and After: America, 1945–1960* (1960) is a classic account of the United States at home and abroad in the years following the end of World War II. Goldman shows how, after much debate and disagreement, the United States continued on the economic and social revolution it had embarked on in the previous two decades. This continuation was achieved by extensions of the welfare state (a system in which government strives to create economic and social benefits for all its citizens) and other policies. Goldman also shows how the United States continued the policies mapped out in the immediate postwar years for containment of the Soviet Union and co-existence with it.

---

returns to start up a business in Sarkhan and puts up the small amount of capital required himself. It should be noted that this is private enterprise in action, not a big government-funded project, and it will rely on local free market forces to prosper.

Colvin again shows what he is made of after Deong gets the better of him, and the mob of women beat him. Ambassador Sears only manages to send Colvin home over his vigorous objections (Colvin says, with great intensity, "I won't go"). But Gilbert MacWhite sends for him again, and this time Colvin's persistence pays off. Within a year or so, his project is a success, and the local economy benefits from his innovation. Thus Colvin demonstrates qualities that the authors believe represent core American values: initiative, self-reliance, business acumen, determination, perseverance, and personal and civic responsibility.

The preeminent example of the ideal American character in action is Homer Atkins. Although he is the "ugly American" of the title, his rough outward appearance does not reflect the inner core of the man. As a blunt-spoken inventor and engineer, Atkins has no patience with intellectual theories or with men who dress in nice suits, wear after-shave lotion, and sit around conference tables. Atkins travels to Vietnam and then, at MacWhite's request, to Sarkhan, as a private individual. He certainly does not need the money, since he has been highly successful in his career and is worth $3 million (a huge fortune in 1958 dollars). He enjoys the challenge of new projects, but he is only interested in things that will be immediately useful for the local people. He is a realist and has no time for grandiose dreams. When it comes to setting up his business in Sarkhan, he presents a textbook example of how foreign aid programs should be conducted. He provides the expertise and the creative mind (in consultation with the local man, Jeepo), but all the materials he uses for the water pump he invents are local: pipes made from bamboo, pistons adapted from the pistons of old jeeps, and power from the drive mechanism of bicycles. Everything is cheap and easily available, and nothing has to be imported. Atkins then employs local labor, and they all work eighteen to twenty-hour days to get the business off the ground. Then those who make the product get the chance to sell it and make money. It is an ideal set-up all round, and its success is due to the sturdy good sense, ingenuity, hard work, and benevolence of Atkins.

Homer's wife Emma is another example of this sturdy American character. She is happy to live in a simple cottage in Sarkhan with relatively primitive facilities: "pressed earth floors, one spigot of cold water, a charcoal fire, two very comfortable hammocks, a horde of small, harmless insects." She does not for a moment miss the amenities of a modern American kitchen or the luxuries that are available in an advanced civilization. Indeed, in their simple, self-reliant way of living, Homer and Emma Atkins resemble not so much a modern American couple but a throwback to earlier times, the nineteenth century or even the colonial period. As John Hellmann points out in his book *American Myth and the Legacy of Vietnam*, the Americans who have the right approach in *The Ugly American* represent ideas about the American character and about the nation's role in the world that go back to colonial times. One of these myths is of the frontier hero, with the frontier displaced in the novel from the American West onto the landscape of Southeast Asia.

Seen in this light, *The Ugly American* is not only an indictment of the ineffectiveness of U.S. policy in Southeast Asia, it is also a wake-up call to Americans to rediscover their own best qualities and values. The authors return to this theme in their "Factual Epilogue," in which they write:

> We have so lost sight of our own past that we are trying to sell guns and money alone, instead of remembering that is was the quest for the dignity of freedom that was responsible for our way of life.

The authors' conclusion, in which they write, "All over Asia we have found that the basic American ethic is revered and honored and imitated when

possible," sends a very clear message. As long as Americans remain true to themselves and their values, they have nothing to fear from communist aggression; they will surely prevail.

Source: Bryan Aubrey, Critical Essay on *The Ugly American*, in *Novels for Students*, Thomson Gale, 2006.

John Hellmann

In the following essay excerpt, Hellmann examines the socio-political environment in which The Ugly American *was published, and posits that the novel is a form of the American Jeremiad, a form of "political-sermon" dating back to the Puritans.*

The Ugly American appeared in the wake of such influential analyses of postwar American society as David Riesman's *The Lonely Crowd* (1950), William H. Whyte, Jr.'s *The Organization Man* (1956), and John Kenneth Galbraith's *The Affluent Society* (1958). These books were widely discussed and alluded to in reviews, columns, and articles. They had such impact because they articulated in persuasive detail suspicions voiced through the decade with steadily increasing anxiety. These suspicions had in common a fear that trends in contemporary American society were fundamentally altering the American character. Conservatives usually focused upon "socialistic" tendencies toward conformity and mediocrity within a network of dependence on the large organizations of government, business, and unions now dominating American life. Liberals more typically emphasized the corrupting effects of a cynical, materialistic consumer society. Underlying these critiques was a shared suspicion that Americans were becoming too "soft," immoral, and greedy to survive the Soviets' dedicated pursuit of world communism.

In 1952, for instance, Louis B. Seltzer, the editor of the *Cleveland Press*, asked in an editorial "What is wrong with us?" and provided an answer that would be received with a torrent of approving telephone calls, letters, and personal congratulations on the street:

> We have everything. We abound with all of the things that make us comfortable. We are, on the average, rich beyond the dreams of the kings of old. . . . Yet . . . something is not there that should be—something we once had. . . .
>
> Are we our own worst enemies? Should we fear what is happening among us more than what is happening elsewhere? . . .
>
> No one seems to know what to do to meet it. But everybody worries.

Forty-one publications all over the country would reprint the editorial. At the end of the decade novelist John Steinbeck received a similar response to the publication of his letter to Adlai Stevenson in which he declared that if he wanted to ruin a nation "I would give it too much and I would have it on its knees, miserable, greedy, and sick. . . . [In rich America] a creeping, all pervading, nerve-gas of immorality starts in the nursery and does not stop before it reaches the highest offices, both corporate and governmental." Steinbeck's letter was also reprinted many times and discussed throughout the country. Luxuriating in a landscape of tailfins, lawn sprinklers, and gray flannel suits, thoughtful Americans were uneasily considering what they had lost in their character and what they might be on their way to losing in the world at large.

Lederer and Burdick's novel presented Americans with confirmation of these fears in melodramatic terms charged with American mythic conceptions. Unlike *The Quiet American,* it attacked not the American character but the failure of many contemporary Americans to retain that character. Presenting confirmation of suspected corruption, *The Ugly American* echoed a traditional American message extending back to the New England Puritans. In *The American Jeremiad,* Sacvan Bercovitch has shown that the political-sermon form of the Puritans known as the jeremiad survived in the political rhetoric of the formative years of the republic, and has continued to be a central ritual of American culture. Combining a criticism of contemporary errors and vision of future disaster with an affirmation of the correctness of the traditional character and purpose of the American "errand," the American jeremiad has enabled speakers and writers to exert a power at once conservative and progressive, demanding of each generation that they return to the way of the fathers and rededicate themselves to the special mission of the culture.

In *The Ugly American* the authors explicitly make this ritualistic call in the epilogue. After finishing their claims for the book's factual basis, the authors begin the ritual with the traditional cry of doom:

> The picture as we saw it, then, is of an Asia where we stand relatively mute, locked in the cities, misunderstanding the temper and the needs of the Asians. We saw America spending vast sums where Russia spends far less and achieves far more. The result has been called "an uneasy balance," but actually it is nothing of the sort. We have been losing—not only in Asia, but everywhere.

> " In its attacks on American policies and personnel in Asia, *The Ugly American* shows its American readers a mirror of their own 'ugliness.'"

> If the only price we are willing to pay is the dollar price, then we might as well pull out before we're thrown out. If we are not prepared to pay the human price, we had better retreat to our shores, build Fortress America, learn to live without international trade and communications, and accept the mediocrity, the low standard of living, and the loom of world Communism which would accompany such a move.

The authors follow this grim assessment with assurance that the future nevertheless remains conditional, since the responsibility for this imminent catastrophe lies in the present attitude of American society:

> Actually, the state in which we find ourselves is far from hopeless. We have the material, and above all the human resources, to change our methods and to win. It is not the fault of the government or its leaders or any political party that we have acted as we have. It is the temper of the whole nation.

They follow this denunciation of the present "temper of the whole nation" with an explanation that the problem lies in a deviation from the past mythos of the nation: "We have so lost sight of our own past that we are trying to sell guns and money alone, instead of remembering that it was the quest for the dignity of freedom that was responsible for our own way of life." Finally, they reassure readers that success is preordained if they will simply return to American principles:

> All over Asia we have found that the basic American ethic is revered and honored and imitated when possible. We must, while helping Asia toward self-sufficiency, show by example that America is still the America of freedom and hope and knowledge and law. If we succeed, we cannot lose the struggle.

The fictional text of *The Ugly American* is a narrative version of this jeremiad: its structure of parabolic tales induces anxiety by showing imminent communist victory in Asia, places the blame upon the lapse of the majority of Americans serving there, and offers visions of the completed errand through small but exemplary successes won by a few virtuous Americans. The story then ends with an apocalyptic challenge to the reader in the form of the Secretary of State's rejection of the heroic few on the grounds that not enough Americans would be willing to make the sacrifices necessary for such policies. The characters of this drama symbolize the concepts intrinsic to the jeremiad from Puritan times to the nineteenth century: the Asian villagers are the American Indians or the Chinese, living in a *terra profana,* to be converted to the Forces of Light; the Soviet agents the clever and ruthless Forces of Darkness; the Viet Minh guerrillas the "savage" Indians manipulated by the Dark Forces; the British and French colonial officials the "dead hand of the European past"; the "ugly" Americans the Chosen who have fallen away from the errand; and the few "non-ugly" Americans, as Lederer and Burdick referred to them in a subsequent *Life* article, the traditional heroes of American mythic history.

The resulting allegory is played out upon an Indochina as much imagined as observed, an Indochina overlaid with the mythic landscapes represented in the American mind by the frontiers of the American West and nineteenth-century China. Set in the invented nation of Sarkhan and such actual nations as Vietnam, Burma, and Cambodia, *The Ugly American* imposes upon an exotic but generalized Southeast Asian topography and demography the "moral geography" characterizing American thought since the colonial period. The dominating features of the resulting symbolic landscape are the classic images of city and country, embodying the stark opposition between civilization and wilderness, Europe and America, technology and nature, the conscious and unconscious, that such critics of classic American literature as D. H. Lawrence and Leslie Fiedler have identified as obsessions of the American psyche. The power of the book lies in its presentation of the struggle in Indochina, and by extension the global cold war, in images holding mythic resonance.

In their prefatory note Lederer and Burdick protest that "what we have written is not just an angry dream, but rather the rendering of fact into fiction." But, however strong the basis of *The Ugly American* in actuality, its fictional power is precisely that of dream, the collective dream of authors and readers in a text based in shared myth. The vivid but formulaic prose, the alternately sentimental and horrific plot, and the sharply drawn but stereotypical characters call easily upon cultural memory. We can compare *The Ugly American* in this aspect to such myth-laden children's tales as Parson Weems' fable of George Washington and the Cherry Tree, which presented generations of American schoolchildren with a symbolic resolution of the psychological conflict of a culture both revolutionary and conservative in its origins. Though it functions as a jeremiad as opposed to the celebration of Weems' fable, *The Ugly American* possesses a similar power and method in its symbolic, ultimately uncritical, presentation of American cultural conflict.

In the symbolic landscape of *The Ugly American,* the success of the external struggle with Soviet agents and their "savage" Asian army of Viet Minh depends upon the outcome of an internal struggle taking place within the American psyche and the American society. The crucial conflict in *The Ugly American* is thus between two types of Americans. The "ugly" Americans, far from being simply incompetent diplomats, represent the "temper of the whole nation" that is in error. They present grotesque reflections of those contemporary Americans who have fallen away from American virtue and mission. In the moral geography of American myth found in the novel, the journey of the ugly Americans west to Asia is ironically a spiritual flight east back to Europe. The targets of the exposé in *The Ugly American*—narrow careerists in the diplomatic service, pleasure-seeking staff members, and "big" foreign-aid projects conferring wealth and status on the native elite without actually helping the people—are the means by which the book indirectly points its accusing finger at the loss of the frontier virtues in postwar society.

In its attacks on American policies and personnel in Asia, *The Ugly American* shows its American readers a mirror of their own "ugliness." Lederer and Burdick depict Americans in Washington being recruited to service overseas with assurances that they will "be living with a gang of clean-cut Americans" on "the high American standard," for even "in Saigon they stock American ice cream, bread, cake, and, well, anything you want." A friendly Asian leader observes that "something happens to most Americans when they go abroad. . . . Many of them, against their own judgment, feel that they must live up to their commissaries and big cars and cocktail parties." Readers in 1958 and later could recognize in these images the pervasive conformity, affluence, and status-seeking characterizing their postwar society.

Source: John Hellmann, "Entering a Symbolic Landscape," in *American Myth and the Legacy of Vietnam*, Columbia University Press, 1986, pp. 19–24.

Edward W. Mill

In the following review of The Ugly American, Mill provides background on U.S. policy and presence in Asia, and examines the novel's "aim to point the way to a stronger and more effective American policy."

American concern with the destinies of the peoples and countries of Asia continues to increase as baffling new problems are encountered in the area and many of our most dedicated efforts often seem to add up to little. From a relatively small coterie of scholars writing of this area, we have moved to the point where books on the region with a wide appeal are now increasingly appearing. Two books in this category are *The Ugly American* by William J. Lederer and Eugene Burdick and *Friend to Friend* by Carlos P. Romulo and Pearl S. Buck.

The setting for these two books is a world of great change. Asia has emerged since the Second World War, as Africa is emerging today, as a region of many newly independent states; this is particularly true of Southeast Asia, which serves as the main locale for the Burdick-Lederer book. With independence has come a radical disruption of old patterns of life and an often frenzied desire to catch up with the twentieth century. While the old imperialism of the West was being chopped or whittled away, a newer imperialism, that of the Communists, began to appear, and to make claims to being a first cousin of the forces of nationalism in each country. American foreign policy, forced to face world-wide challenges, has sometimes been slow to react to the portentous changes in Southeast Asia. Our granting of independence to the Philippines in 1946 was an event of signal success for both Americans and Filipinos, but we have moved very cautiously elsewhere in the area. As the years have passed, we have constantly sought higher and firmer ground in our relations with Southeast Asia.

Burdick and Lederer's book suggests that the process of moving to firmer and higher ground is not an easy one. Through a series of fictional characters, such as Ambassador "Lucky Louis," Joe Bing, John Colvin, Father John Finian, Marie MacIntosh, Col. Edwin B. Hillandale, "The Ugly American" (Homer Atkins), and Captain Boning, they present a telling, if sometimes overdone, story of some of the weaknesses of our efforts in the newly independent lands of Southeast Asia. Though ostensibly fiction, the authors—one a Navy captain and author and the other a professional political scientist—are at pains to stress that the book is largely based on fact. To one who has served in the area in recent years both as a governmental official and as a teacher there are all too many similarities to actual situations and people to contradict them.

The reader is introduced at the beginning of the book to Ambassador "Lucky Louis" Sears, a mythical American Ambassador to the state of "Sarkhan," which is "a small country out toward Burma and Thailand." "Lucky Louis" sits grimacing in his Embassy office as he dwells upon a cartoon in one of the local newspapers which is obviously a sarcastic caricature of him. Sears, a political appointee, "wished to hell some American in the Embassy could read Sarkhanese" so he could get at the bottom of this sort of thing. A misfit and a blunderer from the beginning of his lame-duck appointment, he is ill suited to appreciate the mood and temper of the new age that is dawning in Sarkhan and the other countries of Southeast Asia. He is contrasted unfavorably with the rival Russian Ambassador, Louis Krupitzyn, who has come to his post in Sarkhan schooled in the languages and customs of the area and highly motivated to do his job. "Lucky Louis" has some parallel companions in ineffectiveness in George Swift and Joe Bing. Bing is a classic prototype too often found abroad. He is "the operator," "the man who knows his way around," who has "friends everywhere," but who all too often lacks even an elementary understanding of the deep underlying forces at work in Asia today.

Along with the misfits mentioned, there are also the hardworking and able. Ambassador Gilbert MacWhite is a career man who succeeds "Lucky Lou" in Sarkhan. He has originality, imagination, drive, and a certain amount of valuable humility. He has an eagerness to come to grips with fundamentals that promises rich dividends for his country. He even hies himself off to North Vietnam where, very unpretentiously, he gains useful insights into the military tactics of Mao Tse-tung and Ho Chi Minh. MacWhite has his military counterpart in Colonel Edwin B. Hillandale, "The Ragtime Kid," whose real-life counterpart will hardly be missed by those with field experience in Asia. "The Ragtime Kid," nick-named such by Filipino musicians for his harmonica playing and other abilities, is an almost incredible character who thrives on direct contact with the people wherever he is, though he is hardly *persona grata* to the Counselor at the American Embassy. Major Tex Wolchek is a hard-fighting Texan who comes to know the realities of Communist guerrilla warfare in Vietnam. The Ugly American of the title is a Homer Atkins, who,

" There can be little denying that they aim to point the way to a stronger and more effective American policy."

together with his wife, is brought to Sarkhan by Ambassador MacWhite and proves remarkably adept in improvising simple engineering devices, such as a new pumping system, for the people in Sarkhan; his success suggests that what Asia so often needs are not large-scale, costly economic projects but more simple, down-to-earth technical assistance and small-scale economic projects.

But if there are able and imaginative Americans particularly attuned to the needs and aspirations of Southeast Asia—and there are a great many such Americans—the disturbing thesis developed by Burdick and Lederer is that too often these men receive little recognition and are, in fact, many times penalized. The hard-working, imaginative Ambassador MacWhite of the story is, in the end, more or less forced to resign for speaking out frankly, and in his stead, who comes but good old Joe Bing, everybody's friend, who has toed the line but who hardly has an inkling of the real challenge represented by his job.

Burdick and Lederer, while employing fictional sketches of overseas Americans as their main device, are concerned that some of the serious questions they raise be answered in strictly non-fictional terms. In a rather unusual "Factual Epilogue" at the end of their book, they seek to face up to the questions raised. They repeat, "each of the small and sometimes tragic events we have described has happened . . . many times. Too many times. We believe that if such things continue to happen they will multiply into a pattern of disaster." What can be done to develop a more effective overseas group of official Americans? Certainly, a key answer to the question is training, the most effective possible training for such individuals. The authors stress the need of training in languages and the customs of the people. They indicate the need for an almost missionary zeal on the part of those who serve. The reviewer would suggest that all this involves much greater support and understanding from the American people and their Congress; it indicates also a

need for more alertness to the needs of the hour by more of our colleges and universities. If the American people want to be represented by the MacWhites and the Hillandales instead of "Lucky Lou" and the Joe Bings, they will have to make their wishes clear.

The book by Carlos Romulo and Pearl Buck makes for excellent reading along with *The Ugly American,* for here, in non-fictional form, some of the basic issues involved in the American relationship with Asia are dealt with in succinct and stimulating fashion. General Romulo, whose devotion to freedom and friendship with the United States hardly need to be mentioned to an American audience, writes "frankly and from the heart, not in criticism nor in disparagement of America, but out of my abounding admiration and affection for the American people." He is vitally concerned that the American people come to appreciate more the matter of their relations with the peoples and countries of Asia and Africa. He feels that we are "behind" in our understanding of these new relationships. He urges that we face up to the fact that we are living in a vastly transformed age.

What can America do to win the respect and the affection of the people of Asia and Africa? Why do so many of our acts of generosity in the world go seemingly unappreciated? Among the first things we should attempt to do is dispel a number of "myths" to which we cling. For example, the idea that no matter what the enemies of freedom do, freedom is bound to triumph in the end; or the belief that progress is not possible without freedom. He stresses also the need for our working always to narrow the gap between American profession and American performance, particularly in the field of race relations. The dilemma often posed for us of seeming to have to choose between the older colonial powers and the newly independent nations in matters of international contention is a problem that can only be resolved by adherence to principle. And America should seek vigorously "to take the initiative in making peace proposals and not to allow Soviet Russia, with its phony peace aims, to be always on the offensive." If we base our actions on these principles of policy, Ambassador Romulo is convinced that we will be acting in the best interest of mankind and specifically in our own best interests. Asia and Africa, he believes, cannot help reacting favorably.

From the views of a leader of Southeast Asia and of the United Nations, we turn then in *Friend to Friend* to consider the views of an American, whose years of service in and writing about China make her very well known to the American people. Pearl Buck, writing in the second half of this book, feels that we are, in some ways, a "lonely" people, who have not always found it easy to project our best image abroad. Like Romulo, she feels it is urgent to examine our situation with respect to the new Asia. She believes that the Soviet Union has often beaten us to the punch in winning over the independence movements of this area. She criticizes the lack of effectiveness of many of our overseas operations and personnel; these pages ring clear to the theme of *The Ugly American*; her lament about "the arrogance of Americans as they see and hear us abroad" parallels Romulo's rejoinder about what some Asians have termed "American swagger." Her comment that "neutralism" "is in reality anti-Americanism" would be denied by many Asian leaders and scholars in this country though perhaps not by many members of our Congress.

Pearl Buck feels that we are often our own worst enemies in dealing with the peoples of Asia. We shrink too often from accepting the responsibility that is now ours as a great world power. We tend also to judge other peoples by our own personal standards; we forget that in many ways, geographically, economically, and perhaps politically, we are unique and that it may be impossible for others to follow our exact path.

In the latter portion of her essay Pearl Buck very commendably balances her analysis with some suggestions for Asia also. She asks Asia to face up to the question of what it can do to help us act more effectively in Asia. She points out that all the inconsistencies are not on the American side. India has to deal with a Soviet Union on her borders which may not always allow her the freedom of action she would like, as, for example, in connection with Hungary. Also, prejudice against people anywhere, whether it be in China or Indonesia or in Little Rock, is an assault on the human spirit. America, too, has made great progress in race relations, and while the failures cannot be overlooked, the strides ahead must be recognized for their worth. Mutual understanding of each other's problems should help to lead to greater appreciation and tolerance. Lastly, Mrs. Buck afffirms with conviction that Asia can trust us for the future. Why? Because "we have a conscience." We want to hear and we want to learn if Asia will only join us in speaking to us as *Friend to Friend*.

One of the great attributes of the American democracy is its willingness to face up to constructive criticism and to seek improvement. At times in our history it would appear that we have almost prostrated ourselves in our eagerness for self-examination and condemnation of our failures. There are many who fear that we go too far in this direction, and some of them would point to the book, *The Ugly American,* for proof of the point. Some may even feel that the much milder *Friend to Friend* deals with us rather severely.

But whatever the personal reaction of the individual reader may be to these books, there can be little denying that they aim to point the way to a stronger and more effective American policy and American operation in Asia. Most Americans will have little quarrel with this goal.

Source: Edward W. Mill, "A New Diplomacy for Asia," in *Yale Review*, Spring 1959, pp. 431–36.

Sources

Abrams, M. H., *A Glossary of Literary Terms*, fourth edition, Holt, Rinehart and Winston, 1981, p. 6.

Buss, Claude A., *Southeast Asia and the World Today*, D. Van Nostrand, pp. 92–93.

Hatch, Robert, "Books in Brief," in *The Nation*, October 4, 1958, p. 199.

Hellmann, John, *American Myth and the Legacy of Vietnam*, Columbia University Press, 1986, p. 17.

Lederer, William J., and Eugene Burdick, *The Ugly American*, Norton, 1958.

Mill, Edward W., "A New Diplomacy for Asia," in *Yale Review*, Spring 1959, p. 434.

Trumbull, Robert, "The Ambassador Who Didn't Read Sarkhanese," in *New York Times Book Review*, October 5, 1958, p. 38.

Vandenbosch, Amry, "Our Friends and Antagonists in Southeast Asia," in *Southeast Asia in the Coming World*, edited by Philip W. Thayer, Johns Hopkins Press, 1953, p. 47.

Williams, Lea E., *Southeast Asia: A History*, Oxford University Press, 1976, p. 266.

Further Reading

Allen, Richard, *A Short Introduction to the History and Politics of Southeast Asia*, Oxford University Press, 1970.
    This concise survey of Southeast Asia is very useful for understanding the political situation in that region in the 1950s. Especially interesting is Allen's discussion of the French involvement in Indochina and their defeat at Dien Bien Phu in 1954, which sheds light on the episodes involving Major Monet and Major Wolchek in *The Ugly American*.

Christie, Clive, *"The Quiet American" and "The Ugly American": Western Literary Perspectives on Indo-China in a Decade of Transition, 1950–1960*, University of Kent at Canterbury, Centre of South-East Asian Studies, Occasional Paper No. 10, 1989.

Christie discusses Graham Greene's *The Quiet American*, *The Ugly American*, the memoirs of Dr. Thomas Dooley, a U.S. Navy doctor who worked in Vietnam and Laos in the 1950s, and French literature about the war in Indochina. Christie analyzes these works in the context of the struggle with communism in Southeast Asia and prevailing Western political attitudes toward Asia.

Kuhn, Delia W., "Bagging Asia," in *Saturday Review*, October 4, 1958, pp. 32–33.

In this review of *The Ugly American*, Kuhn, like some other reviewers, criticized what she regarded as shallow characterization. But she also expressed respect for the authors' direct experience of their subject while remaining skeptical of any belief that somehow the United States could save Asia.

Steel, Ronald, *Pax Americana: The Cold War Empire and the Politics of Counterrevolution*, revised edition, Penguin, 1970.

In this widely read book, first published in 1967, Steel discusses the idea of a "Pax Americana" (Latin for "American peace"), which for him was based on a benevolent imperialism with a noble purpose. Steel's chapter on U.S. foreign aid and how it serves the purposes of imperialism has great relevance for *The Ugly American*. In the revised edition, published when the United States was heading for defeat in Vietnam, Steel modified his views, arguing that it was not so easy to claim that U.S. foreign policy was designed to promote liberty.

Winter in the Blood

James Welch

1974

Winter in the Blood (1974), the first novel by James Welch, is set on the Fort Belknap Indian Reservation in Montana, which is located forty miles south of the Canadian border and twenty miles north of the Missouri River. It is the fourth largest Indian reservation in Montana; more than five thousand people live there. The protagonist and narrator of the novel is a thirty-two-year-old Blackfeet Indian whose name is never revealed. He lives on a cattle ranch with his mother and stepfather, but he is an alienated individual who feels little affection for his family. The narrator seems to have no purpose or direction in life, and when he visits the small towns that border the reservation in search of his girlfriend, he gets drunk in bars and indulges in meaningless sex with women he picks up there. However, the narrator also has significant encounters with an old Indian named Yellow Calf, through which he learns more of his family heritage.

With its sharp poetic imagery and its realistic portrayal of life on a Montana reservation, *Winter in the Blood* is considered one of the most important works of the movement known as the Native American Renaissance. This refers to works published from the late-1960s onwards, when Native American writers began to become more prominent in the American literary landscape.

Author Biography

James Welch was born on November 18, 1940, on the Blackfeet reservation in Browning, Montana.

"Our Lady of the Little Rockies," a familiar site in Hays, Montana, on the Fort Belknap Indian Reservation © Dave G. Houser/Corbis

His father, a welder, hospital administrator, and later rancher and farmer, was a Blackfeet Indian. His mother, who trained as a stenographer, was a member of the Gros Ventre tribe.

Welch was raised as a Catholic and attended schools on the Blackfeet and Fort Belknap reservations before moving with his family to Minneapolis. He graduated from high school in 1958 and briefly attended the University of Minnesota before returning to Montana. He graduated from the University of Montana in 1965 with a bachelor's degree in liberal arts. He began writing poetry and entered the master of fine arts program, but he did not complete the degree. In 1968, he married Lois Monk, a university teacher. The following year, Welch was awarded a National Endowment for the Arts grant. This led to the publication of his first collection of poems, *Riding the Earthboy 40: Poems* (1971).

Riding the Earthboy 40: Poems was followed by the publication of Welch's first novel, *Winter in the Blood*, which he wrote between 1971 and 1973 and which was published in 1974. Critical reception of the novel was enthusiastic. Welch's second novel, *The Death of Jim Loney* (1979), also featured an alienated protagonist; it was about an alcoholic half-Indian, half-white man. Welch's

third novel represented a departure from his previous work. *Fools Crow* (1986) was a historical novel that told the story of the Blackfeet Indians in the 1860s, culminating in the massacre on the Marias River in 1870. *Fools Crow* was awarded the *Los Angeles Times* Book Prize and Pacific Northwest Booksellers Association Book award in 1987. Welch's fourth novel was *The Indian Lawyer* (1990), about an Indian attorney and congressional candidate who served on the Montana prison parole board (as did Welch). The attorney gets involved with the wife of a prisoner and is blackmailed, forcing him to return to practice law on the reservation.

For his next project, Welch collaborated with filmmaker Paul Stekler on the PBS documentary about the battle of Little Bighorn in 1876, in which the Seventh Cavalry under General George Custer was annihilated by Sioux Indians. Welch then published his own account of the battle from an Indian point of view, *Killing Custer: The Battle of the Little Bighorn and the Fate of the Plains Indians* (1994).

Welch's final novel, *The Heartsong of Charging Elk* (2000), was a historical novel about a Sioux Indian who as a child witnessed the battle of Little Bighorn. The protagonist of this novel joined Buffalo Bill's Wild West Show, which toured Europe, and was left behind in France recovering from an injury. Remaining in France, he had to make his way in an alien culture.

Welch was a Visiting professor at the University of Washington and Cornell University. In 1997, he received a Lifetime Achievement Award from the Native Writers Circle of the Americas.

Welch died on August 4, 2003, of a heart a tack, at the age of sixty-two.

Plot Summary

Part One

Winter in the Blood begins on an Indian reservation in Montana sometime in the 1960s. It is summer. The narrator, a thirty-two-year-old Blackfeet Indian, comes home after a drinking spree in town, where he got into a fight with a white man in a bar. When he arrives at the cattle ranch where he lives—with his mother, Teresa, and his grandmother—he finds that Agnes, his Cree girlfriend, who had been living with them for three weeks, has left. She has taken his gun and electric razor.

The narrator goes fishing and comes home with Teresa's friend, Lame Bull. After supper, he reads and listens to the radio with his grandmother. Lame Bull and Teresa go away for three days. When they return, they report that they got married in Malta, one of the small towns that border the reservation.

The next day, the narrator helps Lame Bull on the ranch. In conversation with Teresa, he recalls events from his childhood, such as the day he accidentally drowned five ducks he had won at a fair and the death of his father ten years ago, who froze to death returning home drunk one winter's night.

Lame Bull hires Raymond Long Knife to work on the ranch, but Raymond is dissatisfied with the pay. Lame Bull punches him on the nose and takes him back to town.

After a night in which the narrator recalls stories told by his grandmother and his dead brother, Lame Bull gives the narrator a ride to Dodson. The narrator then takes a bus to Malta, fifty miles from his home, to find Agnes, even though he claims she is not worth the trouble. In a bar, he meets Dougie, Agnes's brother. Dougie gets the narrator to help him rob a white man who is drunk and passed out.

At a bar in a hotel, the narrator meets a man from New York, who tells him he has left his wife and intended to fly to the Middle East but instead drove out west. He tells the narrator he wants to go fishing and insists on it even when he is told there are no fish in the river. The man talks to the barmaid, thinking he knows her. She tells the narrator that she used to be a dancer, and the man paid her to dance for him. He recognizes her and rushes out of the bar.

The narrator wakes up the next morning with a hangover. He goes to another bar and remembers that the barmaid was with him in his hotel room the previous night.

Part Two

The narrator rides his horse, Bird, to visit an old blind man, Yellow Calf, who lives in a shack three miles away. They drink coffee and Yellow Calf comments that the world is "cockeyed."

Lame Bull drives with Teresa and the narrator to Harlem, where the narrator gets talking to a woman named Malvina in a bar. He spends the night sleeping on the couch in Malvina's house. In the morning, she rejects his sexual advances and tells him to go away.

The narrator travels to Havre, since he has been told that Agnes is there. In a restaurant, he again encounters the man he met in Malta. The man thinks an old man at the bar is eavesdropping on them, and he wants the narrator to meet him at the Legion Club. After the man leaves, the old man's face plunges into his oatmeal. The narrator realizes he is dead.

At the Legion Club, the mysterious man wins several boxes of chocolate-covered cherries and a teddy bear at a punchboard. He says he is going to Canada to escape the FBI. He wants the narrator to accompany him by car to Calgary and then return alone with the car, which would be his to keep.

They walk through the streets of Havre, the narrator carrying the teddy bear. The man buys a hunting knife and a used Ford Falcon. As they drive downtown, the narrator spots Agnes standing in the street next to her brother.

The narrator and the mysterious man plan to start for Canada at midnight. That evening, the narrator goes out to walk, and a movie house showing old Westerns jogs his memory. He is taken back to his childhood. On a winter's day twenty years ago, when he was twelve and his brother Mose fourteen, their father sent them to bring the cows in. They rode out on horseback at dawn and, by lunchtime, had gathered over half of the seventy-eight cows and three bulls.

The narrative returns to the present. The narrator finds Agnes in a bar, but Dougie and his friends beat him up. The narrator ends up on the street with a broken tooth. A woman named Marlene helps him, and he goes back to a bar and has a whiskey. He then observes the man who wants to go to Canada being arrested and taken away in a police car. He meets Marlene again, and they spend the night together in a hotel. He leaves around mid-morning and decides he has had enough of Havre.

Part Three

The narrator hitchhikes a ride home with a man in an Oldsmobile. When he arrives home, no one is there, not even his grandmother. He assumes she must have died, which is confirmed when Teresa and Lame Bull return in the evening. They took the body to Harlem for preparation before burial. They drink a glass of wine. The next day, they dig her grave.

The narrative returns to the narrator's memories of herding the cows with Mose. It was getting dark, and they had to get the cows across the highway. A calf broke away, and the narrator's horse, Bird, gave chase. A car went past them, and hit Mose, killing him.

Back in the present, after the grave has been dug, the narrator rides to visit Yellow Calf.

Part Four

Yellow Calf talks about the narrator's grandmother, whom he knew when he was young. She was the youngest wife of Standing Bear, a Blackfeet. Yellow Calf recalls a terrible winter of starvation, when they had to run from the soldiers. Standing Bear was killed in battle with the Gros Ventre. The Blackfeet turned against the narrator's grandmother, blaming her for bringing them despair and death. She was left to fend for herself, surviving only because Yellow Calf brought her food. The narrator suddenly realizes that Yellow Calf is his grandfather, not Doagie, a man of mixed race, as he had formerly believed.

The narrator returns home, thinking about the affair between his grandmother and Yellow Calf and wondering how it could have remained hidden for so long.

Ferdinand Horn and his wife visit to offer their condolences. The narrator then struggles, with the help of Bird, to free a cow that is lying on its side in mud. The cow is freed, but the effort kills Bird.

Epilogue

The next day, Teresa, Lame Bull, and the narrator bury the old lady. The narrator's thoughts stray to his future. He will have to see a doctor about his injured knee. He also thinks he may start again with Agnes and perhaps even marry her.

Characters

Agnes

Agnes is a slender young Cree woman from Havre. She is the narrator's girlfriend, who lives with him and his family for three weeks. The narrator's grandmother hates her because she is Cree. Agnes walks out on the narrator, stealing his gun and electric razor. He meets her again in Havre, where she appears to live an aimless life, full of drinking and promiscuity.

Airplane Man

The unnamed man meets the narrator in Malta and then again in Havre. He comes from New York, where he left his wife, apparently taking some of her money. He says the FBI is looking for him. He intended to fly to the Middle East, but at the last minute tore up his plane ticket and drove out west. He persuades the narrator to accompany him by car to Canada, but his scheme fails when he is arrested in Havre.

Doagie

Doagie was a half-white drifter who lived with the narrator's grandmother. The narrator was told that Doagie was his grandfather, but it later transpires that this is not the case.

Dougie

Dougie is Agnes's brother. In Malta, he gets the narrator to help him rob a drunken white man. In Havre, Dougie and his friends beat the narrator up.

First Raise

First Raise was the narrator's father. He was good with machinery and could repair almost anything. He was often away from home, drinking in the bars in town, and Teresa describes him as a foolish man. First Raise's dream was to go on an illegal hunt for elks, but he never got to make the trip to Glacier National Park. One winter night ten years before the story begins, he was on his way home drunk after spending an evening in a bar in Dodson, when he fell down, passed out, and froze to death.

Grandmother

The narrator's Blackfeet grandmother lives with him, Teresa, and Lame Bull. She is old and blind and does not speak. She dies while the narrator is away in Havre and is buried on the family property. As a young woman, she was the wife of Standing Bear and was known for her beauty. After Standing Bear was killed in battle, she was scorned by the Blackfeet, except for Yellow Calf, who brought her the food that enabled her to survive a harsh winter. For years, the narrator believed that his grandmother remained alone for twenty-five years following the death of Standing Bear, until she began living with the drifter Doagie. The narrator later learns that his grandmother was close to Yellow Calf, and that Yellow Calf, not Doagie, is his grandfather.

Larue Henderson

Larue Henderson is an acquaintance of the narrator in Harlem. He manages an auto repair garage.

Ferdinand Horn

Ferdinand Horn is a friend of the narrator's family.

Lame Bull

Lame Bull is Teresa's friend who becomes her husband early in the novel. He is forty-seven years old, eight years younger than Teresa. Part of the reason he married Teresa was so he could own some of the best land in the valley. Being a prosperous cattleman makes him happy. He is efficient, practical, and crafty, although Teresa complains about his sloppy habits.

Raymond Long Knife

Raymond Long Knife is a white man who comes from a long line of cowboys, but he is lazy and does not like to work. Lame Bull employs him for a couple of days to help stack hay bales.

Malvina

Malvina is a woman the narrator meets in a bar in Harlem. He stays the night at her house.

Marlene

Marlene is the woman the narrator meets in Havre. They spend the night together in a hotel.

Mose

Mose was the narrator's elder brother. Mose was fourteen when he was killed by a car as the two boys were driving the cows home one early evening in winter. The brothers were close, and the narrator often remembers the enjoyable times he had with Mose.

The Narrator

The unnamed narrator is a thirty-two-year-old Blackfeet Indian who lives on a ranch with his mother Teresa and her husband Lame Bull. He lives an aimless, unfulfilling life, hanging around the bars in the small towns that border the reservation, getting drunk, picking up women, and getting into fights. The great tragedy in his life was the loss of his brother Mose when the narrator was twelve and Mose was fourteen. In the accident that killed Mose, the narrator smashed his knee, which has never fully recovered. Even though he is intelligent and capable, the narrator has never had much of a career. He worked in a rehabilitation clinic in Tacoma, Washington, for two years, although his mother claims that he was there for much less than that. Then, he spent most of his time in bars in Seattle. Although, during the course of the novel the narrator does nothing of note, he does gain some dignity and self-respect when he discovers that he is the grandson of Yellow Calf, not the half-breed Doagie.

Teresa

Teresa is the narrator's mother. She is a widow who marries Lame Bull. Although she is Indian, she speaks disparagingly of other Indians. She is also a Catholic. Teresa is a rather bitter woman who is not known for her generosity of spirit. The narrator says he never expected much from her and nor did anyone else. Teresa was disappointed in her first marriage. She refers to her late husband as a fool. Teresa is also disillusioned about her son. She regrets that he has not made anything of his life, and she criticizes him for his failure. She does not like having him hang around the ranch and tries to get him to start looking for a job.

Yellow Calf

Yellow Calf is an old blind man who lives in a shack three miles from the narrator's home. He lives a spartan life in tune with nature. After he tells the narrator about the severe winter the Blackfeet endured when he was a boy, and tells what he knows about the narrator's grandmother, the narrator realizes that Yellow Calf is his grandfather.

Themes

Alienation

The narrator is in an alienated state of mind, closed off from his own emotions. He does not feel affection for his family or for his girlfriend. Neither

Topics for Further Study

- What do you think is the cause of the narrator's alienation? Is his alienation mostly his own psychological problem, or are there wider social causes of it, such as the difficulties of Indians living in a dominant white culture? Does the narrator grow and change during the course of the novel? If so, in what ways? Or, does he stay much the same?

- Research Native American religion and spirituality. What are its main characteristics, and how does it differ from the Judeo-Christian tradition?

- Research what current conditions are like on Native American reservations. Has life on reservations changed much in the thirty years since the novel was written? What are the main issues facing Native Americans living on reservations today, and how are those issues being addressed?

- Research the history of the Blackfeet and Gros Ventre tribes, and other tribes of the Great Plains, during the nineteenth century. How were they were forced onto reservations? What was the Dawes Act of 1887, and why did most Indian leaders oppose it?

does he feel any other emotions for them, such as hatred or guilt. His emotional life is simply flat. In the first chapter, which sets the tone for the novel, he refers to this state of mind as "distance," and says it has been growing in him for years. Part of this distance can be explained by the narrator's loss of his father and brother, both long dead. He comments toward the end of the novel that these two were the only people he ever loved. Since then, it appears, he has been unable to find his way in life and connect with others. He lacks self-knowledge and a sense of identity, which may explain why he remains unnamed. He does not really know who he is, and as a result, his life lacks purpose and direction. He hangs around the ranch even though his mother would sooner he went out and looked for a job. When he goes on small expeditions to the local towns, he never connects with anyone in a meaningful way. He drinks too much and the one-night stands he has with the women he picks up in bars are depressing affairs. When Marlene, one of the women, starts sobbing, the narrator cannot respond with an iota of empathy. He simply stares at her, and the image that comes to his mind is devoid of humanity:

> I was staring at the sobbing woman with the same lack of emotion, the same curiosity, as though I were watching a bug floating motionless down an irrigation ditch, not yet dead but having decided upon death.

The narrator is also alienated from the wider community in which he lives and from his cultural heritage. Culturally, as an Indian he is part of a minority group that is mistrusted by the white majority. When he returns home at the beginning of the novel, the narrator has just been in a fight with a white man in a bar, and in Havre, he feels "that helplessness of being in a world of stalking white men." But this is not a novel about the subjugation of Native Americans. The narrator does not get on any better with the Indians he meets in the towns, one of whom, Agnes's brother, beats him up. He admits, referring to Indians as well as whites, that "I was a stranger to both and both had beaten me."

Re-integration

Breaking through the prevailing mood of distance, alienation and separation, the narrator gains at least one moment when he feels more integrated with himself and his world. It comes when Yellow Calf, in telling the story of himself and the narrator's grandmother, obliquely hints that he, Yellow Calf, is the narrator's true grandfather. This is a moment of revelation for the narrator because up to that point, he has believed that a "half-breed" drifter named Doagie was his grandfather. Discovering an important fact about his true origins re-connects him to his family and perhaps also to his Indian cultural heritage, represented by the wise old Yellow Calf. When the narrator realizes the truth, he instinctively knows the importance of what has transpired, and he starts to laugh: "It was the laughter of one who understands a moment in his life, of one who has been let in on the secret through luck and circumstance."

Welch is a subtle writer, and he does not suggest that the narrator's life will now suddenly change for the better. But the ending of the novel does show the narrator in a positive frame of mind, ready to take more decisive action than he has in the past. He seems to be more in touch with his emotions also. When Ferdinand Horn's wife tells him that she has seen Agnes in Havre, it is "a stab in the heart" for the narrator. He realizes that he does feel something for her after all. Then in the final scene, as he stands at the graveside of his grandmother, he is still thinking of Agnes. He decides that "Next time I'd do it right. Buy her a couple of crèmes de menthe, maybe offer to marry her on the spot." Although the tone, in keeping with the rest of the epilogue, may not be entirely serious, the narrator seems now to be a changed man from the disaffected individual presented in the first chapter, who had no feelings for his girlfriend and was "as distant from [him]self as a hawk from the moon."

Style

Metaphor

The novel is structured around the metaphor of a journey, which represents the need to come home—to oneself and to one's family and heritage. It is a difficult journey, as the narrator himself announces in chapter 1, when he returns home from a night on the town: "Coming home was not easy anymore." After the first homecoming, the narrator goes away again, to Malta to find his girlfriend. Part 2 sees him back on the ranch, and then journeying once more, to Harlem and Havre. In part 3, he returns home again. Within this structure of departure and return, two more journeys are embedded in the form of flashbacks. These flashbacks are mental journeys made first by the narrator, as he recalls the events leading up to the tragic death of his brother, and second by Yellow Calf, as he recalls the terrible winter of starvation endured by the Blackfeet when Yellow Calf was in his teens.

Another way of understanding the journey metaphor is to see these journeys as episodes on the path of the most fundamental journey of all, the one that begins with birth and ends with death.

In part 4, the wise man Yellow Calf calls this the only cycle he knows. As if to remind the reader of the ultimate destination of all journeys, the novel begins and ends with the focus on death. First, the narrator sets the scene by referring to the grave of the Earthboys, a local family. More significantly, he also refers to the "borrow pit" (a place from which the earth has been excavated and used for other purposes) where—it is later disclosed—the narrator's father died. Then the novel ends with the burial of the narrator's grandmother.

Imagery

The image of blood that appears in the title of the novel represents passion, life energy, and connection to family, culture and race. Winter in the blood suggests that the blood in the narrator runs thin; he suffers from a kind of spiritual and mental anemia. The blood image returns at a significant moment in part 4, after the narrator's sudden realization that Yellow Calf is his grandfather. This realization was "as though it was his blood in my veins that had told me." In other words, Yellow Calf awakens the cultural and family blood that runs within the narrator, suggesting that the winter in the blood may be at an end.

The suggestion of regeneration is conveyed by another image, that of rain. At the end of part 4, after his strenuous struggle to free the calf, and Bird's collapse, the narrator lies on the ground, feeling the summer rain fall on his face. His thoughts turn to his dead brother and father, and for the first time in the novel they are peaceful rather than troubled thoughts. He thinks that First Raise and Mose will like the rain: "they were that way, good to be with, even on a rainy day." The peaceful nature of this scene is a marked contrast to the chilly wind and falling sleet that occurred as the narrator knelt before the dead body of his brother twenty years ago. The final paragraph of this scene, that concludes part 4, has an unmistakable feeling of something having been washed clean by the rain:

> Some people, I thought, will never know how pleasant it is to be distant in a clean rain, the driving rain of a summer storm. It's not like you'd expect, nothing like you'd expect.

Historical Context

Native Americans in 1960s and 1970s

Taking their cue from the civil rights and "black power" movements, Native Americans in the 1960s

Compare
&
Contrast

- **1970s:** The American Indian, Eskimo, and Aleut population numbers 827,000, which is 0.4 percent of the population of the United States. This represents an increase from 1950, when the Indian population numbered 343,410, which is only 0.2 percent of the population.

    Today: According to the 2000 census, there are more than 2.4 million American Indians and Alaska Natives (Eskimo and Aleut).

- **1970s:** The federal government takes action to preserve Indian rights and culture by promoting Indian self-determination. In 1975, Congress passes the Indian Self-Determination and Educational Assistance Act, under which Indian tribes may administer their own social programs such as housing and education. Congress also passes the Indian Child Welfare Act and the American Indian Religious Freedom Act in 1978.

    Today: Native American tribal governments have large responsibilities for the administration of their land. This includes protection of hunting and fishing rights, water rights, religious traditions, and cultural heritage. Many tribal governments have taken advantage of the 1988 Indian Gaming Regulatory Act, which permits gaming on tribal lands. Nearly 130 tribes in twenty-four states are involved in some kind of gaming.

- **1970s:** Large numbers of Native Americans live in poverty on Indian reservations. But because of growing Indian militancy, mainstream society and American policy-makers are forced to take notice of their plight.

    Today: The U.S. Civil Rights Commission reports to Congress in July 2003 that Native Americans still suffer high rates of poverty, poor educational achievement, substandard housing, and high rates of disease and illness. Native Americans continue to rank at or near the bottom of nearly every social, health, and economic indicator.

---

and 1970s became more assertive in their efforts to preserve their culture and improve their economic situation. In 1969, more than two hundred Native Americans from a group called Indians of all Tribes took over Alcatraz Island, the former federal penitentiary in San Francisco Bay. They used their occupation, which lasted until June 1971, to protest the conditions on Indian reservations.

There was plenty to protest. Native Americans were lower on the socio-economic ladder than any other minority group in the United States. In 1970, the median income of Indians was half that of whites, and over one-third of all Indians lived below the official poverty level. Housing conditions on many reservations were unsanitary, with some dwellings little better than shacks with no running water, sewers or electricity. Life expectancy for Indians was forty-four years, compared to sixty-six years for the general population; infant mortality was three times the national average; and teenage suicide was five times the national average. In 1973, the unemployment rate on Indian reservations averaged 37 percent.

There were more examples of Indian militancy in the early 1970s. A group of Native Americans established a settlement at Mount Rushmore in South Dakota to demonstrate their claims to the Black Hills. In November 1972, members of the American Indian Movement (AIM) occupied the Bureau of Indian Affairs building in Washington, D.C., to publicize their grievances. In 1973, AIM received national attention when two hundred of its members mounted an armed occupation of the town of Wounded Knee on the Pine Ridge Indian Reservation in South Dakota. Wounded Knee was the site of a massacre of three hundred Sioux Indians by U.S. soldiers in 1890.

The Native American Renaissance

Although Native American culture traditionally emphasized oral storytelling, works of fiction

Bison on the Fort Belknap Indian Reservation © Dave G. Houser/Corbis

by Indian writers existed from the early twentieth century. But it was not until the late 1960s that Indian literature began to blossom in unprecedented ways, as Native American writers developed a body of written work that helped to preserve and extend knowledge of Indian life and culture. A landmark event in what came to be known as the Native American Renaissance was the novel *House Made of Dawn* (1968) by N. Scott Momaday, a Kiowa, which was awarded the Pulitzer Prize for Fiction in 1969. The novel tells the story of a Native American who grows up on a reservation in New Mexico, fights in World War II, and then moves to Los Angeles, where he forgets his Native American roots in the harsh city environment.

During the 1970s, as more notable literature was produced by Native Americans, mainstream literary culture became more accepting of books which presented the Native American experience. The major publisher Harper & Row, for example, began a Native American Publishing Program, and the third book in that program was Welch's *Winter in the Blood*. Other important Native American works of the period include Leslie Marmon Silko's novel *Ceremony* (1977), Jo Harjo's poetry collection, *The Last Song* (1975), and *Voices from Wah'kon-tah* (1974), an anthology of Native American poetry.

Critical Overview

Winter in the Blood received warm praise from reviewers on publication. Reynolds Price, in a front-page review in the *New York Times Book Review*, was so impressed he argued that the novel should not be classified as an "Indian novel." He described it instead as "a nearly flawless novel about human life." Price commented on the way in which the narrator's life, so enclosed and self-defeating for most of the novel, was transformed at the end: "it opens onto light—and through natural, carefully prepared, but beautifully surprising narrative means: a recovery of the past; a venerable, maybe lovable, maybe usable past." In *Newsweek*, Margo Jefferson described the novel as "beautiful and austere." She commented that its "power lies in the individual scenes, with their spare dialogue and piercing detail, and in the atmosphere Welch . . . creates."

Winter in the Blood soon came to be considered a classic of Native American literature. In 1977, the Modern Language Association of America held a seminar on the novel at its annual convention. Arising from that session, an entire issue of *American Indian Quarterly* in 1978 was devoted to essays on the novel. Since that time, it has been the subject of much scholarly interest, with whole dissertations being devoted to it. Scholars have interpreted the novel in various ways. Some have placed it within the European literary tradition; others have examined its place within the Native American tradition, in the context of the myths and religions of the Blackfeet and Gros Ventre tribes. The tone of the novel has been variously interpreted as comic, tragic or satiric, and there has been discussion about whether the novel presents a negative picture of Indian life or offers the possibility of spiritual redemption.

Criticism

Bryan Aubrey

Aubrey holds a Ph.D. in English and has published many articles on twentieth century literature. In this essay, Aubrey analyzes the importance of Native American consciousness in the novel, as seen in the characters of the narrator and Yellow Calf.

Welch once commented that the reason he did not give his protagonist a name was because "he didn't do anything significant enough to give him a name" (quoted in Mary Jane Lupton's *James Welch: A Critical Companion*). Insignificant the narrator may in many ways be, but lying behind his ordinariness and the apparent meaninglessness of his existence are glimpses of something that is not ordinary and certainly not meaningless. As another critic, William Bevis, has pointed out, the narrator possesses "a very sophisticated consciousness . . . so sensitive, so observant, so intelligent, so articulate, so verbal" (quoted in *Understanding James Welch*, by Ron McFarland). MacFarland might well have added that even though Welch commented that he wrote within the "Western, European-American tradition" (quoted in McFarland), there is a distinctive Native American tinge to the way the narrator perceives the world; his poetic images and metaphors suggest a way of experiencing life that is quite different from the dominant Western view. When this is viewed in conjunction with the wisdom of old Yellow Calf, the novel reveals the presence of a Native American consciousness that still, even after centuries of domination and invalidation by the Eurocentric West, remains intact and is ready to reaffirm itself.

One of the major differences between the scientific, materialist worldview that has dominated Western thought for more than three hundred years and the Native American view is the relationship between humans and the rest of creation. In the scientific view, consciousness resides only in humans; the material world of rocks, earth, plants, and trees is essentially dead. And to the extent that the traditional Christian worldview has survived the onslaught from scientific rationalism, Westerners regard humans as quite distinct from the animal kingdom, since only humans have been endowed by their Creator with an immortal soul. However, this way of thinking is foreign to the Native American, for whom the entirety of creation is alive, and everything is connected in a web of interacting relationships.

Carol Lee Sanchez, herself a Native American, describes the difference between the two worldviews in her essay, "Animal, Vegetable, and Mineral: The Sacred Connection":

> Most Euro-American or Euro-Western peoples tend to separate themselves from "nature" and to rank humans above animals, plants, and minerals in hierarchical fashion, and so it is not easy for them to perceive or accept a *personal* relationship with what they describe as the "natural world." Native Americans believe themselves to be an integral part of the natural world. When we speak of "nature," we are also including ourselves.

Welch is not a didactic writer; he does not write specifically to express or promote the Native American worldview, and so the narrator in *Winter in the Blood* does not act as a mouthpiece for the Indian way. After all, he is drifting through life with no firm compass, alienated as much from Indians as from whites. But just as a man raised in the Deep South cannot wholly erase his southern accent no matter how long he has lived in New York, the narrator cannot entirely hide who he is and the culture he represents. This is particularly noticeable in his descriptions of animals and birds. As Mary Jane Lupton puts it, Welch characterizes "animals as near humans, by naming them and giving them histories. Animal references appear with great consistency, either as metaphors or as genuine presences." An example of this occurs when the narrator remembers the six ducks that drowned when he was a boy. He not only remembers the exact place it happened, he also observes that "The weeds grew more abundant there, as though their spirits had nourished the soil." It appears that even the lowly duck has a spiritual significance and a continuing connection to the place where it lived its earthly life. The circumlocution "as though" or "as if" is a frequent device the narrator uses in his descriptions of animal life, as if he feels the need to draw back from the full implications of his words and suggest they are merely metaphors. Be that as it may, he seems to be able to divine in non-human creatures a capacity for relationships with humans that are more than merely poetic. Arresting details

What Do I Read Next?

- Welch's *Killing Custer: The Battle of the Little Bighorn and the Fate of the Plains Indians* (1994) is his retelling of the story of the massacre of General Custer and the Seventh Cavalry by Sioux warriors at Little Bighorn in 1876, the aftermath of the battle, and Welch's experience of making the documentary film *Last Stand at Little Bighorn* with Paul Stekle for PBS in 1992.

- *Growing Up Native American: An Anthology* (1995), edited by Patricia Riley, includes writings by twenty-two Native American authors in which they tell stories of oppression and survival, of heritage denied and reclaimed.

- *The Lone Ranger and Tonto Fistfight in Heaven* (1993), by Spokane Indian writer Sherman Alexie, is a well-reviewed collection of twenty-two interconnected stories about life in and around the Spokane, Washington, Indian Reservation.

- *The Ancient Child: A Novel* (1990), by N. Scott Momaday, shapes the Kiowa myth of a boy who turned into a bear into a novel about Set, a Native American boy in search of his identity. Set was raised far from a reservation and, when he returns to Indian lands, he meets a young medicine woman named Grey, who reconnects him to his cultural heritage.

---

surface from time to time in this respect. At the end of part 4, when the narrator struggles to free the cow from the mud, a magpie alights on a fence post and "then squatted to watch." After the cow has been freed, the magpie flies closer, and "his metallic *awk! awk*! was almost conversational." It is just a hint, but here is a glimpse of a world in which all creatures are interrelated and have something to say to each other.

The most notable example of this is the narrator's old horse Bird, whom he has owned since he was a boy and who is a character in the novel in his own right. Long years of association between them enable the narrator to converse with Bird, and Bird has a range of personal responses to his words. When Bird gets tired and the narrator teases him, Bird "flicked his ears as if in irritation." When the narrator tries to free the cow and Bird for a moment does not cooperate, the narrator chides him and a repentant Bird "nodded his agreement." But the most remarkable moment between them comes as the narrator ponders the story he has just been told by Yellow Calf, about the winter of starvation endured by the narrator's grandmother. As the narrator thinks the story over, "Bird farted," and at that moment, the narrator suddenly realizes that Yellow Calf is his grandfather:

> And it came to me, as though it were riding one moment of the gusting wind, as though Bird had had it in him all the time and had passed it to me in that one instant of corruption.

Here, wind, horse, and human mind seem to come together in one stunning moment of secret communication and understanding. It is appropriate that this happens in the presence of Yellow Calf, because he is the wise old man of this tale. In Yellow Calf, the Native American worldview that hovers at the margins of the narrator's consciousness is seen in its fullest form. He appears in only two scenes in the novel, but his importance to its underlying theme is immense. When the narrator first visits Yellow Calf, in part 2, he tells the old man that no one should live alone, but Yellow Calf says that the deer provide him company in the evening. He talks to them and understands what they talk about amongst themselves. He says he understands other animals too, although some more than others. This shows that for Yellow Calf, in keeping with Native American tradition, there is a fluid interplay between the human and the nonhuman worlds. Understanding the animals comes perfectly naturally to him. He does not think it in any way remarkable. As Sanchez says regarding her Native American beliefs: "We are as familiar with the natures and aspects of our local animal populations

---

> **This pure quality of Yellow Calf's life is part of what the narrator calls his 'distance'; it is a distance from all corruption, superficiality and pettiness, and quite different from the distance that separates the narrator from himself and his environment."**

as we are the natures and personalities of our sisters, brothers, and cousins—because we believe all things are our relatives."

Yellow Calf says the deer are not happy because things on the earth have changed: "They know what a bad time it is. They can tell by the moon when the world is cockeyed." The narrator pokes fun at him, but if for a moment one puts aside culturally based beliefs that one cannot hold a conversation with a deer, Yellow Calf's gnomic comment is full of meaning. It suggests another level of alienation in the novel, beyond the merely personal condition of the narrator. In part 1, it is revealed that there are no longer any fish in the river that runs by Teresa's ranch, due to industrial pollution. It appears that Yellow Calf can sense the disturbance in the environment from the deer's reaction to it; the phrase "the world is cockeyed" suggests a pervasive condition of which a polluted river may be only one symptom. And when he says, cryptically, "sometimes it seems that one has to lean into the wind to stand straight," he again hints at some large disturbance of the environmental balance. He is the wise man who, despite his blindness, sees further than other men.

The second scene in which Yellow Calf appears, in part 4, is notable for the way in which the narrator seems to perceive Yellow Calf in terms of the old man's union with the natural world. At one point, Yellow Calf's "shoulders squared and hunched like the folded wings of a hawk"; and the narrator senses that behind his unseeing eyes, Yellow Calf lives in a world "as clean as the rustling willows, the bark of a fox or the odor of musk during mating season."

This pure quality of Yellow Calf's life is part of what the narrator calls his "distance"; it is a distance from all corruption, superficiality and

pettiness, and quite different from the distance that separates the narrator from himself and his environment. Yellow Calf lives deeply within himself and is on good terms with everything in the universe. At one point, the narrator remarks, "A mosquito took shelter in the hollow of his cheek, but he didn't notice." Needless to say, mosquitoes are not usually perceived as "taking shelter" on human skin. There is something remarkable, something unshakeable, about Yellow Calf that suggests a way of experiencing the world undreamed of by the impoverished Western imagination. It gives us the clue that, lying just beneath the surface of this rather bleak tale is something far more rich and strange than the dispiriting escapades of an aimless drunk.

Source: Bryan Aubrey, Critical Essay on *Winter in the Blood*, in *Novels for Students*, Thomson Gale, 2006.

Jim Charles and Richard Predmore

In the following essay excerpt, Charles and Predmore describe aspects of Winter in the Blood *amenable to formalistic analysis and crossliterary teaching.*

New Critical Approach: A Close Reading of Winter in the Blood

There are two main reasons for approaching American Indian literatures from a traditional literary critical standpoint. First, if you want to make the case that a novel like *Winter in the Blood* should be taught not only in an American Indian literatures course but also in a course on the contemporary American novel, then it would be smart to show that the novel contains all the complexity and richness of great literature. The best way to demonstrate this is to subject American Indian literature to formalistic analysis. Secondly, failing to combine formalistic literary analysis with a sociocultural critical approach can lead to mistakes and misemphases, which can be demonstrated through a careful analysis of the main character of *Winter in the Blood.*

On an obvious level there are aspects of the novel other than the main character and the story of his full development that are amenable to formalistic analysis. The five-part structure of the novel correlates with the developmental stages of the protagonist. Welch's "sparse" style is darkly, grotesquely, and absurdly comic. In addition, there are numerous stylistic connections to Eliot's "The Wasteland" in *Winter in the Blood*. These include the identity-changing consciousness of the no-name narrator, allusions to dryness and the coming rain, environmental pollution, alienation, the emptiness of modern urban life, and innumerable references to fishing. Other features of the novel lending themselves to formalistic analysis include the abundance of minor characters used by the author to develop the character of the protagonist as well as Welch's use of imagery and symbolism. For example he uses dryness, the color blue, fishing, scatology, coldness, and distance as major symbols in the novel.

Velie, in his criticism mentioned earlier, misses the main point of *Winter in the Blood* when he states, "There is no resolution at the end of the novel, the narrator does not find himself, or develop a new sense of identity." *Winter in the Blood* is built around the Blackfeet tradition of the narrator protagonist, who goes on a vision quest and takes a wife, enterprises that imply character development. For much of the novel, the protagonist quests in the wrong places—the nameless wasteland towns of northcentral Montana—and he quests for the wrong things: the gun and the razor stolen by his Cree girlfriend.

A complex array of problems besets the protagonist. He is battered by the white world, the "great earth of stalking white men." From a drunken white man, the protagonist receives his "wounded knee." The narrator protagonist suffers from guilt related to the death of his brother Mose. He has an on-again-off-again relationship with his father and a cold mother. His Cree girlfriend has left him.

A good portion of the novel is devoted to describing how lost the narrator is. At home, he is lost in his relationship with his mother and her new husband, Lame Bull. In the towns, he is surrounded by absurd conversations, nihilistic events (death in a bowl of oatmeal, for example), and sterile sexual encounters.

In the beginning of Part II, the narrator visits Yellow Calf, old and blind, and jokingly referred to as a "wise man." But Yellow Calf proves to be wise, and the wisdom he imparts to the protagonist provides direction for the protagonist's impending regeneration. First, the narrator comments on how "clean and spare" the old man's shack is (in marked contrast to the other indoor locations in the novel that are described as messy). Yellow Calf says, "It's easier to keep it sparse than to feel the sorrows of possessions." The deficiency of material possessions is a lesson that comes relatively easily to the narrator who says to Yellow Calf, "'Possessions can be sorrowful.' I agreed, thinking of my gun and electric razor." The dawning growth in character contrasts sharply with the possessiveness of Lame Bull. Secondly, through Yellow Calf, the narrator

> *Winter in the Blood* is built around the Blackfeet tradition of the narrator protagonist, who goes on a vision quest and takes a wife, enterprises that imply character development."

is exposed to Welch's suggestion of a traditional American Indian outlook on nature. This culminates with the narrator's recognition of Yellow Calf's ability to understand animals: "Yellow Calf was facing off toward the river, listening to two magpies argue." The old man's third lesson is the simplest of them all. He tells the narrator, "You must say hello to Teresa for me. Tell her that I am living to the best of my ability." In contrast, as he wanders through the wasteland towns, the narrator does not live to the best of his ability.

Distance is a metaphor that Welch uses to describe modern alienation: "none of them counted; not one meant anything to me. And for no reason. I felt . . . nothing but a distance that had grown through the years." Distance is a condition of life in northern Montana. According to the narrator: "The country had created a distance as deep as it was empty, and the people accepted and treated each other with distance." This distance dominates the lives of the people in the town sections of the novel. The sordid Malvina keeps photos on her night table, "all [of which] were of Malvina alone in various places." The man in the khaki suit, with whom the narrator spends the most time in the town passages of the novel, is most often identified as "the man who tore up his airplane ticket." We cannot figure out where he really comes from, who is family is, or why he wants to go to Canada, if indeed he really does. One of the first things he says to the narrator is about fishing: "I'll take you out with me tomorrow and if we don't catch any fish, I'll buy the biggest steak in—where are we?—Malta!"

In the town sections, the Cree girl represents the opposite pull from the distance and coldness of the man who tore up his airplane ticket. In her eyes the narrator sees "the promise of warm things, of a spirit that went beyond her miserable life of drinking

Street in Malta, Montana © Sheldan Collins/Corbis

and screwing and men like me." The narrator increasingly realizes that if he should go with the airplane man, he "would become somebody else, and the girl would have no meaning for me." He says, "I wanted to be with her, but I didn't move." In a signal moment in the novel, in Havre the narrator sees the airplane man standing in front of the Palace Bar and then sees the entrance to Gable's Bar, into which the Cree girl has just gone. The narrator throws the keys to the Falcon into the air, indicating the narrator's choice. Tossing the keys signals his growth and development: he steps toward the warmth and closeness of a relationship with the Cree girl.

There are clear indications that the narrator is on the mend, that his quest is leading him out of the wasteland. He leaves town and drives to his mother's farm, where he describes bathing himself, a cleansing of the towns from his life. By this time, he has ceased worrying about his gun and razor. Cold and unemotional to this point in the novel, the narrator demonstrates, true feelings—for Marlene, for the Cree girl, and for the professor's daughter. He sees their childlike vulnerability.

In the episode where the narrator and Bird pull the cow out of the mud, the protagonist gets mad for the first time in the novel. Immediately following his healthy outburst, he says, "I crouched and

spent the next few minutes planning my new life." Through memory, he relives the death of Mose and seems to be making progress in ridding himself of the "final burden of guilt." The narrator has warm and loving memories of both First Raise and Mose. He throws his grandmother's old medicine pouch into her grave, an act of closeness to the distant old woman. Another indication of the narrator's growth is indicated in the story of his favorite horse, Bird. He explains how brutal the training was and how hard Bird's life was. In his own way, the narrator, like Yellow Calf, respects the life and wisdom that animates nature: "You have grown old, Bird, so old this sun consults your bones for weather reports." The narrator no longer mocks the old man's sympathetic relationship with nature, and he certainly has outgrown the Michigan professor who "spoke about the countryside as if it were dead."

Given the tough life the narrator describes as the old cow horse's lot, and given Bird's valiant work and sacrificing his life to pull the stupid cow out of the mud, it is clear that the narrator is thinking about Yellow Calf's earlier advice about living life to the best of one's ability. His hard work to save the cow represents a change for him because it is only the second time in the novel readers have seen him work.

After his grandmother's death, the protagonist rides the three miles to inform Yellow Calf.

In his third conversation with the wise man, he learns that Yellow Calf was his grandmother's lover, which makes Yellow Calf the father of the narrator's mother; it makes Yellow Calf the narrator's grandfather. The narrator's growth here parallels the growth of Jack in *All the King's Men*. Both learn their real lineage. Just as important, the narrator learns his grandmother's full story, that she was widowed as a young woman during the brutal winter of 1883–84 and was ostracized from the tribe. It was the teenaged Yellow Calf who hunted game for her through the winter, insuring her survival.

The best way to see the narrator's growth is to realize that his Cree girlfriend is just as lost and ostracized and just as in need of help in the Montana towns as the grandmother was during the desperate winter of 1883. At the end of the novel, when he thinks of marrying the Cree girl, the narrator is obviously thinking of following in his grandfather's footsteps.

Finally, the meaning of temperature and distance and the title of the novel are all made clear. The narrator has always seemed to have winter in his blood; that is, his character has seemed as cold and distant as the Montana winter. But what we learn at the end is that Yellow Calf had given "winter in the blood" a different meaning. Yellow Calf's life showed that even in the worst of times, distance and coldness can be overcome by closeness and warmth. The novel demonstrates the narrator's new warmth: he has genuine feelings for the Cree girl, Marlene, and the professor's sickly daughter; he rescues the stupid cow; he loves First Raise and Mose. All these actions and thoughts show that Yellow Calf's "warmth in the blood" runs through the narrator's veins and that he may indeed end up being able to "live to the best of his ability."

Source: Jim Charles and Richard Predmore, "When Critical Approaches Converge: Team-Teaching Welch's *Winter in the Blood*," in *SAIL: Studies in American Indian Literatures*, Vol. 8, No. 2, Summer 1996, pp. 47–60.

Alan R. Velie

In the following essay, Velie describes how Winter in the Blood, *rather than being a "protest novel," meets all the requirements—characterization, ending, and tone—that define a dramatic comedy.*

If my students are any indication, many white American readers expect any novel written by an Indian, about an Indian protagonist who meets hard times, to be a bitter protest about white oppression of noble red men. Although *House Made of Dawn* and *Winter in the Blood* are by Indians, about

> " Welch's humor varies from raucous farce to subtle satire, and it informs every corner of the novel."

Indians who are pretty well buffered by life, they are not protest novels, though they are often read that way. In my opinion to read them as protest novels is to reduce complex books into simplistic melodramas based on racial stereotypes of noble savage and white oppressor.

It seems to me that there is something condescending and even bigoted about not allowing blacks and Indians to determine their own attitudes about life in America. Too often we expect, even demand, that they be furious with whites and concentrate their efforts on reviling them. Black poet Al Young ridicules this attitude:

> Dont nobody want no nice nigger no more
> these honkies man that put out
> these books & things
> they want an angry split
> a furious nigrah
> they dont want no bourgeois woogie
> they want them a militant nigger
> in a fiji haircut
> fresh out of some secret boot camp
> with a bad book in one hand
> & a molotov cocktail in the other
> subject to turn up at one of their conferences
> or soirees
> & shake the s—— out of them

Like Young, James Welch deplores this attitude on the part of those whites who consider themselves sympathetic to the Indian plight. In explaining why he thinks only an Indian can write honestly about Indians, he says:

> I have seen poems about Indians written by whites and they are either sentimental or outraged over the condition of the Indian. . . . For the most part only an Indian knows who he is—an individual who just happens to be Indian. . . . And hopefully he will have the toughness and fairness to present his material in a way that is not manufactured by conventional stance.

Welch's writing is certainly not "manufactured by conventional stance." Although he is occasionally outraged, he is never sentimental, and his outrage is selective. He despises bigotry and bigots, and attacks them. In "Harlem, Montana: Just off the Reservation" he derides "Harlem on the rocks, / so bigoted, you forget the latest joke," and in "In My First Hard Springtime" he says Montana bigots "are white and common." But Welch has many other moods and stances as well, and *Winter in the Blood* is in no way a protest novel. Not only is it far more complex, it really is neither bitter nor angry. In fact, although it is powerful and moving in places, it is primarily comic.

Once one abandons the idea that all Indian novels must be angry, it is not surprising to find that *Winter in the Blood* has a strong comic undercurrent. The comic novel is becoming the dominant genre in fiction today. Reed, Pynchon, Barth, Barthelme, Vonnegut, Heller, Roth, and Elkins differ widely from one another, but their vision of the world is fundamentally comic. And Welch, Although he is isolated geographically in Montana, is a writer who is well aware of literary trends. Much of his poetry evinces the influence of the surrealism which Robert Bly and James Wright have imported from South America. In his fiction he employs his own variation of the black humor used by Reed, Pynchon, et al.

Before discussing *Winter in the Blood* as a comic novel, perhaps I had better define the term. Traditionally, dramatic genres have been more sharply defined than fictional ones. The basis for identifying dramatic comedy for thousands of years has been characterization, ending, and tone. Donatus and Evanthius, fourth-century grammarians whose commentaries on Terence were appended to his work, were extremely influential in determining Renaissance ideas of comedy. These ideas, put into practice by playwrights like Shakespeare and Jonson, determined the shape of comedy for centuries. Essentially Donatus and Evanthius defined comedy on the oasis of the modest state of the characters ("mediocrity of human fortune" Evanthius called it), the light tone of the work ("pleasingly witty" is Evanthius' phrase), and its happy ending, which usually involved marriage on the part of the hero and heroine.

These distinctions are less helpful in differentiating types of novels. We cannot identify novels on the basis of ending, for instance. Jane Austen's novels end happily with marriage, but many comic novels today end with the thwarting or discomfiture of the hero. In others, the hero is in no better shape at the end than when we found him at the outset. Nabokov's Pnin has lost his job as well as his wife. Roth's Portnoy is no closer to maturity or stability than he ever was. Heller's Yossarian is literally as well as figuratively at sea. What is more, non-comic novels often end on a positive note—

take, for example, *A Portrait of the Artist as a Young Man*, *House Made of Dawn* and *Ceremony*.

Method of characterization gives us some basis for differentiation between comic and non-comic novels, but only if we discard the notion of status, whether in the sense of rank, as the Romans and Greeks conceived it, or in the sense that Northrop Frye uses it to describe the hero of high and low mimetic mode. Rank is irrelevant not only today, but was so even to Shakespeare, who use a duke as protagonist in *Twelfth Night*. And, as Frye points out, although the low mimetic mode, in which the hero is "one of us," is the mode of most comedy, it is also the mode of much realistic fiction. Further, the ironic mode, in which the hero is inferior in power or intelligence to ourselves, can be used not only for farcical comedy, but also for works like *The Scarlet Letter* and *Billy Budd,* in which Hester Prynne and Billy Budd are pharmakoi or scapegoats.

The important thing about characterization is the attitude the author takes towards the character—how much dignity he allows him. If the author treats the character with compassion and allows him dignity, whether he is high mimetic like Hamlet, or ironic like Billy Budd, the character has a tragic, or at any rate serious, dimension. If the author undercuts the character's dignity, holds him up to ridicule either by the situation he puts him in or simply by the way he describes him, we have comedy. There is pathos in the situation of Humbert, Yossarian, Portnoy, and Welch's narrator, but all are treated comically.

It is tone, however, that is the primary basis for the general understanding of the term "comic novel." By and large, a comic novel is a longish work of fiction which contains a liberal amount of humor—or, to put it most concisely, a funny book. On the basis of this definition, *Winter in the Blood* qualifies as a comic novel. The first sentence of the book should let us know what sort of novel we will find; "In the tall weeds of the borrow pit, I took a leak and watched the sorrel mare, her colt beside her, walk through burnt grass to the shady side of the log and mud cabin." There is no lofty seriousness here, just a man performing a function everyone, whatever he might protest to the contrary, finds funny and undignified. Scatology, which plays an important part in the novel, as we shall see or the climax of the book, has been an important ingredient of comedy since the dawn of time. Chaucer, Rabelais, and Faulkner use scatology as a way of making man absurd and comical.

Welch's humor varies from raucous farce to subtle satire, and it informs every corner of the novel. The broadest humor is in scenes like the one in which the unknown man dies face down in his oatmeal, or the one in which the narrator and the airplane man march through the streets of Havre, the narrator with a purple teddy bear, the airplane man with five boxes of chocolate covered cherries under his arm.

Most of the humor is verbal, however. Welch makes masterful use of ironic diction to undercut the dignity of his characters. Here, for example, is Lame Bull:

> Lame Bull had married 360 acres of hay land, all irrigated, leveled, some of the best land in the valley, as well as a 2000-acre grazing lease.

> We brought in the first crop, Lame Bull mowing alfalfa, snakes, bluejoint, baby rabbits, tangles of barbed wire, sometimes changing sickles four times in a single day.

> Lame Bull's hand was in a sling made from a plaid shirt. The more he drank the more the sling pulled his neck down, until he was talking to the floor. The more he talked to the floor the more he nodded. It was as though the floor were talking back to him, grave words that kept him nodding gravely.

Welch's general technique, which he uses most skillfully in the final scene of the novel, the grandmother's funeral, is to start a description as if planned to allow a character some dignity, and then to pull the rug out from under him suddenly:

> I had to admit that Lame Bull looked pretty good. The buttons on his shiny green suit looked like they were made of wood. Although his crotch hung a little low, the pants were the latest style. Teresa had shortened the legs that morning, a makeshift job, having only had time to tack the original cuffs up inside the pant legs.

> Teresa wore a black coat, black high heels, and a black cupcake hat. . . . Once again she was big and handsome—except for her legs. They appeared to be a little skinny, but it must have been the dress.

Welch starts out by telling us that both characters look good, but in describing them reveals that Lame Bull's crotch is baggy and Teresa's legs are skinny.

However long a list we make of funny things in *Winter in the Blood,* two questions arise: How much humor is enough to make a novel comic, and what happens if in addition to the humor there is a good deal of pathos? It is impossible to give a quantitative answer to the first question, but both questions can be answered at once if we say that in a comic novel the author plays most key situations for laughs rather than pathos. Hamlet has some funny lines, and so does Mercutio, but in the climactic scenes *Hamlet* and *Romeo and Juliet* are tragic. There is some genuine pathos in *Winter in the Blood,* the most obvious example being the death of Mose. But in the most important scenes, the epiphany in which the hero recognizes his roots, and the funeral, Welch deliberately opts for comedy.

Let us begin with the epiphany, to use Joyce's term, the sudden revelation of truth which transforms the hero's way of looking at the world. The truth that the hero realizes is that Yellow Calf is his grandfather, the man who saved his grandmother from dying of starvation and exposure. The death of the narrator's father and his brother had left him with winter in his blood—he was numbed emotionally, unable to feel love or compassion for anyone. He felt no closeness towards his mother and very little towards Agnes, the Cree girl he brought home and then ignored while he went on a bender for several days. At the beginning of the book he describes his reluctant homecoming: "Coming home to a mother and an old lady who was my grandmother. And the girl who was thought to be my wife. But she didn't really count. For that matter none of them counted; no tone meant anything to me." The "old lady who was my grandmother" becomes more real to the narrator when Yellow Calf tells him the story of how the Blackfeet cast her out to die during a terrible winter. The narrator sees her as a young, beautiful, and vulnerable woman whereas earlier he had thought of her as bloodless and superannuated. In a flash of insight he realizes that Yellow Calf is the hunter who had provided her with meat and kept her alive. The discovery moves the narrator first to laughter, then to tears. It is a special type of laughter that has nothing to do with humor. "It was the laughter of one who understands a moment in his life, of one who has been let in on the secret through luck and circumstance. . . . And the wave behind my eyes broke." This does not sound very funny, and Reynolds Price, after describing the "beautifully surprising narrative means" that Welch uses in the scene, goes on to say of it: "Welch's new version of the central scene in all narrative literature (the finding of lost kin) can stand proudly with its most moving predecessors in epic, drama, and fiction." Perhaps so, but Price is missing a point here: there is key difference from the reunion of Odysseus and Telemachus, for instance, and that is the element of farce that Welch introduces into the epiphany scene:

> I thought for a moment.

> Bird farted.

> And it came to me, as though it were riding one moment of the gusting wind, as though Bird had had it in him all the time and passed it to me in that one instant of corruption.

Welch uses scatology to undercut the sentimentality of the moment.

Perhaps the best, funniest, and most success-ful scene in the novel is the ending. Normally funerals are not the stuff of comedy since death is not something people usually laugh about. If treated properly however, anything, even death, can be a source of humor, and Welch succeeds in making the funeral comic.

Because *House Made of Dawn* also ends with the death of a grandparent of the hero, some inter-esting comparisons present themselves. In both books the grandparents who die serve as the hero's link with the past and with his traditional culture. When Abel's grandfather dies, Abel sees that he is buried in the prescribed Tanoan manner, then goes out to run in the race for good hunting and harvest that his grandfather had won. This marks the first time since his return from the army that Abel had been able to participate meaningfully in a Tanoan ritual, and it marks his reentry into his native cul-ture. In an important sense it is for Abel a happy ending, although it is certainly not comic.

Since Welch's narrator has just learned the story of his grandmother's life and has been moved by it, we might expect Welch to treat the old lady's death and burial seriously showing how the narra-tor had developed closer ties to his culture, or at least that he had a new respect and deeper feelings for his grandmother. This is not the case. The nar-rator feels only ironic detachment towards his grandmother. After describing what Lame Bull and Teresa are wearing the narrator says, "The old lady wore a shiny orange coffin." Welch adds a farcical touch in having Lame Bull and the narrator fail to dig the grave properly. The coffin is too big, and Lame Bull has to climb into the pit and jump up and down on the box.

Lame Bull's eulogy for the old woman is a highly comic masterpiece of left-handed praise: "Here lies a simple woman . . . who devoted her life to . . . rocking . . . and not a bad word about anybody . . . Not the best mother in the world . . . but a good mother, notwithstanding . . . who could take it and dish it out . . . who never gave anybody any crap." As counter-point to lame Bull's speech, we have the random thoughts of the hero, who is not sufficiently interested in the proceedings to keep his mind on them. He thinks that the weather would probably be good for fishing, that maybe he ought to see a doctor for his leg, and that maybe if he got a few drinks into Agnes and proposed to her he might get her back. Obviously Welch is not taking his hero seriously here, nor treating the funeral as a serious occasion. Quite clearly he is presenting the situation comically so that it will amuse the reader.

Winter in the Blood starts and ends on a comic note. In between the tone varies from pathos (in the scene in which Mose is hit by a car) to farce (in the scenes in the hotel bar with the airplane man). It never approaches the stridency and bit-terness of a protest novel. Throughout most of the book and certainly in most of the key scenes, the tone is richly comic.

Source: Alan R. Velie, "*Winter in the Blood* as Comic Novel," in *Critical Perspectives on Native American Fic-tion*, edited by Richard F. Fleck, Three Continents Press, 1993, pp. 189–94.

A. Lavonne Ruoff

In the following essay excerpt, Ruoff analyzes through a cultural context the narrator's "rela-tionships with and characterizations of" the females of Winter in the Blood.

> But the distance I felt came not from country or peo-ple; it came from within me. I was as distant from myself as a hawk from the moon. And that was why I had no particular feelings toward my mother and grandmother. Or the girl who had come to live with me

In the words quoted above, the nameless nar-rator of *Winter in the Blood* summarizes the sense of alienation which plagues him and which must be exorcised before he can become whole within him-self and can close the distance he feels between him-self and the external world. To do so, he undertakes a spiritual and physical journey into experience and memory to find the truth about his own feelings and about his family and girlfriend. Through most of the novel, the only people he really loves are his brother Mose and his father First Raise. After Mose was killed by an automobile on the highway while the two boys were herding cattle back to the ranch, the narrator became a "servant to a memory of death." Though the loss of the brother was immediate, the loss of his father was gradual. Following the acci-dent, First Raise was home less and less often un-til he finally froze to death on a drunken binge. In the ten years since his father's death, the narrator has been able to do nothing of consequence. The closeness he feels to them contrasts with the dis-tance he feels from the females in the novel— human and animal. The purpose of this paper will be to examine the causes and resolution of the narrator's sense of alienation through an analysis of the cultural context—traditional as well as contemporary—of his relationships with and char-acterizations of these females.

The chain of circumstances which ultimately leads to the narrator's feeling of separateness begins with his grandmother, who is at once the unwitting cause of the family's isolation from the Blackfeet tribe and the means by which the narrator can partially learn about them and his family. Despite the many stories about her early life which the grandmother told her young grandson, she revealed only part of the truth about her life with Standing Bear's band of Blackfeet. In order for the narrator to determine the truth about her life and about the identity of his own grandfather, he must obtain the other parts of the story from blind, old Yellow Calf after his grandmother's death.

A beautiful girl thirty years younger than her husband, she slept with Chief Standing Bear only to keep him warm and to sing softly in his ear. The "bad medicine," which isolated not only the grandmother but also her descendants, began with the migration of her husband's band of Blackfeet from their traditional hunting grounds. After moving into Gros Ventre territory, they endured one of the hardest winters in memory. The details of the starvation winter of 1883–84 come from Yellow Calf, who lost all of his family to starvation or pneumonia.

After Standing Bear's death in a raid on the Gros Ventres, the young widow of not yet twenty was made an outcast by the band. The grandmother attributed their action to the women's envy for her dark beauty and to the men's fear of the women's anger if they helped her as well as to their own reticence because of her position as Standing Bear's widow. However, Yellow Calf attributes the mistreatment to a combination of physical, psychological, and religious causes: "She had not been with us more than a month or two, maybe three. You must understand the thinking. In that time the soldiers came, the people had to leave their home up near the mountains, then the starvation and death of their leaders. She had brought them bad medicine." Her beauty, which had been a source of pride, now mocked them and their situation. Thus, in the case of the grandmother, the source of alienation was external, resulting from circumstances beyond her control. Her isolation from the band became permanent when they were driven like cows by the soldiers to the new Blackfeet Reservation, established in 1888 at the same time as that for the Gros Ventres and Assiniboins at Fort Belknap. Because the band did not mention her to the soldiers and because she had moved a distance from the band in the spring, the soldiers thought she was Gros Ventre.

In addition to attempting to determine the facts about the band's treatment of his grandmother, the narrator also tries to find out who hunted for her. Frustrated by yellow Calf's refusal to answer his questions, the narrator suddenly realizes—at the

> **However, his wanting a close relationship with a woman, even if he has to commit himself to marriage, demonstrates how far he has progressed from the distance he felt within himself and from the women in his life which he expressed at the beginning of the novel."**

moment his horse Bird farts—that Yellow Calf was that hunter. Solving his puzzle also solves those of the identity of his grandfather and of his own tribal heritage. At the beginning of the novel, the narrator explains that his grandmother "remained a widow for twenty-five years before she met a half-white drifter named Doagie, who had probably built this house where now the old lady snored and I lay awake thinking that I couldn't remember this fact." However, he does remember the rumors that Doagie was not his real grandfather.

Between the time she was abandoned by the Blackfeet band and the time she took in Doagie, the grandmother continued to live in isolation, separated by three miles from Yellow Calf, her secret visitor. Despite his realization of his grandfather's identity, the narrator cannot explain the distance between Yellow Calf and his grandmother: why the two waited twenty-five years after Standing Bear's death to procreate a child or why they continued to live separately afterward. Certainly the respect both had for Standing Bear is a very important part of the explanation. Their separation prior to the conception of Teresa may also be partially explained as an allusion to one of the myths about the origin of the Blackfeet. Although men and women lived separately at one time, Old Man (Na'pi), a creator-trickster figure in Blackfeet mythology, brought them together so that they could continue and so that the men would abandon their lazy dissolute ways and learn from the women's example of orderly self-government and mastery of agriculture and domestic arts. The theme of the separation of males and females is repeated in the relationships between Teresa and First Raise and between the narrator and Agnes.

A third part of the explanation may be found in the traditional Blackfeet taboo against intermarriage within the band. Because the male members of the band were considered relatives, there was an old law against such intermarriage. By the time the bands were settled on the reservation, intermarriage was no longer considered a crime but was still bad form. Consequently, when the grandmother (then about forty-five) and Yellow Calf conceived a child almost at the last opportunity before the onset of her menopause, they were violating a taboo in order to recreate a new race of Blackfeet in an alien land. Having done this, however, they chose to remain apart and the grandmother chose to obscure the fatherhood of the child through living with Doagie. Nevertheless, this violation of custom was one more portion of the bad medicine passed on to the daughter Teresa.

The unwitting cause of the family's isolation from other Blackfeet, the grandmother still serves as its link to the tribe's culture and history. The power of the oral tradition she transmits is retained in the memory of the narrator. Advancing age has not diminished the strength of her contempt for those who made her an outcast or her hatred for such old enemies as the Crees. Too weak and feeble now even to chew regular food or to go the toilet by herself, she is still fierce enough to wear a paring knife in her legging and plot ways to slit the throat of Agnes, her grandson's Cree girlfriend. Almost a hundred years old when the novel opens, the grandmother now communicates with her family with an occasional "ai" or squeak of her rocker.

In her silent old age, she must endure the vulgar teasing of Lame Bull, in violation of the old Blackfeet taboo that a man should not speak to his mother-in-law or even look at her, which was equally binding on her. Also violated is the taboo that although a mother-in-law might be supported by her son-in-law, she must live not in the same tepee with him but rather in a smaller one set up some distance away. She must also endure the disinterest of her grandson, who usually regards her as a subject for bad jokes or detached curiosity. His treatment of her is a deviation from the traditional respect children were expected to show elders.

Though she clung to the old ways in life, she is denied them in death by Teresa, who insists that she be properly prepared for burial by the undertaker in near-by Harlem. Ironically, she is sealed up in her shiny coffin so that no one gets to see his handiwork. Her funeral is neither Catholic nor traditional Blackfeet. Only her grandson observes a bit of the old burial customs by throwing onto her

grave her one surviving possession from the old life—the tobacco pouch with its arrowhead. Having reached the end of his odyssey to find the truth about himself and his background, the narrator casts away the bundle containing the bad medicine which has plagued the family.

Teresa combines her mother's solemn dignity and fierce determination to survive with her own alienation from Blackfeet traditions. Because she rejected these in favor of acculturation, she is alienated both from the beliefs of her mother and from the dreams and desires of her first husband and sons. The most valuable material possessions passed on to Teresa by her mother are the land acquired through mistaken identity and a house built by a man she wrongly believed to be her father. Although the ranch supports the family, it has destroyed what has been traditional Blackfeet role structure by making the male financially independent on the female and by forcing the male to give up hunting for ranching to provide for his family. For solace and understanding, she turns to Catholicism and to friendship with the Harlem priest, who makes Indians come to "his church, his saints and holy water, his feuding eyes."

The differences between Teresa and the men in her family are revealed in her son's description of her as having always had "a clear bitter look, not without humor, that made others of us seem excessive, too eager to talk too much, drink too much, breathe too fast." She approves hard work on the ranch and disapproves foolishness and fighting. Whatever natural intolerance she possessed has been sharpened by her experiences with First Raise and her son. As a result, she has developed the ability to interpret things as she wishes to see them and to ignore what she does not, as her memories of First Raise demonstrate. At the same time that she tells her son that his father was not around enough, she insists that he accomplished what he set out to do. When her son points out her inconsistency, she merely says that he has mixed his father up with himself. Her only explanation of why First Raise stayed away so much is that he was a "foolish man" who "could never settle down"—a wanderer just like her son and "just like all these damned Indians."

Because Teresa is primarily concerned with doing what has to be done in order to provide for her family and to keep the ranch going, she marries Lame Bull shortly after her son arrives home from his latest spree in town. Clearly, she has no illusions about Lame Bull, whose advances she has previously resisted. When he jokes that her son has said she is ready to marry him, she replies in her clear, bitter voice that "my son tells lies that would make a weasel think twice. He was cut from the same mold as you." Although after their marriage she complains about Lame Bull's sloppy habits and his teasing of her mother, she is obviously sexually attracted to him. Lame Bull responds to her complaints only by grinning a silent challenge, and "the summer nights came alive in the bedroom off the kitchen. Teresa must have liked his music."

Her relationship with her son is complicated both by her own personality and by his inner turmoil. Like his father, whom he describes as "always in transit" before his death, the narrator can neither live with Teresa nor leave her permanently. The conflict between mother and son is clear from Teresa's first words after he arrives home. Immediately accosting him with the news that his "wife" Agnes took off with his gun and electric razor shortly after he left for town, she simultaneously urges him to get his property back and defends herself for not stopping the girl: "What did you expect me to do? I have your grandmother to look after, I have no strength, and she is young—Cree!" Her tactic of squeezing into one breath as much advice, criticism, and self-defense as possible only antagonizes and further alienates her son. Because she feels that her son's only real problems are that he is a wanderer like all Indians and that he is too sensitive, she cannot understand why he did not stay on at the Tacoma hospital, where he was offered a job after having an operation on his leg. His explanation that he was hired only as a token Indian male to help the hospital qualify for grant money does not penetrate her consciousness. His bitterness at her lack of understanding is summed up in his comment that "I never expected much from Teresa and never got it. But neither did anybody else. Maybe that's why First Raise stayed away so much."

The narrator's discussion with Teresa about his pet duck, Amos, which precedes their discussion of First Raise and of the narrator himself, dramatically reveals the nature and possible consequences of their conflict. It is Teresa who reminds her son about Amos, and her habitually negative recollections become a springboard for her running commentary about her first husband, sons, and Indians in general. She recalls that First Raise won Amos pitching pennies at the fair when "he was so drunk that he couldn't even see the plates" and that the other ducklings drowned because her sons did not keep the tub full of water for them—"You boys were like that." When the narrator tries to explains that Amos, who had remained perched on the edge

of the tub while his siblings plunged to the bottom, survived because he was smarter than the other ducklings, she dismisses his theory with the remark that "He was lucky. One duck can't be smarter than other. They're like Indians." As far as she was concerned, the other ducks were crazy.

Like the narrator, Amos inexplicably survived a disastrous accident which killed his siblings. While the narrator is just as unable to solve this puzzle as he is that of his own survival when Mose died, he does, in the course of this conversation with Teresa, learn that she killed Amos—a truth so horrifying that he desperately tries to avoid comprehending it. When he realizes that the answer to the question of who killed Amos, one he did not want to ask, is going to be either his mother or first Raise, the implications so traumatize him that he tries to suggest, instead, that one or the other of them killed the hated turkey which used to attack him, not Amos, who must have been killed by the bobcat. Matter-of-factly leading her son to a truth he does not want to face, Teresa quietly confesses that she did indeed kill Amos. In her own eyes, she has done what her husband and sons could not do—sacrifice sentiment for practicality by killing the pet duck for Christmas dinner. Her act symbolizes the reversal of traditional male and female roles: because the hunter now can only dream of bringing elk meat home from Glacier Park, the mother is forced to provide food by whatever means available. Although the narrator is reacting to what he feels is the deliberate murder of Amos by his mother and to becoming an accomplice when he unknowingly eats his pet, he does not yet really perceive that the power of life and death Teresa held over Amos is held over him as well. This realization is revealed symbolically as he recalls his dream after the sexual encounter with the barmaid from Malta.

The conflict between mother and son is intensified by the intrusion of the opposite sex. Although Teresa treats Agnes with cold politeness because she thinks the girl is her son's wife, she does not hesitate to point out that the girl is not happy and belongs in town, which the narrator realizes means Agnes belongs in bars. Consequently, she disapproves of her son's wanting to bring Agnes back. Teresa's marriage to Lame Bull and her friendship with the Harlem priest increase the narrator's hostility toward his mother. He cannot bear to see his father replaced by Lame Bull, whom he detests as a crafty, vulgar down and whom he thinks married his mother for her ranch. Realizing that marriage to Lame Bull means that her son must leave, Teresa tells her son to start looking around because there is not enough for him on the ranch. The narrator also cannot bear his mother's drinking partnership with the priest. When the latter sent Teresa a letter, the narrator wants to read it, "to see what a priest would have to say to a woman who was his friend. I had heard of priests having drinking partners, fishing partners, but never a woman partner." Instead, because he cannot even bring himself to see her name inside the envelope, he tears the letter up between his legs.

The Oedipal jealousy he feels is part of his inability to separate himself from her and to see himself and his mother as they really are rather than as his distorted perception makes them seem. Welch provides evidence that the narrator's view is not held by everybody. When the bartender in Malta comments that Teresa is "a good one—one of the liveliest little gals I know of," the narrator wryly comments that "She is bigger than you are, bigger than both of us put together." The best example of the tender side of her nature is her care and love for her mother. The narrator is so distanced from himself and her that he has no perception of how hard the physical and psychological drain of running the ranch, raising her family, and caring for an aged mother have been on Teresa. Now fifty-six years old, she is worn down by the endless demands on her by a mother almost a hundred years old and son of thirty-two whose chief occupation seems to be getting drunk, laid, and beaten up. Her acts of genuine caring and her grief at the death of her mother contrast with the behavior of both the narrator and Lame Bull. Rather than join her new husband and her son in drinking "Vin Rose" after the grandmother's grave is dug, she walks into her bedroom to be alone. During the bizarre funeral, she falls to her knees in grief. The narrator's slowly increasing perception of the hard lives of both his grandmother and mother is reflected in his growing awareness of the fact that Teresa has come to resemble her mother. How much she differs from his one-night stands is revealed in his comment, made while digging the grandmother's grave, that "from this distance she looked big and handsome, clean-featured, unlike the woman I had seen the night before."

Deprived of the affection he needs from Teresa, the narrator seeks it in a misplaced attachment to Agnes and in casual sexual encounters. Because Agnes is a Cree from Havre, scorned by the reservation people, a permanent union with her would continue the bad medicine passed down from the narrator's grandmother. The narrator vividly recalls the stories she has told him about the Crees, who

were good only for the whites who had slaughtered Indians, had served as scouts for the soldiers, and "had learned to live like them, drink with them, and the girls had opened their thighs to the Long Knives. The children of these unions were doubly cursed in the eyes of the old woman."

The contempt of the Blackfeet for the Crees was based not only on their long-standing warfare and on the Crees' close interaction with the whites but also on their strikingly opposed attitudes toward female sexual morality. Among the Crees, chastity was desirable but not essential, and illegitimacy was not a cause of great concern. An adulterous wife might be given to the lover in exchange for a gift, and wife exchange operated similarly. Among the Blackfeet, chastity was of supreme importance. Because illegitimate pregnancy was regarded as a severe family disgrace, young girls were closely watched by their mothers and married off as soon as possible after puberty. Women's prayers uniformly began with the declaration of their purity; and the most important ceremonial, the Sun Dance, began with the vow of a virtuous woman for the recovery of the sick. On the other hand, the Blackfeet male's efforts at seduction were actively encouraged by his family. Perhaps because of this double standard, the Blackfeet traded with the Crees for love medicine, which the former called Ito-wa-mami-wa-natsi (Cree medicine.)

Agnes' conduct, as well as her tribal background, reinforces the conclusion that the narrator has made a disastrous choice. Agnes is interested only in exchanging sex for a good time and whatever she can get or steal. As the narrator puts it, she is "a fish for dinner, nothing more." When she grew bored reading movie magazines and imagining she looked like Raquel Welch, she took the narrator's gun and electric razor and headed for Malta, where she quickly found a new man. Despite his recognition that she is "Cree and not worth a damn," the narrator is haunted by the image of her body by moonlight, a memory stronger than the experience itself. Because he cannot get her out of his blood, he hesitatingly decides to go after her. Like the medicine man Fish, whose interpretation of the signs after Standing Bear's death was partially responsible for making the grandmother an outcast from her band, Agnes possesses a power which cannot be withstood: her "fish medicine" is strong enough to separate the narrator from his grandmother and mother. He longs to recapture what he has convinced himself that he and Agnes had together before she left. But when the narrator finally finds her in Havre, he ducks so that she cannot see him: "I wanted to be with her, but I didn't move. I didn't know how to go to her. There were people counting on me to make her suffer, and I too felt that she should suffer a little. Afterwards, I could buy her a drink."

This same ambivalence is demonstrated in his physical descriptions of her. He is attracted by her combination of open sexuality and childlike innocence. When he meets her in a bar, she is wearing a dress cut almost to the waist in back and pulled up over her thighs. Nevertheless, her eyes "held the promise of warm things, of a spirit that went beyond her miserable life of drinking and screwing men like me." Because of his growing desire to reform himself and to believe that she really is capable of warmth and affection, he tries to persuade her to settle down by learning a trade like shorthand. Although she curtly rejects his advice in disbelief, his attempt to reform her is an essential step toward achieving his own regeneration because he had expressed concern for the welfare of someone with whom he wants a close relationship; "I was calm, but I didn't feel good. Maybe it was a kind of love." Unfortunately, Agnes' reaction to his plaintive confession that he is not happy leaves no doubt that he will get even less sympathy from her than he has from Teresa: "That's a good one. Who is?"

Neither her rejection of his suggestion for a new life nor the beating administered by her brother breaks the bond which ties him to her. Although he lies to his inquisitive neighbor Mrs. Frederick Horn when he tells her that Agnes came back with him, he obviously intends to try to fulfill this wish. By the end of the novel, he has healed enough internally to think about going to a doctor about his injured knee but not enough to risk losing Agnes by taking the time necessary to recover from surgery. His need to end the spiritual and emotional pain of his longing for her is stronger than his need to end the physical pain in his knee: "Next time I'd do it right. Buy her a couple of cremes de menthe, maybe offer to marry her on the spot." Given the evidence about Agnes' attitudes and behavior, his wish for stability and closeness through marriage is not likely to be fulfilled. He may catch his "fish" again, but he probably will not be able to hang onto her. However, his wanting a close relationship with a woman, even if he has to commit himself to marriage, demonstrates how far he has progressed from the distance he felt within himself and from the women in his life which he expressed at the beginning of the novel.

Source: A. Lavonne Ruoff, "Alienation and the Female Principle in *Winter in the Blood*," in *Critical Perspectives on Native American Fiction*, edited by Richard F. Fleck, Three Continents Press, 1993, pp. 195–208.

Kathleen M. Sands

In the following essay, Sands describes how Welch develops and communicates the narrator's "sense of dislocation and alienation through the episodic nature of the narrative" and the incompleteness of the storytelling in Winter in the Blood.

The narrator of James Welch's *Winter in the Blood* suffers the malaise of modern man; he is alienated from his family, his community, his land, and his own past. He is ineffective in relationships with people and at odds with his environment, not became he is deliberately rebellious, or even immaturely selfish, but because he has lost the story of who he is, where he has come from.

Welch's narrator is an American Indian, but one who suffers more than the tensions of living on the margins of conflicting societies. He is an Indian who has lost both tribal identification and personal identity because he is cut off from the tradition of oral narration which shapes consciousness, values, and self-worth. He is a man whose story is confused, episodic, and incomplete because he has never received the story of those who came before and invested the landscape and the people with significance and meaning. Storytelling keeps things going, creates a cultural matrix that allows a continuum from past to present and future; but for the deliberately nameless narrator of *Winter in the Blood,* there is no past, no present, and certainly no future, only the chaos of disconnected memories, desperate actions, and useless conversation.

His dilemma is clear from the beginning of the novel. Welch is blunt as he reveals the barrenness of the narrator's perceptions of himself and his environment. As he walks toward his mother's ranch the narrator reflects, "Coming home was not easy anymore." The land he crosses is empty and abandoned:

> "The Earthboys were gone" (p. 1). The ranch buildings have caved in. Even at this own ranch, there is a sense of emptiness, especially in his relationships with his family: "none of them counted; not one meant anything to me. And for no reason. I felt no hatred, no love, no guilt, no conscience, nothing but a distance that had grown through the years" (p. 2). In fact, he reveals he no longer has feelings even about himself.

There is little for him to feel but pain. His injured knee aches; he is bruised and hung over; his woman has run off, taking his rifle and razor; his mother is abrupt and self-concerned; his ancient grandmother is silent. His memories give him no comfort: his father drunk and grotesquely frozen to death, his brother mangled on the road, his own bitter realization that

> "The narratives in *Winter in the Blood* are broken. Those which do come together are painful for teller and reader alike, and they do not promise a happy future."

his red skin, not his skill, had been the reason he got a job in the Tacoma hospital. Memory fails him totally as the events of the past stream through his mind in a nightmare collage. The story of his life is disordered, chaotic, and finally, to him, meaningless. As the narratives are broken, so is the man.

Welch develops the intensity of the narrator's sense of dislocation and alienation through the episodic nature of the narrative. In the first encounter between Lame Bull and the narrator, they recall a flood on the stream where the narrator is fishing. Lame Bull insists that it occurred when the narrator was not much more than a gleam in his father's eye. The narrator counters, "I remember that I was almost twenty." The story is brief and terse; conflicting versions result in separation of the men rather than a sharing of a common event. The story does not work because it does not grow out of a shared preception.

Other such episodes in the novel demonstrate the emptiness and distance created by separate stories or conflicting versions of the same one. Teresa and the narrator tell variants of the story of Amos, the one duck that survived the neglected water tub. Teresa's version is skeletal and the narrator becomes confused, mixing up Amos and the turkey. The retelling of the events creates confusion rather than clarity. Then, when the narrator asks his mother why his father stayed away so much, she is defensive and abrupt, switching the focus of the discussion to a recollection of First Raise's death. The narrator admits limply that he has little recollection of the event. The episode results not in shared grief or comfort but in Teresa's accusing her son of being a drifter too. The narrator is alienated again: "I never expected much from Teresa and I never got it. But neither did anybody else. Maybe that's why First Raise stayed away so much." This is a bitter resolution to the question which prompted the brief story.

The stories that might make the narrator understand his family and his history are either incomplete or contradictory. They increase his discomfort, frustrating his attempts to confirm his past and create a continuity of events from which to operate in the present. Even when recollections from the family past nudge his memories to the surface, he is unable to patch together satisfactory narratives within his own mind: "Memory fail."

The one story that he does recall, as he sits in the living room facing his grandmother, is her story. Memory does not fail the narrator here as he recalls in rich detail the circumstances of the telling and the events of the narrative:

> "When the old lady had related this story, many years ago, her eyes were not flat and filmy; they were black like a spider's belly and the small black hands drew triumphant pictures in the air."

Traditional storytelling devices are themselves memorable to the narrator: gesture, animation, drama. And as Welch spins out the memory in the narrator's mind, he enriches the language with detailed images and melodious rhythms. The narrator's memories take on the color, logical sequence, and vitality of the traditional tale, all stylistic characteristics which are deliberately absent from the disturbing episodes which cream conflict and further alienate the narrator. In recalling his grandmother's story of her youth he is struck with a kind of awe because "she revealed a life we never knew, this woman who was our own kin." He is caught up in the mystery of the past, in a yearning to know the complete story, and in a fear that he might lose what part of it he still holds. The memory is incomplete but it is not cause for confusion or recrimination. It is the single intact thread in the torn fabric of his history. It holds a promise of some continuity with the past, of pride in his Blackfeet ancestry. His grandmother, however, is silent now, lost in her own memories and physical frailties, and the narrator's memories of the story she told years before slip away, too fleeting to affect the practiced chaos of his life.

When the narrator heads for town, his confusion and misdirection intensify even more: "Again I felt that helplessness of being in a world of stalking white men. But those Indians down at Gable's were no bargain either. I was a stranger to both and both had beaten me."

The structure of the novel reflects the increased sense of disorientation in the terseness of the language and the separation of incidents. As the narrator's life lacks motivation, direction, continuity, the novel apparently does too. This merging of narrative and form allows the structure of the work to carry the theme as effectively as the narration itself. The airplane man becomes a key figure in the effectiveness of the episodic technique. He is a man with no past, no identity, no future, and, more importantly, no story to tell. "Well, that's another story," he says, but he never tells the story. His hints and contradictions only puzzle the narrator further. The airplane man is the radical extreme of disorientation, dislocation, distrust, disillusionment, and disgust. The narrator is mildly fascinated by his wild plots, but he is also repulsed, instinctively aware of the severity of the man's disorder. The appearance of the airplane man marks the narrator's most frustrating and isolated period in the novel, so that even his encounters with women are without intimacy or emotion. They provide drunkenness without relief or elation, fights without victory. And all the while there are snatches of stories, traces of memories. The incompleteness of the stories and memories that disturbed him acutely at home has intensified so that life becomes a confusing and sterile nightmare; "There were the wanted men with ape faces, cuffed sleeves and blue hands. They did not look directly into my eyes but at my mouth, which was dry and hollow of words. They seemed on the verge of performing an operation. Suddenly a girl loomed before my face, slit and gutted like a fat rainbow, and begged me to turn her loose, and I found my own guts spilling from my monstrous mouth. Teresa hung upside down from a wanted man's belt, crying out a series of strange warnings to the man who had torn up his airplane ticket." The nightmare goes on; images and stories melt into one incomprehensible vision of chaos and mute desperation. The elements of a dozen stories have merged into a bizarre and terrifying reality that follows the narrator from sleep into consciousness. Not until the airplane man is arrested, still without having told his story or revealed his identity, has the narrator had enough of the town, and of himself: "I wanted to lose myself."

The time he has spent in the towns has not been without some benefit, however, for it is there that he is confronted again and again with the memory of his brother's death. The story of Mose's death is crucial to his confrontation with his personal past and the landscape that defines him. The story unfolds slowly in his mind. It is too painful to recall at once, so he pieces it together slowly. It too is episodic, but as with his grandmother's story, it is set apart from the alien world of the present by a detailed narrative and a richness of style absent from the action concerned with his search for his girl friend. The story, however, is left unfinished in the city. Not until the narrator

returns to the reservation and cleanses himself of the town dirt and corruption can he face the pain of the remembered sequence of events that preceded Mose's death.

The final episode in the story is precipitated by two events that enable the narrator to complete the story. First, his grandmother has died during his absence and he shares the task of digging her grave with Lame Bull. As they rest he notices the grave of his father, with its headstone which tells only part of a story: "A rectangular piece of granite lay at the head of the grave. On it were written the name, John First Raise, and a pair of dates between which he had managed to stay alive. It said nothing about how he had liked to fix machines and laugh with the white men of Dodson, or how he came to be frozen stiff as a plank in the borrow pit by Earthboy's."

First Raise had been a man who told stories. Granted, they were stories to entertain the white men in the bars, but he had one story which had given him hope, a reason to live from year to year. Every fall he had planned to go hunting, had made elaborate preparations in his mind, and had told his sons of the deer he would shoot. It was a story to live on, but no gravestone could carry First Raise's story. That was up to the narrator. And Mose, the only other man the narrator was not alienated from, did not even have a grave marker. All that was left was the narrator's memory. Awareness of the grave and his recollection of the bone-chilling cold of winter send his memory back over the last few minutes of his brother's life. Even then, so close to the end, the memory breaks off as the narrator walks out to look at his brother's unmarked grave, returns to the house, picks up the nearly-full bottle of wine, and goes to the corral to saddle Bird. Then, as though some unconscious understanding of the power of the story still permeates his mind, he invents a story for Bird, surmising the terror the horse must have felt when it had been broken, empathizing with the animal fear and sympathizing with the age and loyalty of the animal, which in its terror of man had been conquered only by its comprehension of death: "You ran and ran for what must have seemed like miles, not always following the road, but always straight ahead, until you thought your heart would explode against the terrible constriction of its cage. It was this necessity, this knowledge of death, that made you slow down to a stiff-legged trot, bearing sideways, then a walk, and finally you found yourself standing under a hot sun in the middle of a field of foxtail and speargrass, wheezing desperately to suck in the heavy air of a summer's afternoon . . . A cow horse." In the invention of the story, Bird, the same horse he was riding when his brother was struck and killed, is forgiven for its part in the death through the narrator's comprehension of its instinctive acceptance of its role as cow horse: "No, don't think it was your fault—when that calf broke, you reacted as they trained you." The forgiveness allows the narrator to resume and complete Mose's story, "I didn't even see it break, then I felt your weight settle on your hind legs." At last there is no blame. He has forgiven the horse, helpless to reverse its instincts, and he has forgiven himself in the process. Finally, he can grieve: "'What use,' I whispered, cried for no one in the world to hear, not even Bird, for no one but my soul, as though the words would rid it of the final burden of guilt, and I found myself a child again." A burden does remain, but it is the burden of grief, not guilt; the story has created a catharsis. The pain has been confronted and endured, and again, in the eloquence of the language and the merging of emotion, landscape, and tragedy, Welch has demonstrated that this story, as the story of his grandmother's youth, is essential to the narrator's comprehension of himself and his relationship to all that is past. The narrator's telling of his brother's death has been long and painful, a kind of logo-therapy, at least in part curative of the alienation and bitterness and distance he feels. True, the tears he sheds are solitary, but they are a demonstration of feeling for his brother, and more importantly, for himself.

Having unburdened himself, the narrator moves on toward the isolated cabin Yellow Calf inhabits to tell the blind Indian of his grandmother's death. He had been there twice before, once when he was a child, riding behind First Raise through a snow storm, and again before his trip to town. The first trip had seemed significant at the time, but his understanding of it was incomplete. He had known the old man was important, but he had been too young then to ask the right questions. The questions had lingered all those years though, and now on the third visit, he begins, "Did you know her at all?" Slowly, with prompting from the narrator, Yellow Calf tells the story of the bitter winter, the starvation, the shunning of the then-beautiful young wife of Standing bear, the bad medicine the people associated with her after the chief's death. Finally, with the right questions, Yellow Calf tells how someone became her hunter and protector. The half-formed questions that the narrator has carried over two decades are suddenly answered. At the end of Yellow Calf's story, he thinks for a moment and in that moment the old horse farts: "And it came to me, as though it were riding one moment of the gusting wind, as though Bird had had it in him all the time and had passed it to me in that one instant of corruption. 'Listen, old man' I said, 'It was you—you were old enough to hunt!'" Now he knows: Yellow Calf and his grandmother were both Blackfeet; for twenty-five years they had met and loved; Teresa was their child; he was their grandson. The story that his grandmother had told meshed with the one completed by Yellow Calf, and with the completion the narrator knows himself.

The narrator laughs at Bird's fart, at the revelation of truth, at the amazing simplicity of the mystery of his beginnings which had eluded him for so long: "I began to laugh, at first quietly, with neither bitterness nor humor. It was the laughter of one who understands a moment in his life, of one who has been let in on the secret through luck and circumstance." Yellow Calf joins in the laughter, the laughter of relief that the story is finished and the mystery revealed, that he has lived long enough to pass his memory on to his grandson. It is the mutual laughter of the understanding of just one moment in time, but it is a beginning.

The story has done more than give the narrator a personal identity. It has given him a family, a tribal identity. It has invested the land with history and meaning, for Yellow Calf can still lives in that place of the bitter winter, dwelling in harmony with the earth. The old man makes explicit the continuity of human history and the land; "Sometimes in the winter, when the wind has packed the snow and blown the clouds away, I can still hear the muttering of the people in their tepees. It was a very bad time." But it was also a memorable time, a time of such suffering that the land has taken on a sacred meaning for the old hunter, and in turn for the young man. The oral tradition of the people has been passed on to the alienated, isolated Blackfeet man and given him a continuity of place and character. The images that have lived for decades in the old man's mind have been transferred to the younger man: "And so we shared this secret in the presence of ghosts, in wind that called forth the muttering tepees, the blowing snow, the white air of the horses' nostrils. The cottonwoods behind us, their dead white branches angling the threatening clouds, sheltered these ghosts as they had sheltered the camp that winter. But there were others, so many others." The story merges the past with the present, and the language is detailed and descriptive, at times poetic, meant to make the images indelible in the narrator's mind. Like his grandmother's story, Yellow Calf's story is "literary" in style. This rich style is used by Welch only in the two complete narrations in the novel, Mose's story and the combined stories of the old ones.

The two most important narratives in the novel come to completion in one day, both of them on the land where they began in real experience, and they offer the narrator a balanced and curative release of both tears and laughter, a sense of harmony with the earth, and an understanding of himself. But the reintegration of man into family, society, and the land is not accomplished in a moment, not even a moment of intense revelation; the rent fabric of life is not so easily repaired. Even as the secret of yellow calf is revealed, the narrator realized "there were others, so many others." Yet that very realization is in itself a sign of insight, and what he has learned gives him the capacity of imagination for the first time in the novel: "I tried to imagine what it must have been like, the two of them, hunter and widow. If I was right about Yellow Calf's age, there couldn't have been more than four or five years separating them. . . . It seemed likely that they had never lived together (except perhaps that first winter out of need). There had never been any talk, none that I had heard. . . . So for years the three miles must have been as close as an early morning walk down this path I was now riding." His imagination crosses the boundaries of time, but it is linked to the land as he ponders the knowledge he has gained: "It was a good time for odor. Alfalfa, sweet and dusty, came with the wind, above it the smell of rain. The old man would be lifting his nose to the this odor, thinking of other things, of those days he stood by the widow when everyone else had failed her. So much distance between them, yet they lived only three miles apart. But what created this distance? And what made me think that he was Teresa's father? After all, twenty-five years had passed between the time he had become my grandmother's hunter and Teresa's birth. They could have parted at any time. But he was the one. I knew that. The answer had come to me as if by instinct, . . . as though it was his blood in my veins that had told me." Inevitably there must be doubts left for the narrator, but one crucial question had been asked and firmly answered, opening the possibility for reintegration. If Yellow Calf and his grandmother had closed the distance, perhaps his feelings of distance from his family, his past, his people, his land were not unconquerable.

Two events at the end of the novel demonstrate the positive effect of the narrator's new comprehension of himself and his place within the social and physical environments. As he returns to the ranch, he is met by family friends who have come ostensibly to offer condolences but really to question him about the woman who had run away from him. In response to the query the narrator invents a story, saying that his "wife" had returned from Havre and is in the house. "Do you want to see her?" he challenges. His imagination, once engaged, allows him to create a story of his own, one which at the end of the novel, he seems determined to turn from lie to fact when he says, "Next time I'd do it right. Buy her a couple of cremes de menthe, maybe offer to marry her on the spot." The projection is somewhat tentative, but the intent is to close the literal and emotional distance between himself and the girl and to make his story true.

The other event which dramatizes the effect of his new knowledge is the cow-in-the-mud scene. Despite the fact that he wants to ignore the stupid animal, he does not. He enters into a frantic struggle to save the cow, committing all his strength and energy to the task. In the process the pent up anger that has cut him off from his family and the land is spent. "What did I do to deserve this?" he asks, meaning not just the job of saving the cow but all the suffering he has been through. He goes on. "Ah, Teresa, you made a terrible mistake. Your husband, your friends, your son, all worthless, none of them worth a [s——t] . . . Your mother dead, your father—you don't even know, what do you think of that? A joke, can't you see? Lame Bull! The biggest joke—can't you see that he's a joke, a joker playing a joke on you? Were you taken for a ride! Just like the rest of us, this country, all of us taken for a ride." The narrator's anger is directed at himself, at everyone around him, at society, at the country. It is a bitter anger, but it is anger tempered by a sympathy and passion he had not demonstrated before. Earlier, he could say dryly that he never expected or got much from Teresa, but now he feels something for her, a mixture of anger and sympathy. He sees that she is a victim too. He sees beyond himself. His fury purged, he begins to move again saying, "I crouched and spent the next few minutes planning my new life." Having discovered the distant past in Yellow Calf's and his grandmother's story, having resolved the crucial event in his own past by reliving Mose's story, and now intently engaged in the physical present, he projects into the future. He verbalizes no projections and the dilemma of the moment re-engages him, but the very ability to consider the future is encouraging; coupled with his determination to find the girl who has left him, it signals a coming to terms with life that he has not been capable of before.

On another level the cow-in-the-mud scene reintegrates the narrator with the natural environment in a dramatic way. He has walked and ridden the land but has not been a part of it. Now he is literally sucked into it. As the earth has sucked First Raise and Mose into it, it now draws the narrator, so that symbolically he is linked with those who are now past, those for whom he feels the strongest emotional ties. In triumphing over the earth, he has become one with it. As the rain begins to wash the mud from his face, he wonders "if Mose and First Raise were comfortable. They were the only ones I really loved, I thought, the only ones who were good to be with. At least the rain wouldn't bother them. But they would probably like it; they were that way, good to be with, even on rainy day." Though again he is alone, he is also at one with the earth and at peace with himself and his place on it.

James Welch's use of oral tradition in *Winter in the Blood* is a subtle one. He has adapted the traditional form to suit the needs and style of modern fiction. He has transformed it from an essentially narrative mode to one that carries the theme of reintegration of the alienated contemporary Indian. It is not, however, a simply thematic device to facilitate a positive ending in an essentially ironic, even cynical novel. The function of storytelling in Indian communities is to keep life going, to provide a continuum of the past into the present, to allow for the predication of a future. The narratives in *Winter in the Blood* are broken. Those which do come together are painful for teller and reader alike, and they do not promise a happy future. What they do provide for the narrator is knowledge and insight into the past, a painful acceptance of the present, and maybe, the strength and understanding to build a future.

Source: Kathleen M. Sands, "Alienation and Broken Narrative in *Winter in the Blood*," in *Critical Perspectives on Native American Fiction*, edited by Richard F. Fleck, Three Continents Press, 1993, pp. 181–88.

Sources

Jefferson, Margo, Review of *Winter in the Blood*, in *Newsweek*, November 11, 1974, pp. 115–16.

Lupton, Mary Jane, *James Welch: A Critical Companion*, Greenwood Press, 2004, pp. 37–61.

McFarland, Ron, *Understanding James Welch*, University of South Carolina Press, 2000, pp. 52–83.

Price, Reynolds, Review of *Winter in the Blood*, in the *New York Times Book Review*, November 10, 1974, p. 1.

Sanchez, Carol Lee, "Animal, Vegetable, and Mineral: The Sacred Connection," in *Ecofeminism and the Sacred*, edited by Carol J. Adams, Continuum, 1999, pp. 207–28.

Welch, James, *Winter in the Blood*, Harper & Row, 1974.

Further Reading

Beidler, Peter, G., ed., "Special Symposium Issue on James Welch's *Winter in the Blood*," in *American Indian Quarterly*, Vol. 4, May 1978.
   This includes eight essays on the novel and a preface. Three of the essays, by Kathleen Sands, A. LaVonne Ruoff and Louise K. Barnett, discuss the theme of alienation. Other essays analyze the tone of the novel, including humor, the comic mode, and elegy.

Larson, Charles R., *American Indian Fiction*, University of New Mexico Press, 1978, pp. 140–49.
   Larson praises the novel as almost flawless. He admires its comic elements and also comments on the feeling of goodwill displayed by the author to his characters.

Owens, Louis, "Earthboy's Return: James Welch's Acts of Recovery," in *Other Destinies: Understanding the American Indian Novel*, University of Oklahoma Press, 1992, pp. 128–66.
   Owens discusses the theme of alienation in *Winter in the Blood*, focusing on the narrator's quest for identity. The narrator's recovery from his alienated condition is dependent upon a renewed sense of identity as a Blackfeet Indian, and he makes significant progress toward that goal.

Wild, Peter, *James Welch*, Western Writers Series, Boise State University Press, 1983, pp. 24–38.
   Wild offers a comparison between *Winter in the Blood* and N. Scott Momaday's *House Made of Dawn*. The book reviews the critical response to Welch's novel, and gives his own interpretation of its themes.

Glossary of Literary Terms

A

Abstract: As an adjective applied to writing or literary works, abstract refers to words or phrases that name things not knowable through the five senses.

Aestheticism: A literary and artistic movement of the nineteenth century. Followers of the movement believed that art should not be mixed with social, political, or moral teaching. The statement "art for art's sake" is a good summary of aestheticism. The movement had its roots in France, but it gained widespread importance in England in the last half of the nineteenth century, where it helped change the Victorian practice of including moral lessons in literature.

Allegory: A narrative technique in which characters representing things or abstract ideas are used to convey a message or teach a lesson. Allegory is typically used to teach moral, ethical, or religious lessons but is sometimes used for satiric or political purposes.

Allusion: A reference to a familiar literary or historical person or event, used to make an idea more easily understood.

Analogy: A comparison of two things made to explain something unfamiliar through its similarities to something familiar, or to prove one point based on the acceptedness of another. Similes and metaphors are types of analogies.

Antagonist: The major character in a narrative or drama who works against the hero or protagonist.

Anthropomorphism: The presentation of animals or objects in human shape or with human characteristics. The term is derived from the Greek word for "human form."

Antihero: A central character in a work of literature who lacks traditional heroic qualities such as courage, physical prowess, and fortitude. Antiheroes typically distrust conventional values and are unable to commit themselves to any ideals. They generally feel helpless in a world over which they have no control. Antiheroes usually accept, and often celebrate, their positions as social outcasts.

Apprenticeship Novel: See *Bildungsroman*

Archetype: The word archetype is commonly used to describe an original pattern or model from which all other things of the same kind are made. This term was introduced to literary criticism from the psychology of Carl Jung. It expresses Jung's theory that behind every person's "unconscious," or repressed memories of the past, lies the "collective unconscious" of the human race: memories of the countless typical experiences of our ancestors. These memories are said to prompt illogical associations that trigger powerful emotions in the reader. Often, the emotional process is primitive, even primordial. Archetypes are the literary images that grow out of the "collective unconscious." They appear in literature as incidents and plots that repeat basic patterns of life. They may also appear as stereotyped characters.

Avant-garde: French term meaning "vanguard." It is used in literary criticism to describe new writing that rejects traditional approaches to literature in favor of innovations in style or content.

B

Beat Movement: A period featuring a group of American poets and novelists of the 1950s and 1960s—including Jack Kerouac, Allen Ginsberg, Gregory Corso, William S. Burroughs, and Lawrence Ferlinghetti—who rejected established social and literary values. Using such techniques as stream of consciousness writing and jazz-influenced free verse and focusing on unusual or abnormal states of mind—generated by religious ecstasy or the use of drugs—the Beat writers aimed to create works that were unconventional in both form and subject matter.

Bildungsroman: A German word meaning "novel of development." The *bildungsroman* is a study of the maturation of a youthful character, typically brought about through a series of social or sexual encounters that lead to self-awareness. *Bildungsroman* is used interchangeably with *erziehungsroman*, a novel of initiation and education. When a *bildungsroman* is concerned with the development of an artist (as in James Joyce's *A Portrait of the Artist as a Young Man*), it is often termed a *kunstlerroman*. Also known as Apprenticeship Novel, Coming of Age Novel, *Erziehungsroman*, or *Kunstlerroman*.

Black Aesthetic Movement: A period of artistic and literary development among African Americans in the 1960s and early 1970s. This was the first major African-American artistic movement since the Harlem Renaissance and was closely paralleled by the civil rights and black power movements. The black aesthetic writers attempted to produce works of art that would be meaningful to the black masses. Key figures in black aesthetics included one of its founders, poet and playwright Amiri Baraka, formerly known as LeRoi Jones; poet and essayist Haki R. Madhubuti, formerly Don L. Lee; poet and playwright Sonia Sanchez; and dramatist Ed Bullins. Also known as Black Arts Movement.

Black Humor: Writing that places grotesque elements side by side with humorous ones in an attempt to shock the reader, forcing him or her to laugh at the horrifying reality of a disordered world. Also known as Black Comedy.

Burlesque: Any literary work that uses exaggeration to make its subject appear ridiculous, either by treating a trivial subject with profound seriousness or by treating a dignified subject frivolously. The word "burlesque" may also be used as an adjective, as in "burlesque show," to mean "striptease act."

C

Character: Broadly speaking, a person in a literary work. The actions of characters are what constitute the plot of a story, novel, or poem. There are numerous types of characters, ranging from simple, stereotypical figures to intricate, multifaceted ones. In the techniques of anthropomorphism and personification, animals—and even places or things—can assume aspects of character. "Characterization" is the process by which an author creates vivid, believable characters in a work of art. This may be done in a variety of ways, including (1) direct description of the character by the narrator; (2) the direct presentation of the speech, thoughts, or actions of the character; and (3) the responses of other characters to the character. The term "character" also refers to a form originated by the ancient Greek writer Theophrastus that later became popular in the seventeenth and eighteenth centuries. It is a short essay or sketch of a person who prominently displays a specific attribute or quality, such as miserliness or ambition.

Climax: The turning point in a narrative, the moment when the conflict is at its most intense. Typically, the structure of stories, novels, and plays is one of rising action, in which tension builds to the climax, followed by falling action, in which tension lessens as the story moves to its conclusion.

Colloquialism: A word, phrase, or form of pronunciation that is acceptable in casual conversation but not in formal, written communication. It is considered more acceptable than slang.

Coming of Age Novel: See *Bildungsroman*

Concrete: Concrete is the opposite of abstract, and refers to a thing that actually exists or a description that allows the reader to experience an object or concept with the senses.

Connotation: The impression that a word gives beyond its defined meaning. Connotations may be universally understood or may be significant only to a certain group.

Convention: Any widely accepted literary device, style, or form.

D

Denotation: The definition of a word, apart from the impressions or feelings it creates (connotations) in the reader.

Denouement: A French word meaning "the unknotting." In literary criticism, it denotes the resolution of conflict in fiction or drama. The *denouement* follows the climax and provides an outcome to the primary plot situation as well as an explanation of secondary plot complications. The *denouement* often involves a character's recognition of his or her state of mind or moral condition. Also known as Falling Action.

Description: Descriptive writing is intended to allow a reader to picture the scene or setting in which the action of a story takes place. The form this description takes often evokes an intended emotional response—a dark, spooky graveyard will evoke fear, and a peaceful, sunny meadow will evoke calmness.

Dialogue: In its widest sense, dialogue is simply conversation between people in a literary work; in its most restricted sense, it refers specifically to the speech of characters in a drama. As a specific literary genre, a "dialogue" is a composition in which characters debate an issue or idea.

Diction: The selection and arrangement of words in a literary work. Either or both may vary depending on the desired effect. There are four general types of diction: "formal," used in scholarly or lofty writing; "informal," used in relaxed but educated conversation; "colloquial," used in everyday speech; and "slang," containing newly coined words and other terms not accepted in formal usage.

Didactic: A term used to describe works of literature that aim to teach some moral, religious, political, or practical lesson. Although didactic elements are often found in artistically pleasing works, the term "didactic" usually refers to literature in which the message is more important than the form. The term may also be used to criticize a work that the critic finds "overly didactic," that is, heavy-handed in its delivery of a lesson.

Doppelganger: A literary technique by which a character is duplicated (usually in the form of an alter ego, though sometimes as a ghostly counterpart) or divided into two distinct, usually opposite personalities. The use of this character device is widespread in nineteenth- and twentieth-century literature, and indicates a growing awareness among authors that the "self" is really a composite of many "selves." Also known as The Double.

Double Entendre: A corruption of a French phrase meaning "double meaning." The term is used to indicate a word or phrase that is deliberately ambiguous, especially when one of the meanings is risqué or improper.

Dramatic Irony: Occurs when the audience of a play or the reader of a work of literature knows something that a character in the work itself does not know. The irony is in the contrast between the intended meaning of the statements or actions of a character and the additional information understood by the audience.

Dystopia: An imaginary place in a work of fiction where the characters lead dehumanized, fearful lives.

E

Edwardian: Describes cultural conventions identified with the period of the reign of Edward VII of England (1901–1910). Writers of the Edwardian Age typically displayed a strong reaction against the propriety and conservatism of the Victorian Age. Their work often exhibits distrust of authority in religion, politics, and art and expresses strong doubts about the soundness of conventional values.

Empathy: A sense of shared experience, including emotional and physical feelings, with someone or something other than oneself. Empathy is often used to describe the response of a reader to a literary character.

Enlightenment, The: An eighteenth-century philosophical movement. It began in France but had a wide impact throughout Europe and America. Thinkers of the Enlightenment valued reason and believed that both the individual and society could achieve a state of perfection. Corresponding to this essentially humanist vision was a resistance to religious authority.

Epigram: A saying that makes the speaker's point quickly and concisely. Often used to preface a novel.

Epilogue: A concluding statement or section of a literary work. In dramas, particularly those of the seventeenth and eighteenth centuries, the epilogue is a closing speech, often in verse, delivered by an actor at the end of a play and spoken directly to the audience.

Epiphany: A sudden revelation of truth inspired by a seemingly trivial incident.

Episode: An incident that forms part of a story and is significantly related to it. Episodes may be either self-contained narratives or events that depend on a larger context for their sense and importance.

Epistolary Novel: A novel in the form of letters. The form was particularly popular in the eighteenth century.

Epithet: A word or phrase, often disparaging or abusive, that expresses a character trait of someone or something.

Existentialism: A predominantly twentieth-century philosophy concerned with the nature and perception of human existence. There are two major strains of existentialist thought: atheistic and Christian. Followers of atheistic existentialism believe that the individual is alone in a godless universe and that the basic human condition is one of suffering and loneliness. Nevertheless, because there are no fixed values, individuals can create their own characters—indeed, they can shape themselves—through the exercise of free will. The atheistic strain culminates in and is popularly associated with the works of Jean-Paul Sartre. The Christian existentialists, on the other hand, believe that only in God may people find freedom from life's anguish. The two strains hold certain beliefs in common: that existence cannot be fully understood or described through empirical effort; that anguish is a universal element of life; that individuals must bear responsibility for their actions; and that there is no common standard of behavior or perception for religious and ethical matters.

Expatriates: See *Expatriatism*

Expatriatism: The practice of leaving one's country to live for an extended period in another country.

Exposition: Writing intended to explain the nature of an idea, thing, or theme. Expository writing is often combined with description, narration, or argument. In dramatic writing, the exposition is the introductory material which presents the characters, setting, and tone of the play.

Expressionism: An indistinct literary term, originally used to describe an early twentieth-century school of German painting. The term applies to almost any mode of unconventional, highly subjective writing that distorts reality in some way.

F

Fable: A prose or verse narrative intended to convey a moral. Animals or inanimate objects with human characteristics often serve as characters in fables.

Falling Action: See *Denouement*

Fantasy: A literary form related to mythology and folklore. Fantasy literature is typically set in non-existent realms and features supernatural beings.

Farce: A type of comedy characterized by broad humor, outlandish incidents, and often vulgar subject matter.

Femme fatale: A French phrase with the literal translation "fatal woman." A *femme fatale* is a sensuous, alluring woman who often leads men into danger or trouble.

Fiction: Any story that is the product of imagination rather than a documentation of fact. Characters and events in such narratives may be based in real life but their ultimate form and configuration is a creation of the author.

Figurative Language: A technique in writing in which the author temporarily interrupts the order, construction, or meaning of the writing for a particular effect. This interruption takes the form of one or more figures of speech such as hyperbole, irony, or simile. Figurative language is the opposite of literal language, in which every word is truthful, accurate, and free of exaggeration or embellishment.

Figures of Speech: Writing that differs from customary conventions for construction, meaning, order, or significance for the purpose of a special meaning or effect. There are two major types of figures of speech: rhetorical figures, which do not make changes in the meaning of the words, and tropes, which do.

Fin de siecle: A French term meaning "end of the century." The term is used to denote the last decade of the nineteenth century, a transition period when writers and other artists abandoned old conventions and looked for new techniques and objectives.

First Person: See *Point of View*

Flashback: A device used in literature to present action that occurred before the beginning of the story. Flashbacks are often introduced as the dreams or recollections of one or more characters.

Foil: A character in a work of literature whose physical or psychological qualities contrast strongly with, and therefore highlight, the corresponding qualities of another character.

Folklore: Traditions and myths preserved in a culture or group of people. Typically, these are passed on by word of mouth in various forms—such as legends, songs, and proverbs—or preserved in customs and ceremonies. This term was first used by W. J. Thoms in 1846.

Folktale: A story originating in oral tradition. Folktales fall into a variety of categories, including legends, ghost stories, fairy tales, fables, and anecdotes based on historical figures and events.

Foreshadowing: A device used in literature to create expectation or to set up an explanation of later developments.

Form: The pattern or construction of a work which identifies its genre and distinguishes it from other genres.

G

Genre: A category of literary work. In critical theory, genre may refer to both the content of a given work—tragedy, comedy, pastoral—and to its form, such as poetry, novel, or drama.

Gilded Age: A period in American history during the 1870s characterized by political corruption and materialism. A number of important novels of social and political criticism were written during this time.

Gothicism: In literary criticism, works characterized by a taste for the medieval or morbidly attractive. A gothic novel prominently features elements of horror, the supernatural, gloom, and violence: clanking chains, terror, charnel houses, ghosts, medieval castles, and mysteriously slamming doors. The term "gothic novel" is also applied to novels that lack elements of the traditional Gothic setting but that create a similar atmosphere of terror or dread.

Grotesque: In literary criticism, the subject matter of a work or a style of expression characterized by exaggeration, deformity, freakishness, and disorder. The grotesque often includes an element of comic absurdity.

H

Harlem Renaissance: The Harlem Renaissance of the 1920s is generally considered the first significant movement of black writers and artists in the United States. During this period, new and established black writers published more fiction and poetry than ever before, the first influential black literary journals were established, and black authors and artists received their first widespread recognition and serious critical appraisal. Among the major writers associated with this period are Claude McKay, Jean Toomer, Countee Cullen, Langston Hughes, Arna Bontemps, Nella Larsen, and Zora Neale Hurston. Also known as Negro Renaissance and New Negro Movement.

Hero/Heroine: The principal sympathetic character (male or female) in a literary work. Heroes and heroines typically exhibit admirable traits: idealism, courage, and integrity, for example.

Holocaust Literature: Literature influenced by or written about the Holocaust of World War II. Such literature includes true stories of survival in concentration camps, escape, and life after the war, as well as fictional works and poetry.

Humanism: A philosophy that places faith in the dignity of humankind and rejects the medieval perception of the individual as a weak, fallen creature. "Humanists" typically believe in the perfectibility of human nature and view reason and education as the means to that end.

Hyperbole: In literary criticism, deliberate exaggeration used to achieve an effect.

I

Idiom: A word construction or verbal expression closely associated with a given language.

Image: A concrete representation of an object or sensory experience. Typically, such a representation helps evoke the feelings associated with the object or experience itself. Images are either "literal" or "figurative." Literal images are especially concrete and involve little or no extension of the obvious meaning of the words used to express them. Figurative images do not follow the literal meaning of the words exactly. Images in literature are usually visual, but the term "image" can also refer to the representation of any sensory experience.

Imagery: The array of images in a literary work. Also, figurative language.

In medias res: A Latin term meaning "in the middle of things." It refers to the technique of beginning a story at its midpoint and then using various flashback devices to reveal previous action.

Interior Monologue: A narrative technique in which characters' thoughts are revealed in a way that appears to be uncontrolled by the author. The interior monologue typically aims to reveal the inner self of a character. It portrays emotional experiences as they occur at both a conscious and unconscious level. Images are often used to represent sensations or emotions.

Irony: In literary criticism, the effect of language in which the intended meaning is the opposite of what is stated.

J

Jargon: Language that is used or understood only by a select group of people. Jargon may refer to terminology used in a certain profession, such as computer jargon, or it may refer to any nonsensical language that is not understood by most people.

L

Leitmotiv: See *Motif*

Literal Language: An author uses literal language when he or she writes without exaggerating or embellishing the subject matter and without any tools of figurative language.

Lost Generation: A term first used by Gertrude Stein to describe the post-World War I generation of American writers: men and women haunted by a sense of betrayal and emptiness brought about by the destructiveness of the war.

M

Mannerism: Exaggerated, artificial adherence to a literary manner or style. Also, a popular style of the visual arts of late sixteenth-century Europe that was marked by elongation of the human form and by intentional spatial distortion. Literary works that are self-consciously high-toned and artistic are often said to be "mannered."

Metaphor: A figure of speech that expresses an idea through the image of another object. Metaphors suggest the essence of the first object by identifying it with certain qualities of the second object.

Modernism: Modern literary practices. Also, the principles of a literary school that lasted from roughly the beginning of the twentieth century until the end of World War II. Modernism is defined by its rejection of the literary conventions of the nineteenth century and by its opposition to conventional morality, taste, traditions, and economic values.

Mood: The prevailing emotions of a work or of the author in his or her creation of the work. The mood of a work is not always what might be expected based on its subject matter.

Motif: A theme, character type, image, metaphor, or other verbal element that recurs throughout a single work of literature or occurs in a number of different works over a period of time. Also known as *Motiv* or *Leitmotiv*.

Myth: An anonymous tale emerging from the traditional beliefs of a culture or social unit. Myths use supernatural explanations for natural phenomena. They may also explain cosmic issues like creation and death. Collections of myths, known as mythologies, are common to all cultures and nations, but the best-known myths belong to the Norse, Roman, and Greek mythologies.

N

Narration: The telling of a series of events, real or invented. A narration may be either a simple narrative, in which the events are recounted chronologically, or a narrative with a plot, in which the account is given in a style reflecting the author's artistic concept of the story. Narration is sometimes used as a synonym for "storyline."

Narrative: A verse or prose accounting of an event or sequence of events, real or invented. The term is also used as an adjective in the sense "method of narration." For example, in literary criticism, the expression "narrative technique" usually refers to the way the author structures and presents his or her story.

Narrator: The teller of a story. The narrator may be the author or a character in the story through whom the author speaks.

Naturalism: A literary movement of the late nineteenth and early twentieth centuries. The movement's major theorist, French novelist Emile Zola, envisioned a type of fiction that would examine human life with the objectivity of scientific inquiry. The Naturalists typically viewed human beings as either the products of "biological determinism," ruled by hereditary instincts and engaged in an endless struggle for survival, or as the products of "socioeconomic determinism," ruled by social and economic forces beyond their control. In their works, the Naturalists generally ignored the highest levels of society and focused on degradation: poverty, alcoholism, prostitution, insanity, and disease.

Noble Savage: The idea that primitive man is noble and good but becomes evil and corrupted as he becomes civilized. The concept of the noble savage originated in the Renaissance period but is more closely identified with such later writers as

Jean-Jacques Rousseau and Aphra Behn. See also Primitivism.

Novel of Ideas: A novel in which the examination of intellectual issues and concepts takes precedence over characterization or a traditional storyline.

Novel of Manners: A novel that examines the customs and mores of a cultural group.

Novel: A long fictional narrative written in prose, which developed from the novella and other early forms of narrative. A novel is usually organized under a plot or theme with a focus on character development and action.

Novella: An Italian term meaning "story." This term has been especially used to describe fourteenth-century Italian tales, but it also refers to modern short novels.

O

Objective Correlative: An outward set of objects, a situation, or a chain of events corresponding to an inward experience and evoking this experience in the reader. The term frequently appears in modern criticism in discussions of authors' intended effects on the emotional responses of readers.

Objectivity: A quality in writing characterized by the absence of the author's opinion or feeling about the subject matter. Objectivity is an important factor in criticism.

Oedipus Complex: A son's amorous obsession with his mother. The phrase is derived from the story of the ancient Theban hero Oedipus, who unknowingly killed his father and married his mother.

Omniscience: See *Point of View*

Onomatopoeia: The use of words whose sounds express or suggest their meaning. In its simplest sense, onomatopoeia may be represented by words that mimic the sounds they denote such as "hiss" or "meow." At a more subtle level, the pattern and rhythm of sounds and rhymes of a line or poem may be onomatopoeic.

Oxymoron: A phrase combining two contradictory terms. Oxymorons may be intentional or unintentional.

P

Parable: A story intended to teach a moral lesson or answer an ethical question.

Paradox: A statement that appears illogical or contradictory at first, but may actually point to an underlying truth.

Parallelism: A method of comparison of two ideas in which each is developed in the same grammatical structure.

Parody: In literary criticism, this term refers to an imitation of a serious literary work or the signature style of a particular author in a ridiculous manner. A typical parody adopts the style of the original and applies it to an inappropriate subject for humorous effect. Parody is a form of satire and could be considered the literary equivalent of a caricature or cartoon.

Pastoral: A term derived from the Latin word "pastor," meaning shepherd. A pastoral is a literary composition on a rural theme. The conventions of the pastoral were originated by the third-century Greek poet Theocritus, who wrote about the experiences, love affairs, and pastimes of Sicilian shepherds. In a pastoral, characters and language of a courtly nature are often placed in a simple setting. The term pastoral is also used to classify dramas, elegies, and lyrics that exhibit the use of country settings and shepherd characters.

Pen Name: See *Pseudonym*

Persona: A Latin term meaning "mask." *Personae* are the characters in a fictional work of literature. The *persona* generally functions as a mask through which the author tells a story in a voice other than his or her own. A *persona* is usually either a character in a story who acts as a narrator or an "implied author," a voice created by the author to act as the narrator for himself or herself.

Personification: A figure of speech that gives human qualities to abstract ideas, animals, and inanimate objects. Also known as *Prosopopoeia*.

Picaresque Novel: Episodic fiction depicting the adventures of a roguish central character ("picaro" is Spanish for "rogue"). The picaresque hero is commonly a low-born but clever individual who wanders into and out of various affairs of love, danger, and farcical intrigue. These involvements may take place at all social levels and typically present a humorous and wide-ranging satire of a given society.

Plagiarism: Claiming another person's written material as one's own. Plagiarism can take the form of direct, word-for-word copying or the theft of the substance or idea of the work.

Plot: In literary criticism, this term refers to the pattern of events in a narrative or drama. In its simplest sense, the plot guides the author in composing the work and helps the reader follow the work. Typically, plots exhibit causality and unity and have a beginning, a middle, and an end. Sometimes, however, a plot may consist of a series of disconnected events, in which case it is known as an "episodic plot."

Poetic Justice: An outcome in a literary work, not necessarily a poem, in which the good are rewarded and the evil are punished, especially in ways that particularly fit their virtues or crimes.

Poetic License: Distortions of fact and literary convention made by a writer—not always a poet—for the sake of the effect gained. Poetic license is closely related to the concept of "artistic freedom."

Poetics: This term has two closely related meanings. It denotes (1) an aesthetic theory in literary criticism about the essence of poetry or (2) rules prescribing the proper methods, content, style, or diction of poetry. The term poetics may also refer to theories about literature in general, not just poetry.

Point of View: The narrative perspective from which a literary work is presented to the reader. There are four traditional points of view. The "third person omniscient" gives the reader a "godlike" perspective, unrestricted by time or place, from which to see actions and look into the minds of characters. This allows the author to comment openly on characters and events in the work. The "third person" point of view presents the events of the story from outside of any single character's perception, much like the omniscient point of view, but the reader must understand the action as it takes place and without any special insight into characters' minds or motivations. The "first person" or "personal" point of view relates events as they are perceived by a single character. The main character "tells" the story and may offer opinions about the action and characters which differ from those of the author. Much less common than omniscient, third person, and first person is the "second person" point of view, wherein the author tells the story as if it is happening to the reader.

Polemic: A work in which the author takes a stand on a controversial subject, such as abortion or religion. Such works are often extremely argumentative or provocative.

Pornography: Writing intended to provoke feelings of lust in the reader. Such works are often condemned by critics and teachers, but those which can be shown to have literary value are viewed less harshly.

Post-Aesthetic Movement: An artistic response made by African Americans to the black aesthetic movement of the 1960s and early '70s. Writers since that time have adopted a somewhat different tone in their work, with less emphasis placed on the disparity between black and white in the United States. In the words of post-aesthetic authors such as Toni Morrison, John Edgar Wideman, and Kristin Hunter, African Americans are portrayed as looking inward for answers to their own questions, rather than always looking to the outside world.

Postmodernism: Writing from the 1960s forward characterized by experimentation and continuing to apply some of the fundamentals of modernism, which included existentialism and alienation. Postmodernists have gone a step further in the rejection of tradition begun with the modernists by also rejecting traditional forms, preferring the anti-novel over the novel and the antihero over the hero.

Primitivism: The belief that primitive peoples were nobler and less flawed than civilized peoples because they had not been subjected to the tainting influence of society. See also Noble Savage.

Prologue: An introductory section of a literary work. It often contains information establishing the situation of the characters or presents information about the setting, time period, or action. In drama, the prologue is spoken by a chorus or by one of the principal characters.

Prose: A literary medium that attempts to mirror the language of everyday speech. It is distinguished from poetry by its use of unmetered, unrhymed language consisting of logically related sentences. Prose is usually grouped into paragraphs that form a cohesive whole such as an essay or a novel.

***Prosopopoeia*:** See *Personification*

Protagonist: The central character of a story who serves as a focus for its themes and incidents and as the principal rationale for its development. The protagonist is sometimes referred to in discussions of modern literature as the hero or antihero.

Protest Fiction: Protest fiction has as its primary purpose the protesting of some social injustice, such as racism or discrimination.

Proverb: A brief, sage saying that expresses a truth about life in a striking manner.

Pseudonym: A name assumed by a writer, most often intended to prevent his or her identification as the author of a work. Two or more authors may work together under one pseudonym, or an author may use a different name for each genre he or she publishes in. Some publishing companies maintain "house pseudonyms," under which any number of authors may write installations in a series. Some authors also choose a pseudonym over their real names the way an actor may use a stage name.

Pun: A play on words that have similar sounds but different meanings.

R

Realism: A nineteenth-century European literary movement that sought to portray familiar characters, situations, and settings in a realistic manner. This was done primarily by using an objective narrative point of view and through the buildup of accurate detail. The standard for success of any realistic work depends on how faithfully it transfers common experience into fictional forms. The realistic method may be altered or extended, as in stream of consciousness writing, to record highly subjective experience.

Repartee: Conversation featuring snappy retorts and witticisms.

Resolution: The portion of a story following the climax, in which the conflict is resolved. See also *Denouement*.

Rhetoric: In literary criticism, this term denotes the art of ethical persuasion. In its strictest sense, rhetoric adheres to various principles developed since classical times for arranging facts and ideas in a clear, persuasive, appealing manner. The term is also used to refer to effective prose in general and theories of or methods for composing effective prose.

Rhetorical Question: A question intended to provoke thought, but not an expressed answer, in the reader. It is most commonly used in oratory and other persuasive genres.

Rising Action: The part of a drama where the plot becomes increasingly complicated. Rising action leads up to the climax, or turning point, of a drama.

Roman a clef: A French phrase meaning "novel with a key." It refers to a narrative in which real persons are portrayed under fictitious names.

Romance: A broad term, usually denoting a narrative with exotic, exaggerated, often idealized characters, scenes, and themes.

Romanticism: This term has two widely accepted meanings. In historical criticism, it refers to a European intellectual and artistic movement of the late eighteenth and early nineteenth centuries that sought greater freedom of personal expression than that allowed by the strict rules of literary form and logic of the eighteenth-century neoclassicists. The Romantics preferred emotional and imaginative expression to rational analysis. They considered the individual to be at the center of all experience and so placed him or her at the center of their art. The Romantics believed that the creative imagination reveals nobler truths—unique feelings and attitudes—than those that could be discovered by logic or by scientific examination. Both the natural world and the state of childhood were important sources for revelations of "eternal truths." "Romanticism" is also used as a general term to refer to a type of sensibility found in all periods of literary history and usually considered to be in opposition to the principles of classicism. In this sense, Romanticism signifies any work or philosophy in which the exotic or dreamlike figure strongly, or that is devoted to individualistic expression, self-analysis, or a pursuit of a higher realm of knowledge than can be discovered by human reason.

Romantics: See *Romanticism*

S

Satire: A work that uses ridicule, humor, and wit to criticize and provoke change in human nature and institutions. There are two major types of satire: "formal" or "direct" satire speaks directly to the reader or to a character in the work; "indirect" satire relies upon the ridiculous behavior of its characters to make its point. Formal satire is further divided into two manners: the "Horatian," which ridicules gently, and the "Juvenalian," which derides its subjects harshly and bitterly.

Science Fiction: A type of narrative about or based upon real or imagined scientific theories and technology. Science fiction is often peopled with alien creatures and set on other planets or in different dimensions.

Second Person: See *Point of View*

Setting: The time, place, and culture in which the action of a narrative takes place. The elements of setting may include geographic location, characters' physical and mental environments, prevailing cultural attitudes, or the historical time in which the action takes place.

Simile: A comparison, usually using "like" or "as," of two essentially dissimilar things, as in "coffee as cold as ice" or "He sounded like a broken record."

Slang: A type of informal verbal communication that is generally unacceptable for formal writing. Slang words and phrases are often colorful exaggerations used to emphasize the speaker's point; they may also be shortened versions of an often-used word or phrase.

Slave Narrative: Autobiographical accounts of American slave life as told by escaped slaves. These works first appeared during the abolition movement of the 1830s through the 1850s.

Socialist Realism: The Socialist Realism school of literary theory was proposed by Maxim Gorky and established as a dogma by the first Soviet Congress of Writers. It demanded adherence to a communist worldview in works of literature. Its doctrines required an objective viewpoint comprehensible to the working classes and themes of social struggle featuring strong proletarian heroes. Also known as Social Realism.

Stereotype: A stereotype was originally the name for a duplication made during the printing process; this led to its modern definition as a person or thing that is (or is assumed to be) the same as all others of its type.

Stream of Consciousness: A narrative technique for rendering the inward experience of a character. This technique is designed to give the impression of an ever-changing series of thoughts, emotions, images, and memories in the spontaneous and seemingly illogical order that they occur in life.

Structure: The form taken by a piece of literature. The structure may be made obvious for ease of understanding, as in nonfiction works, or may be obscured for artistic purposes, as in some poetry or seemingly "unstructured" prose.

Sturm und Drang: A German term meaning "storm and stress." It refers to a German literary movement of the 1770s and 1780s that reacted against the order and rationalism of the enlightenment, focusing instead on the intense experience of extraordinary individuals.

Style: A writer's distinctive manner of arranging words to suit his or her ideas and purpose in writing. The unique imprint of the author's personality upon his or her writing, style is the product of an author's way of arranging ideas and his or her use of diction, different sentence structures, rhythm, figures of speech, rhetorical principles, and other elements of composition.

Subjectivity: Writing that expresses the author's personal feelings about his subject, and which may or may not include factual information about the subject.

Subplot: A secondary story in a narrative. A subplot may serve as a motivating or complicating force for the main plot of the work, or it may provide emphasis for, or relief from, the main plot.

Surrealism: A term introduced to criticism by Guillaume Apollinaire and later adopted by Andre Breton. It refers to a French literary and artistic movement founded in the 1920s. The Surrealists sought to express unconscious thoughts and feelings in their works. The best-known technique used for achieving this aim was automatic writing—transcriptions of spontaneous outpourings from the unconscious. The Surrealists proposed to unify the contrary levels of conscious and unconscious, dream and reality, objectivity and subjectivity into a new level of "super-realism."

Suspense: A literary device in which the author maintains the audience's attention through the buildup of events, the outcome of which will soon be revealed.

Symbol: Something that suggests or stands for something else without losing its original identity. In literature, symbols combine their literal meaning with the suggestion of an abstract concept. Literary symbols are of two types: those that carry complex associations of meaning no matter what their contexts, and those that derive their suggestive meaning from their functions in specific literary works.

Symbolism: This term has two widely accepted meanings. In historical criticism, it denotes an early modernist literary movement initiated in France during the nineteenth century that reacted against the prevailing standards of realism. Writers in this movement aimed to evoke, indirectly and symbolically, an order of being beyond the material world of the five senses. Poetic expression of personal emotion figured strongly in the movement, typically by means of a private set of symbols uniquely identifiable with the individual poet. The principal aim of the Symbolists was to express in words the highly complex feelings that grew out of everyday contact with the world. In a broader sense, the term "symbolism" refers to the use of one object to represent another.

T

Tall Tale: A humorous tale told in a straightforward, credible tone but relating absolutely impossible events or feats of the characters. Such tales were commonly told of frontier adventures during the settlement of the west in the United States.

Theme: The main point of a work of literature. The term is used interchangeably with thesis.

Thesis: A thesis is both an essay and the point argued in the essay. Thesis novels and thesis plays share the quality of containing a thesis which is supported through the action of the story.

Third Person: See *Point of View*

Tone: The author's attitude toward his or her audience may be deduced from the tone of the work. A formal tone may create distance or convey politeness, while an informal tone may encourage a friendly, intimate, or intrusive feeling in the reader. The author's attitude toward his or her subject matter may also be deduced from the tone of the words he or she uses in discussing it.

Transcendentalism: An American philosophical and religious movement, based in New England from around 1835 until the Civil War. Transcendentalism was a form of American romanticism that had its roots abroad in the works of Thomas Carlyle, Samuel Coleridge, and Johann Wolfgang von Goethe. The Transcendentalists stressed the importance of intuition and subjective experience in communication with God. They rejected religious dogma and texts in favor of mysticism and scientific naturalism. They pursued truths that lie beyond the "colorless" realms perceived by reason and the senses and were active social reformers in public education, women's rights, and the abolition of slavery.

U

Urban Realism: A branch of realist writing that attempts to accurately reflect the often harsh facts of modern urban existence.

Utopia: A fictional perfect place, such as "paradise" or "heaven."

V

Verisimilitude: Literally, the appearance of truth. In literary criticism, the term refers to aspects of a work of literature that seem true to the reader.

Victorian: Refers broadly to the reign of Queen Victoria of England (1837–1901) and to anything with qualities typical of that era. For example, the qualities of smug narrowmindedness, bourgeois materialism, faith in social progress, and priggish morality are often considered Victorian. This stereotype is contradicted by such dramatic intellectual developments as the theories of Charles Darwin, Karl Marx, and Sigmund Freud (which stirred strong debates in England) and the critical attitudes of serious Victorian writers like Charles Dickens and George Eliot. In literature, the Victorian Period was the great age of the English novel, and the latter part of the era saw the rise of movements such as decadence and symbolism. Also known as Victorian Age and Victorian Period.

W

Weltanschauung: A German term referring to a person's worldview or philosophy.

Weltschmerz: A German term meaning "world pain." It describes a sense of anguish about the nature of existence, usually associated with a melancholy, pessimistic attitude.

Z

Zeitgeist: A German term meaning "spirit of the time." It refers to the moral and intellectual trends of a given era.

Cumulative Author/Title Index

Cumulative Author/Title Index

Cumulative Nationality/Ethnicity Index

Adams, Richard
  Watership Down: V11
Austen, Jane
  Emma: V21
  Persuasion: V14
  Pride and Prejudice: V1
  Sense and Sensibility: V18
Ballard, J. G.
  Empire of the Sun: V8
Blair, Eric Arthur
  Animal Farm: V3
Bowen, Elizabeth Dorothea Cole
  The Death of the Heart: V13
Brontë, Charlotte
  Jane Eyre: V4
Brontë, Emily
  Wuthering Heights: V2
Brookner, Anita
  Hotel du Lac: V23
Burgess, Anthony
  A Clockwork Orange: V15
Burney, Fanny
  Evelina: V16
Carroll, Lewis
  *Alice's Adventurers in
    Wonderland:* V7
Chrisite, Agatha
  Ten Little Indians: V8
Conrad, Joseph
  Heart of Darkness: V2
  Lord Jim: V16
Defoe, Daniel
  Moll Flanders: V13
  Robinson Crusoe: V9
Dickens, Charles
  A Christmas Carol: V10
  Great Expectations: V4
  Hard Times: V20
  Oliver Twist: V14
  A Tale of Two Cities: V5
du Maurier, Daphne
  Rebecca: V12
Eliot, George
  Middlemarch: V23
  The Mill on the Floss: V17
  Silas Marner: V20
Fielding, Henry
  Tom Jones: V18
Foden, Giles
  The Last King of Scotland: V15
Forster, E. M.
  A Passage to India: V3
  Howards End: V10
  A Room with a View: V11
Fowles, John
  The French Lieutenant's Woman:
    V21
Golding, William
  Lord of the Flies: V2
Graves, Robert
  I, Claudius: V21
Greene, Graham
  The End of the Affair: V16

Hardy, Thomas
  Far from the Madding Crowd: V19
  The Mayor of Casterbridge: V15
  The Return of the Native: V11
  Tess of the d'Urbervilles: V3
Huxley, Aldous
  Brave New World: V6
Ishiguro, Kazuo
  The Remains of the Day: V13
James, Henry
  The Ambassadors: V12
  The Portrait of a Lady: V19
  The Turn of the Screw: V16
Kipling, Rudyard
  Kim: V21
Koestler, Arthur
  Darkness at Noon: V19
Lawrence, D. H.
  Sons and Lovers: V18
Marmon Silko, Leslie
  Ceremony: V4
Maugham, W. Somerset
  The Razor's Edge: V23
Orwell, George
  1984: V7
  Animal Farm: V3
Rhys, Jean
  Wide Sargasso Sea: V19
Rushdie, Salman
  The Satanic Verses: V22
Sewell, Anna
  Black Beauty: V22
Shelley, Mary
  Frankenstein: V1
Shute, Nevil
  On the Beach: V9
Spark, Muriel
  The Prime of Miss Jean Brodie:
    V22
Stevenson, Robert Louis
  Dr. Jekyll and Mr. Hyde: V11
Swift, Graham
  Waterland: V18
Swift, Jonathan
  Gulliver's Travels: V6
Thackeray, William Makepeace
  Vanity Fair: V13
Tolkien, J. R. R.
  The Hobbit: V8
Waugh, Evelyn
  Brideshead Revisited: V13
  Scoop: V17
Wells, H. G.
  The Time Machine: V17
  The War of the Worlds: V20
Woolf, Virginia
  Mrs. Dalloway: V12
  To the Lighthouse: V8

European American

Hemingway, Ernest
  The Old Man and the Sea: V6

Stowe, Harriet Beecher
  Uncle Tom's Cabin: V6

French

Camus, Albert
  The Plague: V16
  The Stranger: V6
Dumas, Alexandre
  The Count of Monte Cristo: V19
  The Three Musketeers: V14
Flaubert, Gustave
  Madame Bovary: V14
Gide, André
  The Immoralist: V21
Hugo, Victor
  The Hunchback of Notre Dame:
    V20
  Les Misérables: V5
Japrisot, Sébastien
  A Very Long Engagement: V18
Leroux, Gaston
  The Phantom of the Opera: V20
Sartre, Jean-Paul
  Nausea: V21
Voltaire
  Candide: V7

German

Hesse, Hermann
  Demian: V15
  Siddhartha: V6
Mann, Thomas
  Death in Venice: V17
Remarque, Erich Maria
  All Quiet on the Western Front:
    V4

Hispanic American

Cisneros, Sandra
  The House on Mango Street: V2
Hijuelos, Oscar
  *The Mambo Kings Play Songs of
    Love:* V17

Hungarian

Koestler, Arthur
  Darkness at Noon: V19

Indian

Markandaya, Kamala
  Nectar in a Sieve: V13
Roy, Arundhati
  The God of Small Things: V22
Rushdie, Salman
  Midnight's Children: V23
  The Satanic Verses: V22

Subject/Theme Index